BRITAIN AND THE
LAST TSAR

BRITAIN AND THE LAST TSAR

British Policy and Russia
1894–1917

KEITH NEILSON

CLARENDON PRESS · OXFORD
1995

Oxford University Press, Walton Street, Oxford OX2 6DP
Oxford New York
Athens Auckland Bangkok Bombay
Calcutta Cape Town Dar es Salaam Delhi
Florence Hong Kong Istanbul Karachi
Kuala Lumpur Madras Madrid Melbourne
Mexico City Nairobi Paris Singapore
Taipei Tokyo Toronto
and associated companies in
Berlin Ibadan

Oxford is a trade mark of Oxford University Press

Published in the United States
by Oxford University Press Inc., New York

British Library Cataloguing in Publication Data
Data available

Library of Congress Cataloging in Publication Data
Neilson, Keith.
Britain and the last tsar: British policy and Russia, 1894–1917 /
Keith Neilson.
p.   cm.
Includes bibliographical references (p.   ) and index.
1. Great Britain—Foreign relations—Russia. 2. Great Britain—
Foreign relations—1901–1936. 3. Great Britain—Foreign
relations—1837–1901. 4. Russia—Foreign relations—Great Britain.
5. Russia—Foreign relations—1894–1917. I. Title.
DA47.65.N45   1995
327.41047—dc20   95–20059

ISBN 0–19–820470–1

1 3 5 7 9 10 8 6 4 2

Typeset by Best-set Typesetter Ltd., Hong Kong
Printed in Great Britain
on acid-free paper by
Biddles Ltd.
Guildford and King's Lynn

Acknowledgements

THIS book has been a long time in the making. During that time, I have incurred numerous debts of gratitude. A Leave Fellowship from the Canadian Social Sciences and Humanities Research Council made it possible for me to spend a year doing research in Britain, while the Academic Research Programme of the Royal Military College of Canada provided funding for several subsequent trips. Numerous individuals—J. O. Baylen, Michael Dockrill, John Ferris, Greg Kennedy, Paul Kennedy, Brian McKercher, Ian Nish, John Orbell, Donald Schurman, and Zara Steiner—have given me advice and encouragement. In particular, I would like to thank David French and Arnd Bohm: the former for reading the entire manuscript and making valuable comments on it, and the latter for helping to shrink an earlier, even longer version of this book to its present size. None of the above are responsible for what follows, and any errors of fact or interpretation are my own.

The following have graciously given me permission to quote from the material to which they own the copyright: Ms Jane Bonham-Carter; Viscount Esher; Lord Howard of Penrith; the Marquess of Salisbury; the Earl of Selborne; the Trustees of the National Library of Scotland and the holder of the copyright of Field Marshal Earl Haig; the Syndics of Cambridge University Library; the School of Slavonic and East European Studies; the Trustees of the Liddell Hart Centre for Military Archives; the Trustees of the Imperial War Museum; the British Library; the Master, Fellows and Scholars of Churchill College, Cambridge in the University of Cambridge; Baring Brothers; and Vickers plc. Crown copyright material is reproduced by permission of the Controller of Her Majesty's Stationery Office. My sincere apologies are due to anyone whose copyright I may have infringed unwittingly.

My greatest debt is owed to my family. My wife, Joan, has helped in innumerable ways. Her help and understanding make all things possible, and the book is dedicated to her. Our children, Anne, David, and Susan, are in no way responsible for what is in this book but are in part the reason why it has taken so long to write.

Contents

List of Maps

List of Abbreviations

AHR	*American Historical Review*
AJPH	*Australian Journal of Politics and History*
ASEER	*American Slavonic and East European Review*
BIHR	*Bulletin of the Institute of Historical Research*
BJIS	*British Journal of International Studies*
CEH	*Central European History*
CJH	*Canadian Journal of History*
CMRS	*Cahiers du monde russe et soviétique*
CSP	*Canadian Slavonic Papers*
CSS	*California Slavic Papers*
EconHR	*Economic History Review*
EEQ	*East European Quarterly*
EHR	*English Historical Review*
ESR	*European Studies Review*
HJ	*Historical Journal*
HR	*Historical Research*
IHR	*International History Review*
INS	*Intelligence and National Security*
IZ	*Istoricheskie zapiski*
JAH	*Journal of Asian History*
JBS	*Journal of British Studies*
JCH	*Journal of Contemporary History*
JEEH	*Journal of European Economic History*
JEH	*Journal of Economic History*
JICH	*Journal of Imperial and Commonwealth History*
JMH	*Journal of Modern History*
JSAHR	*Journal of the Society of Army Historical Research*
JfGOE	*Jahrbücher für Geschichte Osteuropas*
JSS	*Journal of Strategic Studies*
MAS	*Modern Asian Studies*
MES	*Middle Eastern Studies*
MM	*Mariner's Mirror*
OSP	*Oxford Slavonic Papers*
PHR	*Pacific Historical Review*
RIS	*Review of International Studies*
RH	*Russian History*
RR	*Russian Review*
SEER	*Slavonic and East European Review*

SR	Slavic Review
VI	Voprosy istorii
VIZ	Voenno-istoricheskii zhurnal
VS	Victorian Studies
WS	War and Society

Introduction

'I don't understand you,' said Alice. 'It's dreadfully confusing!'

'That's the effect of living backwards,' the Queen said kindly: 'it always makes one a little giddy at first—'

'Living backwards!' Alice repeated in great astonishment. 'I never heard of such a thing!'

'—but there's one advantage in it, that one's memory works both ways.'

'I'm sure *mine* only works one way,' Alice remarked. 'I can't remember things before they happen.'

'It's a poor sort of memory that only works backwards,' the Queen remarked.

(Lewis Carroll, *Through the Looking Glass*, Chapter 5)

HAVING 'a poor sort of memory' is not the problem for historians. Indeed, the problem is rather the reverse. Like the White Queen's, historians' memories work in two directions; they know in advance how the events they study turn out. Thus, they often find themselves drawn to the conclusion that what did happen was inevitable. But such foreknowledge was denied to those who participated in the events themselves. The latter, like Alice, lived in a world where time's arrow pointed in only one direction. Thus, when attempting to discover the 'why' of history as well as the 'what' it is essential to approach events chronologically in order to understand the actions of the participants in these events.

Such general considerations are particularly significant for the examination of British foreign policy before the First World War. The war has cast a retroactive shadow over historical studies. The knowledge that Britain went to war in August 1914 against the Central Powers and the search for the origins of that war have meant, in particular, that Anglo-German relations have been given greater emphasis for the period before 1914 than they deserve.[1] While not denying the validity of

---

[1] The obvious starting point for such an assertion is P. Kennedy, *The Rise of the Anglo-German Antagonism 1860–1914* (London, 1980), but it permeates all the literature. Even Z. Steiner's admirable *Britain and the Origins of the First World War* (London, 1977), which pays attention to the other aspects of British foreign policy, concentrates on the German menace. This bias is even more noticeable in studies that focus on defence: see M. Howard, *The Continental Commitment: The Dilemma of British Defence Policy in the Era of Two World Wars* (London, 1972); S. R. Williamson, Jr., *The Politics of Grand Strategy: Britain and France Prepare for War, 1904–14* (pbk. edn., 1990; first pub. Cambridge, MA, 1969), and A. Marder, *From the Dreadnought to Scapa Flow*, i, *1904–14: The Road to War* (London, 1961).

such an approach, it is necessary to remember that those who made British policy before the war did not *know*—like Alice—that a conflict with Germany would break out in 1914. Thus, they did not formulate their policy on this basis. Instead, they created a policy designed to prevent war generally, while at the same time safeguarding Britain's interests against *all*-comers. It is the primary contention of this book that, in the period from 1894 to 1914, Russia was considered to be at least as great a threat to Britain and to British interests as was Germany.

Proving this contention has involved structural as well as historical considerations. Like all Gaul, *Britain and the Last Tsar* is divided into three parts. Part I results from the belief that the relationship between countries involves more than what is traditionally encompassed by the term 'foreign policy' and far more than what one clerk said to another.[2] Instead, it is important to consider a wider spectrum of relationships—cultural, economic, financial, strategic and so on—when attempting to discover the 'why' behind foreign policy. Accompanying this belief are two assumptions. The first is that particular individuals—a foreign-policy-making élite—shaped Britain's policy towards Russia and that a knowledge of their 'unspoken assumptions' is essential.[3] The second is that such decisions were made within a certain context that makes up what has been called the 'realities behind diplomacy'.[4] Discovering these matters is the substance of Part I. Those who prefer their history free of what an unkind critic has called 'the murky world of perception' may omit Part I and go directly to Parts II and III.

Parts II and III are chronological. They outline the formal relations between Britain and Russia during the reign of Nicholas II (1894–1917). The choice of beginning and end dates was arbitrary, but not whimsical. I have chosen the reign of Nicholas because, in a country where the personality of the monarch was important for the formation of foreign policy, it forms a discrete unit. By happy

[2] Certainly, I make no claim to originality here. Such books as Kennedy's *The Rise of the Anglo-German Antagonism* (to which the present study, although it disagrees profoundly with Kennedy's conclusions, owes its inspiration) deal extensively with the wider aspects of foreign policy.

[3] J. Joll, *1914: The Unspoken Assumptions* (London, 1967). On the importance of individuals, see D. C. Watt, *What About the People? Abstractions and Reality in History and the Social Sciences* (London, 1983). The concept of the foreign-policy-making élite, is derived from Watt's seminal essay, 'The nature of the foreign-policy-making élite in Britain', in id., *Personalities and Politics: Studies in the Formulation of British Foreign Policy in the Twentieth Century* (London, 1965), 1–15. Watt has expanded on this in his *Succeeding John Bull: America in Britain's Place 1900–75* (Cambridge: Cambridge University Press, 1984), 1–24. The essential starting point for the study of the British Foreign Office in this period is Z. Steiner, *The Foreign Office and Foreign Policy 1898–1914* (Cambridge, 1969) and her 'Elitism and Foreign Policy: The Foreign Office Before the Great War', in B. J. C. McKercher and D. J. Moss (eds.), *Shadow and Substance in British Foreign Policy 1895–1939: Memorial Essays Honouring C. J. Lowe* (Edmonton, Alta., 1984), 19–56. Also of value is R. A. Jones, *The British Diplomatic Service 1815–1914* (Waterloo, Ont., 1983).

[4] My debt here is to P. Kennedy, *The Realities Behind Diplomacy: Background Influences on British External Policy, 1865–1980* (London, 1981).

coincidence, Nicholas's reign also neatly defines a specific period in Anglo-Russian relations. The outbreak of the Sino-Japanese War some three months before Nicholas came to the throne began a period of instability in the Far East that provided the focus of Anglo-Russian relations for the next decade. Nicholas's abdication in 1917 occurred just months before the Bolshevik revolution ended Anglo-Russian relations and ushered in a new era of Anglo-Soviet relations.

The chronological portion is divided into two sections: Part II covers the period from 1894 to 1905 and Part III deals with the period from 1905 to the end of the Romanov dynasty in 1917. This division was made for two reasons. First, from 1894 to 1905, Anglo-Russian relations were strained, while from 1905 to 1917 Anglo-Russian relations were much improved (although still occasionally tense). Second, Anglo-Russian relations in the first period focused primarily in the Far East, while relations in the second period centred on Persia and the Balkans. The Russo-Japanese War and the events in Russia that accompanied it were both the cause of this shift and the reason for the thaw in Anglo-Russian relations. Utilizing this point of division also has yielded a certain serendipity. The end of the Russo-Japanese War roughly coincided with the end of the Unionist government in Britain and the coming to power of the Liberals. Therefore, the bulk of Part II of *Britain and the Last Tsar* examines relations between Russia and a Unionist government, while Part III deals with relations between Russia and a Liberal government.

This is a long book, and it is perhaps useful to outline here some of its conclusions. The first, mentioned above, is that Russia was the most significant long-term threat to British interests in the twenty years before the First World War and that a driving force—perhaps *the* driving force—in British diplomacy was the effort to reach an accommodation with Russia. The Anglo-German antagonism here is relegated to the status of a short-term threat to Britain, of major—but not exclusive—importance in the period after 1906. The coming of the First World War is not regarded as the inevitable outcome of pre-war diplomacy, nor is it assumed that foreign policy makers shaped their policy with full foreknowledge of the war. Britain is not regarded here as a nation in decline, whose foreign policy was determined by the need to commit herself to alliances to meet the challenge posed by the rising power of Germany, but rather as the pre-eminent global power, whose foreign policy was determined by her worldwide interests.[5]

Looked at from this vantage point, the standard interpretations of British foreign policy fade away like the Cheshire cat. Events take on a new appearance. The Anglo-Japanese Alliance becomes an anti-Russian agreement, whose naval considerations were shaped by the dictates of naval technology and doctrine, not naval

[5] I have made this argument elsewhere, and it is implicit throughout what follows: see K. Neilson, ' "Greatly Exaggerated": The Myth of the Decline of Great Britain before 1914', *IHR* 13 (1991), 695–725.

weakness. The Entente Cordiale with France was not an anti-German arrangement for the British, but one designed to end colonial frictions with France and made in the hope of attaining some measure of indirect influence over Russia. The first Moroccan crisis, when considered in the context of the Russo-Japanese War, was less significant for the way in which it underlined the solidarity of the Anglo-French entente against Germany and more significant for the way in which it definitively tipped Russia away from Germany and towards Britain. The Anglo-Russian Convention of 1907 was neither a departure in British foreign policy, nor a sign of the formation of a Triple Entente aimed at the Triple Alliance. Instead, it was the culmination of British efforts stretching back at least to 1894 to reach an agreement with Russia. It was the change in *Russian* foreign policy following the Russo-Japanese War that resulted in Britain's overtures to Russia finally being accepted. Further, 1907 did not usher in a period when Europe was frozen into a pattern where Triple Alliance faced Triple Entente, with both sides awaiting the inevitable war. Instead, Anglo-Russian relations soured progressively towards 1914. Only the outbreak of the war prevented a likely breakdown of the Convention and a possible return to a period of Anglo-Russian diplomatic hostility.

My insistence on the importance of Russia for British foreign policy is not completely novel. Several recent works in German, albeit for widely differing reasons, also have done so.[6] So, too, has the work of Keith Wilson.[7] However, *Britain and the Last Tsar* approaches the subject from rather a different perspective than do these studies, and, for reasons both methodological and interpretative, does not support many of their conclusions.[8] For example, it requires neither '[t]he invention of Germany' nor the existence of a two-faced Sir Edward Grey to argue for the primacy of Russia in British foreign policy.[9] It will be for the reader to decide whether my argument for the centrality of Russia is more convincing and my appreciation of Germany's role in British policy more satisfactory.

The above outlines what *Britain and the Last Tsar* intends, but it is perhaps as important to indicate what it does *not* intend. The book is not a balanced look at

---

[6] See, for example, K. Wormer, *Grossbritannien, Russland und Deutschland: Studien zur britischen Weltreichspolitik am Vorabend des Ersten Weltkriegs* (Munich, 1980) who argues the domestic political reasons for Britain to follow a policy of coming to terms with Russia and E. Hölzle, *Die Selbstentmachtung Europas: Das Experiment des Friedens vor und im Ersten Weltkrieg* (Göttingen, 1975) who emphasizes that Britain refused to restrain Russia in Europe in order to protect British Imperial interests. For this reason, Hölzle argues, Britain must share in the blame for the origins of the First World War.

[7] Most comprehensively in his *The Policy of the Entente: Essays on the Determinants of British Foreign Policy, 1904–1914* (Cambridge, 1985). Many of his articles listed below in the bibliography also argue in this direction.

[8] I return to these matters in the conclusion.

[9] The quotation is a chapter title in Wilson, *Policy of the Entente*; the concept of a malevolent Grey is the thrust of Wilson's chapter, 'Grey' in id. (ed.), *British Foreign Secretaries and Foreign Policy: From Crimean War to First World War* (London, 1987), 172–97.

Anglo-Russian relations. For reasons of space, sources, and personal preference, *Britain and the Last Tsar* focuses on Britain's policy towards Russia and on how and why that policy was formulated. As a result, Russia's policy towards Britain is here presented in two guises: first, as the policy that British contemporaries suspected Russia of pursuing; second, as the policy that subsequent scholarship has suggested Russia actually pursued. The juxtaposition of the two occasionally suggests both some ideas about Russian foreign policy and some judgments on the secondary literature about it; however, I leave the wider issue of the interpretation of Russian foreign policy to pens sharper than mine.[10]

There are several standard technical concerns when dealing with Russian history. With respect to transliteration, in general I have employed the Library of Congress system, although I have omitted diacritical marks. Nor have I always used the Library of Congress system. For example, I have not changed the spelling of Russian names in contemporary quotations and, when a Russian name has a well-known form in English, I have utilised the latter at the expense of consistency. With respect to dates, as this is primarily a study of British foreign policy towards Russia, all are given in the Gregorian calendar despite the fact that Russia employed the Julian calendar throughout the reign of Nicholas II. Those who prefer their Russian history free from such anachronism may subtract the requisite twelve days for dates in the nineteenth century and thirteen days for dates in the twentieth century.

---

[10] In particular, D. Geyer, *Russian Imperialism: The Interaction of Domestic and Foreign Policy, 1860–1914*, trans. B. Little (Leamington Spa, 1987), which also introduces the earlier literature. D. M. McDonald, *United Government and Foreign Policy in Russia, 1900–14* (Cambridge, MA, 1992) is important in itself, and discusses and evaluates subsequent work.

PART I

SETTING THE STAGE

I

Power and Personality

BRITISH policy toward Russia in the period from 1894 to 1917 was made by a small group of men, who constituted the foreign-policy-making élite.[1] This group had several levels, from senior politicians to shapers of public opinion. In between were officials at the Foreign Office, diplomatists, various military and naval officers, bankers, businessmen, and academics. This élite was not solely concerned with Russia, for they directed British foreign policy generally. Foreign policy making was centred in the Cabinet and determined almost exclusively by the secretary of state for foreign affairs. However, his ability to make policy depended upon his relative authority within the Cabinet and, in particular, upon his relationship with the prime minister. Often enough, other ministers exercised a telling influence. The chancellor of the exchequer frequently had a significant voice when foreign policy decisions had important financial implications. So, too, did the service ministers, since foreign policy often needed the backing of force. In addition, the central position that India played in Anglo-Russian relations meant that the secretary of state for India was also a major figure. Of course, others in the Cabinet could affect foreign policy upon occasion. In the twenty years before the First World War, a prime example was Joseph Chamberlain, colonial secretary from 1895 to 1903. Less frequently, groups of MPs outside the Cabinet, such as the Radical wing of the Liberal party, also had an impact on foreign policy, although this influence was generally transitory or else mediated through sympathetic Cabinet members.

The second level of decision-making involved the civil servants, primarily in the Foreign Office but occasionally in other departments of state, who provided ministers with advice and information. At the Foreign Office, Russia was the province of the Eastern Department, headed by a senior clerk and manned by a handful of junior clerks. The Eastern Department, however, was just one of a number of departments in the Foreign Office. Above the Eastern Department's senior

[1] D. C. Watt, *What About the People? Abstractions and Reality in History and the Social Sciences* (London, 1983); Z. Steiner, *The Foreign Office and Foreign Policy 1898–1914* (Cambridge, 1969). The concept of the foreign-policy-making élite is derived from D. C. Watt, 'The nature of the foreign-policy making élite in Britain', in id., *Personalities and Politics: Studies in the Formulation of British Foreign Policy in the Twentieth Century* (London, 1965), 1–15.

clerk was an assistant under-secretary, and above him was the permanent under-secretary (PUS), who was the chief civil servant at the Foreign Office and the man who dealt directly with the secretary of state.

The British representatives in Russia were the third level of the foreign-policy-making élite. The British ambassador at St Petersburg and his staff gathered a wide range of information about Russia and helped to shape perceptions of Russia, since they could decide what information was important and how it should be presented to London. Further, the diplomatic staff implemented and evaluated British policy at St Petersburg.

The fourth level of this élite stood outside the charmed circle of government. Because Russia was beyond the normal experience of politicians and Britons generally, British policy towards Russia was influenced by an eclectic group of authorities. These 'old Russia hands' possessed an expertise concerning Russia as a result of various circumstances: long residence, linguistic aptitude, specialized study, business dealings, and so on.[2] They reported, usually informally, about Russia to the other members of the élite and helped to create the interpretative sieve through which that information was strained.[3] This group also helped to shape the public's views of Russia with books and articles and, thus, to set limits on what was publically acceptable for Britain's policy towards Russia.

THE POLITICIANS

Between 1894 and 1917, Britain had six different prime ministers, and five different foreign secretaries. However, two of the prime ministers, Lord Rosebery and David Lloyd George, each held that office for only one year in this period as did their foreign secretaries, respectively Lord Kimberley and Arthur Balfour. The period thus may be divided into two sections: the years of Unionist government, from mid-1895 to the end of 1905, and then the years of Liberal government to the end of 1916. In this twenty-one-year span, foreign policy was the central responsibility of four men: Lord Salisbury, as prime minister from 1895 to 1902 and foreign secretary from 1895 to 1900; Lord Lansdowne, as foreign secretary from November 1900 to December 1905; Arthur Balfour, as prime minister from 1902 to 1905, and Sir Edward Grey as foreign secretary from 1905 to 1916. Their views of Russia and Britain's relations with her are thus central to an understanding of Anglo-Russian relations, but it would be wrong to ignore either Lord Kimberley,

---

[2] The obvious example of this was China; see N. A. Pelcovits, *Old China Hands and the Foreign Office* (2nd edn.; New York, 1969).

[3] K. Neilson, *Strategy and Supply: The Anglo-Russian Alliance 1914–17* (London, 1984), 1–42.

foreign secretary from March 1894 to June 1895, or Arthur Balfour, who succeeded Grey in December 1916.

Kimberley's year as foreign secretary was the culmination of a long career, much of it concerned with Russia. During the Crimean War, he had served as under-secretary of state for foreign affairs in both Aberdeen's coalition government and Palmerston's first ministry. In 1856, he was appointed British minister to St Petersburg, a post he held until 1858. As secretary of state for India from 1882 to 1885, Kimberley was prominent in the decision to resist Russian encroachments in Afghanistan, the so-called Penjdeh crisis. The India Office was Kimberley's portfolio twice more (February to August 1886 and 1892 to 1894), and in the latter period another quarrel with Russia—the Pamirs crisis—was centre stage.

Rosebery's career was intimately linked with that of Kimberley from the latter's time as secretary of state for India. Almost twenty years Kimberley's junior, Rosebery became foreign secretary in Gladstone's brief government in 1886 and held that post again from 1892 until Gladstone resigned in 1894. At that point, Rosebery succeeded to the premiership and Kimberley became foreign secretary. While Rosebery's experience of Russia was shorter than Kimberley's, it had been intense. In 1886, Rosebery had inherited the dangerous Bulgarian situation from Salisbury, and, like his predecessor, decided to support Bulgarian unification against Russia's wishes. When this policy succeeded, the Russians declared that the port of Batoum was no longer open to the commerce of all nations and would be fortified, both moves in contradiction of the Treaty of Berlin. For Rosebery, the act's symbolic significance far outweighed its actual import.[4] He was not willing to bend to Russian pressure in the Near East: his response was firm and immediate; the Russian response was capitulation.

When Gladstone formed his last government in 1892, Rosebery again became foreign secretary. He was immediately faced with the Pamirs boundary crisis. Relatively trivial in itself, the dispute was tied up with the new diplomatic situation in Europe resulting from the Franco-Russian rapprochement. If Russian incursions were to be resisted, the British had to decide not only whether this was best done through the application of military force on the Indian frontier or by diplomatic threat in Europe, but also whether the latter alternative still existed.[5] The growth of the Russian Black Sea fleet and the possibility of the French fleet being added to the equation meant that Rosebery needed a new policy. He adopted one of bluff and bluster. Britain threatened to send an expedition to the Pamirs. The result was a signal success, although a settlement was not signed until early in 1895.

[4] G. Martel, *Imperial Diplomacy: Rosebery and the Failure of Foreign Policy* (Kingston, Ont., 1986), 50.
[5] Martel, *Imperial Diplomacy*, 68–72.

But, by the time that Kimberley became foreign secretary in 1894, Rosebery's policy of avoiding a dependence on either the Triple Alliance or the Franco-Russian grouping was difficult to adopt. Increasing tension between Britain and Germany forced Rosebery and Kimberley to focus their efforts on establishing better relations with Russia. As Rosebery wrote early in 1895, with the Pamirs settlement clearly in sight: 'It is a great pleasure to begin a new and clean slate with Russia, and I am determined to work loyally with her so long as she will let me.'[6] The end of Rosebery's government six months later left moot the question of whether that could happen.

When Salisbury returned to office in 1895, he did so after a long career in foreign policy, much of it concerned with Russia.[7] He had been secretary of state for India from 1874 to 1878 and foreign secretary three times (April 1878 to April 1880, June 1885 to January 1886 and January 1887 to June 1892) and prime minister twice (June 1885 to January 1886 and August 1886 to June 1892). In each instance, relations with Russia had been a principal focus of British foreign policy. While at the India Office, Salisbury had pushed to establish indirect control over Afghanistan as a bulwark against Russian expansion towards India.[8] At the Congress of Berlin in 1878, Salisbury's goal had been to prop up the Ottoman Empire by limiting the size of Bulgaria, by taking Cyprus for Britain and by reforming the government of Egypt.[9] The first two goals put British foreign policy firmly in opposition to that of Russia. But Salisbury was adamant that Russia must be blocked and formulated his policy on the basis of co-operation with other Powers, particularly Austria-Hungary.

When he returned to office—this time as both prime minister and foreign secretary—in June 1885, Salisbury did so in the midst of the crisis with Russia involving the Afghan border town of Penjdeh.[10] To protect British interests and to deflect criticism from his government, Salisbury turned once more to co-operation with a Great Power—this time, Germany—to halt Russian encroachment. The

---

[6] Rosebery to Lascelles, 6 Jan. 1895, Lascelles Papers, FO 800/16.

[7] Lord Blake and H. Cecil (eds.), *Salisbury: The Man and his Policies* (London, 1987) introduces the literature; see especially the contribution of A. N. Porter, 'Lord Salisbury, Foreign Policy and Domestic Finance, 1860–1900,' 148–84.

[8] J. L. Duthie, 'Some Further Insights into the Working of Mid-Victorian Imperialism: Lord Salisbury, the "Forward" Group and Anglo-Afghan Relations: 1874–1878', *JICH* 8 (1980), 181–208; his 'Pragmatic Diplomacy or Imperial Encroachment?: British Policy towards Afghanistan, 1874–9', *IHR* 5 (1983), 475–95.

[9] C. J. Lowe, *The Reluctant Imperialists* (2 vols.; London, 1967), i. 22–43; B. Williams, 'The Approach to the Second Afghan War: Central Asia during the Great Eastern Crisis, 1875–8'; *IHR* 2 (1980), 216–38.

[10] R. L. Greaves, *Persia and the Defence of India 1884–92: A Study in the Foreign Policy of the Third Marquis of Salisbury* (London, 1959), 70–84.

opportunistic nature of Salisbury's policy towards Russia showed especially clearly in the Bulgarian crisis in the autumn of 1885. Realizing that Bulgaria was a barrier against Russian incursions into the Ottoman empire, Salisbury reversed the stand that he had taken in 1878, and supported the unification of Bulgaria. In his third tenure as foreign secretary, Salisbury would be again faced by Russia. The issue, the limitation of Russian influence in the Ottoman Empire, was the same as it had been in 1878 and 1885, but changed circumstances—the British occupation of Egypt in 1882 and the new Bulgarian situation—meant that Salisbury needed a new diplomacy.[11] By concluding the Mediterranean Agreements in 1887, he was able to work closely with Italy—and, by extension, with the Triple Alliance which Germany and Austria-Hungary formed with Italy—to ensure that Russia would not predominate over the Ottoman Empire in the eastern Mediterranean.

Salisbury's last term in office continued the pattern of controlling Russian expansion. Armenia was the issue. What Salisbury wanted to do was clear. As he told Sir Thomas Sanderson, the PUS, 'the great problem of modern diplomacy— [is] how to exclude the Turk from any kind of power in provinces of the Turkish Empire, while strenuously maintaining its independence & integrity.'[12] Russia was central to the issue. But, circumstances had changed since the 1880s. By 1895, because of changes both in technology and in the relative strength of the British fleet, it was impracticable for the British to force the Straits. As a result, coercing the Turks, or threatening coercion, depended on the concurrence of allies. While in his previous dealings with Russia, Salisbury had found other Powers willing to work with Britain to counter St Petersburg, Germany was now hostile to intervention, unless Britain were willing to commit herself formally to a wider anti-Russian coalition, and Austro-Hungarian support blew hot and cold. Russia's own diplomatic position had strengthened; the 1894 agreement ensured that France would not support any measure that Russia opposed. With a Cabinet that shrank from using force against the Porte, Salisbury was denied the means to bend the Turks to his will. The result was failure.

Finally, but not least, Britain's interests clashed directly with those of Russia in the Far East. Because France, Germany, and Russia had combined in 1896 to limit the extent of Japan's victory over China—the so-called triple intervention—Britain found herself without European allies in her attempts to limit *Russian* advances in Korea and the Liaotung peninsula. Given this, Salisbury realized he had to come to terms with Russia diplomatically. He certainly did not expect any altruism in Russian foreign policy. He thought Russian intentions in the Far East were positively acquisitive: 'Of course she intends to swallow Corea if she can: & we

---

[11] C. J. Lowe, *Salisbury and the Mediterranean 1886–96* (London, 1965), 1–25.
[12] Salisbury to Sanderson, 23 Apr. 1897, Sanderson Papers, FO 800/2.

cannot stop her by "representations" at St P. Much stiffer instruments will be required.'[13] It was with an awareness that such 'stiffer instruments' were in short supply that Salisbury opened his ill-fated negotiations with Russia in 1897. But Salisbury's hold over his Cabinet was weakening due to his own illness. Early in 1898 he was obliged to turn over foreign affairs, and the duties of the premiership generally, to his nephew, Arthur Balfour. Balfour and some other members of the Cabinet, Joseph Chamberlain among them, preferred to attempt to block Russia in the Far East rather than to negotiate.[14] This led to a collapse of the Anglo-Russian negotiations. Upon his resumption of duties Salisbury immediately repudiated Balfour's initiatives and renewed Anglo-Russian negotiations, albeit for a more limited agreement.[15]

Salisbury's last two years as foreign secretary were marked by a growing pessimism and what many perceived as a policy of drift. Even before the outbreak of the Boer War, with its paralysing effect on British foreign policy, colleagues noticed that the Foreign Office were becoming 'difficult to deal with' as they had '[n]o clear and definite policy before them, except it be to keep the peace'.[16] Only Salisbury's 'position, reputation, and intellectual subtlety . . . makes it possible for him to carry on this form of diplomacy with an authority and apparent success that a lesser man could not attempt'. Much of this undoubtedly resulted from personal matters, including Lady Salisbury's lingering illness and subsequent death in 1899. But some of Salisbury's attitude grew out of an awareness that Britain's international position was weakening, and that this would affect her diplomacy. In 1901 he observed that the British unwillingness to spend money and the growing influence of other powers overseas would cause British influence to decline.[17] Notably, Salisbury did not advocate increased expenditures to support foreign policy initiatives. In fact, he opposed any raising of taxes, for this could be done at the expense only of the rich.[18] Salisbury realized the limitations that parsimony placed on Britain's power. Certainly, Sanderson felt that such considerations were at the bottom of Salisbury's policy towards Russia in 1897–98. As the former PUS remarked, on the eve of the signing of the 1907 Anglo-Russian Convention, about Salisbury's earlier initiative: 'The reason [for it] is an obvious one—the process of working in constant antagonism is too expensive.'[19]

[13] Salisbury's undated minute on Bertie to Salisbury, 6 Nov. 1897, Bertie Papers, FO 800/176.

[14] J. A. S. Grenville, *Lord Salisbury and Foreign Policy: The Close of the Nineteenth Century* (London, 1964), 145–7.

[15] Salisbury to Balfour, 9 Apr. 1898, Balfour Papers, Add MSS 49697; Grenville, *Lord Salisbury*, 146.

[16] Hamilton (secretary of state for India) to Curzon (viceroy, India), 17 Aug. 1899, Curzon Papers, MSS Eur F111/158.

[17] Salisbury to Curzon, 23 Sept. 1901, Curzon Papers, MSS Eur F111/223.

[18] Porter, 'Lord Salisbury, Foreign Policy and Domestic Finance, 1860–1900', 148–84.

[19] Sanderson to Spring Rice, 6 Aug. 1907, Spring Rice Papers, FO 800/241.

Salisbury's foreign policy with respect to Russia must be seen in the context of his foreign policy generally.[20] He was no exponent of 'splendid isolation' and held no illusions about Russia.[21] He tried to work within the existing state system to protect Britain's interests. For Salisbury, foreign affairs had to reflect the realities both of power and of domestic circumstances. Britain had been compelled to oppose Russia in certain situations and for the achievement of certain goals. In the period from 1895 to 1900, Salisbury achieved only limited success in his policy towards Russia. It would be up to others to see whether they could do more.

The general success of his first successor, Lord Lansdowne, in resetting British policy towards Russia was a feat of no mean proportion. Lansdowne was foreign secretary from November 1900 to December 1905, coming directly from the War Office, where he had presided over the first year of the British war effort against the Boers.[22] Lansdowne had ample experience of Anglo-Russian relations before coming to the Foreign Office. He had been viceroy of India from 1888 to 1893, and his knowledge of Russian affairs had led to Rosebery's offering him the ambassadorship to Russia in December 1893. While Lansdowne's emergence as foreign secretary was not met with wide public approval, it found at least limited favour within the hierarchy at the India Office. Lord George Hamilton, the secretary of state for India, stressed that the Foreign Office under Lansdowne would give 'prompt' replies, a welcome change from the situation in the last years of Salisbury's tenure.[23]

Lansdowne inherited two main difficulties in British relations with Russia. The first concerned the Far East. While joint European intervention had been necessary to deal with the Boxer rebellion, the subsequent Russian refusal to evacuate from China was a constant menace. The second concerned Persia, where Russian attempts to gain predominance threatened the north-west frontier. But it was not until late in 1901 that Lansdowne could turn away from the maintenance of Britain's position during the Boer War to shore up Britain's global position generally. There were a number of options available. In the autumn of 1901, the possibility of some sort of arrangement with each of Germany, Russia, and Japan was considered. The German card had been considered before but had proven to be

---

[20] For a brief survey of Salisbury's foreign policy, D. Gillard, 'Salisbury', in Wilson, K. (ed.), *British Foreign Secretaries and Foreign Policy: From Crimean War to First World War* (London, 1987), 119–37.

[21] It is doubtful whether 'splendid isolation' ever really existed; C. H. D. Howard, *Splendid Isolation: A Study of Ideas Concerning Britain's International Position and Foreign Policy During the Later Years of the Third Marquis of Salisbury* (London, 1967).

[22] On Lansdowne as foreign secretary, G. Monger, *The End of Isolation: British Foreign Policy 1900–7* (London, 1963). P. J. V. Rollo, 'Lord Lansdowne', in Wilson, K. (ed.), *British Foreign Secretaries*, 159–71, is superficial; the only biography, Lord Newton, *Lord Lansdowne* (London, 1929) is dated. The literature is introduced in B. J. C. McKercher, 'Diplomatic Equipoise: The Lansdowne Foreign Office, the Russo-Japanese War of 1904–5, and the Global Balance of Power' *CJH* 24 (1984), 299–339.

[23] Hamilton to Curzon, 8 Nov. 1900, Curzon Papers, MSS Eur F111/147.

unplayable.[24] It was with this in mind that Lansdowne simultaneously pursued coming to terms with either Japan or Russia. His efforts emerged out of a re-consideration of British policy in the region. Lord Selborne, the first lord of the admiralty, had produced a paper on the 'Balance of Naval Power in the Far East'.[25] In it, he argued that an Anglo-Japanese alliance would allow Britain to maintain a safe naval margin over the combined Franco-Russian fleet in the Far East. This could be done without Britain's having either to move naval forces to those waters or to increase the size of her fleet, an important financial consideration. With this in mind, Lansdowne renewed the earlier negotiations with Japan and began new ones with Russia. The latter failed, collapsing essentially over the issue of a joint loan to Persia, while the former ended with the signing of the Anglo-Japanese alliance early in 1902. But, the idea of a Russian arrangement had not been discard-ed by Lansdowne. In the latter months of 1903, with tension increasing in the Far East, concern growing about the state of Macedonia and revolt on Crete, Lansdowne was only too ready to agree to a Russian proposal to begin wide-ranging discussions.[26]

The negotiations of 1903 did not come to fruition. The outbreak of the Russo-Japanese war meant that Lansdowne's focus was now on maintaining a strict neutrality, while not harming Britain's own vital interests—her position in China and the principle of freedom of the seas. The tensions in Anglo-Russian relations caused by the war, and the poor showing of the Russians in the fighting, made Lansdowne more cautious about discussing any arrangement with Russia. Further, as he told the British ambassador to Paris, any understanding with Russia, while not 'impossible', would be difficult as the 'Russian diplomatic currency has become debased and discredited'.[27] The chaos in Russia in the autumn of 1905, meant that Anglo-Russian negotiations could not progress. Lansdowne's own time in office also was coming to an end, as the Liberals seemed likely to win the elections scheduled for December. In these circumstances, Lansdowne tried to preserve his Russian policy.[28] He did this by confirming that Sir Charles Hardinge would become PUS when Sanderson retired at the beginning of 1906 and by appointing Sir Arthur Nicolson to succeed Hardinge at St Petersburg.[29] Both diplomats were

[24] P. M. Kennedy, 'German World Policy and the Alliance Negotiations with England, 1897–1900', *JMH* 45 (1973), 605–25.

[25] 'Balance of Naval Power in the Far East', Selborne, 4 Sept. 1901, Cab 37/58/81.

[26] Lansdowne to Spring Rice (British chargé d'affaires, St Petersburg), confidential, desp. 307, 7 Nov. 1903; Lansdowne to Spring Rice, very confidential desp. 334, 25 Nov. 1903, both FO 65/1658. The Cabinet authorized 'informal' talks on 16 Nov.: Balfour to the King of that date, Sandars Papers, MS Eng. hist. *c.*715.

[27] Lansdowne to Bertie, 19 Jan. 1905, Lansdowne Papers, FO 800/126.

[28] Wilson, K., *The Policy of the Entente: Essays on the Determinants of British Foreign Policy, 1904–14* (Cambridge, 1985), 17–20.

[29] Steiner, *Foreign Office and Foreign Policy*, 70–82; K. Neilson, ' "My Beloved Russians": Sir Arthur Nicolson and Russia, 1906–16' *IHR* 9 (1987), 524–5.

strongly in favour of an Anglo-Russian understanding, and their offices should ensure that their views were known to and given consideration by Lansdowne's successor. In addition, Lansdowne lobbied to ensure that Grey, whose views on foreign policy were favourable to a continuation of Lansdowne's policies would become foreign secretary in a Liberal government.

In fact, Sir Edward Grey became foreign secretary in December 1905 at the relatively young age of forty-three. Grey and his policy have remained as enigmatic to historians as they were to his contemporaries.[30] In contrast to Salisbury and Lansdowne, whose careers before taking on the Foreign Office had been concerned largely with Russia as Britain's principal rival, Grey's period as parliamentary under-secretary for foreign affairs from 1892 to 1895 was filled with colonial quarrels with Germany and France.[31] For Grey, the lessons of those years were clear: Britain's position as a global power could best be maintained through the balance of power and this balance seemed to depend on Russia. While in opposition, Grey made his preference for an arrangement with Russia clear. During the Armenian crisis of 1895, he argued that 'a bold & skilful Foreign Secretary might detach Russia from the number of our active enemies without sacrificing any very material British interests.'[32] During the debate in 1899 over Anglo-Russian relations in China, Grey noted that 'I shall never believe that a Russian understanding about the Far East is impossible, till I see it proved in black & white'.[33]

Grey had done well as parliamentary under-secretary.[34] Even when there was criticism from his fellow Liberals over his firm stance against French encroachments on the Upper Nile in 1895, Rosebery supported him.[35] Grey had also impressed the members of the Foreign Office with whom he worked. Towards the end of Unionist rule, as rumours abounded as to who would be the Liberals' foreign secretary, Grey was the first choice at the Foreign Office. Valentine Chirol, the foreign editor of *The Times* and formerly a member of the Foreign Office, wrote to Sir Charles Hardinge, the British ambassador at St Petersburg, that the Foreign Office would 'have a jolly time if its [the Liberal party's] radical tail wags the next

---

[30] For Grey, K. Robbins, *Sir Edward Grey: A Biography of Lord Grey of Fallodon* (London, 1971), replacing G. M. Trevelyan, *Grey of Fallodon* (London, 1948). Grey's foreign policy in Hinsley, F. H. (ed.), *British Foreign Policy Under Sir Edward Grey* (Cambridge, 1977). Revisionism in K. Wilson, 'Grey', in id. (ed.), *British Foreign Secretaries*, 172–97; some of the articles in K. Wilson, *Empire and Continent: Studies in British Foreign Policy from the 1880s to the First World War* (London, 1987); Wilson, *Policy of the Entente*.

[31] Lowe, *Reluctant Imperialists*, i. 166–95; Martel, *Imperial Diplomacy*.

[32] Grey to Buxton, 31 Dec. 1895, cited, H. C. G. Matthew, *The Liberal Imperialists: The Ideas and Politics of a Post-Gladstonian Élite* (London, 1973), 204.

[33] Grey to Brodrick (Unionist parliamentary under-secretary for foreign affairs), 11 Mar. 1899, Midleton Papers, PRO 30/67/4; Selborne to Curzon, 23 Mar. 1899, Curzon Papers, MSS Eur F111/229.

[34] Robbins, *Grey*, 38–55.

[35] Rosebery to Kimberley, 2 Apr. 1895, Rosebery Papers 10070; Martel, *Imperial Diplomacy*, 237–41.

administration', but also noted that 'of course if he [Grey] & his friends were certain to rule the roost . . . there would not be much cause for anxiety'.[36] Louis Mallet, Lansdowne's précis writer, was similarly optimistic. Grey, Mallet noted, believed in the continuity of foreign policy.[37] Grey did so even at the risk of breaking with Rosebery. While Rosebery argued in opposition that the Anglo-French Entente was not good policy, Grey did not. 'Edward Grey', Chirol wrote in September 1905, 'at any rate says quite openly that Rosebery's views about the entente have made him quite impossible for the F.O. & that it is absurd to propose that a Liberal Govt. will drop the French entente which has always been a Liberal rather than a Conservative plank.'[38] On another occasion, Mallet put it more simply: 'Of course Grey is quite sound.'[39]

Grey took office in troublous times. Russia was in chaos and Europe was in the midst of the Moroccan crisis. Just eleven days after coming to office, Grey made it clear that he saw Russia as a key to bringing order to Europe. Writing to the British first secretary at St Petersburg, Grey noted that he hoped that Russia's domestic unrest would soon end, as 'I want to see Russia re-established in the councils of Europe, and I hope on better terms with us than she has been yet'.[40] In January 1906, when the Algeciras conference opened, Grey did not hide his views concerning either Germany's intentions or Russia's importance. Writing to Sir Arthur Nicolson, the British representative at Algeciras, on 12 February, Grey doubted whether Germany wanted a diplomatic solution, 'which is acceptable to France on the lines of our Entente with her', as such a solution 'would be regarded as a diplomatic defeat of Germany'.[41] He was optimistic about France's position, an optimism that hinged on Russia: 'in any case time may be on the side of France; for the recovery of Russia will change the situation in Europe to the advantage of France; and it is the situation in Europe that will in the long run decide the position of France & Germany in Morocco.' Grey concluded on a positive note: 'I am in hopes that when Russia recovers we may get & keep on good terms with her; if so this also will count on the side of France.'

Over the course of the next twenty months, Grey and his advisors achieved the foreign secretary's goal of getting on 'good terms' with Russia by signing the Anglo-Russian Convention in August 1907. It was not an easy task. Grey's efforts were complicated by the instability in Russia and by those in his own party who disliked Russia on principle. Even small gestures of Anglo-Russian goodwill, such

[36] Chirol to Hardinge, 24 July 1905, Hardinge Papers, vol. 7.
[37] Mallet to Sandars (Balfour's private secretary), 21? Mar. 1905, Sandars Papers, MS Eng. hist. c.749.
[38] Chirol to Lascelles (British ambassador, Berlin), 17 Sept. 1905, Lascelles Papers, FO 800/12.
[39] Mallet to Hardinge, 4 Apr. 1905, Hardinge Papers, vol. 7.
[40] Grey to Spring Rice, 22 Dec. 1905, Spring Rice Papers, FO 800/241.
[41] Grey to Nicolson, 12 Feb. 1906, Nicolson Papers, FO 800/338.

as the proposed visit of the fleet to Russia in 1906, raised some British hackles.[42] While Grey was alive to such feeling, he did not allow it to undermine his policy. For example, when Edward VII paid a visit to Nicholas II at Reval in June 1908, Grey took little notice of such worthies as the International Arbitration and Peace Association (Inc), who wrote to the foreign secretary that they 'emphatically repudiate[d] the doctrine that the internal affairs of a country have nothing to do with this country's relations to it'.[43] Grey noted wryly that '[t]hey lay themselves open to the retort that they either have not read my speech or cannot understand it, but it is better to leave them alone'.

The challenge was more serious when such criticisms surfaced in the Cabinet or among his own party in Parliament. Grey was not optimistic that he could convince his opponents either of the necessity of dealing with Russia or of the rough-and-tumble nature of international politics generally.[44] In private correspondence and conversation with leading Liberals and with those who had an opportunity to shape Liberal public opinion, Grey endeavoured to show that his policy was principled, practical, and pacific. When the Liberal chief whip, the Master of Elibank, returned from a visit to Russia in 1909, Grey wrote to him that 'I am sure that things in Russia are improving', but cautioned that 'it is no use expecting too much in a short time'.[45] Still, Grey concluded: 'As long as they [affairs in Russia] are moving in the right direction, that is something to the good, and we should recognize it when we can.' On another occasion, he took pains to convey to C. P. Scott, the influential editor of the liberal *Manchester Guardian*, the essence of British Persian policy and argued that this policy would not result in, as some Liberals feared, an Anglo-Russian partition of Persia.[46]

Grey could also be firm with his critics. When Lewis Harcourt, the colonial secretary, complained in January 1914 that Grey's use of the term 'Triple Entente' implied a closer relationship with France and Russia than existed, Grey did not give an inch.[47] After informing Harcourt that no such implication existed and, indeed, that the lack of definite British support for Russia was a sore point for the latter, Grey made a veiled threat: 'I begin to think there is more divergence of view between us about Foreign policy than I had thought, but if any decision is necessary I will bring it before the Cabinet before taking any step that commits the Cabinet to action.'[48] This hint of making the issue a clash of political wills sent Harcourt scuttling. 'I am afraid I did not express myself well,' the colonial secretary re-

[42] Chirol to Nicolson, 3 July 1906, Nicolson Papers, FO 800/338.
[43] Their letter to Grey, 10 June 1908, FO 371/517/20641 and minutes.
[44] Grey to Sanderson, 12 Sept. 1908, Grey Papers, FO 800/111.
[45] Grey to Elibank, 1 Feb. 1909, Grey Papers, FO 800/90.
[46] Grey to C. P. Scott, 21 Sept. 1912, Grey Papers, FO 800/111.
[47] Robbins, *Grey*, 270–1.
[48] Grey to Harcourt, 11 Jan. 1914 and reply, Grey Papers, FO 800/91.

sponded meekly three days later, 'I have the most complete confidence in your action and intentions.' Grey's control of foreign policy and his relative strength in the Cabinet was clear.

Although Grey was regarded highly for his honesty and the simplicity of his character, he was not without a devious side. Russian affairs exposed this trait. 'Grey has constantly, during the past year', Sir Charles Hardinge, the PUS, wrote late in 1908, 'had to appear in the House of Commons as the advocate of the Russian Government. We have had to suppress the truth and to resort to subterfuge at times to meet hostile public opinion.'[49] Nor did Grey confine his efforts to suppressing the truth; he was not above doctoring it. Just before Nicholas II's visit to Cowes, Grey wrote to Sir Arthur Nicolson, the British ambassador at St Petersburg, that '[i]f there has been recently a marked falling off in the number of executions for political and other offenses and a general cessation of martial law throughout Russia, it would be desirable that you should address to me an official despatch on the subject'.[50] Nicolson's reply duly reported that the average Russian citizen was now less likely than before to be the victim of arbitrary action by the Russian government.[51] Given the prompting, Grey's minute on this report—'A very good & wise despatch'—seems ironical, if not cynical.

The foreign secretary was by no means a Russophile, and had no illusions about the nature of Russian government. When a prominent Russian statesman made some disparaging remarks in 1907 about the state of France, Grey's response was acerbic: 'Some of M. Kokovtsoff's [the Russian finance minister] criticisms upon France may be discounted by a Russian's natural incapacity to understand that a free country is not necessarily in a state of dissolution.'[52] Like most of those who made British policy, Grey hoped that Russia would reform herself politically, since a reactionary Russia made good Anglo-Russian relations difficult, whereas a reformed Russia would be both easier to deal with and a better-governed country. As he noted during the First World War, 'if the Emperor would only trust moderate & capable men he would make his country great and have the adoration of his people! The contrast between what he might do & what he is doing is intolerable.'[53] While some of this reflected a frustration with Russia's war effort and the effect that this might have on the Entente, it also stemmed from Grey's belief in the superiority of British institutions.

[49] Hardinge to Nicolson (British ambassador, St Petersburg), 28 Oct. 1908, Nicolson Papers, FO 800/341, excised from the pub. version; see Temperley, H. and Gooch, G. P. (eds.), B[ritish] D[ocuments on the Origins of the War, 1898–1914] (11 vols. in 13; London, 1926–38), v, doc. 414 (see BD hereafter).

[50] Grey to Nicolson, private tel., 8 June 1909, Grey Papers, FO 800/73.

[51] Nicolson to Grey, confidential disp. 376, 15 June 1909, FO 371/732/23026 and Grey's undated minute.

[52] Grey's undated minute on Nicolson to Grey, disp. 520, 14 Oct. 1907, FO 371/327/35455.

[53] Grey to Crewe, 24 July 1916, Crewe Papers, C/17.

Neither Grey nor Nicholas II lasted the war. In late 1916, Arthur Balfour became foreign secretary. Nearly seventy years old at the time, Balfour had enjoyed a long political career. He had been a mainstay of Salisbury's last government and had succeeded his uncle as prime minister in 1902, remaining in power until the end of 1905. Forced out as leader of the Unionist party in 1911, Balfour had acted as an informal conduit between Asquith's wartime Liberal government and the Opposition until 1915, when he became first lord of the admiralty in the coalition. When Asquith fell, Balfour became foreign secretary. But the position was much diminished. Balfour was not a member of Lloyd George's inner War Cabinet, and the Welshman had only disdain for traditional diplomacy. Besides, with Russia as an ally, Anglo–Russian relations were confined mainly to working out the mechanics of the military, economic, and financial co-operation necessary to win the war. Internal changes in Russia during 1917 left little scope for any initiatives in Anglo–Russian affairs beyond cautious efforts to ensure that Russia remained in the war.

But Balfour's tenure as foreign secretary was only a small phase of his time as a member of the élite. His impact on British policy towards Russia is best considered in another context: that of the relationship between foreign secretaries and their prime ministers. In each administration, this relationship was a different one. Both Kimberley and Balfour were overshadowed by a prime minister who tended to make his own foreign policy. As for Salisbury's time at the Foreign Office, he was his own prime minister. Thus, it is the relationship between Lansdowne and Balfour, and Grey and his two leaders that require further study.

That Lansdowne became foreign secretary in 1900 was no surprise. The 'Hotel Cecil', as detractors called the Cabinet that held two of Salisbury's nephews and his son-in-law, was noted for its social homogeneity.[54] Lansdowne, in addition to his extensive political experience and his obvious social standing, had close personal links to the Cecil family. He was a frequent guest at Hatfield and had attended Eton with Balfour, Salisbury's nephew. Lansdowne had, in fact, been 'fag master' to Balfour at Eton. The two men were close friends, and Balfour normally wrote to Lansdowne as 'my dear Clan', a salutation reflecting the fact that, while they were at Eton together, Lansdowne was Viscount Clanmaurice.

As prime minister, Balfour's focus was on the interlinked issues of foreign policy and national defence, on which he had strong opinions.[55] They were often expressed in his correspondence with Lansdowne. When Lansdowne outlined the proposed Anglo-Japanese alliance to the Cabinet in late 1901, Balfour reacted with a long disquisition, to which Lansdowne replied. Whereas Balfour's analysis was

[54] J. P. Cornford, 'The Parliamentary Foundations of the Hotel Cecil', in R. Robson (ed.), *Ideas and Institutions of Victorian Britain: Essays in Honour of George Kitson Clark* (London, 1967), 268–311.
[55] R. F. Mackay, *Balfour: Intellectual Statesman* (New York, 1985), 156–94; R. Williams, *Defending the Empire: The Conservative Party and British Defence Policy 1899–1915* (New Haven, 1991).

wide-reaching and general, Lansdowne's was much more limited and specific.[56]
The discussions between Balfour and Lansdowne on the eve of the Russo-Japanese
war concerning Britain's policy during such a conflict emphasize the fact that the
views of both Balfour and Lansdowne need to be considered when discussing
foreign policy in the period from 1902 to 1905.[57]

The situation from 1906 to 1916 was quite different. Neither Sir Henry Campbell Bannerman, prime minister from 1906 to 1908, nor Herbert Asquith, his
successor and prime minister to 1916, had a great interest in foreign affairs.[58] In
addition, Grey had a strong position within the Liberal party. He, Asquith and R.
B. Haldane (the secretary of state for war in the Liberal government) were the
essence of the imperialist faction in the party, and had agreed in September 1905
(the so-called Relugas compact) that either Grey or Rosebery must hold the foreign
secretaryship in any future government.[59] While Campbell-Bannerman's control
over the party was unshaken, the prominence of the Liberal imperialists was
sufficient to ensure that Grey's hold on the reins of foreign policy was a tight one.[60]
When Asquith became prime minister in 1908, Grey's position was strengthened;
criticism of, or influences on his foreign policy would come from either the Cabinet
or the party, not from the prime minister.

In addition to the foreign secretaries, both the secretary of state for India and the
viceroy had an important voice on Anglo-Russian relations. Two of the various
tandems of secretaries of state and viceroys in the period bear close scrutiny here.
The first was that between Lord George Hamilton (secretary of state for India from
1895 to 1903) and George Curzon (viceroy from 1898 to 1905). The second was
that between John Morley (secretary of state for India from 1905 to 1910) and Lord
Minto (viceroy from 1905 to 1910).

The Hamilton and Curzon combination was between two men who had differences of opinion about Russia and Russian intentions but worked closely together.
Their correspondence was both intimate and discursive on matters of policy. They
agreed on the untrustworthiness and low moral quality of Russian diplomacy. As
Hamilton put it in 1901 concerning Russia's assurances with respect to China: 'The
lying is unprecedented even in the annals of Russian diplomacy.'[61] Curzon put it
even more plainly and more generally: 'Russia's diplomacy', he wrote in 1903, 'as

---

[56] Lansdowne to Balfour, 12 Dec. 1901, Balfour Papers, Add MSS 49727.

[57] McKercher, 'Diplomatic Equipoise', 305–9.

[58] J. Wilson, *C. B.: a life of Sir Henry Campbell-Bannerman* (London, 1973); Roy Jenkins, *Asquith*
(2nd edn.; London, 1978).

[59] Wilson, *Policy of the Entente*, 20–2; T. Boyle, 'The Liberal Imperialists, 1892–1906', *BIHR* 52
(1979), 48–82 and Matthew, *Liberal Imperialists*.

[60] For Campbell-Bannerman's strength in the Liberal party; G. L. Bernstein, 'Sir Henry Campbell-
Bannerman and the Liberal Imperialists', *JBS* 23 (1983), 105–24; D. W. Gutzke, 'Rosebery and
Campbell-Bannerman: The Conflict over Leadership Reconsidered', *BIHR* 54 (1981), 241–50.

[61] Hamilton to Curzon, 15 Mar. 1901, Curzon Papers MSS Eur F111/148.

you know is one long and manifold lie.'[62] Curzon, among the élite the most consistent and outspoken critic of Russia, went further, condemning Russia's expansion in Asia in unsparing terms. Rejecting arguments that Russia, being semi-Asiatic herself, was better suited than other European powers to assimilate subject peoples, Curzon graphically described the Russian advances as follows: 'Russia hammers and slaughters . . . the violence, the drunkenness, and the lust of the Russians are a triple terror wherever they go.'[63]

However, the two differed on the policy that Britain should follow. On the whole, Hamilton believed that Russia's military star was rising. As he told Curzon in 1899, 'I have felt for a very long time past that we must, so far as Russia is concerned, acknowledge the changed conditions that the extension of railroads has made in the relative fighting power of Great Britain and of Russia . . . [and thus] any tug of war on land between Russia and England must result to our disadvantage'.[64] Given this, Hamilton argued, firmly and repeatedly, in favour of a territorial agreement with Russia.[65] But Curzon viewed the idea of an arrangement with Russia as a chimera and was not willing to accept Hamilton's contention that Russia was stronger than Britain.[66] In a typically outspoken letter in 1901, Curzon told the first lord of the admiralty that 'I should be prepared to meet & contest Russia on any field of conflict in the world: partly because I think her diplomacy blustering & bad, still more because, though I admit that She has every card of vantage in her possession, I should not fear to meet her forces, military or naval, in any part of the globe.'[67] Rather letting the metaphors get the better of him, Curzon made the same point to the permanent under-secretary at the India Office: 'I see no reason why we should tremble like an aspen leaf at every faint growl that emanates from the bear's den. Sometimes they are only the stertorous breathings of physical repletion and obesity, frequently the premeditated snarl that is merely intended to warn the rival denizens of the forest away.'[68] While Curzon's time in India would end on a sour note, he remained an acknowledged authority on India and Indian defence, even after 1905.

Minto and Morley, whose relationship was not always friendly, also differed on matters Russian. A devout disciple of Gladstone, Morley symbolized the great Liberal traditions, with a devotion to free trade and a belief that reasonable men could come to reasonable decisions. His reputation as the Liberal of the Liberals

---

[62] Curzon to Selborne, 4 May 1903, Selborne Papers 10.
[63] Curzon to Hamilton, 14 May 1903, Curzon Papers MSS Eur F111/162; R. K. I. Quested, *'Matey' Imperialists? The Tsarist Russians in Manchuria 1895–1917* (Hong Kong, 1982), 12–17.
[64] Hamilton to Curzon, 2 Nov. 1899, Curzon Papers, MSS Eur F111/144.
[65] Hamilton to Curzon, 7 Nov. 1901, 19 Feb. 1903, Curzon Papers, MSS Eur F111/150 and 162.
[66] Curzon to Lansdowne, 16 Mar. 1902, Curzon Papers, MSS Eur F111/161.
[67] Curzon to Selborne, 29 May 1901, Selborne Papers 10.
[68] Curzon to Godley, 23 Mar. 1905, Curzon Papers, MSS Eur F111/164.

was important in Anglo-Russian relations, for Morley's 'unimpeachable record', as Grey termed it, made him the only man who could defuse the Radicals' criticism that no arrangement with Russia was acceptable.[69] Grey's opinion was widely shared. Lord Roberts, the former commander-in-chief of the British army, put it clearly in the wake of the signing of the Anglo-Russian Convention. 'It is lucky Morley is at the India Office,' Roberts wrote to the commander of the Indian army, '[f]ew men would have behaved so firmly or withstood the attack of Radical supporters so well as he has. Fortunately, they look upon him as one of themselves, and he is consequently able to make them accept views which it would be hopeless for some of the other Ministers to attempt to do so.'[70]

One of Morley's greatest obstacles was Minto, who had a pathological distrust of Russia. Morley initially attempted to persuade the viceroy of the need for an arrangement with Russia and later *informed* him that such was government policy. The opening positions were established early in 1906, as the Liberals came to power. Morley mentioned to Minto the likelihood of an Anglo-Russian agreement; the viceroy countered that any such agreement was impossible due to the nature of the Russian government.[71] For the next five months Morley wrote endlessly, attempting to break down Minto's resistance to negotiations—to no avail. By July, Morley had had enough. Within the India Office, he spoke 'disparagingly' of Minto, and made it clear that he regarded the viceroy and the government of India generally as 'agents, no better informed, & less well-qualified to form an opinion than H.M.G.'[72] On 6 July, Morley made this point to Minto. 'You argue' he told the viceroy, 'as if the policy of entente with Russia were an open question. This is just what it is not. H.M.'s Government, with almost universal support in public opinion, have decided to make such attempts ... Be they good or bad, right or wrong, that is our policy ... it is for their [the government's] agents and officers all over the world to accept it.'[73] Morley's influence with respect to Anglo-Russian relations concerning India did not end in 1907. When Minto was about to leave office in 1910, the secretary of state worked hard to safeguard that Minto's successor was not a man who opposed the Convention.[74]

Morley's efforts to ensure the succession of Hardinge, the PUS at the Foreign Office, as viceroy, reflected the former's belief in the primacy of the Foreign Office in determining Britain's external policy. Morley made this broader

---

[69] Esher journal entry, 29 Sept. 1908, Esher Papers, ESHR 2/11.
[70] Roberts to Kitchener, 9 Sept. 1907, Kitchener Papers, PRO 30/57/28.
[71] Morley to Minto, 25 Jan. 1906, Morley Papers, MSS Eur D573/1; Minto to Morley, 15 Feb. 1906, Morley Papers, MSS Eur D573/7.
[72] Hirtzel (Morley's private secretary at the India Office) diary entries, 2 and 4 July 1906, Hirtzel Papers, MSS Eur D1090.
[73] Morley to Minto, 6 July 1907, Morley Papers, MSS Eur D573/1.
[74] S. E. Koss, *John Morley at the India Office* (New Haven, 1969), 118–22.

point evident in 1909. Discussing the defence of the Persian Gulf, Morley put the matter to Minto:

in essence Gulf questions are inextricably bound up with questions of European diplomacy. These arise from, and are settled by, circumstances over which the Indian Secretary has no control; which the G.[overnment] of I.[ndia] is in no position fully to comprehend or rightly measure, mainly because it is too far off the moving forces . . . Mark you I preach no dogma about *British* interests in the Gulf; I only contend that they *are* British, and not Indian (unless very secondarily) and that therefore they should be dealt with by the F.O.[75]

After Morley resigned from the India Office in 1910, he maintained his interest in foreign policy. As lord president of the council from 1910 to his resignation on the outbreak of war in 1914, he often acted as foreign secretary in Grey's absence.

The impact of other members of the cabinet on Britain's policy toward Russia was sporadic, but not negligible. Indeed, it could be very important, as the actions of Chamberlain and Hicks Beach in late 1897 and early 1898 illustrate. Hicks Beach was 'very strongly for' an arrangement with Russia, as this would secure British interests in China.[76] While Salisbury took up Hicks Beach's idea by opening negotiations with Russia for a general agreement on 17 January 1898, Hicks Beach proceeded in a different fashion. In a speech in Wales, he stated that Britain would, 'at the cost of war', maintain her trading rights in China.[77] The Russian ambassador in London was reported to have been 'excited' by Hicks Beach's remarks, and Sanderson had to explain that 'Hicks Beach had a sort of recognized privilege of blurting out disagreeable sentences—but that I did not see why any particular Govt. should try to fit the cap to its head, unless it wished to exclude British trade from China.'[78] Although this intervention eventually came to nought, with respect to financial matters, Hicks Beach was often paramount.[79]

Early in February 1898, Chamberlain complained that Russia was bullying British interests in China and advocated strong action to make Russia open her ports in China. Chamberlain also believed that Britain should pursue other avenues to help control Russia. He suggested that Balfour should meet the German ambassador, reflecting Chamberlain's interest in an Anglo-German alliance.[80] A month and a half later, Chamberlain made another foray into diplomacy. In a public speech on 13 May, he announced that any British agreement with Russia over China would have to be obtained cautiously, noting intemperately, that 'who sups

[75] Morley to Minto, 15 Apr. 1909, Morley Papers, MSS Eur D573/4.
[76] Salisbury to Curzon, 2 Jan. 1898, Curzon Papers, MSS Eur F112/1b.
[77] Lady V. Hicks Beach, *Life of Sir Michael Hicks Beach, Earl St Aldwyn* (2 vols.; London, 1932), ii. 59.
[78] Sanderson to O'Conor, 19 Jan. 1898, O'Conor Papers, OCON 6/25.
[79] The negotiations for a Persian loan in 1901: Selborne to Curzon, 24 Apr. 1903, Curzon Papers MSS Eur F111/229.
[80] Balfour to Salisbury, 14, Apr. 1898, Balfour Papers, Add MSS 49691.

with the devil must have a very long spoon'.[81] This had immediate repercussions in Russia.[82]

The final source of political influence upon foreign policy was Parliament. Given that British foreign secretaries were fond of claiming that Parliament would not stand for some policy or the other, it may seem strange to leave this topic to the last. But, Parliament did not generate foreign policy. At most, Parliament could, and did, act as a brake upon foreign policy, setting limits beyond which a foreign secretary could not go. Thus, British foreign policy was not the product of domestic politics except insofar as political realities occasionally restricted the foreign secretary's freedom of manœuvre.[83]

The principal political group outside the cabinet affecting foreign policy was the Radical faction of the Liberal party. Led by men like H. N. Brailsford, E. D. Morel and the Buxton brothers, these 'troublemakers' endeavoured to shape Liberal foreign policy according to their own vision of the proper world order.[84] While their focus was diffuse—Morel, for example, was interested in the Congo and Morocco, while most of the others focused on Persia—they held much in common.[85] A strong belief was that foreign policy should be made more openly. To borrow a later phrase, the Radicals believed in open covenants, openly arrived at. Russia and Anglo-Russian relations were particular targets of the Radicals. Brailsford, who had made his early reputation as a specialist on the Balkans, was a virulent critic of the Tsarist regime in a succession of liberal newspapers, particularly the *Daily News* and *The Nation*. Brailsford took his hostility to Tsarism a step too far in 1905 when he naïvely obtained false passports for some Russian revolutionaries.[86] Not all took direct action, but Brailsford's attitudes were characteristic. Charles Trevelyan exemplified the position of the Radicals; for him 'nothing less than the expulsion of the Russian Government and the Tsar beyond the pale of human society was fit reward for their black iniquities'.[87] Not surprisingly, their moralistic and simplistic

---

[81] *The Times*, 14 May 1898.

[82] O'Conor to Sanderson, 2 June 1898, O'Conor Papers, OCON 3/15; Sanderson to Scott (British Ambassador, St Petersburg), 7 Dec. 1898, Scott Papers, Add MSS 52298.

[83] M. R. Gordon, 'Domestic Conflict and the Origins of the First World War: The British and German Cases', *JMH* 46 (1974), 191–226; D. French, 'The Edwardian Crisis and the Origins of the First World War,' *IHR* 4 (1982), 207–21.

[84] A. J. P. Taylor, *The Troublemakers: Dissent over Foreign Policy 1792–1939* (Harmondsworth, 1985); D. McLean, 'English Radicals, Russia, and the Fate of Persia 1907–13', *EHR* 93 (1978), 338–52; H. S. Weinroth, 'British Radicals and the Balance of Power, 1902–14', *HJ* 13 (1970), 653–82; D. McLean, 'A Professor Extraordinary: E. G. Browne and His Persian Campaign 1908–13', *HJ* 21 (1978), 399–408.

[85] Summarized in 'Liberals and Foreign Affairs' unsigned, undated enclosure in Noel Buxton to A. Ponsonby, 17 Apr. 1913, Ponsonby Papers, MS Eng. hist. *c*.659.

[86] Sanderson to Hardinge, 21 Mar. 1905, Hardinge Papers, vol. 7.

[87] A. J. A. Morris, *Sir Charles Trevelyan 1870–1958: Portrait of a Radical* (New York, 1977), 103. Generally, A. J. A. Morris, *Radicalism Against War 1906–14: The Advocacy of Peace and Retrenchment* (Totowa, NJ, 1972), 59–64.

approach to foreign affairs infuriated many. As Chirol warned Hardinge in 1905: 'Charlie Trevelyan, one of the leading spirits of the "young Radicals" was down here yesterday, & his ignorance of foreign affairs was only equalled by his cocksure-ness. "All that we want is peace, & all that is needed to secure peace is an unaggress-ive foreign policy. All this talk about the hostility of foreign countries is rubbish. If it exists, we have brought it on ourselves & it serves us right . . .". You will have a jolly time if its radical tail wags the next administration.'[88]

Russia provided the Radicals with a continuous series of targets, and could on occasion make Grey's position difficult. As Nicolson put it in 1912 about Grey's Persian policy: 'There is a very unpleasant agitation among the extreme wing of the Liberal party against the policy of Grey, largely based upon ignorance'.[89] While there is little evidence for A. J. P. Taylor's assertion that 'the Dissenters had won' and that Grey's foreign policy after 1911 was in reality their policy, it is clear that he could not ignore them.[90]

THE CIVIL SERVANTS

The key figures among the civil servants who dealt with Britain's foreign policy in the period from 1894 to 1917 were three PUSs: Sir Thomas Sanderson (1894 to 1906), Sir Charles Hardinge (1906 to 1910 and again from 1916 to 1920), and Sir Arthur Nicolson (1910 to 1916).[91] Sir Thomas Sanderson has never been accused of being an *éminence grise*, but shaped policy to a considerable extent.[92] He entered the Foreign Office at the age of eighteen in 1859, and made his way to the top through diligence, discretion, and a flair for drafting agreements.

Sanderson and Salisbury proved well matched in their views about policy. Both believed that every situation had to be seen in its proper perspective and dealt with as it arose. 'Do not over-fag yourself in the quest for information,' Sanderson wrote to the British chargé d'affaires in Russia on one occasion, '[o]ne runs the risk of losing a clear sight of the general trend of events if one watches too eagerly every oscillation of the political seismograph.'[93] On another occasion Sanderson made his position with regard to hypothetical questions equally clear: 'nothing [is] less *fin* than *finesse* which discusses things that do not exist.'[94] This attitude reflected both

---

[88] Chirol to Hardinge, 24 July 1905, Hardinge Papers, vol. 7.
[89] Nicolson to Buchanan (British ambassador, Russia), 17 Jan. 1912, Nicolson Papers, FO 800/353.
[90] Taylor, *Troublemakers*, 125.
[91] Steiner, *Foreign Office*, 33–7, 56–9; 91–152.
[92] Ibid., 33–7; A. Ramm, 'Lord Salisbury and the Foreign Office', in R. Bullen (ed.), *The Foreign Office 1782–1982* (Frederick, MD, 1984), 46–65.
[93] Sanderson to Spring Rice, 2 May 1905, Spring Rice Papers, FO 800/241.
[94] Sanderson to Scott, 18 July 1900, Scott Papers, Add MSS 52298.

personal belief and Sanderson's appreciation of how British policy was formulated: 'We never look more than 3 inches beyond our noses.'[95] Sanderson had little fondness for Russians, few illusions about Russian foreign policy, and considerable scepticism about Russian veracity. Commenting on a rumour started by the Russian ambassador to Turkey, Sanderson noted of it that '[t]his is the difficulty with Russians. When sober they tell us less than the truth, when tipsy they tell us more than the truth.'[96] He believed that this prevaricating approach dominated Russian diplomacy. As he put it in June 1903 after the Russian foreign minister had invented a British offer to Japan: 'The Russians do not see any harm in these deviations from the brutal facts . . . That . . . Russian diplomacy will not take every advantage they can within those limits is, I fear, not to be expected—and a certain amount of deception is part of their ordinary stock in trade.'[97] Sanderson was also very much aware of the Russian tendency to seize on anything written as being official. 'I think I should endeavour to transact as much business as possible *viva voce* either personally or by Secretaries,' he advised the British ambassador at St Petersburg on one occasion, 'leaving only small "bouts de papier" with a few words scribbled on them and if any objections were raised I should say that the replies received to your formal memoranda were so abominably rude that I was ashamed to send them home.'[98]

Despite his reservations about Russian methods, Sanderson favoured an Anglo-Russian agreement.[99] The principal barriers to such an agreement in the past, Sanderson felt, were cultural differences—'our methods of thought were too diametrically opposed to make an understanding easy'—and the fact that Russia felt that she had little to gain. Sanderson made the point in 1902: 'We have been inviting such an [Anglo-Russian] understanding constantly and it is the Russian Govt. which has kept us off, no doubt because they thought it suited their interests better. Until they see that we can take our pigs to other markets we are not likely to bring them to book and I think the [Anglo-Japanese] Agreement tends rather to promote than to discourage our chance of some definite [Anglo-Russian] understanding.'[100]

These attitudes, compounded of cynicism and pragmatism, coloured Sanderson's approach to a possible arrangement. He did not anticipate the millennium to result from any agreement, and was not willing to base any arrangement on trust.[101]

[95] Sanderson to O'Conor, 15 Apr. 1896, O'Conor Papers, OCON 6/9.
[96] Sanderson to Scott, 26 Apr. 1899, Scott Papers, Add MSS 52298.
[97] Sanderson to Scott, 17 June 1903, Scott Papers Add MSS 52299.
[98] Sanderson to Scott, 7 May 1902, Scott Papers, Add MSS 52299.
[99] Sanderson to Spring Rice, 6 Aug. 1907, Spring Rice Papers FO 800/241.
[100] Sanderson to Scott, 12 Feb. 1902, Scott Papers, Add MSS 52299.
[101] Sanderson to Spring Rice, 18 Nov. 1903, Spring Rice Papers, FO 800/241; Satow diary entry, 13 May 1903, in Lensen, G. (ed.), *Korea and Manchuria Between Russia and Japan 1895–1904: The*

Instead, he wanted the two countries to co-operate on the basis of their shared interests, in Asia as well as in Europe, but not at any price. This left Sanderson at odds with the Germanophobes in the Foreign Office who advocated a Russian alliance as a check to Germany. 'I wish we could make the lunatics here', Sanderson told the British ambassador to Berlin in early 1905, 'who denounce Germany in such unmeasured terms & howl for an agreement with Russia, understand that the natural effect is to drive Germany into the Russian camp & encourage the Russians to believe they can get all they want at our expense & without coming to any agreement with us.'[102]

Sanderson's role in Anglo-Russian relations did not end with retirement, for he maintained his interest in foreign affairs, especially those pertaining to Russia. As Baron Sanderson of Armthorpe, he spoke in favour of the Anglo-Russian Convention in the House of Lords in 1908 and worked to promote informal Anglo-Russian relations.[103] In 1909, he helped organize a visit of Russian Duma members to Britain, and of a reciprocal British delegation three years later. Sanderson also encouraged the academic study of Russia, stating on one occasion that the founding of a journal devoted to Russia 'really tends more to the promotion of international harmony than many more pretentious schemes'.[104]

Sanderson was succeeded by Sir Charles Hardinge.[105] In 1896, when Hardinge, then thirty-eight, became first secretary of the legation in Teheran, his career had been successful, but unexceptional. In 1898, he was appointed secretary of embassy at St Petersburg, in 1903 he became an under-secretary at the Foreign Office and in 1904 returned to St Petersburg as ambassador. This meteoric rise was based on several things: Hardinge's own ability and hard work; the Hardinges' royal connections, and the indefatigable championing of his cause by Francis Bertie, an influential under-secretary at the Foreign Office, and by King Edward VII's private secretary, Francis Knollys.[106] In each of his posts, Hardinge found himself faced with Russian matters. When Hardinge arrived in St Petersburg in 1898, he brought

---

Observations of Sir Ernest Satow British Minister Plenipotentiary to Japan (1895–1900) and China (1900–6) (Tallahassee, 1966), 30 (hereafter, *Satow Diary*); Sanderson to Clarke (secretary, CID), 10 Nov. 1905, Cab 17/60.

[102] Sanderson to Lascelles, 3 Jan. 1905, Lascelles Papers, FO 800/12.

[103] Sanderson to Nicolson, 3 Mar. 1908, Nicolson Papers, FO 800/341.

[104] Sanderson to Tyrrell, 14 June 1911, Grey Papers, FO 800/110.

[105] C. Hardinge, *My Indian Years, 1910–16* (London, 1948); C. Hardinge *Old Diplomacy* (London, 1947); B. C. Busch, *Hardinge of Penshurst: A Study in the Old Diplomacy* (Hamden, 1980); J. D. Goold, '"Old Diplomacy": The Diplomatic Career of Lord Hardinge, 1910–22', Ph.D. thesis (Cambridge University, 1976); his two articles, 'Lord Hardinge and the Mesopotamia Expedition and Inquiry, 1914–17', *HJ* 19 (1976), 919–45 and 'Lord Hardinge as Ambassador to France, and the Anglo-French Dilemma over Germany and the Near East, 1920–22', *HJ* 21 (1978), 913–37.

[106] Busch, *Hardinge*, 43–71; R. A. Jones, *The British Diplomatic Service 1815–1914* (Waterloo, Ont., 1983), 192–4.

ample experience of the cutting edge of Anglo-Russian relations in Asia, including border incidents caused by Russian cossacks during his time in Teheran. In St Petersburg, he protested when Russian troops lingered in China after the Boxer rebellion. His concern for all the manifestations of status extended to diplomatic decorum. When the Russian government failed to enquire after Edward VII's health when the latter was in hospital, he wrote to the Russian government thanking them 'for the kind inquiries after the King's health which they never made, and I hope that Lamsdorff, when he reads it, will appreciate the full measure of his shortcomings'.[107] During his tenure as first secretary at St Petersburg, Hardinge learned about the evasiveness and frequent dishonesty of Russian officials.[108] Even official Russian budgets were often fabricated, and information generally was difficult to gather.[109] Hardinge came away with one conviction: Russia needed 'peace and money'.[110]

When he left Russia early in 1903 to become an under-secretary in the Foreign Office, Hardinge had no inkling that he would soon return. The complicated bureaucratic manœuvrings that returned him as ambassador in May 1904 are well-known.[111] For the next sixteen months he dealt with Anglo-Russian affairs in the strained atmosphere of the Russo-Japanese war. His tasks were simple—maintaining Britain's position of strict neutrality while ensuring that her own interests were not affected by the hostilities—but carrying them out was not. Hardinge had gone to Russia convinced that, when the issue of war or peace was in the balance, '[t]he responsibility seems to me to rest entirely with the Russians who have shown their usual bad faith throughout'.[112] But neither this conviction nor ideological grounds interfered with Hardinge's duties. For him, foreign policy was to be made solely according to considerations of state. As he once noted on a letter excoriating Britain for giving 'our moral and material support' to the Russian government's 'barbarous methods of repressing popular rights': 'Foreign policy based on sentiment can only end in disaster.'[113]

Hardinge, in fact, had been an advocate of an Anglo-Russian understanding from his time in Persia. He made this manifest in a letter to Nicolson in 1907 on the signing of the Anglo-Russian Convention. 'I have been so imbued with the import-

[107] Hardinge to Sanderson, 17 July 1902, Hardinge Papers, vol. 3.

[108] Hardinge to Sanderson, 9 Oct. 1901, Hardinge Papers, vol. 3; Hardinge to Bertie, 8 Nov. 1901, Bertie Papers, FO 800/176.

[109] Hardinge to Sanderson, 24 Nov. 1900; Hardinge to Sanderson, 28 Nov. 1901, both Hardinge Papers, vol. 3.

[110] Hardinge to Lansdowne, disp. 280, 28 Sept. 1901, FO 65/1622.

[111] See Busch, *Hardinge*, 68–9; Jones, *British Diplomatic Service*, 193–4; Steiner, *Foreign Office*, 71–4.

[112] Hardinge to Bertie, 8 Feb. 1904, Bertie Papers, FO 800/176.

[113] Hardinge's undated minute on F. W. Read (South Park Ethical Society) to Grey, 19 June 1907, FO 371/324/20563.

ance of an agreement with Russia that it was one of the reasons which induced me to give up the Embassy at St. P. since I felt that I could do more by impressing my views on people at home.'[114] Hardinge advocated an agreement because Anglo-Russian friction limited Britain's diplomatic freedom of manœuvre, and it was expensive. The Anglo-Russian accord, as Hardinge explained to Nicolson in November 1907, solved many problems:

Russia will inevitably be drawn into paying greater attention to her position in the Near East & there she will constantly find herself in conflict with Germany and not in opposition to us. People say I am an optimist but I have always been hopeful of our having the best possible relations with Russia, which are and must always be of the greatest advantage to us. Anyhow during the eight years that I was connected with St. Petersburg I had a very practical object lesson of the disadvantages of unfriendly relations politically . . . I should be very sorry to see those days return.[115]

This thinking guided Hardinge's views of Anglo-Russian relations throughout his career. As viceroy, he continued to put great value in the Convention, since it guaranteed Britain's imperial position. When discussions between Britain and Russia arose in 1913, Hardinge wrote to Nicolson that 'I do trust that in handling Russia in the Tibetan and Persian questions, nothing will happen to impair our good relations with her in Asia. Good relations with Russia is [*sic*] of vital necessity to India, and in that course alone lies peace on our frontiers and strength in our internal administration.'[116] By no means was Hardinge willing to accept *any* Russian actions for the sake of maintaining the Convention; as viceroy Hardinge continued to advocate hitting the Russians hard when their actions transgressed against British interests.[117]

Hardinge did not advocate an agreement with Russia solely to help maintain Britain's position in Asia.[118] In a long memorandum written in the aftermath of the Bosnian crisis, he saw Russia as central to the European balance of power.[119] If a 'reactionary' government—one that would follow a 'foreign policy more in accordance than now with German arms in Europe'—came to power in Russia as a result of the Bosnian humiliation, should Britain agree to support Russia if requested to do so? His reply was prescient and unequivocal. First, he assumed that in a European war, 'Germany may accordingly be regarded as our only potential enemy in Europe', that Austria-Hungary would support Germany and that 'Italy may be

---

[114] Hardinge to Nicolson, 4 Sept. 1907, Nicolson Papers, FO 800/339.
[115] Hardinge to Nicolson, 25 Nov. 1907, Nicolson Papers, FO 800/340.
[116] Hardinge to Nicolson, 28 Apr. 1913, Hardinge Papers, vol. 93.
[117] Goold, 'Old Diplomacy', 62–6.
[118] The thrust of Wilson, *Policy of the Entente*, 82–4.
[119] 'Memorandum by Sir Charles Hardinge on the Possibility of War', *BD*, v, app. III, 823–6; the original, dated 4 May 1909, is in FO 371/773/41171. Quotations are from the pub. version, except for the minutes by Grey and Asquith.

regarded, as far as England, France and Russia are concerned as a neutral quantity in any conflict in the near future'. With Russia weakened by the Russo–Japanese War and without British support, 'it is almost inevitable that Russia would be compelled by her military weakness to come to terms with Germany'. This would, in turn, drive France into Germany's arms and leave England isolated. Such a circumstance would be acceptable to Britain only if she remained in complete command of the seas; otherwise, an alliance with France and Russia was necessary. Hardinge was not unaware of the political ramifications of such an argument. 'For such an alliance however', he went on, 'public opinion in England is not at present prepared and there is a very large section of the population who would resent an alliance with Russia while under the rule of a reactionary Gov[ern]ment.' Thus, he concluded, an alliance with Russia at present was politically impossible. But at some future point Hardinge had no doubt that it should be made. His was a clear statement of purpose, balanced by considerations of the political limitations of the intended audience. As such, it found wide favour. Grey minuted on it: 'I agree with this paper which is very ably stated: it must be brought up if the question arises.' Asquith's response was supportive, but more guarded: 'This is an able paper, worth thinking over: especially the last two pages.' The fact that the last two pages dealt with the political ramifications of an alliance underscored the difficulties that any agreement with reactionary Russia posed for a Liberal government.

Nicolson succeeded Hardinge in the autumn of 1910.[120] At the age of sixty-one, Nicolson was at the peak of his career. Like Hardinge, Nicolson had served in Persia early in his career, and like his predecessor as PUS had gained there an appreciation of the difficulties that Russia could cause for Britain. But separating Nicolson's time in Persia and his appointment as ambassador to St Petersburg in late 1905 were nearly eighteen years of relatively minor posts in Hungary, Constantinople, Bulgaria, and Tangiers, capped by a brief time as ambassador to Madrid. In 1903, Hardinge considered Nicolson, whom he had known when they were both juniors at Constantinople, 'the most likely candidate' to succeed Sir Charles Scott as ambassador to St Petersburg.[121] While it turned out that Hardinge himself obtained the post, Nicolson's later appointment as Hardinge's successor was both logical and unexceptionable. Nicolson went to Russia with several advantages. The first was that Hardinge, now PUS, and he agreed completely on the proper course of British policy towards Russia. The second was that Grey, who became foreign secretary just after Nicolson was appointed to St Petersburg, gained an immediate favourable impression of Nicolson due to the latter's adroit handling of British affairs at the Algeciras conference.

[120] H. Nicolson, *Sir Arthur Nicolson, Bart. First Lord Carnock: A Study in the Old Diplomacy* (London, 1930) and Neilson, '"My Beloved Russians"'.
[121] Hardinge to Bertie, 4 Dec. 1903, Bertie Papers, FO 800/163.

Nicolson went to Russia in May 1906. During the next fifteen months, he worked hard at improving Anglo-Russian relations, culminating in the signing of the Anglo-Russian Convention at the end of August 1907. During this time Nicolson formed his opinions about Russia.[122] The chaos in the wake of the Russo-Japanese war led him to accept that Russia must be governed firmly, but he did not feel her government exemplary. 'As we find it necessary to govern India by an autocracy,' Nicolson wrote in his diary, 'so it is necessary to govern Russians, but in India it is an enlightened & benevolent autocracy & hitherto this cannot be said in respect to this country.'[123] Guided by such people as Sir Donald Mackenzie Wallace, the prominent British expert on Russia and a trusted advisor in the past, Nicolson put his faith in gradual reform, personified by Petr Stolypin, the chairman of the Russian council of ministers from 1906 to 1911. Nicolson's reaction upon Stolypin's assassination—'I shall deeply regret his loss as we were great friends, and I had the greatest admiration for him. He will be difficult to replace'[124]— summarized his attitude. Nicolson worked hard to ensure that good relations between the two countries continued after the signing of the Convention. He encouraged the formation of an Anglo-Russian Chamber of Commerce and supported creating a school for Russian studies at the University of Liverpool, arguing that '[a]ll that brings the two peoples together in various spheres is all to the good'.[125] Nicolson carried on this policy as PUS, in 1911 strongly advocating reciprocal parliamentary visits between Russia and Britain.

On balance, Nicolson's view of the Anglo-Russian relationship was very similar to that of Hardinge. Nicolson valued the Convention for its effect on the British position in Asia:

The chief advantage of our Conventions, to my mind, is that we keep Russia at a distance from our land frontiers, and bind her to pacific engagements. This is important, as on land she might conceivably be stronger than we are and cause us serious embarrassments. But as regards the Gulf it seems to me that our position is thoroughly assured so long as we retain our sea supremacy: and if we lose our sea supremacy we lose our Empire.[126]

It was a view he retained until his retirement in 1916. Nicolson was unwilling to accede to unreasonable Russian demands in Asia, but saw a Russian alliance as essential to the wider, European aspects of British policy. Concerns about the balance of power emerged in 1911, when Grey's policy over Persia was under attack

---

[122] Neilson, '"My Beloved Russians"', 526–36.
[123] Nicolson diary entry, 27 July 1906, Nicolson Papers, PRO 30/81/13.
[124] Nicolson to Grey, memo, 18 Sept. 1911, Grey Papers, FO 800/93.
[125] Nicolson to Revelstoke (managing director, Baring Brothers), 21 Sept. 1909, Barings Papers, Barings Partners' filing/209; Nicolson to Revelstoke, 4 Nov. 1911, Barings Papers, Barings Partners' filing/212; Nicolson to Pares (British academic), 8 Apr. 1911, Pares Papers, 61.
[126] Nicolson to Hardinge, 19 June 1907, Nicolson Papers, FO 800/337.

and the advocates of naval talks with Germany were at their most vocal. In a letter to the British ambassador at Vienna, Nicolson argued that those who wished to reject the Russian alliance because of Persia did not understand the realities of power.[127] 'I consider', he wrote of Russia in 1913, 'that she is for us at any rate a most formidable factor in European politics, and it is of the highest, and indeed of essential importance, that we should remain on the best of terms with her.' In order to accomplish this, Nicolson preferred an Anglo-Russian alliance. After the Bosnian crisis, he advised Grey that it would be wise to bind Russia firmly to Britain by making the *entente* 'nearer to the nature of an alliance', to prevent Russia's seeking a closer relationship with Germany.[128] Such concerns continued to shape Nicolson's views down to 1914. 'I do not know for how much longer', Nicolson wrote to the British ambassador in Russia in April 1914, 'we shall be able to follow our present policy of dancing on a tight rope and not be compelled to take up some definite line or other. I am also haunted by the same fear as you lest Russia should become tired of us and strike a bargain with Germany.'[129] It is no surprise that during the July crisis Nicolson advocated strongly that Britain join on the side of France and Russia.[130]

Throughout the war, Nicolson remained steadfast in his conviction that Russia would both stay loyal to the entente and be the decisive military factor in the conflict.[131] But Nicolson's power and influence waned during the war, because of the declining influence of the Foreign Office during the conflict, the lessening of Grey's own influence as a result of his poor health and despair over the outbreak of war, and the increasing influence of other departments of state.[132] It was also in part due to Nicolson's own poor health, a fact evident as early as 1912. Also, Grey seemed less inclined than before to listen to Nicolson's advice. Beginning in 1911, a gap had developed between Grey and his PUS, not over Russia, but instead from a difference of opinion over defence spending and contingent policy issues. Nicolson believed in strength at any cost, but Grey was politically committed to economy. Further, there seems to have been a growing lack of intimacy between Grey and Nicolson. Grey, as a senior member of the cabinet, was very much concerned with party politics in the period while Nicolson was PUS. This was evident during the coal strike in 1912. 'Poor Nicolson is in despair', a mutual friend wrote to

[127] Nicolson to Goschen, 28 Feb. 1911, Nicolson Papers, FO 800/347; Nicolson to Goschen, 8 Apr. 1913, Nicolson Papers, FO 800/365.

[128] Nicolson to Grey, 24 Mar. 1909, *BD*, v, doc. 764.

[129] Nicolson to Buchanan, 21 Apr. 1914, Nicolson Papers, FO 800/373; Neilson, ' "My Beloved Russians" ', 546–8.

[130] Nicolson to Grey, memo, 1 Aug. 1914; Nicolson to Grey, 5 Aug. 1914, both Grey Papers, FO 800/94.

[131] Neilson, ' "Beloved Russians" ', 549–50.

[132] R. Warman, 'The Erosion of Foreign Office Influence in the Making of Foreign Policy, 1916–18' *HJ* 15 (1972), 133–59. For the early part of the war, the idea of 'decline' is overstated.

Hardinge in March, 'for he can hardly ever get hold of his Chief for five minutes together, and when he does, his Chief's mind is still monopolised by the strike.'[133] Other issues, particularly Ireland, persuaded Nicolson that his views were 'so entirely divergent with those of the present Government that I think it better to limit myself to talking on those matters which are strictly within my own province'.[134] The thought may not have guided his discretion; some felt that he had been already far too prone to express his views, to the detriment of his influence with Grey.[135]

Nicolson's case shows that the influence of an individual PUS could wax and wane. In fact, the wider issue of the influence of the views of the PUSs on policy generally is a difficult one and offers no simple solution. Sanderson's career makes this manifest. The paucity of his private papers and the infrequency of minutes in Foreign Office files prior to the 1906 reforms makes any judgement of his impact necessarily incomplete. None the less, it is evident that Sanderson's influence was not markedly inferior, at least concerning Anglo-Russian relations, to that of Hardinge or Nicolson. The difference between their regimes reflected more the fact that both of the latter favoured actively pursuing Russia, whereas Sanderson advocated offering British 'pigs' to all 'markets'. This was quite in keeping with Salisbury's and Lansdowne's views. The decline of Nicolson's influence after 1912 partly resulted from the fact that Grey, too, became unwilling to give Russia an exclusive contract for British swine. In short, it would be wrong to dismiss Sanderson's influence as inconsequential simply because he shared the views of Salisbury and Lansdowne, both of whom wished for a Russian agreement but were unable to obtain it. Equally, it would be wrong to overrate the influence of Hardinge and Nicolson, simply because they held office in the period when the Anglo-Russian Convention existed.

Below the level of the PUS, a number of other officials at the Foreign Office had a significant impact on British policy towards Russia. Most, but not all, of them were in the Eastern Department of the Foreign Office. For example, Richard Ponsonby Maxwell was acting supervising clerk in the Eastern Department from 1900 to 1905 and then supervising clerk in that department until his retirement in 1913. Francis Bertie, in contrast, who headed the African and Asiatic Departments as an assistant under-secretary from 1894 until his appointment as ambassador at Rome in 1903, had his influence by dint of the strength of his personality, his excellent royal connections, and the fact that both Salisbury and Lansdowne accorded him substantial autonomy in dealing with Russian matters as they impinged on China.[136]

---

[133] Chirol to Hardinge, 15 Mar. 1912, Hardinge Papers, vol. 92.
[134] Nicolson to Hardinge, 15 Jan. 1914, Hardinge Papers, vol. 93.
[135] Chirol to Hardinge, 22 May 1914, Hardinge Papers, vol. 93.
[136] K. Hamilton, *Bertie of Thame: Edwardian Ambassador* (London, 1990).

Maxwell remains a man of mystery. Educated at Winchester and St John's College, Cambridge, he entered the Foreign Office in 1877. In 1881 he was a colleague of Hardinge's at Constantinople, where the men became friends. Maxwell served as Sanderson's private secretary from 1894 to 1896, became an assistant clerk in the latter year and acted as the secretary to the British delegation to the Hague in 1899. Despite the sketchiness of the record concerning Maxwell, there are signs that he was well-regarded. For example, when Hardinge's appointment to St Petersburg as ambassador was in the air, the latter noted that he 'should not be surprised' if Maxwell succeeded him.[137] This did not occur, but should not be taken as a sign that Maxwell was not highly regarded, for he later refused promotion when it was offered.[138] Although he was at the centre of the reform of the Foreign Office between 1904 and 1906, Maxwell was very much a clerk of the old school. It appears from these few instances where he expressed an opinion that Maxwell favoured the retention of Lamsdorff as Russian foreign minister in 1906, and deprecated the latter's supersession by Izvolskii.[139] Still, there is no reason to doubt Zara Steiner's contention that Maxwell 'was an acknowledged master in his own area'.[140] Hardinge's remark on Maxwell's retirement—'He is a dear creature and will be a great loss'[141]—was a fitting epitaph to Maxwell's career.

There is little mystery about Bertie's views; he was never loathe to air them. The second son of the Earl of Abingdon, Bertie entered the Foreign Office in 1863 after attending Eton. His leap from the Foreign Office to the rank of ambassador at Rome was due largely to royal patronage, leaving room for substantial doubts about his fitness for the post. Lansdowne's letter to Balfour recommending Bertie has an ambivalent tone: 'Bertie is as well known to you as to me, and I need not enlarge on his merits or his defects. He is shrewd enough to keep his temper in control when he is transacting international affairs.'[142] Sanderson, who did not like Bertie (a dislike that was reciprocated), put it more directly. 'Bertie is to be the new Ambassador at Rome,' Sanderson wrote at the end of 1902. 'Between ourselves it is not to my mind an ideal selection—but we must hope that in the Italian climate and with much less work some of the asperities from which we have suffered will disappear.'[143] But everyone acknowledged that Bertie was capable and hard working.[144] Another sign that Bertie's capabilities were recognized was that, when

[137] Hardinge to Bertie, 24 Dec. 1903, Bertie Papers, FO 800/163.
[138] Steiner, *Foreign Office*, 120–1.
[139] Maxwell's undated minutes on Spring Rice to Grey, disp. 216, 28 Mar. 1906, FO 371/121/11175 and Spring Rice to Grey, secret tel. 82, 4 May 1906, FO 371/121/151278.
[140] Steiner, *Foreign Office*, 121.
[141] Hardinge to Alwyn Parker (assistant clerk, FO), 18 Aug. 1913, Hardinge Papers, vol. 93.
[142] Lansdowne to Balfour, 22 Dec. 1902, Balfour Papers, Add MSS 49727.
[143] Sanderson to Lascelles, 31 Dec. 1902, Lascelles Papers, FO 800/11.
[144] Lansdowne to Balfour, 22 Dec. 1902, Balfour Papers, Add MSS 49727.

Sanderson was ill in 1904, Bertie temporarily acted as PUS. And while Bertie could be an abrasive superior, some at the Foreign Office found him a pleasant change from Sanderson's sometimes autocratic style. 'I shall be sorry to lose Bertie', Maxwell wrote to Hardinge, 'who has been most pleasant. He does not fuss, & never rings that bell.'[145] Bertie's views on foreign policy were quite straightforward. In response to a charge that he was anti-German, Bertie once wrote: 'I am not Germanophobe, I am Anglomane.'[146] By 'Anglomane', Bertie meant that he favoured British interests before those of any other government. In practical terms, this amounted to his being both anti-German and anti-Russian.[147] To ally with Germany would be to give up having good relations with either France or Russia. Besides, Bertie had a very low opinion of German foreign policy. 'Your letter . . . breathes distrust of Germany', Bertie wrote to a colleague at the Foreign Office, 'and you are right. She has never done anything for us but bleed us. She is false and grasping.'[148] With respect to Russia, he believed that Russian diplomacy was both muddled in its organization and dishonest in its implementation. As he told the French foreign minister on one occasion, the difficulty in trying to arrange any Anglo-Russian *rapprochement* was the fact that 'at Petersburg agreements were not interpreted in the same way as they would be in London or Paris, at one moment assurances given by the Emperor of Russia were not to be considered those of the Russian Government and vice versa'.[149] He was not impressed by Russia's military strength and did not feel that a Russian alliance was an absolute necessity to safeguard British interests.

The two men who served successively as Grey's private secretary, Louis Mallet (1906–7) and William Tyrrell (1907–15), both played an important role in the formation of British policy towards Russia.[150] From 1902 to 1905, Mallet had been Lansdowne's précis writer, and from 1907 to 1913 he supervised the Eastern Department as an assistant under-secretary and then become ambassador to Turkey. Mallet's abilities were widely recognized.[151] He was one of those at the Foreign Office who found German diplomatic methods and goals distasteful. During the Russo-Japanese war, Mallet believed that Germany was attempting to create an

[145] Maxwell to Hardinge, 28 Nov. 1904, Hardinge Papers, vol. 7. Sanderson used the 'bell' to summon people to his office.

[146] Bertie to Grey, 21 Dec. 1911, cited, K. Wilson, 'The Question of Anti-Germanism at the British Foreign Office before the First World War', *CJH* 18 (1983), 40.

[147] His memo on the possibility of an Anglo-German alliance, 9 Nov. 1901, Lansdowne Papers, FO 800/115.

[148] Bertie to Mallet, 11 June 1904, Bertie Papers, FO 800/170.

[149] Bertie to Lansdowne, 17 Jan. 1905, Lansdowne Papers, FO 800/126.

[150] On Mallet and Tyrrell, Steiner, *Foreign Office*; E. T. Corp, 'Sir William Tyrrell: The *Eminence Grise* of the British Foreign Office, 1912–15', *HJ* 25 (1982), 697–708.

[151] Lansdowne to Bertie, 28 June 1903, Bertie Papers, Add MSS 63015: Hardinge to Bertie, 11 Jan. 1904 and Reginald Lister to Bertie, 12 Dec. 1905, both Bertie Papers, FO 800/163.

anti-British coalition. 'History repeats itself', Mallet noted, harkening back to similar German attempts during the Boer war, '& German methods are always the same . . . I confess that the present attitude of the Germans fills me with suspicion & [I] am strongly of opinion that we should be prepared for an eventuality if by some unlucky chance Russia forces war on us.'[152] Mallet was particularly anxious about matters in 1906 and 1907, when he feared that Russia's weakness after the Russo-Japanese conflict might force her into the German camp.[153] Britain should not allow domestic events in Russia to force her to draw back from her negotiations with Russia for a general agreement, lest Russia 'be thrown into the arms of Germany'.[154] In his view, the two barriers to a Russo-German *rapprochement* were that the Franco-Russian alliance was bound together both by financial necessity and the need to maintain the European balance and that for the Slavs a 'struggle with the Teutons [will be] inevitable in the future'.[155]

These barriers did not mean that Britain could take the existence of good relations with both France and Russia for granted. Though Mallet could crow in 1908 that '[i]t is a remarkable achievement on the part of Germany to have united against her Englishman, Slav and Frenchman in the space of a very few years', he was always suspicious that something would occur to undermine the unity of that opposition.[156] He made this point firmly in 1910 over the interest that Germany expressed in Persia. Echoing Nicolson's assessment, Mallet argued that Germany was attempting to drive a wedge between Britain and Russia in a fashion similar to the attempt to sunder the Anglo-French entente on the issue of Morocco in 1905.[157] 'It is of the utmost importance from an international point of view', Mallet opined, 'that the Entente with Russia should be maintained[.] Our position in Europe would be much weakened morally, if the German move were successful, and the defection of France would probably follow,' While Nicolson did not support Mallet, their ideas on Anglo-Russian relations ran parallel.

Not so the views of Nicolson and Tyrrell.[158] 'Willie' Tyrrell had served as private secretary to Sanderson from 1896 until 1903, had been briefly secretary to the CID and had spent 1904 as second secretary at the embassy in Rome. When Grey took office, Tyrrell became his précis writer and succeeded Mallet as private secretary in 1907. Championed by Hardinge, who had helped get him the position, Tyrrell

---

[152] Mallet to Sandars, 11 Nov. 1904, Balfour Papers, Add MSS 49747.

[153] Mallet to Bertie, 8 Nov. 1906, Bertie Papers, FO 800/177.

[154] Mallet's undated minute on Nicolson to Grey, tel. 100, 16 June 1907, FO 371/324/19792.

[155] Mallet's undated minutes on O'Beirne to Grey, disp. 402, 6 Aug. 1907, FO 371/327/27708; on Nicolson to Grey, disp. 294, 8 May 1909, FO 371/730/18279; on O'Beirne to Grey, disp. 257, 2 June 1908, FO 371/517/19623.

[156] Mallet's undated minute on O'Beirne to Grey, disp. 256, 2 June 1908, FO 371/517/19622.

[157] Mallet's undated minute (but Mar. 1910), Grey Papers, FO 800/93.

[158] Steiner, *Foreign Office*, 118–20 and 147–52.

was powerfully placed to affect policy.[159] This position strengthened after Hardinge left the Foreign Office and Nicolson failed to establish the same warm personal relationship with Grey that Hardinge had enjoyed. Particularly after the death of Grey's brother, the foreign secretary found Tyrrell's charm and intelligence congenial.

Tyrrell advocated a policy towards Russia directly opposite to that espoused by Nicolson. His views may be glimpsed in 1907 in letters written to his close friend, Sir Cecil Spring Rice, at that time the British minister at Teheran. Tyrrell did not believe that an agreement with Russia would be lasting. Any agreement with her depended on 'Russian assurances' and these, he argued 'are reliable it seems to me as long as Russia continues in her present condition of impotency with regard to any offensive policy'.[160] Since Britain 'had lacked the means' to enforce her policy in Persia, the Russian agreement 'is an attempt to cut our coat according to our cloth'. Tyrrell disliked this. 'Alliances can never be substituted', he argued, 'for a sound army or navy or in other words we cannot relieve ourselves of our duties of defence by relying on other nations to fight our battles. It is a stupid & demoralising policy.' Tyrrell saw Russia as having a better position: 'In the nature of things Russia can still think & act impersonally, whilst our horizon's confined to Westminster & it is almost on the sly that now & then we can pursue a statesmanlike policy.'[161] However, in an ironic twist, given the usual importance that British observers accorded to the Duma as the touchstone of Russian constitutional development, Tyrrell noted wittily that 'I console myself by looking forward to the time when Russia will be blessed with Parliamentary institutions which in the region of foreign politics are certainly a blessing in disguise'.

Despite such cynicism, Tyrrell's position was clear. Only a weak Russia could be trusted. British interests had to be safeguarded through strength, and the differences in the two systems of government meant that Britain struggled under a handicap. The growth of Russian power immediately before 1914 meant that Britain had to reconsider her relationship with that country.[162] The improvement of Anglo-German relations in 1912 provided Tyrrell with a chance to put his views forward cogently. Britain, he argued, no longer had to accept Russia's actions uncritically.[163] In the improved international situation, with the balance of power tipped less in Germany's favour, this could be done without imperilling the solidarity of Britain's relationships with France and Russia. Britain no longer had 'to leave

[159] Hardinge had known Tyrrell all the latter's life; Hardinge, *Old Diplomacy*, 228; Hardinge to Ponsonby (equerry and private secretary to Edward VII), 7 May 1911, Hardinge Papers, vol. 92.

[160] Tyrrell to Spring Rice, 15 May 1907, Spring Rice Papers, FO 800/241.

[161] Tyrrell to Spring Rice, 18 Feb. 1907, Spring Rice Papers, FO 800/241.

[162] Corp, 'Tyrrell', 701–2; K. Neilson, 'Watching the "Steamroller": British Observers and the Russian Army before 1914', *JSS* 8 (1985), 199–217.

[163] Chirol to Hardinge, 10 Apr., 18 Apr. and 23 May 1913, all Hardinge Papers, vol. 93.

the Russians to pipe the tune and us to dance to it, whatever it may be'. This policy of firmness found wide support. Sir George Buchanan, the British ambassador at St Petersburg, argued in similar terms, and Hardinge did not view Tyrrell's suggestions as being in the nature of a 'new orientation' in British policy.[164] In fact, by 1914, Nicolson also had come to the reluctant conclusion that the Anglo-Russian Convention needed adjustment.

If the difference between Tyrrell and Nicolson concerning Russia was one of degree, it was magnified by the complicated politics within the Foreign Office surrounding Nicolson's departure as PUS. The competition for succession was simplified somewhat when Mallet went to Constantinople. This left two principal contenders, Tyrrell and Eyre Crowe, the Foreign Office's expert on Germany and the assistant under-secretary supervising both the Western and Eastern Departments.[165] Their contest for supremacy was deferred due to the outbreak of war and Nicolson's extension as PUS, but even in November 1914, one diplomat could write that 'there is a struggle for power between Tyrrell & Crowe, & that each hides things from the other'.[166] Tyrrell's breakdown in 1915 ended his influence until the latter part of the war. But for the crucial period from 1912 until 1915, 'Willie' Tyrrell was clearly an essential figure in Anglo-Russian affairs.

So, too, was Crowe.[167] Educated in Germany and France, he joined the Foreign Office in 1885 and by sheer ability rose to be a senior clerk in 1906. His fluency in languages, hard work, and clear thinking aided in his rise. Although Crowe was passed over in favour of Mallet in 1907, the death of Francis Campbell allowed him to become an assistant under-secretary in 1912. He took charge of the Western Department, where his expertise on matters German could have full play. But when Mallet was transferred to Constantinople in June 1913, Crowe also assumed the Eastern Department, with its responsibility for Russia. Crowe held both positions until the outbreak of war when they were merged into the War Department, with Crowe as its head. For reasons administrative and personal, Crowe ceased to be in charge of the War Department in September 1914 and, instead, was given responsibility for contraband.[168] It was not until 1918 that Crowe returned full time to political work—a return that presaged his appointment as PUS in 1920.

[164] 'Memorandum by Sir G. Buchanan on Anglo-Russian Relations', 19 May 1913, Grey Papers, FO 800/74; Grey to Crewe, 20 May, Crewe Papers C/17; Hardinge to Chirol, 8 May 1913, Hardinge Papers, vol. 93.

[165] Mallet to Hardinge, 11 Aug. 1913, Hardinge Papers, vol. 93.

[166] Findlay (British Minister, Christiania) to Howard (British Minister, Stockholm), 14 Nov. 1914, Howard Papers, DHW 4/Official/6.

[167] On Crowe, Steiner, *Foreign Office*, 108–18, 140–7, 156–65; R. A. Cosgrove, 'The Career of Sir Eyre Crowe: A Reassessment', *Albion*, 4 (1972), 193–205; E. T. Corp, 'Sir Eyre Crowe and the Administration of the Foreign Office, 1906–14', *HJ* 22 (1979), 443–54; E. T. Corp, 'The Problem of Promotion in the Career of Sir Eyre Crowe, 1905–20', *AJPH* 28 (1982), 236–49.

[168] Corp, 'Crowe and Administration', 453 n. 69.

While Crowe's influence was greatest in the period from 1912 to 1914, his views had been formed much earlier. As is well-known, Crowe was prominent among the so-called anti-Germans at the Foreign Office. His famous memorandum of 1 January 1907 is often taken as definitive of that group's views on German foreign policy.[169] But Crowe's policy was not so much anti-German as it was, like Bertie's, Anglomane. Crowe believed that Britain should oppose vigorously all challenges, whether they came from Berlin or elsewhere. St Petersburg did not escape his censure. During the Dogger Bank incident, he was one of the few at the Foreign Office who advocated war should Russia refuse to apologize. Crowe's truculence remained evident when, as head of the Eastern Department, he maintained strongly that Britain needed to take a firm line with Russia. By the early summer of 1914, Crowe was advocating that Britain and Russia partition Persia. 'Persia is not capable of acting as a buffer', Crowe told the British minister to Sweden, 'and the sooner we recognize that fact, the clearer and healthier will be the situation.'[170]

In this respect Crowe agreed with Tyrrell. However, in addition to contending for the succession to the position of PUS, they differed over the extent of Britain's commitment to France and Russia.[171] While Tyrrell attempted to find some means of steering Britain into a neutral path by confining the war to an Austro-Russian one, Crowe argued passionately that Britain must come to the aid of France.[172] While Crowe admitted that 'there is no written bond binding us to France', he maintained that 'the Entente has been made, strengthened, put to the test, and celebrated in a manner justifying the belief that a moral bond was being forged'. Britain could not 'repudiate it without exposing our good name to grave criticism'. On the political side, he argued that if 'England cannot engage in a big war [it] means her abdication as an independent State. She can be brought to her knees and made to obey the behest of any Power or group of Powers who *can* go to war, of whom there are several.' While Crowe's influence on Anglo-Russian relations diminished after he became responsible for matters dealing with blockade, his importance in 1913 and 1914 is undoubted.

Men like Hardinge, Nicolson, Maxwell, Bertie, Tyrrell and Crowe operated at the highest levels of the Foreign Office. Others, who functioned at lower levels, cannot be disregarded. The most significant of these was Herman Cameron Norman. Norman, after schooling at Eton and Trinity College, Cambridge, had joined the diplomatic service in 1894, and served in Cairo, Constantinople, and Washington before being transferred to St Petersburg in 1903 as second secretary

---

[169] K. Wilson, 'Sir Eyre Crowe on the Origin of the Crowe Memorandum of 1 January 1907', *BIHR*, 55 (1983), 238–41.

[170] Crowe to Howard, 27 June 1914, Howard Papers, DHW 4/Official/18.

[171] Corp, 'Tyrrell', 705; Nicolson favoured Crowe for PUS, but Hardinge favoured Tyrrell: cf. Nicolson to Hardinge, 21 May 1913; Hardinge to Chirol, 6 May 1914, both Hardinge Papers, vol. 93.

[172] Crowe's memo, private, 31 July 1914, Grey Papers, FO 800/94.

to the embassy. After three years in Russia, Norman was moved to the Foreign Office. Assigned to the Eastern Department, he became an acting assistant to Maxwell in 1911. That appointment was made permanent a year later, and Norman remained in that post until early in 1914. Norman was the Eastern Department's leading expert on Russia. While in St Petersburg, where he served under both Hardinge and Nicolson, he became fluent in Russian. Both Hardinge and Nicolson praised his hard work, his linguistic abilities, and his knowledge of the Russian scene.[173] By the time of his transfer to Tokyo in 1914, Hardinge wrote that 'I do not know how the Eastern Department could well get on without . . . Norman'.[174]

Although Norman served under two permanent under-secretaries—Hardinge and Nicolson—who had extensive personal knowledge of Russia, they did not have his detailed grasp of Russian domestic politics. Whereas the PUS had all of British foreign policy as his ambit, Norman could focus his attention on Russia. Norman kept in close touch with those in Britain—particularly Bernard Pares—who had expert knowledge of Russia, read the Russian newspapers regularly and subscribed to an English-language newsletter produced in St Petersburg.[175] Norman was perhaps the Foreign Office's greatest supporter of the Duma. He termed 'absurd' the electoral laws adopted by the Russian government after the dissolution of the First Duma, and opined that they had been adopted solely to 'secure a majority in the Douma'.[176] He discounted the Russian government's contention that the Second Duma had been dissolved due to the existence of an anti-government plot among the more extremist parties in the Duma.[177] Norman deprecated the anti-Duma forces in Russia. These 'courtiers', he observed, 'are the only people to whom reaction could be a benefit'.[178] Norman's position put him in conflict with Hardinge, whose view of the Duma was much more in line with that of official Russia.[179] Overall Norman found the Russian government, particularly the foreign ministry, incompetent, the Russian people (and Slavs generally) incapable of sound organization, and the Russian legal system one that 'outrages Western ideas of justice'.[180] This did not mean, however, that he opposed the alignment of Britain with Russia. Instead, Norman put his faith in the gradual reform of Russia, and

---

[173] Hardinge to Grey, disp. 44, 12 Jan. 1906, FO 371/121/2107; Nicolson to Grey, 1 Sept. 1906, disp. 574, FO 371/128/30503.

[174] Hardinge to Oliphant, 16 Mar. 1914, Hardinge Papers, vol. 93.

[175] Norman's minute (19 July) on O'Beirne to Grey, disp. 432, 15 July 1909, FO 371/726/27032.

[176] Norman's minute (18 Mar.) on Nicolson to Grey, disp. 115, 1 Mar. 1907, FO 371/321/8591.

[177] His minute (29 June) on Nicolson to Grey, disp. 340, 22 June 1907, FO 371/324/21209.

[178] Norman's minute (8 May) on Nicolson to Grey, tel. 240, 7 May 1909, FO 371/729/17374.

[179] Hardinge's minutes in the two preceding notes.

[180] His minute (17 Sept.) on Nicolson to Grey, disp. 460, FO 371/327/30830; his undated minute on Woodhouse (British consul, Riga) to Grey, disp. 8, 27 May 1907, FO 371/324/17702; his undated minute on O'Beirne to Grey, disp. 257, 2 June 1908, FO 371/517/19623; for his quoted remark, his minute (28 May) on Nicolson to Grey, disp. 323, 20 May 1909, FO 371/726/19356.

favoured those in Russia who pursued co-operation with the Duma and a foreign policy aligned with France and Britain.[181] Norman's views, quite naturally given his relatively low rank in the Foreign Office, did not determine policy, but there is no doubt that they were considered carefully by those people who did. On questions of detail and on matters dealing with the personalities of those in Russia with whom the embassy came in contact, Norman's knowledge was invaluable.

Clearly, there was not any unity of opinion about Russia at the Foreign Office. What did exist was a spectrum of opinion ranging from Nicolson at one extreme to Tyrrell at the other. Nicolson, personally fond of Russia and Russians, believed that Britain should pursue a formal alliance with Russia in order to safeguard British interests in both Asia and Europe. To obtain this alliance, he was willing to put up with Russia's often difficult behaviour in Persia and her maltreatment of nationalist minorities within Russia. Tyrrell did not put such great stock in a Russian alliance. He believed that Russia had few alternatives but to align with Britain. Britain, on the other hand, held the balance of power. Between these two extremes lay the views of the other civil servants who made up the foreign-policy-making élite.

THE REPRESENTATIVES

There were six British ambassadors to Russia from 1894 to 1917. Two of them, Hardinge and Nicolson, went on to become PUS, and their views have been discussed above. It is the other four who concern us here. Sir Frank Lascelles was ambassador at St Petersburg for just over a year, from mid-1894 to the autumn of 1895. In 1879 he became British agent and consul general in Bulgaria, where he remained until early 1887. At that post, he earned high marks from Salisbury for the way in which he represented Britain during the crisis caused by the Russian kidnapping of Prince Alexander, the Bulgarian ruler, in 1885. When he left Bulgaria, he became minister to Rumania and in 1892 was appointed minister at Teheran. Thus, when he arrived in St Petersburg in July 1894, he came with good knowledge of Russian foreign policy. The Russians also had ample knowledge of Lascelles. The Russian foreign minister, N. N. Giers, told the British ambassador at their first interview that his reputation of being 'very well disposed towards Russia' had preceded him.[182] While Lascelles agreed that such indeed was his attitude, he also noted that 'I could not but remember that at one time I had the misfortune of bearing a very different reputation'. This alluded to Lascelles's time

---

[181] His minute (7 June) on Nicolson to Grey, disp. 327, 23 May 1909, FO 371/731/21127.
[182] Lascelles to Kimberley, disp. 163, 23 July 1894, FO 65/1473.

in Bulgaria when, as one friend put it, 'some of your old Panslavist friends had painted you "black upon black"'.[183] Lascelles had to deal with the matters raised by the Sino-Japanese War as well with the opening stages of the Armenian crisis. The lingering illnesses and subsequent deaths of both Alexander III and Giers, complicated matters. In such circumstances, Lascelles often found it difficult to discern Russia's policy. But he could see that the Russian government was inchoate, with ministers competing for the ear of the Emperor and that Anglo-Russian relations were a difficult matter to put on a good footing.[184] 'I must confess', he wrote to Salisbury shortly before leaving Russia, 'that my hope of seeing a really satisfactory understanding between the two countries seems as far as ever from realisation.'[185]

Lascelles would spend twelve years, the rest of his career, at Berlin as British ambassador. His influence on Anglo-Russian relations diminished, but did not end. He kept a personal interest in Russian affairs because his daughter Florence was married to Sir Cecil Spring Rice, and the latter's career was intertwined with Russia. But Russian affairs also had a very significant impact on his official work at Berlin. At Berlin, Lascelles was 'very pro-German', as one who did not share his views put it; he deprecated the 'anti-German current in the [Foreign] Office' and favoured closer Anglo-Russian relations only if they could be achieved without alienating German affections.[186]

Lascelles was replaced at St Petersburg by Sir Nicholas O'Conor, who had succeeded Lascelles before at Sofia in 1887. From Bulgaria, O'Conor had gone to Peking as envoy to both the Emperor of China and the King of Korea. He handled British interests in the Sino-Japanese War so well that Kimberley recommended him for the KCB. O'Conor served in Russia from April 1896 until July 1898. While he 'heartily rejoice[d] at getting away from this frozen region where I have never felt really well', O'Conor noted that 'with the exception of Paris I have never left a post with more regret', for the O'Conors found Russia and the Russians very hospitable.[187] This was particularly important, since O'Conor's wife, Minna, was 'subject to strange moods which make her quite impossible'.[188] This meant, as a friend noted sympathetically, that O'Conor was 'never likely to get a post where court & social functions play an important part'. The warmth of Russian hospitality undoubtedly took some of the cold out of the Russian winter.

---

[183] Chirol to Lascelles, 24 Aug. 1894, Lascelles Papers, FO 800/15.
[184] Lascelles to Salisbury, 3 July, 25 Sept. 1895, both Lascelles Papers, FO 800/17.
[185] Lascelles to Salisbury, 28 Aug. 1895, Lascelles Papers, FO 800/17.
[186] Mallet to Sandars, 11 Nov. 1904, Balfour Papers, Add MSS 49747; Lascelles to Fitzmaurice (parliamentary under-secretary, FO), 28 Sept., 2 June 1906, both Lascelles Papers, FO 800/19.
[187] O'Conor to Sanderson, 16 and 30 June 1898, both O'Conor Papers, OCON 3/15.
[188] Chirol to Lascelles, 5 Oct. 1904, Lascelles Papers, FO 800/12.

O'Conor attempted to carry out Salisbury's instruction to improve relations with Russia.[189] This proved difficult to do, particularly over the issue of China. Even though O'Conor told Sanderson in May 1896 that British interests in China were best protected 'by not making ourselves disagreeable over things wh.[ich] are not of real importance to us', he could make little headway in his efforts to improve Anglo-Russian relations.[190] The final straw was the Russian seizure of Port Arthur. The Russian foreign minister, Muravev, assured O'Conor that Russia's occupation was only temporary and that the port would be open to all nations. This proved a lie; O'Conor was furious. Salisbury offered him Constantinople, telling O'Conor that '[i]f Mouravieff has the slightest vestige of shame left, the sight of you must bring disagreeable reflections to his mind . . . the sight of you should be a reproach to him'.[191] It is clear that Salisbury's remarks were more a sop to the outraged sensibilities of O'Conor than an expression of true indignation. There is a certain dry humour—'Mouravieff's peculiarities may not startle you as much as they did the present Ambassador'—in Salisbury's offer of St Petersburg to O'Conor's successor, Sir Charles Scott.[192]

Scott received the offer of St Petersburg 'one bright Summer morning in June 1898'.[193] He found the offer 'entirely unexpected', as he was sixty years old and had been passed over for promotion on previous occasions. He accepted with reservations, for he was keenly aware both of the 'difficulties of the post' and of 'the financial worries which so expensive a residence would necessarily entail on an Ambassador like myself with no private fortune & with a large family to provide for'. Why he was offered the post is obscure. Perhaps, given the imbroglio between O'Conor and Muravev and the collapse of Anglo-Russian talks, Salisbury simply wanted a safe man in the post. Besides, Scott had spent the previous five years as British minister at Copenhagen, where, as Salisbury noted, 'your experience . . . may have given you some lights upon the Russian imperial family, besides, I believe, securing that you should be *persona grata*'.[194]

Scott was not completely without experience of Russia. He had been second secretary and head of chancery at St Petersburg from 1874 to 1877. Upon his arrival at St Petersburg in 1898, Scott noted that '[c]oming back here after 21 years['] absence I have been startled at finding so little progress made in the development of natural resources'.[195] He was to find similarly little progress in Anglo-Russian relations. A brightening came with the signing of the Chinese railway agreement in

---

[189] O'Conor to Sanderson, 22 Apr. 1896, O'Conor Papers, OCON 3/14.
[190] O'Conor to Sanderson, 7 May 1896, O'Conor Papers, OCON 3/14.
[191] Salisbury to O'Conor, 6 May 1898, O'Conor Papers, OCON 6/25.
[192] Salisbury to Scott, 28 May 1898, Scott Papers, Add MSS 52297.
[193] Scott's diary entry, 'June' 1907, Scott Papers, Add MSS 52305.
[194] Salisbury to Scott, 28 May 1898, Scott Papers, Add MSS 52297.
[195] Scott to Sanderson, 22 Sept. 1898, Scott Papers, Add MSS 52298.

April 1899, but this proved to be a false dawn. Anglo-Russian relations in the Far East continued to be cloudy, and Scott left with the embassy's being boycotted by Russian society at the beginning of the Russo-Japanese War.[196] Many of Scott's difficulties resulted from his own personality. He was 'straightforward and extremely honest', one of the junior members of the St Petersburg embassy wrote later, '[but] perhaps too inclined to judge others by his own high standard'.[197] Scott wrote bluntly to Salisbury: 'I am convinced that as regards Russians subtlety & diplomatic strategy can best be met by frankness & straightforwardness although confidence is absent, for at the former game English diplomacy would I believe be beaten.'[198] Both Muravev and his successor, Lamsdorff, took advantage of Scott's approach to diplomatic relations to the detriment of his reputation.

Scott's decline also resulted from Bertie and Hardinge's efforts. Bertie primed the King against Scott, while Hardinge, who was first secretary in Scott's embassy from 1898 to 1903, on at least one occasion sent to London evaluations of events in Russia directly counter to those of Scott.[199] Sanderson, who retained confidence in Scott, warned him: 'If I might venture to make a suggestion', Sanderson sent in mid-1903, 'I think it would be better if you avoided in your Despatches such strong expressions of confidence in Lamsdorff's straightforwardness. It drives the King wild.'[200] Even Lansdowne felt it necessary to chide Scott's unblinking faith in Lamsdorff's veracity.[201] Ironically, considering these private assaults, a virulent public attack on him by *The Times* in June 1903—over the failure to take what that newspaper considered adequate steps against the Russian government when the latter expelled *The Times'* correspondent—may have extended Scott's tenure, as the government did not wish to appear to bow to public pressure.[202]

By July 1903, Lansdowne informed Scott that he would not be kept in Russia past the winter.[203] At the end of 1903, it seemed to one of Scott's subordinates at the embassy that the ambassador had 'been made to feel that he is a superfluous person'.[204] In a final irony, Hardinge, who had done so much to undermine Scott, succeeded him. Hardinge wrote Scott that 'I fear that I shall be coming at a difficult

---

[196] The Earl of Onslow, *Sixty-Three Years: Diplomacy, the Great War and Politics, with Notes on Travel, Sport and Other Things* (London, 1944), 109.

[197] Sir H. Beaumont, 'Diplomatic Butterfly', unpub. MS, n.d., Imperial War Museum, 189.

[198] Scott to Salisbury, private and confidential, 14 Dec. 1899, Salisbury Papers, A129.

[199] Bertie to his wife, 3 Aug. 1902; Knollys to Bertie, 20 Aug. 1902, both Bertie Papers, Add MSS 63011; Hardinge to Sanderson, 7 Mar. 1901, Hardinge Papers, vol. 3.

[200] Sanderson to Scott, 17 June 1903, Scott Papers, Add MSS 52299; Bertie to Hardinge, 6 Nov. 1901, Hardinge Papers, vol. 3.

[201] Lansdowne to Scott, 23 Apr. 1901, Lansdowne Papers, FO 800/140.

[202] Hardinge to Bertie, 15 June 1903, Bertie Papers, Add MSS 63015.

[203] Barrington (Lansdowne's private secretary) to Scott, 15 July 1903, Scott Papers, Add MSS 52302.

[204] Spring Rice to Villiers, 9 Dec. 1903, Villiers Papers, FO 800/23.

time, but I have had the advantage of nearly five years at St. P. under you and consequently it is not a "terra incognita"'.[205] At the same time, Hardinge wrote to Bertie that 'Old Scott . . . still hangs on. His indecision is greater than ever and his movements slower.'[206] Hardinge told Bertie sneeringly that he had refused to buy any of Scott's accoutrements of office: 'As for their carriages they were veritable rattletraps. Fancy old Scott wanting me to buy his State liveries which had been O'Conor's before him! Thank Heaven I have some pride.'[207]

Sir George Buchanan was ambassador to Russia from 1910 until early 1918. The quintessential British diplomat, fluent in French, German, and Italian, Buchanan possessed the tact, discretion, honesty, and appearance that a career in diplomacy required. Buchanan joined the diplomatic service in 1876. At Sofia he acted as British Consul General and Agent from 1904 to 1909 and dealt successfully with the complex situation surrounding the Bosnian crisis.[208] In 1910, Buchanan was leap-frogged over '18 of his colleagues' and made ambassador to Russia.[209] Hardinge made clear just why in a letter to Nicolson: 'I am glad to hear that Buchanan is doing well in St Petersburg. I felt sure he would as he is a gentleman and quite sensible although not overburdened with brains.'[210] What he meant was that Russia required someone of breeding and tact; equally someone who believed in good Anglo-Russian relations.

While Buchanan frequently suffered from ill health in Russia and did not find either the embassy or the climate to his liking, by early 1911 he was firmly established, demonstrating his diplomatic skills. 'I must say', Nicolson wrote admiringly in 1914, 'Buchanan has the gift of using forcible language without causing the slightest irritation in Sazonoff's [the Russian foreign minister's] mind.'[211] The Foreign Office shared the belief expressed after the war by a member of the St Petersburg embassy that 'so long as he was dealing with a world he understood, his judgment was never wrong'.[212] Buchanan's opinion of events in Russia was readily accepted in London until 1917, when the revolution created a world that he was thought not to understand. But Buchanan proved this assessment wrong. His putative successor, the Labour member of Lloyd George's War Cabinet, Arthur Henderson, found him valuable, and the ambassador stayed until 1918.

[205] Hardinge to Scott, 16 Feb. 1904, Scott Papers, Add MSS 52302.
[206] Hardinge to Bertie, 22 Apr. 1904, Bertie Papers, FO 800/176.
[207] Hardinge to Bertie, 20 Mar. 1904, Bertie Papers, FO 800/183; Busch, *Old Diplomacy*, 94–7.
[208] Sir G. Buchanan, *My Mission to Russia and Other Diplomatic Memories* (2 vols.; London, 1923), i. 86.
[209] Goschen's diary entry, 9 July 1910, in Howard (ed.), *Goschen diary*, 208.
[210] Hardinge to Nicolson, 29 Mar. 1911, Nicolson Papers, FO 800/348.
[211] Nicolson to Goschen (British ambassador, Vienna), 18 May 1914, Nicolson Papers, FO 800/374.
[212] H. J. Bruce, *Silken Dalliance* (London, 1946), 173; Neilson, *Strategy and Supply*, 25.

Besides the ambassadors there were others in the embassy whose views were given careful consideration. Among them was Sir Cecil Spring Rice. When Spring Rice became first secretary at the St Petersburg embassy in 1903, he was perhaps the most promising young man in the diplomatic corps. Possessed of a sharp mind and a sharper tongue, 'Springy' was a favourite of many of his colleagues.[213] Scott greeted Spring Rice's appointment with enthusiasm, and Hardinge, when he succeeded Scott, found Spring Rice invaluable.[214] Spring Rice, though, did not enjoy his time in St Petersburg. He found the country 'ugly', the climate 'intolerable', and the people 'accustomed to misery'.[215] He also had a low opinion of the Russian government and Russian foreign policy.[216] As to the possibility of good Anglo-Russian relations, Spring Rice was not sanguine. While he believed that 'it is most desirable to do what we can, to soften our relations with Russia,' he also argued that 'a definite & permanent agreement seems impossible'. His reasoning was straightforward. 'The only possible agreement' Spring Rice concluded in April 1904, 'is one which Russia cannot break because she has not the power to break it—because we have the force'.[217]

Such views did not end when Spring Rice left Russia. In 1906 he was made British minister at Teheran. From there, Spring Rice wrote prolifically, opposing 'root and branch' the Anglo-Russian negotiations leading to the 1907 Convention.[218] Even after the Convention was signed, Spring Rice continued to oppose the policy of close ties with Russia, on his assumption that the tsar's regime was not to be trusted. 'The Russians are wonderful people', he wrote in 1908, 'but their eagle is double-headed; one for Europe and one for Asia; one to "explain" and one to "perform".'[219] His opposition was discounted at the Foreign Office, and attributed to his well-known tendency to be somewhat overly imaginative and dramatic in his observations.[220] Though his views were disregarded on this issue, Spring Rice himself was not. Grey and Tyrrell wrote soothing letters, assuring him that his career was not being sidetracked in Persia, and in 1908 he was made

[213] D. H. Burton, *Cecil Spring Rice: A Diplomat's Life* (London, 1990).

[214] Scott to Sanderson, 5 Feb. 1903, Scott Papers, Add MSS 52304; Hardinge to Grey, disp. 44, 12 Jan. 1906, FO 371/121/2107.

[215] Spring Rice to his sister Margaret, 24 Nov. 1903, in Gwynn, S. (ed.), *The Letters and Friendships of Sir Cecil Spring Rice: A Record* (2 vols; London, 1929), i. 369–70.

[216] Beaumont, 'Diplomatic Butterfly', 202; Spring Rice to John Hay (American secretary of state), 31 Aug. 1904, in Gwynn (ed.), *Letters and Friendships*, i. 424–6.

[217] Spring Rice to Mallet, 13 Apr. 1904, Lansdowne Papers, FO 800/115.

[218] O'Beirne to Bertie, 28 May 1907, Bertie Papers, FO 800/176.

[219] Spring Rice to Cromer (British Agent and Consul-General, Egypt), 11 Sept. 1908, Cromer Papers, FO 633/14.

[220] Sanderson to Spring Rice, 4 Nov. 1903, Spring Rice Papers, FO 800/241; Chirol to Lascelles, 18 Apr. 1905, Lascelles Papers, FO 800/11; Hardinge to Nicolson, 23 Jan. 1907, Nicolson Papers, FO 800/339.

minister to Sweden.[221] He continued his denunciations, blaming Russia's policy towards Finland for Sweden's pro-German tendencies.[222] Spring Rice thus belonged with Bertie and Curzon as leading opponents of close Anglo-Russian relations.

Hugh O'Beirne's entire career centred around Russia. He began his diplomatic career as an attaché in St Petersburg in 1892 and died on board H.M.S. *Hampshire* on his way to Russia in 1916. From 1906 until 1915 he was councillor at the embassy in St Petersburg. As early as 1895 Lascelles told Sanderson 'to keep an eye on him [O'Beirne] as one of the future lights of the diplomatic service' and fourteen years later Hardinge rated him one of the top two councillors in the diplomatic service.[223] When Buchanan had to take leave in 1911 just as Balkan affairs were at a boil, Grey wrote that this would not matter so much as 'O'Beirne is good & knows the business & people at St Petersburgh'.[224] In 1915, O'Beirne was sent on a special mission to the Balkans in an attempt to bring about an anti-German coalition of the neutral states in that region. The task was near-impossible, but two able observers felt that O'Beirne might have been able to accomplish it had he been sent sooner.[225]

In Russia, O'Beirne became the most knowledgable man in the diplomatic service about that country. Fluent in Russian, he made a particularly close study of the Russian economy, and his opinion on it was sought both by those in the Foreign Office and by those in British financial circles.[226] He also had important views on other aspects of affairs in Russia. An Irish landowner, O'Beirne felt a certain sympathy for the harsh measures undertaken by Petr Stolypin, the Russian chairman of the Council of Ministers, against unrest in the Russian countryside, but his sympathies did not lie unreservedly with Stolypin. 'No doubt he would have made a good sort of satrap', O'Beirne wrote of Stolypin in 1906, 'but the liberals here do not like him much, because his notions of government are the good old fashioned Russian bureaucrat's ideas, i.e. to pack you into prison or remove you to Siberia if you oppose the Government.'[227]

[221] Grey to Spring Rice, 30 Nov. 1906, 15 Apr. 1907; Tyrrell to Spring Rice, 18 Feb. and 15 May 1907, all Spring Rice Papers FO 800/241.

[222] Spring Rice to Bertie, 30 Aug. 1910, Bertie Papers, FO 800/179.

[223] Lascelles to Sanderson, 22 May 1895, Lascelles Papers, FO 800/17; Hardinge to Graham (acting British agent and consul-general, Cairo), 28 Oct. 1909, Hardinge Papers, vol. 17.

[224] Grey to Nicolson, 21 Sept. 1911, Nicolson Papers, FO 800/350.

[225] Chirol to Hardinge, 25 June 1916, Hardinge Papers, vol. 22; Sir V. Chirol, *Fifty Years in a Changing World* (London, 1927), 312; H. D. Napier, *The Experiences of a Military Attaché in the Balkans* (London, 1923), 12–15.

[226] Revelstoke (head and managing director, Baring Brothers) to O'Beirne, 10 Sept. 1908, Barings Papers, Barings Partners' filings/209.

[227] O'Beirne to Nicolson, 6 Oct. 1907, Nicolson Paper, FO 800/340; quotation from O'Beirne to Bertie, 2 Dec. 1906, Bertie Papers, FO 800/177.

THE OLD RUSSIA HANDS

While the official British representatives in Russia provided London with much of the information for making decisions, that information was not always generated by them. They often relied on people outside the official circles of the British government. Although such sources had an indirect influence, their ideas about Russia had a twofold importance: they reached not only the policy-making élite, but also the British public. Here, only their connection to the élite will be discussed; their views of Russia will be discussed in Chapter three.

Sir Donald Mackenzie Wallace was the father of Russian studies in Britain. From the publication of his *Russia* (1887), Wallace was the acknowledged expert, one well connected politically.[228] It was during Nicolson's time as ambassador that Wallace had his greatest influence. Nicolson had met Wallace in the early 1880s, when Wallace was *The Times'* correspondent at Constantinople and Nicolson a junior member of the embassy there. When Nicolson was the British representative at Algeciras, he had confided in Wallace and had found the latter's opinion 'worth having'.[229] It was not surprising, then, that the ambassador invited Wallace to come to Russia. During the next few months, Wallace lived at the embassy and studied the new Russian political situation that had emerged after 1905. His influence on Nicolson was subtle, yet profound. Nicolson found congenial Wallace's ideas of gradual reform, rather than revolution, in Russia, and Wallace's subsequent trips to Russia helped to reinforce his influence with the ambassador. Certainly Nicolson always lauded Wallace's knowledge of Russia and recommended to his superiors at the Foreign Office that they find time to listen to Wallace's views.[230] Wallace's influence on Nicolson was widely known in diplomatic circles, leading Bertie to remark on one occasion that 'it is evident Nicolson accepts Donald Mackenzie Wallace's views in regard to Russia'.[231] While some—notably Sanderson—were less impressed by Wallace's opinions about Russia than was Nicolson, nevertheless Sir Donald was an important member of the old Russia hands.[232]

If Wallace began Russian studies in Britain, then Bernard Pares must be seen as the man who made them part of academe. In 1898, at the age of thirty-one, he travelled to Russia and became enamoured of the country and its history. Pares had been an extension lecturer with Cambridge since 1895, and he soon parleyed this and his expertise about Russia into a readership in modern Russian history at the

[228] D. G. Morren, 'Donald Mackenzie Wallace and British Russophilism, 1870–1919', *CSP* 9 (1967), 170–83.
[229] Cited, Nicolson, *Lord Carnock*, 171.
[230] Nicolson to Spring Rice, 26 Aug. 1906, Spring Rice Papers, FO 800/241; Nicolson to Grey, disp. 667, 2 Oct. 1906, FO 371/129/34610; Nicolson to Hardinge, 2 Jan. 1908, Hardinge Papers, vol. 12.
[231] Bertie to Mallet, 23 Oct. 1906, Bertie Papers, FO 800/177.
[232] Sanderson to Hardinge, 19 Sept. 1905, Hardinge Papers, vol. 7.

University of Liverpool. By 1908 he was professor of Russian history, language, and literature. In 1919, after spending time as an official British representative to Admiral Kolchak's White regime, Pares moved to London and was director of the School of Slavonic and East European Studies of the University of London from 1922 to 1939.

While Pares certainly lacked Mackenzie Wallace's social connections and easy access to the prominent, he was well-known to those both at the British embassy in St Petersburg and at the Foreign Office. Perhaps his warmest supporters were Nicolson and Norman who were impressed by his wide knowledge of and impartiality towards Russian affairs.[233] Hardinge's views were more complex. On the one hand, Hardinge found Pares 'rather a bore' and felt that he had 'always thrown in his lot with the Cadets' to the detriment of his objectivity.[234] On the other hand, Hardinge accepted that Pares was well informed.

Journalists provided another source of information about Russia. Easily the most prominent among them was the mysterious Dr E. J. Dillon, the *Daily Telegraph*'s long-term correspondent in Russia and a frequent contributor on foreign affairs to the *Contemporary Review*. Born in Ireland, he had studied on the Continent, spoke as many as twenty-six languages and had lived in Russia since the 1880s. He was a close friend of Sergei Witte, the Russian finance minister, and was viewed by the British representatives as being the latter's creature.[235] Hardinge found Dillon odd: 'He is clever & interesting', Hardinge told Sanderson in 1905, 'but very weird, & altho' an Irishman, a great patriot.'[236] Dillon's importance fluctuated. Until 1909, he frequented the British embassy in St Petersburg and his views were given close attention. But eventually he was deemed to have been converted to a pro-Hapsburg position by the flattery of Baron Alois Aehrenthal, the Austro-Hungarian foreign minister. His opinions were discounted at the Foreign Office. Dillon had now become, in Hardinge's words, 'a most unreliable scoundrel', and the PUS scathingly condemned Dillon's 'impertinence' in attempting to get permission for his son to sit the Foreign Office entrance examination.[237] By 1911 Buchanan was describing Dillon as 'dogmatic, and I might add as tiresome, as usual'.[238]

The Times' correspondents in Russia were of particular influence, since *The Times* occupied a special place among British newspapers. As Sanderson told Scott in 1903: 'The Times is to us a constant and fertile source of aggravation. It is always

[233] Norman's minute (19 Sept.) on Pares' memo, 4 Sept. 1908, FO 371/512/30901; Nicolson to Grey, disp. 394, 23 June 1906, FO 371/126/21893.
[234] Hardinge to Nicolson, 6 Feb. 1907, Nicolson Papers, FO 800/339; undated minute (Hardinge) on Nicolson to Grey, disp. 161, 11 Mar. 1909, FO 371/726/7777.
[235] Spring Rice to Lansdowne, 22 July 1905, Lansdowne Papers, FO 800/116.
[236] Hardinge to Sanderson, 15 Feb. 1905, Hardinge Papers, vol. 6.
[237] Hardinge to Nicolson, 10 Nov. 1909, Nicolson Papers, FO 800/342.
[238] Buchanan to Nicolson, 23 Mar. 1911, Nicolson Papers, FO 800/348.

attacking some foreign Power or lecturing it on the inequity and perversity of its ways, and generally at the same moment condemning the Foreign Secretary and his unfortunate department for ineptitude and weakness.'[239] George Dobson was *The Times'* man in Russia from the mid-1870s until he was forced to retire in 1901 because of illness. He was very well-regarded, not only by the British embassy in St Petersburg but also by the Russian authorities.[240] In 1901, Dobson was replaced by Dudley Braham, whose career in Russia was tumultuous. In 1903 he was expelled from Russia as a result of his reportage of revolutionary events.[241] This resulted in *The Times'* declaring war on Russia, and the paper had no regular correspondent in Russia until 1906 when Robert Wilton, formerly the *Glasgow Herald's* correspondent in Russia, took the position. Wilton was *The Times'* correspondent in Russia on a regular basis until 1910 and then, intermittently, until 1913. When the war began, he went to Russia full-time. Wilton had covered the Portsmouth Conference for *The Times* before going to St Petersburg, and had impressed his editor, Valentine Chirol, as being 'better than Braham, but he does not quite come up to the standard'.[242] This view came to be the accepted one at the embassy. In 1909, Nicolson lamented the lack of 'a better band of correspondents' in St Petersburg. 'Wilton, the "Times" man', the ambassador wrote, 'is a good creature but obtuse—and seems incapable of grasping a subject properly. He usually conveys quite a wrong impression.'[243] The embassy often found correspondents a hindrace to maintaining good relations with the Russian government, since the reporters often had sympathies for the liberal movement.[244] The British idea of fair reportage found little sympathy in Russia. Even during the war Wilton's condemnation of 'unduly optimistic' reports concerning Russia's war effort was viewed by the Russian censors as 'tantamount to treason'.[245]

Two other journalists require mention. W. T. Stead, the founder and editor of the *Review of Reviews*, was the leading advocate of a better Anglo-Russian understanding from 1870 until his death on board the *Titanic* in 1912.[246] Under the influence of the Russian Slavophile propagandist, Madam Olga Novikova, Stead preached the need for liberal reform, but always supported the tsars themselves.

[239] Sanderson to Scott, 2 May 1903, Scott Papers Add MSS 52299.
[240] Scott to Lansdowne, 11 June 1903, Lansdowne Papers, FO 800/140.
[241] *The Times, The History of The Times: The Twentieth Century Test 1884–1912* (New York, 1947), 382–8.
[242] Chirol to Hardinge, 22 Aug. 1905, Hardinge Papers, vol. 7.
[243] Nicolson to Hardinge, 18 Jan. 1909, Nicolson Papers, FO 800/337.
[244] Hardinge's undated minute on Nicolson to Grey, disp. 340, 22 June 1907, FO 371/324/21209.
[245] Wilton to Northcliffe (owner of *The Times*), 1 Nov. 1915, Northcliffe Papers, Add MSS 62253.
[246] For Stead, J. O. Baylen's articles: 'W. T. Stead, Apologist for Imperial Russia, 1870–80', *Gazette: International Journal for Mass Communications Studies*, 6 (1960), 281–97; 'The Tsar and the British Press: Alexander III and the *Pall Mall Gazette*, 1888', *EEQ* 15 (1982), 425–39; 'W. T. Stead and the Russian Revolution of 1905', *CJH* 2 (1967), 45–66.

The British representatives in Russia half resented the fact that Stead was able to arrange personal interviews with Nicholas II, and they felt that his influence among liberals had been compromised completely by his support for the tsar in 1905. None the less, he was not thought to be harmful to Anglo-Russian relations. As Scott put it in 1898 when Stead came to Russia to 'practise amateur diplomacy . . . his notorious Russophilism can, I imagine, only do good & no harm here'.[247] Much more significant was Valentine Chirol, the director of *The Times'* foreign department from 1899 to 1912. Chirol had served briefly in the Foreign Office in the 1870s, and was a personal friend to both Hardinge and Nicolson. 'He is as intimate in the Foreign Office', Spring Rice wrote to Theodore Roosevelt in November 1904, 'as anyone can be, and absolutely trusted.'[248] Chirol maintained an extensive correspondence with many British diplomatists, and his letters are filled with wide-ranging discussions of foreign policy. Everyone acknowledged his expertise, not only about Germany (where he had been a correspondent in the 1890s), but also about foreign affairs generally.

The general characteristics of the British policy-making-élite who determined the course of Anglo-Russian relations in the reign of Nicholas II should come as no surprise. But for the 'old Russian hands', its members came from the same social classes that dominated British government generally. With the exception of Eyre Crowe, whose unusual background was an anomaly, the distinctions within the élite were more a matter of gradations—and certainly these could be wide and important—within a class. Intimate links of family, schooling and shared experience ensured that the élite remained homogeneous.

Another unifying factor was experience of either India or Persia. Salisbury and Kimberley had each been secretary of state for India; indeed Kimberley held the office three times. Lansdowne had been briefly under-secretary of state for India and was viceroy from 1888 to 1894. Only Grey among the foreign secretaries had no link with the subcontinent. Outside the political ranks, other members of the élite had ties to India. Curzon and Hardinge, for example, were both viceroys. At the Foreign Office and among the diplomatists, time in Persia distinguished many of those who affected Anglo-Russian relations. Both Hardinge and Nicolson had spent time as secretaries in Teheran. Lascelles had been minister there immediately before he came to St Petersburg, and Spring Rice was briefly secretary of legation in 1900 and, after his time in Russia, became minister at Teheran. This meant that many of the élite had first-hand experience of the cutting edge of Anglo-Russian relations on the north-west frontier of India.

[247] Scott to Sanderson, 20 Oct. 1898, Scott Papers, Add MSS 52298.
[248] Spring Rice to Roosevelt, Nov. 1904, in Gwynne (ed.), *Letters and Friendships*, i. 436–7; L. B. Fritzinger, 'Friends in High Places: Valentine Chirol, *The Times*, and Anglo-German Relations, 1892–6', *Victorian Periodicals Review*, 21 (1988).

This shared experience of Russia did not mean that the élite agreed about Anglo-Russian relations. At one extreme were men like Curzon, Bertie, and Spring Rice, who saw Russia as an implacable foe. In their opinion, efforts to come to an understanding with her were doomed to failure, since the interests of the two countries were irreconcilable and, in any case, Russia could not be trusted to observe any undertaking that she made. At the other extreme was Nicolson, who believed both that an understanding with Russia was essential and that Russia could be trusted. The other members fell somewhere between these two extremes. The interplay between their ideas, the positions of power that they held, and the degree of influence that they enjoyed determined the shape of British policy towards Russia after Nicholas II came to the throne.

The élite can be divided on another basis: that of generations. The first, who might be termed the 'Victorians', were born mainly in the 1830s and early 1840s; the second, the 'Edwardians', were born mainly in the 1850s and early 1860s. Such labels are terms of convenience, for the future Edward VII was born in 1841, the same year as several prominent 'Victorians'. But the 'Edwardians' came to occupy positions of power roughly contemporaneously with Edward VII's accession to power upon the death of Victoria, and the terms evoke the wider change of sensibilities in society, a change that was mirrored in foreign policy.[249]

A number of things divided the 'Victorians' and the 'Edwardians'. For the most part, the 'Victorians'—men like Salisbury (born 1830), Scott (born 1838), Sanderson and Lascelles (both born 1841) and O'Conor (born 1843)—reached their political maturity before the unifications of Italy and Germany. Generally, German unification was regarded favourably by Britain.[250] Germany, it was hoped, would form a natural ally for Britain; one that would balance the French and Russian threat to Europe. The 'Victorians' were not marked by the prevalent anti-Germanism of later generations. Russia was the enemy for the 'Victorians. For them the Crimean War was a vivid memory, together with the mutiny, and the Russian expansion into Central Asia a fact of everyday political life.

The 'Edwardians' saw matters differently. Men like Nicolson (born somewhat early for an 'Edwardian' in 1849), Asquith (born 1852), Buchanan (born 1854), Hardinge (born 1858), Spring Rice and Curzon (both born 1859), and Grey (born 1862) had their formative political experiences much later. The idea of Germany as Britain's natural ally seemed absurd to those who had observed the scramble for Africa and who had to deal with the erratic Wilhelm II. Instead, they saw Germany

---

[249] W. E. Houghton, *The Victorian Frame of Mind 1830–70* (New Haven, 1973); S. Hynes, *The Edwardian Turn of Mind* (Princeton, 1968); J. Rose, *The Edwardian Temperament 1895–1919* (Athens, OH, 1987).

[250] W. E. Mosse, *The European Powers and the German Question 1848–71: With Special Reference to England and Russia* (repr. edn. New York, 1981), 359–60.

as the enemy, and Russia—while autocratic, still a possible threat to Britain, and allied to Britain's traditional foe, France—as the potential answer to the problem posed by Germany's perceived determination to dominate Europe.

There is yet another matter that divides the two groups. For want of a more precise name, it may be termed 'attitude'. The 'Victorians' among the élite took a more detached, less interventionist attitude towards foreign policy than did the Edwardians. Salisbury and Sanderson exemplify this approach. This is not to suggest that this duo did not work hard to protect British interests. Rather, it is to assert that they felt that there were clear limits to foreign policy. Sanderson's warning to Spring Rice that '[o]ne runs the risk of losing clear sight of the general trend of events if one watches too eagerly every oscillation of the political seismograph' was more than advice; it was a statement of principle. Salisbury was convinced that no long-term policy was possible, as all depended on the 'swing of the pendulum at home. It may be taken I think for an axiom', Salisbury opined in 1897, 'that no foreign or external policy can succeed unless it can be completed within one beat of the pendulum.'[251] As a result of such thinking, Salisbury could argue as early as 1877 that 'English policy is to float lazily downstream, occasionally putting out a diplomatic boat-hook to avoid collisions'.[252] Salisbury and Sanderson were never reluctant to put out 'boat-hooks', but neither felt that such 'boat-hooks' could be extended at will or by preordained plan.

The attitude of the 'Victorians' stemmed partly from a confidence in Britain's strength and partly from the disunity of her potential enemies. Both beliefs came under challenge in the 1890s.[253] 'Edwardians' saw Britain as a nation under assault. The manifest growth of German economic and military strength, the potential power of such continent-spanning states as Russia and the United States, and the tendency of the powers to band together into blocs, all posed potential threats to Britain. The responses were diverse. Men like Chamberlain called for imperial federation; others felt 'national efficiency' and an increased commitment to military service would maintain Britain's position.[254] Whatever the response, it was always motivated by a belief that it was both possible and necessary to take action, in foreign policy as well as in other spheres of activity.

Thus, such men as Hardinge, Bertie, and Curzon proposed an active, often combative foreign policy. Foreign threats should be met both by increased British military and naval strength and by firm and principled diplomatic opposition. In

---

[251] Salisbury to Curzon, 23 Dec. 1897, Curzon Papers, MSS Eur F112/1b.

[252] Salisbury to Lytton, 9 Mar. 1877, cited, Lowe, *Reluctant Imperialists*, i. 19.

[253] Howard, *Splendid Isolation*.

[254] G. R. Searle, *The Quest for National Efficiency: A Study in British Politics and British Political Thought, 1899–1914* (Oxford, 1971); A. L. Friedberg, *The Weary Titan: Britain and the Experience of Relative Decline 1895–1905* (Princeton, 1988); P. Kennedy, *The Rise and Fall of the Great Powers* (New York, 1987), 224–32.

practice, this attitude meant different things when applied to different countries. Accommodation with France was possible; accommodation with Germany was not. Russia was an enigma. Some 'Edwardians', like Curzon, felt that an Anglo-Russian arrangement was impossible. Others, like Nicolson, were convinced that it was not only possible but essential. Grey occupied a middle ground, as did Hardinge. But for all of the 'Edwardians', a policy of 'boat-hooks' was temperamentally impossible.

This division into 'Victorians' and 'Edwardians' either by birth date or by attitude should not be taken too far. There are obvious anomalies. Bertie, for example, was by birth (1844) firmly in the 'Victorian' camp, along with men like O'Conor; however, it is clear that by attitude, Bertie clearly belongs with 'Edwardians' like Hardinge. And such a division leaves out men like Balfour (born 1848) and Lansdowne (born 1845), whose birth dates and attitudes straddle the division between 'Victorians' and 'Edwardians'. Equally, circumstance affected what London could (and, perhaps more importantly, could not) do to determine the nature of Anglo-Russian relations.

All foreign secretaries from 1894 onwards wished to come to some arrangement with Russia. But it was only after the Russo-Japanese war that Russian statesmen were willing to do so on terms acceptable to Britain. Coincidentally, this change in Russian attitudes occurred just as there was a generational change in the British élite from the 'Victorians' to the 'Edwardians'. Also, at this time the Liberals came to power in Britain, bringing a change in the composition of the political élite. To complete this collocation of events, the reform of the Foreign Office, which gave greater influence to its members, occurred at this time. For these reasons, the period from 1904 to 1906 was pivotal in Anglo-Russian relations.

British policy towards Russia in the period from 1894 to 1917 was formed by a relatively small number of people. United by class, wealth, upbringing, and schooling, they were divided by party affiliation, responsibility of position, generational beliefs, and opinions. Their views of Russia and individual Russians are extremely important, for they were guided by 'mental maps' of Russia's political landscape when they made policy.[255] The contours of that 'mental map' are essential to an understanding of Anglo-Russian relations.

---

[255] A. K. Henrikson, 'The Geographical "Mental Maps" of American Foreign Policy Makers', *International Political Science Review*, 1 (1980), 498–500; D. C. Watt, *Succeeding John Bull: America in Britain's Place 1900–75* (Cambridge, 1984), 16–17; Z. Steiner, 'Elitism and Foreign Policy: The Foreign Office in the Great War', in B. J. C. McKercher and D. J. Moss (eds.), *Shadow and Substance in British Foreign Policy 1895–1939* (Edmonton, Alta., 1984), 25–6; 44–5.

2

The Élite's Russia

RUSSIA had many facets for those who served Britain in that country. It was not only a political system and a collection of personalities, but also a place to live and a stage in their careers. As a posting, Russia was clearly important. One of the eight—nine, after Japan was accorded such status—ambassadorial posts before 1914, St Petersburg was avidly coveted. While Paris was the plum, in the twenty years before 1914, St Petersburg and Berlin undoubtedly ranked as the second-most prestigious embassies and vied with each other as being the most important politically. A look at the appointments to St Petersburg underlines the significance of Russia. This is especially obvious when it is remembered that consecutive ambassadors to Russia—Hardinge and Nicolson—were successively PUS. Hardinge, indeed, was the clearly the brightest star of the diplomatic service. The long tenure of Hardinge and Nicolson as PUS (and it is significant that Hardinge became PUS again in 1916) meant that Russia was always to the fore in discussions of British foreign policy.

Russia itself was an alien, exotic place to British diplomats. On entering Russia, one diplomat noted in his memoirs, 'one has the sensation of leaving Europe and being in quite another world'.[1] From the symbolic uncoupling of the railway coaches in Warsaw in order to change to the wider Russian gauge to the 'famous Russian smell', Russia presented new experiences for those steeped in Europe. For one thing, the scale was different. The very size of the country came as a shock to British diplomats, and society offered such unusual activities as going bear hunting on the vast estates of the Russian nobility.[2] 'St. Petersburg itself', one diplomat recalled, 'was grandiose, everything was on a big scale: the principal streets, the palaces and the churches.'[3] Society life was equally unusual. The highlights of the season were the three great court balls held in January and February. Their

---

[1] Sir H. Beaumont, 'Diplomatic Butterfly', TS MS, Imperial War Museum, 172; subsequent quotation from Sir W. Hayter, *A Double Life* (London, 1974), 29. Hayter's comments reflect earlier views.

[2] The Earl of Onslow, *Sixty Three Years: Diplomacy, the Great War and Politics, with Notes on Travel, Sport and Other Things* (London, 1944), 94–6; Sir N. Henderson, *Water Under the Bridges* (London, 1945), 24–46.

[3] Sir J. Tilley, *London to Tokyo* (London, 1942), 72. The quotation reflects Tilley's impressions of Russia in 1910.

splendour made an indelible impression on those who attended, and these events clearly seemed extraordinary even to diplomatists accustomed to pomp and circumstance.[4] Equally extraordinary were the hours kept. 'Unless one happened to be asked for dinner', Neville Henderson, whose first posting was to St Petersburg, wrote in his memoirs, 'one went to a party at midnight and it usually lasted to three or four in the morning, often till much later.'[5] This was followed by smaller groups going to restaurants to listen to gypsy music and to dance. Obviously this life took its toll on ambassadors, whose age generally meant that such activities were left to the more junior members of their staff, although there were exceptions. 'I admire your courage', Nicolson wrote to Buchanan in 1911, 'in falling in with the late hours which society are so fond of. I was unable to fall in with these habits but I had not a young lady to take out into the world.'[6]

Pre-1914 Russia was also the Russia of the ballet. At least one member of the diplomatic corps, the head of the chancery at the British embassy, Henry Bruce, took the ballet so seriously that he courted and married Tamara Karsavina, the prima ballerina of the Diaghilev company.[7] For those who preferred their pursuits outdoors, there was polo. This activity, which attracted Hardinge as well as the younger members of his staff, was an interesting social mixer. Even during the boycott of the British embassy by most members of Russian society during the Russo-Japanese War, Prince Sergei Beloselsky, an 'enthusiastic polo player', kept up his regular attendance with the British equestrians.[8] Unfortunately, St Petersburg was such an expensive post that Henderson was able to keep up his string of ponies only through his winnings at bridge; by 1913 polo could be played only by using cheaper, Caucasian steeds. The high cost of living meant that junior members of the embassy, on whom fell many of the social duties, often found their resources stretched to the breaking point.[9] Even ambassadors had to give thought to the cost of living in Russia.[10]

But it was with Russia's government that the British representatives had to deal. That government was intensely personal in nature. As Salisbury wrote in Novem-

[4] Beaumont, 'Diplomatic Butterfly', 215–17; Onslow, *Sixty Three Years*, 94–6; A. Hardinge, *A Diplomatist in Europe* (London, 1927), 90–2.

[5] Henderson, *Water Under the Bridges*, 44; R. H. B. Lockhart, *British Agent* (New York, 1933), 54–62. Such practices remained until the very end of the regime; Clive diary entries, 3 and 5 Feb. 1917, Clive Papers.

[6] Nicolson to Buchanan, 14 Feb. 1911, Nicolson Papers, FO 800/347. The 'young lady' was Buchanan's daughter Meriel; see M. Buchanan, *The Dissolution of an Empire* (London, 1932), 12–25.

[7] H. J. Bruce, *Thirty Dozen Moons* (London, 1949), 1–10; T. Karsavina, *Theatre Street* (New York, 1931).

[8] Henderson, *Water Under the Bridges*, 26, 37–8; Beaumont, 'Diplomatic Butterfly', 193–4; Onslow, *Sixty Three Years*, 98.

[9] Tilley, *London to Tokyo*, 72–3.

[10] Scott's retrospective diary entry, June. 1907, Scott Papers, Add MSS 52305.

ber 1896, 'I think there is more human nature in the Russian Government that in any other.'[11] Autocratic Russia was governed differently from any other great power. The Russian emperor, until the creation of the Duma, had powers that in theory were unlimited and in practice were very wide. Those who administered departments of state were directly responsibly to the sovereign. They owed their positions to the emperor, and were often summarily dismissed. It was a government, in short, that Salisbury's great ancestor, Lord Burghley, would have found perfectly intelligible.

In such a system, the character of individuals loomed large. In the months preceding the death of Alexander III, there was much speculation among British diplomatists about the nature of the heir apparent.[12] Nicholas II would prove enigmatic, to his contemporaries and to historians.[13] A first glimpse of his style of government was given early in 1895 when he dismissed A. V. Krivoshein, the minister of ways and communications.[14] Lascelles then offered a judgement of Nicholas: 'a man of liberal ideas and very conscientious, but would be likely to shrink from any change which could be interpreted as a reproach upon his Father. I do not know who advises him or indeed whether he consults any one. Giers [minister of foreign affairs] is too ill to go to him, and it would seem that the other ministers are too much afraid for their positions to be able to offer suggestions.' However, on 29 January 1895 Nicholas made a speech deprecating any idea that he might share his power and reaffirming his dedication to the concept of autocracy.[15] This, Lascelles wrote, 'has taken people by surprise'.[16] 'It certainly seems at variance', the ambassador went on,'with the supposed liberal character of the Emperor's character, but I know too little yet either of His Majesty's character or of reasons which may have induced him to use such language.' After recounting various explanations that had been put forward for the tone and content of Nicholas's speech, Lascelles could only note that 'the opinions I have heard expressed are so contradictory that it is difficult to ascertain the truth'.[17]

When Salisbury returned to office, Lascelles immediately attempted to explain what he knew about Nicholas. He might be 'a thoroughly honest and well-meaning Sovereign but he is young and inexperienced and so far as I am able to judge has no

[11] Salisbury to O'Conor, 11 Nov. 1896, Salisbury Papers, A129.
[12] Lascelles to Gosselin, 25 Oct. 1894, Lascelles Papers, FO 800/17.
[13] On Nicholas II's influence, cf. A. Verner, *The Crisis of Autocracy: Nicholas II and the 1905 Revolution* (Princeton, 1990) and D. M. McDonald, *United Government and Foreign Policy in Russia 1900–14* (Cambridge, MA., 1992). By far the best biography is D. Lieven, *Nicholas II: Emperor of All the Russias* (London, 1993), which presents Nicholas II in a balanced, sensible fashion.
[14] Lascelles to Sanderson, 16 Jan. 1895, Lascelles Papers, FO 800/17.
[15] Lascelles to Kimberley, disp. 31, 31 Jan. 1895, FO 65/1490.
[16] Lascelles to Kimberley, 31 Jan. 1895, Lascelles Papers, FO 800/17; Medhurst (British consul, Moscow) to Lascelles, 5 Feb. 1895, Lascelles Papers, FO 800/16.
[17] Lascelles to Kimberley, confidential disp. 37, 12 Feb. 1895, FO 65/1490.

one in whom he has sufficient confidence to rely on in the event of an emergency'.[18] A month later, the Emperor's abrupt and somewhat ruthless dismissal of P. N. Durnovo as minister of the interior underlined that Nicholas was capable of decisive action in the defence of his prerogatives as autocrat.[19] The idea grew that Nicholas lacked competent, trustworthy advisers: 'Much of what I hear confirms the idea that the Emperor is influenced by the arguments of his last adviser, but at the same time I am inclined to think that as he has not much confidence in his own judgment he is sensible enough to rely upon one or other of his Ministers—and today it seem to be M. de Witte.' Several weeks later O'Conor suggested that the Emperor did not know 'on whom to lean' among his officials.[20]

Many were willing to believe that, given his youth and inexperience, Nicholas was educating himself slowly in the intricacies of autocratic rule. Madame Staal, the wife of the long-time Russian ambassador to Britain and who possessed good ties to the Romanov court, leaned to this view, as did Sir Charles Scott.[21] Once Scott had gained more first-hand knowledge of Nicholas' character, he was less charitable. In May 1899, Scott remarked on 'the diffidence, or weakness, or conscious inexperience or call it what you like, of the Emperor who wants to do his best, but he is far from having the iron will of his father, and is full of filial respect, and ambitions of a quiet life'.[22] Nicholas wanted to be the dutiful son, and 'not to make his mother cry'.[23] Lacking firm leadership, Nicholas's ministers 'constantly disagree and bicker'. Scott gradually came to believe that the Emperor lacked any ability to make difficult decisions, especially when he was urged by his military advisers to be more aggressive. At the beginning of 1900, with a more active military role for Russia being advocated at court, Scott suggested that 'His Majesty has not all the firmness of purpose which one could wish'.[24] Although Scott was convinced of the pacific nature of Nicholas' foreign policy in China, the ambassador realized that 'his character may not be a very strong one, & his deference to military views at time greater than that of the late Emperor in similar cases'.[25] By 1902, this had become a maxim with Scott.[26]

Countervailing the aggressive polices in Asia advocated by Nicholas' military advisers were the views of the Empress Alexandra, Nicholas' wife. Hardinge felt

[18] Lascelles to Salisbury, 3 July 1895, Lascelles Papers, FO 800/17.

[19] Lascelles to Salisbury, 14 Aug. 1895, Salisbury Papers, A129.

[20] O'Conor to Salisbury, 3 Dec. 1896, Salisbury Papers A129.

[21] Esher journal entry, 8 May 1898, Esher Papers, ESHR 2/10; Scott to Sanderson, 26 Jan. 1899; Scott was rebutting the views of Wilhelm II; see L. Cecil, 'William II and his Russian "Colleagues"', in C. Fink, I. V. Hull, and M. Knox (eds.), *German Nationalism and European Response, 1890–1945* (Norman, OK, 1985), 95–134.

[22] Scott to Sanderson, 4 May 1899, Scott Papers, Add MSS 52303.

[23] Scott to Lascelles, 4 May 1899, Lascelles Papers, FO 800/15.

[24] Scott to Salisbury, 11 Jan. 1900, Salisbury Papers, A129.

[25] Scott to Lansdowne, 27 Dec. 1900, Lansdowne Papers, FO 800/140.

[26] Scott to Lansdowne, 22 Jan. 1902, Lansdowne Papers, FO 800/140.

that she was a firm adherent of a Russian policy of co-operation with England.[27] Her opinion was doubly important 'with a man of weak disposition like the Emperor'. Scott shared his subordinate's views, and added to them the importance of the pacific influence of the Dowager Empress Marie.[28] In December 1903, Scott outlined his views clearly to Lansdowne. The 'dangerous situation' in Asia, Scott wrote, was 'further complicated by the indecision of character of the Emperor Himself, which displays itself particularly at critical moments, when he has a difficulty presented to him in the form of a Gordian Knot which he is called upon to cut by the exercise of his Autocratic decisions'.[29] This quirk of character was telling: 'In another country this symptom might have less serious consequences but here, where there are no Constitutional resources to fall back upon, it tends to render Autocracy a misnomer, & might even constitute a grave national danger.'

Sir Charles Hardinge, Scott's successor, served in St Petersburg during the difficult days of the Russo-Japanese War. To some extent, Hardinge shared Scott's view that the Emperor was bombarded by conflicting advice. But Hardinge thought it likely that Nicholas received this advice only from those closest to him: 'Unfortunately neither M. Witte, nor any of the Ministers except, perhaps, M. Plehve, has any weight with the Emperor, who is said to be influenced chiefly by his surroundings, and more particularly by the Grand Duke Alexander Michailovitch, a clever and ambitious man, the husband of the Emperor's favourite sister, and a partisan of Admiral Alexeieff.'[30] Hardinge was convinced that the autocratic style of government was doomed.[31] As the war progressed and Russia was swept by internal disorders, Hardinge began to have serious doubts about the Emperor's capacity to rule. In the aftermath of Bloody Sunday, Nicholas seemed 'impervious to everything, sees nobody and spends his time playing with the baby. I am beginning to think', Hardinge told Bertie, 'that he does not realise the extreme gravity of both the external and internal situations.'[32] Hardinge was nonplussed by such an attitude, and advanced the opinion that 'I can only explain by that mystic fatalism which is deeply imbued in his nature, together with the idea that a miracle will be performed & that all will come right in the end'.[33] Even when the military situation looked darkest, Nicholas remained, on the basis of a 'message from St. Seraphim', confident of victory.[34]

---

[27] Hardinge to Sanderson, 1 Nov. 1900, Hardinge Papers, vol. 3.
[28] Scott to Lansdowne, 18 Apr. 1901, Lansdowne Papers, FO 800/140.
[29] Scott to Lansdowne, 10 Dec. 1903, Lansdowne Papers, FO 800/140.
[30] Hardinge to Lansdowne, very confidential disp. 327, 29 June 1904, Lansdowne Papers, FO 800/140.
[31] Hardinge to Lansdowne, confidential disp. 548, 31 Oct. 1904, FO 65/1730.
[32] Hardinge to Bertie, 14 Feb. 1905, Bertie Papers, FO 800/176.
[33] Hardinge to Sanderson, 15 Feb. 1905, Hardinge Papers, vol. 6.
[34] Hardinge to Lansdowne, 1 Aug. 1905, Lansdowne Papers, FO 800/141.

The winding down of the war gave Hardinge other opportunities to glimpse the various facets of Nicholas's perplexing personality. Early in April 1905, Hardinge detected a lessening in the trend towards a negotiated peace, one he attributed to Nicholas. Hardinge now suspected that Nicholas 'can hardly be as humane as he has the reputation of being, & it is said that he is warmly supported by the young Empress'.[35] In June some documents leaked from the Russian foreign ministry revealed the extent to which Nicholas himself had played an important role in the prewar negotiations with Japan.[36] That same month, Nicholas's unexpected acceptance of President Roosevelt's peace initiative led Hardinge to speculate that the Emperor's 'complete volte face' was the result of 'the dislike of a weak man to say "no" when face to face with a person in the position of a foreign Amb:'.[37] Returning to what O'Conor had suggested in 1896, Hardinge argued that 'the person who sees him [Nicholas II] last is likely to have the most influence upon him'.[38] While Hardinge favoured Witte's appointment as the Russian plenipotentiary to the Portsmouth peace conference, he noted that 'one cannot sufficiently condemn the duplicity of the Minister of the Court [who had misled Nicholas in the affair], and this story affords a striking instance of the manner in which the Empr: is served by his Ministers'.[39]

Hardinge's views were reinforced by the reports of Spring Rice, who was chargé d'affaires at St Petersburg for six months after Hardinge left for London, a time full of violence and tension in Russian politics. As the Emperor was closeted at Tsarskoe Selo behind, as Hardinge had reported in July 1905, 'a network of barbed wire reaching 10 ft. high above the already existing spiked railings', Spring Rice was hard-pressed to discover the true state of matters.[40] With the Duma not yet functioning properly, Spring Rice looked with despair on governmental affairs. For him, the central problem remained the Emperor. The chargé made his views clear in a long letter to Grey at the beginning of March 1906:

But he [Nicholas II] has no initiative and no courage of the active character. It is possible to make him understand but difficult to make him act. He would like to work with the moderate men of the Zemstvos but is afraid that they will know nothing of business and that they will be unable to manage the administrative machine. So he folds his hands, tell them very nice speeches, and does nothing.[41]

---

[35] Hardinge to Lansdowne, 12 Apr. 1905, Lansdowne Papers, FO 800/141.
[36] Hardinge to Lansdowne, secret disp. 362, 5 June 1905, FO 65/1701; F.A. Campbell's minute (12 June).
[37] Hardinge to Knollys, 21 June 1905, Hardinge Papers, vol. 6.
[38] Hardinge to Sanderson, 21 June 1905, FO 65/1701.
[39] Hardinge to Knollys, 19 June 1905, Hardinge Papers, vol. 6.
[40] Hardinge to Sanderson, 19 July 1905, Hardinge Papers, vol. 6.
[41] Spring Rice to Grey, 1 Mar. 1906, Grey Papers, FO 800/72.

Spring Rice also found the Emperor preoccupied with his domestic life, noting in April 1906 that 'the Emperor is perfectly happy at Tsarskoe where he leads the life which suits him best, playing with his children, and only seeing the people he wishes to see'.[42] The unfortunate part about this, Spring Rice went on, was that Nicholas 'hears what his entourage wishes him to hear'. Nor were such reports without effect in London. Tyrrell wrote to Spring Rice at the beginning of May that 'the Emperor is the personality [in Russian politics] which makes one inclined to chuck up the sponge whether one is Russian or foreigner'.[43]

When Nicolson arrived at St Petersburg at the end of May, Nicholas seemed 'invisible & silent'.[44] At the beginning of June, Nicolson presented his credentials, and obtained a first-hand impression of the monarch. Nicolson found the emperor both well disposed towards England and well prepared for the audience.[45] This surprised Nicolson, for he had been told by the French and Austro-Hungarian ambassadors to Russia that, while Nicholas was well intentioned, he was badly informed.[46] This incident shows how stereotypes of Nicholas II were perpetuated, for they had also told Nicolson that the Emperor was 'fatalistic' and determined to maintain his own prerogatives. Furthermore, Nicholas was thought to be influenced substantially by his wife, who, Nicolson professed himself 'surprised' to hear, was considered to be inclined to 'the reactionary party'. The Empress was deemed also to be a woman of extreme 'religious fervour', a condition that 'exercises a bias on her judgement'. Although Nicolson prefaced this account with the disclaimer that 'of course I have no opinion myself having so recently arrived', these received views soon became largely his own.

One reason for this was, as Nicolson noted, that 'it is exceedingly difficult to know what passes at Peterhof'.[47] Five months after he arrived, the ambassador admitted that 'as to the views of the Emperor, I cannot speak with certainty. I have not seen him since first audience.'[48] Denied any opportunity to form his own first-hand impressions, Nicolson was reduced to sifting through the opinions of others. The snippets gathered reinforced Nicolson's initial impressions and were supported by Spring Rice. Throughout the complicated negotiations leading to the signing of the Anglo-Russian Convention, Nicolson had almost no opportunity to form an opinion of Nicholas.

The fact that the Convention was signed convinced many that Nicholas II was firm in his desire for good relations with Britain. Morley was certain that Nicholas

[42] Spring Rice to Grey, 18 Apr. 1906, Grey Papers, FO 800/72.
[43] Tyrrell to Spring Rice, 1 May 1906, Spring Rice Papers, FO 800/241.
[44] Nicolson diary entry, 30 May 1906, Nicolson Papers, PRO 30/81/13.
[45] Nicolson to Grey, 6 June 1906, Nicolson Papers, FO 800/337.
[46] Nicolson to Knollys, 6 June 1906, Nicolson Papers, FO 800/337.
[47] Nicolson to Hardinge, 6 July 1906, Nicolson Papers, FO 800/337.
[48] Nicolson to Grey, 7 Nov. 1906, Grey Papers, FO 800/72.

had pushed the Convention past the determined opposition of the 'military party' in Russia.[49] And when Nicolson had an audience of the Emperor in October 1907— his first personal contact with the Emperor in well over a year—the ambassador noted that Nicholas 'may be relied upon' to adhere to the Convention.[50] But, even in the more relaxed atmosphere of post-revolutionary Russia, Nicolson was unable to see Nicholas often.[51] Nicholas continued to live 'cooped up in the Palace & park at Peterhof surrounded by Cossacks and sentries on every side'.[52] Despite this, by the end of 1908, Nicolson had arrived at a final, enduring opinion of Nicholas. Included among what Nicolson described to Grey as 'undoubted facts' was the belief that 'the Emperor is loyally and sincerely determined to cooperate with us on all matters'.[53] Further, Nicolson asserted, the Emperor is 'a very straightforward, honest man'.[54] But this could change. On 21 April 1909, Nicolson outlined his fears about the future course of Anglo-Russian relations.[55] Should Izvolskii be removed as minister for foreign affairs, Nicolson thought it likely that Russia would slowly drift towards Germany if the new minister argued that Britain could not be relied upon as an ally and that Russia ought to seek other alliances. Much depended on the Emperor's political servants: 'it is inevitable that his judgment and views must be considerably influenced by those who advise him on foreign affairs'.[56] Thus, Nicholas's shufflings of his ministers were scrutinized with the utmost care.

When Nicolson returned to London in 1910, Sir George Buchanan replaced him. Buchanan and Nicolson tended to see eye to eye about the character and intentions of Nicholas. Even so, Nicolson repeatedly emphasized the importance of the Emperor as the final arbiter in foreign affairs.[57] When Norman suggested, early in 1912, that Nicholas's 'distrust of Germans is perhaps a little uncalled for' with regard to the von Sanders mission to Turkey, Nicolson would have none of it.[58] This reflected not only his suspicion of Germany, but also his strong determination to defend the Emperor and, not incidentally, Nicolson's own authority as a judge of character.

[49] Morley to Minto, 19 Sept. 1907, Morley Papers, MSS Eur D573/2.

[50] Nicolson to Hardinge, 24 Oct. 1907, Nicolson Papers, FO 800/337.

[51] Nicolson to Hardinge, 12 Feb. 1908, Hardinge Papers, vol. 12.

[52] Hardinge to Nicolson, 2nd, 19 Feb. 1908, Nicolson Papers, FO 800/341. Peterhof (modern Petrodvorets) was one of the five palace complexes near St Petersburg.

[53] Nicolson to Grey, 4 Nov. 1908, Grey Papers, FO 800/73.

[54] Nicolson to Villiers, 5 Nov. 1908, Villiers Papers, FO 800/22.

[55] Nicolson to Hardinge, 21 Apr. 1909, Nicolson Papers, FO 800/337.

[56] Nicolson to Hardinge, 25 Feb. 1914, Hardinge Papers, vol. 93.

[57] Nicolson to Stamfordham (George V's private secretary), 2 Oct. 1912, in H. Temperley, and G. P. Gooch, (eds.), B[ritish] D[ocuments on the Origins of the War] (11 vols. in 13; London, 1926–38), ix, p. 1, doc. 807 (see BD hereafter); Nicolson to de Bunsen, 16 Feb. 1914, Nicolson Papers, FO 800/372.

[58] Minutes by Norman (27 Feb.) and Nicolson (n.d.) on Buchanan to Grey, secret disp. 66, 24 Feb. 1912, FO 371/1467/8486.

Thus, much remained constant in the British interpretation of Nicholas. One of the most important of these beliefs was that the Emperor was susceptible to the influences of those surrounding him. Who were they? In the sense outlined by Dominic Lieven, one group may loosely be called 'the Court': including not only 'the officials of the Emperor's household but also all those relatives, friends and acquaintances of the monarch who had access to him', but *not* Nicholas' ministers.[59] In considering 'the Court', it is important to remember that their influence waxed and waned. Not only did Nicholas become more confident in his own abilities, but also some members of his entourage and family either died or became incapacitated.

For example, the Emperor's four uncles held important military and bureaucratic positions early in Nicholas's reign, but by 1909 three were dead. None the less, their close proximity to the Emperor early in his reign meant that the British thought it necessary to keep a close eye on them. The Grand Duke Sergei Aleksandrovich, who served first as governor general of Moscow and later as commander-in-chief of the Moscow military district, was widely considered by the British to be a 'well-known reactionary'.[60] He was, as Hardinge put it in 1904, 'strongly opposed to any sort of concession or reform'.[61] Sergei also was considered to be a man of considerable influence. Early in 1905, Hardinge felt that the Grand Duke was responsible for the appointment of General D. F. Trepov, a firm advocate of law and order, as governor general of St Petersburg. Hardinge also believed that Sergei was instrumental in the selection of A. G. Bulygin as the new minister of the interior, replacing the more liberal Prince Sviatopolk-Mirskii. The British ambassador contended that Sergei Aleksandrovich's 'paramount' influence was 'unfortunate for everybody as he is reactionary and stupid, but with character'.[62] But the Grand Duke's putative influence ended when he was assassinated in mid-February 1905.

Of the Emperor's other three uncles, one, Pavel Aleksandrovich, was of little account. Due to a morganatic marriage, he resided in Paris and could exert little influence.[63] The Grand Duke Vladimir Aleksandrovich was equally insignificant. While considered 'by far the most intelligent of the Grand Dukes', he was not overly interested in public affairs.[64] The remaining uncle, Aleksei Aleksandrovich, was more important. As minister of marine before and during the Russo–Japanese War, he had a significant voice in military matters. In Hardinge's view, however,

[59] D. C. B. Lieven, *Russia and the Origins of the First World War* (London, 1983), 69.

[60] Hardinge to Lansdowne, disp. 118, 18 Feb. 1905, FO 65/1699.

[61] Hardinge to Knollys, 8 Dec. 1904, Hardinge Papers, vol. 6.

[62] Hardinge to Lansdowne, 8 Feb. 1905, Lansdowne Papers, FO 800/141.

[63] R. A. Esthus, *Double Eagle and Rising Sun: The Russians and Japanese at Portsmouth in 1905* (Durham, NC 1988), 4.

[64] Hardinge to Sanderson, 18 Oct. 1900, Hardinge Papers, vol. 3; Nicolson to Grey, confidential disp. 673, 7 Oct. 1906, FO 371/129/34616. But cf. Esthus, *Double Eagle and Rising Sun*, 44–5.

Aleksei was a 'person who has no weight, and only serves as a figure-head and as a prop to the Admiralty in its relations with the Emperor'.[65] Moreover Aleksei was 'entirely engrossed by his relations with an actress of the French theatre', a fact that was so notorious, Hardinge cuttingly remarked, that the Grand Duke has been 'hooted in public . . . and a Russian public is not very particular as to morals'.

The Grand Duke Nicholas Nikolaevich, grandson of Nicholas I and cousin of Nicholas II, was the most important soldier in the royal family. His father, also Nicholas Nikolaevich, had been commander-in-chief of the Russian army in 1877–8 and the son had served on his father's staff at that time. From 1895 to 1905, Nicholas the younger was inspector general of cavalry. He commanded both the St Petersburg military district and the Guards from 1905 to 1914. In June 1905 he had also been appointed by Nicholas II to head the Council for State Defence, a special body created to reform the Russian military establishment in the aftermath of the Russo-Japanese War.[66] As a final token of the esteem in which he was held, Nicholas Nikolaevich was made commander-in-chief of the Russian army upon the outbreak of war in 1914. British observers were well aware of the Grand Duke's status, but less than impressed with the quality of the man. Hardinge dismissed him as a 'somewhat clever but disagreeable soldier who speaks all the time through his teeth. Looked very smart & tall'.[67] With respect to domestic Russian politics the Grand Duke was considered an extreme reactionary.[68] Nor was he considered an overly competent soldier.[69] Equally, he had an 'overbearing manner in his relations with his subordinates', which was felt to be one of the principal reasons for his fall from favour, as marked by his removal as head of the Council for State Defence in 1908.[70] 'It is difficult', it was noted on Nicholas Nikolaevich's assuming command in 1914, 'to imagine the appointment to be a worse one.' The British were equally unimpressed with the Grand Duke's morals. The divorce of Princess Anastasie, the daughter of the King of Montenegro, from the Duc de Leuchtenberg in order to marry Nicholas Nikolaevich was termed a 'disgraceful affair'.[71] More dangerously, however, it was felt that Anastasie would 'increase the evil spiritualist, bigoted and reactionary influences of the Emperor's entourage'.[72] With Nicholas Nikolaevich's brother, the Grand Duke Peter, married to Anastasie's equally spiritualist and pan-

---

[65] Hardinge to Lansdowne, 6 Dec. 1904, Lansdowne Papers, FO 800/141.

[66] M. Perrins, 'The Council for State Defence 1905–1909: A Study in Russian Bureaucratic Politics', *SEER* 58 (1980), 370–98.

[67] Hardinge diary entry, 13 June 1904, Hardinge Papers, vol. 5.

[68] Spring Rice to Grey, disp. 324, 24 May 1906, FO 371/125/18151; O'Beirne to Grey, disp. 357, 13 Aug. 1908, FO 371/519/28444.

[69] Nicolson to Grey, confidential disp. 673, 7 Oct. 1906, FO 371/129/34616.

[70] O'Beirne to Grey, disp. 357, 13 Aug. 1908, FO 371/519/28444; Knox to MO 3, disp. LX, 3–4 Aug. 1914, WO 106/1044.

[71] Hardinge to Nicolson, 8 Jan. 1907, Nicolson Papers, FO 800/339.

[72] Bertie to Grey, private and confidential, 15 Nov. 1906, Grey Papers, FO 800/49.

Slav sister, this concern had force, and Buchanan reported in 1912 on the 'Chauvinistic influence' which the Grand Duke had on Nicholas II.[73]

The Grand Duke Sergei Mikhailovich, another cousin of Nicholas II and the Inspector General of Artillery from 1904 until 1916, was a man of a different stamp. Sergei Mikhailovich was perceived as a military man; a 'good officer' as Hardinge remarked on his appointment.[74] Two years later, Nicolson echoed this assessment, but added that the Grand Duke was 'not disposed or perhaps qualified to take any prominent part' in affairs of state.[75] Despite the quarrels and misunderstandings over the supply of munitions between the British and the Russians during the First World War, incidents in which Sergei Mikhailovich figured prominently, the British continued to respect his competence.[76]

Not all of the Grand Dukes were in the army. Aleksandr Mikhailovich, the son of a brother of Alexander II and the husband of Nicholas II's sister Xenia, was the second of the so-called naval Grand Dukes. Aleksandr Mikhailovich was a particular *bête noire* of the British. During the Russo-Japanese war, Hardinge viewed Aleksandr Mikhailovich as 'the evil spirit' of Nicholas II.[77] Aleksandr Mikhailovich was the 'cleverest & most influential' of the grand ducal circle surrounding the Emperor, and counselled the latter in ways that had brought about the war.[78] In addition, as Minister of Ports and Commercial Navigation, Aleksandr Mikhailovich was intimately connected with the Russian Volunteer Fleet and with the Prize Courts set up during the conflict with Japan. There were bitter quarrels between the Russian and British governments over these two matters. Worst of all, Aleksandr Mikhailovich was thought to be a bitter Anglophobe.[79] Fortunately, the naval debacles of the Russo-Japanese war weakened the influence of the naval grand dukes. Although Aleksandr Mikhailovich remained personally close to the Emperor, he and Aleksei Aleksandrovich lost their positions.

Beyond specific individuals, it was 'the Court' in general that concerned the British élite. As Salisbury summed it up: 'they can hardly fail, in so despotic a country, to affect the Administration.'[80] The Court was felt to be anti-British and

---

[73] Buchanan to Nicolson, 24 Dec. 1912, Nicolson Papers, FO 800/361.

[74] Hardinge to Knollys, 13 Oct. 1904, Hardinge Papers, vol. 6.

[75] Nicolson to Grey, confidential disp. 673, 7 Oct. 1906, FO 371/129/34616.

[76] A. L. Sidorov, 'Otnosheniia Rossii s souiznikami i innostranye postavki vo vremia pervoi mirovoi voiny 1914–17 gg.' *IZ* 15 (1945), 128–79; W. H-H. Waters, *'Secret and Confidential': The Experiences of a Military Attaché* (London, 1926), 341.

[77] Hardinge to Knollys, 21 July 1904, Hardinge Papers, vol. 6.

[78] Hardinge to Sandars (Balfour's private secretary), 21 July 1904, Sandars Papers, MS Eng. hist. *c.*748.

[79] Hardinge's undated minute on Nicolson to Grey, disp. 673 confidential, 7 Oct. 1906, FO 371/129/34616; cf. Scott to Lansdowne, 19 Mar. 1903, Lansdowne Papers, FO 800/140.

[80] Salisbury to Curzon, 2 Nov. 1897, Curzon Papers, MSS Eur F112/1b.

often pro-German.[81] The anti-British faction was referred to variously as 'the military party', 'the reactionaries', 'the chauvinists', the 'Chauvinist Military Party' or some other combination, often linked with the 'grand-ducal brood'.[82] None the less, the Court was not monolithic. Scott could refer to the 'battle of cross currents' around the Emperor, and Nicolson recorded in 1906 that one prominent observer felt that the 'idea of a Gd Ducal party is a myth, partly because they all quarrel among themselves'.[83] And there was also an 'English' party at Court, one that centred around such prominent families as the Benckendorffs, the Dolgorukovs, and the Naryshkins.[84] Overall, the Court was felt to be an influence on politics, hidden from public scrutiny, and one rarely good for Anglo-Russian relations.

Considerable concern centred around the spiritualism rampant among the royal family. Nicolson's remark that the Emperor 'will not derive much useful counsel or assistance from planchette or spirit rapping' indicates how serious and how pernicious this mysticism was felt to be.[85] Both the Empress and her sister, the wife of the Grand Duke Sergei Aleksandrovich, were known to be tinged, and Nicolson reported that their 'spiritualistic tendencies did not create a very invigorating atmosphere at Peterhof'.[86] The Montenegran princesses were also thought to have introduced the Empress to Rasputin. Buchanan was well informed about what he called 'the gossip about the influence which Rasputin has obtained over the Empress'.[87] Noting that the Empress had 'always taken a great interest in occultism and magnetism', Buchanan went on to note that Rasputin had played on the fears of this 'nervous, hyper-sensitive woman' to increase his own influence at court. 'The worst of it all', Buchanan concluded delicately, 'is that Rasputin's reputation is so bad . . . that the masses place the most unjustifiable construction on his relations with the Empress.' But Rasputin was just the most notorious of the religious mystics who surrounded the court. Another was 'Father John of Cronstad' who 'went about dressed in goatskins, with bare legs, bare arms and tousled head. In his hand he carried the branch of a tree, and if you got near him . . . the smell of

---

[81] With good reason, see, D. Lieven, 'Pro-Germans and Russian Foreign Policy 1890–1914', *IHR* 2 (1980), 44–5.

[82] Scott to Salisbury, 1 Dec. 1898, Scott Papers, Add MSS 52297; Scott to Sanderson, n.d. (but Dec. 1899), Scott Papers, Add MSS 52303; Hardinge to Sanderson, 21 July 1904, Hardinge Papers, vol. 6; Hardinge to Lansdowne, 8 Feb. 1905, Lansdowne Papers, FO 800/141; Nicolson to Grey, 16 June 1906, disp. 370 most confidential, FO 371/126/21434; O'Beirne to Grey, 2 June 1908, disp. 256, FO 371/517/19622; Nicolson to Hardinge, 23 Feb. 1910, *BD*, ix, pt. 1, doc. 115; O'Beirne to Grey, disp. 207, 5 July 1912, FO 371/1469/29840; 'grand-ducal brood' in Hardinge to Bertie, 14 Feb. 1905, Bertie Papers, FO 800/176.

[83] Scott to Sanderson, n.d. (but Dec. 1899), Scott Papers, Add MSS 52303; Nicolson diary entry, 7 Oct. 1906, Nicolson Papers PRO 30/81/13.

[84] Nicolson to Grey, 16 June 1906, disp. 370, most confidential, FO 371/126/21434.

[85] Nicolson to Hardinge, 21 June 1906, Nicolson Papers, FO 800/337.

[86] Nicolson to Hardinge, 24 Sept. 1906, Nicolson Papers, FO 800/337.

[87] Buchanan to Nicolson, 4 Apr. 1912, Nicolson Papers, FO 800/356.

Goatskin and human being was overpowering'.[88] While this was very much in the Russian tradition of the *starets*—the elderly holy man and spiritual adviser—it was not likely to provide any assurance to the British of the modern nature of the country.[89]

The Court was also thought to be corrupt. The Grand Dukes were known to be involved in the hunt for timber concessions on the Yalu, often given as a cause of the Russo-Japanese War. Three years later, discussing what the British considered another potential Russian diplomatic blunder, Tyrrell noted that 'there must be a limit to the follies the St. Petersburg Govt are capable of & there is no Yalu timber concession in Persia which might tempt the appetite of a Russian Grand Duke'.[90] Military contracts were of course susceptible. During the international competition in 1913 for the lucrative contract to build a munitions complex at Tsaritsyn, Buchanan reported that the representative of Schneider-Creusot, the French contender, was staying at the home of the Grand Duchess Marie Pavlovna. In exchange for her efforts to lobby the ministry of marine, Schneider-Creusot was paying the Grand Duchess three million francs.[91] Nor was corruption limited to the quasi-respectable arena of 'introductions'.[92] Peculation was a way of life in the armed forces generally. A pungent minute on the Russian naval estimates for 1914 encapsulates the British view: 'No doubt much of the money voted goes into the pockets of G__d D_ k_s.'[93]

While the attitudes of the Court and royal family remained obscured by the isolation of the royal residences and the formalities of court life, the same was not true concerning the Emperor's principal ministers. This was particularly the case with the occupants—Nicholas II's foreign ministers—of the *Pevcheski most* (the Singers' Bridge, the site of the Russian foreign ministry). Generally, British diplomats saw the Russian foreign ministers on a regular basis, usually once a week. However, when the Emperor was away from St Petersburg, the foreign minister often accompanied him, and on such occasions the British spoke with the deputy foreign minister. The British representatives soon developed definite opinions about these men.

Before 1914, Nicholas II was served by six foreign ministers. The first three— Nikolai Karlovich Giers (1882–95), Aleksei Borisovich Lobanov-Rostovskii

---

[88] Onslow, *Sixty-Three Years*, 106.

[89] R. D. Warth, 'Before Rasputin: Piety and the Occult at the Court of Nicholas II', *Historian*, 476 (1985), 323–37; N. Challis and H. W. Dewey, 'The Blessed Fools of Old Russia, *JfGOE* 22 (1974), 1–11.

[90] Tyrrell to Spring Rice, 7 Aug. 1907, Spring Rice Papers, FO 800/241.

[91] Buchanan to Grey, secret disp. 95, 20 Mar. 1913, FO 371/1743/13418.

[92] K. Neilson, 'Russian Foreign Purchasing in the Great War: A Test Case', *SEER* 60 (1982), 572–90.

[93] Crowe's minute (25 Oct. 1913) on O'Beirne to Grey, disp. 308, 16 Oct. 1913, FO 371/1747/47540; Hardinge, *Diplomatist in Europe*, 137–9.

(1895–6) and Mikhail Nikolaevich Muravev (1897–1900)—had short tenures in office. The last three—Vladimir Nikolaevich Lamsdorff (1900–6), Aleksandr Petrovich Izvolskii (1906–10) and Sergei Dimtrievich Sazonov (1910–16)—had longer stays. Regardless of the duration of their time in power, these men were considered pivotal when it came to evaluating Russian foreign policy.

Giers scarcely outlived Alexander III. By October 1894, he was 'very feeble and unable to walk', and even his Russian subordinates felt that it was 'hopeless' to expect any decisions from him.[94] He was unable to give much guidance before he died in January 1895. His successor's credentials were impressive. From a distinguished family, Lobanov had been in the diplomatic service for nearly fifty years, except for fifteen years spent in the ministry of the interior. Since 1879, he had been successively ambassador at London, Vienna, and Berlin. Lascelles found him 'charming', but added that many held him to be 'extraordinarily lazy'.[95] After having been misled in May and June 1895 by Lobanov about Russia's involvement in loans to China, Lascelles decided that he was not to be trusted.[96] Despite this Lascelles argued that Lobanov was 'far and away the best Foreign Minister that could be found for Russia', as he wanted peace and tranquillity.[97] On the other hand, Sanderson argued in mid-April 1896 that Lobanov was 'at heart unfriendly' to Britain and possibly believed her to be pursuing some sort of 'evil design'. Lobanov was, Sanderson added, a man 'perfectly regardless of truth'.[98] After months of tortuous negotiation with Lobanov over China and Armenia, O'Conor felt that Lobanov's policy had 'for its key almost a diseased mistrust of England and of British machinations not only at Constantinople but well nigh over the world'.[99] At the India Office, Hamilton put it more succinctly. Lobanov had been, the Indian secretary wrote, 'a bitter enemy to this country'.[100]

There was an interregnum at the *Pevcheski most* after the death of Lobanov. Various names were bandied about, but by the beginning of 1897 O'Conor reported that Muravev, the Russian minister at Copenhagen, seemed the likely replacement, and he was indeed appointed.[101] Twenty-one years younger than Lobanov, Muravev had established a reputation as a high liver early in his career. As San-

[94] Lascelles to Kimberley, disp. 220, 17 Oct. 1894, FO 65/1473; Lascelles to Kimberley, 10 Oct. 1894, Lascelles Papers, FO 800/17.
[95] Lascelles to A. Wodehouse (Kimberley's private secretary), 28 Feb. 1895, Lascelles Papers, FO 800/17.
[96] Lascelles to Kimberley, 19 June 1895; Lascelles to Salisbury, 28 Aug. 1895, both Lascelles Papers, FO 800/17.
[97] Lascelles to Salisbury, 3 July 1895, Lascelles Papers, FO 800/17.
[98] Sanderson to O'Conor, 15 Apr. 1895, O'Conor Papers, OCON 6/9.
[99] O'Conor to Salisbury, confidential disp. 194, 7 Sept. 1896, FO 65/1515.
[100] Hamilton to Elgin (British viceroy, India), 2 Sept. 1896, Hamilton Papers, MSS Eur C125/1.
[101] O'Conor to Salisbury, disp. 252, 12 Nov. 1896, FO 65/1517; O'Conor to Salisbury, private tel., 12 Nov. 1896, FO 65/1516.

derson wrote, at the Hague Muravev had been reputed 'to drink 3 bottles of champagne a day and complain of his nerves'.[102] O'Conor needed no briefing on the new minister, for they had been colleagues at both Berlin and Paris where they, as O'Conor told Lascelles, 'used to go about occasionally together'.[103] O'Conor characterized Muravev as 'not . . . without ability, but inordinately conceited & vain as a woman, hardly likely to take a strong line of his own'. Further, O'Conor felt that Muravev would take a pro-German line in foreign policy and would likely fall under the influence of the powerful Sergei Witte, the Russian finance minister. By the summer of 1897, opinions about Muravev had hardened.[104] O'Conor's opinion of Muravev did not improve in the new year. 'He is generally very fitful', the ambassador wrote to Salisbury on 26 January 1898, '& I fear his veracity is nearly on the level of Prince Lobanoff's.'[105] From Berlin, where he was now ambassador, Lascelles cautioned that 'I confess I do not feel inclined to place much confidence in Mouravieff'.[106]

When Scott became ambassador in the summer of 1898, there was a brief change in the embassy's feelings towards Muravev. Scott reported in September that Muravev's 'evident desire to cultivate the most friendly & confidential relations with me' was a precursor to establishing 'a good understanding with England'.[107] Hardinge felt that Scott was being taken in by Muravev: 'Mouravieff lies very pleasantly and it would be almost amusing if one could banish the thought of possible consequences.'[108] Hardinge, with his 'Edwardian' attitudes, was temperamentally less akin to Muravev than was the 'Victorian' Scott. The latter, who placed great importance on personal relations, found the congenial Russian a 'most accessible & conciliatory' man.[109] When Muravev died suddenly in June 1900, even Scott could not be completely charitable. In summing up Muravev's career, Scott concluded that the former 'may not have been a good friend to English policy . . . [and] was an Ultra Conservative & had no sympathy with liberal aspirations'. At the India Office, Hamilton was again harsher: '[h]e will be no loss as far as this country is concerned, for he was an incurable intriguer, apparently without principle or any definite policy.'[110]

The next foreign minister, V. N. Lamsdorff, was well-known to British representatives in Russia. A long-time protegé of Giers, Lamsdorff had been

[102] Sanderson to Lascelles, 13 Jan. 1897, Lascelles Papers, FO 800/15; Lascelles to Salisbury, 23 Jan. 1897, Lascelles Papers, FO 800/17.
[103] O'Conor to Lascelles, 28 Jan. 1897, Lascelles Papers, FO 800/15.
[104] O'Conor to Salisbury, disp. 213, 26 Aug. 1897, FO 65/1533.
[105] O'Conor to Salisbury, 26 Jan. 1898, Salisbury Papers, A129.
[106] Lascelles to Sanderson, 29 Jan. 1898, Lascelles Papers, FO 800/17.
[107] Scott to Salisbury, 8 Sept. 1898, Salisbury Papers, A129.
[108] Hardinge to Sanderson, 29 June 1899, Hardinge Papers, vol. 3.
[109] Scott's diary entry, 21 June 1900, Scott Papers, Add MSS 52305.
[110] Hamilton to Curzon, 21 June 1900, Curzon Papers, MSS Eur F111/146.

Muravev's deputy and trusted assistant. Whenever the latter had been ill or un-
available, the British had dealt with Lamsdorff and had found him very capable. In
fact, O'Conor had once concluded that, of the two, Lamsdorff was 'much the abler
man'.[111] Scott, too, had been impressed by Lamsdorff's 'manner & way of doing
business'. When there was momentary doubt as to whether Lamsdorff would
succeed Muravev, Scott noted that 'if Lamsdorff remains I shall be delighted'.[112]
Scott wrote that Lamsdorff 'will be safer at any rate than a new hand who would
have a name to make for himself' and added that the new foreign minister's
long experience in the foreign ministry would ensure a certain continuity in
policy.[113]

However, Lamsdorff proved to be a heavy burden for Scott. The new Russian
minister led the British ambassador a merry chase over China, although Scott
continued to report that 'I confess I believe in his sincerity'.[114] Sanderson warned
Scott to watch 'out for a sly dig in the ribs' when dealing with Lamsdorff and not
to accept the latter's constant 'use of the Emperor's sceptre to beat you about the
head' when he wished to dodge responsibility for Russian actions.[115] But Scott
continued to believe in Lamsdorff, and to accept Lamsdorff's protestations that
much of his seeming lack of straightforwardness resulted from Nicholas II's tepid
support.[116] With Hardinge's reporting to the King that Lamsdorff's actions were
duplicitous, Scott's own position was weakened. Sanderson gently pointed out to
Scott that, while Lamsdorff might be pro-English in his policy, 'he certainly does
not stick at an occasional fib'.[117]

The outbreak of the Russo-Japanese War swung British opinion around towards
Lamsdorff. Scott felt that Lamsdorff was to be 'pitied' and might be made a 'scape
goat' for anything that went wrong in the progress of hostilities.[118] But it was
Hardinge who underwent a notable conversion. After succeeding Scott, Hardinge
advanced the idea that while Lamsdorff was 'miserably weak and dare not commit
himself to anything without first consulting the Emperor, he is an element of law
and order and is, I really believe, well disposed towards us'.[119] During the Dogger
Bank incident, despite the fact that Lamsdorff resorted to 'undignified shifts and
wrigglings' in an attempt to dodge blame, Sanderson also argued that 'it is worth
while to let him down as easily as is compatible with the maintenance of our own

[111] O'Conor to Salisbury, 10 Feb. 1898, Salisbury Papers, A129.
[112] Scott to Sanderson, private and confidential, 12 July 1900, Scott Papers, Add MSS 52303.
[113] Scott to Sanderson, 8 Aug. 1900, Scott Papers, Add MSS 52303.
[114] Scott to Lansdowne, 18 Apr. 1901, Lansdowne Papers, FO 800/140.
[115] Sanderson to Scott, 24 Apr. and 17 July 1901, both Scott Papers, Add MSS 52299.
[116] Scott to Sanderson, 6 Mar. 1902; Scott to Lansdowne, private and personal, 8 Jan. 1903, both
Scott Papers, Add MSS 52304.
[117] Sanderson to Scott, 17 June 1903, Scott Papers, Add MSS 52299; Hardinge to Bertie, 14 Nov.
1901, Bertie Papers, FO 800/176.
[118] Scott to Lansdowne, 18 Feb. 1904, Lansdowne Papers, FO 800/115.
[119] Hardinge to Lansdowne, 6 Dec. 1904, Lansdowne Papers, FO 800/141.

contentions' for the simple reason that 'he is well-intentioned'.[120] And, as the seriously ill Lamsdorff's time in office drew to a close, the British observers became quite laudatory.[121]

Aleksandr Izvolskii, who took office as foreign minister in 1906, had already spent thirty-one years in the Russian diplomatic service. His last post had been as Russian minister to Denmark. When Izvolskii was appointed, London was immediately flooded with opinions of him. Sir A. Johnstone, the British minister at Copenhagen, who had been a colleague of Izvolskii's for two years at Rome in the late 1890s and had been 'very intimate' with the Russian, sent an evaluation that was widely circulated. Johnstone felt Izvolskii to be a 'man of much intelligence and a very hard worker', generally pro-British but someone who had attacked the Anglo-Japanese Treaty. Izvolskii was 'fond of society, and perhaps the weak spot in his character is his susceptibility to flattery'.[122] Sir Edward Goschen, who had known Izvolskii at Copenhagen, had described the Russian in 1903 as 'very clever—but very conceited', and Spring Rice wrote from St Petersburg that Izvolskii was 'vain and very sensitive to flattery'.[123] With respect to policy, most agreed with Johnstone that Izvolskii would follow a pro-British course.[124]

Nicolson and Izvolskii worked together from 1906 to 1910. Initially, Nicolson was not impressed by Izvolskii, finding him 'timorous & afraid of responsibility', as the latter seemed unwilling to begin negotiations for improved Anglo-Russian relations.[125] In reality, this delay owed much to the chaotic nature of events in Russia and to Izvolskii's desire to begin simultaneous parallel discussions with Japan and Germany. In time, Nicolson began to like Izvolskii. By the autumn of 1906, Nicolson reported that the Russian was 'quick & intelligent & a delightful man with whom to do business', although 'disinclined to submit to any drudgery or to carefully examine papers'.[126] Equally important, Nicolson began to realize that Izvolskii's position as minister was not secure; that he had 'many enemies here . . . among the bureaucracy and military party' who viewed him, because of his long service abroad, 'as a foreigner and a westerner, and as not being thoroughly Russian at heart'.[127] By the end of the year, Nicolson and Hardinge were both

---

[120] Sanderson to Hardinge, 29 Nov. 1904, Hardinge Papers, vol. 3.

[121] Hardinge's undated minute on Spring Rice to Grey, disp. 119, 12 Feb. 1906, FO 371/123/5943; Spring Rice to Lascelles, 25 Apr. 1906, Lascelles Papers, FO 800/13.

[122] Johnstone to Grey, very confidential disp. 56, 9 May 1906, FO 371/125/17344.

[123] Goschen's diary entry, 3 Oct. 1903, in C. H. D. Howard, (ed.), *The Diary of Edward Goschen 1900–14* (London, 1980), 82 (hereafter, *Goschen Diary*); Spring Rice to Grey, 24 May 1906, Grey Papers, FO 800/72.

[124] Hardinge's undated minute on Johnstone to Grey, tel. 6, 7 May 1906, FO 371/121/15601; Spring Rice to Grey, 10 and 24 May 1906, both Grey Papers, FO 800/72.

[125] Nicolson to Grey, 5 July 1906, Nicolson Papers, FO 800/337.

[126] Nicolson to Grey, 12 Sept. 1906, Nicolson Papers, FO 800/337.

[127] Nicolson to Hardinge, 11 Oct. 1906; Nicolson to Hardinge, 6 Dec. 1906, both Nicolson Papers, FO 800/337. Quotation from the former.

convinced, as the former put it, of Izvolskii's 'loyalty and sincerity'.[128] Nicolson also had changed his mind about Izvolskii's diligence.[129]

Throughout the hard months of negotiation in 1907, Nicolson was inclined to accept Izvolskii's explanation that most difficulties arose as a result of the interference of elements in the Russian government hostile to the Convention.[130] Nicolson was pleased with the close co-operation that Izvolskii offered in dealings with the Amir of Afghanistan, and by August of 1908 reported that the Russian foreign minister seemed 'more self confident & firmer generally'.[131] Nicolson claimed that Izvolskii, 'unless he is deceiving me . . . is earnestly desirous of laying Russian foreign policy alongside that of England'. It was deception. Izvolskii was in the midst of a complicated diplomatic manœuvre designed to deliver Constantinople and the Straits to Russia in exchange for Austria-Hungary's annexation of Bosnia and Herzegovina. Despite this, Nicolson rejected the idea that Izvolskii had played him false.[132] Instead, all was attributed to Izvolskii's tendency to be a 'little yielding' in discussions and a 'little too discursive in examining possible compensations'. While Nicolson remained steadfast, others were not so sure.[133] In the aftermath of the eventual Russian humiliation, Grey remarked that Izvolskii's willingness to believe that Britain had suggested unconditional recognition of the annexation meant that he had 'judged us by some low standard of his own'.[134]

But the British did not now wish to be rid of Izvolskii, since his dismissal would be regarded as a triumph for German diplomacy and herald 'a change to Germanophil policy in foreign affairs'.[135] Nicolson agreed: 'with all his defects, I very much doubt if we could find one who would be so willing to work with us as he.'[136] Hardinge demurred on the grounds that if the rest of the Russian government remained in favour of a pro-British foreign policy, Izvolskii's presence was no longer essential. 'He has made an agreement with us, and has been loyal throughout,' the PUS stated realistically, 'but he is not a statesman and his tactics have certainly been bad.'[137] Even Nicolson conceded, as his time in Russia ended, that Izvolskii had 'never lied to him but seldom told him the *whole* truth'.[138]

[128] Nicolson to Hardinge, 11 Oct. 1906, Nicolson Papers, FO 800/337.

[129] Nicolson to Grey, 21 Nov. 1906, Nicolson Papers, FO 800/337. This reflected Izvolskii's circumstances; G. H. Bolsover, 'Izvol'sky and the Reform of the Russian Ministry of Foreign Affairs', *SEER* 63 (1985), 21–40.

[130] Nicolson to Hardinge, 30 Aug. 1907, Nicolson Papers, FO 800/337.

[131] Nicolson to Hardinge, 13 Aug. 1908, Nicolson Papers, FO 800/337.

[132] Nicolson to Grey, 8 Oct. 1908, Grey Papers, FO 800/73.

[133] Balfour to Asquith, 14 oct. 1908, Asquith Papers, I/11; Hardinge to Nicolson, 15 Mar. 1909, Nicolson Papers, FO 800/342.

[134] Grey to Nicolson, 2 Apr. 1909, Grey Papers, FO 800/73.

[135] Hardinge to Nicolson, private tel., 8 Apr. 1909, FO 371/729/13412.

[136] Nicolson to Grey, 8 Apr. 1909, Grey papers, FO 800/73.

[137] Hardinge to Nicolson, 10 May 1909, *BD*, v, doc. 860.

[138] Goschen diary entry, 9 July 1910, Howard, (ed.), *Goschen Diary*, 208, original emphasis.

Izvolskii was replaced in the autumn of 1910 by his deputy, Sergei Dmitrievich Sazonov. Sazonov's career had been linked with that of his chief before; they had served together at the Vatican in the 1890s, and Izvolskii saw him as a man likely to maintain Izvolskii's own pro-British policy.[139] Sazonov was an anglophile, the residue of his two sojourns in London at the Russian embassy: as second secretary from 1890 to 1894 and then as counsellor from 1904 to 1906. Since Sazonov was also the brother-in-law of Petr Stolypin, the Emperor's chief minister, matters seemed propitious for continued warm Anglo-Russian relations. The British, however, were not convinced of Sazonov's abilities. When Izvolskii's removal seemed imminent in 1909, Hardinge had written disparagingly of Sazonov as a possible successor.[140] This view was immediately reinforced when Sazonov travelled to Potsdam for conversations with the German chancellor, Theobald von Bethmann-Hollweg, yielding a Russo-German *rapprochement* that appeared to threaten good Anglo-Russian relations.

This redounded upon Sazonov. By December 1910, Nicolson was reportedly 'rather upset' by Sazonov's actions, and at the New Year, Buchanan described Sazonov's German policy as 'lamentably weak'.[141] The PUS's despair was complete: 'I confess that I am completely bewildered and mystified by the actions and attitudes of Sazonov . . . I cannot understand how he can be so completely blind to the consequences of what he is doing.'[142] Only Sazonov's serious illness, which kept him from acting in his official capacity from February 1911 to the end of that year, managed to rehabilitate him somewhat in British eyes. In April 1911, when it was rumoured that Sazonov had only a fortnight to live, Buchanan wrote that '[h]e will be a great loss to me both officially and as a friend'.[143] The growing tide of anti-Germanism at the Foreign Office after the Moroccan crisis, Sazonov's helpful attitude towards British policy during the Balkan Wars, and his own distancing of Russia from Germany restored the Russian minister to the good books of the British. In fact, when it appeared in 1913 that Sazonov might be removed from office, Buchanan told Nicholas II that 'He was to be congratulated on having had a Minister like Sazonov to carry out His policy during a crisis like that through which we have been passing'.[144] The particular favour in which Sazonov was held was reflected in February 1914, when it appeared that Sazonov might be dismissed.

[139] Nicolson to Grey, 9 Aug. 1910, Grey Papers, FO 800/73.

[140] Cf. Hardinge to Nicolson, 27 Sept. 1909, Nicolson Papers, FO 800/342; Nicolson to Grey, 9 Feb. 1910, *BD*, ix, part 1,119–20.

[141] Goschen's diary entry, 22 Dec. 1910, Howard (ed.), *Goschen Diary*, 229; Buchanan to Grey, 26 Jan. 1911, Grey Papers, FO 800/73.

[142] Nicolson to Cartwright (British ambassador, Vienna), 6 Feb. 1911; *BD*, x, pt. 1, 650–1.

[143] Buchanan to Nicolson, 20 Apr. 1911, Nicolson Papers, FO 800/348; Norman's minute (12 Apr.) on Buchanan to Grey, confidential tel. 83, 12 Apr. 1911, FO 371/1214/13767.

[144] Buchanan to Nicolson, 17 Apr. 1913, Nicolson Papers, FO 800/365.

Buchanan's concern lay not with policy—'his departure . . . will not necessarily entail any change in the course which Russia has hitherto steered'—but with the fact that any successor might pursue Russia's policy 'in a less conciliatory spirit and with a firmer hand'.[145] The man was the thing, as Nicolson's evaluation made clear. 'We all know his defects', the PUS wrote to Hardinge, 'and I must say he has lost few opportunities in displaying them, but at the same time he is a thoroughly sincere adherent to our understanding and is acquainted in a certain measure with the English character and opinions.'[146]

In a government where cabinet solidarity did not exist, many ministers other than the occupant of the *Pevcheskii most* had an opportunity to influence foreign affairs. Sergei Iulevich Witte, minister of finance from 1893 to 1903, Russia's delegate to the Portsmouth peace conference in 1905 and chairman of the council of ministers from October 1905 to May 1906, was one. Certainly, the view of Witte's omnipotence was widespread. In September 1895, Salisbury informed Lascelles that the German emperor, Wilhelm II, felt that Lobanov had no influence in foreign affairs and 'that the whole working of the [governmental] machine was in the hands of Witte . . . & the Empress Mother'.[147] Lascelles disagreed, arguing that the German ambassador to Russia had a 'severe attack of Witte on the brain'.[148] 'No doubt finance covers a very large field', Lascelles concluded, 'but I doubt Witte having such influence on the general direction of affairs.'

O'Conor's initial view of Witte noted only that he was 'a strong and energetic man, absolutely fearless, and of extraordinary initiative power', dominant in financial matters but 'detested by the Court & Society'.[149] Witte soon won over the British ambassador. Nine months later, O'Conor reported Witte's 'considerable kindness' and found his 'frankness' refreshing and unusual among Russians.[150] Nor did he find Witte's views on foreign policy unpalatable. According to Witte, Russia wanted not 'a foot more' territory, 'peace to bring out the wealth of the country', and an improvement in Russia's standard of living.[151] Further, Witte 'saw no reason' why a 'friendly understanding' between Britain and Russia should not be part of Russia's foreign policy. O'Conor felt Witte's affirmations 'no less sincere that they are mainly founded upon the necessity of gaining over the London money market'.[152] The connection between Witte's plans for economic development in the Far East and Anglo-Russian relations in that area meant that Witte became more

[145] Buchanan to Grey, 18 Feb. 1914, Grey Papers, FO 800/74.
[146] Nicolson to Hardinge, 25 Feb. 1914, Nicolson Papers, FO 800/372.
[147] Salisbury to Lascelles, 17 Sept. 1895, Lascelles Papers, FO 800/16.
[148] Lascelles to Salisbury, 25 Sept. 1895, Lascelles Papers, FO 800/17.
[149] O'Conor to Salisbury, 18 Nov. 1896, Salisbury Papers, A129.
[150] O'Conor to Salisbury, secret and confidential disp. 219, 31 Aug. 1897, FO 65/1533.
[151] O'Conor to Salisbury, confidential disp. 15, 24 Jan. 1897, FO 65/1531.
[152] O'Conor to Salisbury, disp. 258, 12 Aug. 1898, FO 65/1555.

central in matters of foreign policy. Upon meeting Witte for the first time in November 1898, Scott was told the same things that O'Conor had reported.[153] Witte's remarks, Scott noted, 'may mean a great deal, or nothing, in accordance to the relative weight to be attached to his professions of Sincerity [*sic*]'. With respect to a loan that the Russian government provided for Persia in 1900, a loan whose existence was denied throughout the negotiation of it, Scott passed on Witte's explanation of events with the caveat that it sounded 'plausible if it can be relied on, which is always open to question'.[154]

As Anglo–Russian relations became more strained after the Boxer rebellion, the British saw Witte as holding a near-impregnable position.[155] Hardinge felt that, in the rivalry for the Emperor's favour between Witte and Plehve, the minister of the interior, 'I should certainly put my money on Witte'.[156] Thus, when Witte was dismissed as minister of finance in August 1903, the British were puzzled.[157] Perhaps the chairman of the committee of ministers, normally an honorific position, was to become something more significant since Witte held it. Indeed, Lansdowne hoped that Witte's change of office might check the expansionist circles in the Russian government and their designs on Manchuria.[158] Witte out of office proved to be less attractive. During the Russo-Japanese War, Witte was considered by the British to be an element of uncertainty, interested solely in his own return to power. 'Once in power he is all right,' Hardinge noted, 'but he fishes for his own advantage in troubled waters, and he is likely to continue to stir up the mud until his position is assured.'[159] But Hardinge was convinced that Witte's machinations were not likely to restore his position, because Witte, 'never . . . able to dissociate statesmanship from intrigue', had alienated both Emperor and reformers.[160] The Emperor considered him a 'dangerous intriguer', and the liberals regarded him as someone who, while mouthing the slogans of reform, was actually bent on preventing them. In addition, Witte's 'overpowering presence . . . rough manner, and . . . brusque speech has made his personality distasteful to the Emperor'.[161]

After Portsmouth, despite the unfavourable Russian public reaction to the peace settlement, Witte's star seemed once more in the ascendant. During the autumn of 1905, he was one of those who persuaded Nicholas II to issue the October

---

[153] Scott to Salisbury, 3 Nov. 1898, Scott Papers, Add MSS 52297.
[154] Scott to Sanderson, 11 Mar. 1900, Scott Papers, Add MSS 52303.
[155] Scott to Sanderson, 6 Mar. 1902, Scott papers, Add MSS 52304; Sanderson to Hardinge, 3 Dec. 1902, Hardinge Papers, vol. 3.
[156] Hardinge to Sanderson, 27 Nov. 1902, Hardinge Papers, vol. 3; E. H. Judge, *Plehve: Repression and Reform in Imperial Russia 1902–1904* (Syracuse, NY, 1983), 63–92, 150–74.
[157] Scott to Lansdowne, disp. 263, 30 Aug. 1903, FO 65/1661.
[158] Lansdowne to Selborne, 2 Sept. 1903, Selborne Papers 34.
[159] Hardinge to Lansdowne, 4 Jan. 1905, Lansdowne Papers, FO 800/141.
[160] Hardinge to Lansdowne, confidential disp. 187, 14 Mar. 1905, FO 65/1699.
[161] Hardinge to Lansdowne, disp. 42, 17 Jan. 1905, FO 65/1698.

manifesto, creating a constitution for Russia. In addition, Witte was made chairman of the council of ministers. But as the country became more stable, Witte's position became less so. By the beginning of 1906, Spring Rice reported that 'Witte is universally condemned', but noted that despite his unpopularity 'he seems, with Durnovo [the minister of the interior] the only man capable of carrying on the government'.[162] Soon it was evident that Witte and Durnovo were locked in a struggle for supremacy, and at the beginning of May Witte was removed from office, never to hold high position again.[163]

Even out of office, Witte generated a good deal of discussion, for his return to a position of authority was often rumoured. From his dismissal until his death in 1915, three things remained constant in the British evaluation of Witte. The first was that he had earned the Emperor's everlasting dislike.[164] The second assumption was that Witte was constantly attempting to work his way back into power.[165] At the Foreign Office such thinking became axiomatic. 'Count Witte is an arch intriguer and entirely unscrupulous and self-seeking', Norman minuted in 1912 on a report that the former minister had taken pains to emphasize to Nicholas II his availability for office.[166] Witte's tendency to intrigue for position was made more distasteful to the British because of the third constant believed about him. This was, as Buchanan noted in March 1914, that Witte felt 'that it should be a fundamental principle of Russia's foreign policy to establish the closest possible relations with Germany'.[167] During the war, it was thought that Witte was the focus for those elements in Russia who favoured a separate peace with Germany.[168] His death in March 1915 occasioned little sorrow among the British élite.

When Witte was forced to resign as chairman of the council of ministers in May 1906, he was replaced by Ivan Logginovich Goremykin. Goremykin, in his mid-sixties, was not unknown to the British. As minister of the interior from 1895 to 1899, he had quarrelled with Witte and been forced to resign. The British considered him a 'marked reactionary', but one whose attitude to England was not 'unfriendly'.[169] Possessed of great personal charm, Goremykin was not overly

---

[162] Spring Rice to Grey, 16 Jan., 16 Feb. 1906, both Grey Papers, FO 800/72.

[163] Spring Rice to Lascelles, 25 Apr. 1906, Lascelles Papers, FO 800/13; H. Heilbronner, 'An Anti-Witte Diplomatic Conspiracy, 1905–6: The Schwanebach Memorandum', *JfGOE* 14 (1966), 347–61.

[164] O'Beirne to Bertie, 2 Dec. 1906, Bertie Papers, FO 800/177; Nicolson to Buchanan, 18 May 1914, Nicolson Papers, FO 800/374.

[165] Hardinge to Nicolson, 24 Dec. 1906, Nicolson Papers, FO 800/338.

[166] Norman's minute (9 Apr.) on Buchanan to Grey, disp. 102, 2 Apr. 1912, FO 371/1468/14640.

[167] Buchanan to Grey, 31 Mar. 1914, *BD*, x, pt. 2, doc. 536.

[168] R. Sh. Ganelin, 'Storonniki separatnogo mira s Germanaiei v tsarskoi Rossi', in E. V. Tarle (ed.), *Problemy istorii mezhdunarodnykh otnoshenii* (Leningrad, 1972) 126–55.

[169] Spring Rice to Grey, disp. 309, 10 May 1906, FO 371/121/16396 and Spring Rice to Grey, tel. 77, 2 May 1906, FO 371/121/14931. Quotation from the latter.

energetic, and his time as chairman of the council was brief, ending in July 1906 with the dissolution of the First Duma. Goremykin, Nicolson noted in his diary, 'treats Duma &c with the greatest disdain—presumptuous professors, ideologues, revolutionaries not at all representative body. Let them babble.'[170] But, unlike Witte, and despite his advanced age, Goremykin was not at the end of his political career. A loyal functionary, Goremykin always retained Nicholas II's confidence, and, in the aftermath of the Bosnian crisis, when Izvolskii's position seemed insecure, it was rumoured that Goremykin might replace him as foreign minister. This was viewed with unease by the British. Goremykin was felt to be a man who favoured aligning Russia's foreign policy with that of Germany, while moving her domestic policy away from liberalism.

Thus, in 1914, when Goremykin once again became chairman of the council of ministers, this move sparked apprehension at the Foreign Office.[171] It was greatly feared that this might presage the dismissal of Sazonov, by now considered a staunch supporter of the entente with Britain. The Foreign Office had to take cold comfort in the hope that Goremykin would not interfere overly in foreign affairs and that his appointment was only a stopgap.[172] However, Goremykin would remain in office until February 1916. Throughout 1915, the British kept a wary eye upon him, reacting with predictable joy when he was thought likely to be replaced and with equally predictable dismay when it was rumoured that he might replace Sazonov as foreign minister.[173] When Goremykin was dismissed, it was a measure of the British dislike of him that Buchanan could write of Boris Stürmer, the successor, that he 'is a great improvement on Goremykin'.[174]

A much greater favourite of the British was Petr Arkadevich Stolypin, the man who succeeded Goremykin as chairman of the council of ministers after the latter's first term. Stolypin took up the post on 22 July 1906, in the midst of political chaos. Stolypin had spent most of his career in Poland, but had been appointed minister of the interior by Goremykin in May 1906 on the strength of his firm handling of unrest in the province of Saratov. This latter suggested to Spring Rice that Stolypin's 'Liberalism is in all probability of a restricted nature'.[175] It was clear,

---

[170] Diary entry, 13 June 1906, Nicolson Papers, PRO 30/81/13.

[171] Minutes by Crowe (12 Feb.) and Nicolson (n.d.) on Buchanan to Grey, tel. 46, 11 Feb. 1914, FO 371/2091/6329.

[172] Buchanan to Grey, tel. 47, 12 Feb. 1914, FO 371/2091/6481; memo (16 Feb.) by Oliphant of a conversation with Poklevski (counsellor, Russian embassy, London), FO 371/2091/8357.

[173] K. Neilson, 'Wishful Thinking: The Foreign Office and Russia, 1907–17' in B. J. C. McKercher, and D. J. Moss (eds.), *Shadow and Substance in British Foreign Policy 1895–1939* (Edmonton, Alta., 1984), 162–4.

[174] Buchanan to Grey, 8 Feb. 1916, Grey Papers, FO 800/75; Macdonogh (DMI) to Grey, 30 Oct. 1916, Macdonogh Papers, WO 106/1511.

[175] Spring Rice to Grey, disp. 309, 10 May 1906, FO 371/121/16396; O'Beirne to Bertie, 2 Dec. 1906, Bertie Papers, FO 800/177.

though, that by dismissing Goremykin and installing Stolypin, 'the Govt have taken off their coats & we must see which party is the stronger'.[176] Over the course of the next few months, Stolypin became a favourite, first with Nicolson and then with the British generally.[177] An assassination attempt against Stolypin in August 1906 won for him Nicolson's admiration.[178] By 1908 Stolypin was seen in London as the man who was carrying on the enormous task of reform largely by himself in the face of a shortage of capable men.[179] And, when his position was threatened by Durnovo and Witte in 1909, the British response was quick.[180] Nicolson made every effort to persuade Nicholas II of Stolypin's worth.[181] When it was learned that Stolypin's position—and that of Izvolskii which had been similarly threatened—was secure, London was relieved. As Norman pointed out, because Stolypin was considered firmly in favour of the alliance with Britain, and should be replaced by such men as Durnovo and Witte, the result would have been to push 'Russia into the arms of Germany'.[182]

Buchanan soon fell under Stolypin's sway: 'the more I see of Stolypin the more I like him,' Sir George reported soon after he came to Russia.[183] But it was evident to British observers that the cares of office had taken their toll on Stolypin and that he had declined in Nicholas II's estimation. In June 1911, O'Beirne reported Stolypin to be 'depressed' and added that 'his position is insecure'.[184] This was correct; however, Stolypin was assassinated in September 1911 while attending the opera in Kiev. Genuine encomia flowed. 'I shall deeply regret his loss', Nicolson wrote to Grey, 'as we were great friends, and I had the greatest admiration for him. He will be difficult to replace.'[185] The foreign secretary shared Nicolson's feelings,

[176] Diary entry, 22 July 1906, Nicolson Papers, PRO 30/81/13.

[177] K. Neilson, '"My Beloved Russians": Sir Arthur Nicolson and Russia, 1906–16', *IHR* 9 (1987), 531–5.

[178] Respectively: diary entry, 6 Sept. 1906, Nicolson Papers, PRO 30/81/13; Nicolson to Hardinge, 12 Sept. 1906, Nicolson Papers, FO 800/337.

[179] Minutes on Nicolson to Grey, disp. 383, 27 Aug. 1908, FO 371/519/30064; A. S. Korros, 'Activist Politics in a Conservative Institution:The Formation of Factions in the Russian Imperial State Council, 1906–7', *RR* 52 (1993), 1–19.

[180] Nicolson to Grey, 8 Apr. 1909, Nicolson Papers, FO 800/337; E. Chmielewski, 'Stolypin and the Russian Ministerial Crisis of 1909', *CSS* 4 (1965), 1–38; A. Ia. Avrekh, 'Tretia Duma i nachalo krizisa treteiunskoi sistemy (1908–9)', *IZ* 53 (1955), 50–109.

[181] Nicolson to Grey, 14 Apr. 1909, *BD*, v, doc. 835.

[182] Norman's minute (6 June) on Nicolson to Grey, disp. 327, 23 May 1909, FO 371/731/21127; undated minutes (Hardinge and Grey) on Nicolson to Grey, tel. 234, 30 Apr. 1909, FO 371/729/16363.

[183] Buchanan to Nicolson, 4 May 1911, Nicolson Papers, FO 800/348.

[184] O'Beirne to Nicolson, 15 June 1911, Nicolson Papers, FO 800/348; E. Chmielewski, 'Stolypin's Last Crisis', *CSS* 3 (1964), 95–126; C. E. Brancovan, 'Grand Duke Nikolay Mikhailovic on the Ministerial and Parliamentary Crisis of March-April 1911. Five Letters to Frédéric Masson', *OSP*, NS, 6 (1973), 66–81, and A. Ia. Avrekh, 'Vopros o zapadnom zemstve i bankrotstvo Stolypina', *IZ* (1961), 61–112.

[185] Nicolson to Grey, memo, 18 Sept. 1911, Grey Papers, FO 800/93.

replying that the 'death of Stolypin is a great blow to Russia and to *her* friends: I am very sorry.'[186]

Stolypin was succeeded by Vladimir Nikolaevich Kokovtsov, who became chairman of the council of ministers after a long career in the imperial bureaucracy, with most of his early time spent in the ministry of justice and in the imperial chancery. He had made his name, however, in the ministry of finance, where he had been minister from February 1904 to October 1905 and then again from 1906 to the death of Stolypin. There he had initially been responsible for negotiating foreign loans, and had gained great expertise in this regard. Upon Kokovtsov's reappointment as finance minister in 1906, Spring Rice had noted that his 'politics are Conservative', an opinion that two years later had been transformed at the Foreign Office into the view that he was both 'rather reactionary and rather optimistic'.[187] Izvolskii had told Nicolson in 1910, when the former was on the verge of resigning, that he hoped to be succeeded by Kokovtsov, a man Izvolskii described as 'clear-headed [and] wide-minded'.[188] As to his politics, Nicolson mentioned that Kokovtsov 'was always profuse . . . in regard to his friendship for England—but his professions are to rebut assertions to the contrary, and therefore subject to discount'.[189] None the less, the PUS found Kokovtsov 'able', 'inclined to the Right', but lately of 'more liberal tendencies'.

Thus, when Kokovtsov succeeded Stolypin in September 1911, he was a known entity. Not surprisingly, given his background, he soon developed the reputation as a man for whom 'foreign affairs are entirely a matter of finance', as O'Beirne put it in 1913.[190] This had two effects. First, as O'Beirne noted in the same letter, Kokovtsov would be a 'strong influence . . . in favour of a pacific policy at any price', since war would mean financial chaos. Second, since Kokovtsov made finances paramount, 'he is more difficult to influence in questions that either directly or indirectly affect Russia's economic interests'.[191] There was often friction between Sazonov and Kokovtsov over foreign policy on this account, and rumours frequently circulated that either Kokovtsov would replace the foreign minister or Kokovtsov would become ambassador to Paris.[192] The important thing in British eyes was that Kokovtsov was in favour of good Anglo-Russian relations.[193]

[186] Grey to Nicolson, 19 Sept. 1911, *BD*, ix, pt. 1, doc. 231.
[187] Spring Rice to Grey, disp. 309, 10 May 1906, FO 371/121/16396; minute (28 Oct.) by Norman on Nicolson to Grey, disp. 520, 14 Oct. 1907, FO 371/327/35455.
[188] Nicolson to Grey, 9 Aug. 1910, Grey Papers, FO 800/73.
[189] Nicolson to Grey, memo, 21 Mar. 1911, Grey Papers, FO 800/93; undated minute (Maxwell) on Buchanan to Grey, tel. 60, 21 Mar. 1911, FO 371/1214/10340.
[190] O'Beirne to Nicolson, 18 Sept. 1913, Nicolson Papers, FO 800/370.
[191] Buchanan to Nicolson, 21 Sept. 1911, Nicolson Papers, FO 800/350.
[192] Buchanan to Nicolson, 24 Jan., 21 Mar. 1912 and 17 Apr. 1913, Nicolson Papers, FO 800/353, 354 and 365.
[193] Nicolson to Goschen, 18 Nov. 1913, Nicolson Papers, FO 800/371.

Kokovtsov's fall in February 1914, a result of his liberalism and the dislike of other ministers, disappointed the British, although it did not surprise them.

A variety of other figures commanded attention, because of their position, because political events had thrust them to the fore of public attention, or because they were known socially to the British representatives. Ministers of the interior fell into the first two categories, particularly during the violent period from 1902 through 1906, when two of them were assassinated while applying the repressive measures that brought worldwide publicity. The British attitude towards these men was a mixture of disdain for their methods and sympathy for their task. D. S. Sipiagin, who served as minister from 1899 until his death in 1902, was described as 'a typical representative of the Old Russian School and an unyielding advocate of repressive measures' whose actions had gained him the 'special detestation of the nihilists' who eventually killed him.[194] Sipiagin was also thought to be politically under the sway of Witte.[195] V. K. Plehve, Sipiagin's successor and minister until his own assassination in 1904, was a more complicated man. Central in the push to oust Witte, Plehve was recognized by the British as a powerful infighter in Russia's tangled government. Plehve's firm hand resulted in his being termed '[t]he best hated man in Russia', but the British did not dismiss him as a mere reactionary.[196] They were aware that he had advocated a policy of 'reform and education', albeit 'from above and [with] order restored first', and knew that, because his ideas had been blocked, his policy had thus ended 'in a regime of pure repression and enforced ignorance'.[197]

Certainly the need for strength in dealing with Russia's turbulent conditions was realized by the British. Their attitudes to Plehve's successor, Prince P. D. Sviatopolk-Mirsky, make this clear. Mirsky was personally attractive, but his tenure in office was brief.[198] Hardinge's evaluation was an indictment: 'Circumstances however were too strong for Prince Mirsky and being an amiable gentlemen of no great force of character the impetus he gave to the reform movement by his liberal tendencies set forces in motion which were beyond his power to control unaided.'[199] Nor would his successor fare much better. General A. F. Bulygin, formerly governor of Moscow, was thought an 'absolute cypher', whose appointment owed

---

[194] Scott to Lansdowne, disp. 132, 14 Apr. 1902, FO 65/1641.

[195] Scott to Lansdowne, 8 Jan. 1903, Scott Papers, Add MSS 52304.

[196] Diary entry, 3 June 1904, Hardinge Papers, vol. 5.

[197] Spring Rice to Nicolson, 6 Aug. 1906, Nicolson Papers, FO 800/338.

[198] Diary entry, 4 Oct. 1904, Hardinge Papers, vol. 5.

[199] Hardinge to Lansdowne, disp. 8, 4 Jan. 1905, FO 65/1698; D. Turnbull, 'The Defeat of Popular Representation, December 1904: Prince Mirskii, Witte, and the Imperial Family', *SR* 48 (1989), 54–70; F. S. Zuckerman, 'Political Police and Revolution: The Impact of the 1905 Revolution on the Tsarist Secret Police', *JCH* 27 (1992), 281–2.

much to the Grand Duke Sergei Aleksandrovich.[200] Much more impressive was P. N. Durnovo, who had been assistant minister under Mirsky and who was appointed acting minister succeeding Bulygin in October 1905.[201] While Durnovo succeeded Plehve as 'the best hated man in Russia', he was also 'efficient in his duties' in contrast to his immediate predecessors.[202] He, along with his assistant minister, General D. F. Trepov—'a far more efficient police officer than is usually found among Russian officials'—stemmed the tide of revolution that many thought Mirsky's reforming bent had stimulated.[203] Unlike Trepov, who was assassinated in September 1906, Durnovo continued to attempt to act as an adviser to the Emperor and was an active participant in the making and unmaking of ministers.[204] Often working in unison with A. F. Trepov, the brother of the late general, Durnovo was thought, for example, to be at the centre of the 'cabal of reactionaries' who nearly toppled Stolypin from office in 1911.[205]

Two other Russian officials deserve notice: Baron Staal was Russian ambassador to London from 1884 to 1902 and Count Alexander Benckendorff, his successor, held the post from 1903 until his death in 1917. Staal established an 'exceptional position' in London over the course of his eighteen years there.[206] Suggestions that he be moved elsewhere were resisted by the British, in one instance at the behest of Queen Victoria. Sanderson found Staal of great value, since the PUS was 'sure [that] he does all he can to keep matters smooth and remove the prejudices of his Government'.[207] However, by 1901, many in London came to believe that Staal was too old for the job: 'De Staal is delightful, but completely played out' and '[h]e is a mere figure-head: he neither knows what is going on, nor, as I understand it, does the Foreign Office in St. Petersburg pay very much attention to his representations.'[208]

Benckendorff was even more highly-regarded. He and Scott had served overlapping times as ministers at Copenhagen and had become friends.[209] Scott noted that Benckendorff was 'an ardent advocate of a good understanding with England', a

---

[200] Hardinge to Sanderson, 15 Feb. 1905, Hardinge Papers, vol. 6; Hardinge to Lansdowne, disp. 86, 6 Feb. 1905, FO 65/1698.

[201] D. Lieven, 'Bureaucratic Authoritarianism in Late Imperial Russia: The Personality, Career and Opinions of P.N. Durnovo', *HJ* 26 (1983), 391–402.

[202] Spring Rice to Grey,disp. 51, 15 Jan. 1906, FO 371/121/2402.

[203] Nicolson to Grey, disp. 626, 16 Sept. 1906, FO 371/138/32909.

[204] Lieven, *Russia and the Origins of the First World War*, 76–82; his *Russia's Rulers under the Old Regime* (New Haven, 1989), 216–30.

[205] Buchanan to Nicolson, 23 Mar. 1911, Nicolson Papers, FO 800/348.

[206] Lascelles to Kimberley, very confidential disp. 108, 22 Apr. 1895, FO 65/1490.

[207] Sanderson to O'Conor, 27 Apr. 1898, O'Conor Papers, OCON 6/25.

[208] Hamilton to Curzon, 25 Apr. 1901, Curzon Papers, MSS Eur F111/148; Hamilton to Curzon, 17 Oct. 1901, Curzon Papers, MSS Eur F111/150.

[209] Scott to Lansdowne, 25 Dec. 1902, Lansdowne Papers, FO 800/140.

fact that likely made his appointment a welcome one.[210] Benckendorff was also a 'sincere Anglophile' and had access to Nicholas II himself.[211] Benckendorff was a thoroughly westernized Russian. He spoke several languages better than he did Russian—the legend that he spoke no Russian was not true—and had picked up liberal views that one of his colleagues later wrote would have been 'criminal heresy' in Russia.[212] In fact, Hardinge once noted of Benckendorff's candour and willingness to see Russia from the perspective of an outsider: 'I could hardly realise that he is a Russian.'[213] Benckendorff and his family moved effortlessly in English society.[214] For example, 'the Bencks' were frequent guests of the Asquiths and their circle.

Benckendorff was always willing to turn his desire for good Anglo-Russian relations into concrete acts. During the Dogger Bank incident, he worked hard to prevent an open rupture between the two countries, a fact that drew praise from Lansdowne.[215] Early in 1905, while on leave in Russia, Benckendorff attempted to organize a peace party to push the Russian government to seek a compromise settlement with Japan.[216] Perhaps most important for the British, Benckendorff worked assiduously in favour of the Anglo-Russian Convention. During its negotiation in 1907, while again on leave, Benckendorff did 'capital work' in 'allaying the fears and jealousies of the Military Party' who opposed the Convention.[217] In fact, he once urged Hardinge to 'flatly reject' a Russian proposal as it would then be withdrawn. 'Rather amusing,' Hardinge wrote, 'is it not, to get such advice from such a quarter?'[218] While Benckendorff's influence waned over time, his very presence in London meant that one aspect of Anglo-Russian relations remained on a friendly and intimate basis.

The creation of the Duma in 1905 gave the British another range of political action to consider. From the very first, there was an underlying conviction that the development of parliamentary institutions in Russia must follow a course of gradual

[210] Scott to Sanderson, undated (but Dec. 1899), Scott Papers, Add MSS 52303; O'Conor to Sanderson, 21 Apr. 1898, O'Conor Papers, OCON 3/15.

[211] Scott to Salisbury, 14 Dec. 1899, Salisbury Papers, A129; Hardinge to Knollys, 13 June 1905, Hardinge Papers, vol. 6; Nicolson diary entry, 16 Jan. 1907, Nicolson Papers, PRO 30/81/13; Lieven, *Russia's Rulers*, 139, 146–7 and 157–8.

[212] Marsden (British journalist) to Nicolson, 17 July 1911, Nicolson Papers, FO 800/346; D. I. Abrikossow, *Revelations of a Russian Diplomat* (Seattle, 1964), 110; C. Nabokoff, *Ordeal of a Diplomat* (London, 1921), 34. Quotation from the latter.

[213] Hardinge to Lansdowne, 8 Feb. 1905, Lansdowne Papers, FO 800/141.

[214] See the picture of 'the Bencks' in M. Brock and E. Brock (eds.), *H. H. Asquith: Letters to Venetia Stanley* (Oxford, 1982); esp. 117.

[215] Lansdowne to Benckendorff, 28 Oct. 1904, FO 65/1729.

[216] Hardinge to Lansdowne, 8 Feb. 1905, Lansdowne Papers, FO 800/141.

[217] Nicolson diary entry, 9 Feb. 1907, Nicolson Papers, PRO 30/81/13; Morley to Minto, 7 Mar. 1906, Morley Papers, MSS Eur D573/2.

[218] Hardinge to Nicolson, 2 Apr. 1907, Nicolson Papers, FO 800/339.

arrogation of power to the Duma. For example, when details of the new governmental process that the calling of the First Duma would initiate were announced,
it was noted in London that 'The bureaucracy has hedged itself in with every sort
of safeguard but the Duma will necessary [*sic*] grow in power and will in time
remove them and dictate their own constitution.'[219] This belief persisted, but could
not ensure that the path was straightforward, or even always promising in the eyes
of the British. The British saw the First Duma as definitely opposed to the existing
government.[220] And, while Nicolson considered the Constitutional Democrats (or
Cadets) as the dominant party in the Duma, he felt that this was not likely to last,
as the Cadets—'for the most part respectable, intelligent, & cultivated men'—
would prove ineffectual as an administration and would soon be replaced by less
moderate types.[221] While the dissolution of the Duma raised a great hue and cry in
England, Nicolson viewed it calmly. For him, the need was for strong government
in the face of the chaos existing in Russia.

But the ambassador did not close his eyes to the steps taken by the Russian
government to ensure that the elections to the Second Duma returned a body less
radical than the First had proved. In the run-up to the election, the embassy
reported that the new electoral laws 'have obviously been framed to hamper the
propaganda of all parties belonging to the "Left" and to place the "Centre" and
"Right" parties in a privileged position'.[222] When even these methods failed to
produce a suitably subservient Duma, opinion at the Foreign Office was properly
cynical.[223] Even Stolypin's speech to the Second Duma on 19 March 1907, in which
he promised that the government would act within clearly defined legal limits, did
not dispel doubts. 'This is the most satisfactory declaration which has been made
by the Russian Govt since the issue of the Manifesto [granting the Duma] itself: but
they have so often expressed their intention of carrying out the provisions of that
Manifesto and so often failed to do so that even now it is hard to help feeling
sceptical in spite of appearances.'[224]

Nicolson was not optimistic. The Second Duma proved to be as contumacious as
the First, and simply refused to accept the limits on debate that Stolypin wished to
impose. This, Nicolson felt, would result in dissolution, causing the Foreign Office
to regard the future of liberty in Russia as dim.[225] But when dissolution actually

[219] Undated minutes (Eldon Gorst and Hardinge) on Spring Rice to Grey, disp. 177, 8 Mar. 1906,
FO 371/124/8658; minutes on Spring Rice to Grey, disp. 189, 14 Mar. 1906, FO 371/122/9508.
[220] Nicolson to Grey, disp. 346, 6 June 1906, FO 371/122/19858.
[221] Nicolson to Hardinge, 4 July 1906, Nicolson Papers, FO 800/337.
[222] Fortnightly report in Nicolson to Grey, disp. 9, 3 Jan. 1906, FO 371/318/578.
[223] Norman's minute (18 Mar.) on Nicolson to Grey, disp. 115, 1 Mar. 1907, FO 371/321/8591.
[224] Norman's minute (25 Mar.) on Nicolson to Grey, disp. 149, 21 Mar. 1907, FO 371/322/9659.
[225] Nicolson's disps. 162, 170 and 187, 27 and 29 Mar. and 4 Apr. 1907, FO 371/322/10354, 11880
and 11890 and the minutes.

occurred, the ambassador did not feel that a regime of reaction was necessarily sure to follow. 'It would be most unfortunate', he reported on 17 June 1907, 'if any serious impediment were placed in the way of the constitutional development of the country, slow, laborious and chequered as it undoubtedly is and will be.'[226] The elections, held in the autumn of 1907, for the Third Duma, showed him to have been perspicacious. The parties of the left, which had dominated the first two Dumas, were substantially reduced in numbers, but even a Duma more of the political right found it difficult to co-operate with the Russian government. 'The third Duma', Nicolson wrote early in 1908, 'was the touchstone by which the possibility of permanently establishing representative institutions was to be tested' and its failure to work with the government presaged a possible 'serious situation' in Russia. 'The third Duma', it was wittily noted at the Foreign Office, 'instead of providing "a touchstone" . . . seems rather to be qualifying itself to act as their tombstone.'[227] Grey, also resorting to puns, spread the blame evenly: 'The Russian Government manipulated the Constitution in order to secure a tame Duma & have apparently got a dummy.'

By the summer of 1908, when the Duma's session ended, the Third Duma was looked on more favourably. The fact that it had managed to pass legislation, albeit at the last minute, led Norman to state that it had 'shown a good deal of independence and good sense'.[228] Near the end of 1909, the Third Duma seemed to be 'settling down to real hard work'.[229] This was seen as part of a larger trend. 'It is satisfactory', Norman wrote, 'that the youth of the country should be becoming more practical because the tendency to do nothing but talk and the passion for abstraction and ideals has always been too prominent in the minds of the educated classes in Russia.'[230] Events proved that the British observers had misjudged the Duma. Elements of the extreme right, whose most violent faction, the Union of Russian People, had been characterized by Hardinge as early as 1906 as 'officially recognised hooliganism', decided to bring a halt to the development of parliamentary government.[231] When the Third Duma came to an end in June 1912, O'Beirne summed up its achievements.[232] What he felt was its 'key-note', especially under Guchkov, 'was the determination to avoid conflict with the Government'. This left the Duma 'open to the reproach of excessive subservience'. Many of its actions,

---

[226] Nicolson to Grey, disp. 325, 17 June 1907, FO 371/324/20722; Mallet's undated minute.
[227] Nicolson to Grey, disp. 44, 26 Jan. 1908, FO 371/512/3630; Kilmarnock (Eastern Department clerk, FO) minute (2 Feb.). The next two sentences and the quotation are from the minutes.
[228] Norman's undated minute on O'Beirne to Grey, disp. 326, 16 July 1908, FO 371/512/25036.
[229] Norman's minute (25 Nov.) on Nicolson to Grey, disp. 613, 18 Nov. 1909, FO 371/726/42641.
[230] Norman's minute (26 Dec.) on Nicolson to Grey, disp. 630, 16 Dec. 1909, FO 371/726/44305.
[231] Hardinge's undated minute on Bagge (acting British consul-general Odessa) to Grey, disp. 60, 15 Oct. 1906, FO 371/129/35819.
[232] O'Beirne to Grey, disp. 200, 27 June 1912, FO 371/1470/27680; Norman's minute (3 July).

especially those dealing with Finland and local government in western Russia, were 'harsh and illiberal' to ethnic minorities. Norman's evaluation of this report—'it is hard to imagine a clearer and more concise history of the Third Duma'—reflected the fact that the easy optimism of 1906 was finding actual conditions in Russia disappointing.

The Fourth Duma, from the autumn of 1912 until the end of the Tsarist regime, featured an even more right-wing composition, and foundered on growing opposition. At the end of the first session of the Fourth Duma, in July 1913, Buchanan summarized its achievements as 'practically . . . nil'.[233] When the Duma's final prewar session began in October 1913, the situation was reminiscent of 1904, and Kokovtsov was felt likely to be unable to obtain a working majority in the Duma.[234] Only Nicolson refused to accept such pessimism. 'I doubt if the Duma', the PUS minuted on O'Beirne's despatch, 'will be curtailed in its functions and rights, but it is quite probable that it has not realized all the hopes of the advocates of parliamentary Gov't—but Russia is not unique in that respect.' Rumours in early 1914 about the possibility of a 'coup' against the Duma, wherein the latter would be dissolved without a re-assembly date, strengthened the pessimists.[235] While the coup turned out merely to be the dismissal of Kokovtsov and his replacement by Goremykin, this did not cheer the Foreign Office. The attempt in the spring by the government to prosecute a Georgian Menshevik deputy, Chkheidze, for advocating a republic led to scenes in the Duma 'unparalleled in [its] history . . . and disorderly to a degree never attained in the revolutionary second Duma'.[236] By the eve of war, in the view of the Foreign Office, the Russian constitutional experiment was exceedingly fragile.

How, then, was Russia perceived by the British élite? It is evident that a close eye was kept on individual Russians and on Russian politics generally. The Russian autocracy was seen to be an old-fashioned kind of government, one that put great emphasis on individuals rather than on institutions or process. As Hardinge put it, the autocracy was 'an anachronism existing now only in semi-civilised & barbarous states, & must inevitably be modified to meet the requirements of the great advance in civilisation made in Russia during the past 20 years'.[237] In this system, hard evidence about events and people was difficult to obtain. Although the Emperor was away at Livadia for months and sequestered as Tsarskoe Selo in the years following 1905, rumour and conversation revealed a great deal and were extremely

---

[233] Buchanan to Grey, disp. 226, 23 July 1913, FO 371/1743/34606.
[234] O'Beirne to Nicolson, 16 Oct. 1913, Nicolson Papers, FO 800/371; O'Beirne to Grey, disp. 360, 25 Nov. 1913, FO 371/1743/54107. The next quotation from Nicolson's undated minute on the latter.
[235] Pares' memo on Russian affairs, 13 Jan. 1914 and minutes, FO 371/2090/3312.
[236] Buchanan to Grey, disp. 138, 6 May 1914, FO 371/2093/20884.
[237] Hardinge to Knollys, 8 Feb. 1905, Hardinge Papers, vol. 6.

valuable. As Hardinge noted in 1905 about events in Russia: 'nothing remains secret here long . . . the difficulty here is to sift the truth from the lies.'[238] None the less, the quality of the information provided by the embassy in St Petersburg was impressive. With extensive contacts in Russian society, the British were attuned to the undertones of Russian politics, and their knowledge compares favourably with modern research.[239] And when Russian foreign policy is considered, the range and depth of material gathered is even more impressive.

But, in Russia, as elsewhere, foreign statesmen were judged by British standards. Grey, for example, noted in 1908 that several prominent European statesmen, including Stolypin, 'would hold their own in English public life', but that several others, including Izvolskii, would not.[240] The obvious inference was that foreigners were rarely up to the mark. This was particularly evident concerning personal honesty and forthrightness. A remark in 1901 by Curzon—'Russian statesmen are such incurable liars. I have now followed the careers of at least four: Giers, Loba-noff, Mouravief, Lamsdorff. They all lied, and lied shamelessly'—was extreme, but there is little doubt that more moderate versions of this statement were widely accepted.[241] Such opinions were shared even by some prominent Russians. Benck-endorff, it was reported, stated that while Lord Lansdowne had never lied to him, he wished that the reverse were true![242] Such beliefs spilled into the arena of policy-making. During the preliminaries of the negotiations for the Anglo-Russian Con-vention, Lord Minto spoke directly to this point. 'I am afraid', he wrote to Morley, 'I have always been very doubtful as to the reliability of the professions of Russian diplomatists.'[243] In every circumstance, there was the underlying British perception that Russians prevaricated at best and lied at worst. This was bound to affect relations.

It is also evident that Russian statesman were judged more by their Anglophilia than by any standards of professional competence. Lamsdorff, Izvolskii, and Sazonov were all judged as not overly capable when they took office, but their faults were overlooked the more they followed a foreign policy in line with Britain's. Muravev, on the other hand, never became a British favourite, and it was no coincidence that his time in office was one marked by unrelenting ill feelings between the two countries. Lobanov's brief time in office did not provide time for him to be judged. Witte's career shows the changing nature of British assessments most clearly. Lauded as a great man and a statesman when he favoured a pacific

---

[238] Hardinge to Campbell, 29 Mar. 1905, FO 65/1699.
[239] Cf. the Embassy's reports and G. A. Hosking, *The Russian Constitutional Experiment* (Cambridge, 1973); V. S. Diakin, *Samoderzhavie, burzhuaziia i dvorianstvo, 1907–11 gg.* (Leningrad, 1978).
[240] Esher's diary entry, 27 Sept. 1908, Esher Papers, ESHR 2/11.
[241] Curzon to Selborne, 29 May 1901, Selborne Papers, 10.
[242] Hardinge to Sanderson, 15 Feb. 1905, Hardinge Papers, vol. 6.
[243] Minto to Morley, 15 Feb. 1906, Morley Papers, MSS Eur D573/7.

policy in the Far East, a policy that dovetailed nicely with British interests, he became known as a place seeker and a renegade after 1905 when he advocated a policy of closer Russo-German alignment, a policy judged inimical to Britain's position.

The problems of evaluation were never more obvious than with respect to Nicholas II. Quite rightfully, the British noted that '[t]he Emperor is the all important factor' in foreign policy.[244] But they were never able to come to grips with the personality of the elusive monarch. In such a circumstance, wishful thinking could take over. Since close Anglo-Russian relations were desired, the best possible interpretation was put on Nicholas's every utterance and action. Perhaps unconsciously sharing the traditional view of the Russian peasantry that all ills could be attributed to the Tsar's officials rather than to the monarch himself, the British tended to view Nicholas as influenced by the last person who advised him. This allowed them to ignore the fact that Nicholas very much ran his own ship, something that the peace negotiations in the Russo-Japanese War underlined.[245] It was not until during the First World War that Robert Bruce Lockhart, the acting British consul in Moscow, got closer to the truth: 'the Emperor is by no means stupid, talks well and to the point, and is fully aware of what he is doing . . . he is obstinate and vindictive, and quite obsessed with the idea that autocracy is his and his children's by Divine right.'[246] But to have accepted this view would have run counter to the British belief—hope may be more accurate—in Nicholas II as a closet liberal. Nicholas's evident disregard for the Duma, a body which for the British was the touchstone of a favourable future for Russia, was largely ignored or blamed on the machinations of his advisors. The required Nicholas became the accepted one.

For better or worse, then, Russia was regarded by British decision makers not as she actually may have been, but as she was thought to be. British policy towards Russia was based on the élite's beliefs about the nature of Russia, Russian policy, and the attitudes of individual Russians. The correctness of these beliefs is open to challenge, but the significance of them is not. Only by understanding them can an accurate appreciation of Anglo-Russian relations be obtained.

[244] Nicolson to Stamfordham, 2 Oct. 1912, *BD*, ix, pt. 1, doc. 807.
[245] R. A. Esthus, 'Nicholas II and the Russo-Japanese War', *RR* 40 (1981), 396–411.
[246] Lockhart to Grey, disp. 2, 22 Jan. 1916, FO 371/2745/25836; D. R. Jones, 'Nicholas II and the Supreme Command: An Investigation of Motives', *Sbornik*, 11 (1985), 47–83.

3

The Public's Russia

'I WISH indeed', Sir Arthur Nicolson, the Permanent Undersecretary (PUS) at the Foreign Office, wrote in April 1914, 'that we could bring the feelings of the public in this country into a similar state towards Russia as they are towards France, but this will take some time to effect as there is so much misrepresentation in regard to Russia being circulated through many circles in this country and also such complete ignorance of Russia herself.'[1] Nicolson then went on to outline his optimism about the future:

Englishmen are going more frequently to Russia and British capital is very largely invested in various Russian enterprises, while, you may laugh at me for saying so, both the Russian ballet and Russian opera have done good. Knowledge of Russian literature too is tending to show that the Russians are not such barbarians as most people tend to think.

But he concluded his letter pessimistically: 'To change the present attitude of mind prevalent in this country towards Russian affairs will take a long time, and until such a change is produced I very much fear that it would be difficult for any Government to enter into closer and more precise and definite relations with Russia.'

Nicolson's remarks make evident the need to consider a range of matters wider than what one clerk said to another when discussing Anglo-Russian relations. Foreign policy is not made in a vacuum; those who make it are not divorced from the currents of thought in their society. While diplomats, with their long years abroad, their fluency in foreign languages and their specialized knowledge, were perhaps something of an exception to this generalization, others were not.[2] The views held of Russia by the wider public exerted a definite, if subtle and hard-to-quantify influence on the general relations between the two

---

[1] Nicolson to Goschen (British ambassador, Berlin), 27 Apr. 1914, Nicolson Papers, FO 800/373.

[2] B. Porter, '"Bureau and Barrack": Early Victorian Attitudes towards the Continent', *VS* 27 (1984), 407–33; J. Buzard, 'A Continent of Pictures: Reflections on the "Europe" of Nineteenth-Century Tourists', *PMLA* 108 (1993), 30–44; V. G. Kiernan, 'Diplomats in Exile', in R. Hatton and M. S. Anderson (eds.), *Studies in Diplomatic History: Essays in Memory of David Bayne Horn* (London, 1970), 301–21; N. Brailey, 'Sir Ernest Satow, Japan and Asia: The Trials of a Diplomat in the Age of High Imperialism', *HJ* 35 (1992), 115–50.

countries.[3] It is important to understand what is meant here by 'public'. What follows is not a study of public opinion in the modern sense. When considering a time when public-opinion polls did not exist, it is impossible retrospectively to obtain such information.[4] Even the meaning of the word has shifted. Before the First World War, a clear distinction was made between 'public' and 'popular' opinion: the former suggested the views of the educated and influential who played a prominent role in public life; the latter referred to the passions of the multitudes who, generally speaking, did not.[5] It is the views of the public, defined in this sense, that concern us here.

What Victorian and Edwardian Britons thought of Russia is difficult to know.[6] What is clear is that these thoughts were never far from political considerations. Popular views of Russian life, literature, and culture were linked to the fact that Russia was Britain's principal enemy from the 1830s onward.[7] They tended to focus on the darker and more unpleasant aspects of Russian life: Russia was brutally governed, semi-civilized, and alien to the European mind; Russia itself was 'eternal snow, sledges and wolves'.[8] Little illustrates this better than Victorian adventure and spy fiction.[9] While Germany has been the focus of most of the scholarly work done on this genre, it is important to note that such emphasis does not represent the historical reality. Following the political verities of the time, Russia and France were the favourite opponents of Britain in imaginary wars from 1893 until at least 1905.

Perhaps no author is as readily identifiable with such novels as is William Le Queux.[10] From 1890 to his death in 1927, Le Queux wrote nearly two hundred

---

[3] Grey to Nicolson, 24 Feb. 1908, Nicolson Papers, FO 800/341.

[4] C. J. Lowe, *The Reluctant Imperialists*. (2 vols.; London, 1967), i. 11–12; P. M. H. Bell, *John Bull and the Bear: British Public Opinion, Foreign Policy and the Soviet Union 1941–5* (London, 1990), 17–24.

[5] Chirol to Hardinge, 1 Nov. 1904, Hardinge Papers, vol. 7.

[6] M. S. Anderson, *Britain's Discovery of Russia 1553–1815* (London, 1958); A. G. Cross: 'British Knowledge of Russian Culture (1698–1801)', *Canadian-American Slavic Studies*, 13 (1979), 412–35 and his introductions to id. (ed.), *Russia Under Western Eyes 1517–1815* (London, 1971), 13–47 and id. (ed.), *The Russian Theme in English Literature from the Sixteenth Century to 1980: An Introductory Survey and a Bibliography* (Oxford, 1985), 1–82. Two articles with the same title by G. Phelps: 'The Early Phases of British Interest in Russian Literature', in *SEER* 36 (1958) 418–33 and *SEER* 38 (1960), 415–30; distinguished below as 'Early Phases' 1 and 2 respectively.

[7] Contentious since France and a French invasion were also of prime consideration; J. H. Gleason, *The Genesis of Russophobia in Great Britain* (Cambridge, MA., 1950); H. Orel, 'English Critics and the Russian Novel: 1850–1917', *SEER* 33 (1995) 457–69.

[8] Phelps, 'Early Phases 2', 430.

[9] K. Neilson, 'Tsars and Commissars: W. Somerset Maugham, *Ashenden* and Images of Russia in British Adventure Fiction, 1890–1928', *CJH* 27 (1992), 475–500; I. F. Clarke, *Voices Prophesying War, 1763–1964* (London, 1966), D. Stafford, *The Silent Game: The Real World of Imaginary Spies* (Toronto, 1988) and W. K. Wark (ed.), *Spy Fiction, Spy Films, and Real Intelligence* (London, 1991).

[10] Stafford, *Silent Game*, 14–29.

novels. But the novel that catapulted him to fame was *The Great War in England in 1897* published in 1894.[11] The subject of *The Great War* was a Franco-Russian invasion of England. Le Queux's Russian invasionary force—'the grey-coated hordes'—was the picture of savagery. Upon landing, the Russians attacked Eastbourne, showing 'no quarter' and 'robbery, outrage, and murder ran riot in the town'.[12] Le Queux highlighted the brutality of Russian behaviour by emphasizing the Englishness of the victims. By doing so, he was able to portray the Russian army as an alien, nearly inhuman, force: 'Horrible were the deeds committed that night,' runs a typical passage, 'English homes were desecrated, ruined and burned. Babes were murdered before the eyes of their parents, many being impaled by gleaming Russian bayonets; fathers were shot down in the presence of their wives and children, and sons were treated in a similar manner.' Not just the actions of the Russian troops, but the manner of their actions was vile. 'The soldiers of the Tsar, savage and inhuman, showed no mercy to the weak and unprotected. They jeered and laughed at piteous appeal, and with fiendish brutality enjoyed the destruction which everywhere they wrought.'[13] The words 'fiendish' and 'brutality' were a stock-in-trade for Le Queux.

A second matter that Le Queux emphasized was the size of the Russian army. This was not without its political point. In his preface to *The Great War*, Le Queux made clear his hope that this book would alert British public opinion to the 'gigantic Armies' possessed by the Continental Powers. Throughout the novel, Le Queux deliberately drove this home. Thus, he referred to the 'grey-coated masses of the Russian legions', the 'dense grey white masses of the [Russian] enemy', the 'enormous [Russian] forces', and, on a more encouraging note, as the inevitable Anglo-Saxon victory begins to unfold, the 'appalling losses' that the Russians suffered in the battle of Birmingham.[14] The Russian army was so gigantic and so brutal that it could best be compared to a natural catastrophe. As Le Queux put it in his usual florid prose: 'Throughout the land the grey-coated hordes of the White Tsar spread like locust—their track marked by death and destruction.'[15] In another instance, the Russian troops were compared to 'packs of wolves', lying in wait to attack honest English villages.[16] By comparing the Russians to beasts, Le Queux was rendering them less than human and all the more frightening.

These images were not exclusive to Le Queux's works; they were the stock images of the stage Russian throughout such literature. In another invasion thriller,

[11] W. Le Queux, *The Great War in England in 1897* (London, 1894).
[12] Ibid. 65–6.
[13] Ibid. 67.
[14] Ibid. 50, 142, 125, and 153 respectively. Le Queux editorialized broadly on the minuscule size of the British forces; see 71–2.
[15] Ibid. 137.
[16] Ibid. 50. The use of 'wolves' harkened back to the earliest portrayals of Russia.

The Final War (1896), Louis Tracy put a similar emphasis on the nature of the Russian forces.[17] In a war between Britain and a Continental coalition of France, Germany, and Russian, it was the latter that posed the greatest threat to Britain and her Empire. Initially standing aloof from the French and German assault on Britain, Russia—'with her armies uncountable, and her fleets, which might sweep unquestioned through the Baltic and break into the charmed waters of the North Sea, a power irresistible and invincible'—entered the war late.[18] It was St Petersburg's ostensible intent to seize Constantinople and the Ottoman empire. The real goal of perfidious Russia was, however India. Here were Victorian fears at their worst. But, the Russian onslaught was turned back by 'all that was most brilliant and most resolute in the British military genius'—the army of India.[19] Although heavily outnumbered, the Indian army emerged victorious, due both to this 'genius' and to the fact that 'Generalship can dispense with multitudes when Asiatics are in front'.[20] This latter remark, with racist overtones common at the time, is revealing, for it linked Russia with Asia—and as such extra-European and alien—and the latter's teeming populations and traditional disregard for human life.[21]

The goals of Russian foreign policy in popular fiction of the time did not stray far from what seemed likely to contemporaries. In George Griffith's *The Outlaws of the Air* (1897), an Anglo-Russian war broke out over the Russian seizure of 'Port Lazareff' in China, a clear extrapolation from the actual German acquisition of Kiaochow and a prescient anticipation of the actual Russian appropriation of Port Arthur.[22] Nor was Griffith's peace settlement unrelated to British fears. In defeat, Russia was forced to abandon 'all her pretensions in Central Asia south of the 40th parallel of north latitude, the crossing of which, on any pretence, by her troops or allies was for ever considered as a declaration of war'.[23] The era certainly provided a number of plausible reasons for an Anglo-Russian war. In another book, Griffith had such a conflict begin over a border incident in the Hindu Kush, while a different author anticipated the Boer War and followed this with a Franco-Russian ultimatum demanding that Britain evacuate Egypt.[24] Clearly, Russia was seen as a worldwide threat to British interests.

---

[17] L. Tracy, *The Final War* (New York, 1896).
[18] Ibid. 136.
[19] Ibid. 83.
[20] Ibid. 225.
[21] K. Ballhatchet, *Race, Sex and Class under the Raj: Imperial Attitudes and Policies and Their Critics, 1793–1905* (London, 1980).
[22] G. Griffith, *The Outlaws of the Air* (London, 1897), 141.
[23] Griffith, *Outlaws of the Air*, 372.
[24] G. Griffith, *The Angel of the Revolution: A Tale of the Coming Terror* (London, 1893), 101; C. Gleig, *When All Men Starve: Showing how England Hazarded her Naval Supremacy, and the Horrors which Followed the Interruption of her Food Supply* (New York, 1898).

But the Russia of late nineteenth-century pulp novels was not just a military threat. Just as significantly, Russia was also a source of nihilism and anarchism.[25] These two movements had a particular significance for the British in the half century before the First World War. Beginning in the 1880s, Victorian England felt itself threatened from two quarters. One quarter—the Fenian bomb outrages—was concrete; the other—what Bernard Porter has termed 'the changing political and social ethos in Britain'—was much more nebulous.[26] But, however nebulous, the latter threat was intimately bound up with Russia. From the large number of Jewish—mostly Russian Jewish—immigrants in the East End of London to the anarchist and nihilist threat to the existing order both in Britain and Europe, Russia seemed to be at the bottom of much of what threatened Victorian stability.[27] The presence of considerable numbers of Russian political refugees in Britain, many of whom had links to anarchist and nihilist groups, only underlined this belief.[28]

Although there was generally a public revulsion against anarchists and nihilists, this was tempered by a belief that many of their activities—when carried out abroad and particularly in Russia—were justified by the behaviour of the repressive regimes that had spawned the movements.[29] Particular anarchists could even be appealing. The favourable reception in Britain of Peter Kropotkin, the so-called prince of anarchists, underlined the fact that personal qualities could lift an anarchist above the general condemnation of the breed in the public's mind.[30] There was a long tradition of sympathy in Britain for those persecuted by the Tsarist regime. English radicals gave a warm welcome to those Polish exiles who had left after the uprisings in 1830–1 and 1863.[31] Such Russian revolutionary luminaries as

[25] B. A. Melchiori, *Terrorism in the Late Victorian Novel* (London, 1985), 122–89.

[26] B. Porter, *The Origins of the Vigilant State: The London Metropolitan Special Branch before the First World War* (London, 1987), 19, 98–113; H. Shpayer-Makov, 'Anarchism in British Public Opinion 1880–1914', *VS* 31 (1988), 487–516.

[27] B. Gainer, *Alien Invasion: The Origins of the Aliens Act of 1905* (New York, 1972). On anti-Semitism in Britain, G. C. Lebzelter, *Political Anti-Semitism in England 1918–39* (London, 1978); C. Holmes, *Anti-Semitism in British Society, 1876–1939* (New York, 1979).

[28] B. Porter, *The Refugee Question in Mid-Victorian Politics* (Cambridge, 1979). The Russian exiles were a particular aspect; J. Slatter (ed.), *From the Other Shore: Russian Political Emigrants in Britain, 1880–1917* (London, 1984); M. A. Miller, *The Russian Revolutionary Emigres 1825–70* (Baltimore, 1986).

[29] R. B. Jensen, 'The International Anti-Anarchist Conference of 1898 and the Origins of Interpol', *JCH* 16 (1981), 323–47.

[30] H. Shpayer-Makov, 'The Reception of Peter Kropotkin in Britain 1886–1917', *Albion*, 19 (1987), 373–90.

[31] P. Brock, 'Polish Democrats and English Radicals 1832–62: A Chapter in the History of Anglo-Polish Relations', *JMH* 25 (1953), 139–56; id., 'Joseph Cowen and the Polish Exiles', *SEER* 32 (1953), 52–69; J. F. Kutolowski, 'Polish Exiles and British Public Opinion: A Case Study of 1861–2', *CSP* 21, 1 (1979), 45–65, and id., 'Victorian Provincial Businessmen and Foreign Affairs: The Case of the Polish Insurrection, 1863–4', *Northern History*, 21 (1985), 236–58.

Alexander Herzen were listened to carefully.[32] This linkage took on new force in December 1889 when the prominent Russian revolutionary Sergei Mikhailovich Stepniak-Kravchinsky (generally known as Stepniak) and Robert Spence Watson (a leading Liberal who was the president of the National Liberal Federation from 1890 to 1902) formed the Society of Friends of Russian Freedom (SFRF).[33] The SFRF published a journal, *Free Russia*, from 1890 to 1915, under the editorship of Stepniak and, after his death in 1895, another Russian émigré, Felix Volkhovsky. The purpose of the SFRF was manifold: to provide accurate information in Britain about Russia, to counter the favourable propaganda about the Tsarist regime provided by such Tsarist apologists as Madame Olga Novikova, to organize protests against specific actions of the Russian government, and to agitate generally in favour of reform in Russia.[34] Stepniak was ideally suited through his wide range of contacts among English socialists and Liberals, to ensure that the misdeeds of Tsarist Russia did not go unnoticed.

Perhaps the most famous episode involving Russian revolutionaries in Britain occurred in 1898. In that year, Vladimir Burtsev, a Russian revolutionary living in London, was arrested at the behest of the Russian government for advocating, in his terrorist journal, *Narodovolets*, the assassination of Nicholas II.[35] Burtsev was supported strongly by the SFRF. They raised money for his defence, and rallied public opinion on his behalf. While the Crown's case involved only whether Burtsev had indeed written and sold the offending journal, the defence used the opportunity to make wide-ranging attacks on Tsarism and the autocratic system in Russia. Burtsev was found guilty and sentenced to eighteen months at hard labour, but the legal victory had been won at the cost of embarrassing publicity for the Russian government.

[32] M. Partridge, 'Alexander Herzen and the English Press', *SEER* 36 (1958), 454–70 and id., 'Alexander Herzen and the Younger Joseph Cowen, M. P.: Some Unpublished Material', *SEER* 41 (1962), 50–63.

[33] D. Senese, *S. M. Stepniak-Kravchinskii: The London Years* (Newtonville, MA, 1987), 46–108; id., 'Felix Volkovsky in London, 1890–1914', *Immigrants and Minorities*, 2 (1983), 67–78; B. Hollingsworth, 'The Society of Friends of Russian Freedom: English Liberals and Russian Socialists, 1890–1917', *OSP*, NS, 3 (1970), 45–64; D. B. Saunders, 'Stepniak and the London Emigration. Letters to Robert Spence Watson, 1887–90', *OSP*, NS 13 (1980), 80–93; J. Slatter, 'Stepniak and the Friends of Russia', *Immigrants and Minorities*, 2 (1983), 33–49; G. M. Hamburg, 'The London Emigration and the Russian Liberation Movement: The Problem of Unity, 1889–97', *JfGOE* 25 (1977), 321–39; R. Grant, 'The Society of Friends of Russian Freedom (1890–1917): A Case Study in Internationalism', *Journal of the Scottish Labour History Society*, 3 (1970), 3–24.

[34] J. O. Baylen, 'Madame Olga Novikov, Propagandist', *ASEER*, 10 (1951), 255–71 and id., 'Madame Olga Novikov: Defender of Imperial Russia, 1880–1900', *Historia*, 1 (1951), 133–56.

[35] A. Kimball, 'The Harassment of Russian Revolutionaries Abroad: The London Trial of Vladimir Burtsev in 1898', *OSP*, NS, 6 (1973), 48–65; D. Saunders, 'Vladimir Burtsev and the Russian Revolutionary Emigration (1888–1905)', *ESR* 13 (1983), 39–62; F. S. Zuckerman, 'Vladimir Burtsev and the Tsarist Political Police in Conflict, 1907–14', *JCH* 12 (1979), 193–219.

Given the prominent activities of Russian political exiles in Britain, it was not surprising that Russia was a constant theme in Victorian adventure novels dealing with terrorists and anarchists. The portrayal of these types was a mixture of revulsion and sympathy. This was clear in George Griffith's *The Angel of the Revolution*. In this novel, an anarchist, Maurice Colston, took off his shirt to reveal 'the sign-manual of Russian tyranny—the mark of the knout!'[36] But, this was not enough; Colston had also been flogged. Not only was the flogging brutal, but also it 'was my [Colston's] reward for telling the governor of a petty Russian town that he was a brute-beast for flogging a poor decrepit old Jewess to death'. Colston was not the only person flogged by the Russian government, so, too, was Radna Michaelis, a member of the Inner Circle of the Brotherhood (as Colston's anarchist organization is called). A portrait of her, naked to the waist while being whipped, hangs in the Brotherhood's headquarters, no doubt to stimulate both the reader's revulsion and a certain prurience.[37] While the Brotherhood was supposedly above politics and nationalism, it was not without a certain British bias. Its chief was Lord Alanmere, a graduate of Trinity College, Cambridge, and now a member of the British embassy at St Petersburg. At the end of the novel, when the Brotherhood had triumphed over the evil Russian forces, the Brotherhood was dissolved in favour of world domination by an Anglo-Saxon League under Alanmere's benevolent leadership. The contrast between good—Anglo-Saxons under an English aristocrat—and evil—Russians led by the autocratic Tsar—could not be more plain.

Russian nihilists were an essential part of the background for most novels dealing with the adventures of Britons in Russia. When Duckworth Drew, Le Queux's archetypal British secret agent, travelled on a mission to St Petersburg, his contact there was a nihilist.[38] Drew's attitude towards the nihilists was ambivalent. On the one hand—'Such persons were by no means desirable companions, but it was not the first time that necessity had brought me into queer company'—he was critical of them; on the other—the nihilists were 'the conspirators of the cause of Russian freedom' whose help he readily accepted—he found them sympathetic.[39] Significantly, Drew's nihilists supported a pro-British, rather than a pro-German tilt to Russian foreign policy because England 'had offered so many of their refugees hospitality'.

In fact, Russian nihilists were often viewed simply as those who are struggling to reform Russia. In Tracy's *The Final War*, Captain Ponchowski, the 'Supreme Head

---

[36] Griffith, *Angel of the Revolution*, 14.

[37] N. Hiley, 'Decoding German Spies: British Spy Fiction, 1908–18', in Wark (ed.), *Spy Fiction*, 55–79.

[38] W. Le Queux, *Secrets of the Foreign Office: Describing the Doings of Duckworth Drew, of the Secret Service* (London, 1903), 73. This book is a collection of short stories featuring Drew.

[39] The quotations are from ibid. 81.

of the Nihilist Party' that was attempting to overthrow Tsardom, put himself on the side of the angels when he noted that his force must make common cause with England against Russia: 'If England is beaten', Ponchowski orated, 'we are all beaten, humanity is beaten with her. The light of freedom goes out; man crawls back into his chains; the dungeon once more gapes open.'[40] Given a man of such obvious discriminating good taste, how could any Englishman resist supporting his cause? In another novel, an Englishwoman who was in love with a Russian nihilist put it all more simply. When her family and friends expressed concern about her lover's politics, she dismissed it: 'Nihilist, if you like. It's a ridiculous name of course. In Russia nowadays it simply means a person who has the wrong opinions.'[41] A similar note was struck by Henry Seton Merriman, the author of many novels dealing with the Russian theme.[42] In *Prisoners and Captives*, published in 1891, Merriman expatiated at length upon nihilism and nihilists:

This is no political pamphlet, and the writer is no Nihilist . . . a Nihilist is not a Terrorist, nor a Socialist, nor an Atheist, but merely, if you please, a politician—a man who loves his country sufficiently well to risk all for her sake . . . To-day the Nihilists are criminals, some day they will be heroes. To-day Nihil merely represents the fruit that they gather from their seed, but in times to come one cannot help hoping that there will be a mighty harvest.[43]

Besides the obvious sympathy for nihilism, this passage was interesting in that Merriman carefully separated the nihilists from terrorists, socialists, atheists, all figures designed to raise the hackles of conservative Victorians. Instead, like Tracy, he aligned the nihilists with the search for liberty. The fact that the ends of the nihilists—and in this context the term also meant revolutionaries generally—were viewed as laudable, stemmed from the general perception of the Russian government found in these novels.[44] In general, it was viewed as autocratic, repressive and corrupt. One of Merriman's characters put it succinctly in *Prisoners and Captives*: 'The state of Russia and her system of government is a disgrace to the whole world—yet the whole world closes its eyes to the fact.'[45] A common feature in these novels was the arbitrary nature of Russian government and the possibility of sudden arrest on charges either trifling or non-existent.

For Duckworth Drew, Russian justice was an open book. 'To act the spy in Russia is practically to invite confinement in a fortress for the rest of one's life . . . When the Russian police detect a spy they make very short work of him— arrest and prompt consignment to a fortress without any trial beyond the secret

---

[40] Tracy, *The Final War*, 310.
[41] E. L. Voynich, *Olive Latham* (Philadelphia, 1904), 39.
[42] Cross, *The Russian Theme in English Literature*.
[43] H. S. Merriman, *Prisoners and Captives* (London, 1891), 230.
[44] Melchiori, *Terrorism*, 150–89 informs the discussion below.
[45] Merriman, *Prisoners and Captives*, 84.

court-martial.'[46] While such a procedure might have been just acceptable to Le Queux's readers—after all, Drew *was* a spy even though he was an Englishman—in other cases it was not. In G. A. Henty's *Condemned as a Nihilist*, his English hero, Godfrey Bullen, was arrested in Russia.[47] Released from custody, one of his Russian friends told him that only his English nationality prevented his stay from being indefinite. 'The wonder is [that the authorities] made any inquiries at all. If you had been a Russian the chances are that your family would never have heard of you again . . . and you would have been sent to Siberia for life.'[48] And this theme was repeated by others, including Merriman.[49]

Once put in a Russian prison, the fate of the incarcerated was generally regarded as sealed. The gruesome literary images of being 'sent to Siberia' have their origins well before their current association with Solzhenitsyn's world of the Gulag. After his arrest in Russia, one of Le Queux's characters was sent east: 'In chains with a convoy of convicts he crossed the Urals, and tramped for weeks on the snow-covered Siberian Post Road.'[50] An even more vivid account may be found in *Prisoners and Captives*. 'There is a certain excitement', Merriman stated near the end of the novel, 'in imagining a snow-covered plain traversed by one dirty, deeply-rutted road, and to set thereon a string of miserable human beings, dragging one leg after another—their backs turned towards home and all they love, their horror-stricken eyes looking on hopeless exile.'[51] The reader must guard against this sentiment, Merriman concluded, '[for] there is no excitement in standing at the edge of the road and watching with living eyes those same poor human beings in the flesh. There is no dramatic thrill in standing at the side of a miserable pallet infested with vermin, reeking with damp, and watching the last throes of a repulsive heap of dirt and rags which was once a comely, fair young girl.'

This led into a common sub-plot in such stories: the fate of women condemned to prison in Russia. Russian gaols provided a fertile ground for the Victorian fate-worse-than-death theme. As Griffith put it vividly in *The Outlaws of the Air*, when Natasha, the nihilist heroine of the piece, was captured:

Not one of those who heard but had good reason to know what it meant for a revolutionist to fall into the hands of Russia. For a man it meant the last extremity of human misery that flesh and blood could bear, but for a young and beautiful woman it was a fate that no words could describe—a doom that could only be thought of in silence and despair . . .[52]

    [46] Le Queux, *Secrets of the Foreign Office*, 71.
    [47] G. A. Henty, *Condemned as a Nihilist: A Story of Escape from Siberia* (New York, 1897); P. A. Dunae, 'Boy's Literature and the Idea of Empire, 1870–1914', *VS* 24 (1980), 109–11.
    [48] Henty, *Condemned as a Nihilist*, 12.
    [49] See his *The Sowers* (New York, 1968; first pub. 1895). This repr. edn. has a useful discussion of the reception of the book.
    [50] Le Queux, *The Great War*, 29.
    [51] Merriman, *Prisoners and Captives*, 231.   [52] Griffith, *Outlaws of the Air*, 65.

Natasha was soon 'brutally searched', tried, and condemned by administrative order (again the arbitrary nature of the Tsarist state) to exile for life in Sakhalin. But a much worse fate awaits her. 'You know what that means for a beautiful woman like Natasha. She will not go to Sakhalin. They do not bury beauty like hers in such an abode of desolation as that. If she cannot be rescued, she will only have two alternatives before her. She will become the slave and plaything of some brutal governor or commandant at one of the stations, or else she will kill herself. Of course, of the two she would choose the latter—if she could and when she could.'[53]

Natasha's situation was not unique. In *Olive Latham*, Wanda Slavinski, the girlfriend of a suspected nihilist, was arrested shortly after her lover is gaoled.[54] When he emerged from prison, Wanda was nowhere to be found. 'Then the hushed-up story leaked out bit by bit. Wanda had been a pretty girl, and a new gaoler, appointed during her second year in the prison, had an eye for pretty girls. No actual outrage had been committed; but the girl had not dared to sleep, and her nerves had broken down under the strain of watching and nightly dread.' The inevitable result was Natasha's preferred solution: suicide.

Taken collectively, British adventure fiction painted a black image of Russia. Russia was a military threat to Britain and her Empire, a despotic land ruled by an arbitrary and brutal government and the home of new creeds that threatened the established order. The impact of such fiction on British public opinion is difficult to quantify. Certainly, there were sufficient real-life episodes of a nature similar to those portrayed above to give credence to the fictional accounts of Russian life. But, it is not possible to demonstrate concrete linkages between fiction and British policy. However, several incidents are suggestive. Erskine Childers's fictional account of a German invasion of Britain, *The Riddle of the Sands*, was a case in point. The book generated enough public interest that Lord Selborne, the first lord of the admiralty wrote to the director of naval intelligence that 'it is remarkable how many people have been struck by it and who constantly come to me about it', and had the latter read the novel, if only to rebut its premise.[55] The memoirs of Robert Bruce Lockhart, who went to Russia as British vice-consul at Moscow in 1912, give another indication of the impact of fiction. When he heard of his posting to Russia, Lockhart wrote: 'Moscow! Like a flash the Russia of Seton Merriman—the only Russia I knew—passed before my eyes. Adventure, danger, romance photographed themselves in my mind.'[56] The adventure novel had left its mark.

[53] Ibid. 66.
[54] Voynich, *Olive Latham*, 42–3.
[55] Selborne to Battenberg, 27 Apr. 1904; Battenberg to Selborne, 23 Feb. 1904, both Selborne Papers 44.
[56] R. H. B. Lockhart, *British Agent* (New York, 1933), 48.

Popular views of Russia did not derive entirely from adventure fiction. Occasionally, more serious novels took up the Russian theme. Undoubtedly the most famous of these was Joseph Conrad's *Under Western Eyes*, published in 1911.[57] While *Under Western Eyes* was a far more sophisticated novel than those discussed above, its views of Russia were remarkably similar. The speech of the political assassin, Haldin, could easily be mistaken for anything found in the nihilist novels:

You suppose that I am a terrorist, now—a destructor of what is. But consider that the true destroyers are they who destroy the spirit of progress and truth, not the avengers who merely kill the bodies of the persecutors of human dignity. Men like me are necessary to make room for self-contained, thinking men like you ... And, besides, an example like this is more awful to oppressors when the perpetrator vanishes without a trace. They sit in their offices and palaces and quake.[58]

Razumov, the protagonist, who turns Haldin over to the authorities, cannot hide from himself the true nature of Russia: 'Everything was not for the best. Despotic bureaucracy ... abuses ... corruption ... and so on.'[59] For Conrad, Russia was the antithesis of all things English. His earlier spy novel, *The Secret Agent* (1907), made this evident. With its Mr Vladimir, the sinister Russian representative in London, *The Secret Agent* reflected, as Thomas Mann later observed, 'the whole conflict between the British and the Russian political ideology'.[60] Even the sophisticated reader must have found Russia a land of political reaction and despair.

The writings of journalists were also of great significance in shaping the public's views of Russia. People like Stead, Mackenzie Wallace, and Dillon wrote extensively about international affairs, and both the public and members of the élite paid close attention to their views.[61] Stead's views of Russia have been the subject of extensive study.[62] He was an advocate of an Anglo-Russian *rapprochement*. Begin-

[57] J. Conrad, *Under Western Eyes* (London, 1947; first pub. 1911); Cross, *Russian Theme in English Literature*, 57–8; L. M. Magill, 'Joseph Conrad: Russia and England', *Albion*, 3 (1971) 3–8; T. C. Moser, 'An English Context for Conrad's Russian Characters: Sergey Stepniak and the Diary of Olive Garnett', *Journal of Modern Literature*, 11 (1984) 3–44.

[58] Conrad, *Under Western Eyes*, 19–20.

[59] Ibid. 35, original ellipsis.

[60] J. Conrad, *The Secret Agent* (London, 1907); the quotation is from Thomas Mann's introduction to the German translation: see T. Mann, 'Joseph Conrad's *The Secret Agent* (1926)', in I. Watt, (ed.), *Conrad: The Secret Agent: A Casebook* (London, 1973), 102.

[61] Scott to Sanderson, 4 May 1899, Scott Papers, Add MSS 52303; Scott to Lansdowne, private and personal, 8 Jan. 1903, Scott Papers, Add MSS 52304; Scott to Sanderson, 17 Mar. 1903, Lansdowne Papers, FO 800/115; Hardinge to Sanderson, 27 July 1904, Hardinge Papers, vol. 6; Sanderson to Hardinge, 3 Feb. 1905, Hardinge Papers, vol. 7, and Hardinge to Sanderson, 15 Mar. 1905, Hardinge Papers, vol. 6.

[62] J. O. Baylen, 'W. T. Stead, Apologist for Imperial Russia, 1870–80', *Gazette: International Journal for Mass Communications Studies*, 6 (1960), 281–97; id., 'W. T. Stead and the Russian Revolution of 1905', *CJH* 2 (1967), 45–66; id., 'The Tsar and the British Press: Alexander III and the *Pall Mall Gazette*, 1888', *EEQ* 15 (1982), 425–39.

ning in the 1870s, he argued that Britain and Russia should collaborate, not compete, in Central Asia. During the Russo-Turkish War, Stead anticipated Gladstone's support for the Bulgarian Christians (and, willy-nilly, Russia), and portrayed the Russian peace terms at San Stefano as moderate. Even at the height of the Penjdeh incident, Stead struck a pro-Russian stance. He was not, however, an unqualified supporter of Russia. Stead opposed Russia's assimilationist policy in Finland, although his tone was more one of sorrow than of anger. During the revolution of 1905, Stead called upon Nicholas II to free himself from his bureaucracy and use the opportunity to modernize Russia. Not even the repressive actions of the Tsarist regime could dissuade Stead that Nicholas II was essential to the future of Russia, and Stead insisted that Russia's reform must be gradualist rather than revolutionary in nature.

Mackenzie Wallace was another moderating force in British public opinion. Wallace's long career in matters Russian, and the influence of his two-volume study, *Russia*, which first appeared in 1877 and emerged in new editions in 1905 and 1911, gave his voice a special authority in Russian issues.[63] His attitudes towards Russia were particularly evident during the events of 1905–7. Wallace went to Russia in 1906 and again in 1907 with a serious purpose in mind. His second edition of Russia had underestimated the revolutionary potential in that country— as Sanderson waspishly remarked of the new edition at the end of 1905: 'Mackenzie Wallace has not shown himself a very astute prophet.'[64] Wallace was thus determined to regain his credibility. His view of events was in many ways similar to that of Stead. Wallace felt that Nicholas II had been justified in dissolving the Duma, since the latter was too revolutionary. Wallace believed that, as Russia was not yet ready for British parliamentary-style government, reform must be gradual lest revolution occur. Wallace was concerned that his 'Liberal friends' in Russia were acting 'very foolishly. Instead of accepting and trying to develop workable moderate reforms, they are rushing recklessly into revolution, of which no one can foresee the terrible consequences.'[65] This led some to see Mackenzie Wallace as an apologist for Tsarism: as Spring Rice put it, 'Mackenzie Wallace . . . is always on the side of the King and the nobles against the vulgar.'[66] But, in the long term, Wallace was not optimistic that Russia could or would be reformed.

Dillon's views of Russia were unique. Dillon's 'Foreign Affairs' feature in the *Contemporary Review* and his reportage for the *Daily Telegraph* gave him important

---

[63] D. G. Morren, 'Donald Mackenzie Wallace and British Russophilism, 1870–1919', *CSP* 9 (1967), 170–83; W. Harrison, 'Mackenzie Wallace's View of the Russian Revolution of 1905–7', *OSP*, NS, 4 (1971), 73–82; id., 'The British Press and the Russian Revolution of 1905–7', *OSP*, NS, 7 (1974), 75–96.

[64] Sanderson to Hardinge, 19 Sept. 1905, Hardinge Papers, vol. 7.

[65] Wallace to Nicolson, 28 June 1906, Nicolson Papers, FO 800/338.

[66] Spring Rice to Nicolson, 21 Aug. 1906, Nicolson Papers, FO 800/338.

platforms from which to espouse his views. As Count Witte's confidant, Dillon had a vested interest in his mentor's career. Thus, until Witte was no longer a likely candidate for the post, Dillon favoured the appointment of a 'strong man' at the head of Nicholas II's government in order to give it some direction.[67] His opinions were based, in part, on his mystic view of Russia and Russians. 'After ages of spiritual stagnation and politico-social bondage', Dillon argued, 'the Russian man is still half a child and half an imperfectly tamed beast.'[68] But, beyond this, Dillon was convinced that Russia needed firm government and that the revolutionary movement was dangerous.[69] In general, Dillon supported the autocracy, even to the extent that he felt that the policy of Russification in Finland was justified by the actions of the Finns.[70]

Thus, three of the most prominent journalist writing about Russia generally took a line towards that country that ran somewhat counter to the rampant anti-Tsarism prevalent in much of popular writing about Russia. None the less, while they might have been—as a result of their specialized knowledge of Russia and their own prejudices—less inclined to condemn the Russian government root and branch, all of them felt that Russia needed reforming. Even the most conservative of British readers could not escape the view that Russian government was in a state of disrepair.

The public's knowledge and images of Russia did not come exclusively from British writing about Russia. Russian authors themselves offered the literate public views of Russia. The novels of Turgenev and Tolstoy were popular well before the First World War, while Dostoevsky's popularity had to wait until 1912 and the translation of his work by Constance Garnett (whose sister-in-law was a close confidante of Stepniak).[71] By 1930, an anonymous writer in the *Times Literary Supplement* could state that 'the Russian fever' that swept English letters had begun in 1912.[72] While this may have been true of the fever, the Russian infection had started much earlier. Russian novels were commonly discussed in periodicals by 1870, and by 1900 most educated readers would have been familiar with at least some Russian works. Indeed, in 1893 a group, the Anglo-Russian Literary Society (ARLS), was founded in London with the object of promoting the

---

[67] Spring Rice to Nicolson, 11 July 1906, Nicolson Papers, FO 800/338; Nicolson's diary entry, 19 Aug. 1906, Nicolson Papers, PRO 30/81/13.

[68] E. J. Dillon, *The Eclipse of Russia* (London, 1918), 13. His entire chapter, 'The Russian Mind', 11–26, is full of such half-baked nonsense.

[69] Nicolson to Hardinge, 29 Jan. 1908, Nicolson Papers, FO 800/337.

[70] Nicolson to Grey, disp. 132, 10 Mar. 1910, FO 371/975/8702.

[71] Moser, 'An English Context for Conrad's Russian Characters'; Johnson, B. C. (ed.), *Tea and Anarchy! The Bloomsbury Diary of Olive Garnett 1890–3* (London, 1989).

[72] 'Dostoyevsky and the English Novel', *Times Literary Supplement*, 5 June 1930, cited, Phelps, 'Early Phases 1'. The following is based on Phelps's two articles and Orel, 'English Critics'.

study of Russian language and literature.[73] But, while there was widespread interest in Russian literature, it was how to read Russian novels that caused problems. Since Russian novels were highly politicized, English audiences found them difficult to interpret.

Tolstoy's didactic tone found opposition from those who did not agree with his message; the suffering in Dostoevsky's writings made him unpalatable to others. What did remain was the idea that Russia was somehow different, in, but not of Europe, and, above all, a place of sorrow and suffering. This point was commented on by Maurice Baring, the author of one of the earliest attempts to make Russian literature intelligible to English readers and a man well-qualified to pontificate on Russia.[74] Baring, the son of Edward Baring, first Baron Revelstoke (of Baring Brothers Bank), had entered the diplomatic service in 1898, but resigned in 1904. He was a war correspondent in Manchuria in 1904 and then special correspondent for the *Morning Post* in Russia from 1905 to 1908. An intimate friend of the Benckendorffs, Baring published eight books on Russia and Russian literature in the period from 1905 to 1914. In a letter to his uncle, Lord Cromer, the long-term British consul-general in Egypt, Baring noted 'the flashes of ignorance' shown by politicians towards Russia.[75] While agreeing that Russia was 'neither East nor West', Baring deprecated the general interpretations of Russia as gleaned from Russian novels.

Taking the whole subject broadly, I think people who haven't lived in Russia, would necessarily derive from any books on Russia, especially novels, a far too gloomy impression. If the gloom were as 'inspissated' as all that life wouldn't be tolerable. But when we go there what do we find? People of all classes enjoying themselves very much, having a good time generally, and *enjoying their enjoyment*, attaching importance to the fact that from time to time a man should, if possible, have a *very good time*, get drunk, do anything.

While Baring might have disagreed with the usual reading of Russian literature, his remarks attested to the fact that it existed.

But the obvious point was that the existence of such literature destroyed the idea that Russia was a land without civilization or culture. This new belief was reinforced on other artistic fronts. There was an efflorescence of interest in Russian culture just before the First World War.[76] As Samuel Hynes put it: 'Russian literature, Russian modes of dress, Russian drama, Russian opera, and Russian ballet all had vogues between 1910 and 1914.' The Ballets russes burst on to the London scene in 1911, two years after its triumph in Paris. The Russian impres-

---

[73] D. Galton, 'The Anglo-Russian Literary Society', *SEER* 48, (1970), 272–82.

[74] In his *Landmarks of Russian Literature* (London, 1910); E. Letley, *Maurice Baring: A Citizen of Europe* (London, 1991).

[75] Baring to Cromer, 22 Mar. 1913, Cromer Papers, FO 633/22.

[76] S. Hynes, *The Edwardian Turn of Mind* (Princeton, 1968), 335–45. Quotation from 336.

ario, Sergei Diaghilev, brought the leading dancers of the day, Nijinskii and Kar-savina, to Covent Garden on 26 June 1911 for George V's coronation gala. It was an enormous success: 'Thus, in one evening', Diaghilev noted, 'the Russian ballet conquered the whole world.'[77] With its revolt against accepted form, and its exotic and colourful sets designed by Leon Bakst, the Russian ballet dominated the season. Bakst's fashions, in fact, inspired a 'Russian-cum-Oriental style' of dress among the smart set.[78] Russian-ness itself became the mode. When to this was added the growing admiration for Chekhov among a theatre-going élite and the impact of Russian visual artists—Alexander Archipenko, the first Cubist sculptor; Marc Chagall, whose paintings of Russia were a sensation in Paris in 1911; Wassily Kandinsky, who created the Abstrationist school of painting in 1909, to name only a few[79]—Russia clearly had become a substantial cultural force in Europe.

Culture was not the only link between Britain and Russia. There were also economic ties that helped determine public awareness of the Tsarist state. In general, Britain was Russia's second-largest trading partner well behind Ger-many.[80] From 1894 to 1913, British exports to Russia rose from 132.8 million rubles to 173.0 million. These two figures represented, respectively, 21.7 per cent and 12.6 per cent of Russia's imports. British imports from Russia show a similar pattern. Britain was Russia's second-largest export market, again behind Germany. British imports from Russia amounted to 173.5 million rubles in 1894 (out of Russian total exports of 668.6 million) and 267.8 million in 1913 (out of 1520.1 million). Exports to Britain thus accounted for 25.9 per cent of Russian exports in 1894 and 17.6 per cent in 1913. Clearly Britain was an important, if declining, trading partner for Russia. The reverse was not true. Total British exports in 1894 were worth £216 million, while imports were valued at £416 million.[81] This meant that only 3.4 per cent of British imports by value came from Russia in 1894, while British exports to Russia amounted to 8.8 per cent of Britain's total.[82] By 1913, the situation had not changed much except that Russia's proportion of British exports had fallen. Total British exports in that year amounted to £525 million, while imports reached £769 million. The Russian market thus took 3.6 per cent of British exports in 1913, while Russia provided 3.8 per cent of British imports the year before the war.

[77] Cited, M. Eksteins, *The Rites of Spring: The Great War and the Birth of the Modern Age* (Toronto, 1989), 26–7.

[78] J. B. Priestley, *The Edwardians* (London, 1970), 238. Quotation from 236.

[79] Some idea of the vitality and influence of Russian art can be seen in J. -L. Ferrier (ed.), *Art of Our Century: The Chronicle of Western Art 1900 to the Present*, trans. W. Glanze (New York, 1989).

[80] Derived from D. Geyer, *Russian Imperialism: The Interaction of Domestic and Foreign Policy, 1860–1914*, trans. B. Little (Leamington Spa, 1987), 164.

[81] British trade from B. R. Mitchell, *European Historical Statistics 1750–1970* (London, 1978), table E 1. I have converted the ruble to pounds sterling using the ratio 9.2 rubles = £1.

[82] This latter figure would be even smaller if re-exports were included in the total of British exports.

Nor was Russia a primary area for British investment. The related issues of where and how much British capital was invested abroad and how much foreign capital was invested in Russia are matters of contention.[83] Most scholars, however, agree that Russia required substantial amounts of foreign capital from about 1890 onwards in order to modernize her economy.[84] Determining how much British capital was invested in Russia is difficult, and estimates for the 1913 total range from £66.6 million to £110 million.[85] These figures may be too high, given that both take Russian issues placed on the London market as being wholly subscribed by English capital. In either case, they do not amount to a great deal when taken in the context of a British overseas investment of at least £2.6 billion and possibly as much as £4 billion.[86]

But if Russia were not the centre of the British economic and financial world, that does not mean that *individual* firms did not have significant stakes in Russia. While Anglo-Russian trade links reached back to Elizabethan times, it was not until the nineteenth century that British firms and British capital began to take a particular interest in Russia.[87] That interest was initially confined to a few industries, such as textiles and metallurgy.[88] But, by the end of the nineteenth century, British

---

[83] D. C. M. Platt, *Britain's Investment Overseas on the Eve of the First World War* (London, 1986). As to where such investment went and whether it should have gone there, cf. L. E. Davis and R. A. Huttenback, *Mammon and the Pursuit of Empire: The Political Economy of British Imperialism, 1860–1912* (Cambridge, 1986) and S. Pollard, 'Capital Exports, 1870–1914: Harmful or Beneficial?', *EconHR*, 2nd ser., 38 (1985), 489–514. Davis and Huttenback have generated controversy; see A. Porter, 'The Balance Sheet of Empire, 1850–1914', *HJ* 31 (1988), 685–99 and A. G. Hopkins, 'Accounting for the British Empire', *JICH* 16 (1988), 234–47. On the Russian side, P. V. Ol', *Foreign Capital in Russia*, trans. G. Jones and G. Gerenstain (New York, 1983); M. Falkus, 'Aspects of Foreign Investment in Tsarist Russia', *JEEH* 8 (1979), 5–36.

[84] P. Gatrell, *The Tsarist Economy 1850–1917* (London, 1986), 222–9. Two exceptions are D. C. M. Platt, *Foreign Finance in Continental Europe and the United States, 1814–70* (London, 1984), 75 and H. Barkai, 'The Macro-Economics of Tsarist Russia in the Industrialization Era: Monetary Developments, the Balance of Payments and the Gold Standard', *JEH* 33 (1973) 360. Barkai's contentions have been challenged: P. R. Gregory and J. Sailors, 'Russian Monetary Policy and Industrialization, 1861–1913', *JEH* 36 (1976), 836–51.

[85] Platt, *Britain's Investment Overseas*, 91.

[86] The smaller figure is that of Platt; the larger that of Feis, see Platt, *Britain's Investment Overseas*, 31–60.

[87] T. S. Willan, *The Muscovy Merchants of 1555* (Manchester, 1953); C. Dunning, 'James I, The Russia Company, and the Plan to Establish a Protectorate Over North Russia', *Albion*, 21 (1989), 206–26; D. K. Reading, *The Anglo-Russian Commercial Treaty of 1734* (New Haven, 1938); H. H. Kaplan, 'Russia's Impact on the Industrial Revolution in Great Britain during the Second Half of the Eighteenth Century: The Significance of International Commerce', *Forschungen zur osteuropäischen Geschichte*, 29 (1981), 7–59; id., 'Observations on the Value of Russia's Overseas Commerce with Great Britain during the Second Half of the Eighteenth Century', *SR* 45 (1986), 85–94; P. H. Clendenning, 'William Gomm: A Case Study of the Foreign Entrepreneur in Eighteenth Century Russia', *JEEH* 6 (1977), 533–48.

[88] S. Thompstone, 'Ludwig Knoop, "The Arkwright of Russia"', *Textile History*, 15 (1984), 45–73; for metallurgy, T. H. Friedgut, *Iuzovka and Revolution*, i, *Life and Work in Russia's Donbass, 1869–1914* (Princeton, 1989); for grain, see S. Fairlie, 'Shipping in the Anglo-Russian Grain Trade, to 1870: Part

firms were part of the growing number of foreign entrepreneurs seeking profits in Russia, particularly in the oil fields at Baku.[89] The totality of Anglo-Russian economic and financial relations is beyond the scope of this study. However, two case studies, significant in themselves, throw light on the broader aspects of the subject. The first study involves the Russian activities of the British arms manufacturer, Vickers Limited; the other involves the activities of the British banking firm, Baring Brothers.[90]

After 1906, the Russian government began a determined effort to restore Russian's navy.[91] While there were substantial pressures in Russia to give contracts to Russian firms—both private and state-controlled—the need to keep costs low and to have access to the most modern technology led to foreign firms becoming involved.[92] Vickers' first step in this market was not auspicious. The building of the cruiser *Riurik*, which Vickers had contracted in 1906 for delivery in 1907, was plagued by quarrels concerning design and capability between the firm and the Russian government. When the ship was finally delivered in 1909, the Russian admiralty attempted to impose a large fine for late delivery, an issue not cleared up until 1913.[93] In 1912, Vickers became 'technical advisers' to a French consortium, La Société des Ateliers et Chantiers de Nicolaieff that obtained contracts for constructing several Russian naval vessels at Nikolaev. This project ran into difficulties. Vickers was slow to produce designs for the Russian ships, and constructed

One', *Maritime History*, 1 (1971), 158–75 and id., 'Shipping in the Anglo-Russian Grain Trade, to 1870: Part Two', *Maritime History*, 2 (1972), 31–45.

[89] J. P. McKay, *Pioneers for Profit: Foreign Entrepreneurship and Russian Industrialization 1885–1913* (Chicago, 1970). Case studies include R. W. Tolf, *The Russian Rockefellers: The Saga of the Nobel Family and the Russian Oil Industry* (Stanford, CA, 1976); K. H. Kennedy, *Mining Tsar: The Life and Times of Leslie Urquhart* (London, 1986), and R. Munting, 'Ransomes in Russia: An English Agricultural Engineering Company's Trade with Russia to 1917', *EconHR*, 2nd ser., 31 (1978), 257–69. For a survey, see F. V. Carstensen. 'Foreign Participation in Russian Economic Life: Notes on British Enterprise, 1865–1914', in G. Guroff and F. V. Carstensen (eds.), *Entrepreneurship in Imperial Russia and the Soviet Union* (Princeton, 1983), 140–58.

[90] C. Trebilcock, *The Vickers Brothers: Armaments and Enterprise, 1854–1914* (London, 1977), 119–41; E. R. Goldstein, 'Vickers Limited and the Tsarist Regime', *SEER* 58 (1980), 561–71. On Barings, P. Ziegler, *The Sixth Great Power: Barings, 1762–1929* (London, 1988); J. Orbell, *Baring Brothers & Co., Limited. A History to 1939* (London, 1985). I would like to thank Dr Orbell for his help in using the Barings archives.

[91] K. F. Shatsillo, *Russkii imperializm i razvitie flota nakanune pervoi mirovoi voiny (1906–14)* (Moscow, 1968); id., 'O disproportsii v razvitii vooruzhennyk sil Rossii nakanune pervoi mirovoi voiny (1906–14 gg.)' *IZ* 83 (1969), 123–36. Ramifications are in P. Gatrell, 'After Tsushima: Economic and Administrative Aspects of Russian Naval Rearmament, 1905–13', *EconHR*, 2nd ser., 43 (1990), 255–70.

[92] W. H. McNeill, *The Pursuit of Power: Technology, Armed Force, and Society since A.D. 1000* (Chicago, 1982), 285–94; K. F. Shatsillo, 'Inostrannyi kapital i voenno-morskie programmy Rossii nakanune pervoi mirovoi voiny', *IZ* 69 (1961), 72–4.

[93] M. Perrins, 'The Armored Cruiser *Riurik* and Anglo-Russian Naval Co-operation 1905–9', *Defense Analysis*, 8 (1992), 173–8.

a slipway that was one-third underwater on the mistaken 'supposition that the waters of the Black Sea are tidal'.[94] The British Foreign Office placed the blame squarely on Vickers, and informed the firm that 'it will be useless to ask for our assistance [in getting contracts] in the future unless they are better able to look after their own interests'. But Vickers had its own explanation for delays. As they were acting only as 'advisers', they did not have the power to ensure that their advice was followed.[95] Equally, the workforce was 'entirely inexperienced', the management 'very antagonistic to any new methods', the organization of the shipyard 'not what it should be', and the entire project plagued by inefficiency and sloth. The result was that, when the Russian minister of the marine visited Nikolaev in August 1913, he 'expressed great dissatisfaction at the progress of the work'.

Despite these complaints and the attitude of the British Foreign Office, in 1913 Vickers was able, with the support of the embassy, to garner a much more lucrative contract in Russia.[96] This was for the creation of a new gunworks at Tsaritsyn (modern-day Volgograd). At Tsaritsyn, Vickers' stake was substantial: the company put up nearly one-quarter of the 13 million rubles invested and promised to provide the plant's required technology for fifteen years. In exchange, Vickers would get a fee for their engineering advice and 10 per cent of the profits accruing over the first ten years of production.[97] But, just as at Nikolaev, Vickers found Russian management and workers difficult. The detailed plans for the gunworks sent from Vickers' Sheffield plant to Tsaritsyn in 1913 were rejected by the Russian engineers on the spot, and the latter also proposed alternatives that Vickers found unfeasible.[98] While things progressed more smoothly after that, the legacy of distrust between Vickers and the Russian government had serious repercussions during the First World War.[99]

Baring Brothers' involvement in Russia stretched back to the early nineteenth century.[100] In the 1820s and in the period from 1850 to 1870, Barings had helped to

[94] Grenfell's disp. 13, confidential, 4 Sept. 1912 in Buchanan to Grey, disp. 274, 5 Sept. 1912, FO 371/1469/37774 and Mallet's minute.

[95] C. Evans (Vickers Commission, Nikolaev) to Vickers, 16 Nov. 1912; T. Jones (Vickers commission, Nikolaev) to Vickers, 19 July 1913; T. Jones to T. G. Owen (Vickers), 29 Aug. 1913, all Vickers Papers R214.

[96] Barker (Vicker's representative, Russia) to Buchanan, 7 and 27 May 1913, Vickers Papers, R214; C. Trebilcock, 'British Armaments and European Industrialization, 1890–1914', *EconHR*, 2nd ser., 26 (1973), 265–7.

[97] This was typical: C. Trebilcock, 'British Multinationals in Japan, 1900–41: Vickers, Armstrong, Nobel, and the Defense Sector', in T. Yuzawa and M. Udagawa (eds.), *Foreign Business in Japan before World War II* (Tokyo, 1990), 89–100; the chart on 93.

[98] W. Clark (director, Vickers Sheffield) to Barker, 7 Oct. 1913, Vickers Papers, R215.

[99] N. Robinson (Vickers, St Petersburg) to Vickers, 20 Nov. 1913, Vickers Papers, R215; A. L. Sidorov, 'Otnosheniia Rossii s soiuznikami i innostranye postavki vo vremia pervoi mirovoi voiny 1914–17 gg.' *IZ* 15 (1945), 128–79.

[100] Ziegler, *Sixth Great Power*, 95, 170–6.

float both Russian loans and Russian issues on the London market. This relationship was not always fruitful. In 1890, the withdrawal of Russian government funds that had been deposited with Barings in London was one of the catalysts that had threatened the overextended firm with bankruptcy.[101] None the less, Barings and the Russian government had a longstanding, if not always close relationship. In the period from 1894 to 1914, this was particularly evident at the end of the Russo-Japnese War. As that war drew to a close, Russian finances were in tatters. The Russian government had borrowed heavily during the war, and required a large loan at its conclusion in order to stabilize the Russian gold standard.[102] The need was widely anticipated in banking circles. By 10 September, a representative of the Russian ministry of finance was in London, along with Edouard Noetzlin, a director of the Banque de Paris et des Pays-Bas, to consult Barings about raising a Russian loan. John Baring, second Baron Revelstoke and a managing director of Barings, immediately asked Lansdowne whether the latter approved of such a move.[103] Lansdowne replied that he did not object, and underlined the political significance that this particular loan had.[104] Since Lansdowne wished to reopen negotiations for a general agreement with Russia, this was not surprising. For the rest of September, the loan hung fire. In France, Noetzlin had several conversations with Sergei Witte, the latter on his way home to Russia from his negotiations at Portsmouth.[105] By 3 October, all was settled. Revelstoke immediately took two steps. First, he began negotiations in Holland and the United States to make the loan an international one. Second, he wrote to Charles Hardinge, an old friend as well as British ambassador to Russia, to apprise him of the negotiations. Revelstoke also enquired whether the ambassador would be in St Petersburg during Revelstoke's proposed visit.[106]

Revelstoke departed for Russia on 14 October.[107] At St Petersburg, he stayed at the embassy, no doubt pleased to be able to combine a small family reunion—his first cousin, Rowland Baring (Viscount Errington) was third secretary at the embassy—with business. By 25 October the bare bones of an agreement had been reached, but the civil unrest that accompanied the end of the Russo-Japanese War

---

[101] Ibid. 245–6; Orbell, *Baring Brothers*, 58.

[102] The Russian war loans totalled nearly £120 million, see Hardinge to Lansdowne, disp. 507, 26 Aug. 1905, FO 65/1702; Ziegler, *Sixth Great Power*, 312–15; R. Girault, *Emprunts russes et investissements français en Russie, 1887–1914* (Paris, 1973), 435–43.

[103] E. Noetzlin to Revelstoke, 9 Sept. 1905; Revelstoke to Lansdowne, confidential, 11 Sept. 1905; Lansdowne to Revelstoke, tel., 12 Sept. 1905, all Barings Papers, Barings Partners' filing/206.

[104] Lansdowne to Revelstoke, 12 Sept. 1905, Barings Papers, Barings Partners' filings/206.

[105] Noetzlin to Revelstoke, 20 Sept. 1905, Barings Papers, Barings Partners' filings/206.

[106] Kidder-Peabody (Boston banking firm and collaborator with Barings in America) to Barings, confidential tel., 6 Oct. 1905; Revelstoke to R. Winsor (Kidder-Peabody), tel., 6 Oct. 1905; Revelstoke to Hardinge, confidential, 5 Oct. 1905, all Barings Papers, Barings Partners' filings/206.

[107] 'Emprunt Russe 1905', 10 Oct. 1905, Barings Papers, Barings Partners' filing/206.

and was to culminate in Nicholas II's granting a constitution, led to a flight of the international bankers and the suspension of the loan talks.[108] From the political point of view, Lansdowne was pleased with the Russian loan negotiations.[109] However important they were to the Foreign Office, there was not yet a financial return for Barings. Over the course of the winter of 1905–6, while the domestic situation gradually calmed in Russia, the British embassy in St Petersburg kept Revelstoke in touch with the Russian political and financial scene.[110] Thus, when the Russian ambassador to Britain, Count Benckendorff, officially asked Revelstoke on 18 March 1906 to participate in renewed loan negotiations, Barings were ready.[111] Revelstoke immediately began a correspondence both with Noetzlin about the loan and with the Foregn Office about the official attitude towards one.[112] Both Noetzlin and Grey were in favour, although the loan was politically awkward for Grey, as there was substantial opposition to the loan from liberals in Britain, France and Russia, who felt that the loan appeared to provide a financial prop for the maintenance of the autocratic regime.[113] The loan was concluded on 16 April, with Revelstoke's receiving praise for his contribution to good Anglo-Russian relations from the Foreign Office.[114]

Over the next three years, Revelstoke and Barings kept in touch with Russian affairs. During August and September of 1908, Revelstoke engaged in discussions, both with Noetzlin and with Kokovtsov, the Russian finance minister, all the while keeping the Foreign Office closely advised.[115] A chief concern for Revelstoke was that not too many Russian issues should be offered simultaneously. But, as had been the case in 1905, the new Russian loan was affected by politics. The Bosnian crisis, with its fear of an attendant Austro-Russian war, nearly torpedoed the

[108] Spring Rice to Lansdowne, disp. 642, 30 Oct. 1905, FO 65/1703.

[109] Lansdowne to Spring Rice, 7 Nov. 1905, Lansdowne Papers, FO 800/141.

[110] Spring Rice to Revelstoke, 2 Dec. 1905, 3 Apr. 1906, Barings Papers, Barings Partners' filing/206 and 207.

[111] Benckendorff to Revelstoke, 18 Mar. 1906, Barings Papers, Barings Partners' filing/207.

[112] Revelstoke to Noetzlin, private and confidential, 20 Mar. 1906; Noetzlin to Revelstoke, private and confidential, 21 Mar. 1906; Revelstoke to Grey, 6 Apr. 1906 and reply, all Barings Papers, Barings Partners' filing/207.

[113] Grey to Bertie, disp. 204, 6 Apr. 1906, FO 371/124/12335; J. W. Long, 'Organized Protest Against the 1906 Russian Loan', *CMRS* 13 (1972), 24–39; O. Crisp, 'The Russian Liberals and the 1906 Anglo-French Loan to Russia', *SEER* 39 (1961), 497–511; Grey to Campbell-Bannerman, 6 Apr. 1906, Campbell-Bannerman Papers, Add MSS 52514.

[114] Spring Rice to Revelstoke, 27 Apr. 1906; Hardinge to Revelstoke, 3 May 1906, both Barings Papers, Barings partners' filing/207.

[115] 'Memorandum of a conversation with Mr. E. Noetzlin after he had seen Mr. Kokovtzoff at Homburg on the 4th instant.' Revelstoke, 6 Aug. 1908; Revelstoke to Kokovstov, personal and confidential, 8 Sept. 1908; Revelstoke to O'Beirne (British counsellor, St Petersburg), 10 Sept. 1908; all Barings Papers, Barings Partners' filing/207; also Hardinge's minute on Bertie to Grey, disp. 355, 18 Sept. 1908, FO 371/518/32691; Errington to Revelstoke, confidential, 29 Sept. 1908 and reply, both Barings Papers, Barings Partners' filing/209.

transaction; however, by January 1909 an agreement had been reached for a loan of approximately £50 million. Barings placed some £6 million on the London market.[116] The 1909 loan was the last big Russian issue that Barings consummated before the outbreak of the First World War. Nevertheless, Barings always kept a weather eye on Russian opportunities. Revelstoke met with Kokovstov on occasion and Revelstoke's brother, Cecil, travelled to St Petersburg in 1910 in order to ensure a close liaison between Barings and the Russian finance minister.[117] In late 1909, at Kokovstov's suggestion, Revelstoke created a syndicate of British bankers interested in Russian issues; this 'to ensure that Russian Government business should be strongly centralized'.[118] While one member of the syndicate, Lloyds, dropped out of the arrangement in 1910, this syndicate was still active in late 1913 to early 1914, when it was involved in negotiations for a Russian state railway loan in the sum of 600 million francs.[119]

Doing business in Russia was often difficult. A contract to electrify the Moscow tramway illustrates this nicely.[120] The two chief contenders were a British firm, Bruce, Peebles & Company, and a German competitor. The Moscow town council hinted that the contract would be awarded to Bruce, Peebles in the event of a favourable issuance of Moscow municipal bonds on the London market. While Revelstoke did not feel that the Moscow bonds would do well, by February 1908 he was moving towards doing so (perhaps only to block the efforts of a British rival to establish itself in Russia). The British consul in Moscow supported issuing the bonds only if a British firm were guaranteed the electrification contract.[121] Bruce, Peebles rejected this arrangement on the grounds that it would irritate Barings. Besides, Bruce, Peebles had another backer willing to float the bond issue, and this backer had a signed agreement with the Moscow town council to that effect. All went sour. Ignoring their signed agreement, the Moscow town council dealt with Barings, who placed (but did not participate in the transaction themselves) the bond in London. With money in hand, and with Bruce, Peebles' own finances weak, the Moscow town council did its own work. Comment at the Foreign Office on this deal said a good deal about British business efforts in Russia. 'Messrs Bruce, Peebles & Co.', Norman wrote, 'appear to have neglected their own interests to an astonishing extent and the Moscow Town Council have acted as Russian business

---

[116] Revelstoke to Noetzlin, very confidential, 15 and 17 Oct. 1908; Revelstoke to Hope (Dutch banker), confidential, 14 Nov. 1908; Revelstoke to Barings, tel., 13 Jan. 1909, all Barings papers, Barings Partners' filing/209.

[117] Revelstoke to Kokovstov, 2 Feb. 1910, Barings Papers, COF/05/6/9.

[118] Revelstoke to Kokovstov, 3 Dec. 1909, Barings Papers, Barings Partners' filing/212.

[119] Revelstoke to Noetzlin, 1 Nov. 1911, Barings Papers, COF/05/6/9.

[120] Grove (British consul, Moscow) to Nicolson, 11 and 17 Sept. 1907, both Nicolson Papers, FO 800/340; Grove's desp. 1, 28 Mar. 1908, FO 368/216/13350.

[121] Grove to Foreign Office, tel., 4 Feb. 1908, FO 368/216/4052; Bruce, Peebles to Foreign Office, 5 Feb. 1908, FO 368/216/4185; Mallet's minute (20 Sept.), FO 368/455/34891.

people too often do. It should be a lesson to all intending investors in Russia.'[122] This view was not new, nor confined to the Bruce, Peebles case. A year earlier, it had been noted at the Foreign Office that 'the abstention of British capital from municipal enterprises in Russia is perhaps due to the unsatisfactory business methods of municipalities'.[123]

Despite such difficulties, efforts were made, both officially and unofficially, to improve Anglo-Russian trade. Beginning in 1907, Henry Cooke was appointed commercial attaché in Russia, with a brief to divide his time between Russia and British companies interested in doing business in the former.[124] The need for this was obvious. By 1909, Cooke could report that companies in the City of London felt that 'there is now no difficulty whatever in finding capital for investment in Russia'.[125] Indeed, the growth of British interest in Russia led Cooke in 1910 to complain that he should be in either Russia or Britain full-time.[126] The Foreign Office agreed, and Cooke remained in Britain, with the embassy's translator in St Petersburg given additional salary to take over Cooke's work in Russia. Cooke's appointment was not the only effort to improve trade. In 1908, a group of Russian and British businessmen established an Anglo-Russian Chamber of Commerce in Russia, despite the tepid support given to it by the British colony in St Petersburg who feared that their own exclusive position in Russia might be undermined.[127] The idea of the Chamber was supported by the British embassy. In recognition of his interest in promoting closer Anglo-Russian relations, Nicolson was made an honourary member in 1909.[128] But while the embassy wanted trade to improve, and was willing to support the attempts of British firms to garner contracts, this did not mean that there was any direct government assistance to these firms.[129] British firms were expected to sink or swim on their own merits. And, at the Foreign Office, there was a general belief that the majority of these firms would sink.

This was seen as the result of the low level of competence of British sales representatives in Russia. In late 1910, the British vice-consul at Moscow travelled

---

[122] Norman's minute on Grove to FO, disp. 1, FO 368/216/13350.

[123] Barrington's (assistant under-secretary, FO) minute (7 Mar.), on Nicolson to Grey, disp. 27, 4 Mar. 1907, FO 368/123/7439.

[124] His report, 6 Jan. 1908, FO 368/216/754.

[125] Cooke's minute, 15 May 1909, FO 368/324/18379.

[126] Cooke to Law (senior clerk, Commercial Department, FO) 12 May 1910 and Law's undated minutes, all FO 368/453/16991.

[127] Woodhouse (British consul, St Petersburg), disp., 29 Oct. 1908, in Nicolson to Grey, disp. 116 commercial 5 Nov. 1908, FO 368/218/38895 and minutes; Cooke's disp., 17 Dec. 1908, in Nicolson to Grey, disp. 148, FO 368/218/44406.

[128] Nicolson to Revelstoke, 21 Sept. 1908, Barings Partners' filing/209; Timioriseff (president of the Anglo-Russian Chamber of Commerce) to Nicolson, 24 Apr. 1909, Nicolson Papers, FO 800/342.

[129] For the Foreign Office's attitude, see the minutes on Boulton Brothers & Company to Nicolson, 3 May 1911, FO 371/1217/16739.

to the west and south of Moscow to survey the opportunities for British firms.[130] He reported ample business possibilities, but added that 'there is no evidence of any effort on the part of British firms to push their goods in any way'. British commercial travellers were few; their 'price-lists' and correspondence ('in the rare cases in which they write') were in English. All of this, the survey concluded, 'seems to show that they have no serious interest in increasing their hold on the Russian market'. This was not an isolated opinion. A few months later, the British consul in Batoum made similar comments, which were greeted at the Foreign Office with the remark: 'This is the time-honoured complaint of the refusal of the British manufacturer to send out competent travellers.'[131] Some in the Foreign Office believed that British trade in Russia could be enlarged by an improvement in the British consular representation in that country, but such improvement was expensive.[132] Others believed that trade could be enlarged only by the efforts of traders. As the Board of Trade tended to favour the latter view, nothing very significant was done to improve consular services in Russia.[133]

Businessmen, academics, journalists, novelists, and financiers all had their views of Russia. These categories were not as autonomous as they might seem. One of the most interesting things about the public's awareness of Russia was the fact that those who shaped it often knew each other. Two examples make such linkages clear. The first involved Barings. When Barings made their financial decisions concerning Russia, they had access to a particular and exclusive body of information. Lord Revelstoke was a personal friend of both Charles Hardinge and Lord Lansdowne, and often visited the latter at his country estate. Revelstoke's younger brother, Maurice, was Britain's leading expert on Russian literature, a former member of the Foreign Office, a close friend of the Benckendorffs, and a sometime newspaper correspondent in Russia. Revelstoke's uncle, the Earl of Cromer, was British agent and consul-general in Egypt (a post of some significance in Anglo-Russian relations during the Russo-Japanese War), while Cromer's son, Rowland, was a member of the diplomatic service in Russia from late 1904 to 1906 and later Hardinge's private secretary. It is hard to imagine that Revelstoke could have been better situated to receive accurate information about Russia.

The Barings circle was much more circumscribed than the one which revolved around Bernard Pares. Pares seems to have known almost everyone who was concerned with Russia. His connections to the élite have been discussed above, but it is important to examine his links to the wider public. From his university posts

---

[130] Grove (British consul, Moscow) to Grey, disp. 2, 21 Jan. 1911, FO 368/575/2954, enclosing Vice-Consul Bosanquet's memo.

[131] Stevens (British consul, Batoum) to Grey, disp. 5, 30 Mar. 1911, FO 368/577/13287 and minute.

[132] Minutes on Pares to Norman, 10 Mar. 1911, FO 371/1214/9310.

[133] G. J. Stanley (Board of Trade) to Foreign Office, 29 Aug. 1911, FO 371/1214/34234 and minutes.

at Cambridge and Liverpool, Pares was instrumental in spreading a wider knowledge of Russia in Britain. In 1907, he published *Russia and Reform*, the aims of which were avowedly didactic.[134] *Russia and Reform*, was an attempt to 'summarise the chief things which Englishmen ought to know, if they wish to form an intelligent judgment of what is now taking place in Russia'. His efforts did not end with his writing. In 1909, Pares co-ordinated a visit of leading Russian politicians to England, ensuring that they met their English counterparts.[135] A reciprocal visit of Englishmen to Russia took place in 1912. Again, Pares was the organizing force on the English side.[136] The English representatives were mostly drawn from the Anglo-Russian Friendship Committee that Pares had established after the 1909 exchange. Its membership was an impressive amalgam of members of both Houses of Parliament, English churchmen, businessmen, and pressmen.[137] While members of the élite initially did not believe that such visits were very significant, the enormous public success of the exchange changed many opinions. Buchanan spoke for many when he wrote that '[t]he English visit has been a wonderful success and has, I think, served to create a friendly feeling towards England such as has never before existed in this country'.[138]

Pares had other links to Russia. One was his membership in the ARLS. Another resulted from his publishing efforts. In 1911, Pares proposed a journal, the *Russian Review*, the purpose of which was to create a forum for the discussion of Russian affairs.[139] By 1912, Pares' had garnered the support of such people as Sanderson, Nicolson, and Buchanan for his project, and the *Review* had begun its long career. In the following year, Pares became part of the group organizing an Anglo-Russian Exhibition, scheduled to take place in London in 1915.[140] This Exhibition brought together the Anglo-Russian Chamber of Commerce, the Anglo-Russian Committee, various individual businessmen and those interested in the arts. While the outbreak of war (coupled with difficulties concerning finances) prevented the Ex-

---

[134] B. Pares, *Russia and Reform* (London, 1907), pref.

[135] A circular outlining the purpose of the visit and an undated memo by Pares giving biographical details of the leading Russian delegates, both Pares Papers, 59; Sanderson to Tyrrell, 4 June 1909, and H. Montgomery (Grey's précis writer) to Grey, 5 June 1909, both Grey Papers, FO 800/93.

[136] 'Visit of Representative Englishmen to Russia', Pares, private and personal, Apr. 1911, Pares Papers, 61. Pares own account in his *A Wandering Student* (Syracuse, NY, 1948), 168–73.

[137] The list of those going is in an undated memo by Pares [but *c.* Nov. 1911], giving an itinerary for the trip, Pares Papers, 61; Sanderson to Hardinge, 12 Jan. 1912, Hardinge Papers, vol. 92.

[138] Cf. Buchanan to Nicolson, 8 Feb. 1912, Nicolson Papers, FO 800/353 and Asquith to Grey, 3 Jan. 1912, Grey Papers, FO 800/100; Nicolson to Hardinge, 20 Dec. 1911, Nicolson Papers, FO 800/352.

[139] Sanderson to Tyrrell, 14 June 1911, Grey Papers, FO 800/110.

[140] Lord Weardale (Anglo-Russian Committee) to Pares, 19 Apr. 1913, Pares Papers 62; Pares to Nicolson, 22 June 1913, FO 368/857/30541; Grove (British consul, Moscow) to Norman, 25 June 1913, FO 368/857/30541; Buchanan to Grey, disp. 188, 25 Aug. 1913, FO 368/857/39672; Homyakov (Nicholas Khomiakov, former president of the Duma; president of the Russian branch of the Anglo-Russian Committee) to Pares, strictly confidential, 17 Mar. 1914, Pares Papers 62.

hibition from taking place, its organization underlined the wide range of prominent people, in both Britain and Russia, who knew Pares. While it is difficult to demonstrate, the existence of such groupings as those around Barings and Pares undoubtedly had an important impact on the public's general knowledge of Russia.

General knowledge of Russia meant little by itself. Facts needed to be interpreted. And there were at least two overarching visions of Russia that aspired to provide the interpretive framework on which the British public mind could hang such information. One, deriving from tradition and the political left, portrayed Russia as alien, extra-European, politically despotic, and uncivilized. For convenience, it shall be termed the 'autocratic' school. The other, stemming from the cultural élite and the business and financial community, saw Russia as an emerging European country, full of opportunities for profit and possessed of a powerful and unique culture. For convenience, it shall be referred to as the 'Ballets russes' school. The two schools created images of Russia that were both overlapping and complementary. Both tended to see Russia as in great need of political reform. The 'Ballets russes' school preferred reform to be gradualist, so that the achievements of Russia would not be swept away with the regime itself. The supporters of the 'autocratic' school—and this group would have included the Radicals within the Liberal party and much of its rank-and-file generally—wished for the immediate destruction of the Tsarist system (although they had no idea of just what revolution entailed in a practical sense). These two divisions should not be taken as mutually exclusive. Many who held to the 'autocratic' image of Russia undoubtedly were at the forefront of the cultural élite who cleaved to the products of Russian high culture—one of the leading elements helping to establish the 'Ballets russes' school. Far from creating any dissonance, this dichotomy no doubt reinforced the views of the political left, who attributed the positive aspects of Russia to a new, emerging group of Russians—people undoubtedly much like themselves—who rejected traditional Russian government. The treatment of Russian nihilists and anarchists, in both literature and real life, as political reformers rather than as terrorists underlines this point. And, those who held to the 'Ballets russes' school undoubtedly often accepted, just as easily as did the advocates of 'autocratic' Russia, the brutal and threatening nature of the Tsarist regime.

But, however they interpreted Russia, it is clear that the British public had definite views of that country. For the most part, these views were unfavourable. This meant that the public had to be convinced that any improvement in Anglo-Russian relations entailed distinct advantages to Britain, advantages that overcame a natural repugnance to treat with a society seen as antithetical to British sensibilities. Spring Rice caught the flavour of this during the negotiations for the Anglo-Russian Convention: 'It was easy for two civilized and liberal nations like France and England to come to terms and act together; but common action between an English Liberal and a Russian bureaucracy is a pretty difficult thing to manage. A wild ass and a commissary mule make a rum team to drive.'[141] Close Anglo-Russian relations required a skilful driver.

[141] Spring Rice to Cranley (private secretary successively to Hardinge and Nicolson at St Petersburg, now British embassy, Berlin), 28 Mar. 1907, in S. Gwynn (ed.), *The Letters and Friendships of Sir Cecil Spring Rice: A Record* (2 vols.; London, 1929), ii. 95.

4

The Bear and the Whale: Russia in British Defence Planning

IN February 1910, the prominent Russian newspaper, *Novoe vremia*, characterized the nineteenth century as one full of Anglo-Russian quarrels, and termed them 'the great struggle between the bear and the whale'.[1] The metaphor was apt. Russia, Europe's most formidable land power for much of the nineteenth century, represented the greatest threat to Britain's largely sea-based global pre-eminence. Indeed, much of British defence planning in the century after Waterloo can be interpreted as an attempt to discover a way to check the burgeoning Russian menace.[2] This was important for Anglo-Russian relations. Behind the niceties of diplomacy lay the menace of force, and no examination of Anglo-Russian affairs can be complete without a knowledge of the military and naval balance between the two countries.

Britain's defence concerns were peculiar. British defence planners needed to consider not only home defence (and its relation to the balance of power on the Continent), but also imperial defence. Thus, Britain's defence policy was necessarily Janus-like. The link between home and imperial defence was the Royal Navy, which ensured that Britain could not be invaded, provided for the security of the Empire, and protected essential trade routes. Russia's place in British defence planning was a mixture of the commonplace and the unique: Russia was a major player in the balance of power on the Continent, a significant factor to be considered in the maintenance of British naval supremacy, and a threat to the Empire in a variety of locales (particularly in India). With respect to the balance of power, Russia was treated no differently than was any other potential British rival. Britain had no intention to act unilaterally against an attempt by *any* power to achieve hegemony on the Continent; therefore her brief concerning Russia in this regard was simple.[3] Britain would observe and evaluate the Russian threat to Europe and

---

[1] Nicolson to Grey, disp. 70, 5 Feb. 1910, FO 371/978/4743.
[2] A. Lambert, *The Crimean War: British Grand Strategy, 1853–56* (Manchester, 1990), pp. xvi–xxi; 1–8.
[3] The theme of D. French, *The British Way in Warfare 1688–2000* (London, 1990).

deal with it by means of alliances as necessary. Russian naval power was also considered in the usual fashion. The Royal Navy was intended to deal with all possible opponents, and the Russian threat was evaluated on its merits. From 1893 to about 1905, this meant that Russia was central to British naval planning. It was with respect to imperial defence that geography and circumstance made Russia a unique and particularly difficult problem. Unlike the cases with respect to either France or Germany (Britain's other two most likely foes), the Russian threat to the British Empire was overland. Here, and particularly with the rise of railways, the Royal Navy was of limited value. India, in particular, could be defended *directly* against Russia only by military means, and the cost of doing so was enormous. Given the nature of the Russian problem, the élite decided that Russia would have to be dealt with on a worldwide basis, and, if possible, in the context of a European alliance. This ensured that for most of the twenty years before the First World War, Russia was at the centre of British defence planning and British foreign policy generally.

British naval policy towards Russia had two aspects. The first consisted of wide-ranging efforts, both naval and diplomatic, to limit Russia's access to the high seas. The second involved the consideration of Russia's naval power in the context of British naval policy generally. While linked, these two aspects are most easily examined separately. Until just after 1900, British policy focused on containing Russia's sea power, something evident as early as the Crimean War. Despite the geographic implications of the name of this conflict, Britain had fought Russia globally.[4] The cumulative effect of these campaigns, not just the amphibious operation at Sevastopol, resulted in an Allied victory in 1856.[5] The Treaty of Paris underlined the British commitment to restrain Russia. The demilitarization of the Black Sea prevented Russia from menacing the British position in the eastern Mediterranean and opened the possibility that, in times of tension, a British fleet could threaten Russia's southern flank. Similarly, the separate but related provisions of 1856 that provided for the demilitarization of the Åland islands ensured that Russia's Baltic fleet could neither menace Sweden nor turn the eastern Baltic into a *mare clausum* against Britain.[6] This situation lasted until the 1870s, when

[4] Lambert, *Crimean War*, pp. xvi–xxi, 158–76, 269–80; id., 'Preparing for the Russian War: British Strategic Planning, March 1853–March 1854', *WS* 7 (1989), 15–39; J. B. Conacher, 'The Asian Front in the Crimean War and the Fall of Kars', *JSAHR* 58 (1990), 169–87; C. I. Hamilton, 'Sir James Graham, the Baltic Campaign and War-Planning at the Admiralty in 1854', *HJ* 19 (1976), 89–112; E. Anderson, 'The Role of the Crimean War in the Baltic', *Scandinavian Studies*, 41 (1969), 263–75; and J. J. Stephan, 'The Crimean War in the Far East', *MAS* 3 (1969), 257–77.

[5] H. Strachan, 'Soldiers, Strategy and Sebastopol,' *HJ* 21 (1978), 303–25; on Paris and the naval situation, C. I. Hamilton, 'Anglo-French Seapower and the Declaration of Paris', *IHR* 4 (1982), 166–90; J. C. K. Daly, *Russian Seapower and 'The Eastern Question', 1827–41* (London, 1991).

[6] J. Barros, *The Åland Islands Question: Its Settlement by the League of Nations* (New Haven, 1960), 1–19.

several circumstances changed to Britain's disadvantage. First, Russian expansion in Central Asia enhanced the Russian threat to India.[7] Second, in 1870 Russia had taken advantage of the international situation during the Franco-Prussian war to abrogate the Black Sea provisions of the Treaty of Paris.[8] Finally, by that time, the growth of railways in Europe had lessened both the logistical advantages accruing to and the threat to trade exerted by naval supremacy. With the rise of steam power, the development of ironclads, and the improvement in naval gunnery, British naval strategy and tactics were in flux, while British naval expenditure fell sharply from 1861 to 1885.[9] Thus, by the mid-1870s, Britain faced an awkward circumstance should relations with Russia turn sour.

This occurred in 1877. The end of the Russo-Turkish War faced Britain with a number of unpleasant possibilities. The Treaty of San Stefano raised the likelihood of a Bulgaria dominated by Russia and the possibility of a subsequent Russian descent on Constantinople. In either case, Russia would be a Mediterranean naval power. At the Congress of Berlin, Salisbury and Disraeli successfully rolled back the Russian tide. The British statemen obtained the reduction of Bulgaria and the cession of Cyprus to Britain. By means of the former, Russia could be kept distant from Constantinople; by means of the latter, Britain could keep the Russian fleet penned up even should the Tsarist state escape the strictures of Berlin. Salisbury faced a similar problem in 1885, this time in Central Asia. While the Penjdeh crisis was resolved without recourse to war, the difficulties of fighting Russia unaided were evident.[10] Salisbury attempted to eliminate Anglo-Russian quarrels by means of finding a political accommodation with Russia, but by 1888 this had proven impossible. The British diplomatic position instead was bolstered by means of the Mediterranean agreements with Austria-Hungary, which

[7] E. Ingram, *In Defence of British India: Great Britain in the Middle East, 1775–1842* (London, 1984), id., *Commitment to Empire: Prophecies of the Great Game in Asia 1797–1800* (Oxford, 1981); id., *The Beginning of the Great Game in Asia, 1828–34* (Oxford, 1979); M. Yapp, *Strategies of British India: Britain, Iran and Afghanistan 1798–1850* (Oxford, 1980); G. J. Alder, 'India and the Crimean War', *JICH* 2 (1973), 15–37.

[8] W. E. Mosse, 'Public Opinion and Foreign Policy: The British Public and War-Scare of November 1870', *HJ* 6 (1963), 38–58; id., 'The End of the Crimean System: England, Russia and the Neutrality of the Black Sea, 1870–1', *HJ* 4 (1961), 164–90; N. S. Kiniapina, 'Borba Rossii za otmenu ogranichitelnykh uslovii parizhskogo dogovora 1856 goda' *VI* 8 (1972), 35–51.

[9] C. J. Bartlett, 'The Mid-Victorian Reappraisal of Naval Policy', in K. Bourne and D. C. Watt (eds.), *Studies in International History* (London, 1967), 189–208; C. I. Hamilton, *Anglo-French Naval Rivalry 1840–70* (Oxford, 1993), 64–105; id., 'The Royal Navy, *la Royale*, and the Militarisation of Naval Warfare, 1840–70', *JSS* 6 (1983), 182–212; id., 'Naval Power and Diplomacy in the Nineteenth Century', *JSS* 3 (1980), 74–88; B. Ranft, 'The protection of British seaborne trade and the development of systematic planning for war, 1860–1906', in id. (ed.), *Technical Change and British Naval Policy 1860–1939* (London, 1977), 1–22; J. F. Beeler, 'A One Power Standard? Great Britain and the Balance of Naval Power, 1860–80', *JSS* 15 (1992), 548–75; D. M. Schurman, *The Education of a Navy: The Development of British Naval Strategic Thought, 1867–1914* (Chicago, 1965).

[10] R. L. Greaves, *Persia and the Defence of India, 1884–92* (London, 1959), 70–84; 85–120.

also provided a check to Russian ambitions in both the Balkans and the Mediterranean.[11]

By 1894, the dimensions of the Russian threat to Britain were clear, as was the limited nature of possible British responses.[12] In 1877, Salisbury had written that Russia was 'unassailable by us' and noted that there was 'absolutely no point at which we could attack her with any chance of doing serious injury'. The Russo-Turkish war had forced the British to review their worldwide security, and it was evident that the lines of imperial communication with India could not be easily maintained.[13] Writing in 1884, the Intelligence Branch at the War Office was bleak in its assessment of the ways in which Britain could strike an effective blow against Russia.[14] Only the Black Sea port of Batum, given to Russia after the Russo-Turkish war but required to be kept unfortified under the terms of the treaty of Berlin, was felt susceptible to British naval power. And, in 1886, the Russian abrogation of Article 59 of the treaty and the port's subsequent fortification, ended even that possibility.[15] In 1887, 1892, and 1894, expert military and naval opinion war unanimous in stating that Britain could no longer hope either to pin the Russian fleet in the eastern Mediterranean or to attack Russia herself via the Black Sea.[16]

Despite this, when the Armenian crisis began in 1895, Constantinople and the Straits remained the centre of British strategic planning for the defence of the eastern Mediterranean and the Suez Canal.[17] Contrary to the advice of his naval experts, Salisbury wanted to send the British fleet into the Straits to forestall a

[11] C. J. Lowe, *Salisbury and the Mediterranean 1886–96* (London, 1965).

[12] B. Jelavich, 'British Means of Offence against Russia in the Nineteeth Century', *RH* 1 (1974), 119–35; Salisbury to Lytton (Viceroy, India), 22 June 1877, cited, B. J. Williams, 'The Approach to the Second Afghan War: Central Asia during the Great Eastern Crisis, 1875–8', *IHR* 2 (1980), 216.

[13] D. M. Schurman, 'The Imperial Crisis of 1878', unpub. paper; id., 'Imperial Defence 1868–87: A Study in the Decisive Impulses Behind the Change from "Colonial" to "Imperial" Defence', Ph.D. thesis (Cambridge University, 1955).

[14] 'England's Means of Offence against Russia', Major J. S. Rothwell, DAQMG, Intelligence Branch, in B. Jelavich, *The Ottoman Empire, the Great Powers, and the Straits Question 1870–87* (Bloomington, IN, 1973), 189–98; D. R. Gillard, 'Salisbury and the Indian Defence Problem, 1885–1902', in Bourne and Watt (eds.), *Studies in International History*, 239–41.

[15] B. Jelavich, 'Great Britain and the Russian Acquisition of Batum, 1878–86', *SEER* 48 (1970), 44–66.

[16] 'Brackenbury memorandum', Major General Henry Brackenbury (director of military intelligence), 25 Jan. 1887; memo by E. F. Chapman (director of military intelligence) and Cyprian A. G. Bridge (director of naval intelligence), 18 Mar. 1892, both in C. J. Lowe, *The Reluctant Imperialists* (2 vols.; London, 1967), ii. 45–7, 85–91. Untitled memo by Sir John Ardagh (of the directorate of military intelligence), Oct. 1894, Rosebery Papers, 10135; K. Neilson, ' "Greatly Exaggerated": The Myth of the Decline of Great Britain before 1914', *IHR* 13 (1991), 710–13.

[17] K. Wilson, 'Constantinople or Cairo: Lord Salisbury and the Partition of the Ottoman Empire 1886–97', in id. (ed.), *Empire and Continent: Studies in British Foreign Policy from the 1880s to the First World War* (London, 1987), 1–30; A. G. Hopkins, 'The Victorians and Africa: A Reconsideration of the Occupation of Egypt, 1882', *Journal of African History*, 27 (1987), 363–91.

Russian descent on the Ottoman capital.[18] Failing to find support for such a policy within the Cabinet, Salisbury sought to contain Russia by diplomatic means. By October 1896, the director of military intelligence, Sir John Ardagh, was suggesting that, as Britain could no longer either force the Straits or prevent the Russians from seizing them and making the Black Sea a *mare clausum*, it would be better if they were opened to all nations.[19] This would allow the Sultan to be coerced more easily by the British and ensure that a '*coup de main* by Russia [was] rendered impossible'. Thus, as 1896 drew to a close, British opinion was becoming inured to the fact that the defence of Constantinople would not be possible by military and naval means. Lord George Hamilton, the secretary of state for India, was not entirely displeased by this event. 'Russia, as mistress of Constantinople,' he wrote in October, 'would be more formidable to Austria and France than to us, and, though I should prefer the neutralization of the Straits and Constantinople, I do not believe that, either strategically or politically, the consequences of Russian predominance would seriously affect us.'[20] Salisbury was equally resigned, but more pessimistic. 'As time goes on,' the Prime Minister wrote to his ambassador at Constantinople, 'the prospect that we shall ultimately keep the Straits out of the hands of Russia becomes fainter and fainter. But we must continue to hold the old language for though our hopes may be fainter our views of policy are unaltered.'[21] But, with Russian foreign policy increasingly directed towards the Far East, the Straits became less of an issue. From 1896 to just before the outbreak of the Russo-Japanese War, the matter of defending British interests at Constantinople was raised only sporadically.[22]

The formation of the Committee of Imperial Defence (CID) in 1902, created a new forum for the discussion of a possible seizure of the Dardanelles by Russia.[23] On 11 February 1903, the CID concluded that should Russia seize the Straits, 'it would not fundamentally alter the present strategic position in the Mediterranean'.[24] While Russia would gain the tactical advantage of no longer having to force the Straits and would have moved her forward naval base some 400 miles

[18] T. J. Spinner, Jr., *George Joachim Goschen: The Transformation of a Victorian Liberal* (London, 1973), 198–9.

[19] 'The Eastern Question in 1896' Ardagh, secret, Oct. 1896, Ardagh Papers, PRO 30/40/14.

[20] Hamilton to Elgin (viceroy, India), 8 Oct. 1896, Hamilton Papers, MS Eur C125/1.

[21] Salisbury to Currie, 23 Nov. 1896, cited, Wilson, 'Constantinople or Cairo', 11.

[22] O'Conor to Salisbury, confidential disp. 49, 25 Feb. 1897; O'Conor to Cromer, private and secret, 8 Jan. 1900, O'Conor Papers, OCON 3/16; Scott to Sanderson, 8 Mar. 1900, Scott Papers, Add MSS 52303; M. Allen, 'Rear Admiral Reginald Custance: Director of Naval Intelligence 1899–1902,' *MM* 78 (1992), 61–75.

[23] N. d'Ombrain, *War Machinery and High Policy: Defence Administration in Peacetime Britain 1902–14* (London, 1973).

[24] 'Report on the Conclusion arrived at on the 11th February in reference to Russia and Constantinople', Balfour, 14 Feb. 1903, Cab 4/1/1B.

closer to the Mediterranean, 'these advantages, though not to be ignored, do not constitute, so far as we are concerned, any fundamental, or even very important, change in the naval problem'. Nor, did such a change indicate the need for 'any substantial alteration in the number and distribution of our Mediterranean Fleet'. Given this, the CID rejected the idea of either landing a force at the Dardanelles or seizing Lemnos on a permanent basis. As a corollary, Balfour pointed out that 'the maintenance of the *status quo* as regards Constantinople is not one of the primary interests' of Britain.

This decision was a ringing renunciation of the position that Britain had taken with respect to the Straits since 1856, but one that recognized certain vital facts. The first was that Russia would attempt such an action only in concert with the French. In a war against a Russo–French coalition, the closure of the Straits was not vital. Second, the CID's findings reflected the simple fact that a Russian seizure of the waterway could not be opposed. Finally, the decision revealed the greater sophistication of thinking about naval power that was coming into existence around the turn of the century.[25] Fleets did not have to be everywhere powerful; a Russian fleet at Constantinople would still have to defeat the Royal Navy in battle before it became anything more than a temporary, local nuisance.[26] Similarly, the value of gunboat diplomacy, with its requisite of a 'fleet-in-view', was declining. New technologies had changed the situation. As Sir John Fisher, the commander-in-chief, Portsmouth and future first lord of the admiralty, told Balfour early in 1904: 'The Russians are welcome to Constantinople if we bag Lemnos and infest the Dardanelles from there with submarines!'[27] The strategic value of Constantinople and the Straits had diminished.

This was underlined during the discussions leading to the signing of the Anglo-Russian Convention of 1907. In November 1906, Hardinge wrote a long memorandum concerning the feasibility of conceding passage of the Straits to Russia.[28] Reiterating the arguments that had been made in 1903, he concluded that they were still valid and that 'it is, if desirable, possible to make an important concession to Russia in relation to the Dardanelles without fundamentally altering the present strategic position in the Mediterranean'. This thinking was reinforced by the near-contemporaneous considerations of the CID about the means available to exert pressure on Turkey. In February 1907, the CID concluded that 'landing an expeditionary force on or near the Gallipoli Peninsula would involve great risk, and

[25] Hamilton, 'Naval Power and Diplomacy', 74–88; P. Kennedy, 'The Influence and the Limitations of Sea Power', *IHR* 10 (1988), 2–17.

[26] '[The effect on our Naval Strategic Position in the Mediterranean of a Russian occupation of Constantinople]', Battenberg (DNI), 7 Feb. 1903, Cab 4/1/2B.

[27] Fisher to Balfour, 5 Jan. 1904, Balfour Papers, Add MSS 49710.

[28] 'Memorandum respecting the Passage of Russian War Vessels through the Dardanelles and Bosphorus', Hardinge, 16 Nov. 1906, Grey Papers, FO 800/92.

should not be undertaken if other means of bringing pressure to bear on Turkey were available'.[29] If it were hazardous to attempt to force the Dardanelles against the resistance provided by the Turks, how much more difficult would it be to attempt such an action if the Russians held the Straits?

During the negotiations for the Anglo-Russian Convention, Russia made several attempts to bring the Straits into the discussions, but these were resisted by the British for diplomatic, not strategic, reasons.[30] This point can be seen in 1908 when Izvolskii, desperate to obtain something for Russia as compensation for the Austro-Hungarian seizure of Bosnia and Herzegovina, attempted to persuade London to accept the free passage of Russian warships through the Straits. Grey informed the Russian that if the Turks agreed to such a course, Britain would not raise any objections.[31] Arthur Balfour, now the leader of the Opposition, who had also been canvassed by the Russian foreign minister, outlined the hard facts of the situation: 'Whatever the public law of Europe with regard to the Straits, we never could risk a fleet inside the Dardanelles, unless we were sure of the friendship of Turkey.' The irony of this statement, given the Dardanelles campaign of 1915, is evident; but so, too, is the clear fact that the Straits agreement with Russia of that same year was merely the culmination of strategic and political decisions taken as early as 1903.[32]

Russian expansion in China also raised naval problems for Britain. While Russia's taking of Port Arthur late in 1897 did not have the momentous implications of a seizure of Constantinople, it did affect the naval balance of power in the region.[33] The China Station of the Royal Navy had always existed to protect trade, but, towards the end of the century, Great-Power rivalry in the region had meant that larger ships had been stationed there. With Germany's obtaining a lease at Kiao-chow and Russia's acquisition of Port Arthur, Britain's ability to maintain a two-power standard against any European combination was in doubt. With two potential naval rivals in the area improving their position by the acquisition of bases, the British turned their eyes to Wei-hai-wei on the Shantung peninsula.

---

[29] Minutes of the 96th meeting of the CID, 28 Feb. 1907, Cab 2/2; 'The Possibility of a Joint Naval and Military Attack Upon the Dardanelles', General Sir N. G. Lyttleton (CGS) and the DNI, 20 Dec. 1906, Cab 4/2/92B.

[30] Nicolson to Grey, 27 Mar. 1907, Nicolson Papers, FO 800/337; Grey to Nicolson, 1 Apr. 1907, Nicolson Papers, FO 800/339; Nicolson to Grey, 11 Apr. 1907, Grey Papers, FO 800/72.

[31] Balfour to Lansdowne, [15] Oct. 1908, Balfour Papers, Add MSS 49729.

[32] Grey later felt bound by his remarks of 1908 to support Russia's having free passage of the Straits; Grey to Buchanan, 7 Apr. 1913, Grey Papers, FO 800/74; Bertie's memo, 18 Dec. 1914, Bertie Papers, Add MSS 63035.

[33] M. H. Murfett, 'An Old Fashioned Form of Protectionism: The Role Played by British Naval Power in China from 1860–1941', *American Neptune*, 50 (1990), 178–91; I. H. Nish, 'The Royal Navy and the Taking of Weihaiwei, 1898–1905', *MM* 54 (1968), 39–54; 'British and Foreign Fleets on China Station', G. J. Goschen (First Lord of the Admiralty), 1 Feb. 1898, Cab 37/46/17.

Wei-hai-wei was not the only alternative for the Royal Navy. In the mid-1880s, at the height of the Penjdeh incident, the British had occupied briefly Port Hamilton (modern Komundo) in Korea as a counterbalance to a feared Russian acquisition of Port Lazaref.[34] Earlier in 1897, O'Conor had advised that 'if things go to the mischief in China we must lose no time in laying claim to Chusan'.[35] Although Wei-hai-wei had serious deficiencies as a naval port—it was too shallow, it was exposed to northerly winds and it had a limited capacity[36]—the British government obtained a lease on the port on 3 April 1898. The reasons for this were evident. As Balfour informed the House of Commons at the end of the month, the Russian acquisition of Port Arthur needed to be counterbalanced, and the British agreement with China—the formal lease was signed on 1 July 1898 and gave Britain the right to occupy Wei-hai-wei for twenty-five years or until Russia left Port Arthur—served that purpose.[37]

Both Constantinople and the Straits and Wei-hai-wei need to be seen in the wider context of the British naval position and its relationship to Russia. Since 1889, Britain had abided by the so-called two-power standard.[38] Initially, this standard was aimed at a combination of France and Italy, but, by the end of 1893, the growth of the Russian navy and the creation of the Franco-Russian alliance meant that the British yardstick became the naval strength of the latter two powers.[39] Indeed, the Russian component became the drive wheel of British building programmes towards the end of the century. In February 1898, the British embassy in St Petersburg reported that the Russian government had decided to increase its naval strength.[40] In March, George Goschen, the first lord of the admiralty, told Hicks Beach of 'the remarkable growth of Russian expenditure on Naval Ordnance', a clear warning that British costs might also rise.[41] By May, the earlier reports of increases in Russian naval expenditure had been confirmed.[42] The British response was quick. 'I am compelled by the action of Russia', Goschen wrote on 6 June 1898, 'to bring the question of naval construction before the Cabinet as a matter for most serious and urgent consideration.'[43] The Russian decision to build

[34] J. E. Hoare, 'Komundo-Port Hamilton', *Asian Affairs*, 17, pt. III (1986), 298–308.
[35] O'Conor to Bertie, 14 Jan. 1897, FO 65/1531.
[36] Nish, 'Royal Navy and Weihaiwei', 52.
[37] Ibid. 48; *Parl Debs*, 4th ser., vol. 60, cols. 647–8.
[38] A. J. Marder, *From the Dreadnought to Scapa Flow*, i, *1904–14: The Road to War* (London, 1961), 123–5.
[39] 'Spencer Memorandum', Spencer (first lord of the admiralty), 8 Dec. 1893, Cab 37/34/57.
[40] O'Conor to Salisbury, disp. 52, 10 Feb. 1898, enclosing Waters (military attaché), disp. 5 confidential, 8 Feb. 1898, FO 65/1552.
[41] Goschen to Hicks Beach, 4 Mar. 1898, Hicks Beach Papers, D2455, PCC/83.
[42] O'Conor to G. J. Goschen, 18 May 1898, O'Conor Papers, OCON 3/15; Goschen to Hicks Beach, 6 June 1898, Hicks Beach Papers, D2455, PCC/87.
[43] 'Russian Naval Construction', G. J. Goschen, 6 June 1898, Cab 37/47/39.

four new battleships in 1898, and possibly two more the following year, forced Goschen to revise his earlier estimate of British requirements.[44] This meant that Britain would have to build seven new battleships to maintain the two-power standard. This was not all, for the Russians began to construct two new cruisers, with the promise of more to come.[45] As a result, Goschen was forced in July to lay supplemental naval estimates before Parliament amounting to about £2 million: four extra battleships and four first-class cruisers.[46] In January 1899, Goschen argued that the Russian cruiser threat had to be countered if British commerce were to be secured. Franco-Russian military spending 'runs our army and navy estimates here', Lord George Hamilton informed Curzon in February 1899, 'up to an appalling figure'.[47]

The British were careful to keep the Russians informed about the increases in the estimates, particularly in the light of the Tsar's call for international disarmament (which was to culminate in the First Hague conference).[48] Goschen told the Russians that the new battleships in the estimates for 1899–1900 were to be built 'in the main, to balance the further construction of battleships which has been announced from Russia'.[49] When Scott raised the matter in Russia, the Tsar's response was equivocal.[50] He appreciated the British confidence, but did not feel that the time was ripe for 'exchanging views about a mutual curtailment of Naval Programmes'. Only the fact that the Russians would find it difficult to procure the money to carry out their ambitious building programme gave the British hope. The evident point, was that Russia, not Britain, was forcing the pace of naval construction.[51]

By the beginning of 1901, there was substantial naval pressure on Britain. Selborne, the new first lord of the admiralty, made this evident.[52] First, he reconsidered the notion of the two-power standard. Noting the rise of three 'new navies'—those of the United States, Germany and Japan—since 1895, Selborne argued that it would be a 'hopeless task' for Britain to attempt to match them.

[44] 'Navy Estimates and Ship-building Programme, 1898–9', G. J. Goschen, 17 Feb. 1898, Cab 37/46/20.

[45] G. J. Goschen to Hicks Beach, 20 July 1898, Hicks Beach Papers, D2455, PCC/83.

[46] 'Navy Estimates, 1899–1900', G. J. Goschen, 31 Jan. 1899, Cab 37/49/7; cf. G. J. Goschen to Hicks Beach, 20 July and two of 21 July 1898, all Hicks Beach Papers, D2455, PCC/83.

[47] Hamilton to Curzon, 10 Feb. 1899, Curzon Papers, MSS Eur F111/142; Hicks Beach to Salisbury, 27 and 30 Jan. 1899, Hicks Beach Papers, D2455, PCC/34.

[48] D. L. Morrill, 'Nicholas II and the Call for the First Hague Conference', *JMH* 46 (1974), 296–313, does not discuss naval arms limitation.

[49] Goschen to Salisbury, confidential, 1 Mar. 1899, Scott Papers Add MSS 52297.

[50] Scott to Salisbury, 9 Mar. 1899, Salisbury Papers, A129; Scott to Goschen, 9 Mar. 1899, Scott Papers, Add MSS 52303.

[51] Hicks Beach to Salisbury, 24 Jan. 1900, Hicks Beach Papers, D2455, PCC/34.

[52] 'Navy Estimates 1901–2', Selborne, 17 Jan. 1901, Cab 37/56/8; Selborne to Hicks Beach, 29 Dec. 1900 and reply, 2 Jan. 1901, both in D. G. Boyce (ed.), *The Crisis of British Power: The Imperial and Naval Papers of the Second Earl of Selborne, 1895–1910* (London, 1990), 105–7.

Therefore, Selborne proposed that the Royal Navy be considered 'almost exclusively' on the basis of its 'relative strength to that of France and Russia combined'. Nor was this specific definition of the two-power standard to be based only on simple 'numerical equality', but on creating a Royal Navy 'such as will enable us to have a reasonable expectation of beating France and Russia'. Selborne's ideas about how to achieve this were wide-ranging. The first lord argued that, while the navy could 'reasonably expect' to have better crews than did Russia and also to enjoy a technological superiority in gun and ship design, the same advantages could not be expected against France. The dispositions of the fleets of the two rivals complicated the situation. Russia's despatch of substantial forces to the Far East had to be met by Britain's sending a 'corresponding number' of ships there. And, Britain could not prevent the junction of the Russian and French fleets in the Mediterranean, because there was 'no serious military impediment' to Russia's ships passing the Straits 'at any moment they choose'. It would be unwise to risk the Royal Navy's being caught 'in greatly inferior numbers' between the converging fleets.

Finally, Selborne pointed out that naval losses would not entail the same risks for France and Russia as they would for Britain. Britain could never invade the two Continental powers, but 'the loss of a few battle-ships by us after starting with an exact equality of numbers might make just the difference between the possibility of an invasion of England'. With battleships increasingly vulnerable to such innovations as the submarine and the gyroscopically controlled torpedo, the situation was dangerous. 'I am therefore of opinion', the first lord concluded, 'that it is no longer safe for this country to rest content with a simple equality of numbers in battle-ships as compared with France and Russia.' In addition, as France and Russia were building a 'swarm' of armoured cruisers to attack British merchantment, Britain would have to build sufficient cruisers to defend her commerce.

It is in this light that Wei-hai-wei and the signing of the Anglo-Japanese Alliance of 1902 need to be seen. In September 1901, Selborne circulated a memorandum entitled 'Balance of Naval Power in the Far East.'[53] Generally regarded as the document from which the Anglo-Japanese alliance sprang, Selborne's paper reiterated much of what he had argued in January.[54] He emphasized the impact that Russia's building programme would have on the British position in the Far East, and pointed out that a defeat in those waters would eliminate the British trading position in China. Despite eventual naval victory elsewhere over the Franco-Russian combination, the loss of trade would be hard to reverse. While home waters and the Mediterranean remained the predominant concerns, care needed to be

---

[53] Selborne, 4 Sept. 1901, Cab 37/58/81, in Boyce (ed.), *Crisis of British Power*, 123–6.
[54] I. H. Nish, *The Anglo-Japanese Alliance: The Diplomacy of Two Island Empires 1894–1907* (London, 1966), 174–5; Z. Steiner, 'Great Britain and the Creation of the Anglo-Japanese Alliance', *JMH* 31 (1959), 29–31.

taken of the Far East. For Selborne, the most effective and least expensive means of so doing was an Anglo-Japanese alliance. The need to consider cost was paramount. Hicks Beach, the chancellor of the exchequer, was concerned about Britain's financial position, particularly in light of the cost of the Boer War.[55] In October, Hicks Beach called for a reduction in the naval estimates.[56] Selborne riposted with a 'rather formidable document', which 'sets out (clearly I hope) my naval policy' and the means to deal with Hicks Beach's concerns.[57] Selborne's memorandum began with the argument that naval strength and credit—'the two main pillars on which the strength of this country rests'—were linked. Without money the navy could not be maintained; without the navy Britain's trade (and, hence, her financial position) could not be protected. The navy, therefore, needed to be strong enough in battleships to win any war and to possess sufficient cruisers to protect trade.[58] Selborne countered Hicks Beach's contention that too much had been spent on the navy in the last five years by pointing out that the 'growth of the Naval Estimates has been caused solely by the efforts of France and Russia to establish a naval superiority over this country'. And, over a longer time period, the excess of British naval spending over the combined Franco-Russian total amounted to about £250,000 per year, an inconsiderable sum when it was remembered that Britain's seaborne trade was more than double the combined Franco-Russian total and that her merchant fleet was about six times larger. For these reasons, Selborne concluded that 'I can hold out no hopes of such a slackening of our efforts as the Chancellor of the Exchequer suggests'.

As against whom Britain's naval building was directed, Selborne was candid. A four- or three-power standard was 'unnecessary and impossible'. Britain would frame her naval policy against France and Russia, since a war with them was 'less improbable than any other naval war which we can foresee' and because those two powers—'France practically exclusively, and Russia largely'—shaped their naval

[55] A. L. Friedberg, *The Weary Titan: Britain and the Experience of Relative Decline, 1895–1905* (Princeton, 1988), 106–20; id., 'Britain Faces the Burdens of Empire: The Financial Crisis of 1901–5', *WS* 5 (1987), 15–37; J. T. Sumida, *In Defence of Naval Supremacy: Finance, Technology and British Naval Policy, 1899–1914* (London, 1989), 3–36.

[56] 'Financial Difficulties: Appeal for Economy in Estimates', Hicks Beach, Oct. 1901, Cab 37/58/109; Hicks Beach to Salisbury, 13 Sept. (twice) and 16 Sept. 1901, all Hicks Beach Papers, D2455, PCC/34; Hicks Beach to J. Chamberlain, 2 Oct. 1901, Hicks Beach Papers, D2455, PCC/86.

[57] Selborne to Salisbury, 31 Oct. 1901, in Boyce (ed.), *Crisis of British Power*, 128–9; Selborne's memo in draft form printed in ibid. 129–36. The quotations in the rest of this paragraph are from the revised version: 'The Navy Estimates and the Chancellor of the Exchequer's Memorandum on the Growth of Expenditure', Selborne, 16 Nov. 1901, Cab 37/59/118.

[58] For modern comment, S. R. B. Smith, 'Public Opinion, the Navy and the City of London: The Drive for British Naval Expansion in the Late Nineteenth Century', *WS* 9 (1991), 29–50; B. Ranft, 'Parliamentary Debate, Economic Vulnerability, and British Naval Expansion, 1860–1905' in L. Freedman, P. Hayes, and R. O'Neill (eds.), *War, Strategy, and International Politics: Essays in Honour of Sir Michael Howard* (Oxford, 1992), 75–93.

policies with Britain in mind. As to the new naval powers, Japan's naval policy was directed solely against Russia, and no one, not 'even the Americans themselves' knew 'what is the exact naval policy of the United States'. German policy was 'definite and persistent' and designed to make Germany a world power, an event that would be hastened should 'ever we find ourselves at war with France and Russia'. Thus, the Anglo-Japanese Agreement of 1902 was shaped by naval considerations largely caused by Russia's ambitious building programme and was directed against that country.[59] Both Britain and Japan hoped to check Russia's burgeoning naval strength in the Far East. To ensure this, Selborne went to extraordinary lengths to determine the nature and extent of the Russian building programme.[60] The Russian actions left the British financially pressed but determined. By the end of 1903, Selborne professed himself in 'despair about the financial outlook . . . but these cursed Russians have actually begun four of the new battleships . . . This leaves us 3 battleships behind the two Power standard and everybody knows it would be quite impossible to defend any slacking off in building.'[61] Concern about a German threat was for the future, after the events of the Russo-Japanese War had given a setback to Russia's naval ambitions.[62]

Meanwhile, Indian defence took centre stage.[63] After the Crimean War, the Russian threat to India had remained, but its focus became Afghanistan.[64] Defence schemes abounded.[65] The arguments over them were complicated by the fact that

[59] Nish, *Anglo-Japanese Alliance*, 229–47; id., 'Naval Thinking and the Anglo-Japanese Alliance 1900–4', *Keio Hogaku Kenkyu*, 56 (1983), 5–14.

[60] Captain C. L. Ottley (British naval attaché, St Petersburg) to Selborne, 16 Sept., 3 Oct., 21 Oct. 1901, Selborne Papers 29; Sanderson to Scott, secret, 12 Feb. 1902, Scott Papers, Add MSS 52299; Sanderson to Selborne, secret, 24 Apr. 1902, Selborne Papers 33.

[61] Selborne to Balfour, 28 Oct. 1903, Sandars Papers, MS Eng. hist. *c*.745.

[62] The German fleet had been considered earlier: Lansdowne to Lascelles, secret, 22 Apr. 1902, Lascelles Papers, FO 800/11; Lascelles to Lansdowne, 25 Apr. 1902, Lascelles Papers FO 800/18; 'Navy Estimates, 1903–4', Selborne, 10 Oct. 1902, Cab 37/63/142; Selborne to Curzon, 4 Jan. 1903, Curzon Papers, MSS Eur E111/229. This meant that there could be no 'peace dividend' in the form of reduced British naval expenditure due to the Russian misfortunes; see Selborne's memo, '[Naval Estimates 1904–5: possible reduction.]', 26 Feb. 1904, Cab 37/69/32; 'Memorandum', Selborne, 12 May 1904, Balfour Papers, Add MSS 49707.

[63] J. Gooch, *The Plans of War: The General Staff and British Military Strategy c.1900–16* (London, 1974), 198–237; Friedberg, *Weary Titan*, 209–78.

[64] A. P. Thornton, 'Afghanistan in Anglo-Russian Diplomacy, 1869–73', *Cambridge Historical Journal*, 11 (1954), 204–18; G. J. Alder, *British India's Northern Frontier 1865–95* (London, 1963), 165–205; three articles by J. L. Duthie: 'Some Further Insights into the Working of Mid-Victorian Imperialism: Lord Salisbury, the "Forward" Group and Anglo-Afghan Relations: 1874–8', *JICH* 8 (1980), 181–208; 'Pressure From Within: The "Forward" Group in the India Office During Gladstone's First Ministry', *JAH* 15 (1981), 36–72; 'Pragmatic Diplomacy or Imperial Encroachment?: British Policy towards Afghanistan, 1874–9', *IHR* 5 (1983), 475–95; J. Ferris, 'Lord Salisbury, Secret Intelligence, and British Policy toward Russia and Central Asia, 1874–8', in K. Neilson and B. J. C. McKercher (eds.), *Go Spy the Land: Military Intelligence in History* (New York, 1992), 115–52.

[65] Three articles by A. Preston: 'Frustrated Great Gamesmanship: Sir Garnet Wolseley's Plans for War against Russia, 1873–80', *IHR* 2 (1980), 239–65; 'Sir Charles Macgregor and the Defence of India,

the Victorian army contained competing theoretical and practical 'patterns of thought'.[66] These patterns divided military thinkers into two general camps. The first wished to defend India on the north-west frontier; the other felt that such a defence was impossible and, instead, favoured a worldwide campaign (utilizing both Britain's diplomatic and amphibious capabilities) against Russia. But changing technology made combined operations against Russia more difficult than they had been in Crimean times, and, since the early 1890s, there had been little serious examination of the subject.[67] However, with the outbreak of the Boer War, the British began to fear that Russia might take advantage of their preoccupation in South Africa. This situation was complicated by the growth of the Russian railway system into Central Asia, which meant that Russia would have 'better military access' to India than did Britain.[68] Curzon, the new viceroy, was not indifferent. In 1899, he argued for a forward policy in the Persian Gulf. London's response was bleak. Lord George Hamilton argued that while Britain could strike effectively against either France or Germany during a crisis, 'Russia is practically invulnerable to attack'.[69] In fact, he argued that, 'if you come to analyse the instruments or materials upon which we should have to rely if our Persian policy is ever seriously put to the test in a time of emergency, you will find that it rests almost entirely upon bluff'.[70] This took on particular significance early in 1900. A Russian loan to Persia led the British to reconsider their policy. In February, the director of military intelligence, Sir John Ardagh, argued that Britain must now lose no time in discussing tripartite (British, Russian, and Persian) control of a proposed railway from the Caspian Sea to the Persian Gulf, a course he had rejected a month earlier.[71] The reasons were evident. Ardagh noted that the War Office had long realized that '[a]s regards Northern Persia we have long admitted that the establishment of Russian predominance was only a question of time, as no efforts or

---

1857–87', *HJ* 12 (1969), 58–77; 'The Eastern Question in British Strategic Policy During The Franco-Prussian War', *Historical Papers* (Canadian Historical Association), 1972, 55–88; J. L. Duthie, 'Sir Henry Creswicke Rawlinson and the Art of Great Gamesmanship,' *JICH* 11 (1983), 253–74.

[66] H. Bailes: 'Patterns of Thought in the Late Victorian Army', *JSS* 4 (1981), 29–45; 'Technology and Tactics in the British Army, 1866–1900', in K. Neilson and R. G. Haycock (eds.), *Men, Machines & War* (Waterloo, Ont., 1988), 21–48.

[67] The last study had been in 1893; app. II 'Military Needs of the Empire In a War with France and Russia', Intelligence Department, War Office, 12 Aug. 1901, Cab 3/1/1A.

[68] Godley (permanent under-secretary, India Office) to Curzon, 10 Nov. 1899, Curzon Papers, MSS Eur F111/144; Salisbury to Queen Victoria, tel., 30 Oct. 1899, Midleton Papers, PRO 30/67/4; Sanderson to Scott, 3 Jan. 1900, Scott Papers, Add MSS 52298.

[69] Hamilton to Curzon, 11 Nov. 1899, Curzon Papers, MSS Eur F111/144.

[70] Hamilton to Curzon, 23 Nov. 1899, Curzon Papers, MSS Eur F111/144.

[71] 'An Understanding with Russia on Persian Matters', Ardagh, 3 Feb. 1900, and an earlier paper (23 Jan. 1900) with the same title, both Ardagh Papers, PRO 30/40/4.

preparations which the people of this country would be willing to undertake, could avert it'.[72]

This gloomy view was unacceptable to Curzon. But his attempts to inspire a more forceful policy were met with contrary and varied arguments. At the India Office, the permanent under-secretary decried the possibility of 'that foolish & vacillating individual, the man in the street' ever being willing to support a firm policy against Russia.[73] Hamilton believed that Russia would not lightly 'pick a quarrel with us' unless the European situation were to her advantage.[74] In that case, the British fleet would have 'a very tough job at the outset of a war' and fears of an invasion of Britain would necessitate the retention of troops there. Without knowing the 'existing conditions at the same time in Europe' any discussion of what aid Britain could give India against a Russian descent would be academic.[75]

By the middle of 1901, better, although not particularly comforting, information was available.[76] Without reinforcements, the Indian army 'would be unable to maintain those positions which both politically and strategically it would be advisable to occupy'. As long as Britain was involved militarily in South Africa, she was a 'third-rate power', despite her 'enormous strength, both effective and latent', due to the wide dispersal of her forces. An extensive study (of a war against the Franco-Russian alliance) done by the War Office in August 1901 argued the case explicitly.[77] To defend India, a further 30,000 British troops were required, while the defence of the United Kingdom itself demanded a home defence force of 350,000. There was no means of offence against Russia, as the traditional venues—Central Asia, the Caucasus, the Black Sea and Russian naval bases in the Far East—were all considered either impracticable or else unlikely to produce any decisive result. The one ray of hope was financial pressure: 'Russia's only weak point is her poverty.' The War Office argued that the British should concentrate on defeating France; this for two reasons. The first was that France was more vulnerable to Britain than was Russia; the second was that by defeating France, Britain would deprive Russia of Gallic financial assistance.[78]

---

[72] 'Russia—Increase of Military Force in Central Asia during the Boer War', Ardagh, secret, 5 Feb. 1900, Ardagh Papers, PRO 30/40/4.

[73] Godley to Curzon, 9 Apr. 1900, Curzon Papers, MSS Eur F111/145.

[74] Hamilton to Curzon, 27 Apr. 1900, Curzon Papers, MSS Eur F111/145.

[75] Hamilton to Curzon, 17 May 1900, Curzon Papers, MSS Eur F111/145.

[76] Hamilton to Curzon, 13 June, 4 July and 11 July 1901, all Curzon Papers, MSS Eur F111/149.

[77] 'Military Needs of the Empire in a War With France and Russia', n. 67 above.

[78] A French invasion could not be overlooked; 'The Military Resources of France, and Probable Method of Their Employment in a War Between France and England.' W. R. Robertson, AQMG, secret, 27 Dec. 1901, Cab 3/1/4A.

In a war with Russia alone, British options were much more limited.[79] The War Office discounted any efforts to put economic pressure on Russia, since, unless 'the land frontiers of Russia should be closed', naval blockade would be ineffectual. So, too, would be any amphibious action in the Baltic. On the other hand, Russia could utilize her ability to threaten the north-west frontier of India to paralyse Britain and thus seize Constantinople and the Straits. Britain's range of alternatives against Russia would be determined primarily by Russia's and Britain's relations with the other powers. In the detailed military and naval discussions with Japan following the signing of the Anglo-Japanese alliance, the possibility of joint Anglo-Japanese military action against Russia in the Far East was discussed.[80] The British were cool to a Japanese suggestion that a combined Anglo-Japanese army should operate in Manchuria, citing the need to consider the defences of India first. Instead, the British were prepared to give naval logistical aid to the Japanese army. Any possible means of striking at Russia needed to be considered.[81]

This meant India. The subject had been looked at carefully six months earlier, as a result of fears about Russia's taking advantage of Britain's preoccupation in South Africa.[82] The report concluded that Russia could put as many as 200,000 men into Central Asia within four to five months, with 120,000 of them in Transcaspia and the Herat theatre, although such numbers were deemed unlikely until Russia could complete the railroad from Orenberg to Tashkent. As 'any hopes of indirectly assisting India by expeditions against Russia in other parts of the world would prove illusory', and as the Admiralty would not guarantee that reinforcements could be transported safely to India according to specific schedules, India required a 'permanent increase' in her British garrison. The increase was estimated to be in the neighbourhood of 50,000 men, although a final figure of 100,000 was bruited. As to where the Russian threat should be met, the report favoured a forward policy of occupying either Kandahar or Jalalabad, an action that made the attitude of the Afghans crucial.

Thus, when Balfour became prime minister in July 1902, the means of how to defend India were both undecided and pressing. Debate over it was the centre-piece of defence planning for the next two years. This debate took place in a changed atmosphere. First, Balfour's coming to power meant that matters concerning defence took on a higher priority, as the prime Minister had long held a strong

---

[79] 'The Military Resources of Russia, and Probable Method of Their Employment in a War Between Russia and England', W. R. Robertson, AQMG, secret, 17 Jan. 1902, WO 106/48/E3/1.

[80] 'Report of Conference between Military Representatives of Great Britain and Japan . . . to discuss Concerted Military Action in War', 8 July 1902, Cab 37/62/122.

[81] An Anglo-German agreement to check Russia in Persia was also bruited; W. R. Robertson (AQMG) to DGMI, secret, 10 Nov. 1902, Robertson Papers, I/2/4.

[82] 'Report of a Committee Appointed to Consider the Military Defence of India', 24 Dec. 1901, Cab 6/1/1D.

interest in the subject.[83] Second, the political atmosphere was more congenial to such matters. The end of the Boer War in May meant that the time was ripe for investigations designed to prevent a repetition of the poor British showing in that struggle. Finally, the heavy hand of Hicks Beach was removed from the Exchequer. While Balfour had endeavoured to keep 'Black Michael' at the Treasury, and while his successors, C. T. Ritchie and Austen Chamberlain, were equally committed to keeping government expenditures under control, the former did not have Hicks Beach's political clout and the latter did not have an ideological antipathy to tariff reform. If the senior leadership of the government wished it, money might be found. And, with Balfour as prime minister, Lansdowne as foreign secretary, Selborne as first lord of the admiralty and St John Brodrick at the War Office, a new generation had come to power.[84] The 'Edwardians' were in the ascendent. The changed atmosphere did not mean that all political impediments to a new (and necessarily expensive) defence policy had been removed. Balfour's Cabinet was riven by the debate over free trade, an issue that eventually smashed the government.[85] Ritchie, a dedicated believer in free trade, would not countenance any protective measures beyond the corn duty that Hicks Beach had reluctantly imposed in 1902.[86] For Ritchie, the prudent action was to reduce expenditure. The obvious target—given that Ritchie accepted Selborne's arguments concerning the growth of foreign fleets—was the army.[87] This placed the defence of India in an awkward position. As of the summer of 1902, the best military advice called for an increased garrison for India (at an increased cost). The best financial advice called for decreased expenditures (with the likely corollary of a decreased garrison for India). This dilemma faced the newly created CID in December 1902.

Selborne outlined the difficulties early in the new year.[88] After noting that the naval estimates for 1903–4 would necessarily rise—this 'a simple question of national existence'—Selborne went on to argue that 'it is possible that the Army should continue to increase pari passu'. This possibility was the result of 'three exceptions to our naval & insular character': the need to defend Canada against the

---

[83] R. F. Mackay, *Balfour: Intellectual Statesman* (Oxford, 1985), 59, 61 and 66–9; R. Williams, *Defending the Empire: The Conservative Party and British Defence Policy 1899–1915* (New Haven, 1991), *passim*.

[84] The close personal ties between these men cannot be overstated. Balfour and Lansdowne had been at Eton together, Selborne was married to Salisbury's daughter and was, in addition, Balfour's cousin. Brodrick was, along with Balfour, one of the 'Souls': N. W. Ellenberger, 'The Souls and London "Society" at the End of the Nineteenth Century', *VS* 25 (1982), 133–60.

[85] Cf. P. Fraser, 'Unionism and Tariff Reform: The Crisis of 1906', *HJ* 5 (1962), 149–66; D. Dutton, 'Unionist Politics and the Aftermath of the General Election of 1906: A Reassessment', *HJ* 22 (1979), 861–76.

[86] Friedberg, *Weary Titan*, 107–20; Mackay, *Balfour*, 136–55.

[87] 'Our financial position.' Ritchie, 21 Feb. 1903, Cab 37/64/15.

[88] Selborne to Curzon, 4 Jan. 1903, Curzon Papers, MSS Eur F111/229.

United States, the hostility of the Boers in South Africa, and the fact that 'Russia is Russia in Central Asia.' Two of these threats could be managed. Diplomacy should solve the first; the Dutch republics were broken.[89] This left only Russia. 'It is a terrific task', Selborne wrote plaintively, 'to remain the great Naval Power when Naval Powers are year by year increasing in themselves in naval strength and at the same time to be a military power strong enough to meet the greatest military power in Asia', especially when 'financial stability & sound credit is the only foundation of national strength'. Still, Selborne was confident that 'Arthur's cabinet will not drift without a definite policy' concerning the defence of India, however handicapped Britain was by financial stringencies: 'A pretty problem truly; yet it can't be insoluble.'

This optimism aside, answers were not immediately evident. After three meetings of the CID, Hamilton informed Curzon that 'all Imperial members of that Committee are greatly impressed with the dimensions of the territory which, in certain contingencies we may have to protect'.[90] The bright spot was that the CID was proving to be an important venue for co-ordinating the differing perspectives of the departments involved. Selborne's frustration—'Indian govt, I.[ndian] O.[ffice], Minister at Teheran, F.[oreign] O.[ffice], Cabinet Committee, Treasury, Cabinet. Bah! The Russians *ought* to walk round us every time.'—with the complexities of making a policy for the north-west frontier, was eased by the fact that the CID permitted the entire question to be studied 'in a way in which they have never been studied in this country before by any authentic body'.[91] Perhaps most importantly, Balfour himself was becoming immersed in the problem. By the middle of April 1903, Godley noted that 'it gives me the greatest satisfaction to know that the Prime Minister is concentrating his attention upon questions of imperial defence'.[92]

But even Balfour's lucid intellect found the problems inherent in Indian defence largely intractable, on occasion leaving him 'fairly puzzled'.[93] The prime minister summed up the CID's discussions in three consecutive memoranda, written in the late spring and early summer of 1903.[94] The defence of India was best served by a

---

[89] It is instructive to see the differences ascribed to the American and Russian governments: first, the Americans did not want to invade Canada, whereas the Russians had designs on India; second, the Americans 'have a conscience, and a sense of right and wrong, which Russia has not'. Godley to Curzon, 17 Feb. 1903, Curzon Papers, MSS Eur F111/161.

[90] Hamilton to Curzon, 19 Mar. 1903, Curzon Papers, MSS Eur F111/162.

[91] Selborne to Curzon, 24 Apr. 1903, Curzon Papers, MSS Eur F111/229.

[92] Godley to Curzon, 23 Apr. 1903, Curzon Papers, MSS Eur F111/162.

[93] Roberts (British C.-in-C.) to Kitchener (British C.-in-C., India), 21 May 1903, Kitchener Papers, PRO 30/57/28.

[94] 'Indian Defence. First instalment of a draft by the Prime Minister', Balfour, 28 Apr. 1903; 'Second Instalment of Draft Conclusions on Indian Defence by Mr. Balfour, dealing chiefly with Seistan', Balfour, 20 May 1903; 'Memorandum to be sent to Lord Curzon and Lord Kitchener with (corrected copies of first two instalments of Prime Minister's Memorandum)', Balfour, 2 July 1903, Cab 6/1/12D, 19D and 28D.

maintenance of the *status quo*, a situation in which Afghanistan and Persia would serve as 'non-conducting' buffers between the Russian and British empires. However, given the growth of Russian railways into these areas, this situation was unlikely to last. Thus, the key defensive positions became, for Afghanistan, the line from Kabul to Kandahar, and, for Persia, the area of Seistan. Any 'Russianization' of Persia or Afghanistan that would threaten these two vital areas would have to be met by similar 'Anglization' of the two countries. This was a political question. The military dimensions of the situation led to three conclusions. First, as the Admiralty could not promise prompt reinforcement of the British position in India, the Indian garrison must be sufficient to hold its own initially.[95] Second, a close eye needed to be kept on any Russian efforts to improve her railways (particularly the line from Orenberg to Tashkent) in the area. Third, 30,000 reinforcements would be needed within the first four months of the war and a further 70,000 men would be required within six months.

These were considerable figures, with considerable attendant costs, but even they were deemed insufficient by the authorities in India.[96] Disputing the CID's conclusions as to the number of Russian troops that could be launched against India, Curzon and Kitchener refused to accept that body's figures for reinforcements pending the outcome of a war game that Kitchener proposed to look into the entire question. And even before this was done, there was scepticism about Britain's ability to checkmate Russia. It was 'universally admitted', Hamilton wrote to Curzon in April 1903, that Russia could not be prevented from taking Herat and hence establishing herself in northern Afghanistan.[97] Britain's best response was the traditional one: 'to make [it] known to Russia that a movement of this kind entails war in all parts of the world with Great Britain.' However, given that military and naval opinion over the previous ten years had been increasingly negative about the possibility of striking at Russia anywhere other than the north-west frontier, this must have seemed cold comfort. While Kitchener pondered his war game, everything in London stopped for politics. In September and October, Balfour had to reconstruct his government.[98] The clash between free traders and tariff reformers—personified by Joseph Chamberlain's actions—was too strong for the Cabinet to be held together. This had its impact on defence. One of the bones of contention was the budget. Ritchie's steadfast objection to increases in the

---

[95] 'Memorandum on the Dispatch of Reinforcements from the United Kingdom to India', Intelligence Department, Admiralty, secret, 12 May 1903, Cab 6/1/15D; 'Defence of India. Memorandum . . . on the Possible Difficulties of Transporting Reinforcements from South Africa to India in the Event of War', Roberts, secret, 21 May 1903, Cab 6/1/17D.

[96] Kitchener to Roberts, 23 July 1903, Kitchener Papers, PRO 30/57/29; 'Memorandum by the Viceroy and the Commander-in-Chief on the Provisional Report of the Defence Committee on Indian Defence', Curzon and Kitchener, 7 Aug. 1903, Cab 6/1/30D.

[97] Hamilton to Curzon, 24 Apr. 1903, Curzon Papers, MSS Eur F111/162.

[98] Mackay, *Balfour*, 144–55.

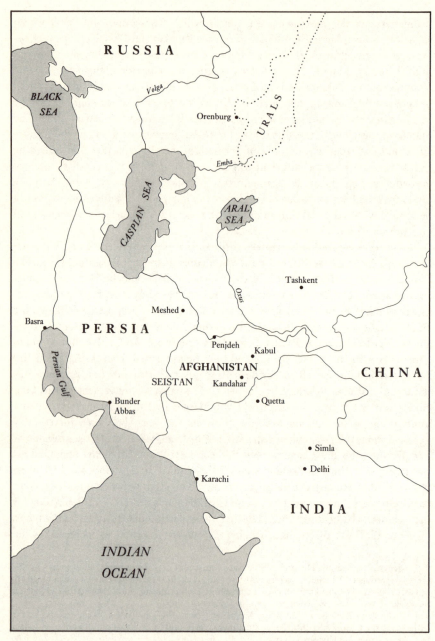

MAP 4.1 Persia and the north-west frontier

defence estimates was linked to his free trader's opposition to raising revenue via tariffs. Brodrick's plans for army reform, made more necessary by the perceived needs of Indian defence, required more money.[99] What Balfour required was a secretary of state for war who could offer an army (and, hence, Indian defence) on the cheap and a chancellor of the exchequer who could raise money and not irrevocably split the Unionist party. The answers were H. O. Arnold-Forster at the War Office and Austen Chamberlain at the exchequer.[100]

By December 1903, events in the Far East had strong repercussions for British defence policy. The possibility of a Russo-Japanese conflict in Korea created the likelihood that Britain, because of the Anglo-Japanese alliance, might become involved. This came at a particularly delicate time, for Lansdowne had just initiated discussions aimed at an Anglo-Russian diplomatic agreement.[101] Both impinged on the financial situation and the debate on Indian defence. Chamberlain spoke directly to these latter concerns on 7 December. Echoing his predecessors, he called for naval and military cuts. 'Our defensive strength rests', the Chancellor argued, 'upon our financial not less than upon our military and naval resources, and I am bound to say that in the present condition of our finances it would, in my opinion, be impossible to finance a great war except at an absolutely ruinous cost.'[102]

These were firm words, but they could not halt events. The growing Russo-Japanese tension had already had an impact on Chamberlain's estimates. Late in November the British government had purchased two battleships being built on Tyneside for the Chilean government, pre-empting a Russian purchase of the ships. This had been done in order to prevent 'the balance of Naval Power in the Far East . . . [from being] seriously modified'.[103] Selborne responded immediately to Chamberlain's memorandum, arguing that both the increases in Russian naval spending and the new threat posed by the German fleet meant that no naval cuts could be contemplated for the sake of 'national safety'.[104] With Selborne's strong position in the Cabinet and the long-standing adherence to the two-power standard, naval cuts were unlikely. This left only the army and the defence of India. At the beginning of February 1904, the Indian government made it plain that in its view the defence of the subcontinent was both open-ended with respect to the

[99] L. J. Satre, 'St John Brodrick and Army Reform', *JBS* 15 (1976), 117–39.

[100] A. Tucker, 'The Issue of Army Reform in the Unionist Government, 1903–5', *HJ* 9 (1966), 90–100; I. Beckett, 'H. O. Arnold-Forster and the Volunteers', in I. Beckett and J. Gooch (eds.), *Politicians and Defence: Studies in the Formulation of British Defence Policy 1845–1970* (Manchester, 1981), 47–68; D. Dutton, *Austen Chamberlain: Gentleman in Politics* (Bolton, 1985), 31–7; Friedberg, *Weary Titan*, 122–3.

[101] B. J. C. McKercher 'Diplomatic Equipoise: The Lansdowne Foreign Office, the Russo-Japanese War of 1904–5, and the Global Balance of Power', *CJH* 24 (1989), 299–339.

[102] 'The Financial Situation', A. Chamberlain, 7 Dec. 1903, Cab 37/67/84.

[103] Balfour to the King, 27 Nov. 1903, Sandars Papers, MS Eng hist *c*.715.

[104] 'Navy Estimates, 1903–4', Selborne, 17 Dec. 1903, Cab 37/63/142.

number of troops required and extended far beyond the borders of India itself into Persia.[105] This entailed an increased estimate in the number of troops required. Simultaneously, the Cabinet cast about for means to strike at Russia should the latter attempt to offset any losses against Japan by threatening India.[106] The CID met six times in March largely to consider both these issues.[107] The results were pessimistic. Lord Roberts 'hope[d] that no move will be made by Russia for some time to come, for we are certainly not prepared', while Selborne noted that the members of the CID 'must be impressed with the great weakness which accrues to the British Empire from the fact that, whereas Russia can strike at us when she pleases through Afghanistan, we apparently can hit back at her nowhere'.[108]

This was typical of expert opinion. With the admiralty's assertion that Russia was 'very un assailable [*sic*] to a sea power with a small army' that left only dubious schemes about the possibility of fomenting unrest among the national groups within the Tsarist empire.[109] The Indian insistence that the Afghan 'non-conducting' buffer could not be created diplomatically meant that only military means could ensure the security of that area. This attitude irritated some. As far as Selborne was concerned, the 'complete & total failure of Indian diplomacy' was evident in such attitudes.[110] Balfour was more resigned.[111] The prime minister was not optimistic that the Afghans could be dealt with in any fashion; instead, he hoped that their fissiparous tendencies would render them the equivalent of neutral. As to Russia, Balfour stated that 'I do not personally believe that Russia is vulnerable in any mortal spot except her Exchequer, and this I hope will be seriously weakened by the present hostilities.' By the end of April, the prime minister seemed to be moving towards the idea that diplomacy, not 'preparations on the frontier' must solve the problem of Indian defence.[112]

The last six months of 1904 were filled with debate centring around transportation and its implications for the number of troops Russia could deploy and the number of reinforcements Britain would have to send to India to counter them.[113] The foci of these debates were many and varied: the carrying capacity of Russian

[105] Gooch, *Plans of War*, 208–19.

[106] Widely rumoured: Scott to Lansdowne, disp. 71, 18 Feb. 1904, FO 65/1678; Clarke (Secretary, CID) to Selborne, 25 Apr. 1904, Selborne Papers 45.

[107] 32nd–37th meetings of the CID, 2, 4, 10, 16, 24, and 30 Mar. 1904, Cab 2/1.

[108] Roberts to Kitchener, secret, 30 Mar. 1904, Kitchener Papers, PRO 30/57/28; Selborne to Kerr (First Sea Lord), secret, 1 Apr. 1904, Selborne Papers 39; Kitchener to Roberts, 27 Apr. 1904, Kitchener Papers, PRO 30/57/29.

[109] Kerr to Selborne, 2 Apr. 1904; Selborne to Balfour, 5 Apr. 1904, both Selborne Papers 39; Arnold-Forster diary entry, 28 Nov. 1903, Arnold-Forster Papers, Add MSS 50335.

[110] Selborne to Balfour, 3 Apr. 1904, Balfour Papers, Add MSS 49707.

[111] Balfour to Selborne, 6 Apr. 1904, Selborne Papers 1.

[112] Arnold-Forster diary entry, 28 Apr. 1904, Arnold-Forster Papers, Add MSS 50337.

[113] Gooch, *Plans of War*, 213–19; Friedberg, *Weary Titan*, 253–5.

railroads, the speed of construction of British railways in India, the need (or lack of need) to defend Seistan, and so on. But the unifying factor was the rising number of men required. By July, Kitchener was calling for 135,614 reinforcements within nine months; by November he wanted 143,686 in the same period; and, early in 1905, the general staff argued that at least 211,824 troops could be required between the eighth and fifteenth months.[114] Many, like Sir George Clarke, the newly-appointed secretary of the CID, believed that these projections were excessive: 'Sooner or later', he wrote on 18 November, 'this Govt. will be forced to put its foot down on India.'[115]

Such demands also meant expense. In November 1904, Chamberlain warned that it might prove impossible to provide such extravagant numbers.[116] As Arnold-Forster was proving unable to reform the army at the same time as controlling costs, Chamberlain's concerns were more than a routine restatement of the need to retrench.[117] In February 1905, he placed them squarely before the Cabinet.[118] Chamberlain carefully distanced himself from Arnold-Forster's ideas on reform, reminded his colleagues of the difficulties inherent in raising revenues and pointed out that financial resources were as important to defence as were naval and military ones. India could not be permitted to drain these financial resources without end. Counter-attacks also were brewing against India's insatiable demands for troops. By November 1904, Balfour had changed his mind about the British ability to strike at Russia elsewhere than in India.[119] While he admitted that it might be difficult 'to find a proper "Prize-ring" in which England and Russia were to fight out their differences, it was impossible that, in a state of war, there would not be developments—financial, military, or naval—which would not be sufficient to prevent the contest ending in a mere stale mate [*sic*]'. Clarke pointed out that the relatively weak state of the Russian army in Central Asia, meant that 'we cannot endorse K[itchener]'s exaggerated alarms'.[120] Even Roberts, who agreed with Kitchener's requests for troops, pointed out the opposition to spending such large sums on Indian defence.[121]

The continued failure of Russian arms, both at sea and on land, meant that arguments about the need to spend vast sums to ensure India's security lost their

---

[114] 'Estimate of Forces required for the Defence of India during the First Year of a War with Russia, by Colonel H. Mullaly, R. E. With comments by Viscount Kitchener', 28 July 1904, Cab 6/2/64D; 'Cavalry, Artillery and Infantry Reinforcements for India', Adjutant General (WO), Cab 6/2/73D; 'Demands for Reinforcements by the Government of India', WO, 20 Feb. 1905, Cab 6/2/74D.

[115] Clarke to Esher, 18 Nov. 1904, Esher Papers, ESHR 10/34.

[116] 58th meeting of the CID, 22 Nov. 1904, Cab 2/1.

[117] Friedberg, *Weary Titan*, 126–7.

[118] 'Army Estimates', Chamberlain, 3 Feb. 1905, Cab 37/74/21.

[119] Balfour to Brodrick, 10 Nov. 1904, Balfour Papers, Add MSS 49721.

[120] Clarke to Esher, 12 Dec. 1904, Esher Papers, ESHR 10/34.

[121] Roberts to Kitchener, 23 Dec. 1904, Kitchener Papers, PRO 30/57/28.

force, despite occasional attempts to use the Russian bogey to justify further spending.[122] Gradually, it came to be believed that the Russian threat was diminished and that other means could be found to defend India. One involved the Anglo-Japanese alliance, which was being renegotiated in the spring of 1905.[123] Two papers written in April advocated extending the alliance to cover the defence of India.[124] The arguments for such a renewal were straightforward. The alliance as it currently existed had been of great value to Britain. It had allowed Japan to fight her war against Russia successfully, and, by so doing, had 'greatly benefitted' Britain both by 'crippling' Russia's navy and by maintaining the open door in China. All of this had been done 'without extra financial expenditure on our part'. However, these benefits were tangential. Japan, on the other hand, had a firm assurance of naval support if attacked by two other powers. A renewed Anglo-Japanese alliance, one that committed Japan to sending troops to defend India, would have enormous advantages for Britain. Russia would be deterred from attacking India, and both Britain and Russia would cease having to intervene in Afghanistan. The Russians would still be able to annex the northern provinces of Persia 'whenever they choose', but the British, freed of anxieties about India, could 'easily hold our own' in the south.

This aspect of the linkage between the negotiations for the second Anglo-Japanese Alliance and the defence of India is relatively well-known.[125] However, there were also anti-Russian naval considerations behind the discussions.[126] The director of naval intelligence (DNI) pointed out that if the Anglo-Japanese alliance were simply renewed, it would serve as a '*direct stimulus to Russian naval recuperation*'. This was because the alliance guaranteed that Britain would aid Japan only if the latter were attacked by two powers; '[h]ence Russia's one and only chance of success at sea is to build ships against Japan, and to fight her single-handed'. Even worse, the fact that Russia would concentrate such a fleet in the Far East would mean that Britain would have to counter it. This would be an 'entire waste of force' should Britain be involved in a war with any other of the large naval powers: Germany, France, or the United States. 'For these reasons', the DNI concluded, 'it appears that under any circumstances it will be preferable that Russia's new fleet (if and when she builds it) should be stationed in Home Waters and Baltic rather than

---

[122] Clarke to Chirol, 2 Apr. 1905, Sydenham Papers, Add MSS 50832.

[123] 70th meeting of the CID, 12 Apr. 1905, Cab 2/1.

[124] Untitled memo, Clarke, Apr. 1905, Cab 17/54 (before 20 Apr., as it is partly reproduced in Clarke to Esher, 20 Apr. 1905, Esher Papers, ESHR 10/35); 'Renewal of the Anglo-Japanese Alliance', C. L. Ottley (DNI), 9 May 1905 (largely presented to the Admiralty on 8 Apr.), Cab 17/67.

[125] Nish, *Anglo-Japanese Alliance*, 317–35.

[126] 'Renewal of the Anglo-Japanese Alliance', n. 124 above, emphasis original. Nish, *Anglo-Japanese Alliance*, 313, mentions Ottley's discussion of the naval implications, but does not view them as important.

in China.' This could be achieved by creating a new Anglo-Japanese alliance that provided for Britain's aiding Japan whenever the latter was attacked by any *single* power. As Russia 'could not reasonably hope to outrival Japan and Great Britain combined', such a treaty 'might conceivably lead to an indefinite abandonment of her aspirations to sea power'. Even if it did not, Russia would have to concentrate her naval efforts in such locales as the Mediterranean, where 'we should find the sympathy of the principal European Powers on our side instead of hers'.

The anti-Russian purport of the new alliance was clear. In exchange for giving Japan more comprehensive naval support (a move that also furthered British interests), Britain would get India defence on the cheap. While the negotiations were on with Japan, Balfour also made certain that the Russians understood the British determination to defend India. During a debate in the Commons, the prime minister gave an important speech on defence policy.[127] He warned the Russians that continuing to build strategic railways in Central Asia would be met by uncompromising British efforts to defend India. This had its effect in Russia, where the speech was generally regarded as being 'due to a desire to take advantage of Russia's present difficulties'.[128] Balfour would not accept this view: 'I am at a loss to understand', he wrote in rebuttal, 'how Russia can feel injured at our discussing problems of *defence*.' There was more than just a hint of disingenuousness in both the Russians' and Balfour's remarks. But Balfour had staked out the British position clearly, and he reiterated the defensive nature of the new alliance to the Cabinet at the end of May 1905, when the Japanese accepted the British proposals.[129]

With the Japanese acceptance in hand, the Russian Baltic fleet at the bottom of the straits of Tsushima, and the Russo-Japanese War running down (President Roosevelt sent invitations for a peace conference to both belligerents on 8 June), Indian defence lost some of its urgency. This did not mean that all was resolved. Kitchener argued in July that Russia's defeat in the Far East made it more likely that she would attempt to regain her prestige by threatening India.[130] At the CID, Clarke repeatedly rebutted this contention. He emphasized two points: first, that Russia had been weakened sufficiently that India stood in no danger for some time to come; second, that in any case the 'defence of India lies mainly with the F.[oreign] O.[ffice]'.[131] With the unsettled political situation during the last few months of the Unionist government, the question of India did not arise. And when

---

[127] *Parl Debs*, 4th ser., vol. 146, cols. 78–84; Mackay, *Balfour*, 209–11.

[128] Spring Rice to Lansdowne, private tel., 18 May 1905, Lansdowne Papers, FO 800/141 and Balfour's undated minute.

[129] [Untitled memo on the renewal of the Anglo-Japanese alliance], Balfour, 31 May 1905, Cab 1/5.

[130] Gooch, *Plans of War*, 235.

[131] Clarke to Kitchener, 7 July 1905, Kitchener Papers, PRO 30/57/34; Clarke to Esher, 16 Aug., 1 Sept. and 11 Sept. 1905, Esher Papers, ESHR 10/37.

the new Liberal government came to power in 1905, it immediately found itself in the midst of the Moroccan crisis, which deflected military thinking towards the Continent.[132]

There still remained two unfinished matters: the possible use of Japanese troops in India under the provisions of the new alliance and the linked issue of Britain's naval responsibilities to Japan. The naval aspect was decided quickly. At a meeting of the CID on 1 February 1906, the committee accepted the Admiralty's view that the new Anglo-Japanese agreement was likely to come into play only against a grouping of Russia, France, and Germany.[133] In such circumstances, the Admiralty argued that Britain's responsibility was to maintain the two-power standard, while Japan built to the level of the third strongest power. The British fleet should not attempt to be 'unnecessarily strong' in one place (here, the Far East) if that meant risking being 'undesirably weak' in another (here, European waters). The War Office had second thoughts concerning the use of Japanese troops in India. A fortnight after the Admiralty's arguments on naval position had been adopted, the CID accepted the War Office's contention that to use Japanese troops on the north-west frontier would both be logistically difficult and 'not be consistent with either our dignity or self-respect'.[134] Only should Britain face Russia in combination with another power could Japanese military aid be countenanced. There were second thoughts about this in April 1907, just prior to talks with the Japanese aimed at defining the military aid that the two powers owed each other under the terms of the 1905 treaty. At that time it was decided to enquire whether the Japanese would provide aid against Russia in Persia or, *in extremis*, in India itself.[135] But this came to nought, as the Japanese declined to be drawn into Indian defence.[136]

The new Anglo-Japanese alliance reflected the changes that had occurred since 1902. The changes centred on Russia. In 1902, the burgeoning Russian fleet in the Far East was an expensive menace to both Britain and Japan. By 1905, it had been extensively damaged and Russia was on the verge of financial failure. In 1902, Russia was firmly allied to France, and Anglo-French relations were tepid. By

---

[132] Gooch, *Plans of War*, 225.

[133] 83rd meeting of the CID, 1 Feb. 1906, Cab 2/2; 'Anglo-Japanese Agreement of August 12, 1905. Proposals for Concerted Action.—Memorandum by the Admiralty', Admiralty, secret, 7 Dec. 1905, Cab 4/2/70B.

[134] 84th meeting of the CID, 15 Feb. 1906, Cab 2/2; 'Anglo-Japanese Agreement of August 12, 1905. Proposals for Concerted Action.—Memorandum by the General Staff', secret, Nov. 1905, Cab 4/1/68B.

[135] 97th meeting of the CID, 25 Apr. 1907, Cab 2/2; K. Wilson, 'The Anglo-Japanese Alliance of August 1905 and the Defending of India: A Case of the Worst Scenario', *JICH* 21 (1993), 334–56.

[136] Nish, *Anglo-Japanese Alliance*, 357–8; 'Conclusions of a Conference held at 2 Whitehall Gardens on May 29th, June 1st and 6th, between the Military representatives of Great Britain and Japan . . .', NS, n.d., WO 106/48.

1905, the Anglo-French entente had been signed and had proved compatible with the Franco-Russian alliance during the Russo-Japanese War. In 1902, the Boer War and its aftermath were at the centre of British defence thinking. By 1905, the defence of India occupied that spot. Thus, when the new alliance was being negotiated, the British wanted to ensure two things. First, they did not want to channel future Russian naval building towards the idea of *revanche* against Japan. With war against the Franco-Russian coalition having been shown to be unlikely by the events of 1904–5, Britain was willing to guarantee Japan support against any single power in order to deter Russia's attempting to regain her position in the Far East. Second, the British hoped to yoke this guarantee to a complementary Japanese commitment to defend India. These two aims would have the added benefit of keeping British defence spending within acceptable limits, a principal concern for a government ideologically wedded to fiscal orthodoxy.[137]

With the twin issues of British naval responsibility to Japan and the use of Japanese troops in India decided, this left only the final determination of the number of reinforcements that Britain would provide India should Russia invade. The estimated requirements had not diminished. Early in 1906, the director of military operations (DMO), Major-General J. M. Grierson, posited that India would require 187,100 troops in the first year of a war with Russia and the phenomenal numbers of 21,000 officers and 514,000 men in two years' time.[138] There were several things working against the acceptance of such figures. First, the new Liberal government was committed to expensive social reforms and possessed a strong pacifist wing. R. B. Haldane, the new secretary of state for war, was no less constrained by financial pressures than had been Brodrick and Arnold-Forster.[139] Second, Russia was weakened by the Russo-Japanese War and racked by internal difficulties; thus her threat to India was lessened. Third, at the CID Sir George Clarke continued to produce papers undermining the logistical basis of Kitchener's plans for the defence of the north-west frontier.[140] All pushed the question of the defence of India towards a diplomatic solution. And the latter was itself the final factor. Grey's intention to effect an Anglo-Russian *rapprochement* ensured that increased expenditure on the Indian army would be the second option for securing

---

[137] 'Note on the Anglo-Japanese Treaty of 1905', Clarke, 15 Dec. 1906, Cab 17/67.

[138] 'Memorandum upon the Military Forces Required for Over-Sea Warfare', Grierson, secret, 4 Jan. 1906, Robertson Papers, I/2/6.

[139] E. M. Spiers, 'Haldane's Reform of the Regular Army: Scope for Revision', *BJIS* 6 (1980), 73–4; J. Gooch, 'Haldane and the "National Army"', in Beckett and Gooch (eds.), *Politicians and Defence*, 74–5; H. S. Weinroth, 'Left-Wing Opposition to Naval Armaments in Britain before 1914', *JCH* 6 (1971), 93–120.

[140] 'Suggestions as to a basis for the calculation of the required transport of an Army operating in Afghanistan, 7 June 1905', Clarke, 7 June 1905, Cab 6/3/82D; 'Number of Troops That Can be Maintained by a Single Line of Railway', Clarke, secret, 20 May 1906, Cab 6/3/93D.

the north-west frontier.[141] Thus, when the CID met on 25 May 1906, the number of reinforcements for India was left open, and the issue was left to a special subcommittee of the CID which met in 1907.[142] Written under the shadow of the Anglo-Russian negotiations, the report of the subcommittee did not provide a definitive answer, although the figure of 135,500 put forward by the chief of the Indian general staff was not dismissed. Instead, the subcommittee simply noted that the ability to send 100,000 troops to India within a year was a 'military necessity'; beyond that, any speculation as to numbers 'would be neither practical nor fruitful'. With the signing of the Anglo-Russian Convention, the matter was not discussed again before 1914.[143]

After 1907, Russia ceased to be discussed as a potential enemy in British war planning. This should not be read as meaning either that the problems of defending India had been solved or that Russia was considered a negligible quantity in a military or naval sense. In fact, more than thirty years of discussion had come to the same conclusion: Russia was largely invulnerable to anything that Britain could manage single-handed. Instead, Britain was to threaten Russia with the death of a thousand cuts through a worldwide assault on the peripheries of the Russian empire. Any serious Russian challenge would be met either by diplomatic deterrence or by coalition warfare. The exception to this was the defence of India. Here, Britain would be unlikely to be able to enlist any European allies and would have to face Russia alone. By 1907, it was clear that India could not be defended within the limits imposed by the politics of both finance and manpower. The Anglo-Russian Convention, although not dictated primarily by British military concerns, provided an answer, albeit a temporary one, to this seemingly insoluble problem.[144] While never accepted by military men in India, the defence of India lay with the Foreign Office.

Though Russia was no longer discussed as a military threat, this does not mean that her military and naval prowess was not evaluated. On the contrary, with Russia as a possible ally and a chief player in the European balance of power, the efficiency of her armed forces and the expenditures on them remained an essential matter. Of course, such an interest in Russia's prowess in the European theatre had not begun only after the Russo-Japanese War and the signing of

[141] 'Anglo-Russian Relations as Affecting the Situation in India', Clarke, secret, 16 July 1906, Cab 17/60.

[142] Gooch, *Plans of War*, 227–32; 'The Military Requirements of the Empire as Affected by the Defence of India', Morley, 1 May 1907, Cab 16/2.

[143] The figure of 100,000 reinforcements for India was used in subsequent planning: 'Report of the Standing Sub-Committee ... appointed to enquire into the question of the Oversea Transport of Reinforcements in Time of War', Esher, 22 Mar. 1910, Cab 4/3/116B.

[144] D. McLean, *Britain and Her Buffer State: The Collapse of the Persian Empire, 1890–1914* (London, 1979), 73–6; diary entry, Grant Duff (assistant secretary, CID), 1 Dec. 1911, Grant Duff Papers.

the Anglo-Russian Convention.[145] Russia had figured largely in European military circles and had been a substantial threat to British interests worldwide since at
least the Napoleonic Wars. Generally speaking, the Russian army was viewed
favourably by the British. Just because the Russian army had been defeated by
the Japanese, the War Office argued in 1907, 'it would be a very grave error to
think . . . that the Russian army is bad and to underrate it accordingly'.[146]
The Russian army, despite its officer corps being poor, its men lacking in-
dividuality, and its having flaws with respect to tactics, training, and cohesion
between arms, was 'extremely formidable'. Its enormous size, its indifference to
losses, and the 'undoubted military qualities of the rank and file' gave the Russian
army a particular character and ensured that it would have to be considered
carefully by the British. This was particularly so because 'a quarrel between
Russia and Great Britain must be fought out upon the north-west frontier of India,
and . . . we cannot effectively attack Russia in other parts of the world'.

Despite this report, the British were much concerned about the state of the
Russian army after the Russo-Japanese War. In particular, the mutinous and
revolutionary activity within the army during final phases of war raised doubts
as to the army's capacities.[147] However, by 1908, there were assurances from the
British military attaché in Russia that the imperial army could hold its own in a
defensive war. And, while Russia had refused to go to war in 1909 over the Bosnian
crisis, by 1910 the War Office was told that the 'revolutionary propaganda has been
entirely eradicated from the army'.[148] Equally, the 'passive defensive role' that
Russia's military weakness had forced upon her was to be abandoned.[149] Coupled
with the rebound in Russia's finances—severely strained by the Russo-Japanese
War—there was widespread optimism about Russia's military recovery.[150] However, this recovery was not complete. During the Moroccan crisis of 1911, Sir
Henry Wilson, the DMO, told Grey that Russia would be incapable of mobilizing
fast enough to save France should Germany invade, while Lloyd George had to be
informed that Russia was not sufficiently strong to allow her to send troops by sea
to the western front.[151]

[145] K. Neilson, 'Watching the "Steamroller": British Observers and the Russian Army before 1914',
JSS 8 (1985), 199–217.
[146] 'The Military Resources of the Russian Empire', General Staff, WO, 1907, WO 33/419.
[147] J. Bushnell, *Mutiny Amid Repression: Russian Soldiers in the Revolution of 1905–6* (Bloomington,
IN, 1985).
[148] Wyndham (British military attaché, St Petersburg), report, 19 Nov. 1908, FO 371/519/40798; his
contribution in 'Russia. Annual Report, 1910', 22 Mar. 1911, FO 371/1214/11045.
[149] Wyndham's report, 6 Apr. 1910, FO 371/979/12149.
[150] The opinion of the *Times*' military correspondent, Charles Repington, diary entry, 17 Jan. 1911,
Grant Duff Papers.
[151] Wilson, diary entry, 9 Aug. 1911, Wilson Papers; Grant Duff, diary entry, 25 Aug. 1911, Grant
Duff Papers.

The years from 1911 to the outbreak of war found a growing British belief in
Russia's military strength. Much of this reflected the increased Russian expenditure on her armed forces.[152] Spending rose from 608.1 million rubles in 1908 to
959.6 million in 1913, and the percentage of government spending on defence rose
from 23.2 per cent in 1907 to 28.3 per cent in 1913.[153] The British were well aware
of this; in 1912, the military attaché reported that the army budget estimates for
1913 were some 41.5 per cent greater than actual expenditure in 1908.[154] The so-
called great programme of 1914, which called for expanding the standing army
from 1.3 million in 1914 to 1.75 million by 1917 and substantial increases in
artillery procurement, underlined the growing military might of Russia.[155] This was
axiomatic at the War Office. In a widely circulated dispatch written in March 1914,
Lieutenant-Colonel A. F. W. Knox, the British military attaché in Russia, provided
the War Office with his evaluation of the Russian army.[156] He was lavish in his
praise for the quality of the men and lower-ranking officers: they were 'brave to a
fault and . . . never know when they are beaten' and discipline was 'good'. Their
weaknesses stemmed from Russia's history and culture: they were 'deficient in
initiative and decision of character'. While senior officers still suffered from the
careerism and ignorance that had characterized the army before 1905, this was
being remedied by forced retirements and rapid promotion of younger men. Knox
concluded his report on a high note. As the Russian army was 'improving in quality
every day' and as Russia had a high birth rate, ensuring that she could maintain the
enormous size of her standing army, 'it seems only a matter of time till the army
becomes a match for all western Europe'.

Knox's views were accepted at face value at the War Office. Captain Archibald
Wavell, fresh from a brush with the Russian secret police and now dealing with
Russian matters at the War Office, enthusiastically endorsed Knox's opinions.[157]
'Colonel Knox's estimate of the qualities of the Russian army,' Wavell minuted on
the former's report, 'the virtues and defects of the leaders, subordinate officers and
rank & file, agrees exactly with the opinion formed in this section from information
received from other sources.' Wilson's minute underlined the significance of
Knox's report: 'This is a most important Despatch. It is easy to understand now

---

[152] A. L. Sidorov, *Finansovoe polozhenie Rossii v gody pervoi mirovoi voiny (1914–17)* (Moscow,
1960), 14–106.

[153] First figures: P. Gatrell, 'Industrial Expansion in Tsarist Russia, 1908–14', *EconHR*, 2nd ser., 35
(1982), table 4, 105; the second set: P. R. Gregory, *Russian National Income, 1885–1913* (Cambridge,
1982), table F.1, 252.

[154] Knox, report, 14 Nov. 1912, FO 371/1472/48947.

[155] A. Zhilin, 'Bolshaia programma po usileniiu russkoi armii', *VIZ* 16 (1974), 90–7; N. Stone, *The
Eastern Front 1914–17* (London, 1975), 29–43.

[156] 'Army Programme and the Western Frontier', Knox, secret, 19 Mar. 1914, WO 106/1039 and
minutes.

[157] Wavell had been arrested for alleged espionage activities in Russia.

why Germany is nervous about the future & why she may think that it is a case of "now or never".' While there were others who felt that Russia's strength might be undermined by her lack of 'sufficient organization' and the 'corruption which pervades *all* classes', the general belief was that Russia was a formidable land power.[158]

This was not paralleled by views of the Russian navy. While the naval débâcles of the Russo–Japanese War for the most part had destroyed only ships that were either obsolete or obsolescent, the damage to the prestige and confidence of the Russian navy was considerable.[159] To counter this, in 1908 the Russian government launched a building programme designed to reconstitute the fleet.[160] This determination was emphasized in 1912 when a further building programme was approved. Despite the vast sums spent, the British Admiralty, in the person of the British naval attaché in St Petersburg, Commander H. G. Grenfell, was never convinced that Russia would obtain commensurate results.[161] This was due to a number of things. First, the Russian government was determined to build the ships in Russia with Russian resources and this meant that there would be an enormous waste of money both for supplies and in bribes. Second, Russian shipyards took longer to build ships than did their main foreign competitors; thus, the Russian navy would always be obsolescent technologically. Equally, Russian administration was 'still too near her unregenerate past' to be able to undertake such large projects. Finally, the personnel of the Russian navy was not up to the long, sustained hard work necessary to run and build such a fleet.

This pessimistic view was balanced by an optimistic view at the Foreign Office. While not arguing with Grenfell's evaluation of the Russian fleet, the Foreign Office viewed it in the perspective of the strategical–political situation in Europe. While Russia's fleet building might stir up diplomatic problems (since Sweden would be certain to take alarm), a Russian fleet in the Baltic would force Germany to divide her own navy to counterbalance it.[162] Winston Churchill, the first lord of the admiralty, replied, when asked by the Russians in 1911 whether the British favoured the new Russian building programme in the Baltic, that 'the growth and

---

[158] Untitled memo, Bertie, 24 Apr. 1914, Bertie Papers, Add MSS 63032.

[159] K. F. Shatsillo, *Russkii imperializm i razvitie flota nakanune pervoi mirovoi voiny (1906–14)* (Moscow, 1968); id., 'O disproportsii v razvitii vooruzhennyk sil Rossii nakanune pervoi mirovoi voiny (1906–14 gg)', *IZ* 83 (1969), 123–36; P. Gatrell, 'After Tsushima: Economic and Administrative Aspects of Russian Naval Rearmament, 1905–13', *EconHR*, 2nd ser., 43 (1990), 255–70.

[160] O'Beirne to Grey, disp. 213, 2 May 1908, FO 371/516/16030 and minutes.

[161] Grenfell's disps., 22 June 1912, FO 371/1470/27675 and 21 Aug. 1912, FO 371/1470/35876 and Grenfell to Buchanan, 19 Mar. 1914, in H. Temperley and G. P. Gooch (eds.), *B[ritish] D[ocuments on the Origins of the War, 1898–1914]* (11 vols. in 13; London, 1926–38), x, pt. 2, 771–2 (see *BD* hereafter).

[162] Buchanan to Grey, disp. 138, 17 May 1911 and minutes; O'Beirne to Grey, disp. 280, 30 Sept. 1911 and minutes; the German response, I. N. Lambi, *The Navy and German Power Politics, 1862–1914* (London, 1984), 395–9.

revival of the Russian Fleet there would certainly be welcomed by us'.[163] And, as Nicolson pointed out in June 1912, the Russian Baltic fleet was just another reason why Britain should endeavour to maintain her good relations with the Tsarist state, for if a Russo-German *rapprochement* were to take place, Germany could concentrate her entire fleet against Britain, secure in the knowledge that Russia would police the Baltic.[164] This latter concern was instrumental in British thinking concerning a possible Anglo-Russian naval agreement in 1914.[165]

What was the impact of Russia on British defence planning in the generation before 1914? The most obvious point is the tremendous importance of Russia.[166] In 1888, the Stanhope memorandum rated the defence of India as the second priority (behind only aid to the civil power) of the British army; in 1903 Balfour, undoubtedly treating aid to the civil power as a given, placed India first.[167] Only the signing of the Anglo-Russian Convention of 1907 ended the perpetual demand from India for more troops and more money with which to prevent a Russian invasion. And, from 1893 to at least 1904, the Russian fleet was one of the components of the 'two-power' standard that determined the size of the Royal Navy. No other Great Power impinged so directly on British interests as did Russia. Although Britain and France were naval rivals, France could not threaten Britain's colonial empire except by means of amphibious attack. As long as the Royal Navy remained supreme, France's challenge to the British Empire was a nuisance, but nothing more. And France's own overseas empire was similarly vulnerable to British depredations. Germany's threat was even more distant than was that of France. Anglo-German colonial rivalries were trivial in comparison to the Anglo-Russian struggle on the north-west frontier; they were more a product of the growing general misunderstanding between the two powers than the clash of real interests. Certainly, after about 1905, the German fleet became a serious menace to the Royal Navy, but it was not the only one. The Royal Navy built against all potential rivals, for British naval needs were global in nature, reflecting the extent of the Empire.

It was for this reason that Russia, more than any other European power, occupied such a central position in British defence planning. Russia could threaten India, while, as study after study reiterated from the 1870s onward, Britain could not threaten Russia. Unless Russia could be contained by means of a European

---

[163] Churchill to Grey, 28 Nov. 1911, Grey Papers, FO 800/87.

[164] Nicolson to O'Beirne, 18 June 1912, Nicolson Papers, FO 800/357.

[165] Nicolson to de Bunsen (British ambassador, Vienna), 27 Apr. 1914, *BD*, x, pt. 2, 786–7.

[166] S. Mahajan, 'The Defence of India and the End of Isolation: A Study in the Foreign Policy of the Conservative Government, 1900–5', *JICH* 10 (1982), 168–93.

[167] I. F. W. Beckett, 'The Stanhope Memorandum of 1888: A Reinterpretation', *BIHR* 57 (1984), 240–7; id., 'Edward Stanhope at the War Office 1887–92', *JSS* 5 (1982), 278–307; Balfour to Kitchener, 3 Dec. 1903, cited, J. McDermott, 'The Revolution in British Miliary Thinking from the Boer War to the Moroccan Crisis', *CJH* 9 (1974), 167.

alliance, India would have to be defended by Britain alone. This was difficult. First, it was expensive. Neither the Unionist or Liberal governments were willing to spend the amounts that Indian defence required. Only conscription at home could have provided the numbers required to defend India within (possibly) the budgetary limits acceptable to either party. And, conscription itself was anathema politically to all but the 'radical right'.[168] Second, if Britain were involved in a major war on the north-west frontier, her circumstances would resemble those during the Boer War, when she found herself politically impotent in Europe. Finally, the Russian navy was a force to be reckoned with until May 1905. The threat that Russia posed in the Far East, at Constantinople and in the Baltic put a particular strain on the Royal Navy, forcing it to be sufficiently strong in three widely spread locales. This ran counter to the new naval thinking, which considered the seas to be one and called for the concentration of battle fleets to maintain British naval supremacy.[169] A number of things combined to end the policy of checking Russia in these venues. In the Far East, the task was shared with the Japanese via the Anglo-Japanese alliance. At Constantinople and in the Baltic, the Admiralty came to the conclusion that, due in part to new technologies, Russia could not be denied.

Little has been said above about Russia and the European balance of power. Britain did, however, closely consider her in this regard. But, the British were well aware that the best guarantee of the balance was the relative parity between the Franco-Russian and Austro-German groupings. The minuscule size of the British army—and the same objections to expanding it that plagued discussions of the defence of India—meant that Britain could play only a naval and financial role in a European conflict.[170] Whether Britain was committed to maintaining the balance of power by throwing her weight on either side of the two power blocs in Europe is a moot point.[171] Certainly, Britain would endeavour—just as she had in the Napoleonic Wars—to prevent any one power from dominating Europe. However, Britain also had imperial interests and foremost among them was India. A German alliance carried with it the implicit threat to India from a disgruntled or hostile Russia. An alliance with France and Russia did not. But a binding alliance with either grouping would certainly have wrecked the Liberal government. Faced with unpalatable alternatives, Grey walked a middle road. Given the realities of British

---

[168] R. J. Q. Adams and P. P. Poirier, *The Conscription Controversy in Great Britain, 1900–18* (London, 1987), 23–48; R. J. Q. Adams, 'The National Service League and Mandatory Service in Edwardian Britain', *Armed Forces & Society*, 12 (1985), 53–74.

[169] Neilson, '"Greatly Exaggerated"'.

[170] D. French, *British Economic and Strategic Planning 1905–15* (London, 1982).

[171] Cf. K. Wilson, 'British Power in the European Balance, 1906–14', in D. Dilks (ed.), *Retreat from Power: Studies in Britain Foreign Policy of the Twentieth Century*, i, *1906–39* (London, 1981), 21–41; id., 'Imperial Interests in the British Decision for War, 1914: The Defence of India in Central Asia', *RIS* 10 (1984), 189–203; id., *The Policy of the Entente: Essays on the Determinants of British Foreign Policy, 1904–14* (Cambridge, 1985).

military and naval power and their relationship to Russia, this seems to have been
a sensible course.

A detailed look at the Russian aspect of British defence policy before 1914 also
offers some general results. First, it drives a stake through any lingering belief
that the British Expeditionary Force (BEF) was created by Haldane to check the
German menace in Europe.[172] It is evident that the BEF was intended to serve
British interests overseas, *wherever* (including India) they were threatened, and
always within the ambit of an acceptable price. Second, it throws doubt on the
concept that the Royal Navy's policy, since the passage of the German *Novelle* in
1898, was directed against the German menace.[173] Just as the technological under-
pinnings of this theory have been questioned, so, too, should its underlying tele-
ological assumptions of the inevitability of an Anglo-German naval war.[174] It was
the increased expenditure of the *Russian*, not the German, navy in the period from
1898 to 1904 that drove British naval planning. If Britain had been drawn into the
Russo-Japanese war and had faced Russia on the high seas (as conceivably could
have happened either as a result of Russia's blockade policy or the Dogger Bank
incident), then it would be just as logical to assume that British naval planning had
been designed to deal with the inevitable Anglo-Russian war.

And this leads us to a final point: the question of cost. The Russian case
illustrates that much of the debate on British defence policy cannot be explained
without considering expense. Neither the British army nor, to a lesser extent, the
Royal Navy were exempt from the nineteenth century belief in the need for
economy.[175] There was continual intra-departmental wrangling within the British
cabinet concerning military and naval estimates, with successive chancellors of the
exchequer viewing the service estimates as the most likely place to make cuts. But,
just as in the 1920s, when the Treasury attempted to extend its grip over defence
spending, the exigencies of the international situation, with their implications for
Britain's place in the world, tended to override financial concerns when it came to
matters essential to Britain's defence.[176] Russia spoke directly to these essential
matters. No one challenged either the need to defend India or the maintenance of
the 'two-power' standard.[177] The debate was always over ways and means, with the

---

[172] E. W. Spiers, *The Army and Society 1815–1914* (London, 1980), 268–84; id., *Haldane: An Army Reformer* (Edinburgh, 1980), 192–3.

[173] A. J. Marder, *From the Dreadnought to Scapa Flow*, i, *The Road to War, 1904–14* (London, 1961); P. M. Kennedy, *The Rise and Fall of British Naval Mastery* (London, 1976), 205–38.

[174] C. H. Fairbanks, Jr., 'The Origins of the *Dreadnought* Revolution: A Historiographical Essay', *IHR* 13 (1991), 246–72; P. Kennedy, *The Rise of the Anglo-German Antagonism 1860–1914* (London, 1980), 464–70.

[175] Sumida, *Defence of Naval Supremacy*, 37–70; Weinroth, 'Left-Wing Opposition', 93–120.

[176] J. R. Ferris, *Men, Money, and Diplomacy: The Evolution of British Strategic Foreign Policy, 1919–26* (Ithaca, NY, 1989), shows the primacy of defence needs over financial concerns in the early 1920s.

[177] India may have been a strategic liability; K. Jeffery, 'The Eastern Arc of Empire: A Strategic View 1850–1950', *JSS* 5 (1982), 531–45.

hope that such debate could find economies. The concerns of the Treasury were an important retardant to defence planning, but did not control it in the final analysis.

The essential point is that Anglo-Russian relations were never far from matters of defence. The centrality of Russia in British defence planning and the unique way in which Russia affected Britain's position both globally and in Europe meant that Russia occupied a special place in British foreign, as well as in defence, policy. This combined with the high cost of defending British interests against Russian encroachments, meant that there would always be a thrust towards finding a diplomatic agreement with Russia that would solve these intertwined problems. When this could not be achieved, Britain had to contain Russia by means of naval checkpoints, an enhanced military presence in India, and diplomatic manœuvring. Russia could never be ignored.

PART II

RIVALRY 1894–1905

5

Problems Old and New: China and Armenia, 1894–1896

As Alexander III lay dying in the autumn of 1894, Anglo-Russian relations were experiencing one of their periodic outbursts of good will. The policy of *rapprochement* that Lord Rosebery had initiated in 1892 seemed to be paying dividends. The long-standing issue of the Pamirs appeared near solution; no serious quarrel had yet emerged between the two countries over the ramifications of the Sino-Japanese War.[1] Indeed, by the beginning of 1895, Rosebery could write to the British ambassador at Madrid that 'our relations with Russia are, I honestly believe, more cordial than at any period since the German war'.[2] The following decade did not bear out Rosebery's optimistic assessment of Anglo-Russian relations. Instead, and despite British efforts to make it otherwise, Anglo-Russian relations deteriorated.

In the first two years of Nicholas II's reign, Anglo-Russian relations had two centres. The first was the Sino-Japanese War; the second was the Armenian crisis. The Sino-Japanese War was one of the first manifestations of the effect that the emergence of Germany and Japan as Great Powers had on Anglo-Russian relations. In Europe, the growth of Germany's power, coupled with her aspirations for *Weltmacht*, threatened the rough equilibrium established at Vienna in 1815. In the Far East, Japan's rise meant that European powers—particularly Britain and Russia—could gain either an ally or a rival. And, in both Europe and the Far East the likelihood of Britain and Russia's clashing over the interests of third parties grew. The second centre of Anglo-Russian relations—Armenia—was a traditional one, and was representative of the fact that British and Russian imperial interests were worldwide and often in competition with each other. The Sino-Japanese War was new wine in a new bottle; the Armenian crisis was old wine in a changing bottle. Both were potent vintages.

Rosebery and Kimberley had anticipated that the clash of Chinese and Japanese

---

[1] G. J. Alder, *British India's Northern Frontier 1865–95* (London, 1963), 226–86.
[2] Cited, G. Martel, *Imperial Diplomacy: Rosebery and the Failure of Foreign Policy* (Kingston, Ont., 1986), 240.

aspirations in Korea might bode ill for Britain even before the Sino-Japanese War began.[3] On the eve of the war, the two men discussed the increasing tension in the peninsula. For Kimberley, what the British had to decide was 'ought we to interfere most decisively? or shall we let matters take their course?'[4] This question involved Russia. Any British intervention would likely have to take the form of 'armed mediation, and will really be directed against Japan'. To be effective, such a step 'must be in conjunction with Russia', but this would result in the 'disagreeable prospect' that the two intervening powers would have to administer Korea jointly in order to forestall further Japanese and Chinese clashes. This seemed decisive for Kimberley: 'on the whole I incline to leaving the Chinese & Japanese alone as the least of two evils provided the Russians abstain from active interference.' Rosebery readily accepted this view. He doubted whether any of the other powers would join in a British demonstration, and was not convinced that Parliament could be roused to carry out such an action wholeheartedly.[5] Besides, by doing so, Britain 'should weaken and alienate a Power [that is, Japan] of great magnitude in those seas, and which is a bulwark against Russia'. The prime minister also shared Kimberley's abhorrence of an Anglo-Russian condominium in Korea: such an idea was 'in itself enough to deter one from action. It would as a matter of certainty only redound to the advantage of Russia, while it might engage us in great complications.'

During the first months of the Sino-Japanese War, such a policy was followed. Sir Frank Lascelles, whose arrival at St Petersburg as ambassador nearly coincided with the outbreak of the war, reported on 2 August 1894 that the Russians felt that affairs in Korea had gone too far for any 'collective remonstrance' to the belligerents to be effective.[6] On the same day, Kimberley moved to assure the Russians that there would be no independent British diplomatic moves in the matter, and that British representatives abroad would keep their Russian counterparts informed of all discussions.[7] While there were worries on both sides that individual representatives—Russians in China; Britons in Japan—might make policy initiatives without recourse to their own governments, by the middle of August Lascelles discounted them.[8] As he wrote to Kimberley, '[t]here is so little going on here now

---

[3] The Sino-Japanese conflict has not been given much attention by historians who deal with the foreign policies of the European powers. This is not true for historians of Japan; see Munimitsu, M. (ed.), *Kenkenroku: A Diplomatic Record of the Sino-Japanese War, 1894–5*, trans. and ed. G. M. Berger (Tokyo, 1982), pp. xi–xiii; W. G. Beasley, *Japanese Imperialism 1894–1945* (Oxford, 1987), 42–68.

[4] Kimberley to Rosebery, 30 July 1894, Rosebery Papers 10068.

[5] Untitled memo by Rosebery in response to Kimberley's letter, 30 July 1894, Rosebery Papers 10134.

[6] Lascelles to Kimberley, tel. 55, 2 Aug. 1894, FO 65/1474.

[7] Kimberley to Lascelles, tel. 38, 2 Aug. 1894, FO 65/1474.

[8] Kimberley to Lascelles, 7 Aug. 1894, Lascelles Papers, FO 800/15; Lascelles to Kimberley, tel. 55, 2 Aug. 1894, FO 65/1474.

that I am thinking of taking a trip to Finland next week to ascertain by personal experience whether there are trout in that country.'[9] With Alexander III's health deteriorating and no evident progress in the actual fighting between China and Japan, Anglo-Russian relations seemed placid: 'The Russians have been as civil as possible', Lascelles wrote to his colleague in Teheran, 'and as far as I can judge really wish to act with us in the Corean business; I think now they are running straight.'[10]

Circumstances changed. By October, the possibility of a decisive Japanese advance on Peking forced Kimberley to reassess. His first need was to determine the Russian reaction to the Japanese successes; his second was to determine British policy.[11] Kimberley was inclined to accept Japanese assurances that any advance on the mainland would not threaten the British position at Shanghai, but he was not certain how Britain could now interfere to prevent a Chinese defeat without seeming overtly anti-Japanese. This concern was shared by the Russian foreign minister, Giers, who suggested that Britain and Russia 'consult' with the other powers as to a possible course of action.[12] In fact, rumours were rife in St Petersburg that Giers, and the Russian government, had come to terms with the Japanese and thus could face the possibility of a Chinese defeat with equanimity.[13] The British, however, believed that, with Alexander III and Giers both ill and the latter in attendance on the Emperor at Tsarskoe Selo, Russian decision-making was paralysed.[14] This paralysis extended abroad. Francis Bertie informed Rosebery that the Russian ambassador 'has no instructions about China'.[15] Despite these difficulties, Kimberley had a high regard for the need to act in concert with the Russians:'As to China, the point is now I think to persuade Russia to act with us . . . If Russia & we agree & take the lead the others would probably follow.'[16]

By mid-October, the British became more suspicious. Information from Sir Edward Malet, the British ambassador at Berlin, gave new credence to the rumour of a Russo–Japanese agreement.[17] But, while Kimberley felt that this might explain 'Russia['s] holding back' and while he 'greatly mistrust[ed] Russia', the foreign secretary felt that there was 'nothing for the moment but to wait'. In the meantime, the Foreign Office attempted to discover what Japan's terms for ending the war

[9] Lascelles to Kimberley, 15 Aug. 1894, Lascelles Papers, FO 800/17.

[10] Lascelles to Sir Mortimer Durand (British minister, Teheran), 30 Aug. 1894, Lascelles Papers, FO 800/17.

[11] Kimberley to Lascelles, tel. 67, 2 Oct. 1894, FO 65/1474; Kimberley to Rosebery, 3 Oct. 1894, Kimberley Papers 10242.

[12] Lascelles to Kimberley, tel. 82, 4 Oct. 1894, FO 65/1474.

[13] Lascelles to Kimberley, confidential disp. 210, 7 Oct. 1894, FO 65/1473.

[14] Lascelles to Kimberley, 10 Oct. 1894, Lascelles Papers, FO 800/17.

[15] Bertie to Rosebery, 8 Oct. 1894, Rosebery papers 10134.

[16] Kimberley to Rosebery, 8 Oct. 1894, Rosebery Papers 10069.

[17] Kimberley to Rosebery, tel., 13 Oct. 1894, Kimberley Papers, 10242.

might be.[18] All was complicated by circumstances. The illness of both Alexander III and Giers caused what Kimberley termed an 'unfortunate state of things for diplomacy'.[19] Further, Kimberley himself was absent from the Foreign Office on holiday, putting a particular strain on the under-secretaries.[20] This made the wheels of diplomacy turn slowly. It was not until 24 October that Lascelles was able to get a definite reply from Giers about the possibility of joint action.[21] The results did not justify the long wait. Germany's reluctance to join in any coercion of the belligerents led Giers to advocate 'to suspend but not to entirely abandon' negotiations. And, in the British Cabinet, some members had begun to make 'anxious enquiries' about the Far East.[22]

The death of Alexander III on 1 November largely eliminated the paralysis in St Petersburg. When the Chinese government on 3 November appealed to the powers to intervene, the Russian response was prompt, if circumspect. Giers noted that Russia would join, but not lead, the other powers in suggesting peace to Japan.[23] This was good tactics. With such a response, the Russians could ascertain the position of the other powers without committing themselves to definite action. The British reply was similarly evasive. Kimberley informed Staal that, while the British government favoured a joint Anglo-Russian note to Japan, any British action would depend on the attitude of the other powers.[24] In fact, the British favoured concerted action. By 9 November, and despite the lukewarm response of the other powers to the British initiative, the Cabinet had approved joint Anglo-Russian action.[25] Accordingly, the foreign secretary informed the Russians that the British were 'desirous' to end the war, and were ready 'if they [the Russians] will join us' to carry any Chinese peace proposals to the Japanese. The Russians were hesitant. Giers informed Lascelles that it was 'better to wait before taking any action', citing as reasons for the delay the fact that Germany had not yet made her position clear, France had agreed to participate only if all other powers had agreed to and the United States had already offered her good offices to the belligerents.[26] This Russian sluggishness brought Kimberley's attempt to a dead end. The foreign secretary termed Giers's response 'not encouraging', but it was left to the prime minister to sum up the British position: 'we can do nothing, having done our best.'[27]

[18] Bertie to Rosebery, 12 and 17 Oct. 1894, Rosebery Papers, 10134.
[19] Kimberley to Lascelles, 17 Oct. 1894, Lascelles Papers, FO 800/15.
[20] G. H. Murray (Rosebery's private secretary) to Rosebery, 17 Oct. 1894, Rosebery Papers, 10049.
[21] Lascelles to Kimberley, 25 Oct. 1894, Lascelles Papers, FO 800/17.
[22] G. H. Murray to Rosebery, 25 Oct. 1894, Rosebery Papers, 10049.
[23] Giers to Staal, tel., 5 Nov. 1894, copy, FO 65/1481.
[24] Kimberley to Lascelles, disp. 301, 7 Nov. 1894, FO 65/1471.
[25] See Kimberley to Lascelles, tel. 91, 9 Nov. 1894, FO 65/1474.
[26] Lascelles to Kimberley, tel. 121, 11 Nov. 1894, FO 65/1474.
[27] Kimberley to Rosebery, 11 Nov. 1894, Rosebery Papers, 10069; Rosebery to Kimberley, 12 Nov. 1894, Kimberley Papers, 10243.

The matter rested there until the New Year. The inaction was the result of the personal nature of decision-making in Russia. Nicholas II was married on 27 November and was otherwise engaged on his honeymoon. And, even without the Tsar's nuptials, the change of reign and Giers's illness mitigated against a business-like functioning of the Russian foreign ministry. Kimberley was well aware of this situation: 'while the Russians are very friendly . . . with a new and inexperienced Emperor and a Foreign Minister seriously ill, it is difficult to get any business done with them at Petersburg.'[28]

The arrival in Japan of Chinese representatives early in 1895 ended this inaction. On 23 January, the Russians asked Lascelles whether the Chinese visit should be utilized as an opportunity for the British and Russian governments to express their hope that peace should be concluded.[29] This proposal was welcomed in London. Noting that, as it 'is so important to keep on the same line with Russia', Kimberley urged agreement.[30] But Rosebery was not optimistic as to the efficacy of a second Russian proposal: that if the Chinese terms for peace proved unacceptable to the Japanese, then the latter should be pressed to express their own terms. Kimberley and Rosebery had to conduct their negotiations with one eye on the Cabinet. A faction, headed by Sir William Harcourt, the chancellor of the exchequer, felt that previous negotiations had been conducted without consultation. As Kimberley noted to the prime minister: 'you will remember how jealous they were about our earlier proceedings with China & Japan.'[31]

Even the death of Giers on 26 January did not halt the Anglo-Russian efforts. The Russian representative in Japan was told to co-operate with the British minister in Tokyo in urging peace upon the Japan and China.[32] A week later, the Russians repeated this sentiment, and suggested that the two governments have 'an exchange of ideas' to establish the best line to follow in the Far East.[33] Kimberley greeted this cautiously, asking the Russian ambassador to be more specific about what the Russian government wished to discuss.[34] The time taken to clarify this point, the failure of the Chinese to send a representative to Japan with full plenipotentiary powers, and the dilatoriness of the Russian government in appointing a successor to Giers, all delayed further discussion. Kimberley chafed at such inactivity. On 19 February he proposed asking Russia and France whether they would join the

[28] Kimberley to Sir William Harcourt (chancellor of the exchequer), 23 Dec. 1894, Rosebery Papers, 10143.

[29] Lascelles to Kimberley, tel. 5, 23 Jan. 1895, FO 65/1494; Lascelles to Kimberley, confidential disp. 19, 23 Jan. 1895, FO 65/1490.

[30] Kimberley to Rosebery, 24 Jan. 1895, Rosebery Papers, 10069.

[31] Kimberley to Rosebery, 2nd, 24 Jan. 1895, Rosebery Papers, 10069; Martel, *Imperial Diplomacy*, 198–201, 221–2.

[32] Lascelles to Kimberley, confidential disp. 29, 29 Jan. 1895, FO 65/1490.

[33] Lascelles to Kimberley, tel. 11, 2 Feb. 1895, FO 65/1494.

[34] Minute by Kimberley, 3 Feb. 1895, on FO 65/1494.

British in supporting an armistice proposal if one were made by the new Chinese envoy, Li Hung Chang.[35] Russian action made this unnecessary. Four days later, the Russians informed Kimberley that the Chinese had asked St Petersburg to help in obtaining an armistice and that Russia had replied that all she could do was to 'advise Japan to make peace'.[36] By the end of the month, Staal had informed Kimberley that the Russian government 'desired especially' to know whether Britain attached great importance, as did Russia, to Korean independence.[37] Kimberley replied that the British government did hold such an opinion.[38]

While this was going on, a satisfactory ending both to the Sino–Japanese conflict and to the Anglo-Russian sparring over it became more likely. The drawn-out negotiations about the frontier in the Pamirs were concluded. This meant that, despite some outstanding issues (notably the future of Afghanistan and the vexed matter of the Armenian massacres), no feature of Anglo-Russian relations, indeed no matter in British foreign affairs generally, was of any 'special urgency'.[39] With Lobanov-Rostovskii newly installed as Russian foreign minister, a resolution of the Sino-Japanese imbroglio did not seem out of reach. At Lobanov's first interview, he expressed himself pleased with Kimberley's desire for co-operation between Britain and Russia, and added that Russia had no territorial ambitions or desire for compensation in the Far East. Kimberley's pacific view of the international scene did not seem threatened from St Petersburg.

As the peace negotiations between the Chinese and Japanese representatives at Shimonoseki proceeded, the British and the Russians strove to maintain their united front. On 21 March, Lobanov told Lascelles of an unofficial hint from the Japanese minister in St Petersburg that Japan might demand 'one of the peninsulas jutting out into the gulf of Pechili' as part of the peace settlement.[40] This, Lobanov felt, 'would put Pekin [*sic*] completely at the mercy of the Japanese'. While Kimberley likely did not approve of such a Japanese acquisition, his interests lay more with obtaining a settlement. The first step, he felt, was to get the Japanese to outline their peace terms, and he attempted to get the Russians to assist in forcing Tokyo to do so.[41] In addition, Kimberley warned Sir Nicholas O'Conor, the British minister at Peking, to combat any suggestion that the two European powers were not in harmony.[42]

The events of the next month shattered this illusion of harmony. When the

---

[35] Kimberley to Rosebery, 19 Feb. 1895, Kimberley Papers, 10242.

[36] Lascelles to Kimberley, tel. 18, 23 Feb. 1895, FO 65/1494.

[37] Kimberley to Lascelles, disp. 54A, 27 Feb. 1895, FO 65/1489.

[38] Lascelles to Kimberley, disp. 56, 13 Mar. 1895, FO 65/1490.

[39] Kimberley to Rosebery, 8 Mar. 1895, Rosebery Papers, 10069.

[40] Lascelles to Kimberley, tel. 26, 21 Mar. 1895, FO 65/1494.

[41] Kimberley to Rosebery, 22 Mar. 1895, Rosebery Papers, 10069; Kimberley to Lascelles, tel. 30, 23 Mar. 1895, FO 65/1493.

[42] Lascelles to Kimberley, tel. 30, 25 Mar. 1895, FO 65/1494; Kimberley to Lascelles, tel. 33, 26 Mar. 1895, FO 65/1493; Lascelles to Kimberley, 28 Mar. 1895, Lascelles Papers, FO 800/17.

Japanese peace terms were presented to China on 4 April, it became evident that the British and Russian governments had sharply differing views concerning their validity. Russia's initial reaction to the Japanese terms was moderate. The following day, however, the Russian foreign minister began to outline what became the permanent Russian attitude.[43] While not reneging on his previous statement that the Japanese terms were 'not heavier' than expected, Lobanov pointed out that the Japanese claim to the Liaotung peninsula was a 'more serious question'. Although terming his remarks a 'personal opinion', Lobanov stated that a Japanese acquisition of the peninsula would be 'a standing menace to Peking and would compromise the independence of Corea'. Clearly, any British support for the Japanese position would find opposition in Russia.

To complicate matters, at this point British foreign policy became embroiled in a ferocious intra-party debate. Harcourt had long contended that he held a special position within the party, one that entitled him to a virtual veto on any foreign policy pronouncement.[44] On 28 March, Sir Edward Grey, the Liberal parliamentary under-secretary for foreign affairs, had made a statement concerning the British response to French incursions on the Upper Nile. Harcourt took exception, and used this incident to launch a general assault on the primacy of Rosebery and Kimberley in the making of foreign policy. The matter of the British response to the Japanese peace terms quickly was drawn in. Harcourt seized upon Lobanov's first, moderate, response. 'I trust', the chancellor wrote to Kimberley on 5 April, 'therefore that we shall not meddle in this matter in which we have only a very indirect concern—though I know we meddle everywhere—particularly where we have no concern.'[45] After making the logical point that it would be impolitic for Britain to quarrel with Japan, 'the rising power in the East—and allow Russia to appear as her friend', Harcourt returned to his sweeping criticism of Kimberley's (and, indirectly, the prime minister's) foreign policy. 'Is there no pie in the world', the chancellor concluded grandiloquently, 'out of which we can manage to keep our fingers?'

Rosebery was in no mood to bow to the wishes of his intemperate chancellor. The prime minister realized that there were 'deep seated & radical differences' between himself and Harcourt on foreign policy: 'His view', Rosebery wrote to Kimberley, 'is broadly that in questions between G. Britain & Foreign countries, foreign counties are always in the right & G. Britain always in the wrong.'[46] But, even given the 'delicate state of affairs' in domestic politics, where a statement by Harcourt on foreign policy might 'bring about the instant disruption or fall of the

[43] Lascelles to Kimberley, tels. 34 and 35, 4 and 5 Apr. 1895, FO 65/1494; Lascelles to Kimberley, disp. 88, 9 Apr. 1895, FO 65/1490, the following quotations are from the latter.

[44] Martel, *Imperial Diplomacy*, 240–2.

[45] Harcourt to Kimberley, 5 Apr. 1895, copy, Rosebery Papers, 10143.

[46] Rosebery to Kimberley, 5 Apr. 1895, Rosebery Papers, 10070.

Govt.', the prime minister was unwilling to accede to Harcourt's demands. In fact, as Rosebery made clear to his beleaguered foreign secretary, the prime minister would rather resign than allow Harcourt to shape foreign policy.[47]

This did not discourage Harcourt. In a letter that Kimberley termed 'ridiculous' and described as one 'which displays in its worst form his combined ignorance and arrogance in relation to foreign affairs', Harcourt insisted that Britain adopt a stance of 'absolute neutrality' with regard to the negotiations at Shimonoseki.[48] Mixing his metaphors as much as he muddled his thoughts, Harcourt argued the Britain should not pull Russian 'chestnuts out of the fire', especially as it was 'proverbially risky to attempt to take a bone out of the mouth of a hungry dog, and especially such a dog as Japan'.

Kimberley still had to determine British policy. After meeting with both the Russian and German ambassadors, he outlined his concerns to Rosebery on 6 April.[49] There were two questions to be answered: '1. shall we give advice to Japan? 2. if that advice is not followed are we prepared to enforce it?' The first question had two ramifications. The British government could advise Japan either not to annexe Liaotung or not not extend the annexation beyond the peninsula itself. Neither course seemed practical. A limitation of the territory annexed would not reduce the threat either to Peking or to Korea. If Japan rebuffed a British suggestion not to annexe the peninsula at all, 'we could not accept it . . . [and] we might then have to employ force, a most grave step'. These considerations pointed towards non-interference, but Kimberley was aware that such a policy might result either in 'a break up of the Chinese dynasty' or in the creation of a Chinese state 'under the virtual domination of Japan'. Kimberley put little faith in the Japanese assurance that they would respect Korea's autonomy, and argued that a meeting of the Cabinet to determine British policy was essential. The prime minister agreed, but felt that some points were obvious: 'We cannot go to war with Japan unless she directly and immediately threatens British interests. This second indisputable truth is a sure guide to principle. Method requires more consideration.'[50] The Cabinet meeting was set for 8 April 1895.

The Cabinet's decision—that 'H.M. Govt. have no grounds for interference'— must have given Harcourt the illusion that his was the decisive voice.[51] But this decision resulted from the views of those more intimately involved in making foreign policy. When Lascelles had first been approached by Lobanov about

[47] Rosebery to Kimberley, secret, 7 Apr. 1895, Rosebery Papers, 10070.
[48] Kimberley to Rosebery, confidential, 7 Apr. 1895, Rosebery Papers, 10070; Harcourt to Kimberley, 6 Apr. 1895, copy, Rosebery Papers, 10143.
[49] Kimberley to Rosebery, 6 Apr. 1895, Rosebery Papers, 10070.
[50] Rosebery to Kimberley, 6 Apr. 1895, copy, Rosebery Papers, 10070.
[51] Kimberley to Lascelles, tel. 45, 8 Apr. 1895, FO 65/1493.

Britain's possible intervention against the Japanese terms, the British ambassador had stated that 'personally I did not think England would make war on Japan'.[52] Kimberley's doubts about intervention are outlined above, and Rosebery had told his foreign minister the day before the Cabinet meeting that 'the line for us to take up [is] that the Japanese terms are not, under the circumstances, unreasonable'.[53] There were also general foreign-policy reasons for such an approach. Grey's speech about the Nile had been overtly anti-French, with the threat of military force behind it; thus, it was not the time to take on further, possibly military, commitments in Asia.[54]

The Russians did not like the British decision. In London, Staal called at the Foreign Office on both 8 and 9 April. On his first visit, he suggested that the powers 'might express their opinion in the most friendly manner to Japan that the acquisition of Port Arthur would be both a permanent menace to peace in the Far East and obstacle to good relations between Japan and China'.[55] Informed of the British Cabinet's decision not to interfere, Staal returned the next day with reinforcements. The German ambassador, Count Paul von Hatzfeldt, 'pressed' on Kimberley that the support of Germany and 'probably France' for Russia's call for intervention 'created a new situation'.[56] In St Petersburg, similar pressure was applied. On 8 April, when Lobanov was asked by Lascelles whether Russia would go to war to prevent Japan's taking the Liaotung peninsula, the Russian foreign minister replied only that it 'would be a very serious decision to take'. Two days later, Lobanov 'again expressed his regret' at the British decision.[57]

In London, although Kimberley fended off Hatzfeldt's suggestion, he did not do so without reconsidering the reasons for non-intervention.[58] The foreign secretary noted that when the issue had been discussed in Cabinet he had certainly considered that Russia might intervene without British support and 'that our separation from Russia would have an effect on our relations in Europe'. Even so, Kimberley could not see 'what advantage *we* should gain' by pressing Japan, nor was he 'much moved by the eagerness of Germany' to do so. 'On the whole', he concluded, 'I should be inclined to adhere to our decision.' This inclination was reinforced when the French also suggested that Britain advise Japan to revise her peace terms. Kimberley discerned wider motives in the French proposal: 'I perceived in his [the French ambassador's] language a marked desire that Russia[,]

[52] Lascelles to Kimberley, tel. 35, 5 Apr. 1895, FO 65/1494.
[53] Rosebery to Kimberley, confidential, 7 Apr. 1895, Kimberley Papers, 10243.
[54] Martel, *Imperial Diplomacy*, 240.
[55] Kimberley to Lascelles, secret tel. 46, 8 Apr. 1895, FO 65/1493.
[56] Kimberley to Rosebery, 9 Apr. 1895, Rosebery Papers, 10070.
[57] Lascelles to Kimberley, disp. 88, 9 Apr. 1895; Lascelles to Kimberley, secret and confidential disp. 89, 10 Apr. 1895, both FO 65/1490.
[58] Kimberley to Rosebery, 9 Apr. 1895, Rosebery Papers, 10070.

France and England should form a combination. Evidently he was looking more to Europe, and the advantage of diminishing our close relations with the Triple Alliance than to China and Japan.'[59] Since the mainspring of British policy had been to maintain a certain freedom of manœuvre between the Triple Alliance and the fledgling Dual Alliance of Russia and France, the French argument was unlikely to win much favour.

Rosebery agreed with Kimberley. But the prime minister was well aware that Russia must be treated with 'great delicacy' and that Britain should 'not shut the door with a clang, or indeed shut it at all'.[60] Instead, the Russians should be told politely, and with 'boundless expressions of regret', that while Britain was 'above all things anxious to act with Russia & the other Powers . . . we are convinced that popular feeling here would never permit a resort to arms even did we think it expedient'. Realizing the need to sooth Russian *amour propre*, Rosebery went so far as to write a note outlining the British position in order that Kimberley might 'show or read it to Staal'.[61] The note not only was full of 'boundless expressions of regret', but also contained the essence of why Britain refused to push the Japanese. There were three considerations. The first was that if the powers were to attempt to limit Japan's demands, they 'must be prepared to enforce . . . by warlike operations' such a decision on the Japanese forces. For Rosebery, such an extreme step was not warranted. The second consideration was closely related to the first. The prime minister felt that, 'considering the absolute and increasing success of the Japanese', the peace terms were 'not unreasonable'. Moreover, 'they are not so vitally injurious as to justify war'. Finally, Rosebery concluded, no 'amiable expression of opinion' by Britain to Japan would serve any purpose: the threat of force would be required and Britain was not prepared to take this step. A policy of bluff was untenable.

Not even Rosebery's concluding honeyed words, stressing his hope that 'a free interchange of views' between Britain and Russia would result in a continuance of 'close cooperation' between them, could sweeten Staal. The Russian ambassador refused to be mollified. Staal told Kimberley that 'our [the British] attitude must have a very unfavourable effect on our 'entente' generally with Russia which he greatly regrets. The party in Russia which has always been adverse to us, will now exclaim 'Just what we always told you, that England would leave us in the lurch whenever a pinch came." '[62] In St Petersburg, reaction was more muted, but still signalled a cooling in Anglo-Russian relations. Lobanov informed Lascelles that,

---

[59] Kimberley to Rosebery, 2nd, 9 Apr. 1895, Rosebery Papers, 10070.

[60] Rosebery to Kimberley, secret, 9 Apr. 1895, Rosebery Papers, 10070.

[61] Rosebery to Kimberley, 10 Apr. 1895; note by Rosebery, 10 Apr. 1895, both Kimberley Papers, 10243. Quotations from the latter.

[62] Kimberley to Rosebery, 10 Apr. 1895, Rosebery Papers, 10070.

while the British refusal was not unexpected, it was the Russian view that the British action would result in 'encourag[ing] the Japanese in their demands, [and] had greatly complicated the question'.[63] The chief of the Russian foreign office's Asiatic section, Count D. A. Kapnist, was more outspoken. He expressed what Lascelles termed 'vexation' at the British decision.[64] Russian unhappiness seemed ubiquitous.

Lascelles suspected hidden wellsprings. While the ambassador understood and even sympathized with the Russian arguments about the danger of the cession of the Liaotung peninsula, he did nor feel the Russian position to be disinterested. Citing Russia's 'notorious desire' for a warm-water port, Lascelles suggested that the Japanese move to take Port Arthur was seen more as a block to Russian aspirations than as a threat to either Korea or China.[65] The Russian determination to obtain a port, Lascelles feared, might lead to 'very serious complications'. 'Russia', he argued, 'would almost of necessity be compelled to resort to force' unless she could get sufficient compensation from Japan. In a speculative letter, Lascelles embroidered on this theme.[66] Neither 'love of China [n]or fear of Japan' could explain the Russian attitude, Lascelles opined. In addition to reiterating his suspicions about Russia's own desire and her probability of using force to obtain them, the ambassador suggested an equally unpleasant possibility: a Russo-Japanese agreement allotting Russia a port in the north of Korea as compensation for Japan's gains.

Russia's negative response to Britain's even-handed policy 'vexed' Rosebery, but the prime minister had no wish to separate British policy from that of Russia.[67] Realizing that 'we must remember Armenia & Central Asia even in the Far East', Rosebery informed his foreign secretary that, 'rather than separate from her [Russia]', Britain might join the Tsarist government in advising Japan to prolong the armistice. However, it must be made clear to Russia that such a step had been taken only 'to regain the confidence and cordiality of Russia'. At a luncheon with Staal on 13 April, Rosebery put the British case forward.[68] The prime minister's exposition was an ingenious mixture of *realpolitik* and special pleading. Rosebery reiterated the contention that joint representation at Tokyo would be futile and that 'public feeling' in Britain would not allow the government to pursue the alternative course of armed intervention. He then expounded on the particular difficulties posed by Cabinet government. Perhaps, he admitted, the Cabinet should not simply have rejected the Russian proposal that Britain join in coercing Japan, but rather should

---

[63] Lascelles to Kimberley, secret tel. 38, 10 Apr. 1895, FO 65/1494.
[64] Lascelles to Kimberley, disp. 91, 10 Apr. 1895, FO 65/1490.
[65] Lascelles to Kimberley, secret and confidential disp. 89, 10 Apr. 1895, FO 65/1490.
[66] Lascelles to Sanderson, 11 Apr. 1895, Lascelles Papers, FO 800/17.
[67] Rosebery to Kimberley, secret, 11 Apr. 1895, copy, Rosebery Papers, 10134.
[68] Rosebery to Lascelles, 13 Apr. 1895, Lascelles Papers, FO 800/16.

have 'asked a question [of Russia]: "In the event of the failure of the representations what steps do you propose to adopt?" ' But this would have meant another Cabinet session to consider the Russian reply and further questions also requiring answers: in all, 'a slow & unsatisfactory process'. But, Russia should not view Britain as unfriendly, for 'I attach the greatest importance to our joint action, & would willingly prove my sense of it if a practicable opportunity offered'.

The intransigence shown on both the Russian and Japanese sides worried Rosebery. By 16 April the prime minister was afraid that the situation could escalate either into a partition of China or into a 'war between Japan & several of the Western Powers',[69] This apprehension was increased the following day when it was announced that Japan had forced the Chinese government into signing the Treaty of Shimonoseki.[70] Two days later, the Russian government notified the British that a joint French, Russian, and German note was to be given to the Japanese, a note calling on the latter to renounce her claim to the Liaotung peninsula. The British government was again invited to join in this triple intervention.[71] The Russian proposal tested the assurances that Rosebery had made to Staal at their luncheon date. On 21 and 22 April Lobanov stated quite bluntly that, while Russia 'understood' the British position, she was convinced that Japan would back down before the united European powers.[72] Further, Lobanov believed that there was 'no doubt that the decision of Her Majesty's government was an encouragement to Japan . . . and made the situation much more difficult'. Little augured well either for close Anglo-Russian relations or for Britain's diplomatic position generally. Rosebery saw this in sharp relief. '[B]oth Russia and Germany', he wrote on 22 April, 'are disgusted with us for not pulling their Chinese chestnuts out of the fire'.[73] The situation was 'pregnant with possibilities of a disastrous kind; and it might indeed result in an Armageddon between the European Powers struggling for the ruins of the Chinese Empire'. With the Armenian situation (see below) threatening a worldwide call on British resources, Rosebery concluded that 'for me the first necessity is a concentration of power. We must not scatter ourselves: we must be ready at any moment to place our full force in one or both of the regions affected by the Eastern Questions.' Events in the Far East would prove to be the key to the situation.

Such worries must have informed the deliberations of the British cabinet on 23 April. With people like Harcourt firmly opposed to any British interference in the Far East and with the inherent naval and military difficulties involved in pursuing

[69] Rosebery to Sanderson, secret, 16 Apr. 1895, Rosebery Papers, 10070.

[70] I. H. Nish, *The Anglo-Japanese Alliance: The Diplomacy of Two Island Empires 1894–1907* (London, 1966), 26–31.

[71] Lascelles to Kimberley, tel. 43, 19 Apr. 1895, FO 65/1494.

[72] Lascelles to Kimberley, confidential disp. 107, 22 Apr. 1895, FO 65/1490.

[73] Rosebery to Lord Cromer (British agent and consul-general, Egypt), secret, 22 Apr. 1895, Rosebery Papers, 10136.

any intervention there, the government decided to adhere to its previous position. The British non-compliance with the other Powers' message to Japan was communicated directly to Russia.[74] For the next ten days, the British found themselves at the center of an intense lobbying effort. On the one hand, the Russians continued to press Kimberley to add the British imprimatur to the powers'note. On the other, the Japanese attempted to swing the British to a position of disapproval. The Russian efforts were often of a dubious nature. On 24 April, both Lobanov in St Petersburg and Staal in London suggested that 'England should support the diplomatic action of the other Powers on the distinct but secret understanding that she should withdraw if other than diplomatic action became necessary'.[75] Kimberley turned down both this scheme and Lascelles' idea that Britain privately inform Japan of the serious consequences of refusing the Powers' request. As the foreign secretary told his ambassador to Russia, the British government 'could not risk the eventuality, which under present circumstances they consider extremely probable if not certain, of the communication being ignored by Japan'.[76]

The Japanese lobbying efforts were no more successful.[77] Rosebery was not obdurately opposed to joining Japan, but there was no sufficient '*inducement*' to do so.[78] Thus, he continued, 'our policy is quite simple and sincere. We have pursued a benevolent neutrality all along, watching carefully on behalf of our own interests.' Such hypocrisy aside, Rosebery informed Kimberley to advise the Japanese than while the British 'admire the qualities that Japan has displayed and wish her well . . . that we fear her answer will not satisfy the Powers . . . that our great interest is peace; and that we are convinced that Russia at any rate is in earnest'. In order to ensure that the simplicity and sincerity of British policy was appreciated properly, Kimberley also informed the Russians of this communication.[79] Denied any support by the British, on 4 May the Japanese government capitulated, and renounced any claim to the Liaotung peninsula.[80] Lobanov was quick to give credit to the British for their last-minute admonitions to the Japanese. He told Lascelles on 6 May that the Russian government recognized the 'loyalty and straightforwardness' of Britain in the affair, and accepted that the Japanese decision was 'in great measure due to the advice' that Kimberley had given to Japan.[81] This was the public attitude. In reality, the differences over the treaty of Shimonoseki had demonstrated that Anglo-Russian interests in the Far East were

[74] Kimberley to Lascelles, tel. 57, 23 Apr. 1895, FO 65/1493.
[75] Lascelles to Kimberley, 24 Apr. 1895, Lascelles Papers, FO 800/17; Lascelles to Kimberley, 24 Apr., tel. 47, FO 65/1494; Kimberley to Lascelles, disp. 118A, 24 Apr. 1895, FO 65/1489.
[76] Kimberley to Lascelles, tel. 63, 25 Apr. 1895, FO 65/1493.
[77] Nish, *Anglo-Japanese Alliance*, 29–30.
[78] Rosebery to Kimberley, confidential, 28 Apr. 1895, copy, Rosebery Papers, 10070.
[79] Lascelles to Kimberley, tel. 51, 2 May 1895, FO 65/1494; Lascelles to Kimberley, confidential disp. 120, 7 May 1895, FO 65/1491.
[80] Nish, *Anglo-Japanese Alliance*, 32–5.
[81] Lascelles to Kimberley, disp. 119, 7 May 1895, FO 65/1491.

not necessarily congruent, although they might be compatible under certain circumstances.

This did not escape the British. On 1 May, Kimberley wrote a perceptive analysis to Lascelles. 'I am afraid', the foreign secretary penned, 'your relations with Lobanoff must suffer by our not joining Russia in her remonstrance to Japan, and we most sincerely regret that we could not go with her in the matter.[82] However, Kimberley went on, British interests were not imperilled by the Japanese terms. While the Liaotung peninsula was the bone of contention for the Russians, the 'cession of Formosa touches us much more nearly' and even that was insufficient to justify a British intervention. Only should Wei-hai-wei be taken by the Japanese would the British be concerned, for this would 'cut . . . the [Chinese] Empire in half and they [the Japanese] would be in inconvenient proximity to Shanghai and the great trade routes of the Yangtse River'. As such a Japanese acquisition seemed unlikely, and as the Foreign Office had 'not heard a word' from British trade interests about the commercial aspects of the Japanese demands on China, the British position was fixed, at whatever the cost in Russian displeasure.

For the moment, any considerable upheaval in Anglo-Russian relations over the Far East had been avoided. However, this avoidance had not stemmed from the efforts of either the British or the Russian governments. While each had been eager to appear to be co-operating with the other, neither had been willing to give up its goals or compromise its interests in the region for the sake of good relations with the other. Only the Japanese decision to give in to the three-power note had allowed the gap between the Russian and British positions to be bridged, and such an occurrence could not be counted upon in the future. In the spring of 1895, the potential for an Anglo-Russian quarrel in the Far East remained large.

The resolution of the Sino-Japanese War and the collapse of the Liberal government occurred nearly simultaneously. In June 1895, Lord Salisbury, 'somewhat against my will', as he informed George Curzon, returned to the Foreign Office in the joint guise of prime minister and foreign secretary.[83] Salisbury found that the Eastern Question, long at the center of his career, had risen again, this time in Armenia.[84] For the next eighteen months, Salisbury struggled to solve this problem. Co-operation with Russia seemed the most logical means of achieving

[82] Kimberley to Lascelles, 1 May 1895, Lascelles Papers, FO 800/16.

[83] Salisbury to Curzon, 27 July 1895, Curzon Papers, MSS Eur F112/1a.

[84] M. S. Anderson, *The Eastern Question 1774–1923: A Study in International Relations* (London, 1966); J. A. S. Grenville, *Lord Salisbury and Foreign Policy: The Close of the Nineteenth Century* (London, 1964), 24–53, 74–89; A. O. Sarkissian, 'Concert Diplomacy and the Armenians, 1890–7', in id. (ed.), *Studies in Diplomatic History and Historiography in Honour of G. P. Gooch* (London, 1961), 48–75; M. M. Jefferson, 'Lord Salisbury and the Eastern Question, 1890–8', *SEER* 39 (1960), 44–60; R. Douglas, 'Britain and the Armenian Question, 1894–7', *HJ* 19 (1976), 113–33; J. Salt, 'Britain, the Armenian Question and the Cause of Ottoman Reform: 1894–6', *MES* 26 (1990), 308–28.

a solution; however, as had been the case in the Sino–Japanese War, differences in national interests prevented Britain and Russia from working together smoothly.

Salisbury inherited the Armenian problem. Since 1893, there had been rumours of Turkish atrocities against the Armenians, opening what Harcourt termed 'a very ugly aspect' in Anglo–Turkish relations.[85] By December 1894, the rumours had become facts, as the Turkish authorities moved with savagery against the Armenians in the *vilayet* of Bitlis (in south-eastern Turkey). When Kimberley raised the issue of Armenia with Staal, the foreign secretary was met with some indifference. Replete with her own minority group of Armenians the Russian government, 'would not be disposed to do anything at the present time'.[86] The British could not accept this position. The reported massacres of Armenians at Talori had received widespread press coverage in Britain, and the Cabinet had decided late in November 1894 to 'take a strong attitude' about them.[87] Equally, Harcourt attacked both Kimberley and Sir Philip Currie, the British ambassador at Constantinople, for their inaction in the matter. With Armenian affairs tied to British domestic politics, Kimberley moved to have the British consul at Erzerum accompany a Turkish commission of enquiry into the Bitlis massacre. In an attempt to maintain a close working relationship with the Russians, Kimberley enquired whether Russia, too, wished to send her consul. Russian reluctance was evident. Faced with a 'flabby' Russian reply, Kimberley decided on 26 December not to embarrass the Russians by sending the British consul.[88] Instead, he reserved the right to send the consul, and, to placate his domestic critics, Kimberley arranged for a team of British delegates to accompany the Commission.

By March 1895 it was evident that the Bitlis Commission had failed. This was no surprise to Lobanov, who had 'never entertained' much hope for the investigation.[89] The Russians could maintain such an Olympian attitude; the British could not. Faced with pressure from groups like the Women's Liberal and Temperance Associations, the government was 'very hotly pressed' about Armenia.[90] Besides, as Sanderson remarked, 'after what has happened, and with the reports we have as to the intolerable state of things, we cannot without dishonour allow the question to drop'. Domestic pressure and possible dishonour proved irresistible. The British

[85] Harcourt to [Sanderson], note, 5 May 1894, Sanderson Papers, FO 800/1.
[86] Kimberley to Lascelles, disp. 344, 12 Dec. 1894, FO 65/1471.
[87] Cabinet conclusion, 27 Nov. 1894, cited Douglas, 'Britain and the Armenian Question', 117, 115–18; P. Marsh, 'Lord Salisbury and the Ottoman Massacres', *JBS* 11 (1972), 63–84.
[88] Minutes by Sanderson (25 Dec.) and Kimberley (26 Dec.) on Lascelles to Kimberley, tel. 137, 24 Dec. 1894, FO 65/1474.
[89] Lascelles to Kimberley, disp. 59, 13 Mar. 1895, FO 65/1490.
[90] Sanderson to Rosebery, 12 Mar. 1895, Rosebery Papers, 10134; Sanderson to Lascelles, 29 Mar. 1895, Lascelles Papers, FO 800/16; quotation from the latter; A. Nassibian, *Britain and the Armenian Question 1915–23* (London, 1984), 44–6.

managed to get the Tsarist government to agree that the British, Russian, and French ambassadors at Constantinople should work together in an attempt to draw up a proposal for reforms in the Ottoman empire. By the end of March, the Russians had agreed that reforms must be attempted, but Lobanov tended to dwell on the difficulties of the problem, rather than on the possibility of solution.[91]

During April and early May 1895, Kimberley's attention was diverted from Armenia by the Sino-Japanese War. It was clear that the two matters were intertwined and that the common thread was Russia. Describing the situation in the Ottoman empire as one that 'has so long been a terror to European statesmen', Rosebery went on to speak of the 'unprecedented' fact that Britain was faced simultaneously with two 'Eastern Questions'.[92] Both in the Far and Near East, Anglo-Russian co-operation held the key to success. Such co-operation was as difficult to achieve over Armenia as it was over China. However, by the beginning of May 1895, the Armenian issue again demanded to be heard. This resulted from the fact that the three ambassadors—British, French, and Russian—had managed to reach common ground on 19 April. Lobanov's response was cautious. The reform programme, he informed Lascelles on 8 May, was too broad and could be carried out only 'by direct interference in the internal affairs' of the Ottoman empire.[93] This Lobanov was reluctant to do, but he emphasized that this was only his personal opinion; the views of the Russian government would be forthcoming.

A fortnight later, and despite the fact that the ambassadors already had presented the Sultan with the reform programme on 11 May, Lobanov made it clear that the official Russian position was close to that which he had adumbrated to Lascelles. The Russian stance was based on domestic considerations. There was 'great agitation among the Armenians in Russia, who were purchasing arms, and were in communication with the Armenian Committees in London and elsewhere'.[94] This worried Lobanov. Lascelles summed up the situation neatly on 22 May:

The Russians can scarcely be expected to wish that the Armenians in Turkish territory should enjoy greater liberty than the Armenians in Russian territory and they are therefore not likely to press seriously on the Porte reforms which they are not prepared to grant to their own subjects. From the beginning Lobanoff has been, to say the least, lukewarm about Armenian reforms and I am afraid that the prospect of a general insurrection in Asia Minor will make him positively cold.[95]

On 4 June, Lobanov erased any doubts about Russia's stance. The Sultan's

[91] Lascelles to Kimberley, 28 Mar. 1895, Lascelles Papers, FO 800/17.

[92] Rosebery to Lord Cromer (British Agent and Consul-General, Egypt), secret, 22 Apr. 1895, Rosebery Papers, 10136.

[93] Lascelles to Kimberley, disp. 124 confidential, 8 May 1895, FO 65/1491.

[94] Lascelles to Kimberley, disp. 132, confidential, 22 May 1895; Lascelles to Kimberley, disp. 136, confidential, 24 May 1895, both FO 65/1491.

[95] Lascelles to Sanderson, 22 May 1895, Lascelles Papers, FO 800/17.

rejection of the reforms (which had taken place the previous day) did not justify 'using threatening language' to the Porte and the Russian government 'would certainly not join in any coercive measures'.[96] Lascelles reported privately just how hostile the Russian foreign minister was to the idea of coercion.[97] 'I have rather softened down', Lascelles wrote, 'than exaggerated his language. He is full of wrath against the Armenian Committee in London, who, he is convinced, is working for a resolution, which it is evident Russia, on account of her geographical position, must prevent.'[98] This meant, Lascelles concluded, that 'we cannot hope for much support from him in pressing the reforms upon the Sultan'.

The combination of Lobanov's hostility and the appointment of a new Grand Vizier by the Sultan temporarily mollified the British. The Cabinet, in any case just a fortnight away from resignation and riven with internal squabbling, approved a policy of temporization.[99] In the interim, Kimberley attempted to make the British position clear to both Staal and Lobanov.[100] First, he emphasized that British policy towards Armenia was not 'being swayed by the agitators who press that "Armenia" should be . . . practically an autonomous State'. Second, he pointed out that British policy was against the formation of such a state. Finally, Kimberley ventilated his fear that the Sultan would be able to 'snap his fingers at the Powers', secure in the knowledge that Russia would not move against him. While this might be so, it would be disastrous for the Sultan to be aware of it, for he might then act so as to inflame the situation, yielding 'the re-opening of the Eastern Question in an acute form'. Kimberley concluded that Britain and Russia should continue to work together, despite the fundamental differences in their attitudes towards coercing Turkey. This, and the advent to power of Salisbury, softened Lobanov's unhappiness with the British.[101] But Russia's basic position remained unchanged.[102] Salisbury began to cast around for a solution to the Armenian entanglement. His first thought was to intimidate the Sultan through a show of naval force. While a British fleet was moved to Salonika, other schemes involving gunboats on the Tigris and a naval display at Jeddah on the Red Sea were not implemented: in any case, the Sultan remained uncowed.[103] Salisbury thus turned to co-operation with Russia as a means of ending the Armenian imbroglio. As Salisbury wrote to his ambassador

---

[96] Lascelles to Kimberley, tel., 4 June 1895, FO 65/1494.

[97] Lascelles to Kimberley, disp. 142, confidential, 4 June 1895, FO 65/1491.

[98] Lascelles to Kimberley, 6 June 1895, Lascelles Papers, FO 800/17.

[99] Kimberley to Lascelles, draft tel. 106, 11 June 1895, FO 65/1493; P. Stansky, *Ambitions and Strategies: The Struggle for the Leadership of the Liberal Party in the 1890s* (Oxford, 1964), ch. 3; R. Rhodes James, *The British Revolution: British Politics, 1880–1939* (2 vols.; London, 1976), i, *From Gladstone to Asquith. 1880–1914*, 148–55.

[100] Kimberley to Lascelles, 25 June 1895, Lascelles Papers, FO 800/16.

[101] Lascelles to Kimberley, 3 July 1895, Lascelles Papers, FO 800/17.

[102] Lascelles to Salisbury, 3 July 1895, Salisbury Papers, A129.

[103] Grenville, *Lord Salisbury*, 28–9.

in Constantinople at the end of July, 'the key of the situation lies with Russia'.[104] Lobanov proved a jealous turnkey. Sanderson noted at the beginning of July: 'Prince Lobanov continues to be very suspicious of our intentions. He has a nightmare of what he calls an Armenian Bulgaria just outside the Russian frontier.'[105] Salisbury did his best to dispel this nightmare. On 26 July, the prime minister informed Lobanov that the British were not 'urging & do not desire the bestowal of any privileges on the Armenians, but merely justice & the security of life & property'.[106] On 27 July, Salisbury outlined British policy.[107] Noting that he had waited until the present 'in the hopes of our being able to get something out of the Turk', Salisbury enumerated the British desiderata with respect to Armenia:

There are two things we want of Russia in this matter. The first is that she will believe us, that we have no intention whatever of setting up any form of Armenian autonomy—or indeed creating any sort of privileged province . . . We want nothing but moderate security & good government. The other thing we want of her is that she will make up her own mind (& confide the result to us) how far she is prepared to go if the Sultan is utterly obdurate. Is she prepared for any form of coercion? There are of course many grades of coercion from the appearance of three gunboats, belonging to the three Powers, under the windows of Yldiz [the imperial palace at Constantinople], to the less romantic but more lucrative resource of confiscating the proceeds of the Smyrna Customs House. If Russia is adverse to any form of coercion in any case—will she object to the exercise of it by her allies—or even ally? For matters are getting to that point that we must consider how we are to get out of the very boggy lane of policy with which our finer feelings have beguiled us.

By 5 August, with the ambassadors reporting that the Sultan was likely to remain obdurate, Salisbury became more pressing about the need to remove British policy from the boggy lane.

In a telegram to Lascelles, the prime minister pointed out that 'it is now very important to ascertain from Russia how far she is prepared to go in pressing the Sultan. I do not think diplomatic steps will be of much further use.'[108] This blunt telegram forced Lobanov's hand, and made him speak his true thoughts.[109] On 9 August, Lobanov again rejected the proposed reforms in Armenia as 'unworkable', and stated that the Emperor found the idea of the use of force by the

[104] Salisbury to Currie, 27 July 1895, Salisbury Papers, A138.

[105] Undated minute (*c*.8 July 1895), Sanderson, on Lascelles to Salisbury, disp. 173 confidential, FO 65/1491.

[106] Salisbury to Lascelles, draft tel. 138, 26 July 1895, FO 65/1493.

[107] Salisbury to Lascelles, 27 July 1895, Salisbury Papers, A129; partially cited, Grenville, *Lord Salisbury*, 30; Marsh, 'Lord Salisbury', 77–8.

[108] Salisbury to Lascelles, tel. 146, 5 Aug. 1895, FO 65/1493.

[109] Lascelles to Sanderson, 30 July 1895, Lascelles Papers, FO 800/17.

three powers against Turkey 'personally repugnant'.[110] In fact, such action by any single power would be 'equally distasteful' to the Russian government. Lobanov then attempted to honeycoat this blunt refusal. The Russian foreign minister noted that he was pleased that the two governments had the same ends—'moderate security and good government'—in mind for Armenia, and added that he appreciated the fact that Salisbury had ignored the public clamour on behalf of the Armenians.[111]

Lobanov left Salisbury no policy. With Russian co-operation unattainable and naval force either ineffective or unworkable, Salisbury was trying to make bricks without straw. And, the Armenian question had other ramifications. The visit of the German Kaiser to Cowes, beginning on 5 August, added a new dimension.[112] Wilhelm II, due to the misrepresentations of Salisbury's position by the German ambassador to Britain, suggested a partition of the Ottoman empire to the prime minister. Salisbury was not completely adverse to the idea, but recognized that such a course was not practical: Austrian and Russian sensibilities needed to be considered. This left little but bluff and bluster. On 15 August, when Parliament convened, Salisbury spoke harshly of Turkish actions.[113] The speech had little effect on the Turks, but stirred some action in Russia.

By the end of August, Lobanov was moving in favour of an idea that Salisbury had bruited earlier in the month: the creation of 'some sort of "mécanisme de surveillance"' to oversee reform in Turkey.[114] But Salisbury was not impressed with the vague verbal commitments that the Sultan made to such an idea. On 11 September, the prime minister put the matter fully to Lascelles:

There are two methods of attaining this end [a solution to the Armenian problem]. One is that advised by the Ambassadors, which consists in requiring that a proportion of the functionaries of all sorts should be Christians: and that where the high officials are of one religion they should have an assessor of the other. The other consists in allowing the present Moslem machinery to go on under the inspection of a Commission resident in the province, consisting partially of European commissioners, who should be able to report abuses to the Ambassadors. This was our suggestion.

Salisbury concluded that: 'We are willing to negotiate on one or the other form of

---

[110] Lascelles to Salisbury, disp. 196, confidential, 9 Aug. 1895, FO 65/1491.

[111] Lascelles to Salisbury, disp. 197, confidential, 9 Aug. 1895, FO 65/1491; Lascelles to Salisbury, 14 Aug. 1895, Salisbury Papers, A129. Quotation from the latter.

[112] Grenville, *Lord Salisbury*, 31–43; Jefferson, 'Lord Salisbury', 48–51; cf. C. J. Lowe, *The Reluctant Imperialists: British Foreign Policy 1878–1902* (2 vols.; London, 1967), i. 197–8.

[113] *Parl Debs*, 4th ser., vol. 36, cols. 45–52, 15 Aug. 1895.

[114] Lascelles to Salisbury, disp. 196, confidential, 9 Aug. 1895; Lascelles to Salisbury, disp. 209, confidential, 28 Aug. 1895, both FO 65/1491; Salisbury to Lascelles, tel. 164, 1 Sept. 1895, FO 65/1493; Lascelles to Salisbury, disp. 219, confidential, 10 Sept. 1895, FO 65/1492.

guarantees: but at present we have no definite offer of either.'[115] Lobanov shared
Salisbury's anxiety, but did not feel that the Sultan's verbal commitment should be
ignored. Instead, the Russian foreign minister made it clear that 'he thinks it
entirely our fault or rather Philip Currie's that the question has not been settled
before this'.[116]

The situation filled Salisbury with some despair as to Anglo–Russian relations.
Faced with the awkward task of rejecting the German proposal for a partition of the
Ottoman Empire without offending the Kaiser's sensitivities, the prime minister
decided that his policy of co-operation with Russia was bankrupt. He made this
clear to Lascelles: '[w]e may, & I hope shall, retain the friendship of Germany: but
I see very little hope of regaining the friendship of Russia.'[117] The irreconcilable
point between Britain and Russia was Armenia. The prime minister had even
begun to suspect bad faith: 'Russia I fear has become very lukewarm in her
support,—& is probably working against us secretly at C[onstantino]ple. Whether
Lobanoff or Nelidoff [the Russian ambassador at Constantinople] is the sinner I am
not sufficiently informed to be able to guess.' Feeling that Lobanov 'never was
serious from the first—& that the only thing he & his Govt. cared about was the
prevention of too much excitement in their Armenians', Salisbury was prepared to
await a solution: as the Russians wished for peace among their Armenians, 'delay is
consequently one of our weapons'.

The events of October took away this tactic. A renewal of the atrocities against
the Armenians raised a storm of public indignation in Britain. With Gladstone
fulminating against the government's inactivity, Salisbury informed the Russian
government on 23 October that Britain 'trust[ed] that instructions will be sent to
the Ambassadors of the other Powers to join in impressing upon the Porte the
necessity of issuing the most stringent orders to prevent any repetition' of the
massacres.[118] To underline the seriousness of the British concern, Salisbury informed the British chargé d'affaires in St Petersburg, W. E. Goschen, that the
Admiralty were likely to send British warships to Turkey.

This raised two issues: the first military; the second political. Threatening the
Porte with a naval intervention naturally invoked the matter of a Russian response.
Since Russia had made it clear that she was opposed to any attempt to coerce the
Turks, was she capable of opposing it? On this, British military and naval opinion
was firm and consistent. In March 1892, a joint report by the directors of military
and naval intelligence had concluded that Britain alone was unable to prevent

[115] Salisbury to Lascelles, tel. 178, 11 Sept. 1895, FO 65/1493.
[116] Lascelles to Salisbury, 17 Sept. 1895, Lascelles Papers, FO 800/17.
[117] Salisbury to Lascelles, 17 Sept. 1895, Lascelles Papers, FO 800/16.
[118] Salisbury to W. E. Goschen (British chargé d'affaires, St Petersburg), tel. 208, 23 Oct. 1895, FO
65/1493; see R. T. Shannon, *Gladstone and the Bulgarian Agitation 1876* (London, 1963).

Russia from seizing Constantinople.[119] When this same issue had been raised again in October 1894, the conclusion was the same, and it was noted that all Britain could do in retaliation was to seize Gallipoli.[120] This was reiterated on 12 November 1895 by the director of naval intelligence (DNI).[121] The political issues were two-fold: would the other European powers, particularly Russia, now join in coercing the Turks and would the British Cabinet support Salisbury's intention to do so; if need be, alone? In answering these questions, the exact chronology of events is crucial.

Since the beginning of the Armenian crisis, Salisbury's policy had two aims. The first was to persuade—force if necessary—the Turks to reform. The second was to achieve this reform in harmony with Russia. The summer and autumn of 1895 had demonstrated that the first was unlikely without the second. The obvious need was for a lever of some sort with which to compel the Russians to join with Britain. In July and August, Salisbury had repeatedly refused Currie's suggestion to send the fleet unilaterally, all the while trying to get the Russians to agree to joint action. This had failed. So, beginning in August, Salisbury began to threaten the Turks with a British action at Jeddah (on the Red Sea), choosing that spot because, as Jeddah was outside the Mediterranean, an attack there would not challenge Russia's interests at Constantinople directly.[122] But there were other intents. First, so doing might coerce the Sultan into making a firm commitment to reform and solve the entire issue. Second, it might jar the Russians and bring about a change in their policy. The latter was a strong possibility, because British armed interven-tion might result in 'bring[ing] down the Turkish Empire with a run', an event that would likely result in a full-scale revolt of all Armenians (including those in Russia).[123] For her own sake, then, Russia might be forced to take action in concert with Britain. This explains Salisbury's belief in mid-September that 'delay is consequently one of our weapons'.

While the massacres of October temporarily had eliminated Salisbury's Fabian policy, they had brought about new opportunities. First, on 17 October the Sultan had agreed to undertake the reforms suggested by the ambassadors. Second, Lobanov's continued discounting of the possibility that these reforms would actu-ally occur and consequent concern that the civil disturbances in the Ottoman empire

---

[119] Lowe, *Reluctant Imperialists*, ii. 85–91.

[120] Untitled memo, Colonel Sir John Ardagh (the future director of military intelligence—DMI), Oct. 1894, with a covering note, E. F. Chapman (the incumbent DMI), 20 Nov. 1894, Rosebery Papers, 10135.

[121] A. J. Marder, *The Anatomy of British Sea Power* (London, 1942), 247–8.

[122] K. Wilson, 'Constantinople or Cairo: Lord Salisbury and the Partition of the Ottoman Empire 1886–97', in id. (ed.), *Empire and Continent: Studies in British Foreign Policy from the 1880s to the First World War* (London, 1987), 16–17; cf. C. J. Lowe, *Salisbury and the Mediterranean 1886–96* (London, 1965), 101.

[123] Salisbury to Currie, 27 Aug. 1895, cited, Wilson, 'Constantinople or Cairo', 17.

would spread to Russia gave Salisbury a possibility to attract the Russians.[124] In a speech at the Guildhall on 9 November, the prime minister threatened the Sultan on behalf of the Concert of Europe, although carefully ensuring that the details of the threat remained vague.[125] The invitation was obvious. Russia should join Britain in coercing the Turks and hence end her problems with her own Armenian minority.

The speech had unexpected benefits. On 11 November, the Austrian foreign minister, Count Agenor Goluchowski, proposed that Britain, Russia, and Austria should force the Straits.[126] Here was the possibility for which Salisbury had hoped. The following day, the DNI's report, mentioned above, made the situation more obvious. Since Russia could not be denied the Straits by British efforts alone, since continued unrest in the Ottoman empire ran the risk of creating such an uproar that Russia might decide to act against Turkey unilaterally, and since Salisbury did not wish Russia to be able to present the powers with a *fait accompli* at Constantinople, a joint effort by the three powers would serve Salisbury's purposes splendidly. Salisbury's intentions were thwarted by two interconnected facts. First, Lobanov proclaimed himself hostile to the Austrian proposal.[127] As he informed the British chargé d'affaires, the powers must support the Sultan in his attempt to carry out the reforms. A failure to do so would only weaken the Sultan's domestic grip and encourage further revolts. And, in a pointed remark aimed at Salisbury's veiled support for the Armenians, Lobanov observed that '[m]y experience in the East tells me that such disturbances as are now taking place soon die a natural death, except in cases when the opposing elements are stirred up to continued activity by some Power for her own political interests'. The second barrier to Salisbury was the attitude of his own Cabinet. Led by the first lord of the admiralty and a significant number of ministers, the general view was that forcing the Straits was too hazardous except in conjunction with the other powers. In particular, the Cabinet was opposed to giving Currie *carte blanche* to call up the fleet.[128] With Lobanov's outright refusal of Russian support—which soon yielded Austria's dropping her proposal for joint intervention—Salisbury's policy was dead in the water. It was clear, even to the Liberal opposition, that the concert of Europe 'only exists on paper & upon condition that it is not to be turned to any practical purpose'.[129] Salisbury's frustration was evident. The prime minister termed 'theological' Gos-

---

[124] W. E. Goschen to Salisbury, disp. 235, confidential, 4 Nov. 1895, FO 65/1492.

[125] *The Times*, 10 Nov. 1895.

[126] Lowe, *Salisbury and the Mediterranean*, 101–2; F. R. Bridge, *From Sadowa to Sarajevo: The Foreign Policy of Austria-Hungary, 1866–1914* (London, 1972), 213–16.

[127] Lowe, *Salisbury and the Mediterranean*, 102; W. E. Goschen to Salisbury, disp. 270, confidential, 20 Nov. 1895, FO 65/1492.

[128] Wilson, 'Constantinople or Cairo'; Marsh, 'Lord Salisbury', 79–80; T. J. Spinner, Jr., *George Joachim Goschen: The Transformation of a Victorian Liberal* (London, 1973), 198–9.

chen's easy acceptance of the Admiralty's contention that the Royal Navy could not force the Straits, and added that in such circumstances: 'The Eastern question may be summed up thus. It is impossible to mend the lot of the Armenians without coercing or deposing the Sultan. It is impossible to get at the Sultan without quarrelling with Russia, Turkey, France and (now) Austria. So there is *no* practical course open at present.'[130] Salisbury would have to wait for new circumstances to find a solution to the Armenian issue.

Was Salisbury aiming at a partition of the Ottoman empire in 1895? Aspects of his policy are consistent with this interpretation and there is no doubt that the Germans believed this to be so both in the summer of 1895 and again in December of that year. Salisbury was willing to run the risk of a dissolution of the Ottoman realm in order to end the Armenian problem. But the prime minister was not willing to give Constantinople to the Russians. Salisbury's real attachment to the value of Austria as a British ally, and his feeling that Austria 'would [not] acquiesce in any portion of the Straits being surrendered to Russia', made him wish to ensure that any collapse of the Ottoman empire did not begin with a Russian seizure of Constantinople.[131] This would have changed the entire naval balance in the Mediterranean to the benefit of Russia and the detriment of Britain. In 1892, when his military advisors had stated that Britain could no longer hold the Straits against a Russian *coup de main*, Salisbury had concluded that this necessitated removing the British fleet from the Mediterranean and Britain's disavowing any intention to defend Constantinople.[132] But such drastic measures had not been necessary in 1892, and Salisbury was loath to consider anything in 1895 that would give Russia such an advantage.

Among the permanent officials at the Foreign Office, there was no doubt that the German belief in an Anglo-Russian seizure of Constantinople was ludicrous. As Sanderson wrote to the newly installed British ambassador at Berlin on 26 December 1895:

What mortal man can of dreamt of anything so foolish as a *condominium* of Russia and England at Constantinople. And when did we suggest to Austria and Italy that we should jointly force the Dardanelles? and then draw back again. It was the Austrians who made some suggestions tending to that very end and have now dropped the whole concern like a hot potato.[133]

---

[129] Asquith to Rosebery, 8 Dec. 1895, Rosebery Papers, 1001.

[130] Salisbury to Goschen, 18 Dec. 1895, cited, Spinner, *Goschen*, 199.

[131] Salisbury to Curry, 15 Dec. 1896, Salisbury Papers, A138; A. Marsden, 'Salisbury and the Italians in 1896', *JMH* 40 (1968), 91–117.

[132] Salisbury's covering memo in Lowe, *Reluctant Imperialists*, ii. 85–91.

[133] Sanderson to Lascelles, 26 Dec. 1895, Lascelles Papers, FO 800/15; Sanderson to Lascelles, 23 Nov. 1895, Lascelles Papers, FO 800/16; G. H. Villiers (senior clerk, Eastern Department) to Lascelles, 26 Dec. 1895, Lascelles Papers, FO 800/15.

Such a view was shared by Hicks Beach, who believed that Britain was 'alone' among the Powers 'in desiring forcible intervention in Turkey'.[134] Should Britain attempt to coerce the Turks unilaterally, the chancellor felt that she would be opposed by 'Russia, and perhaps also France'. While an Anglo-Russian initiative was thus unlikely—for both British and Russian reasons—this does not rule out the possibility that Salisbury would have preferred a *general*, pan-European solution involving partition. However, opposed by his Cabinet, faced with rejection from the Russians, abandoned by the Austrians, and faced with other difficult foreign policy issues—the Venezuelan crisis and the South African imbroglio—Salisbury saw that the Armenian question had no quick solution.[135]

Despite this, the prime minister continued to push at both Constantinople and St Petersburg. On 15 January 1896, Salisbury proposed that the ambassadors at Constantinople should endeavour 'to cooperate in devising some remedy for the existing state of things in Turkey'.[136] In order to allay Lobanov's suspicions, it was emphasized that this proposal was 'limited to an authorisation to the Ambassadors to discuss the situation' only. Lobanov's reply was polite and pessimistic: 'if trouble is to come in Macedonia and the Balkans it will come in spite of all that the Ambassadors at Constantinople may do or devise.' Staal underlined the Russian refusal on 25 January.[137] Salisbury found the Russian position 'clear enough'. Knowing this attitude to be shared generally in Europe, Salisbury bowed to the inevitable: he 'was fully convinced that the evils which would result from any interruption in the harmonious relations of the Powers, would far outweigh any advantage that could possibly be expected from isolated action'.

Despite further attempts by Goschen to explain that Salisbury's proposals were limited in nature, Lobanov refused to countenance even ambassadorial discussions.[138] As a result, the Armenian question remained quiescent until August 1896, although the revolt on Crete against Ottoman rule in the interim made it clear that the troubles in the Sultan's lands were widespread.[139] On 26 August, a new massacre of Armenians brought the question once more to the fore. The Russian reaction was obscured by events. Nicholas II had left St Petersburg the previous day, destined for Vienna as part of his tour of European capitals. Accompanied by Lobanov, the Emperor was en route when the crisis broke. And,

[134] Hicks Beach to Salisbury, 20 Dec. 1895, Hicks Beach Papers, D2455, PCC/35.
[135] Marsh, 'Lord Salisbury', 80; Salisbury to Hicks Beach, 2 Jan. 1896, Hicks Beach Papers, D2455, PCC/69; Hicks Beach to Salisbury, 5 Jan. 1896, Hicks Beach Papers, D2455, PCC/33.
[136] W. E. Goschen to Salisbury, disp. 11, very confidential, 16 Jan. 1896, including Goschen to Lobanov, note, 15 Jan. 1896, both FO 65/1514.
[137] Salisbury to Goschen, disp. 22, 29 Jan. 1896, FO 65/1513.
[138] W. E. Goschen to Salisbury, disp. 18, confidential, 30 Jan. 1896, FO 65/1514.
[139] D. Dakin, *The Greek Struggle in Macedonia 1897–1913* (Thessalonika, 1966), 34–9.

just as the imperial party left Vienna, Lobanov suffered a fatal stroke and died on 30 August.

While the death of this 'bitter enemy' to Britain was not lamented in London, it did make it difficult for Salisbury to obtain the views of the Russian government.[140] But, the crisis in Turkey was ended without the Russian government's espousing any formal position, for the Russian ambassador at Constantinople, A. I. Nelidov, threatened a Russian bombardment of the city unless the Sultan put an end to the atrocities.[141] By mid-September, when things had calmed down, the *official* Russian position was announced. Despite Nelidov's strong words, Russian policy was much as it had been before Lobanov's death. The acting Russian minister for foreign affairs, N. P. Shishkin, announced on 17 September that 'the only course was to maintain as long as possible the existing *Regime*, as any violent alteration might lead to very serious political complications and even to an European war'.[142] In the face of the Russian (and general European) tendency to 'sit still with uplifted hands and say Oh how shocking!', Sanderson professed that he could 'scarcely myself see what is to come of it . . . It looks as if we should have to sit still'.[143]

The Tsar's European tour provided Salisbury with an opportunity. Nicholas' arrival in Scotland on 22 September, en route to Balmoral and a visit with Queen Victoria, seemed an ideal chance for Salisbury to attempt to persuade the young monarch of the need for joint Anglo-Russian action. The British were suspicious that this would be difficult, since it was believed that Russia was working generally to erode the British position in Egypt and 'isolate us from the rest of Europe'.[144] On 27 and 29 September, Salisbury made his pitch.[145] The prime minister's offer was the same as before: the Sultan was incompetent to rule and therefore the European powers must step in and depose him if necessary. Britain was not categorically opposed to Russia's taking Constantinople, but would accept such an occurrence only if the other powers, and particularly Austria, were compensated. With petitions about Armenia 'pour[ing] in by the score' to the Foreign Office, the need for action, or the semblance of action, was essential.[146]

Salisbury was not optimistic that he had won over the Tsar. Three days after Nicholas left England, Salisbury outlined the results to his parliamentary under-

---

[140] Lord George Hamilton to Lord Elgin (viceroy, India), 2 Sept. 1896, Hamilton Papers, MSS Eur C125/1.

[141] Grenville, *Lord Salisbury*, 75.

[142] O'Conor to Salisbury, disp. 208, confidential, 17 Sept. 1896, FO 65/1516.

[143] Sanderson to O'Conor, 15 Sept. 1896, O'Conor Papers, OCON 6/9.

[144] Hamilton to Elgin, 24 Sept. 1896, Hamilton Papers, MSS Eur C125/1; Lowe, *Reluctant Imperialists*, i. 204–14; Grenville, *Lord Salisbury*, 107–21.

[145] Lowe, *Reluctant Imperialists*, i. 78–83; M. M. Jefferson, 'Lord Salisbury's Conversations with the Tsar at Balmoral, 27 and 29 September 1896', *SEER* 39 (1960), 216–22.

[146] Sanderson to O'Conor, 30 Sept. 1896, O'Conor Papers, OCON 6/9.

secretary, George Curzon.[147] Salisbury had proposed that all the powers should support, by force if necessary, the imposition of the reform scheme worked out by the ambassadors. 'The Russian Emperor at Balmoral', Salisbury penned,

seemed to be in its favour: but as it was understood that what he said there did not pledge himself, I do not attach much importance to that indication. He was strongly against meddling with the *status quo* territorially of Turkey. He was not so strong against deposition—at first he was rather in favour of it, but [balked?] at it after reflection & consultation with Staal.

The prime minister now planned to suggest to all the European powers a line of action similar to that outlined above. In the meantime, Curzon should not state in the Commons that any discussion of ousting the Sultan had taken place at Balmoral, 'but a carefully guarded intimation that you believed that the question of deposition had been under discussion between some of the governments might do good'. Also, Curzon should stress 'the impossibility of isolated action' and argue that not to interfere in the Sultan's domain would inevitably lead to the very disorder and collapse that the powers claimed to fear. 'In short', Salisbury concluded, 'professions of loyalty to the Concert of Europe & exhortations to the Concert to look alive, will be the gist of your Foreign Office sentiments.'

On 20 October Salisbury issued a circular dispatch to the powers.[148] This dispatch has been termed 'one of Britain's great state papers'.[149] Such a phrase exaggerates its contents. The circular stated that not to interfere in Turkey would lead to that country's collapse, that the powers should therefore let their ambassadors at Constantinople work together and devise a plan of reform, and that the powers should accept that the ambassadors' 'unanimous decision in these matters is to be final, and will be executed up to the measure of such force as the Powers have at their command'. Salisbury had advocated this since he had returned to office in June 1895. He was not overly sanguine about its probable impact: 'I do not know what effect it will have—possibly none—but it will mark time.'[150] Acceptance of the circular depended on Russia. As Currie wrote from Constantinople, British policy was to 'leave the lead in Russia's hand & be always ready to fall into step. That is what I am trying to do here–lying low.'[151]

The fact that Nicholas was not in St Petersburg delayed the official Russian response, but Shishkin's preliminary observation was that he did 'not anticipate any objections'.[152] A week later the tone had changed. After consulting with the

---

[147] Salisbury to Curzon, confidential, 6 Oct. 1896, Curzon Papers, MSS Eur F112/1a; Salisbury to Hicks Beach, 5 Oct. 1896, Hicks Beach Papers, D2455, PCC/69.

[148] Untitled circular disp., confidential, Salisbury, 20 Oct. 1896, FO 65/1513.

[149] Grenville, *Lord Salisbury*, 83.

[150] Salisbury to Hicks Beach, 5 Oct. 1896, Hicks Beach Papers, D2455, PCC/69.

[151] Currie to O'Conor, 13 Oct. 1896, O'Conor Papers, OCON 6/9.

[152] W. E. Goschen to Salisbury, tel. 57, 26 Oct. 1896, FO 65/1517.

Emperor, Shishkin stated that the Russian government preferred to deal with the Armenian problem by putting controls on the Sultan's finances.[153] The 'idea of coercion . . . was extremely distasteful to the Imperial Govt.' In a secret postscript, Goschen reported that Shishkin's 'tone was not friendly & he said "One does not make diplomatic suggestions with regard to Turkey with a fleet of 40 ships in the Mediterranean"'. On 6 November, Shishkin expanded his remarks. The acting minister 'shuffled about and would not give a plain answer' to Salisbury's proposal.[154] Instead, he questioned British motives: 'England's policy was to search about for weak and undefended places & then use her enormous naval force to seize them.' The fact that Britain had earlier 'annex[ed]' Egypt was advanced as evidence that she contemplated doing the same at Constantinople. Sanderson was contemptuous of this interpretation:

I am afraid that Chichkine spells donkey in Russian. What nonsense to talk about our having 40 ships in the Mediterranean as an obstacle to our making diplomatic proposals about Turkey. How many thousand men has Russia got massed along the Austrian, Roumanian and Turkish frontiers. Does this prevent her from making diplomatic proposals about Turkey or has anyone suggested that it should be so! Perhaps it was merely an effect of ill-temper.[155]

Sanderson's view aside, Salisbury's attitude of a year earlier suggested that Russian suspicions about British motives and the significance of '40 ships in the Mediterranean' were not without foundation. On the other hand, Salisbury's policy was purely defensive, and, unless Russia had designs upon Constantinople, her fears were groundless.

What of Russian plans and capabilities? In October 1896, there was much speculation about them in British circles. Sir John Ardagh, the DMI, drew up a long memorandum entitled 'The Eastern Question in 1896'.[156] After reiterating his view that Russia could take the Straits whenever she chose, Ardagh argued that the Royal Navy alone could not force the Straits as a counterstroke: faced with the opposition of Turkish and 'possibly' Russian troops, the British fleet would need to be supported by at least 10,000 men. The possibility of this number being available, Ardagh saw as minuscule. He then considered the 'effect on British interests of opening the Straits' either to 'all nations' or 'to Russia'. The first he saw as positive, for while it would require the Royal Navy to maintain a larger presence in the eastern Mediterranean, it would also make the Black Sea a theatre of operations, enable all of the powers to coerce the Sultan and free the latter from exclusive Russian influence. More immediately, it would allow the powers to stop the

---

[153] W. E. Goschen to Salisbury, tel. 60, 4 Nov. 1896, FO 65/1517.
[154] Goschen to Sanderson, 7 Nov. 1896, O'Conor Papers, OCON 6/9.
[155] Sanderson to O'Conor, 11 Nov. 1896, O'Conor Papers, OCON 6/9.
[156] 'The Eastern Question in 1896', secret, Ardagh, Oct. 1896, Ardagh Papers, PRO 30/40/14.

Armenian atrocities. The second alternative Ardagh considered inimical to British interests. If Russia alone controlled the Straits, the Black Sea would become a military harbour, Russia would have 'an even more complete command over Turkey' and the Sultan would have 'no alternative but complete subordination to Russia'. Salisbury's idea of a joint intervention by the powers was supported by such an analysis, for such a move would effectively checkmate any potential Russian *coup de main*.

Russia's strength and intentions were also being considered at St Petersburg by the British military attaché, Lieutenant-Colonel W. H-H. Waters. It was, he wrote in October 1896, 'an admitted fact' that the Russian government 'will not permit, if at any cost she can prevent it, the Sea of Marmara falling under the domination of any European Power except herself'.[157] Some in Russia favoured making Constantinople a free city under Russian protection, but others 'boldly declare' that the city and environs should be part of the Russian empire. In a crisis, Waters suggested, 'the probabilities are altogether in favour of the latter party receiving general national support'. While Waters pointed out that the naval and military preparations that had been going on in Russia's Black Sea ports since the beginning of 1896 supported the idea of a Russian descent, he had two caveats. First, he did not feel that the Russian fleet was strong enough to effect an attack; second, he considered that the Russians thought such a course possible only in the context of a European war and that they considered themselves too weak to contemplate the latter. Thus, Russia would find a peaceful policy at Constantinople congruent with her national interests and 'avoid entering prematurely' into a final solution of the eastern question.

With such considerations in mind, Salisbury continued his attempt to win Russian support. Despite Shishkin's remarks, the prime minister was not convinced that Russia would ultimately reject his plan.[158] Given a hint from Staal that sweet words would be well received in Russia, the prime minister pitched his Guildhall speech on 9 November in that direction. Terming 'a superstition' the idea that there should be a 'necessary antagonism' between Britain and Russia, Salisbury suggested that the two countries had ample common ground to arrive at a mutually satisfactory policy about Armenia.[159] This had its implications for Anglo-German relations: 'I went as far as I could', the prime minister informed O'Conor, 'but even that very restrained disclaimer of hostility will bring the wrath of Germany upon me.'[160] Despite Salisbury's efforts, the Russians were

---

[157] Waters to W. E. Goschen, confidential disp., 13 Oct. 1896, in Goschen to Salisbury, disp. 241, 17 Oct. 1896, FO 65/1516.

[158] Salisbury to O'Conor, 11 Nov. 1896, Salisbury Papers, A129.

[159] *The Times*, 10 Nov. 1896.

[160] Salisbury to O'Conor, 11 Nov. 1896, Salisbury Papers, A129.

still opposed to coercion. Although Shishkin stated that Salisbury's Guildhall speech had given him the 'greatest pleasure' and had shown that 'there could no longer be any doubt' that the two countries were working together, the acting foreign minister felt that threats of coercion 'would weaken the authority of the Sultan' to the detriment of reform.[161] Salisbury rejected this. Even Shishkin's statement that Nelidov would inform the Sultan that 'the era of paper reforms was past' was insufficient. Without a definite commitment to action, Salisbury noted on 12 November, it was 'doubtful whether there will be much utility in combined further representations on the part of the Ambassadors'.[162]

But this seemingly categorical rejection of the British circular was not the only evidence before Salisbury. Both Sanderson and O'Conor had been told by highly placed Russians that Shishkin's remarks should not be taken as final.[163] On 18 November, O'Conor attempted to explain the vacillating nature of Russian policy.[164] The explanation centred about the Emperor and the general nature of the decision-making process in Russia. O'Conor stated that 'much of what I hear confirms the idea that the Emperor is influenced by the arguments of his last adviser, but at the same time I am inclined to think that as he has not much confidence in his own judgement he is sensible enough to rely upon one or the other of his Ministers—and today it seems to be M. de Witte'. Witte, the finance minister, and 'the Slavophil Party', O'Conor contended, 'are opposed to all serious reforms in Turkey dictated by the joint pressure of the European Powers'.[165] There were other influences at work. Nelidov had returned to St Petersburg from Constantinople on 15 November and was spreading the gospel that the Ottoman Empire's 'decomposition is complete & the total disruption inevitable at no distant date'.[166] Thus O'Conor saw Nelidov and Shishkin as advocates of accepting Salisbury's proposals, but advocates whose voices were not likely to be the most dominant in the din surrounding the Emperor.[167] Faced with this, Salisbury lapsed into pessimism, feeling it unlikely that Russia could be kept eventually from the Straits, and arguing that the best Austria-Hungary and Britain could hope for in such a case was compensation.[168]

---

[161] O'Conor to Salisbury, tel. 62, 11 Nov. 1896, FO 65/1517.

[162] Salisbury to O'Conor, tel. 196, 12 Nov. 1896, FO 65/1517.

[163] O'Conor to Salisbury, private tel., 12 Nov. 1896, FO 65/1517; Sanderson to Salisbury, memo, 13 Nov. 1896, FO 65/1523; O'Conor to Salisbury, private tel., 14 Nov. 1896, Salisbury Papers, A129.

[164] O'Conor to Salisbury, 18 Nov. 1896, Salisbury Papers A129.

[165] O'Conor to Salisbury, disp. 261, 18 Nov. 1896, FO 65/1516.

[166] O'Conor to Chirol, 19 Nov. 1896, O'Conor Papers, OCON 5/3/2.

[167] Ibid.; O'Conor to Currie, 18 Nov. 1896; O'Conor to Sanderson, 18 Nov. 1896, O'Conor Papers, OCON 3/14.

[168] Salisbury to Currie, 23 Nov. 1896, Salisbury Papers, A138.

Thus, it was a bombshell when, on 25 November, the Russians accepted Salisbury's circular.[169] The exact wording of the acceptance—that the Russian government 'would not refuse to take into consideration the application of coercive measures'—was not all that the British had wished for, but even this was a surprise.[170] O'Conor's attempt to explain the Russian *volte face* reflected the fact that he was unaware of the deeper changes in Russian policy.[171] The ambiguity of the Russian reply was no accident. As the British were to discover only in 1898, in late November and early December 1896 the Russians had decided to resolve the eastern question by force of arms.[172] The arguments in favour stemmed from Nelidov. In a memorandum of 30 November, he made two points: that the Ottoman regime was on the brink of collapse and that the British would attempt to pre-empt the Russians at the Straits. With Shishkin's being generally in favour, it remained only to convince Nicholas II of the wisdom of such a move. In the meantime, Britain was to be persuaded that the Russians contemplated joint, not unilateral action. Nelidov's ability to act out this charade was reflected in O'Conor's remarks of 2 December:

Then again Nelidoff no longer talks of the utter decomposition of Turkey, admits he may probably be wrong and that palliatives must be applied. A radical cure he still holds to be impossible, and hardly conceals that if possible he doesn't care to try it . . . After much shilly shallying they have accepted in principle Ld. Salisbury's proposal resp.[ecting] coercive measures . . .[173]

Three days later, Nicholas II approved a Russian *coup de main* against Constantinople. Only Witte's determined opposition to this decision and the moderating influence of French diplomacy brought about a reconsideration.

But, in 1896, the British were unaware of these Russian machinations. Instead, Salisbury focused on ensuring that the Russian declaration of 25 November was as binding as possible. After some rather careful drafting—with Sanderson's attempting to tone down Salisbury's blunt language—the British reply was issued early in December.[174] Salisbury was determined that the Russian reply must indicate the latter's willingness to use force against the Sultan if necessary. While the

---

[169] O'Conor to Salisbury, tel. 68, 25 Nov. 1896, FO 65/1517; Sanderson to O'Conor, 25 Nov. 1896; Barrington (Salisbury's private secretary) to O'Conor, 25 Nov. 1896, both O'Conor Papers, OCON 6/9.

[170] O'Conor to Salisbury, 3 Dec. 1896, Salisbury Papers, A129.

[171] O'Conor to Salisbury, disp. 266, very confidential, 25 Nov. 1896, FO 65/1516.

[172] O'Conor to Salisbury, very secret, 16 June 1898, Salisbury Papers, A129; W. L. Langer, *The Diplomacy of Imperialism 1890–1902* (2nd edn; New York, 1968), 336–45; Witte, S. I., *The Memoirs of Count Witte*, ed. and trans. S. Harcave (London, 1990), 250–2; V. A. Georgiev *et al.*, *Vostochnyi vopros vo vneshnei politike Rossii* (Moscow, 1978), 268–73.

[173] O'Conor to Currie, 2 Dec. 1896, O'Conor Papers, OCON 3/14.

[174] Salisbury to O'Conor, disp. 302, 25 Nov. 1896 (sent a week later), FO 65/1513 and minutes.

Russians were considering using much more force than the prime minister suspected, he was determined to avoid a continuance of the flabby policy that he had inherited from Kimberley. By the middle of December, Salisbury could rest assured that the Russians were willing to take coercive measures to deal with the Sultan.[175] And, as Salisbury had always felt, with such unanimity among the powers, by February 1897 the ambassadors had agreed upon a wide-ranging plan of reform for the Ottoman empire. Only the outbreak of war between Greece and Turkey over Crete prevented its implementation.

The Armenian crisis of 1895–6 demonstrated a number of things. First, British and Russian interests in the Near East were not congruent. Russia's desire to control Constantinople was incompatible with Britain's desire to keep the Straits in the hands of the Turks. Second, while Salisbury was quite willing to coerce the Sultan, he was not willing to depose him to the exclusive benefit of Russia. To do so would have meant giving up any idea of working with Austria-Hungary in the region, and, while the Mediterranean agreements were not set in stone for Salisbury, he would not abandon them without having some better alternative to hand. Any such alternative would necessarily involve a general agreement with Russia, and the Armenian crisis certainly did not suggest that such an arrangement was possible. With problems in South Africa and the Sudan looming, Salisbury needed to concentrate his diplomacy on maintaining a flexible position for Britain; a Russian settlement would have to wait. In the meantime, Anglo-Russian relations again found their focus in China.

[175] O'Conor to Salisbury, disp. 280, 16 Dec. 1896, FO 65/1516.

6

Concessions, Conflict, and Conciliation: China, 1895–1899

WHILE Salisbury had reason to be unhappy with the position that he inherited in Anglo-Russian relations about Armenia, the same could not be said about the position in China. At the end of the Sino-Japanese War, Anglo-Russian relations in the Far East were on a relatively friendly footing. During the next four years, the situation fluctuated greatly. From 1895 until 1897, the Great Powers sought railway concessions in and the right to make loans to China. This involved the British government to some extent, but it was largely an issue of secondary importance. The Foreign Office had confidence that British commercial interests could hold their own unaided. The German seizure of a naval base at Kiaochow in 1897, which prompted a similar Russian acquisition of Port Arthur, was viewed quite differently. This threatened the strategic balance in the Far East. When these actions were combined with a Russian attempt to gain undue influence over China by means of offering her a big loan, the British had to take action. The result was Salisbury's failed attempt in 1898 to reach a general agreement with Russia. However, while this wider initiative was not successful, in April 1899 Salisbury was able to reassert Britain's influence in the Far East through a limited Anglo-Russian agreement over Chinese railway concessions.

After the successful coercion of Japan by the Great Powers, the immediate question arose: where were the Chinese to obtain the money to pay the indemnity that they owed Japan?[1] The immediate contenders were the Hongkong and Shanghai Banking Corporation, the largest British financial power in the Far East, and the Deutsche-Asiatische Bank, the quasi-state bank created to provide funding for German commercial efforts in China.[2] However, in the wings were both the French and Russian governments, with the latter quite willing to accept the burden of the entire loan in order to strengthen its influence in China. The Hongkong Bank

[1] E. W. Edwards, *British Diplomacy and Finance in China, 1895–1914* (Oxford, 1987), 8–30.
[2] F. H. H. King, *The History of the Hongkong and Shanghai Banking Corporation*, ii, *The Hongkong Bank in the Period of Imperialism and War, 1895–1918: Wayfoong, the Focus of Wealth* (Cambridge 1988), 258–312; R. A. Dayer, *Finance and Empire: Sir Charles Addis 1861–1945* (New York, 1988), 35–46.

turned immediately to the Foreign Office to ensure its interests in the welter of
Great Power politics.

On 7 May 1895, Ewen Cameron, the London manager of the Bank, visited
Sanderson.[3] Cameron explained that the Bank was attempting to raise a loan for
China's indemnity, but was 'apprehensive' that the three coercive powers were
attempting 'to establish some international control of the Customs, and to issue the
loan under their own exclusive patronage'. In order to strengthen its hand further,
the Hongkong Bank also held talks with Lord Rothschild. Rothschild, who was at
once both a prominent banker and Rosebery's father-in-law, took the matter to the
prime minister.[4] Rosebery's policy was clear. The government, far from caring as to
the nature of Cameron's plans for a loan, 'do not wish to interfere for or against'.
And, as Sanderson warned Cameron, any attempt by the Hongkong Bank to
exclude the French and German governments from the Chinese loan would be
difficult to achieve, and 'a failure would have the worst consequences'. In fact, there
was little confidence at the Foreign Office that the Hongkong Bank was capable of
floating such a large loan on its own. Instead, Sanderson told Cameron that a plan
of Rothschild's—that the loan be made an Anglo-Franco-German one, with
Rothschilds' helping the Hongkong Bank to bring out the English portion—'was
such as we could openly work for'. With its domestic life near expired, and not
needing a demanding confrontation over China, the Rosebery administration clearly preferred an international settlement.

The problem was Russia. In mid-May, it became evident that Witte would
attempt to scoop up the entire loan. The response from the Foreign Office was
quick. As Kimberley wired to the British ambassador at Peking, Nicholas O'Conor,
the Chinese 'would be unwise to entertain Russian offer of direct assistance which
would place them in embarrassing position of subserviency and expose them possibly to territorial demands later on'.[5] O'Conor's reply was equally rapid, but
disappointing: 'I believe the Chinese Govt. is aware of [the] danger but they may
not be able to resist pressure of Powers unless they can borrow in open market.'
Unable to thwart the loan in Peking, the British turned to St Petersburg. On 17
May, Kimberley informed Staal that given Britain's 'immense commercial
interests' in China, she expected 'to be consulted' about the terms of any Chinese
loan.[6] Before the issue could be raised directly with Lobanov, good news arrived
from China. O'Conor reported on 18 May that the Chinese government, while
finding the Russian loan difficult to refuse, was 'suspicious of conditions and alive

[3] Sanderson to [Rosebery], memo and enclosures, 7 May 1895, Rosebery Papers, 10134.
[4] Sanderson's memo (13 May 1895) of a conversation with Cameron, with Rosebery's undated
marginalia, in Rosebery Papers, 10134.
[5] Kimberley to O'Conor, private and secret tel., 15 May 1895 and reply, private tel., 16 May 1895,
both Rosebery Papers, 10134.
[6] Kimberley to Lascelles, tel. 81, 18 May 1895, FO 65/1493.

to their consequences'.[7] In addition, the Chinese government had given its assurance 'that no arrangement would be made . . . to [the] exclusion of England'.
O'Conor was overly optimistic. Even as this telegram was received, Ewen Cameron
was informed that the Chinese government had accepted a Russian loan for £8
million. Cameron went at once to the Foreign Office.[8] Kimberley and Sanderson,
upon receipt of this tale, spoke with Rothschild. The banker confirmed that such a
loan would be issued on the Paris market, guaranteed by the Russian government
and the revenues of the Chinese customs.

Kimberley immediately instructed Lascelles to see Lobanov 'at once', and
'without actually mentioning' the facts of the Chinese loans 'you may let him see
that we know what is going on, and that any attempt to exclude us from the loan
negotiations would have a serious effect on public opinion here'.[9] An indirect
attempt to discourage the loan—by informing the Germans that the French and
Russians were attempting to freeze out Berlin—was dismissed as 'too Machiavellian'.[10] The British wanted to prevent the pressure on the Chinese from becoming
overly great lest China be forced into 'a state of subserviency to Russia'. Lobanov
affected to know little. On 19 May, when asked whether he was 'prepared to act in
harmony' with Britain, Lobanov said only that he would have to ask Witte about
the situation.[11] Even when the British made their position very clear, Lobanov
continued to dissimulate concerning Russia's intentions.[12] To the British proposal
that a private international banking consortium handle the Chinese loan, Lobanov
replied that 'how or by whom the loan was to be raised was a matter of perfect
indifference to the Russian government'.[13] This, of course, did not square well with
what the British knew, and Lascelles was puzzled. As he wrote to Sanderson on 22
May:

I cannot quite make out whether Lobanoff is trying to humbug me about the China loan or
whether he does not know about Witte's communication to Rothschilds in Paris. I have not
told him straight out that we know what Witte has been doing, but I should have thought
that he would have guessed, from our insistence on the point, that we had an inkling of what
was going on.[14]

Lascelles was not alone in being duped by Lobanov; the German ambassador to St
Petersburg had received similar professions of Russian indifference about the
loan.[15]

---

[7] O'Conor to Kimberley, private and secret tel., 18 May 1895, Rosebery Papers, 10134.
[8] Sanderson to Rosebery, 18 May 1895, Rosebery Papers, 10134.
[9] Kimberley to Lascelles, secret tel. 82, 18 May 1895, FO 65/1493.
[10] Sanderson to Rosebery, 19 May 1895, Rosebery Papers, 10134.
[11] Lascelles to Kimberley, confidential disp. 128, 21 May 1895, FO 65/1491.
[12] Kimberley to Lascelles, tel. 87, 21 May 1895, FO 65/1493.
[13] Lascelles to Kimberley, disp. 133, 22 May 1895, FO 65/1491.
[14] Lascelles to Sanderson, 22 May 1895, Lascelles Papers, FO 800/17.
[15] Lascelles to Kimberley, 6 June 1895, Lascelles Papers, FO 800/17.

Lobanov's mendacity aside, the negotiations for the loan stalled.[16] It was not until 5 June that the Russians made the Chinese a solid offer: a £16 million loan at 4 per cent, with the interest guaranteed by Russia. On 6 July 1895 the indemnity loan became a reality. During this time, the British worked ineffectually to block it. Their reasons for opposing the loan were straightforward. It was feared that the Russians would obtain wide-ranging concessions in exchange for their loan. Rumours abounded: in mid-June there were noises that Russia would get permission to run the trans-Siberian down the Liaotung peninsula, while a week later there was the horrifying thought that France might be ceded Hong Kong.[17] Further, as Rosebery put it, if the Chinese were to grant substantial concessions to the Russians, Peking might find it difficult to raise further loans, as the Russian position might be seen to have 'impaired and threatened the security she [China] had to offer'. The reasons for the flaccid nature of the British opposition were equally clear. The first was domestic. The Rosebery government collapsed in mid-June, and this was not the time to pursue a marginal foreign-policy issue. The second was related to the events of the previous six months. The British refusal to join in putting pressure on Japan during the settlement of the Sino-Japanese War had put a strain on Anglo-Russian relations. This strain had been partially eased at the end of April and in early May of 1895, and the Foreign Office did not wish to re-aggravate matters over an issue where no distinct British interests were threatened. If there were to be a strong British policy about China, it would have to await concrete Russian moves to utilize their new financial influence in ways detrimental to Britain.

When Salisbury took office in late June, the Chinese loan seemed a small matter in Anglo-Russian relations in comparison to the Armenian question. At the end of his first month in Downing Street, Salisbury wrote to Lascelles that 'I hope that in other matters—Pamir boundaries—& Chinese loans—there is a truce to all discussions with Russia: & we may assume I suppose that even her more fiery spirits will not wish to "set the heather alight" till after the Imperial Coronation'.[18] While Salisbury manœuvred in the autumn of 1895 to induce Russia to join him in a settlement at Constantinople, the heather seemed remarkably fireproof. In the Far East, Salisbury confined himself to settling affairs with France over the latter's imperial aspirations in south-east Asia.[19] By doing so, the prime minister ensured that if events in the Far East came to a head, then the Franco-Russian alliance would not operate closely in tandem; as well, it was a simple recognition that Britain was incapable of dealing with such scattered (and relatively insignificant) matters simultaneously.

[16] D. McLean, 'The Foreign Office and the First Chinese Indemnity Loan, 1895', *HJ* 16 (1973), 315–8.
[17] Ibid. 317; untitled memo by Rosebery, 21 June 1895, Rosebery Papers, 10134.
[18] Salisbury to Lascelles, 27 July 1895, Lascelles Papers, FO 800/16.
[19] L. K. Young, *British Policy in China 1895–1902* (Oxford, 1970), 31–6.

While relations with Russian over China remained calm, they were not without incident. On 25 October 1895, *The Times* published an account of a purported Russo-Chinese treaty, giving Russia the right to build a railway through Chinese territory to Vladivostok and to extend a spur from this line to Port Arthur.[20] The Russians immediately denied that the so-called Cassini convention (named after the Russian minister to Peking) existed: 'there was not a word of truth' in the report, Staal informed Salisbury on 30 October.[21] W. E. Goschen, the British chargé d'affaires at St Petersburg, was inclined to accept this denial, but only as 'strictly accurate'.[22] Goschen concluded that while there was 'every reason to believe that no definite and formal agreement' had yet been signed, 'it [was] by no means so certain that the Russian Government does not contemplate making the Railways in question in the near future'. Salisbury was not concerned. Deeply involved in his intricate manœuvrings over Armenia, the prime minister's first requirement was Russian co-operation. His Guildhall speech on 9 November even made reference to there being room for all in Asia.[23] Any diversion of Russia's effort to Asia was to be welcomed, and Salisbury's attitude nearly paralleled the belief found in Russian newspapers: 'that if the report [of the Cassini convention] is not true, it ought to be true.'[24] This indifference also resulted from the fact that British commercial and economic interests in China were not imperilled. After its failure to secure the first Chinese indemnity loan, the Hongkong Bank had decided to throw in its lot with the Germans. In July 1895, the Hongkong Bank and the Deutsche Asiatische Bank formed a consortium to share Chinese endeavours.[25] This consortium obtained the second Chinese indemnity loans—also for £16 million—in 1896.[26] Not even the creation in late 1895 of the Russo-Chinese Bank, whose purpose was clearly as much political as financial, served to upset Salisbury's view that good Anglo-Russian relations were more important than keeping Russia out of Asia.[27]

The British were naïve about Russian intentions. In February 1896, Goschen

[20] *The Times*, 25 Oct. 1895; W. E. Goschen (British chargé d'affaires, St Petersburg) to Salisbury, confidential disp. 254, 4 Nov. 1895, FO 65/1492.

[21] Salisbury to Goschen, disp. 319, 30 Oct. 1895, FO 65/1489.

[22] W. E. Goschen to Salisbury, 4 Nov. 1895, confidential disp. 254, 4 Nov. 1895, FO 65/1492. W. E. Goschen was the brother of W. J. Goschen, the First Lord of the Admiralty.

[23] *The Times*, 10 Nov. 1895.

[24] W. E. Goschen to Salisbury, confidential disp. 254, 4 Nov. 1895, FO 65/1492.

[25] D. J. S. King, 'The Hamburg Branch: The German Period, 1889–1920', in F. H. H. King (ed.), *Eastern Banking: Essays in the History of the Hongkong and Shanghai Banking Corporation* (London, 1983), 517–45; 519–20.

[26] Edwards, *British Diplomacy and Finance*, 12–16.

[27] Goschen to Salisbury, confidential disp. 287, 19 Dec. 1895, FO 65/1492; Goschen to Salisbury, disp. 5, 4 Jan. 1896, FO 65/1514. R. K. I. Quested, *The Russo-Chinese Bank: A Multinational Financial Base of Tsarism in China* (Birmingham, 1977); O. Crisp, 'The Russo-Chinese Bank: An Episode in Franco-Russian Relations', *SEER* 52 (1974), 197–212.

reported that a Russian survey crew had finished its work in China, supporting the earlier rumour about the purport of the Cassini convention.[28] Sanderson was sceptical about the Russian denials: 'It does not follow that the lines will not be made—and under Russian superintendence.' But there were other rumours concerning Russia's efforts in the Far East that were at least as worrisome, plus a continuing Franco-Russian pressure on the British position in Egypt.[29] The rumours centred around Russo-Japanese relations.[30] There were conflicting counsels in both countries. In Russia, various factions supported improving either Sino-Russian or Russo-Japanese relations. In Japan, various factions supported improving either Russo-Japanese or Anglo-Japanese relations. Goschen informed Sanderson on 12 March that Russia favoured taking a warm-water port in Korea.[31] The chargé saw this in the context of a Russo-Japanese agreement over the hermit kingdom, a possibility that he viewed as 'not at all improbable'. And, he concluded, given that Japan was seriously weakened by her war with China, Tokyo 'unless she saw any reasonable chance of England coming to her assistance—she may, like Turkey, throw herself into the arms of the Power whom she most fears'. This proved to be correct. The Japanese, fearing that Britain was encouraging Russia in the Far East, began negotiations with St Petersburg in March 1896.[32] Despite an abortive attempt by Salisbury to check this Russo-Japanese *rapprochement*, by the middle of May the two powers had agreed to a sharing of predominance in Korea.

At the same time, Russia was posing as the defender of China. In late April, Salisbury obtained a copy of a putative Sino-Russian treaty, one giving the Russians what O'Conor termed 'the objects of Russia's Ambition in the Far East'.[33] O'Conor felt that the treaty was 'in the main apocryphal', and chose not to take up the document with Lobanov since the Russians had recently denied the existence of the treaty. Sanderson felt that the story of the treaty was 'one of a cock and a bull', but the ambassador was less certain.[34] This was particularly true of the provision to shorten the trans-Siberian railway by giving it a terminus on Chinese territory. Li Hung-chang, the Chinese ambassador extraordinary to the Tsar's coronation, was being pressed hard by the Russian authorities, and O'Conor reported that 'the opinion [is] prevalent here that the Russian Government will in one way or another

---

[28] Goschen to Salisbury, secret disp. 31, 27 Feb. 1896, FO 65/1514 and Sanderson's undated minute.

[29] O'Conor to Salisbury, 9 Apr. 1896, O'Conor Papers, OCON 3/14; Sanderson to O'Conor, 28 Apr. 1898, O'Conor Papers, OCON 6/9.

[30] I. H. Nish, *The Anglo-Japanese Alliance: The Diplomacy of Two Island Empires 1894–1907* (London, 1965), 41–5.

[31] W. J. Goschen to Sanderson, 12 Mar. 1896, FO 65/1514.

[32] Nish, *Anglo-Japanese Alliance*, 43.

[33] O'Conor to Salisbury, disp. 82, 6 May 1896, FO 65/1514.

[34] O'Conor to Sanderson, 7 May 1896, O'Conor Papers, OCON 3/14; Sanderson to O'Conor, 13 May 1896, O'Conor Papers, OCON 6/9.

wring this concession from the Chinese'.[35] Sanderson believed that Li would resist Russian blandishments, but O'Conor's opinion proved to be well founded. On 3 June, Li was induced to sign a treaty that provided Russia with the right to build a spur line through Manchuria, but did not provide for an ice-free port.[36] Although O'Conor remained unaware that the treaty had actually been signed, after the coronation he stated that 'my impression confirms the supposition that the basis of some agreement has been come to'.[37] This required a counter. Noting that Li would be in England in late July, O'Conor suggested that the Chinese ambassador be treated to a special naval display in order to 'impress . . . indelibly' the fact of British naval superiority. Thus, while Britain remained officially ignorant of the facts of the Sino-Russian agreement, policy was being made on the supposition that it existed.

Anglo-Russian relations in the Far East were quiet over the next eighteen months. With the Russians moving only slowly to survey their rail routes in Manchuria, there existed just the usual rumours of Russian concession hunting and loans.[38] Instead, the focus of Anglo-Russian relations was in the Near East, on Armenia and the Greco-Turkish War. Only the German seizure of Kiaochow in November 1897 made the Far East again the centre of attention. The British response to the German action was cautious, and reflected Russia's seeming indifference to it.[39] Even the announcement, later in December, that the Russian fleet would spend the winter in Port Arthur did not clarify Tsarist policy, for Muravev told Goschen that the Russian fleet had entered Port Arthur only because there was 'a certain difficulty' in wintering the Russian ships in Japanese harbours as had been the usual practice in the past.[40] Goschen's evaluation of this remark encapsulated the British interpretation of Russian policy in the Far East:

I presume that it [the explanation] may be considered true from the Russian point of view— that is to say just as long as it suits Russia not to precipitate matters and show her full hand

[35] O'Conor to Salisbury, disp. 82, 6 May 1896; O'Conor to Salisbury, confidential disp. 87, 9 May 1896, both FO 65/1514.
[36] Sanderson to O'Conor, 1 June 1896, O'Conor Papers, OCON 6/9; Young, *British Policy in China*, 37.
[37] O'Conor to Salisbury, confidential disp. 112, 12 June 1896, FO 65/1515.
[38] O'Conor to Salisbury, disp. 143, 8 July 1896, FO 65/1515; O'Conor to Salisbury, disp. 231, 5 Oct. 1896, FO 65/1516; O'Conor to Salisbury, disp. 281, 17 Dec. 1896, FO 65/1516; O'Conor to Salisbury, disp. 103, 24 Dec. 1896, FO 65/1516; O'Conor to Bertie, 14 Jan. 1897, FO 65/1531; O'Conor to Salisbury, disp. 3, 25 Feb. 1897, FO 65/1537; O'Conor to Bertie, 17 Apr. 1897, FO 65/1532 and O'Conor to Salisbury, confidential disp. 155, 9 July 1897, FO 65/1533; A. Rosenbaum, 'The Manchurian Bridgehead: Anglo-Russian Rivalry and the Imperial Railways of North China, 1897–1902', *MAS* 10 (1976), 41–64.
[39] Goschen to Salisbury, disp. 277, 1 Dec. 1897, FO 65/1534.
[40] Goschen to Salisbury, tel. 103, 23 Dec. 1897, FO 65/1535; Goschen to Salisbury, confidential disp. 295, 26 Dec. 1897, FO 65/1534.

in the Far East. But there is no reasonable doubt, as Your Lordship is well aware, that, notwithstanding the ice-breaker at Vladivostok, as soon as her Railways are completed and her military strength brought up to the required standard, Russia will endeavour to establish herself definitely in a Port free from ice in the winter—either Port Arthur—or some equally convenient and commanding position in the vicinity.[41]

Until that time, Goschen concluded, Russia was unable and unwilling 'to precipitate matters or to take any step which might possibly involve her in difficulties with Foreign Powers'. Therefore, the Russian government had to explain their occupation of Port Arthur in terms hiding the fact that a trial of strength among the Great Powers in the Far East was occurring. Goschen built upon this analysis to explain the 'spiteful tone' of the Russian press towards England.[42] Initially, the Russian press had been hostile to the actions of Germany. But, since Russia had decided to profit indirectly from Germany's action by acquiring Port Arthur, press attacks on Britain now served as a 'safety valve' for Russian distemper.

In London, Salisbury received advice from a number of sources. O'Conor, home on leave, outlined Witte's view that an agreement between England and Russia was possible.[43] Indeed, throughout 1897, the Russian finance minister had floated trial balloons about such a possibility.[44] Sir C. Smith, the former governor of the Straits Settlement and president of the China Association, also put forward the idea of an Anglo-Russian agreement.[45] Smith argued that, with respect to a possible permanent Russian occupation of Port Arthur:

I do not see how we can object, but as it is of supreme importance to her that we should be her friends rather than her antagonists she would probably be more likely now than at any previous time to enter into a friendly understanding with us—more especially in view of the attitude which Japan is nearly certain to take up,—so our respective spheres of influence might not be interfered with by them.

Salisbury noted on Smith's remarks that '[i]n the main I quite agree with him'. By the beginning of the New Year, matters were coming to a head. In the Cabinet there was pressure for Britain to do something, a move spearheaded by Chamberlain's desire for an approach to Germany. But others felt that an agreement with Russia

---

[41] Goschen to Salisbury, confidential disp. 295, 26 Dec. 1897, FO 65/1534.

[42] Goschen to Salisbury, disp. 296, 27 Dec. 1897, FO 65/1534.

[43] J. A. S. Grenville, *Lord Salisbury and Foreign Policy. The Close of the Nineteenth Century* (London, 1964), 136–7.

[44] O'Conor to Salisbury, confidential disp. 15, 24 Jan. 1897, FO 65/1531; O'Conor to Salisbury, secret and confidential disp. 219, 31 Aug. 1897, FO 65/1533; quoted, A. W. Palmer, 'Lord Salisbury's approach to Russia 1898', *OSP*, NS, 6 (1955), 103–4.

[45] C. Smith to Bertie, 27 Dec. 1897, sent to Salisbury 28 Dec. 1897 with a covering note, both Bertie Papers, Add MSS 63017. Salisbury's undated minute is on Bertie's covering note.

might be more to Britain's advantage. In a letter to Curzon on 2 January 1898, Salisbury put the matter clearly:

The question whether we shall join with Russia is of course the *crux*. Beach is very strongly for it: I am less so, but still I think clearly in its favour. It would be however a grave step as it would leave us near to Russia, further from Germany. However, Macdonald's [Sir Claude, the British minister at Peking] tel. this morning makes it probable that we shall not be able to make a deal with China, unless we agree to Russia 'going snacks'. My own tendency is to believe that our own future interest lies in the valley of the Yangtze and the adjacent seas: & that if we can secure that we should not be wise in spending strength or money . . . [elsewhere].[46]

But the approach to Russia was surrounded by other matters. The third Chinese loan for the indemnity payments was being negotiated at the same time, and these discussions directly affected Anglo-Russian relations generally.

On 22 December, Sir Claude Macdonald had reported that the Chinese government had been offered a £16 million loan by the Russian government.[47] This led to an immediate series of discussions in London concerning the implications of the offer. Salisbury, Sanderson, and Bertie met to discuss the British response, and, on 23 December, O'Conor joined them. Opinions varied. Salisbury wished to avoid taking any Chinese territory unless Russia or Germany annexed a portion of the Celestial Empire. O'Conor was more bellicose. He favoured the occupation of Chusan as a counterweight to the Russian action. There was also the financial aspect of the situation. Hicks Beach was cautious. If the British government were to help China it 'must be part . . . of a much more definite and stronger policy than we have hitherto adopted there'.[48] Hicks Beach preferred that the British government itself should make the loan to China, if possible in concert with Russia and certainly excluding the Hongkong Bank. The result was that Salisbury put forward on 31 December a tentative proposal to Macdonald that Britain and Russia should share in a loan to the Chinese.[49] A swirl of rumour and speculation followed. Lord Rothschild informed Bertie on 6 January that the Russians were moving ahead with their loan offer and that if the British government hoped to act in the matter they should do so 'speedily'.[50] Even the Portuguese were involved, with their representative in Russia inquiring whether the British had plans to occupy Macao as a counterbalance to the German seizure of Kiaochow.[51]

[46] Salisbury to Curzon, 2 Jan. 1898, Curzon Papers, MSS Eur F112/1b.
[47] Young, *British Policy in China*, 51–62.
[48] Hicks Beach to Salisbury, confidential, 26 Dec. 1897, Hicks Beach Papers, D2455, PCC/34.
[49] Salisbury to MacDonald, 31 Dec. 1897, secret tel., Cab 37/46/29.
[50] Bertie to Salisbury, private and confidential, 6 Jan. 1898, Bertie Papers, Add MSS 63017.
[51] Goschen to Salisbury, disp. 8, 9 Jan. 1898, FO 65/1552.

When O'Conor returned to Russia early in 1898, he immediately attempted to discover Russian policy.[52] The ambassador found that Nicholas and the Kaiser had discussed a German acquisition of a coaling station in the Far East during the latter's visit in 1897. Thus, when Germany had taken Kiaochow, the Russian position had been one of grudging acquiescence, much to the discomfiture of Witte. The Russian finance minister's policy, O'Conor argued, was based on the idea 'that Russia should maintain the integrity of China in order to work at Pekin, under cover of this protection, for the establishment of a preponderant influence with the Mandarin Government' and thus obtain concessions for Russian in north China. Muravev, the ambassador reported, was hiding his annoyance at the new line of policy.

O'Conor's analysis was not universally shared. At the Foreign Office, Bertie put forward an alternate explanation. The influential assistant under-secretary argued that the German take-over was the result of a deep-seated Russian plot that had gone wrong.[53] For Bertie, the Russians had intended to seize the Liaotung peninsula after the Sino-Japanese War, but had not done so until it could be ascertained whether the British were likely to support Japan. The German seizure of a base in the north upset all the Russian calculations, Bertie opined, and 'the Russian Government finding that the Czar felt himself bound by his word hoped that we should make objections and are disappointed that we have not done so'. O'Conor's analysis was likely the one accepted in London. For when, on 17 January 1898, Salisbury instructed his ambassador to broach the idea of a working Anglo-Russian agreement, the prime minister suggested that O'Conor do so to *Witte*, not to Muravev.[54] Salisbury's instructions reflected his desire to bring an end to the ongoing quarrels in China. As he put it: 'Our objects are not antagonistic in any serious degree: on the other hand we can both of us do each other a great deal of harm if we try. It is better therefore we should come to an understanding. We should go far to further Russian commercial objects in the North, if we could regard her as willing to work with us.' This approach was not one designed to frustrate, or even to check Russian ambitions. Russia would be allowed, in Salisbury's earlier phrase, to 'go snacks' in northern China in exchange for an acceptance of British predominance in her own sphere.

O'Conor was optimistic. He took up Salisbury's proposal with Muravev on 19 January. '[H]e responded', O'Conor reported, 'more favourably even than I

---

[52] O'Conor to Salisbury, confidential disp. 12, 12 Jan. 1898, FO 65/1552; O'Conor to Sanderson, 13 Jan. 1898 (misdated 1897), O'Conor Papers, OCON 3/15. Quotation from the former.

[53] Bertie's memo for Salisbury, 17 Jan. 1898, Bertie Papers, FO 800/176.

[54] Salisbury to O'Conor, secret tel. 7, 17 Jan. 1898, in H. Temperley and G. P. Gooch (eds.), *B[ritish] D[ocuments] on the Origins of the War* (11 vols. in 13; London, 1926–38), i, doc. 5 (see *BD* hereafter); Sanderson to O'Conor, 19 Jan. 1898, O'Conor Papers, OCON 6/25; Palmer, 'Lord Salisbury's Approach to Russia', 102–14; Grenville, *Lord Salisbury*, 136–43.

expected.'[55] Indeed, with O'Conor's prodding, Muravev seemed interested in expanding Salisbury's suggestion of a limited, regional agreement into a general, wider agreement. The Russian foreign minister called for a 'friendly exchange of general views', and promised to 'take steps' to alter the hostile tone of the Russian press towards Britain. At the same time, however, Muravev revealed that Russia had intended to take Kiaochow herself and that the movement of the Russian fleet to Port Arthur foreshadowed 'a permanent military occupation of a port in the North of China'.[56] When O'Conor spoke to Witte, the latter reiterated his view that Russia's 'true policy is to keep China intact', and seemed quite willing to divide that country into a Russian sphere of influence in the north, a British one on the Yangtze.[57] But, significantly, Witte also enquired as to what Britain's position would be if the Russian fleet's occupation of Port Arthur 'became permanent'.

On 25 January, Salisbury replied to Muravev's call.[58] The prime minister made it clear that he hoped to end the frictions with Russia in both the Chinese and Turkish empires. The essence, Salisbury argued, was 'no partition of territory, but only a partition of preponderance'. Salisbury was striving to achieve a dual condominium, so that England and Russia would cease to 'neutraliz[e] each other's efforts much more frequently than the real antagonism of their interests would justify'. When O'Conor took these ideas to Muravev on 26 January, the ambassador found the Russian's attitude 'not quite so satisfactory as last week'.[59] Noting that Muravev's tendency to lie ('his veracity is nearly on the level of Prince Lobanoff's') tended to obscure matters, O'Conor outlined the Russian objections. There was, the ambassador explained, a 'deep rooted prejudice among the Official & Military classes in regard to our policy' and this would have to be overcome. But the key to the situation remained 'on the way the Emperor looks on the question', and here O'Conor was optimistic. But the general tone of his letter was sombre. The ambassador was convinced that Russian and Japanese interests in the Far East were fundamentally opposed, and he wished to keep the 'Japanese Card' firmly in the British hand. 'The possibility of our alliance with Japan', he wrote, 'haunts them & helps us.' While he had been responsible for introducing the concept of an Anglo-Russian agreement extending beyond China, O'Conor was not convinced that it was possible.[60] With regard to eliminating the British 'popular nightmare' of a Russian

[55] O'Conor to Salisbury, private tel., 19 Jan. 1898, Salisbury Papers, A/129; O'Conor to Salisbury, secret tel. 10, 20 Jan. 1898, *BD*, i, doc. 6. Quotation from the latter.

[56] See O'Conor to Salisbury, disp. 24, 20 Jan. 1898, *BD*, i, doc. 7. O'Conor to Salisbury, disp. 25, 21 Jan. 1898, FO 65/1552.

[57] O'Conor to Salisbury, secret tel. 12, *BD*, i, doc. 8.

[58] Salisbury to O'Conor, secret tel. 22, 25 Jan. 1898, *BD*, i, doc. 9.

[59] O'Conor to Salisbury, 26 Jan. 1898, O'Conor Papers, OCON 3/15.

[60] O'Conor to Sanderson, 27 Jan. 1898, O'Conor Papers, OCON 3/15.

descent upon India, 'it was not very clear how this can be managed'.[61] Of course, O'Conor was too experienced a diplomatist to believe 'that the negotiation of so serious a matter will not in its course encounter considerable opposition from various quarters or that the difficulties in the way of a successful issue can be easily overcome'.[62]

In reality, the possibility of success was small. Russian policy had been determined late in 1897, and was designed to make her position dominant in China.[63] Witte's policy of economic penetration, always backed by force, had not held the day. Instead, the ideas of the naval and military authorities—the seizure of Port Arthur or a port on the Korean coastline—which dovetailed nicely with Muravev's own views, were adopted. The negotiations with Britain were a case of diplomatic camouflage, designed to prevent the British both from seeing the Russian objectives plainly and from looking elsewhere—perhaps to Tokyo—to ensure that their interests were protected.

By the end of January, the proposed Anglo-Russian arrangement was losing support. In London, many were in favour of unilateral British action. On 22 January the Cabinet was, in Hicks Beach's words, 'keen for the Chinese loan for any amount, and on any terms', a policy which the chancellor himself opposed on financial grounds.[64] None the less, Salisbury had made up his mind. On 28 January, he telegraphed MacDonald that should China reject Britain's loan and then accept one from Russia, the British government would necessarily require a series of concessions from China in order to maintain the 'balance of influence' in the region.[65] The following day, in response to Hicks Beach's surprise at the seemingly minatory nature of the telegram, Salisbury outlined his policy clearly.

You did not read my telegram correctly. I am not threatening China with the consequences if she refuses our loan: but if having refused it she accepts a loan from Russia. Take the fact that she formally asked for the loan: that it has been offered on generous terms—that she refuses it (if she does) under the strong protest of Russia because it would destroy the balance of influence in China. If at Russia's instigation she has acted on this view: & *then* gives it to Russia, she will clearly have destroyed the balance of influence the other way: though we have 80 p.[er] c.[ent] and Russia less that 20 p.[er] c.[ent] of the trade. In such a case our position in regard to Russia in China will be one of absolute effacement.[66]

[61] O'Conor to Salisbury, 26 Jan. 1898, O'Conor Papers, OCON 3/15.

[62] O'Conor to Salisbury, secret disp. 32, 26 Jan. 1898, FO 65/1552.

[63] D. Geyer, *Russian Imperialism: The Interaction of Domestic and Foreign Policy, 1860–1914*, trans. B. Little (Leamington Spa, 1987), 197–8; A. Malozemoff, *Russian Far Eastern Policy 1881–1904: With Special Emphasis on the Causes of the Russo-Japanese War* (Berkeley, 1958), 100–10.

[64] Hicks Beach to Salisbury, 23 Jan. 1898, Hicks Beach Papers, D2455, PCC/34.

[65] Salisbury to MacDonald, tel. 23, 28 Jan. 1898, Cab 37/46/29.

[66] Salisbury to Hicks Beach, 29 Jan. 1898; Hicks Beach to Salisbury, 28 Jan. 1898, both Hicks Beach Papers, D2455, PCC/34 and PCC/69.

While this was too much for Hicks Beach, others wanted more. Chamberlain was convinced that Britain was pursuing a feeble line towards Russia generally. Instead of trying to conciliate Russia in any fashion, the colonial secretary believed that Britain should concert with the United States and Germany and insist that all ports taken by European powers in China should be open. And, he concluded, 'if Russia refuses this scheme we should summon her fleet to leave Port Arthur & make her go if necessary'.[67]

In such circumstances, the Chinese indemnity loan took on a greater importance in both London and St Petersburg. If the Russian efforts to prevent the Anglo-German consortium from obtaining the loan were successful, Sanderson felt that '[t]here will be a regular row here . . . [for] the public have set their minds on it'.[68] In St Petersburg, Witte informed O'Conor that there was strong opposition to an agreement.[69] Witte stated that the possibility of an agreement's being reached was 'doubtful', and blamed Muravev for this situation. For his own part, Witte reiterated that he favoured an agreement, but warned that he would no longer 'mix himself up with foreign affairs as whenever he did so of late he had got into trouble'. This was ominous for O'Conor's own hopes, as Witte had been the leading advocate of a settlement with England. A more astute observer would have heard the hint that the Russian finance minister's policy had lost the day, but O'Conor clung to his belief that he could sway Nicholas. At the court ball, held the evening of 1 February, O'Conor found the Emperor's language 'most encouraging'.[70] This feeling was reinforced by a meeting with Muravev two days later. But again there were overtones that should have warned O'Conor that his optimism was misplaced.[71] Both men talked favourably about a general agreement, but when O'Conor chided Muravev about a proposed Franco-Russian loan to China (in opposition to the British loan), the latter feigned an inability to understand the British position. In London, Salisbury grew impatient. On 8 February he instructed O'Conor to determine precisely what the Russian government objected to about the British proposals for a loan to China.[72] At the same time, he informed the Chinese government that Britain would not accept her loan offer being rejected due to the pressure put on China by foreign governments.[73] On 11 February, Salisbury put his views

[67] M. V. Brett and Oliver, Viscount Esher (eds.), *Journals and Letters of Reginald Viscount Esher* (4 vols.; London, 1934–8), i, journal entry, 29 Jan. 1898, 210–11; quotation from Chamberlain to Balfour, secret, 3 Feb. 1898, Balfour Papers, Add MSS 49773.

[68] Sanderson to O'Conor, 28 Jan. 1898, O'Conor Papers, OCON 6/25.

[69] O'Conor to Salisbury, private tel., 31 Jan. 1898, Salisbury Papers, A129.

[70] O'Conor to Salisbury, secret tel., 2 Feb. 1898, *BD*, i, doc. 10.

[71] O'Conor to Salisbury, secret disp. 45, 3 Feb. 1898, FO 65/1552; the version of this in *BD*, i, doc. 12, omits the vital discussion of the Chinese loan.

[72] Salisbury to O'Conor, secret tel. 36, 8 Feb. 1898, *BD*, i, doc. 14.

[73] Young, *British Policy in China*, 62–3.

bluntly to the British minister at Peking: 'We have had some interchange of friendly language at St. Petersburg, but they are insincere and their language is ambiguous.'[74]

The divide between Salisbury and O'Conor was wide. Salisbury had entered the negotiations hoping that general discussions with Russia would help him find a solution to immediate problems, including China. He was not prepared to give up Britain's predominant position in China, nor to agree to a division into spheres of influence (a 'balance of influence' over the Chinese government was another thing). O'Conor had wider visions.[75] O'Conor argued Witte's line that Russia required peace to develop her resources. 'Are we', O'Conor asked rhetorically, 'playing up to Russia by coming to a friendly understanding that will enable her to do all this in safety & then give her irresistible power as against England? or can we assume that the vital interests of both countries are compatible & that she will not fall foul of us when the "entente" has served its purpose?' O'Conor's answer was optimistic. In time, given trade and personal contact, the 'political differences' between the two countries will 'be terribly lessened'. This assumption shaped O'Conor's views. It did not shape Salisbury's. Throughout the first three weeks of February, the prime minister pressed the Russians to make manifest their position on the Chinese loan. When Nicholas II finally made it clear that the Russian terms included a twenty-year lease of Port Arthur in exchange for not opposing the British loan, Salisbury and O'Conor were at opposite poles.[76] Salisbury, O'Conor informed Lascelles, 'thinks we have got most of what we want without a loan & he is doubtful whether to go on with it [the wider Anglo-Russian talks]'.[77] O'Conor believed that Russia would press China no matter what the British did, and that the latter should 'acquiesce in the inevitable', demand compensation when the Russians obtained a lease at Port Arthur, but continue on with the negotiations for a general Anglo-Russian arrangement.[78] For O'Conor, the Chinese loan was secondary.

At 10 Downing Street, there were divided counsels. With Salisbury ill, and recuperating in France, foreign affairs fell to Balfour. The Cabinet meeting on 23 February was, Balfour wrote, 'brief, but important'.[79] Discussion centred on China. It was the opinion of 'many members of the Cabinet' that Britain should not object to the Russian demand for Port Arthur (or, alternatively, Talienwan), 'for it opens ports which are now closed, and it makes it practically impossible for the French,

---

[74] Salisbury to Macdonald, secret tel. 34, 11 Feb. 1898, *BD*, i, doc. 15.

[75] O'Conor to Salisbury, 10 Feb. 1898, Salisbury Papers, A129.

[76] See *BD*, i. 11–15, 19–20.

[77] O'Conor to Lascelles, 23 Feb. 1898, Lascelles Papers, FO 800/6.

[78] Quotation from ibid.; O'Conor to Sanderson, 24 Feb. 1898, O'Conor Papers, OCON 3/15.

[79] Balfour to G. J. Goschen (first lord of the admiralty), 26 Feb. 1898, Balfour Papers, Add MSS 49706.

if they have any aggressive designs on Hainan, to do more than adopt a similar policy of leasing, combined with Free Trade'. This attitude was reinforced by the practical consideration that 'we see no way of preventing the lease'. What did concern the Cabinet was that Russia might close these ports. To prevent this, the Cabinet decided to initiate discussions with the Americans, the latter always concerned over the issue of the 'Open door' in China. The object of these negotiations was to ensure that China was not 'ceded piecemeal' or that, if she were, that British trade was not affected. Balfour noted 'that our desire was to combine the policy of a friendly understanding with Russia with that of a defensive arrangement with the U.S., and as Russia has proposed nothing inconsistent with that arrangement there seems to be no reason why the policies should not properly be run together'. Balfour's disclaimer notwithstanding, the anti-Russian nature of the initiative was evident.

On 26 February, with rumours swirling of China's accepting the British loan, O'Conor called on Lamsdorff (who was acting in Muravev's stead).[80] Lamsdorff played the aggrieved party, asserting that the British had acted falsely by pursuing the China loan, while 'the Russian have held their hand pending the outcome of our [wider] negotiations'. O'Conor realized that his hopes to attain the latter likely had fled, but he carried on the discussion none the less, in the fashion of 'a man who is up a tree and cannot get down without a fall & thought the best thing was to climb up higher and have a look round'. Sanderson stated that the settlement 'does not alter our desire to work on friendly terms with Russia and endeavour to arrange that our respective policies shall not clash',[81] but the proposed Anglo-Russian agreement sank quickly. On 1 March the Chinese government officially accepted the Anglo-German loan. The following day, O'Conor was informed that Nicholas II was 'disappointed' and that the wider negotiations would no longer be pursued.[82] Over the course of March, the Cabinet dithered over the proper response if Russia actually obtained the lease of Port Arthur. This was complicated by the fact that the beginnings of the Fashoda crisis were already evident.[83] O'Conor was not lacking for an opinion. The ambassador believed that 'as nothing short of war will stop Russian Ambition [sic]' in the Far East, Britain must take compensation from China.[84] This would be hard on China; however, that country 'had endless opportunity to harken to our advice but she preferred the hug of the Bear & she must now take the consequences'. O'Conor felt that the British position was strong: 'At heart Russia is in a mortal funk over our Fleet and not at all easy about Japan and we have

---

[80] O'Conor to Sanderson, 26 Feb. 1898, O'Conor Papers, OCON 3/15.
[81] Sanderson to O'Conor, 2 Mar. 1898, O'Conor Papers, OCON 6/25.
[82] O'Conor to Salisbury, secret disp. 71, 3 Mar. 1898, *BD*, i, doc. 22.
[83] Hamilton to Elgin, confidential, 11 Mar. 1898, Hamilton Papers, MSS Eur C125/3.
[84] O'Conor to Sanderson, 10 Mar. 1898, Bertie Papers, FO 800/176.

a big card in our hand which we must not give up unless we can win with our long suit so to say.' In addition, O'Conor recommended to Salisbury that efforts be made to link the British position in Burma with that on the Yangtze.[85] Such sentiments, but with a different target, were shared at the Foreign Office. Bertie argued that Britain must take Wei-hai-wei as a suitable counterpoise to the German and Russian acquisitions.[86] However, as Wei-hai-wei was in Japanese hands, and as the latter were unwilling to stand up to the Russians, this line was impracticable.[87]

With matters in London in a 'distracted condition' due to Salisbury's illness, the British continued to attempt to find a compromise with Russia.[88] On 17 March, Sanderson noted that the British would 'raise no objections' to Russia's taking Port Arthur and Talienwan, providing that British treaty rights were observed and Russia did not 'oppose our obtaining similar concessions elsewhere if we wish it'. Thus, while O'Conor attempted to persuade the Russians that taking Port Arthur and making it a closed port would both irritate Britain and bring about a partition of China, and while the Cabinet discussed what Britain should do if O'Conor's representations failed, all depended on Russia.[89] Balfour put the situation in his characteristic detached fashion: 'I am very curious to see what Russia will do about Port Arthur.'[90] Others did not view the situation with such equanimity. O'Conor feared that even should Russia renounce Port Arthur, this would not augur well for improved Anglo-Russian relations. The ambassador painted a bleak picture of what might happen if he 'succeed[ed] too well' and persuaded Russia not to insist on holding Port Arthur.[91] If this were to occur, Russia would 'pose again as the friend & protector of China' and use this position both to obtain concessions and to block British initiatives at Peking. Further, it was not in Britain's long-term advantage to oppose Russia in the region. This stemmed from Britain's lack of force available in the Far East: 'every year will see the Russians pressing down South more & more till the weight of the mass eventually tells & an inevitable historical episode will be completed.' To attempt to block Russia would, in the short term, lead to renewed Anglo-Russian quarrels: 'In proportion as we cross them in N. China they will harass us in Asia, on the Indian Frontier: in the Persian Gulf. If we squeeze them in N. China, they will bite us where they can & the other Powers will be only too pleased.'

[85] O'Conor to Salisbury, private tel., 12 Mar. 1898, Salisbury Papers, A129.
[86] 'Memorandum by Mr. Bertie', 14 Mar. 1898, *BD*, i, doc. 24; E-T. Z. Sun, 'The Lease of Wei-hai-Wei', *PHR* 19 (1950), 277–83.
[87] Nish, *Anglo-Japanese Alliance*, 53–7.
[88] Sanderson to O'Conor, 17 Mar. 1898, O'Conor Papers, OCON 6/25.
[89] O'Conor to Salisbury, disps. 112 confidential and 121, 21 Mar. and 23 Mar. 1898, FO 65/1553.
[90] Balfour to G. J. Goschen, 23 Mar. 1898, Balfour Papers, Add MSS 49706.
[91] O'Conor to Sanderson, 24 Mar. 1898, Salisbury Papers, A129.

O'Conor's views found mixed support in the Cabinet.[92] Chamberlain was opposed to the idea of annexing Wei-hai-wei as a counter to the Russian actions. Instead, the colonial secretary hankered after a German alliance. Balfour, acting as prime minister in Salisbury's absence, found Chamberlain's sudden awareness of Britain's position amusing: the discussions on China 'had forced on his [Chamberlain's] attention our isolated and occasionally therefore difficult diplomatic position'.[93] Others did not share this apprehension of British weakness. George Goschen, as befitted a first lord of the admiralty who was at this very time endeavouring to counter Russia's newest naval building programme, was disgusted with O'Conor's suggestion that Britain must acquiesce in Russia's eventual domination of China.[94] Finally, and despite Chamberlain's dissent, the Cabinet made up its mind. Taking 'their courage in both hands', they agreed that should Russia seize Port Arthur, Britain should demand Wei-hai-wei as compensation.[95]

On 27 March, Russia announced that she had signed a twenty-five year lease on Talienwan and Port Arthur. The British response was swift. The following day, MacDonald pressed the Chinese government for a similar British lease at Wei-hai-wei. O'Conor was instructed to notify the Russian government that the British regretted the Russian action and 'must retain their entire liberty of action' to protect their own interests.[96] In London, Balfour was forced to explain British policy. Throughout March, *The Times* had published 'nightly articles slashing at the Govt.' over foreign policy, and Balfour needed to put his party's case before the public.[97] This immediately ran into difficulties. On 1 April Balfour telegraphed to St Petersburg that he intended to speak in the House of Commons on the 5th and to 'express entire confidence' in the assurances that the Russian government had made orally to O'Conor promising that Talienwan and Port Arthur would become open ports.[98] He suggested to O'Conor that the ambassador now obtain a written statement from the Russian government to the latter effect. O'Conor rapidly discovered the true Russian position. Muravev's response was that the assurances given on 16 March were merely in the nature of a 'friendly exchange of views' pending the outcome of the Russo-Chinese discussions.[99]

O'Conor was predictably furious: 'I am sorry to be obliged to send home such a history of Chicanery [*sic*] as is disclosed in Mouraveieff's Notes', he wrote to

---

[92] Sanderson to O'Conor, 30 Mar. 1898, O'Conor Papers, OCON 6/25.

[93] Balfour to Salisbury, 14 Apr. 1898, Balfour Papers, Add MSS 49691.

[94] His minute on O'Conor to Sanderson, 24 Mar. 1898, Salisbury Papers, A129.

[95] See n. 93.

[96] Salisbury to O'Conor, disp. 76A, 28 Mar. 1898, *BD*, i, doc. 41.

[97] O'Conor to Lascelles, 7 Apr. 1898, Lascelles Papers, FO 800/16.

[98] Balfour to O'Conor, private and secret tel., 1 Apr. 1898, Salisbury Papers A129; O'Conor to Lascelles, 16 Mar. 1898, Lascelles Papers, FO 800/6; O'Conor to Salisbury, disp. 99, 16 Mar. 1898, FO 65/1553.

[99] O'Conor to Salisbury, disp. 137A, 4 Apr. 1898, FO 65/1553.

Sanderson, and termed Muravev that 'slippery Minister with whom I have to deal daily'.[100] But, O'Conor was relatively satisfied with the actual outcome of events. He had never felt that Britain could stop Russia from taking Port Arthur, and the British lease of Wei-hai-wei was in accord with his advice that Britain should therefore look after her own interests.[101] With respect to the status of Port Arthur and Talienwan, O'Conor felt that pressure from the other powers would force Russia to respect her now-renounced promises. The Cabinet, too, was relatively satisfied, although many in it felt that 'the Russians have treated us very badly'.[102] The important thing, from a political point of view, was to ensure that the government did not appear to be Russia's dupe and that its actions did not seem motivated by popular pressure. In this vein, Salisbury instructed Curzon that the point to be made in Parliament was that 'we only abstained from raising the question of Wei-hai-wei until we knew the attitude of Russia with respect to Port Arthur & that it was not taken up at the last moment under pressure from the Jingo press'.[103] With typically perfect hindsight, and ignoring the shilly-shallying that had characterized their deliberations, the politicians decided to take credit for a firm response to the Russian actions in China. The government had emerged relatively unscathed politically. As Salisbury told Curzon in the middle of April: 'As far as I can judge here the Chinese difficulty has, for the present, passed by. The Liberals say we ought never to have taken W.[ei] H.[ai] W.[ei] & the Jingoes say we ought to have taken it sooner.'[104]

The resolution of the Port Arthur crisis brought Anglo–Russian relations in China to a new departure. While the Russian *coup* had not been blocked, the British response had been firm, and the balance of power in the region maintained. The question was whether Russia would be able to use her acquisition of Port Arthur as a lever with which to pry further concessions from the Chinese. The test case would be railway concessions, and the negotiations over them occupied Anglo–Russian relations for the next year. These negotiations need to be seen in the wider context of the British position in China.[105] Since 1895 there had been a flood of foreigners into China, each trying to obtain concessions. The British interest in railway building was slight, but the Hongkong Bank was keen to obtain concessions for the lucrative construction of public works. By the spring of 1898, the Bank's position had changed. The alliance with Deutsche Bank, which had obtained the third Chinese indemnity loan earlier in the year, had collapsed. While the Hongkong

[100] O'Conor to Sanderson, 7 Apr. 1898, O'Conor Papers, OCON 3/15.
[101] Ibid.; O'Conor to Sanderson, 15 Mar. 1898, O'Conor Papers, OCON 3/15.
[102] Sanderson to O'Conor, 13 Apr. 1898, O'Conor Papers, OCON 6/25.
[103] Salisbury to Curzon, 9 Apr. 1898, Curzon Papers, MSS Eur F112/1b.
[104] Salisbury to Curzon, 15 Apr. 1898, Curzon Papers, MSS Eur F112/1b; Young, *British Policy in China*, 75; Sanderson to O'Conor, 27 Apr. 1898, O'Conor Papers, OCON 6/25.
[105] Edwards, *British Diplomacy and Finance*, 31–7; Young, *British Policy in China*, 77–99.

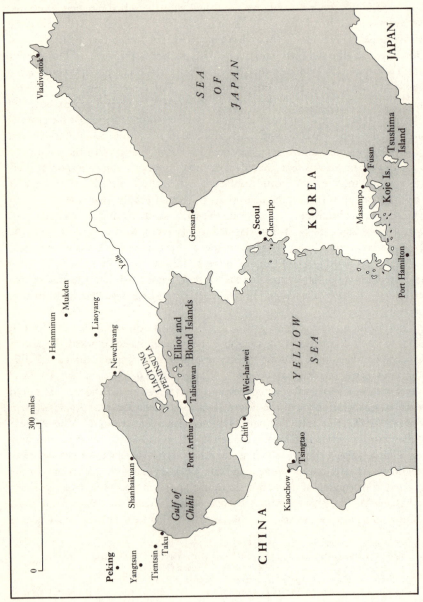

MAP 6.1 The Far East

Bank scrambled to create a new, British group, the Foreign Office found itself in an awkward position. If foreigners obtained concessions in China, they would utilize them to the detriment of British trade. While not opposed to foreign investment in China, Britain would, as Salisbury wrote at the end of May 1898, refuse 'and doubtless continue to refuse, general preferential rights either for Russia in Manchuria, or Germany in Shangtung'.[106] The Foreign Secretary continued that

But we ought to have on the stocks a railway in the Yangtze region: & if any powers resists the concession to us, we ought to resist any concession of any kind that they ask for anywhere. I see no other mode of fighting the matter. The difficulty is to produce a syndicate really willing and able to build a railway in the Yangtze region. I see no signs of that passionate desire to invest in Chinese railways either in this country or in any other—on which the whole of these calculations are built.

And if no British 'patriotic capitalists' could be found, Salisbury wrote a week later, how could the Chinese be prevented from accepting Russian offers? 'I see clearly', he concluded gloomily, 'that our principal diplomatic occupation at Pekin [*sic*], will not be in obtaining concessions of our own, but in blocking other people's.'[107]

In June, part of Salisbury's problem was solved. The Hongkong Bank brought into existence the British and Chinese Corporation (BCC—a conglomerate of British merchant banks and, among other firms, Jardine Matheson), for the express purpose of seeking concessions in China. Operating through the Hongkong Bank, the BCC offered the Chinese government a loan of £2.3 million for the extension of the Peking–Shanhaikuan railway to Hsinminun, with a branch to the port of Newchwang. This loan was to be guaranteed by the Chinese government, but, in addition, the BCC would have first charge on the revenues of the lines constructed and, in the case of default, the entire line would become its property.[108] Here were Salisbury's 'patriotic capitalists', although their activities were not in the Yangtze valley where British interests were centred. However, the BCC's interest in acquiring a line that would compete with Russian projects in Manchuria certainly aided Salisbury in his contention that Russia had no exclusive rights in that area.

By July 1898, Salisbury had decided to use the Newchwang line (the term by which the entire project was generally referred) as a strong point against Russian efforts to secure an exclusive position in Manchuria. When Sir Charles Scott, O'Conor's replacement as British ambassador at St Petersburg, arrived in Russia on 12 August, he was faced immediately with a quarrel over the Newchwang railway. Three weeks earlier, Salisbury had authorized the British minister in Peking, Sir Claude MacDonald, to inform the Chinese government that Britain would support

---

[106] Salisbury to Curzon, 30 May 1898, Curzon Papers, MSS Eur F112/1b.
[107] Salisbury to Curzon, 4 June 1898, Curzon Papers, MSS Eur F112/1b.
[108] Edwards, *British Diplomacy and Finance*, 38; Young, *British Policy in China*, 91.

China against any power 'which commits an act of aggression on China because China has granted to a British subject permission to make or support any railway or similar work' as a bulwark against what were believed to be Russian-inspired efforts to block the Chinese acceptance of the British loan.[109] Salisbury underlined this position on 8 August by informing the Chinese minister in London that 'Russia had no right whatever to object to a mortgage loan being made by the Hong Kong bank to the Newchang [*sic*] railway: and that I strongly advised China to pay no regard to her objection'.[110] In point of fact, Salisbury was not overly concerned that Russia might act over the issue: 'I do not think the Newchwang Railway will come to be a test case for our declaration. That is to say, I do not think Russia will commit any act of aggression upon China, on account of China yielding the right of mortgage & control to the Hong Kong Bank.'[111] What was more likely, Salisbury felt, was that 'China may herself elect to give way'. Certainly, the Russians attempted to per-suade the Chinese not to ratify the loan with the Hongkong Bank.[112]

Even before Scott presented his credentials to Nicholas II, the ambassador found himself immersed in the Newchwang issue. On 18 August, Scott discussed the position thoroughly with Muravev.[113] The Russian minister pointed out that a British line to Newchwang would compete with the Russian terminus at Talienwan and Russian trade would be 'fatally injured'. To forestall this, Russia had signed a secret agreement with China. This did not forbid a line to Newchwang; however, it did provide that it would 'be constructed with China's own money and always remain in Chinese hands and under Chinese control'. This latter had been nego-tiated long before the Hongkong Bank had shown any interest in the project, and was by no means an anti-British stipulation. In London, the Russian attitude was seen favourably, and the secret agreement as just another case of the Chinese government's 'bad faith'.[114] However, the British wished to push Russia into stating her position clearly, in order that Britain might propose a bargain: an abandonment of Newchwang in exchange for recognition of the British position in the Yangtze valley.[115] As Balfour told Salisbury: 'I want to drive them into making a distinct offer of spheres of influence (so far as concessions go)—i.e. Manchuria v. basin of Yangstse.'

[109] Salisbury to MacDonald, tel. 230, 22 July 1898, *BD*, i, doc. 55.

[110] Salisbury's minute (8 Aug. 1898) on MacDonald to Salisbury, tel. 237, 25 July 1898, *BD*, i, doc. 56.

[111] Salisbury to Curzon, 8 Aug. 1898, Curzon Papers, MSS Eur F112/1b.

[112] Balfour to Scott, tel. 215, 17 Aug. 1898, *BD*, i, doc. 57; Young, *British Policy in China*, 93–4; Malozemoff, *Russian Far Eastern Policy*, 113–15.

[113] Scott to Salisbury, confidential disp. 286, 18 Aug. 1898, FO 65/1555.

[114] Unsigned minute on ibid.: 'Count Mouravieff's attitude seems to have been most conciliatory.'; the quotation from Hamilton to Elgin (viceroy, India), 24 Aug. 1898, Hamilton Papers, MSS Eur C125/3/1.

[115] Ibid.; Edwards, *British Diplomacy and Finance*, 40; Balfour to Salisbury, 30 Aug. 1898, Balfour Papers, Add MSS 49691.

By early September, Muravev seemed to have accepted this point. When the Russian minister met with Scott on 8 September, Muravev stated that Russia's interests in China were 'exclusively political & to the north of Pekin [*sic*]'.[116] British interests, Muravev went on, 'were more especially commercial & lying to the S. of Pekin [*sic*]' and Russia was prepared to recognize them. While Scott emphasized that the term 'sphere of influence' was to be used carefully lest it should be thought to adumbrate a partition of China, he was very pleased with Muravev's 'desire to cultivate the most friendly & confidential relations with me, with a view to advancing a good understanding with England'. Others were more cynical. As MacDonald wrote from Peking: 'recent events here' showed that 'you have only to speak firmly to the Russians and they knuckle down'.[117] The arrival of more British warships on the China Station had resulted in an 'effusive cordiality' from the Russians at Peking. None the less, by the end of September, Scott was confident that a solution to the quarrel over concessions could be worked out, a conviction that was shared in London.[118]

This assessment was overly optimistic.[119] What Scott thought had been agreed— a trade-off wherein an agreement favourable to Russia over the Newchwang railway was accepted in return for a recognition of British predominance in the Yangtze valley—turned out to be a chimera. While the Russians warmly agreed to the first part of the deal, they rejected the second, and argued that it was a distinct and separate matter. Sanderson was not dismayed; the PUS pointed out that the complexities of decision-making in Russia made it 'too much' to expect a quick decision.[120] However, Sanderson opined, 'clearly we cannot take the first half of the agreement without the second'. All this was complicated by Chinese politics. The reform programme instituted by the Emperor in the spring of 1898 had resulted in the Dowager Empress Tzu-his' confining the Emperor to his quarters, and there was concern that Russia might take advantage of the situation.[121] In these circumstances, Scott had decided that the best policy was 'to lie by, and at least see whether the Chinese Govt. ratify the contract with the Hongkong Bank'.[122]

At the beginning of November, things began to move. This was largely due to Witte. The Tsarist finance minister had opposed the taking of Port Arthur in the first place; the reaction of foreign powers had only reinforced his views. Equally, Witte could not afford to have his plans for Russian commercial expansion in the

---

[116] Scott to Salisbury, private and confidential, 8 Sept. 1898, Salisbury Papers A129.
[117] MacDonald to Bertie, 18 Sept. 1898, Bertie Papers, Add MSS 63013.
[118] Scott to Sanderson, 22 Sept. 1898; Sanderson to Scott, 28 Sept. 1898, both Scott Papers, Add MSS 52298.
[119] Scott to Sanderson, 6 Oct. 1898, Scott Papers, Add MSS 52298; Scott to Salisbury, disp. 325 very confidential, 6 Oct. 1898, FO 65/1555.
[120] Sanderson to Scott, 12 Oct. 1898, Scott Papers, Add MSS 52298.
[121] Hamilton to Elgin, 4 Oct. 1898, Hamilton Papers, MSS Eur C125/3/1.
[122] Scott to Sanderson, 20 Oct. 1898, Scott Papers, Add MSS 52298.

Far East stymied by the creation of a British commercial rival at Newchwang. For these reasons, he began discussions with Scott. On 2 November, Witte suggested that a general Anglo-Russian agreement be sought, and, as a token of Russian good faith, suggested that Talienwan might be made a free port.[123] This was greeted sceptically at a Foreign Office basking in the glow of the French backdown at Fashoda: Bertie felt that the advantage accruing to British trade would be slight, Salisbury stated that such an agreement would 'be a good deal laughed at', and Balfour noted that 'as at present advised I should insist on the delimitation of spheres of interest for [the] concession which is already agreed to in principle'. However, two facts—that Witte was seen to be 'perfectly sincere' (and very much in need of British capital for investment in Russia) and the soothing words of the Russian foreign office—held out hope that a suitable Anglo-Russian arrangement could be reached.[124] At this point, the Chinese negotiations became entangled with other matters. Muravev's vacation in France raised fears of a combined Russo-French position on Fashoda. Scott ventilated this British concern at St Petersburg: 'it would be fatal to any efforts to come to an understanding on the Chinese question, if we could not be satisfied of the sincerity of Russian professions [on matters generally, here concerning Fashoda].'[125] While both Scott and Sanderson felt that Russia had 'no intention of helping the French to any serious extent in their Upper Nile encroachments', the Chinese negotiations were not carried on in a vacuum.[126]

At the same time, the question of governmental support for the Hongkong Bank was again raised.[127] With the Bank's finding it difficult to raise money on the London market, Cameron wished to have the British government make some heartening statement to support the loan. Bertie agreed. The entire matter had 'become rather a matter of credit for this Country, as well as a trade question, that the Railway should be constructed'. Again, as he had in September, Hicks Beach objected.[128] His argument was simple: it would not do for the British government to give an advantage to investors in the Hongkong Bank's project that was not extended to other investments elsewhere. Faced with such opposition, and with the Russians quiet, the proposed endorsement was not forthcoming.

For the next two months, Scott cooled his heels in St Petersburg. Despite

---

[123] Scott to Salisbury, disp. 355 very confidential, 2 Nov. 1898, FO 65/1556 and minutes; Sanderson to Scott, 9 Nov. 1898, Scott Papers, Add MSS 52298.

[124] Scott to Salisbury, 3 Nov. 1898; Scott to Salisbury, private and confidential 17 Nov. 1898, both Salisbury Papers, A129.

[125] Scott to Salisbury, 17 Nov. 1898, Scott Papers, Add MSS 52297.

[126] Sanderson to Scott, 23 Nov. 1898, Scott Papers, Add MSS 52297; J. Cockfield, 'Germany and the Fashoda Crisis', *CEH* 16 (1983), 256–75.

[127] Bertie's memo for Salisbury, 24 Nov. 1898, Balfour Papers, Add MSS 49691.

[128] His minutes (25 Nov. 1898) on ibid.; Edwards, *British Diplomacy and Finance*, 41.

Muravev's return from Paris, and the fact that he 'abounded in amiability', no concrete Russian proposal over China emerged.[129] In the interim, Scott contented himself with positing differing explanations for the delay. His varying views underline just how difficult it was to read Russian politics. In mid-December, the ambassador informed Salisbury that Muravev 'is evidently very anxious not to repeat his former mistake by committing himself too far until quite sure of the ground on which he & Witte stand with the Emperor on this question, & I do not think it safe to press him, or to let him think that we are in more urgent need than Russia of an agreement'.[130] By the end of the month, Scott had changed his tune. The delay, he now advanced, was due to the Emperor's being absent; without the imperial presence it was impossible to reconcile the differences in policy which Scott now perceived between Muravev and Witte.[131] By the New Year, Scott admitted to Salisbury that 'I wish I could ascertain more clearly how we actually stand with Russia just now'.[132] With the Emperor away from St Petersburg, the machinery of Russian policy-making stood idle. At the end of January it was jolted into action. Cameron and the BCC finally prevailed upon the British government to give a limited public backing to the Newchwang railway project.[133] While Scott was not immediately informed of this fact, the Russians were. Within a week, the long-awaited draft of an agreement on China was in the ambassador's hands.[134] In essence, the Russians proposed that Britain should not block Russian railway building north of the Great Wall, while Russia would behave likewise towards British endeavours in the Yangtze basin. This was coupled to a vague profession of good will between the two countries. Despite this lack of precision, Scott suggested that the Russian proposal be accepted 'as a preliminary agreement' and exact details considered later. With the 'despair' that he had begun to hold about the negotiations dispelled, and his 'very mistrustful' attitude towards the Russians now set aside, Scott was prepared to carry on discussions.[135]

His view found ready acceptance at the Foreign Office. There, Bertie had at last been able to convince the Russian ambassador that the Hongkong Bank's loan for the Newchwang railway did 'not give control of the lines North of the great-wall, nor violate the [Russian secret] agreement with China'.[136] This had seemingly

[129] Scott to Salisbury, disp. 381 very confidential, 26 Nov. 1898, FO 65/1556; quotation from Scott to Salisbury, 1 Dec. 1898, Salisbury Papers A129.

[130] Scott to Salisbury, 15 Dec. 1898, Salisbury Papers A129.

[131] Scott to Sanderson, 29 Dec. 1898, Scott Papers, Add MSS 52298.

[132] Scott to Salisbury, 12 Jan. 1899, Salisbury Papers A129.

[133] Edwards, *British Diplomacy and Finance*, 42.

[134] Scott to Salisbury, disps. 34 and 35 confidential, 2 and 6 Feb. 1899, FO 65/1577; Scott to Salisbury, disp. 40 confidential, 8 Feb. 1899, FO 65/1577; Scott to Salisbury, 9 Feb. 1899, Salisbury Papers A129.

[135] Scott to Lascelles, 9 Feb. 1899, Lascelles Papers, FO 800/15.

[136] Scott to Salisbury, 23 Feb. 1899, Scott Papers, Add MSS 52303.

eliminated the outstanding sore point between the two countries, and Salisbury
agreed that Scott should carry on further discussions using the Muravev proposal
as a preliminary agreement. These proved to be complicated and tedious. As one
member of the British Cabinet put it: 'Mouravieff is a terrible trickster, and always
contrives on some plea or other to put off the final meeting which is to ratify the
principles of the general understanding.'[137] By the end of March, Scott was beginning to show signs of despair and self-pity:

I do think this battle of the Banks is most irritating and fraught with future embarrassment.
It is a thousand pities that our Bank could not have taken some other security for their loan
than one that ostensibly spells 'control' of the Manchurian Line. It seems as if ever since my
negotiations began here, everything possible to cut the ground from under my feet has been
done in China, under the conviction that nothing would come out of the negotiations with
Russia.[138]

The ambassador went on to put blame on MacDonald, the British minister in
Peking, and ended with the admonition that '[t]here's a Russian side to the story
which must not be overlooked'.

This was too much for Sanderson. In a blistering letter, the PUS demolished,
one by one, the Russian allegations of British interference, bad faith, or hostile
intent.[139] Sanderson pointed out that '[a]s a Government we did not originate or
push the matter' of the Newchwang railway, and that it was done by merchants
with commercial intent. The tone of the letter was biting:

Lessar [the Russian chargé d'affaires in London] came here one day when first the Russians
made objections to the loan and talked such outrageous nonsense in explanation of their
objections that it made me quite sick and I scarcely had the patience to answer him. He talked
about our making use of the mortgage to occupy the line with soldiers and attack Russia. I
asked him how he could come with such a story to anybody who had seen a map and knew
our relative military and naval strength.

But, Sanderson continued, the Russian government in February had accepted
the fact that the Hongkong Bank loan would not be used as means to alienate
control of the line from the Chinese. The British government had imposed this
condition on the Hongkong Bank, 'thereby incurring a good deal of attack', and
now the Russians argued that there were other conditions of the secret Russian
arrangement with China that are being violated. 'Can anybody call this straight
forward?' Sanderson asked rhetorically, and added that if the Russians had deliberately concealed provisions of their secret arrangement with China that would vitiate
an agreement with Britain 'it was a piece of odious trickery'. His conclusions were

---

[137] Hamilton to Curzon, 10 Feb. 1899, Curzon Papers, MSS Eur F111/142.
[138] Scott to Sanderson, 23 Mar. 1899, Scott Papers, Add MSS 52303.
[139] Sanderson to Scott, 28 Mar. 1899, Scott Papers, Add MSS 52298.

blunt. The British government were committed to the policy as stated and had not the 'smallest intention' of changing their position. This might lead to a strain in Anglo-Russian relations, but while 'that will be a great misfortune . . . it will not be our fault'.

This broadside, which Sanderson repeated to Staal, and Scott outlined to Muravev, had the desired effect.[140] On 20 April, Scott reported to the PUS that 'some definite agreement with Russia on this tiresome railway question' had at last been reached.[141] Scott was under no illusions that the agreement, which was not actually signed until 28 April, was definitively binding on the Russians. In the same letter to Sanderson, the ambassador noted that adherence depended on community of interest, and noted that 'if there is any secret intention of evading its spirit, no words could have been formed that would not leave some loop hole'. Still, Scott was sanguine that the Russians would observe the agreement, and in any case it was 'far more reliable than mere verbal assurances of intention with which hitherto we have had to deal'. In actual content, the agreement went little beyond Muravev's proposal of February.[142] Britain agreed not to seek railway concessions north of the Great Wall and not to obstruct Russian efforts to obtain them there. Russia agreed to pursue an identical policy with respect to British endeavours in the Yangtze. Both parties agreed not to infringe upon the sovereign rights of China or upon the privileges granted in existing treaties, while a final clause made it clear that the agreement was 'of a nature to consolidate peace in the Far East and to serve the primordial interests of China herself'. In addition to this pious phrase, an additional note stated that the Newchwang line was to be regarded as Chinese, although European engineers could inspect it. Scott's triumph in carrying out this difficult negotiation was duly recognized by his being awarded the GCB in the June honours list.

The Muravev–Scott agreement brought to an end four years of concession hunting in China. Throughout the period, Kimberley and Salisbury had both sought to come to an arrangement with Russia that would regularize their conflicting aspirations in the Far East. The search for this arrangement was complicated by Great Power rivalry. The German seizure of Kiaochow and the Russian taking of Port Arthur turned a colonial and commercial matter into one of prestige and international power. For this reason, British commercial and banking interests in China became identified with British political interests and the wider aspects of British foreign policy. This was not a concerted thrust by British imperialism in the form of the Hongkong Bank's working hand in glove with the Foreign Office.

---

[140] Sanderson to Scott, 29 Mar. 1899, Scott Papers, Add MSS 52298; Scott to Sanderson, 6 Apr. 1899, Scott Papers, Add MSS 52303.
[141] Scott to Sanderson, 20 Apr. 1899, Scott Papers, Add MSS 52303.
[142] Scott to Salisbury, disp. 127, 29 Apr. 1899, FO 65/1578.

Rather, it was a confluence of interests: the Hongkong Bank's desire to get governmental backing for its commercial endeavours; the Foreign Office's reluctant support of the Bank's position in order to apply a brake to Russian expansion into China. The separate natures of the Bank's and the Foreign Office's interests in the railway concessions were clearly illustrated in the summer of 1899. At that time, the Hongkong Bank proposed selling its shares in the Newchwang line to the Russians, since the line was not producing the profits expected.[143] The Foreign Office objected, largely on the grounds of prestige, and the matter was dropped. While frictions remained between the Bank and the Russians, official Anglo-Russian relations in China remained a backwater until the events of the Boxer rebellion and its aftermath brought them again to the fore.

[143] Edwards, *British Diplomacy and Finance*, 44–8.

7

Anglo-Russian Relations, 1899 –1903: China and Central Asia

'THERE has been an epidemic of illness which has affected certain members of the Government,' Hamilton wrote early in 1899, 'Chamberlain is ill with influenza and gout, and both Goschen and Beach are showing evident signs of work and worry. We are none of us getting younger.'[1] The infirmities of the Cabinet were a metaphor for the last days of the 'Victorian' ascendency in British foreign policy. From 1899 to November 1900, the Boer War brought growing discontent with Salisbury's management of foreign affairs. The 'Edwardians' advocated abandoning Britain's diplomatic isolation and re-examining Britain's defence policy.[2] When Lansdowne took over the Foreign Office in November 1900, he spent the next year considering the alternatives—an arrangement with either Germany or Russia— before settling on an Anglo-Japanese alliance. At the same time, and particularly after Balfour assumed the premiership in mid-1902, Britain's military and naval position underwent a thorough re-examination, centred on Russia.[3]

From 1899 to 1903, Anglo-Russian relations focused on China and Central Asia. The Russian refusal to withdraw from Manchuria was a continual irritant. After the Scott–Muravev agreement, Anglo-Russian relations were relatively quiet: the British desired calm in the Far East because of South Africa; the Russians were fearful about British intentions in China. Conversely, the British were concerned that Russia would attempt to advance there. By mid-May 1899, there were rumours that the Russians were trying to extract a concession to build a line from Newchwang to Peking, with possible dire implications for China's sovereignty.[4]

[1] Hamilton to Curzon, 24 Feb. 1899, Curzon Papers, MSS Eur F111/142.
[2] C. H. D. Howard, *Splendid Isolation: A Study of Ideas Concerning Britain's International Position and Foreign Policy During the Later Years of the Third Marquis of Salisbury* (London, 1967).
[3] G. Monger, *The End of Isolation: British Foreign Policy 1900–7* (London, 1963); I. H. Nish, *The Anglo-Japanese Alliance: The Diplomacy of Two Island Empires 1894–1907* (London, 1966); J. Gooch, *The Plans of War: The General Staff and British Military Strategy c.1900–16* (London, 1974); A. L. Friedberg, *The Weary Titan: Britain and the Experience of Relative Decline, 1895–1905* (Princeton, 1988).
[4] Scott to Sanderson, 18 May 1899, Scott Papers, Add MSS 52303; Scott to Salisbury, disp. 160, 23 May 1899, FO 65/1578; Bertie's untitled memo, 19 May 1899 and Salisbury's minute (20 May), both Bertie Papers, FO 800/163.

Salisbury was convinced that the completion of the trans-Siberian alone was enough to put Peking 'in the greatest danger'. He and Bertie suggested to the Chinese that their capital be moved south, where British naval power could counter the Russian threat.[5] The situation in China did not result in any serious Anglo-Russian friction in the summer of 1899. As Scott reported in August: 'Mouravieff's chief desire is, I feel convinced, to keep everything quiet, and to avoid every pretext for raising difficulties or questions in any part of the world, and this is, I am convinced, the desire of the Emperor and Witte.'[6] A month later, with Nicholas II and most of the Russian officials leaving for the Crimea, Scott decided to return to England.[7] In their absence, Scott felt 'that nothing satisfactory (like last year) can be done in the way of work until December'. Although Scott assumed that consequent relations would be uneventful, he was mistaken. Before he returned on 10 December, the Boer War had broken out and Anglo-Russian relations had become strained, to some extent due to the 'bitterness and hostility towards our country' of the Russian press.[8] Rumours were also heard that Russia was attempting to create a combination of European powers against Britain.[9] But Salisbury believed that the likelihood of such a coalition was very unlikely: '[i]t is presumed therefore that Prince Mouravieff wished to address it as a threat or warning to us to make us comply with some demands he intends to make.'[10] Salisbury felt that Muravev hoped to get the Dardanelles opened, but others looked to Persia and Afghanistan as the likely points of Russian advances. Sanderson argued that Russia would 'postpone committing themselves [to any arrangement in Persia] in the hope that we may be more squeezable after further difficulties in South Africa'.[11] Hamilton warned that the British 'have not a friend in Europe' and that, in this circumstance and with the 'extension of [Russian] railroads' towards Persia, sea power might no longer safeguard British interests there. From Constantinople, O'Conor argued that should the Amir of Afghanistan die, Russia might 'make a rush at Herat & trust to her good luck to save her from the consequences'.[12]

Establishing British policy was complicated by the Boer War and the personal circumstances of Lord Salisbury.[13] To many, Salisbury's apparent inaction was

[5] Bertie's untitled memo, 19 May 1899 and Salisbury's minute (20 May), both Bertie Papers, FO 800/163. The Chinese were as wary of the British as of the Russians. Bertie to Salisbury, 21 May 1899, Bertie Papers, Add MSS 63013.

[6] Scott to Salisbury, 10 Aug. 1899, Scott Papers, Add MSS 52303.

[7] Scott to Sanderson, 7 Sept. 1899, Scott Papers, Add MSS 52303.

[8] Hardinge to Salisbury, disp. 313, 18 Oct. 1899, FO 65/1580; Hardinge to Sanderson, 2 Nov. 1899, Hardinge Papers, vol. 3; Hardinge to Salisbury, disp. 361, confidential, 8 Dec. 1899, FO 65/1580.

[9] Hardinge to Salisbury, secret disp. 323, 30 Oct. 1899, FO 65/1580.

[10] Salisbury to the Queen, copy, tel., 30 Oct. 1899, Midleton Papers, PRO 30/67/4.

[11] 'Views of India Govt on Russia', memo, Sanderson, 2 Nov. 1899, Midleton Papers, PRO 30/67/4.

[12] O'Conor to Chirol, 5 Nov. 1899, O'Conor Papers, OCON 5/3/3.

[13] Hamilton to Curzon, 23 Nov. 1899; quotation from Hamilton to Curzon, 1 Dec. 1899, both Curzon Papers, MSS Eur F111/144.

unacceptable. In January 1900, St John Brodrick, the parliamentary under-secretary for foreign affairs, wanted to approach Russia about an understanding over Persia, but noted that 'in L[or]d S.'s present state of feeling' nothing could be done.[14] At the India Office, feelings ran higher.[15] And, in June 1900, Hamilton delivered a comprehensive condemnation:

The Foreign Office at the present moment is in a hopeless state of flabbiness, and I tell you quite frankly that I do not think you will get them to do anything either in connection with Persia or, so far as I can see, anywhere else. To let things drift seems now to be the accepted policy of that Department, or at any rate of its chief, and the misfortune is that time is not on our side, and the longer we drift the worse position we find ourselves in.[16]

Such sentiments would later result in a Cabinet revolt against Salisbury's Victorian policies, but here they created a background of discontent to Anglo-Russian relations.

British fears about possible Russian diplomatic and military initiatives found their first focus in Persia. From India, throughout 1899, Curzon had been urging a firm policy against Russia in Persia.[17] His views were opposed at the India Office, where Godley, the permanent under-secretary, asserted that Russia's 'entry into Persia would be an absolute walk-over: I do not suppose it would even be opposed'.[18] Hamilton was equally blunt; should Russia invade Persia: 'I do not see where the material force [to oppose her] is to come.'[19] Nor would 'popular opinion' in Britain likely sanction war to aid the Shah, 'as the tyranny and misgovernment in Persia is becoming yearly more well-known'. In November, Hardinge reported that the Russians were transferring troops to that region.[20] Sanderson felt that this 'cannot be considered an altogether friendly proceeding' and termed Muravev's policy 'mischievous'.[21] Curzon wished to seize various locales in the Persian Gulf to safeguard the British position, but this was rejected in London.[22] Hamilton and Godley reiterated their view that Britain had few means of blocking Russia's advance, and Godley added that the extension of the Russian railway system made places like India and China less the 'quasi-islands' that they had been, to the detriment of Britain's sea-based power. As Russia was 'practically invulnerable' to any British efforts, Hamilton advocated compromise: he was 'always disposed to

[14] Brodrick to Balfour, 18 Jan. 1900, Balfour Papers, Add MSS 49720.
[15] Godley to Curzon, 19 Jan. 1900, Curzon Papers, MSS Eur F111/145.
[16] Hamilton to Curzon, 6 Jun. 1900, Curzon Papers, MSS Eur F111/146.
[17] D. McLean, *Britain and Her Buffer State: The Collapse of the Persian Empire, 1890–1914* (London, 1979), 29–47.
[18] Godley to Curzon, 3 May 1899, Curzon Papers, MSS Eur F111/143.
[19] Hamilton to Curzon, 23 June 1899, Curzon Papers, MSS Eur F111/143.
[20] Hardinge to Sanderson, 8 and 16 Nov. 1899, both FO 65/1580.
[21] Sanderson to Hardinge, 22 Nov. 1899, Hardinge Papers, vol. 3.
[22] Hamilton to Curzon, 9 Nov. 1899; Godley to Curzon, 10 Nov. 1899, both Curzon Papers, MSS Eur F111/144.

come to some rational agreement with Russia, provided we have reason to think they will adhere to the arrangement'.[23]

Throughout December 1899 and January 1900, reports of Russian troop movements in Central Asia abounded.[24] Scott argued that the 'military party' in Russia was using these rumours as a means both to put pressure upon Britain and to block the pacific policy urged by Muravev and the Emperor. The ambassador advocated accepting Muravev's professions of friendship as sincere.[25] In this, Scott was quite wrong.[26] Russian naval and military men were advocating a descent upon the Dardanelles, but lacked confidence that they had the means to carry it out. Muravev, on the other hand, was urging a push in Central Asia. In the Far East, only considerations of Japan's strength, rather than any concerns about British reactions, tempered Muravev's desire to strengthen Russia's position.[27] Muravev's duplicity was made manifest on 31 January 1900, when a Russian loan of £2.4 million to Persia was announced.[28] The loan, whose terms forbade Persia to borrow further from any foreign sources, was purely political, designed to place Persia firmly in the Russian orbit. Sanderson's reaction was balanced:

The announcement of the Russian loan is rather an eye opener as to the character of our friends. Staal has prudently avoided coming here today. If I see him I shall say that I regret personally these occurrences more because they destroy all confidence here on the possibility of working with the Russian Govt. than on account of their actual importance.[29]

The DMI, Sir John Ardagh, contended that the loan presaged a Russian military advance. For him, the circumstances were doubly galling, since he had recently argued that Britain should not open any discussions with Russia about Persia 'in consequence of our embarrassments in South Africa'.[30] Now, he asserted, Britain must do so immediately.[31] The Persian loan and the movement of Russian troops into Central Asia indicated that the 'anticipation that Russia would profit by our

---

[23] Hamilton to Curzon, 11 Nov. 1899, Curzon Papers, MSS Eur F111/144.

[24] Sanderson to Scott, 3 Jan. 1900, Scott Papers, Add MSS 52298; Scott to Salisbury, disp. 15 secret, 11 Jan. 1900, FO 65/1598; Scott to Salisbury, 11 Jan. 1900, Salisbury Papers, A129.

[25] Scott to Salisbury, disp. 369 very confidential, 14 Dec. 1899, FO 65/1580; Scott to Salisbury, confidential, 14 Dec. 1899, Salisbury Papers A129.

[26] D. Geyer, *Russian Imperialism: The Interaction of Domestic and Foreign Policy, 1860–1914*, trans. B. Little (Leamington Spa, 1987), 201–5.

[27] Hardinge to Sanderson, 30 Nov. 1899, and Sanderson to Hardinge, 6 Dec. 1899, both Hardinge Papers, vol. 3; O'Conor to Sanderson, secret, 10 Jan. 1900, O'Conor Papers, OCON 3/16.

[28] F. Kazemzadeh, *Russia and Britain in Persia, 1864–1914* (New Haven, 1968), 321–6.

[29] Sanderson to Scott, 31 Jan. 1900, Scott Papers, Add MSS 52298.

[30] 'An Understanding with Russia on Persian Matters.' Ardagh, secret, 23 Jan. 1900, Ardagh Papers, PRO 30/40/14.

[31] 'An Understanding with Russia on Persian Matters.' Ardagh, 3 Feb. 1900, Ardagh Papers, PRO 30/40/14.

embarrassments in South Africa is already fully justified'.[32] The fact that Russia had concluded the loan, while pretending to give consideration to a joint Anglo-Russian loan to the Shah, meant that future Russian assurances could not be trusted. This disillusionment was echoed by Scott, whose confidence 'in the value of verbal assurances however positive has received a severe blow, and it never was very strong'.[33]

It was hard to know Russia's intentions. Hamilton doubted that Russia 'wants to pick a quarrel with us: [but] I assume she believes that we are at the present moment so hampered that she may with comparative impunity tread upon our toes'.[34] But the Russian desire to open direct relations with Afghanistan—something denied to her by an Anglo-Afghan agreement reaching back to 1880—again fitted with the rumoured movements of Russian troops.[35] While Muravev repeatedly denied them, Sanderson preferred to put his faith in 'our better success in South Africa' to 'check any adventurous [Russian] policy'.[36] Only the fact that the British military attaché, Colonel Beresford, was permitted to travel to Central Asia, gave any credence to Russian denials.[37] Any warming of relations was prevented by the recriminations that resulted from the Medhurst incident, where the eponymous British consul in Moscow was insulted by a high-ranking Russian official, triggering off a spate of angry telegrams. While military fears about Central Asia began to subside, the mobilization of Russian troops in the Crimea and Caucasus brought new speculation about a possible descent on Constantinople.[38] Sanderson concluded that this mobilization was not a serious threat, and Muravev assured Scott that it was purely routine, but such issues continued to strain Anglo-Russian relations.[39]

But, Britain was in no position to oppose Russia by military means. As Sanderson remarked on 9 May, 'I think that in regard to Persia and indeed all other matters Lord Salisbury wishes to remain as quiet as possible while we have this war on our hands. It is quite natural that everybody should think it a moment at which they ought to get the better of us in any negotiation.'[40] This was entirely agreeable

[32] 'Russia—Increase of Military Force in Central Asia during Boer War.' Ardagh, secret, 5 Feb. 1900, Ardagh Papers, PRO 30/40/14.

[33] Scott to Sanderson, 8 Feb. 1900, Scott Papers, Add MSS 52303.

[34] Hamilton to Curzon, 9 Feb. 1900, Curzon Papers, MSS Eur F111/145.

[35] Scott to Salisbury, disp. 51, 21 Feb. 1900, FO 65/1598; Scott to Sanderson, 22 Feb. 1900, Scott Papers, Add MSS 52303.

[36] Sanderson to Scott, 28 Mar. 1900 (twice), one 'private', one 'secret', Scott Papers, Add MSS 52298; quotation from the latter.

[37] Scott to Salisbury, disp. 63, secret, 7 Mar. 1900, FO 65/1598

[38] Scott to Sanderson, 8, 11 Mar. and 31 May 1900, Scott Papers, Add MSS 52303.

[39] Sanderson to Scott, 14 Mar. 1900, Scott Papers, Add MSS 52298; Scott to Salisbury, disp. 77, 20 Mar. 1900, FO 65/1598.

[40] Sanderson to Scott, 9 May 1900, Scott Papers, Add MSS 52298.

to Scott, who was 'very glad' not to have to raise 'important questions like Persia while we have this war'.[41] And Hamilton reminded Curzon of some hard facts: 'I have got on very little with the Persian question. I own that I do not see, owing to the hesitation of the Foreign Office on the one hand, and the lack of material force behind us in Northern Persia on the other, how we can possibly suggest any course of action which will not die of inanition.'[42] Any British support for the defence of India, could not be known 'until the conditions existing at the same time in Europe could be predicated . . . The keys of India, as "Dizzy" truly said, are in London, and it is impossible to us to disperse our naval and military forces to protect distant parts of our Empire, however valuable they may be in themselves, if we leave the heart of Empire open to attack.'[43]

At the beginning of June, the Boxer rebellion refocused Anglo–Russian attention on the Far East.[44] Salisbury and Muravev initially took an oversanguine view of the situation, each believing that the problem was local and would sort itself out.[45] Until the relief of the foreign Legations on 14 August, Anglo–Russian relations centred on negotiations over the composition and command of the international force raised to defeat the Boxers. Several themes emerged from the event. First, the British, with their forces tied up in South Africa, needed the resources of others to deal with the Boxers. Second, sending Japanese troops to China, which would have been the most logical solution given the geographic propinquities, was precluded by internal Japanese politics and Russian objections.[46] Finally, Russia was financially weak and unprepared for war. At the end of July, Scott reported that the Russians were in a 'terrible fix'.[47]

The situation in China did spark much diplomatic activity. The British ambassador at Madrid reported early in July that there was a general Franco–Russo–German diplomatic agreement resulting from the Boxer rebellion, a rumour that both Sanderson and Scott rejected as implausible.[48] More concrete, but equally obscure, was an overture from the German Kaiser, Wilhelm II.[49] Inspired by his foreign minister, Wilhelm II began tentative negotiations with Britain for an

---

[41] Scott to Sanderson, 17 May 1900, Scott Papers, Add MSS 52303.

[42] Hamilton to Curzon, 10 May 1900, Curzon Papers, MSS Eur F111/146.

[43] Hamilton to Curzon, 17 May 1900, Curzon Papers, MSS Eur F111/146.

[44] J. A. S. Grenville, *Lord Salisbury and Foreign Policy: The Close of the Nineteenth Century* (London, 1964), 303–10; Nish, *Anglo-Japanese Alliance*, 80–95; J. D. Hargreaves, 'Lord Salisbury, British Isolation and the Yangtze Valley, June–September 1900', *BIHR* 30 (1957), 62–75.

[45] Grenville, *Salisbury and Foreign Policy*, 303–10; Scott to Salisbury, disp. 165 confidential, 14 June 1900, FO 65/1599; Scott diary entry, 19 June 1900, Scott Papers, Add MSS 52305.

[46] Nish, *Anglo-Japanese Alliance*, 88–91; Scott to Salisbury, disp. 195, 4 July 1900; Scott to Salisbury, disp. 227, confidential, 23 July 1900, both FO 65/1600.

[47] Scott to Sanderson, 25 July 1900, Scott Papers, Add MSS 52303.

[48] Sanderson to Scott, 18 July 1900, Scott Papers, Add MSS 52298; Scott to Sanderson, 25 July 1900, Scott Papers, Add MSS 52303.

[49] Grenville, *Salisbury and Foreign Policy*, 311–18.

Anglo-German agreement maintaining the 'Open Door' in China and renouncing any intention of annexing further Chinese territory. These negotiations were given concrete form on 24 August, when Wilhelm suggested to the British ambassador at Berlin, Sir Frank Lascelles, that a formal Anglo-German agreement to this effect should be made. This proposal resulted in an Anglo-German agreement over China being signed on 16 October.[50] Between the Kaiser's initiative and the signature of the agreement, the challenge to Salisbury's foreign policy came to a head. The prime minister was suspicious of the Germans: Bertie noted on 20 August that 'Lord Salisbury suspects the Emperor William of big designs in China'.[51] Salisbury was not about to rush into any arrangement with Germany without knowing the exact nature and direction of her diplomacy. Others, such as Chamberlain, Goschen, and Lansdowne saw a possibility of separating Germany from Russia to Britain's advantage.[52]

The difference between the two camps is evident in the contrast between the views of Chamberlain and Salisbury. On 10 September, Chamberlain argued that Russia seemed likely to secure North China in the immediate future:

It is certain that we are not strong enough by ourselves to prevent her from accomplishing such an annexation, and both in China and elsewhere it is in our interest that Germany should throw herself across the path of Russia. An alliance between Germany and Russia, entailing as it would the cooperation of France is the one thing we have to dread, and the clash of German and Russian interests whether in China or Asia Minor would be a guarantee of our safety.

I think then our policy clearly is to encourage good relations between ourselves and Germany, as well as between ourselves and Japan and the United States, and we should endeavour to make use of the present opportunity to emphasize the breach between Russia and Germany and Russia and Japan.[53]

A month later, Salisbury reconsidered the nature of European alignments and Russia's role in them:

I do not feel the same danger in the case of Russia—for though Russia is much more powerful and quite as unscrupulous, she is less likely to a *coup de tête*. As to Germany I have less confidence than you. She is in mortal terror on account of that long undefended frontier of her's [*sic*] on the Russian side. She will therefore never stand by us against Russia: but is always rather inclined to curry favour with Russia by throwing us over. I have no wish to quarrel with her: but my faith in her is infinitesimal.[54]

[50] L. K. Young, *British Policy in China: 1895–1902* (Oxford, 1970), 193–213.

[51] Satow diary entry, 20 Aug. 1900, in G. Lensen (ed.), *Korea and Manchuria Between Russia and Japan, 1895–1904: The Observations of Sir Ernest Satow, British Minister Plenipotentiary to Japan (1895–1900) and China (1900–6)* (Tallahassee, 1966), 11.

[52] Monger, *End of Isolation*, 14–20; Grenville, *Salisbury and Foreign Policy*, 313–16.

[53] Chamberlain memo, 10 Sept. 1900, cited, Monger, *End of Isolation*, 15.

[54] Salisbury to Curzon, 17 Oct. 1900, Curzon Papers, MSS Eur F111/222.

Salisbury would bow to his colleagues' wishes and carry out the negotiations with Germany. But his reservations would be vindicated by the failure of negotiations over the next two years.[55]

In the meantime, relations with Russia continued to worsen, as the issue of the withdrawal of Russian troops from Manchuria came to the fore. Hardinge, acting as chargé d'affaires, was blunt about Russian intentions: 'Now that the Russian campaign in Manchuria is practically over it will be interesting to see how they will maintain their hold over that vast region & at the same time keep up the fiction of withdrawing other troops.'[56] His fears were realized as Russian troops occupied much of the Newchwang railway, and the line was now claimed to be Russian by right of conquest.[57] Hardinge protested formally to the Russian government on 3 November.[58] A resolution was delayed by domestic events. In Britain, the so-called Khaki election occupied nearly a month, and Salisbury's new Cabinet did not take up their positions until 1 November. In Russia, British representatives were frustrated in their attempts to deal expeditiously with matters because Nicholas II, Lamsdorff and many of the other ministers were in the Crimea from the end of September until mid-January 1901.[59] None the less, negotiations continued. Hardinge's protest of 3 November was greeted with 'excitement' at the *Pevcheskii most*.[60] 'In my opinion', Hardinge told Sanderson self-satisfiedly, 'they have rather lost their heads, but it is good that they should realise that we cannot be put off.' The note had been timely. Since the end of September, the Russians had been carrying on two sets of negotiations in China, one at Peking; the other in Manchuria, both designed to ensure that Russia gained considerably from its occupation.[61] The Manchurian negotiations bore the first fruit. On 10 November, the commander of the Russian forces in the Far East, Admiral Alekseev, signed an agreement with Tseng Chi, the governor general of Mukden, giving Russia troops full sway in Manchuria. Three days later, a conference at Livadia between Lamsdorff, Witte, and Kuropatkin, approved the Alekseev–Tseng agreement, and the finance minister obtained the agreement of the other two

[55] Monger, *End of Isolation*, 21–45; Grenville, *Salisbury and Foreign Policy*, 344–69.

[56] Hardinge to Bertie, 20 Sept. 1900, Hardinge Papers, vol. 3.

[57] Hardinge to Salisbury, disp. 323, 6 Oct. 1900; Hardinge to Salisbury, disp. 353, 22 Oct. 1900, both FO 65/1601.

[58] Hardinge to Salisbury, disp. 368, 3 Nov. 1900, FO 65/1602; Hardinge to Salisbury, disp. 353, 22 Oct. 1900, FO 65/1601.

[59] Hardinge to Sanderson, 4 Oct. 1900, Hardinge Papers, vol. 3; Hardinge to Salisbury, disp. 373 confidential, 7 Nov. 1900, FO 65/1602; Hardinge to Sanderson, 15 Nov. 1900, Hardinge Papers, vol. 3; Scott to Lansdowne, 29 Nov. 1900 and Scott to Sanderson, 13 Dec. 1900, both Scott Papers, Add MSS 52304.

[60] Hardinge to Sanderson, 8 Nov. 1900, Hardinge Papers, vol. 3.

[61] A. Malozemoff, *Russian Far Eastern Policy 1881–1904* (Berkeley, 1958), 151–60.

ministers to placing the Chinese Eastern Railway under the control of the Ministry of Finance.[62]

The Russians immediately began to raise a cloud of diplomatic smoke to obscure their aims. Hardinge was given a note on 14 November that, rather than explaining the continuing Russian occupation of the Newchwang line, merely observed that Russia would fulfil the financial obligations of the Scott–Muravev agreement.[63] As no financial obligations existed, London was puzzled, but not taken in. Lansdowne noted on Hardinge's despatch that 'we can't allow matters to drift indefinitely, & if we do not get satisfactory assurances, or practical evidences of good faith, we shall have to return to the charge'. From St Peterburg, Hardinge congratulated Bertie on being the driving force behind a policy of 'firmness', and argued that only such an approach would work with Russia: 'I am *quite* sure that that is the proper way to treat the Russians & the protest I was instructed to make brought them up with a round turn & was admirable in every sense.'[64] Hardinge was not placated either by a Russian agreement to withdraw their troops from the province of Chihli or by honeyed words from the Russian foreign office.[65] He remained certain that the Russians intended to ensure that 'Manchuria, without any formal annexation, will gradually assume the character of a Chinese province under a Russian Protectorate'. The only barrier to this policy was that both the Russian economy and finances remained weak.[66] In London, Lansdowne 'return[ed] to the charge' on 22 November, and rejected the Russian attempts to make the return of the line a matter for negotiation.[67] Thus, when Scott finally returned to Russia on 26 November, he found an unpleasant situation. On the mistaken premise that Lamsdorff opposed any Russian annexations or occupations and that to threaten him was to strengthen the hand of the military hawks in the Russian government, Scott wished to attack Lamsdorff's arguments with logic alone.[68]

The friction between Scott's approach and that favoured by Hardinge and Bertie was soon evident. Scott complained to Sanderson on 13 December that no one at the Foreign Office had informed him of Hardinge's strong protest of 3 November.[69] Bertie, in fact, had 'evidently preferred to have no conversation with me at all'. Sanderson soothed Scott's feelings by noting that the Chinese Department at the

[62] Young, *British Policy in China*, 269–71.

[63] Hardinge to Lansdowne, disp. 386, 14 Nov. 1900 and minutes, FO 65/1602.

[64] Hardinge to Bertie, 15 Nov. 1900, Bertie Papers, Add MSS 63014.

[65] Hardinge to Lansdowne, disp. 389 confidential, 15 Nov. 1900; Hardinge to Lansdowne, disp. 392 confidential, 16 Nov. 1900; Hardinge to Lansdowne, disp. 400, 23 Nov. 1900, all FO 65/1602.

[66] Hardinge to Sanderson, 24 Nov. 1900, Hardinge Papers, vol. 3.

[67] Young, *British Policy in China*, 276.

[68] Scott to Lansdowne, 29 Nov. 1900, Lansdowne Papers, FO 800/140.

[69] Scott to Sanderson, 13 Dec. 1900, Scott Papers, Add MSS 52304.

Foreign Office was 'inclined to be vague' when 'hustled' by events and that 'Bertie's disposition does not tend to excessive communicativeness'.[70] From Bertie's side, a contempt for Scott was manifest: 'Poor Scott swallows everything that Lamsdorff tells him', Bertie wrote in February 1901, 'and deprecates distrust of his assurances!'[71]

Here, again, the 'Edwardian' and 'Victorian' approaches to Russia clashed. Late in 1900, while the Russians negotiated with the Hongkong Bank to buy out the British railway concessions and with Russian troops moving out of Pechihli, Lansdowne favoured the 'Victorian' approach of quiet diplomacy.[72] This was challenged on 3 January 1901 with the publication in *The Times* of a version of the Alekseev–Tseng agreement.[73] Impelled further by a report from China that Russia and Germany had come to an agreement on railway issues, *The Times*' report had a quick impact. First, Scott was told to inquire about the agreement; the Russians replied that any agreement was merely provisional.[74] Second, a meeting between representatives of the British and Chinese Corporation (BCC), Hamilton and Lansdowne was held at the Foreign Office on 8 January. They agreed that Russian claims should be rejected, and the BCC was informed that the British government would not approve of any sale of British interests to Russia. On 12 January, the Japanese government asked Britain to join in a protest against Russia's policy in China. Lansdowne did not concur, but assured the Japanese that the British would not accept the Russian action. However, Lansdowne was 'very anxious to know how Germany regards the Russian landgrabbing', and instructed his ambassador at Berlin to attempt to discover the German position.[75] On 16 January, Chamberlain met socially with the *éminence grise* of the German embassy in London, Baron Hermann von Eckhardstein. Eckhardstein over-represented his conversation with Chamberlain to the German government as being the preliminary to alliance talks, and the arrival of the Kaiser in England to attend at Victoria's final illness meant that talk of an Anglo-German *rapprochement* was everywhere.[76]

In these circumstances, the Russian seizure in mid-January of British railway material at Tientsin raised a chorus of anti-Tsarist sentiment. For Hamilton, the Russian action was the last straw: 'I used to believe that it would be possible to come to some arrangement with Russia as regards the division of our respective spheres

[70] Sanderson to Scott, 19 Dec. 1900, Scott Papers, Add MSS 52298.

[71] Bertie to Lascelles (British Ambassador, Berlin), 27 Feb. 1901, Lascelles Papers, FO 800/10.

[72] Young, *British Policy in China*, 276–7; Scott to Lansdowne, 27 Dec. 1900, Lansdowne Papers, FO 800/140.

[73] Young, *British Policy in China*, 277–81; Monger, *End of Isolation*, 21–4; Nish, *Anglo-Japanese Alliance*, 112–14; Grenville, *Salisbury and Foreign policy*, 329–32 and 336–9.

[74] Scott to Lansdowne, disp. 7, 8 Jan. 1901 and minutes, FO 65/1619.

[75] Lansdowne to Lascelles, secret, 17 Jan. 1901, Lansdowne Papers, FO 800/128.

[76] Scott to Lansdowne, disp. 29 very confidential, 20 Jan. 1901, FO 65/1619.

of influence in Asia,' he wrote to Curzon, 'I have reluctantly been forced to the conclusion that it is impossible; at any rate until there is in Russia an autocrat who can make his policy and promises respected and obeyed by the Military Department and the Generals.'[77] Lansdowne was inclined to go slowly until the attitude of Germany could be ascertained, but had Scott speak sharply to Lamsdorff about the Tientsin incident. Lamsdorff tried to assure the ambassador that Russia would evacuate any territory she now held in China as soon as possible.[78] The assurances were not accepted. 'What ruffians and liars', Hamilton wrote at the end of January, 'these Russian officials are.'[79] And, indeed, while Lamsdorff was attempting to placate Scott, Witte was carrying on parallel negotiations with the Chinese designed to strengthen Russia's position.[80] As in January, it was the Japanese who forced the issue. On 15 February, Count Takaaki Katō, the Japanese foreign minister, informed the British that Japan planned to advise China to resist any further Russian incursions—a broad hint for Britain to do the same.[81] But Lansdowne, still relying on the Anglo-German agreement, did not take up the Japanese suggestion, but temporized, suggesting to the Japanese that everything must await a Chinese approach to the other powers.

Even when the thrust of the Russian terms for an agreement with China became general knowledge, Lansdowne continued to avoid confronting Russia.[82] With characteristic detachment (and insight), Sanderson noted: 'As for the Manchurian Agreement we may I suppose take it for granted that neither the Chinese nor the Russians are particularly careful to tell us the exact truth—it is obviously the game of the Chinese to exaggerate the Russian demands, and that of the Russians to minimise them.'[83] Lansdowne attempted to gather information about Russia's financial situation, particularly Witte's ongoing attempts to raise a loan in Germany.[84] Events forced Lansdowne's hand. On 1 March, Peking officially asked the powers for mediation in the Sino-Russian dispute. Lansdowne now asked for the exact nature of the Russian demands.[85] Scott's interview with Lamsdorff on 7 March was frigid.[86] Lamsdorff took a 'very indignant attitude', despite Scott's

---

[77] Hamilton to Curzon, 18 Jan. 1901, Curzon Papers, MSS Eur F111/148.

[78] Scott to Lansdowne, disp. 28, 19 Jan. 1901; Scott to Lansdowne, disp. 36, 31 Jan. 1901; Scott to Lansdowne, disp. 41, 6 Feb. 1901; Scott to Lansdowne, disp. 48, 15 Feb. 1901, FO 65/1619.

[79] Hamilton to Curzon, 31 Jan. 1901, Curzon Papers, MSS Eur F111/160.

[80] Young, *British Policy in China*, 282–4.

[81] Nish, *Anglo-Japanese Alliance*, 113–4; Young, *British Policy in China*, 283–7; Sanderson to Scott, 13 Feb. 1901, Scott Papers, Add MSS 52299.

[82] Malozemoff, *Russian Far Eastern Policy*, 157–8.

[83] Sanderson to Scott, 27 Feb. 1901, Scott Papers, Add MSS 52299.

[84] Lascelles to Bertie, 22 Feb. 1901, Bertie Papers, Add MSS 63014; Sanderson's memo, 28 Feb. 1901, Lansdowne Papers, FO 800/115; Scott to Lansdowne, disp. 69 confidential, 6 Mar. 1901, FO 65/1620; Hardinge to Sanderson, 7 Mar. 1901, Hardinge Papers, vol. 3.

[85] Monger, *End of Isolation*, 24–32; Grenville, *Salisbury and Foreign Policy*, 336–43.

[86] Scott to Lansdowne, 7 Mar. 1901, Lansdowne Papers, FO 800/140.

repeated efforts to emphasize the benign nature of the British request. Ominously, Lamsdorff argued that there were two courses for the powers to follow: 'either to trust to the loyalty of Russia's intentions, or to continue to distrust them and take whatever steps they thought best to safeguard their own interests, [as] Russia would safeguard hers.' There was little 'trust to the loyalty of Russia's intentions' in London, but few options, given that German support for a strong line against Russia was not forthcoming.[87]

On 10 March, all this seemed to change. The Japanese ambassador to Britain, Count Tadasu Hayashi, informed Lansdowne that the Germans would act as a benevolent neutral in any Russo-Japanese quarrel. What then, Hayashi enquired, would be the British position? Lansdowne jumped at this opportunity. On a personal level, Lansdowne wished to refurbish his reputation, tarnished by the Boer War. But he was also a representative of the 'Edwardians', and their unspoken agenda in forcing the Cabinet reshuffle of November had been to rescue Britain from what they felt was dangerous isolation. Lansdowne's policy with regard to China since November had been restricted by Germany's ambivalent attitude. Hayashi's message seemed to remove these uncertainties. The British failure during the course of the next year to come to terms with Germany both over China and in a general sense is well-known.[88] This is usually considered in the context of Anglo-German relations and seen as part of the 'inevitable' growth of an antagonism between the two countries leading to the First World War. However, in the context of Anglo-Russian relations, Lansdowne's pressing diplomatic problem was how to cope with Russia while Britain was involved in South Africa.[89] This could be done either by direct negotiations with Russia or by joining in some sort of coalition designed to limit Russian aims. In the period from March 1901 to the signing of the Anglo-Japanese alliance in January 1902, Lansdowne attempted both options. Far from being the time in which Britain's diplomacy was put firmly on an anti-German path, it was the time when the means of checking Russian expansion in the Far East was settled.

When Lansdowne presented the text of a proposed Anglo-German declaration of benevolent neutrality in the event of a Russo-Japanese conflict to the Cabinet on 12 March, it was rejected. Until Germany made her position clear, there was a belief that her encouragement of Japan (and, indirectly, Britain) to resist Russia was designed only to embroil Tokyo in a quarrel with St Petersburg to Berlin's benefit. Sanderson also pointed out that a Russo-Japanese war would be dangerous for

---

[87] Hamilton to Curzon, 8 Mar. 1901, Curzon Papers, MSS Eur F111/148.

[88] Monger, *End of Isolation*, 25–45; Grenville, *Salisbury and Foreign Policy*, 336–69; P. Kennedy, *The Rise of the Anglo-German Antagonism 1860–1914* (London, 1980), 244–9.

[89] There were Anglo-American problems. C. S. Campbell, *Anglo-American Understanding, 1898–1903* (Baltimore, 1957); A. E. Campbell, *Great Britain and the United States 1895–1903* (London, 1960).

Britain. In a prescient letter, the PUS noted that a Russo-Japanese conflict would raise 'some very embarrassing questions'—primarily the issue of whether the Russian Black Sea fleet would be permitted to pass through the Straits.[90] By the middle of March, it would be evident that the suspicions concerning Germany's motives were justified. But the heightened state of tension between Japan and Russia in the Far East remained, as did the uncertainty in British policy. Hamilton limned the scene nicely on 15 March:

Independent of our home troubles, foreign affairs are disturbing and restless. The Russian Government are behaving abominably in China. The lying is unprecedented even in the annals of Russian diplomacy; and France sticks inseparably close to the heels of Russia. We have already strained our relations with the Russian Government, and Scott certainly with Lamsdorff, by pressing for explanations, and by constantly addressing to them strong remonstrances.[91]

When Eckhardstein made yet another proposal on 18 March—this time for a general defensive alliance between Germany and Britain—Lansdowne's options seemed few.[92] On the one hand, it was unlikely that the Russians wished to push matters so hard that an Anglo-Japanese grouping opposing them would coalesce; on the other, the war in South Africa and the consequent 'increased taxation and enormous increase of our peace expenditure' deterred Britain from joining Japan.[93]

Lansdowne's best solution seemed an agreement with Russia. On 23 March, he made it clear that Britain had no desire to 'be pedantic about Manchuria. We have already recognized its "gravitation" [towards Russia] for Railway purposes, and we should not fall foul of any reasonable arrangement of the conditions under which the Russian troops might be withdrawn.'[94] However, given Britain's interests in China, Lansdowne could not permit any 'surreptitious bargains' between Russia and China that might 'contain provisions derogatory to our Treaty rights and of a permanent character. With a little bonne volonté', Lansdowne concluded, '& mutual confidence the whole affair might be capable of settlement.' In order to create such good will, Lansdowne made an important speech on Manchuria in the House of Lords on 28 March, designed to reassure Russia and to make British policy clear to Germany.[95] The entire Manchurian situation improved within a week. Scott saw Nicholas II on 3 April, and was informed that Russia was 'sincerely anxious to

---

[90] Sanderson to Lansdowne, 10 Apr. 1901, Lansdowne Papers, FO 800/119.
[91] Hamilton to Curzon, 15 Mar. 1901, Curzon Papers, MSS Eur F111/148.
[92] Lansdowne to Lascelles, secret, 18 Mar. 1901, Lansdowne Papers, FO 800/128.
[93] Hamilton to Curzon, 22 Mar. 1901, Curzon Papers, MSS Eur F111/160.
[94] Lansdowne to Scott, 23 Mar. 1901, Lansdowne Papers, FO 800/140.
[95] *Parl Debs*, 4th series, vol. 92, cols. 15–29; Lansdowne to Lascelles, 4 Apr. 1901, Lansdowne Papers, FO 800/128.

avoid any serious disagreement'.[96] Lamsdorff told Scott the following day that the actions of newspaper correspondents had prevented the Chinese situation from being solved via 'quiet and conciliatory diplomacy'. On 5 April Russia ended its attempt to force China to sign an agreement, although Russian troops would not be withdrawn from Manchuria. Unable to bribe the Chinese into signing, faced with Japan's unrelenting opposition and Germany's meddling, uncertain of Britain's position and in need of a foreign loan, the Russians had decided to adopt a new course.[97]

At Scott's weekly meeting with Lamsdorff on 17 April, the latter was all sweetness and light.[98] There was no problem in Anglo-Russian relations 'that could not be easily reconciled'. All quarrels over China had been the result of misunderstandings, Russia had never reached—had never attempted to reach—a final understanding with China, and the Russian troops would remain in Manchuria only until 'a normal state of affairs had been re-established'. Indeed, the troops there served only the common Anglo-Russian good. Scott regarded Lamsdorff's remarks as a 'decided attempt at an overture for the renewal of the attempt to come to an understanding about China', attributed this change of policy to Nicholas II, and professed a belief in the 'sincerity' of Lamsdorff's motives in making the offer.[99] In London, scepticism prevailed. Lansdowne noted that, while 'I am as ready as you are to give him [Lamsdorff] credit for a desire to pursue a conciliatory policy', Lamsdorff's assurances about China could not be believed.[100] Lansdowne instead credited the change of Russia's attitude to 'the plain speaking of Japan, to our insistence with China, to the attitude of Germany and last but not least to the conduct of the Yangtse Viceroys', the latter having prevented any outbreak of violence in the provinces.[101] Sanderson reiterated and amplified the need for caution in dealing with Russia.[102] While the Emperor might favour Britain, the 'military party' undoubtedly would attempt to 'give us a "nasty one" in return for the check [in China] they have received'. Further, Witte was in Berlin trying to arrange a loan to China backed by a joint Russo-Franco-German guarantee 'out of which the three should pay themselves and leave others to get what they could afterwards'. In these circumstances, the PUS warned, 'you had better look out for a sly dig in the ribs'. Still, he concluded, 'in the long run the policy of trying to work

    [96] Scott to Lansdowne, 4 Apr. 1901, Scott Papers, Add MSS 52304.
    [97] Monson (British ambassador, Paris) to Lansdowne, 17 May 1901, Lansdowne Papers, FO 800/125.
    [98] Scott to Lansdowne, disp. 110 very confidential, 17 Apr. 1901, FO 65/1620.
    [99] Scott to Lansdowne, 18 Apr. 1901, Lansdowne Papers, FO 800/140.
    [100] Lansdowne to Scott, 23 Apr. 1901, Lansdowne Papers, FO 800/140.
    [101] Lansdowne to Hicks Beach, 7 Apr. 1901, Hicks Beach Papers, D2455, PCC/84.
    [102] Sanderson to Scott, 24 Apr. 1901, Scott Papers, Add MSS 52299.

comfortably with Russia is the only sound one—but it must be worked very slowly and cautiously and with the feeling that our friends are the most slippery of customers'.

Anglo–Russian relations for the next four months dealt with how the Chinese were to recompense the European powers for the losses incurred in the Boxer rebellion and what sort of indemnity the Russians were going to pay the British for the supplies seized at Tientsin. While Germany, Russia, and Japan preferred that China raise customs duties to pay compensation, Britain, whose merchants would be adversely affected by such a move, preferred that the Chinese issue bonds backed by the powers, each to the extent of its claim against the Chinese government.[103] This was opposed by Russia and Japan, whose weak international credit meant that they would have to issue the bonds at a higher rate and thus would be unlikely to realize the entirety of their claims. By the end of June, the Russians had agreed to the British bonds proposal, but the 'very disagreeable & tiresome' matter of the Tientsin railroad properties did not admit of solution.[104]

With Russia's acceptance of the bond scheme, Lansdowne explored buying Japanese acquiescence by compensating her for any losses. This was rejected by the Cabinet, probably on financial grounds, but when Japan none the less agreed to the issuance of bonds on 18 July, Lansdowne took the initiative and began discussions towards an Anglo–Japanese understanding.[105] By the end of August, things looked promising: 'I have had some interesting conversations with Hayashi', Lansdowne wrote, 'as to the possibility of a closer understanding between us & I think it not at all improbable that we may succeed in arriving at this.'[106] An Anglo–Japanese alliance could address the threat of Russia and would also improve Britain's naval position *vis-à-vis* the Dual Alliance, without enormously inflating the naval estimates. Thus, the 'Edwardians' could have an alliance, Hicks Beach's ongoing fears about the financial situation could be soothed, and the British position in the Far East could be guaranteed. The British position worldwide would be enhanced. Although the Anglo–Japanese alliance was shaped by both naval and anti-Russian considerations, Lansdowne certainly did not wish to evict Russia from Manchuria, merely to keep her in check there.

As the British discussions with Japan progressed, Anglo–Russian relations once again became strained, because of events in Central Asia and the renewed Russian endeavour to sign a Manchurian convention with China. Then, in mid-October,

---

[103] Nish, *Anglo-Japanese Alliance*, 135–7.
[104] Scott to Lansdowne, 11 July 1900, Lansdowne Papers, FO 800/140; Scott to Sanderson, 25 July 1901, Scott Papers, Add MSS 52304; Sanderson to Scott, 31 July 1901, Scott Papers, Add MSS 52299.
[105] Nish, *Anglo-Japanese Alliance*, 143–62.
[106] Lansdowne to Satow (British minister, Peking), 25 Aug. 1900, Lansdowne Papers, FO 800/119.

the Amir of Afghanistan died, heightening existing British fears that Russia would attempt to open direct relations with that country.[107] However, as Russia's military forces in Central Asia were unprepared, Hardinge felt that Russia would do nothing too precipitate:[108] instead, it was the Persian situation that proved more acute. By 1901, the Persian government had already spent the loan provided by Russia in the previous year.[109] While Lansdowne was 'very unhappy about the prospects of Persia becoming committed to Russia by a further loan'—primarily due to fears that Russia would establish herself on the Persian Gulf (which, indeed, was the Russian intention)—the foreign secretary saw few ways to oppose it.[110] The problem was money: 'after all we have spent in South Africa I doubt the House of Commons finding money for a Persian loan: & under these conditions we may expect sooner or later that Teheran will fall under the virtual protectorate of Russia.'[111]

Russia's own financial weakness provided Lansdowne with his only opportunity to deal with Persia. In September and October, rumours that Witte was seeking a French loan to shore up Russia's finances were current in St Petersburg.[112] Even Hardinge was convinced that Russia might be interested in improved Anglo-Russian relations due to her financial difficulties, for 'every kopeck has to be thought of at the present'.[113] Although unable to get the Imperial Bank of Persia to provide the loan that the Shah required and with the Council of India unwilling (despite Curzon's own position) to put forward the money out of Indian revenues, Lansdowne took a crucial policy initiative.[114] On 29 October, the foreign secretary informed Staal that the British government wished to deal 'frankly and directly' with Russia over matters of mutual interest.[115] Lansdowne did not oppose a Russian commercial interest in the Persian Gulf, but objected to any strategic position being acquired. Britain and Russia, he proposed, should offer a joint loan to Persia, and the foreign secretary suggested the corollary that a similar joint approach should be taken in China. Hamilton thought it unlikely that Russia would accept Lansdowne's proposal, despite the fact that '[t]he moment is in one sense a favour-

[107] Hardinge to Lansdowne, disp. 289, 9 Oct. 1901, FO 65/1623; Hardinge to Sanderson, 9 Oct. 1901, Hardinge Papers, vol. 3.

[108] Hardinge to Bertie, 17 Oct. 1901, Bertie Papers, Add MSS 63014.

[109] Kazemzadeh, *Russia and Britain in Persia*, 352–85.

[110] Hamilton to Curzon, 2 Oct. 1901, Curzon Papers, MSS Eur F111/150; J. B. Kelly, 'Salisbury, Curzon and the Kuwait Agreement of 1899', in K. Bourne and D. C. Watt (eds.), *Studies in International History* (London, 1967), 249–90.

[111] Salisbury to Curzon, 23 Sept. 1901, Curzon Papers, MSS Eur F111/223.

[112] Hardinge to Lansdowne, disp. 280, 28 Sept. 1901, FO 65/1622; Hardinge to Bertie, 17 Oct. 1901, Bertie Papers, Add MSS 63014; Hardinge to Lansdowne, disp. 299, 24 Oct. 1901, FO 65/1623.

[113] Hardinge to Bertie, 30 Oct. 1901, Bertie Papers, FO 800/176.

[114] Monger, *End of Isolation*, 50–6; Grenville, *Salisbury and Foreign Policy*, 401–2.

[115] Lansdowne to Hardinge, disp. 287, 29 Oct. 1901, FO 65/1623.

able one for diplomatic negotiations. Russia is evidently hard up.'[116] Bertie shared his views, and told Hardinge that he (Bertie) had told Lansdowne that any hope for the negotiations depended on them being carried out by Hardinge in Scott's absence.[117]

Such pessimism was well founded. With Witte convinced that plans for the development of the Russian oil industry in Baku depended on the construction of a pipeline to the Gulf, the Tsarist government was not interested in the joint loan. This being so, Lamsdorff endeavoured to turn Lansdowne's initiative to Russia's advantage. On 3 November, after rejecting the idea of a joint loan to Persia, Lamsdorff attempted to read Lansdowne's offer as indicating the disinterestedness of the British government in Manchuria.[118] Hardinge was not deceived, and rapped the Russian foreign minister's knuckles hard: Lamsdorff, he wrote had dug a 'pitfall for me. I was very angry.'[119] But the Russian rejection, having been expected, opened the way for a new policy: 'both Lansdowne and I', Hamilton informed Curzon, 'felt that our hands were freer than before. We had made our offer: the Russian Government had declined it; and we, therefore, felt justified in making an offer ourselves to the Persian Government.'[120] Not incidentally, the Russian rejection of the British offer also meant that the Anglo-Japanese talks could proceed without any fear of a Russian reproach that Britain had chosen Japan without considering Russia, and on 5 November, the Cabinet approved such a course.[121]

In St Petersburg, Hardinge followed up his rebuttal of Lamsdorff's assertions over China by obtaining an interview with Witte to discuss the Persian loan. Witte fully admitted loan discussions with Persia and told Hardinge that Lamsdorff was well aware of them, but continued to maintain the fiction that no pressure was being exerted on the Persian government to accept the loan. Hardinge saw this as evidence that Russian ministers pursued their own policies independently of one another, and Bertie expressed evident glee that Hardinge's visit 'helped to show up both L.[amsdorff] & W.[itte] as liars—much to the distress of Scott'.[122] For the remainder of 1901, Anglo-Russian relations subsided into a state of inactivity. The Persian government refused to make a formal response to the British offer of a loan until early January 1902, although it was clear by the end of November that the

[116] Hardinge to Curzon, 1 Nov. 1901, Curzon Papers, MSS Eur F111/150.
[117] Bertie to Hardinge, confidential, 6 Nov. 1901, Hardinge Papers, vol. 3.
[118] Hardinge to Lansdowne, disp. 313, 3 Nov. 1901; Hardinge to Lansdowne, confidential disp. 316, 4 Nov. 1901, both FO 65/1623; Kazemzadeh, *Britain and Russia in Persia*, 366–7.
[119] Hardinge to Bertie, 8 Nov. 1901, Bertie Papers, Add MSS 63014.
[120] Hamilton to Curzon, 7 Nov. 1901, Curzon Papers, MSS Eur F111/150.
[121] Grenville, *Salisbury and Foreign Policy*, 402–5; Nish, *Anglo-Japanese Alliance*, 180–4.
[122] Hardinge to Bertie, 8 Nov. 1901, Bertie Papers, FO 800/176; Bertie to Hardinge, 20 Nov. 1901, Hardinge Papers, vol. 3.

offer would be rejected due to Russian pressure. In China, the death of Li Hung-chang brought Russian negotiations over Manchuria to a sudden halt. However, the ongoing debate over the general direction of British foreign policy was not without relevance to Anglo-Russian relations. On 9 November, Bertie argued that an Anglo-German alliance—still being considered despite the lack of progress shown in the summer—would irrevocably prevent both good Anglo-French or Anglo-Russian relations; albeit without gaining any German support.[123] This was countered by Balfour's contention in December that an Anglo-Japanese alliance would likely embroil Britain in conflicts with France and Russia without gaining any compensatory advantage against Russian advances against the north-west frontier of India.[124] On the other hand, an alliance with Germany *would* provide support for the British position in India. Lansdowne's reply reflected his limited conception of the Anglo-Japanese alliance.[125] With the geographic extant of the alliance strictly fixed, the possibility the treaty would be invoked were 'much fewer'. Besides, the visit of Marquis Itō, the former Japanese premier, to St Petersburg raised the unpleasant possibility that Japan might turn to Russia should the Anglo-Japanese talks collapse.[126]

In December 1901 and January 1902, while the final details of the Anglo-Japanese alliance were being considered, Anglo-German relations reached a new low.[127] A speech by Chamberlain on 6 January extolled the virtues of splendid isolation, provoking intemperate criticism in the Reichstag. This, in turn, triggered a violent anti-German outburst in the British press. While there was no suggestion in London that the deterioration was irreversible or that Germany was now to be considered an enemy, it ended the alliance talks that had taken place since at least 1900. Nor did Anglo-Russian relations remain unchanged. When the Persian government at last rejected formally the British offer of a loan on 8 January, Arthur Hardinge, the British minister at Teheran, immediately demanded that Persia not permit a Russian pipeline to be built to the Gulf and insisted that the revenues of the strategic province of Seistan not be mortgaged to Russia.[128] What material force backed this demand? Curzon was optimistic; Britain would not always have her

---

[123] Bertie's untitled memo, 9 Nov. 1901, Lansdowne Papers, FO 800/115; Grenville, *Salisbury and Foreign Policy*, 360–1.

[124] Balfour to Lansdowne, 12 Dec. 1901, Balfour Papers, Add MSS 49727.

[125] Lansdowne to Balfour, 12 Dec. 1901, Balfour Papers, Add MSS 49727.

[126] I. Nish, *The Origins of the Russo-Japanese War* (London, 1985), 116–26; Hardinge to Sanderson, 28 Nov. 1901, Hardinge Papers, vol. 3; Hardinge to Lansdowne, confidential disp. 337, 30 Nov. 1901; Scott to Lansdowne, very confidential disp. 343, 11 Dec. 1901; Scott to Lansdowne, very confidential disp. 345, 12 Dec. 1901, all FO 65/1623.

[127] Grenville, *Lord Salisbury and Foreign Policy*, 362–9; Monger, *End of Isolation*, 67–9.

[128] Kazemzadeh, *Russia and Britain in Persia*, 375–7; Scott to Lansdowne, 22 Jan. 1902, Lansdowne Papers, FO 800/140.

forces tied up in South Africa.[129] Instead, Curzon placed the blame on the home government's inability to 'make up their minds, or stick to a policy about anything'. This view was shared at the India Office. Godley lauded the new-found firmness that Lansdowne had demonstrated both in his instructions to Arthur Hardinge and in his public statements, but doubted whether it would last.[130] Like Curzon, Godley believed that Britain could protect her interests: the 'fact of our having the troops, and being thought to be ready to use them, would make war improbable if not impossible.'

Godley and Curzon must have been heartened by Lansdowne's actions early in February. No doubt buoyed by the signing of the Anglo-Japanese alliance on 30 January, Lansdowne instructed Scott on 3 February to raise again the issue of Russia's attempt to enter into direct diplomatic negotiations with Afghanistan.[131] Lansdowne wished to get the Afghanistan matter dealt with before the Anglo-Japanese alliance was officially announced on 11 February, since to do otherwise 'would be like throwing the gauntlet down to Russia'.[132] The Russian government noted that it regretted the specific action that had brought about Lansdowne's protests, but failed to respond regarding direct negotiations with Afghanistan.[133] This was viewed philosophically by Sanderson: 'I do not think that we can reasonably expect the Russian Govt. to do more in an official note than endeavour to explain away . . . [the problem]. It is not their habit to do more nor to consider strict accuracy in statements of fact to be indispensable.'

When the Anglo-Japanese treaty was announced, British public reaction was surprisingly and unexpectedly favourable. The Russian reaction was awaited with apprehension.[134] 'The only doubt that I have in my mind', Hamilton wrote of the alliance, 'is that, if Russia finds that we have by this instrument checked her advance in Manchuria, she may concentrate her attention upon Persia.'[135] Godley was less equivocal: 'As to its effect on India, I suppose we must be prepared for some Russian activity, perhaps on the Afghan frontier. They will give us a dig in return if they can.'[136] Hamilton's worries about Manchuria seemed likely to become

---

[129] Curzon to Godley (permanent under-secretary, India Office), 2 Jan. 1901, Curzon Papers, MSS Eur F111/161.

[130] Godley to Curzon, 24 Jan. 1902, Curzon Papers, MSS Eur F111/161.

[131] Lansdowne to Scott, disp. 31, 29 Jan. 1902, FO 65/1639; Scott to Lansdowne, disp. 29, 3 Feb. 1902, FO 65/1640.

[132] Bertie to Lascelles, confidential, 6 Feb. 1902, Lascelles Papers, FO 800/10.

[133] Scott to Lansdowne, disp. 36, 5 Feb. 1902, FO 65/1640; Scott to Lansdowne, 6 Feb. 1902, Lansdowne Papers, FO 800/140; Scott to Lansdowne, disp. 47, 11 Feb. 1902, FO 65/1640; following quotation from Sanderson's undated minute on the latter.

[134] Sanderson to Scott, 12 Feb. 1902, Scott Papers, Add MSS 52299.

[135] Hamilton to Curzon, 13 Feb. 1902, Curzon Papers, MSS Eur F111/161.

[136] Godley to Curzon, 14 Feb. 1902, Curzon Papers, MSS Eur F111/161.

fact, for, as the head of the Chinese Board of Foreign Relations told the British, 'with a smile of satisfaction', the Anglo-Japanese alliance could be used to 'pare' the Russian demands on Manchuria 'down still more'.[137] Lansdowne was well aware that the Russians might be angered, but defended the even-handedness of his policy. As he wrote to Curzon: 'I hope some day or other to bring out the fact that we offered the Russian Government to play *cartes sûr table* with them about China and Persia, and that they refused.'[138]

The official Russian response was couched in terms of sorrow rather than of anger.[139] Lamsdorff pronounced on the fact that Russia had always followed a pacific policy in the Far East and that, thus, nothing in the Anglo-Japanese agreement could be of detriment to her. He opined that the rapidity and secrecy of the negotiations would naturally confirm the Russian public in its long-standing opinion that Britain was Russia's natural enemy, and argued that actions by Britain (or her agents) in the past had vitiated the continuing attempts of Russia to come to a general understanding with Britain. While Scott would have none of the latter contention, Lamsdorff went on to state that he felt that the Alliance likely precluded any 'eventual frank understanding with us on all questions in Asia'. Although there was an element of threat in this latter remark, Lansdowne noted that the British could not 'complain of the manner in which the question has been officially dealt with'.[140] The unofficial Russian response was much more bitter.[141] Scott was aware that the measured public response only masked anger: 'At present I think we must be prepared to find Russia, even if she takes no more active step, for some time exceedingly unconciliatory & disposed to make herself disagreeable to us all round. They can scarcely disguise their discomfiture at our having stolen a march on them in the matter of this agreement with Japan.'[142] It was not surprising that Russia quickly moved to mend her diplomatic fences. On 20 March, France and Russia signed an agreement promising to work together to maintain the *status quo* in China.[143]

However, the Anglo-Japanese Agreement, combined with other events, wrought a change in Russian policy. Witte had long been calling for the withdrawal of Russian troops from Manchuria. With the Russian economy reeling under the twin

[137] Satow (British minister, Peking) to Lansdowne, 13 Feb. 1902, Lansdowne Papers, FO 800/119.
[138] Lansdowne to Curzon, 16 Feb. 1902, Curzon Papers, MSS Eur F111/161.
[139] Scott to Lansdowne, confidential disps. 56 and 61, 17 and 20 Feb. 1902, FO 65/1640.
[140] Lansdowne to W. E. Goschen, 8 Mar. 1902, Lansdowne Papers, FO 800/122.
[141] W. E. Goschen (British minister, Copenhagen), diary entry 19 Feb. 1902, in C. H. D. Howard (ed.), *The Diary of Sir Edward Goschen 1900–14* (London, 1980), 72; O'Conor (British ambassador, Constantinople) to Sanderson, 24 Feb. 1902, O'Conor Papers, OCON 3/18; Satow (British minister, Peking) to Lansdowne, 5 Mar. 1902, Lansdowne Papers, FO 800/119.
[142] Scott to Sanderson, 6 Mar. 1902, Scott Papers, Add MSS 52304.
[143] Scott to Lansdowne, disp. 88, 20 Mar. 1902, FO 65/1641; Malozemoff, *Russian Far Eastern Policy*, 174–6.

hammers of a poor harvest in 1901 and the effect of the international downturn in trade, Witte required a policy of peace and retrenchment.[144] With Lamsdorff's aid, Witte managed to get support for an agreement with China, signed 8 April, providing for the phased withdrawal of all Russian troops from Manchuria by early October 1903.[145] This was all to the good as far as the British were concerned; however, Witte's own position was not strong. On 15 April, D. S. Sipiagin, the Russian minister of the interior, was assassinated.[146] Sipiagin, a close political ally of Witte, was replaced by V. K. Plehve, one of Witte's bitterest political opponents. This would eventually lead to Witte's downfall, but the initial British concern lay with Russia's stability. While Hamilton argued that the assassination was an individual act, he was concerned that it might mark the 'beginning of a movement [of] which he [Nicholas II] will be either afraid or unwilling to quell, and which may soon attain dangerous dimensions'.[147] Hamilton worried that if the Emperor himself were assassinated, this would mean the coming to power of someone 'very hostile' to Britain.

But the foci of Anglo-Russian relations were in Persia and Afghanistan. In April 1902, the British had complained about the actions of the Russian consul at Seistan.[148] At the beginning of May, Lamsdorff returned an uncompromising reply, arguing that if the British took umbrage at an action that was obviously not threatening, then the Russian government would reply in kind.[149] Scott was taken aback at Lamsdorff's tone, but felt that it reflected the domestic criticism that the Russian government was taking for its foreign policy.[150] The moderated British response was given only verbally to the Russians.[151] The realities of power underpinned British policy: reports were circulating about the rapid extension of Russian railways towards the Indian frontier.[152] In December 1901, the War Office had reported that Russia could, as soon as the railroad from Orenburg to Tashkent were finished, put 200,000 troops on the Afghan border.[153] Thus,

---

[144] Hardinge's report, 22 Feb. 1902, in Scott to Lansdowne, confidential disp. 78, 6 Mar. 1902, FO 65/1640.

[145] Malozemoff, *Russian Far Eastern Policy*, 175; Scott to Lansdowne, 17 Apr. 1902, Lansdowne Papers, FO 800/140.

[146] Scott to Lansdowne, disp. 137 confidential, 16 Apr. 1902, FO 65/1641; E. H. Judge, *Plehve: Repression and Reform in Imperial Russia 1902–4* (Syracuse, NY, 1983), 1–2, 154–9; Malozemoff, *Russian Far Eastern Policy*, 177–207.

[147] Hamilton to Curzon, 17 Apr. 1902, Curzon Papers, MSS Eur F111/161.

[148] Scott to Lansdowne, disp. 119, 4 Apr. 1902, FO 65/1641.

[149] Scott to Lansdowne, disp. 161, 1 May 1902, FO 65/1641; Scott to Sanderson, 1 May 1902, Scott Papers, Add MSS 52304.

[150] Sanderson to Scott, 7 May 1902; Scott to Sanderson, 15 May 1902, both Scott Papers, Add MSS 52299.   [151] Lansdowne to Scott disp. 145, 21 May 1902, FO 65/1639.

[152] Scott to Lansdowne, disp. 188 confidential, 27 May 1902, FO 65/1642.

[153] 'Report of a Committee Appointed to Consider the Military Defence of India', WO, 24 Dec. 1901, Cab 6/1/1D.

despite the end of the Boer War, Hamilton could write that 'the weakness of our position is very apparent. There is no form of coercion or of pressure that we can exercise' that could not be countered by Russia.[154] Still, he felt that once Britain extricated her troops from South Africa, it would be necessary to tell Russia firmly that British interests in Persia would not be compromised.

Despite this, nothing troubled Anglo-Russian relations over the summer of 1902. Balfour's accession to the premiership and Hicks Beach's resignation meant that the 'Edwardians' were ascendant; however, the international situation, in the aftermath of the Boer War, seemed more favourable to Britain than any time since 1899, and no fresh initiatives seemed necessary. With 'no cloud on the political horizon' of Anglo-Russian affairs, Scott left for England on 9 October.[155] However, a new Russian proposal to enter into direct communication with Afghanistan ended this calm. On 31 October, Lansdowne instructed Hardinge, the British chargé d'affaires in St Petersburg, to notify the Russian government of Britain's opposition to any unilateral talks with the Amir.[156] The entire matter, Lansdowne went on, would be taken up when the new Russian ambassador arrived in London to replace Staal. On 19 November, representatives from the Admiralty, the India Office, the War Office and the Foreign Office met to discuss what should be done if Russia attacked Persia or if that country dissolved in chaos.[157] The conference concluded that all that could be done was to hold Seistan and some points on the Gulf. This gloom was partially dissipated by a report from the British military attaché in Russia: Colonel Beresford stated that Russia was in no way prepared to attack Central Asia.[158] This meant that Britain could 'be almost sure that the Russians will not precipitate matters on the Afghan frontier until the completion of the Orenburg–Tashkend Railway, for which $2\frac{1}{2}$ years more are required'.[159] This merely deferred the problem; as Hamilton put it:

Of course we can smash the Amir any day we choose, but would that put us in a better position? The 'Alpha and Omega' of our policy for the last thirty years has been to try and secure the cooperation of the Afghans in the event of a collision with Russia; and yet the restrictions and limitations which we are compelled to impose upon the very inducements we offer to the Amir to come over on our side, are not unlikely to force him over towards the side of our adversary. It is a most difficult and perplexing situation, and one which has caused both Lansdowne and myself considerable anxiety.[160]

[154] Hamilton to Curzon, 6 June 1902, Curzon Papers, MSS Eur F111/161.
[155] Scott to Lansdowne, disp. 325, 7 Oct. 1902, FO 65/1643.
[156] Lansdowne to Hardinge, disp. 278, 31 Oct. 1902, FO 65/1639 and minutes.
[157] 'The Persian Question', 19 Nov. 1902, with Hamilton to Curzon, 2 Dec. 1902, Curzon Papers, MSS Eur F111/161.
[158] Beresford to Hardinge, 20, secret, 20 Nov. 1902, in Hardinge to Lansdowne, disp. 357 very confidential, 24 Nov. 1902, FO 65/1643.
[159] Hardinge to Sanderson, 27 Nov. 1902, Hardinge Papers, vol. 3
[160] Hamilton to Curzon, 27 Nov. 1902, Curzon Papers, MSS Eur F111/161.

For these reasons, if for nothing else, Lansdowne was still hoping that some sort of *modus vivendi* could be worked out with Russia.

The opportunity arose at the end of the year. Scott, taking advantage of the fact that he and Count Benckendorff were old friends, had two long unofficial conversations about Afghanistan with the ambassador-designate before departing for London.[161] Scott's talks were given added importance because *Novoe vremia* had just published a communiqué, purportedly authorized by the Russian Foreign Office, stating that Russia's foreign policy was in no way subservient to that of Britain, and that Russia had 'simply notified' the British of her intention to begin direct relations with Afghanistan.[162] Benckendorff's remarks gave hope that an agreement about Afghanistan on terms acceptable to Britain was possible.[163]

Thus, 1903 began on an optimistic note. It was to end with Britain's making careful calculations about what policy to follow in a Russo-Japanese War—and how best to avoid having to fight Russia in such an eventuality. Balfour's government was determined to come to grips with the enduring problem of Russian pressure. Selborne pointed this out to Curzon early in 1903: 'The Middle Eastern question is the question of the future, Persia & Afghanistan. Right or wrong I feel sure that Arthur's cabinet will not drift without a definite policy on these questions.'[164] Curzon was adamant that no sound policy could be based on an agreement with Russia, as Russia would be certain to break any agreement 'precisely when she chooses'.[165] Godley argued that Britain would be 'compelled . . . to come to an understanding with Russia' over Persia, since '[t]ime is on Russia's side: the longer we delay coming to an arrangement, the worse the settlement for us will be'.[166] 'What I am suggesting will, I know, horrify you', Godley gloomily concluded, 'but can we go on drifting and nailing to our mast a policy that every five years becomes more and more hopeless, and which must lead to a most severe diplomatic and political collapse or to war?' This statement should not suggest that Lansdowne pursued his discussions with Benckendorff either in a weak fashion or from a position of weakness. Throughout February, Lansdowne explained, 'gently but firmly to Benckendorff that Seistan frontier questions are no business of Russia'.[167] While the Cabinet rejected Curzon's proposal that troops should immediately be sent to Tibet, a Russian incursion there was not considered acceptable. To underline this, Lansdowne was authorized to tell Benckendorff that while Britain had 'no territorial ambitions' in Tibet, any appointment of a Russian agent in Lhassa would

[161] Scott to Lansdowne, secret, 25 Dec. 1902, Lansdowne Papers, FO 800/140.

[162] Scott to Lansdowne, disp. 380, 20 Dec. 1902, FO 65/1643; Scott to Lansdowne, 20 Dec. 1902, Lansdowne Papers, FO 800/140.

[163] Lansdowne to Scott, private and personal, 29 Dec. 1902, Lansdowne Papers, FO 800/140.

[164] Selborne to Curzon, 4 Jan. 1903, Curzon Papers, MSS Eur F111/229.

[165] Curzon to Hamilton, 8 Jan. 1903, Curzon Papers, MSS Eur F111/162.

[166] Godley to Curzon, 16 Jan. 1903, Curzon Papers, MSS Eur F111/162.

[167] Sanderson to Scott, 25 Feb. 1903, Scott Papers, Add MSS 52299.

be met by a similar British action, likely accompanied by troops.[168] Curzon's
initiative was rejected for two reasons. First, the distances involved meant that
there was no immediacy to a Russian threat to Tibet. Second, 'there are many
difficult questions pending between us and Russia in connection with Central Asia
ambitions. An arrangement with her is most desirable: but no such arrangement is
possible if we irritate her unnecessarily about Tibet.'

Lansdowne's discussions with Benckendorff came to a halt early in March when
the latter returned to Russia due to his wife's illness. This, coupled with a new
Russian statement—'a very sinister document'—that implied Russia would treat
directly with Afghanistan whenever she chose in the future, meant that Anglo-
Russian negotiations were neither warm nor rapid.[169] Sir Charles Hardinge, now at
the Foreign Office as assistant under-secretary in the Eastern Department, found
the delay galling: 'It is hard work endeavouring to infuse a little energy into this
Office about Persia. Nobody seems to dare to come to any decision & everybody
waits to see which way the cat is going to jump.'[170] This was not surprising. At the
CID on 18 March, its members had been 'greatly impressed with the dimensions of
the territory which, in certain contingencies, we may have to protect', and therefore
it was unlikely that a wider Persian obligation would be undertaken lightly.[171]
Meanwhile, Lansdowne continued to push about Tibet, despite the fact that
Lamsdorff avoided the subject.[172] Benckendorff's return to London permitted the
foreign secretary to insist on the clarification of the Russian position in Central Asia
generally. 'I am extremely anxious', Lansdowne informed Scott, 'to convince the
Russian Govt that we cannot deal with these occurrences as if they were isolated
incidents. If we are to come to an understanding it should have reference to Tibet,
Afghanistan, Seistan, & Persia generally.'[173] By the beginning of April, there were
indications both in St Petersburg and in London that the Russians were willing.[174]
In fact, by 14 April Lansdowne had received 'quite straightforward & satisfactory'
assurances about Tibet from Benckendorff, and told Balfour optimistically that 'I
doubt extremely whether the Russians wish to force the pace anywhere just at
present, and I don't despair of finding a resonable solution of the Russo-Afghan
difficulty, and perhaps of other tiresome questions which concern Russia & us'.[175]

[168] Balfour to the King, 19 Feb. 1903, Sandars Papers, MS Eng. hist. 715; Lansdowne to Benckendorff, 20 Feb. 1903, Lansdowne Papers, FO 800/140.
[169] Sanderson to Scott, 11 Mar. 1903, Scott Papers, Add MSS 52299; Hamilton to Curzon, 13 Mar.
1903, Curzon Papers, MSS Eur F111/162.
[170] Hardinge to Lascelles (British ambassador, Berlin), 18 Mar. 1903, Lascelles Papers, FO 800/14.
[171] Hamilton to Curzon, 19 Mar. 1903, Curzon Papers, MSS Eur F111/162.
[172] Scott to Lansdowne, 19 Mar. 1903, Lansdowne Papers, FO 800/140.
[173] Lansdowne to Scott, 23 Mar. 1903, Lansdowne Papers, FO 800/140.
[174] Scott to Lansdowne, 2 Apr. 1903, Lansdowne Papers, FO 800/140; Sanderson to Scott, Scott
Papers, Add MSS 52299.
[175] Lansdowne to Balfour, 12 Apr. 1903, Balfour Papers, Add MSS 49728.

This optimism let Lansdowne make a strong public statement about Persia on 5 May: 'we should regard the establishment of a naval base or fortified port in the Persian Gulf by any other power', he told the House of Lords, 'as a very grave menace to British interests, and we should certainly resist it with all the means at our disposal.'[176]

An even more serious quarrel with the Tsarist state was about to break out because of earlier events in Russia.[177] In January and February 1903, a series of high-level meetings involving, among others, Witte, Kuropatkin, and Lamsdorff, had decided that the second phase of the Russian withdrawal of her troops from Manchuria would be delayed until China complied with a number of demands.[178] These demands were given to the Chinese government on 18 April, and within a few days reports of them were circulating in London. While the British were suspicious that the Chinese might have exaggerated the Russian demands so as to be able to play the powers off against each other, there was no disguising the potential for Russian bad faith.[179] Both Benckendorff and Lamsdorff assured Lansdowne that the Russian requirements were only temporary and not nearly as onerous as the Chinese made out.[180] Correctly believing that there were divided counsels in the Russian government, Lansdowne easily accepted the idea that the 'military party' in Russia had temporarily overruled Lamsdorff. Thus, the foreign secretary contented himself with attempting to work in concert with the United States in an attempt to ensure that British interests were preserved.[181] Meanwhile, the British assumption, both in London and St Petersburg, was that the Russians had made 'one of their usual tries-on' and that it was 'too early to impute deliberate bad faith or mendacity to Russia' about Manchuria.[182] In fact, the British under-estimated the change that had occurred in Russia's Far Eastern policy. While Scott was aware of the influence of what he called '*unofficial Russia*'—the coterie of Grand Dukes, bankers, and adventurers that surrounded Nicholas II—the ambassador did not realize that they had gained the upper hand.[183] That they had done so reflected also the opposition of other ministers (such as Plehve) and military men (such as Alekseev) to Witte. On 15 May, Nicholas II inaugurated the so-called new

---

[176] *Parl Debs*, 4th series, vol. 121, cols. 1343–53; Hamilton to Curzon, 7 May 1903, Curzon Papers, MSS Eur F111/162.

[177] Nish, *Russo-Japanese War*, 163–78; Malozemoff, *Russian Far Eastern Policy*, 201–7.

[178] Nish, *Russo-Japanese War*, 145–51.

[179] Lansdowne's undated minute on Scott to Lansdowne, disp. 117, 27 Apr. 1903, FO 65/1660.

[180] Lansdowne to Scott, disps. 99 and 102, 29 Apr. and 1 May 1903, both FO 65/1658; Scott to Lansdowne, disp. 126 very confidential, 4 May 1903, FO 65/1660.

[181] Monger, *End of Isolation*, 123–6.

[182] Sanderson to Scott, 6 May 1903, Scott Papers, Add MSS 52299; Scott to Lansdowne, 14 May 1903, Lansdowne Papers, FO 800/140.

[183] Scott to Sanderson, 6 Feb. 1903, Scott Papers, Add MSS 52304; Nish, *Russo-Japanese War*, 164–8.

course in Russian policy in the Far East, appointing Alexander Mikhailovich Bezobrazov, a retired millitary man who had involved himself in numerous concession-hunting efforts in Korea, as a 'state secretary' and gaving Alekseev authority over all the departments of state dealing with the Far East.[184] From this time forward, Russia was committed to an active policy in Manchuria, one that would culminate in war.

In June 1903, Scott spent his time attempting to determine the exact nature of Russian policy at the same time as defending his own credibility. The long campaign that Bertie and Hardinge had waged against him had poisoned the King's mind against the ambassador, Lansdowne was not pleased with Scott's continual defence of Lamsdorff's sincerity, and *The Times* carped at Scott's unwillingness to protest against the expulsion of its St Petersburg correspondent. In a plaintive letter also defending his own actions, Scott argued that Lamsdorff's position was a difficult one, that several of the past deceptions were the result of Witte's machinations, and that nothing was to be gained by always doubting the sincerity of Lamsdorff's professions.[185] 'He is human, & a Russian as well', Scott argued, '& naturally will take any advantage which he properly can, without actually violating any formal engagement or declaration made by him.' In these circumstances, British policy should be 'keeping calm & making our own position strong'. This was wise advice, but Scott's position was irreversibly damaged; on 15 July, he was informed that he would soon be replaced as ambassador.[186] In London, Lansdowne extracted a written statement from Benckendorff on 11 July about Manchuria.[187] The Russian position was that most towns in Manchuria would be gradually opened to foreign trade, but that Harbin would not. Lansdowne's response was cool and measured.[188] The Russian assertions would 'require careful examination', and could not be accepted until the details were known in their entirety. Lansdowne had in practice adopted Scott's policy of 'keeping calm & making our own position strong', the former by deferring any formal response; the latter by opening the negotiations with France that were to lead to the Anglo-French entente some eight months later.[189]

This requires further examination, since the Anglo-French entente is generally seen as part of the British response to the growth of German power.[190] For what the

---

[184] Malozemoff, *Russian Far Eastern Policy*, 179.

[185] Scott to Sanderson, 25 June 1903, Scott Papers, Add MSS 52304.

[186] E. Barrington (Lansdowne's private secretary) to Scott, 15 July 1903, Scott Papers, Add MSS 52302.

[187] Lansdowne to Scott, disp. 184, 11 July 1903, FO 65/1658.

[188] Lansdowne to Scott, disp. 194, 15 July 1903, FO 65/1658.

[189] C. Andrew, *Théophile Delcassé and the Making of the Entente Cordiale* (London, 1968).

[190] Neilson, ' "Greatly Exaggerated": The Myth of the Decline of Great Britain before 1914', *IHR* 13 (1991), 695–6.

negotiations with France actually did was to strengthen Lansdowne's hand against France's erstwhile alliance partner, Russia. The French foreign minister, Théophile Delcassé, visited London at the beginning of July, and told Lansdowne that, should an Anglo–French agreement be reached, 'he [Delcassé] will exercise a restraining influence upon Russia, if not in fact intimate to Russia that, under certain conditions, she could not rely upon French support if she picked a quarrel with us'.[191] One of the main stumbling blocks to Britain's adopting a hard line against Russia in the Far East was the uncertain effect that it would have with regard to France. Considerations of this had been a central argument against concluding the Anglo–Japanese alliance. A conflict against a Franco–Russian combination had serious implications for British defence policy, since the Royal Navy would face two formidable opponents and British land resources would be thinly stretched. An Anglo–French agreement would eliminate this possibility and give Lansdowne a greater flexibility to pursue the global balance of power, long the concern of the 'Edwardians'.[192]

By August, with the French negotiations underway, there was little for the British to do but to sit back and await developments. Besides, domestic British politics were beginning to relegate foreign policy to the rear of the political stage: 'everybody here', Sanderson wrote on 29 July, 'is so absorbed in the Fiscal Policy of the Empire that nothing else excites much attention.'[193] In London, Benckendorff made reassurances that Manchuria would be evacuated and referred to the need for a 'general understanding' between Russia and Britain.[194] Lansdowne refused to be drawn: Britain's attitude to Russia's actions in the Far East would 'remain observant and critical.' This was fortunate. On the day following Benckendorff's assurances, the next step in the Russian 'new course' was announced. On 13 August, Admiral Alekseev was made viceroy of the Far Eastern provinces, with authority over the civil, military, and naval aspects of the Russian government in the region.[195] Scott saw this as the start of a policy in which 'the Emperor has decided to attach greater weight to the views of the military authorities in the Far East than to the diplomatic and financial considerations' of Lamsdorff and Witte.[196] This decision had created, he felt, a situation 'most serious and pregnant with the seed of fresh complications and dangers to the peace of the Far East'. Coupled with the fact that Russia was planning to double her naval strength in the Far East over

---

[191] Hamilton to Curzon, 9 July 1903, cited, Monger, *End of Isolation*, 129.

[192] B. J. C. McKercher, 'Diplomatic Equipoise: The Lansdowne Foreign Office, the Russo–Japanese War of 1904–5, and the Global Balance of Power', *CJH* 24 (1989), 299–339.

[193] Sanderson to Scott, 29 July 1903, Scott Papers, Add MSS 52299.

[194] Lansdowne to Scott, disp. 226, 12 Aug. 1903, FO 65/1658.

[195] Malozemoff, *Russian Far Eastern Policy*, 224–7; Scott to Lansdowne, disp. 234, 13 Aug. 1903, FO 65/1661.

[196] Scott to Lansdowne, disp. 244 very confidential, 20 Aug. 1903, FO 65/1661.

the course of the next year, the implications for British interests were serious.[197] Before the British were able to fathom exactly what Alekseev's appointment meant, another bombshell exploded. On 30 August, Witte was dismissed as finance minister and given the largely ceremonial post as president of the committee of ministers.[198] Scott was certain of its portent: 'It must be regarded as marking a fresh victory for the party and influences now prevailing at Court, which secured Admiral Alexeieff's appointment as Viceroy in the Far East.'[199] The expansionist leaders of the 'military party' had gained the upper hand. Sanderson had no doubt that this meant trouble: 'things do not look favourable to an easy or prompt settlement of our [Anglo-Russian] questions—and I cannot think that the post you hold is likely to be other than a difficult and invidious one—entailing constant struggle with little satisfactory result.'[200]

In London, the collapse of the Unionist government and the restructuring of the Cabinet occupied September. However, urgent events in the Balkans meant that foreign policy could not be ignored completely. A revolt in Macedonia against Turkish rule had broken out in April 1903; by September a war between Turkey and Bulgaria seemed imminent.[201] Since 1897 Russia and Austria-Hungary had worked together to push reforms on the Turks, and their voices were the dominant ones.[202] However, with the chance that Balkan Christians might be attacked came the possibility of the rebirth of the public furore in Britain that had accompanied the Bulgarian 'atrocities' of 1876 and the Armenian 'massacres' of 1894–5.[203] O'Conor, who advocated that Britain follow the line of Russia and Austria-Hungary, had vivid personal memories of the latter event and summed up the situation well: 'The whole question is complicated and the policy of Russia so difficult to understand that it wants very careful handling to prevent affairs getting out of hand. Any mistake might bring about a collapse, and we might be in as great a mess as we were in the Armenian question.'[204] However, besides its diplomatic dimension, the Balkan crisis also contained a strategic element: the question of the Straits.

Thus, the situation was reminiscent of the one that had faced Salisbury over Armenia in 1895. However, in the intervening years, certain factors had changed. The matter of Russia's position at the Straits in connection with Britain's policy in

[197] Scott to Lansdowne, disp. 243, 20 Aug. 1903, FO 65/1661.
[198] Scott to Lansdowne, disp. 263, 30 Aug. 1903, FO 65/1661.
[199] Scott to Lansdowne, disp. 270 confidential, 3 Sept. 1903, FO 65/1661.
[200] Sanderson to Scott, 4 Sept. 1903, Scott Papers, Add MSS 52299.
[201] Monger, *End of Isolation*, 137.
[202] F. R. Bridge, *From Sadowa to Sarajevo: The foreign policy of Austria-Hungary, 1866–1914* (London, 1972), 231–65.
[203] R. T. Shannon, *Gladstone and the Bulgarian Agitation, 1876* (London, 1963).
[204] O'Conor to Sanderson, 25 Sept. 1903, O'Conor Papers, OCON 3/19.

the Balkans generally had been raised in September 1902.[205] At that time, there were reports that the Turks would permit Russian warships through the Straits. As Salisbury had done in 1895, Lansdowne approached Austria-Hungary with a view to establishing an arrangement—a reconstituted form of the Mediterranean agreements—to block Russia. But, by December, Austria-Hungary made it clear that she would not oppose Russia; the diplomatic situation remained much what it had been in 1895. However, in February 1903, the CID concluded that Russia's possession of the Straits would not affect the naval balance in the Mediterranean in any serious fashion. Lansdowne thus found himself in a situation where, although he did not have the diplomatic leverage necessary to oppose Russia, there was no longer any vested British strategic interest in doing so. What he then attempted was to bring an end to the violence without leaving the government open to charges of having 'accept[ed] the extreme anti-Bulgarian view which the two Powers [Austria-Hungary and Russia] have adopted, and of blindly following their lead'.[206]

Lansdowne achieved his goal. The so-called Mürzsteg Punctuation of 2 October, signed by Russia and Austria-Hungary, promised further reforms for Macedonia. While it was not British pressure that brought about Mürzsteg—Russia was attempting to minimize her Balkan problems in order to concentrate on the Far Eastern situation—the signing was beneficial to Lansdowne.[207] By accepting Mürzsteg, with the provision that all the Great Powers be involved in its implementation, a charge of subservience to Russia could be avoided at the same time as the public pressure for action could be reduced. Lansdowne might be criticized for giving way to Russia and for being 'too rigid in his adherence to the European Concert', but he had defused a situation in which British interests were slight and her risks great.[208] The clear link between the situations in the Near and Far East was evident in Lansdowne's intention not to let the Macedonian question escalate into a serious Anglo-Russian quarrel was demonstrated by his pacific policy in Crete. He refused to countenance the suggestion that the settlement forced on Crete in the aftermath of the Greco-Turkish War of 1897 be modified such that the four powers (Britain, France, Italy, and Russia) who supervised the settlement be replaced by Greece. The argument was clear. 'Were we to do so,' Hardinge wrote, 'we should undoubtedly be snubbed by Russia and to make such a proposal at the present moment would raise the Macedonian question in a more acute form . . . When the time comes the first step will be certainly taken by Russia & we shall follow in her wake.'[209]

[205] Monger, *End of Isolation*, 84–7.
[206] Lansdowne to Balfour, 24 Sept. 1903, Balfour Papers, Add MSS 49728.
[207] Nish, *Russo-Japanese War*, 187–8.
[208] Salisbury (4th Marquis) to Balfour, 14 Oct. 1903, Sandars Papers, MS Eng. hist. *c.*745.
[209] Hardinge to E. Howard (British consul-general, Crete), 21 Oct. 1903, Howard Papers, DHW 2/8; B.J.C. McKercher, *Esme Howard: A Diplomatic Biography* (Cambridge, 1989), 38–44.

Although Lansdowne felt that the tension in Russo-Japanese relations in the Far East 'should be capable of satisfactory arrangement', the foreign secretary realized that there were 'disquieting symptoms'.[210] In these circumstances, Lansdowne suggested to Balfour in mid-October that Britain guarantee a loan to Japan for the purchase of two warships from Vickers.[211] Lansdowne had positive expectations: 'Of course the step would be regarded by Russia as openly hostile, but she is behaving so badly to us, that I should not much mind that. The result might be to convince her that she could not safely continue to flout us, and to bring about, what I have always wanted to see, a frank understanding between us as to Manchuria, Thibet, Afghanistan, Persia &c'. The impact of Russo-Japanese relations on Britain's relations with Russia also was raised from other quarters. In St Petersburg, Sir Cecil Spring Rice, Hardinge's successor as first secretary and chargé d'affaires in Scott's absence, suggested at the end of October that a general agreement between Britain, Russia, and Japan was the only way to smooth Anglo-Russian relations.[212] Spring Rice argued that it was the attitude of the Amir that determined the limits of Russian policy. With the Orenberg–Tashkent railway reaching completion, Russia would soon be in a position to menace the Amir more decisively than could Britain; in such circumstances, any Anglo-Russian agreement would, from the Russian point of view, be 'valid as long as it is convenient'. On the other hand, a tripartitite agreement including Japan would ensure Anglo-Russian peace 'for the simple reason that Russia would be very busy for some time in developing the new provinces [in Manchuria] and would also be able to keep her officers on our Indian frontier in order.'

Spring Rice's evaluation assumed both unremitting hostility between Japan and Russia and the likelihood of Japan's going to war to turn the Russians out of Manchuria. In London, Sanderson found the first secretary's analysis 'interesting . . . [but] somewhat imaginative'.[213] For Sanderson, what seemed more likely was Japan's consolidating her position in Korea, with any hostility resulting from a Russian response to this. As to any agreement with the Russians, Sanderson was not sanguine: 'I shall be glad if the Russians will make some show of a desire to behave towards us with more friendliness and civility in regard to various current questions. The negotiations for a general understanding during the Port Arthur Question in 1897–8 were not of a nature to encourage much hope of our getting very far in that direction. They never sign Treaties on such matters.' Whatever the possibilities of conflict in the Far East, Balfour wanted to ensure that the naval

---

[210] Lansdowne to Balfour, 23 Oct. 1903, Balfour Papers, Add MSS 49728.

[211] Ibid.; Lansdowne to Selborne, 16 Oct. 1903, Selborne Papers, 34.

[212] Spring Rice to Louis Mallet (précis writer to Lansdowne), 29 Oct. 1903, Lansdowne Papers, FO 800/140.

[213] Sanderson to Spring Rice, 4 Nov. 1903, Spring Rice Papers, FO 800/241.

balance favoured the Anglo-Japanese combination. As he wrote to the first lord of the admiralty on 30 October: 'If Russia . . . conceives that she has sufficient local strength to crush Japan before we have made up our minds to go to her assistance, she may take a risk which, if we and the Japanese together were obviously too strong for her, she might hesitate to run. It is possible, therefore, that an augmentation of our Eastern Fleet *might* make for peace; as well as be useful in case of war.'[214] In the meantime, Anglo-Russian relations would depend on the attitude of Russia.

On 7 November Benckendorff called on Lansdowne.[215] This was the first meeting between the two since 12 August when the Russian ambassador had assured Lansdowne that Russia would soon evacuate Manchuria. In the interim Benckendorff had returned to Russia for his holidays and to hold discussions at the *Pevcheskii most*. He returned with instructions 'to discuss frankly with me [Lansdowne] the various questions outstanding between Great Britain and Russia, with the object of arriving at an agreement as to the manner in which they should be dealt with'. With his negotiations with France well in hand, Lansdowne accepted Benckendorff's offer from a position of strength. The foreign secretary laid stress on two issues. The first was Russia's refusal to accept that she could not hold direct political discussions with Afghanistan. The second was that Britain was 'constantly placed in an embarrassing position owing to the ignorance in which we were kept as to the actual demands put forward by Russia in her negotiations with Japan and China'. Benckendorff quickly assured Lansdowne that Russia had dropped her demands about Afghanistan, and explained that the problems over the evacuation of China resulted from the divided authority caused by the creation of the Far Eastern viceroyalty. Lansdowne welcomed the first assurance, but noted that the latter circumstance made it difficult for Britain to come to terms with Russia.

Lansdowne immediately took up the Russian initiative. First, at a Cabinet meeting on 13 November, he obtained a 'perfectly unanimous' agreement that the Indian government should avoid irritating Russia by any 'avoidable advance' into Tibet.[216] Three days later, at a second Cabinet, Lansdowne was authorized to 'make informal use' of a dispatch sent to Russia on 5 November protesting vigorously Russia's actions in Afghanistan.[217] If this despatch were shown to Benckendorff unofficially, the Cabinet believed that it 'might convince him of the very serious state of things being brought about by Russia's unfriendly intrigues in Central Asia'. This strong line likely was made possible by the fact that the Anglo-French negotiations, which were also discussed by the Cabinet, were moving towards a

[214] Balfour to Selborne, 30 Oct. 1903, Selborne Papers, 34.

[215] Lansdowne to Spring Rice, disp. 307 confidential, 7 Nov. 1903, FO 65/1658.

[216] Brodrick (secretary of state for India) to Curzon, 13 Nov. 1903, Curzon Papers, F111/162; Balfour to the King, 19 Feb. 1903, Sandars Papers, MS Eng. hist. c.715.

[217] Balfour to the King, 16 Nov. 1903, Sandars Papers, Ms Eng. hist. c.715.

settlement. On 25 November Lansdowne held talks with Benckendorff, and showed him the minatory despatch.[218] Further, the foreign secretary laid out clearly the British desiderata for an agreement with Russia. Russia had to 'recognise in the most formal manner' the fact that Afghanistan was 'entirely within our sphere of influence and guided by us in regard to its external policy'. In return, Britain would agree to 'purely local' and 'non-political' intercourse between Russia and Afghanistan. Britain also expected Russia to recognize that Tibet lay entirely within the British sphere and to cease sending agents there. In the Far East, Britain recognized Russia's 'predominating interest' in Manchuria and Russia's right to take 'any reasonable measures of precaution' to safeguard her railway lines. On the other hand, Britain expected her trading rights to be respected and that Russia should fulfil her pledges to withdraw troops from Manchuria. Lansdowne further informed Benckendorff that Britain acknowledged Russia's 'certain preponderance' in northern Persia and did not wish to prevent her having 'commercial facilities in the south of Persia, and on the Persian Gulf'. As to railway building in that region, Britain acknowledged the ban that Russia had forced on Persia, but noted that the British government expected to be consulted should the ban be lifted. With respect to Seistan, '[w]e should expect the Russian Government to recognise that this province was entirely under British influence, and to abstain from interfering with the trade routes leading through it'.

Lansdowne's offer was far-ranging and reflected both Britain's improved diplomatic position and the realities of power. The British attitude about Seistan and Afghanistan, both deemed essential to the defence of India, was uncompromising. Curzon's desire to include all of southern Persia in the British sphere was rejected, for the simple reason that Britain did not have the means to defend it. As Hamilton had told the viceroy in March 1903, it was unlikely that there would be any political support for defending British interests in Persia beyond 'the angle drawn from Seistan to Bunder Abbas.'[219] In China, Lansdowne's policy was that which had motivated Salisbury—a recognition of Britain's predominant trading interests. But Britain's position had improved since Salisbury's time. With the Boer War over and the Anglo-Japanese alliance in hand, Lansdowne could afford to be firmer. And, while the Russo-French combination was still a possible threat, the British negotiations with France were moving ahead, and the French were unhappy about Russia's intransigence in the negotiations with Japan.[220] While Sanderson had not been hopeful on 18 November that Britain would get 'much out of the Russian professions of friendship but fair words', by 4 December Hardinge could express

---

[218] Lansdowne to Spring Rice, disp. 334 very confidential, 25 Nov. 1903, FO 65/1658.
[219] Hamilton to Curzon, 19 Mar. 1903, Curzon Papers, MSS Eur F111/162.
[220] Hardinge to Bertie, very private, 4 Dec. 1903, Bertie Papers, FO 800/163; Nish, *Russo-Japanese War*, 187–8; Sanderson to Spring Rice, 2 Dec. 1903, Spring Rice Papers, FO 800/241.

guarded optimism about the talks: 'I for the first time believe that it might be possible to come to an agreement.'[221]

Still, the British took precautions that an outbreak of hostilities in the Far East would not redound to their disadvantage. At the Cabinet on 27 November, a Russian offer to buy from Vickers the two warships that Selborne had been 'constantly urging the Japanese to buy' was discussed.[222] Under consideration was the idea that Britain herself should buy the ships. This was a complicated issue. The Russian purchase would have an effect on the naval balance of power in the Far East, but to oppose it would have anti-Russian implications. There were financial complications as well. Selborne had professed himself to be 'in despair about the financial outlook' at the end of October, ironically, due primarily to the fact that 'these cursed Russians' were laying down new battleships that jeopardized the two-power standard.[223] Throughout November he had engaged in a correspondence with the chancellor of the exchequer, Austen Chamberlain, on the topic of increasing the naval estimates.[224] Selborne squared the circle by purchasing the two battleships. For public consumption the purchase was justified as a step to maintain the two-power standard; in reality, the purchase was designed to thwart Russia.

From 1899 to the end of November 1903, the British had attempted to come to terms with Russia over China and Central Asia. For various reasons, the Russians had rejected all British initiatives. However, in this same period, the British bargaining position had improved. The end of the Boer War, the signing of the Anglo-Japanese Alliance, and the opening of negotiations with France, all had strengthened the British hand. Conversely, the Russian position had deteriorated. The slump in the Russian economy, France's growing discontent with Russia's policy in the Far East and Japan's unrelenting hostility had combined to make an agreement with Britain more attractive. The Russo-Japanese War would determine just what direction Anglo-Russian relations would take.

---

[221] Sanderson to Spring Rice, 18 Nov. 1903, Spring Rice Papers, FO 800/241; Hardinge to Bertie, very private, 4 Dec. 1903, Bertie Papers, FO 800/163.

[222] Balfour to the King, 27 Nov. 1903, Sandars Papers, Ms Eng. hist. *c.*715.

[223] Selborne to Balfour, 28 Oct. 1903, Sandars Papers, Ms Eng. hist. *c.*715.

[224] Chamberlain to Selborne, 11 Nov. 1903; Selborne to Chamberlain, 13 Nov. 1903; Chamberlain to Selborne, 24 Nov. 1903, all D. G. Boyce (ed.), *The Crisis of British Power: The Imperial and Naval Papers of the Second Earl Selborne, 1895–1910* (London, 1990), 160–2.

8

The Russo-Japanese War

THE Russo-Japanese War brought about the decisive turning point in Anglo-Russian relations between 1894 and 1914. Before the war, Russia had repeatedly rejected British overtures for a general agreement between the two countries. After the war, as a result of military defeat and internal unrest, Russia attempted to accommodate the Great Powers. The Anglo-Russian Convention of 1907 was the eventual result. Such a result was not preordained. The Russo-Japanese War also marked the nadir of Anglo-Russian relations. Without skilful management and good fortune, the struggle in the Far East could have resulted in a general global conflict between an Anglo-Japanese coalition and the Franco-Russian pairing.

During December 1903, while Russo-Japanese relations soured, the British élite pondered the situation. They focused on two linked issues: the balance of power in the Far East and the British response to any attempt to change it. The first was tied to finance and naval strength; the second to considerations of Britain's interests worldwide. The urgency was evident. On 11 December, the Cabinet authorized unofficially warning the French that a Russo-Japanese War might lead to complications between the two European states, and by 16 December both Russia and Japan were purchasing supplies in London preparatory for war.[1] The British attempted to maintain, at least publicly, an even-handed policy. First, they turned down—on the grounds that it was overtly anti-Russian—an attempt by the Japanese to buy the Chilean battleships.[2] Second, they continued to discuss a general Anglo-Russian agreement, although Hardinge felt that 'it is gradually becoming complicated & too unwieldy to inspire confidence'.

These were holding actions; the pressing need was to decide British policy. On 21 December, a flurry of correspondence began among Balfour, Chamberlain, Lansdowne, and Selborne. Balfour inquired of his military experts what Japan's

---

[1] Balfour to the King, 11 Dec. 1903, Sandars Papers, MS Eng. hist. *c.*715; Sanderson to Scott, 16 Dec. 1903, Scott Papers, Add MSS 52299.

[2] I. H. Nish, *The Anglo-Japanese Alliance: The Diplomacy of Two Island Empires 1894–1907* (London, 1966), 270–3; Lansdowne to Balfour, 17 Dec. 1903; Chamberlain to Lansdowne, 21 Dec. 1903, both Balfour Papers, Add MSS 49728; Hardinge to Bertie, 18 Dec. 1903, Bertie Papers, FO 800/163.

likely 'plan of campaign' might be if negotiations broke down, since a knowledge of it 'might prove most valuable guide to our own diplomacy'.[3] For both the first lord and the chancellor, the issue was to decide Britain's proper response should a Russo-Japanese war break out. Selborne stated that 'we could not afford to see Japan smashed by Russia; but, if that is accepted does it not follow that we cannot wait to make up our minds till after Japan *has* been smashed?'[4] He realized, however, that to intervene might bring in France and lead to a general war; for this reason he wondered whether Britain and France might not act in concert to restrain their allies. Chamberlain was more robust and anti-Russian.[5] He agreed with Selborne's opinion that 'we could not allow Japan to be crushed at sea', but proposed that, should a war break out, 'is not that the proper time for us to secure, and to secure *promptly*, whatever we want in places where Russia is our rival?' As to the effect on the Anglo-Russian negotiations, Chamberlain was blunt, cynical, and realistic: 'I cannot help thinking that if she [Russia] is once free of her anxieties about Japan, her inclination to negotiate a settlement of outstanding questions with us will evaporate, and that we shall find her very troublesome and not a little aggressive for all Benckendorff's smooth words.'

This was supported by Balfour. On 17 December, Lansdowne had sent the prime minister 'a fresh draft' of the British proposals to Russia concerning an agreement.[6] Balfour's comments reflected his scepticism about the possibility of any lasting understanding with Russia.[7] For the present, Balfour argued, with the creation of the Far Eastern viceroyalty, Russian foreign policy was 'divided into two distinct halves, connected only by the Emperor'. Britain could deal through 'diplomatic machinery' with only the western half. Thus, negotiations with Russia were likely to be difficult and unsatisfactory until this duality was removed. But, in any case, the eternal reason why an Anglo-Russian agreement was unlikely resulted from the

little confidence that experience shows can be placed in Russian assurances. They may be sincere at the moment, but they are purely temporary in their operation. Russia always thinks herself absolved from them if she can show, or assert without showing, that circumstances have changed since they were made. She is less fast and loose in her method of regarding formal Treaties, but formal Treaties she is unwilling to make, and even these she has not always been too scrupulous in observing.

---

[3] Balfour to Selborne, 21 Dec. 1903, Selborne Papers 34; Selborne to Kerr, 21 Dec. 1903, Selborne Papers 35; Balfour to Lansdowne, 22 Dec. 1903; Balfour Papers, Add MSS 49728.
[4] Selborne to Lansdowne, 21 Dec. 1903, Balfour Papers, Add MSS 49728.
[5] Chamberlain to Lansdowne, 21 Dec. 1903, Balfour Papers, Add MSS 49728.
[6] Lansdowne to Balfour, 17 Dec. 1903, Balfour Papers, Add MSS 49728.
[7] [Untitled memorandum], n.s. [but Balfour], 21 Dec. 1903, Balfour Papers, Add MSS 49728.

Since Russia desired British territory and Britain did not covet any of the lands of the Tsar: 'We have nothing to give and nothing to take away.' Balfour concluded: 'I am not hopeful of a thoroughly satisfactory permanent arrangement. Temporary arrangements, however, are better that nothing; they smooth things for the time being.'

On 22 December, Lansdowne wrote again to Balfour, this time enclosing Selborne's and Chamberlain's letters.[8] The foreign secretary's accompanying letter was both a commentary on the remarks of his colleagues and a statement of his own position. The situation in the Far East was 'precarious'; Lansdowne hoped to avoid war by working with the French. But, he felt that Selborne espoused the idea of Anglo-French co-operation too much: 'I doubt whether we ought to go the length of telling the French categorically that we shall go to war to save Japan.' Despite this, the foreign secretary had told Paul Cambon, the French ambassador to London, that 'public opinion here would probably not permit us to allow Japan to be smashed'. Chamberlain's letter reminded Lansdowne that there were financial considerations involved in any war, and the foreign secretary adjured Balfour to recall that Chamberlain had stated earlier in December that it was ' "impossible to finance a great war except at an absolutely ruinous cost" '.[9] There were limits to Lansdowne's willingness to let events take their course: 'We should, I take it,' the foreign secretary concluded, 'not allow Japan to be *invaded*.'

In response, Balfour drew up a memorandum encompassing his own views.[10] In his opinion, even though Japan had fewer battleships than did Russia, the most that the Tsarist state could hope to do was prevent Japan's sending troops to Korea.[11] Any invasion of Japan by Russia 'on any important scale is, I believe, impossible'. The result would be that Russia controlled Korea and gained the perpetual enmity of Japan. This was to Britain's advantage:

We, of course, care little for Corea except as it affects Japan. From every other point of view (except trade), there could be nothing better for us than that Russia should involve herself in the expense and trouble of Corean adventure, with the result that at the best she would become possessed of a useless province, which would cost more than it brought in, which could only be retained so long as she kept a great fleet in the Far East, and a large army thousands of miles from her home base, and which would be a perpetual guarantee that whenever Russia went to war with another Power, no matter where or about what, Japan would be upon her back.

[8] Lansdowne to Balfour, 22 Dec. 1903, Balfour Papers, Add MSS 49728.
[9] Ibid. Lansdowne was quoting 'The Financial Situation', secret, Chamberlain, 7 Dec. 1903, Cab 37/67/84.
[10] Balfour to Selborne, 23 Dec. 1903, Selborne Papers 34; 'Memorandum by Mr. Balfour respecting Japan and Russia.', Balfour, 22 Dec. 1903, Cab 37/67/92.
[11] For the naval calculations, I. Nish, *The Origins of the Russo-Japanese War* (London, 1985), 198–9.

Thus Balfour argued that Britain should not risk giving advice to Japan; to do so would be to risk being blamed by the latter for anything that went wrong: 'I should let her work out her own salvation in her own way.'

Balfour's memorandum was sent to Lansdowne, Chamberlain, Selborne, and Arnold Forster.[12] On Christmas Eve, the prime minister's remarks triggered a letter from Selborne to Lansdowne.[13] The first lord argued that Balfour's analysis had two flaws. The first was that Japan 'simply cannot see [the Korean port of] Masampho occupied and fortified by Russia without risking a fleet action'. The second was that, when Russian naval reinforcements from the Mediterranean arrived in the Far East, Russia would be so strong as to ensure that Japan would lose the 'fleet action', and 'I think the disappearance of the Japanese battle fleet would have very serious results for us. It would inevitably entail increased naval expenditure on our part'.

Lansdowne penned his own comment on Balfour's memorandum.[14] The foreign secretary made two important observations: first, that Japan was at present stronger navally in the Far East than was Russia; second, that, in such circumstances, Japan was likely to invade Korea and occupy Masampho. Lansdowne pointed out that the naval situation would *not* change when Russia's reinforcements arrived in the Far East from the Mediterranean, but that, within a year, Russia *would* become dominant. The result would be unpleasant for Britain's interests: 'by next autumn Russia might be mistress of the situation, and might impose terms on Japan which would wipe the latter out as a military power, and obliterate her fleet. If this is true, a war would not only affect Japan "through Corea", but might render her an almost negligible factor in Far Eastern politics, instead of, as at present, a potential ally of great importance to us.' Instead of waiting for this military solution to solve the Far Eastern imbroglio in Russia's favour, Lansdowne favoured (contrary to the prime minister) a diplomatic settlement, and preferably one that involved Britain, Japan, Russia, and the United States. Any resort to arms, Lansdowne believed, created for Britain a 'three-fold risk': Japan might be 'crushed', Britain might be drawn into the war, and the government would see 'the aggravation of our present financial difficulties'.

On Christmas Day, Selborne responded to Lansdowne's remarks and Chamberlain replied to Balfour's memorandum. The first lord thought that Lansdowne was too sanguine about Japan's naval power after Russia's naval reinforcements arrived

---

[12] Balfour to Selborne, 23 Dec. 1903, Selborne Papers 34; Arnold Forster diary entry, 25 Dec. 1903, Arnold-Forster Papers, Add MSS 50335.

[13] Selborne to Lansdowne, 24 Dec. 1903, Cab 37/67/94.

[14] Lansdowne to Balfour, confidential, 24 Dec. 1904, Cab 37/67/93; Lansdowne to Balfour, 25 Dec. 1903, Balfour Papers, Add MSS 49728.

from the Mediterranean.[15] For Selborne, Japan's present naval advantage was a factor urging her towards an immediate war. On the other hand, he agreed with the foreign secretary about the danger of Japan's being weakened in a war with Russia such as 'to upset the balance of power in the Far East altogether'. For this reason, he accepted Lansdowne's views about the value of mediation, but asked, could not France be persuaded 'to put pressure on Russia? France must dread war more than we do.' Selborne's preference for mediation was balanced by Chamberlain's views.[16] The chancellor shared Balfour's assumptions about the dangers of such a course; as long as Japan could hold her own navally against Russia, Britain should not intervene.

The various positions having been aired, Balfour was required to reach a decision. But intervening events also had to be considered. On 28 December, the Japanese minister to Britain, Tadasu Hayashi, called at the Foreign Office.[17] Hayashi inquired as to 'what extent and in what shape' Japan could count on British support in a war against Russia. Lansdowne had little doubt, as he told Balfour, that what Japan desired 'most is money'; this both for general needs and for the purchase of two cruisers being built for Argentina in Italy (a matter that Hayashi had discussed earlier, on 17 December).[18] Lansdowne was in favour of finding money for the Japanese, but the foreign secretary reiterated his belief that Britain should attempt to find a means of mediating the dispute. Despite the fact that a Far Eastern war might 'cripple her [Russia's] resources', a Japanese defeat would mean that Japan was 'deprived of her position as a naval Power in Far Eastern waters and of her value as an ally'.

Balfour was not moved. On 29 December, the prime minister outlined his policy.[19] Outside the formal obligations of the Anglo-Japanese Alliance, British policy should be made 'solely in the light of British interests, present and future'. Balfour agreed that it was not to Britain's advantage that Japan should be 'crushed' by Russia, but argued that the chance of this was '*none*'. The worst that could happen was that Russia would occupy Korea and the port of Masampho. While this would be unpleasant for Japan, it was not equivalent to being 'crushed'. What, then, would this mean for Britain? Balfour's argument on this point cut to the heart

[15] 'Notes on Lord Lansdowne's Comments on Mr. Balfour's Memorandum on the Crisis between Japan and Russia', confidential, Selborne, 25 Dec. 1903, Cab 37/67/95. Selborne sent the substance to Balfour; Selborne to Balfour, 25 Dec. 1903, in D. G. Boyce (ed.), *The Crisis of British Power: The Imperial and Naval Papers of the Second Earl of Selborne* (London, 1990), 164–5.

[16] [Untitled memorandum], confidential, A. Chamberlain, 25 Dec. 1903, Cab 37/67/96.

[17] [Untitled memo], Sanderson, 28 Dec. 1903, Balfour Papers, Add MSS 49739.

[18] Lansdowne to Balfour, 29 Dec. 1903, Balfour Papers, Add MSS 49728; Nish, *Anglo-Japanese Alliance*, 272. The cruisers were purchased by Japan on 29 Dec.; Kerr to Selborne, 29 Dec. 1903, Selborne Papers 35.

[19] [Untitled memo], confidential, Balfour, 29 Dec. 1903, Cab 37/67/97.

of Anglo-Russian affairs, and demonstrated just how much they were involved in the Russo-Japanese quarrel: 'Would Russia, as a world Power,' the prime minister asked rhetorically, 'be stronger all along the vast line of her frontier, from the Baltic to Vladivostock, if she added Corea to her dominions?' His answer to this question was based on the following assumptions: 'Russia's strong point is her vast population and the unassailable character of her territories. Her weak point is finance.' In Balfour's view, a Russian occupation of Korea would only exacerbate Russia's financial weakness and leave her permanently estranged from Japan.

In these circumstances, what should British policy be? Working on the basis of 'a cool calculation of national interests', the prime minister stated that even should Russia defeat Japan—and he felt this 'very doubtful'—Britain should maintain a strict neutrality. The reasons were varied. One involved the general diplomatic and military situation: the 'risk and loss' of becoming involved in a 'world-wide war' with the Franco-Russian alliance. The other referred specifically to Anglo-Russian relations. While a Russian victory in the Far East might make her stronger in that area, 'we have to fear her chiefly as (a) the ally of France; (b) the invader of India; (c) the dominating influence in Persia; and (d) the possible disturber of European peace. For these purposes she will not be stronger but weaker after over-running Corea.' Financially strapped by this effort and faced with a hostile Japan, 'her [Russian] diplomacy, from the Black Sea to the Oxus, might be weakened into something distantly resembling sweet reasonableness'. Here was Balfour at his lucid best; here, indeed, was 'a cool calculation of national interests'.

With policy set, Balfour set about to implement it. First, he rejected the Japanese request for money, arguing that it would be equivalent to an 'act of war' against Russia.[20] Second, he authorized Selborne to circulate to the Cabinet a proposed 'heads of agreement', outlining rough terms for the negotiation of a general Anglo-Russian understanding.[21] Finally, he called a meeting of the Committee of Imperial Defence (CID) on 4 January 1904 to discuss what Britain should do in case of a Russo-Japanese War.[22] At this meeting, three papers were discussed: Balfour's own memorandum of 29 December, a projection by the War Office of the likely military outcome of a Russo-Japanese conflict, and an outline of what action Britain should take if she were drawn into the war as a belligerent.[23] As the War Office saw it, command of the sea was the determining point in a Russo-Japanese conflict, since

[20] Balfour to Lansdowne, 31 Dec. 1903, Balfour Papers, Add MSS 49728.
[21] Balfour to Lansdowne, 2nd, 31 Dec. 1903, Balfour Papers, Add MSS 49728; 'Proposed Agreement with Russia', Lansdowne, 1 Jan. 1904, Cab 37/68/1.
[22] 29th meeting of the CID, 4 Jan. 1904, Cab 2/1.
[23] [Untitled memo], Balfour 29 Dec. 1903; 'Forecast of the First Phase of a War Between Russia and Japan', Intelligence Department, WO, 28 Dec. 1903; 'British Intervention in Far East', E. A. Altham, AQMG, WO, 31 Dec. 1903, Cab 4/1/11B, 12B and 13B.

without it Japan could neither land nor supply troops in Korea. Should Britain enter the war, it was assumed that in all cases (that is, whether or not France was involved) the Anglo-Japanese combination would have command of the sea. Britain's first military concern would then be India, which would require an immediate reinforcement of 30,000 men and a subsequent reinforcement of 70,000 troops. With these considerations in mind, the CID decided both to seek further information from India about the need for reinforcements and to undertake a study of the logistical problems involved.[24]

There were also naval considerations. These involved two sets of issues. The first was legal: the linked questions of the right of the Russian Black Sea fleet to pass through the Dardanelles in time of war and its subsequent right of passage through the Suez Canal.[25] The second was purely strategic: how should Britain act so as to ensure that she controlled the Mediterranean against any possibility, including the menace of a combined Franco-Russian fleet? This latter was not new. The two-power standard was directed against a Franco-Russian menace, and the CID had decided in February 1903 that a Russian seizure of the Straits would not 'fundamentally alter' the naval situation in the Mediterranean.[26] Thus, all that was required was that 'Willie Selborne will have an adequate force in the Eastern Mediterranean'.[27]

The legal question was more complicated. It involved the interpretation of both the Treaty of Paris of 1856 and the Suez Canal Convention of 1888. The 'inner Cabinet' of Arnold-Forster, Balfour, Chamberlain, Lansdowne, and Selborne wrestled with this problem throughout the first half of January 1904.[28] On 19 January, Balfour drew up a memorandum both summarizing his colleagues' views and suggesting a line of policy.[29] The prime minister proposed that Britain should do two things. The first was to warn the Russians that Britain would not acquiesce in the Russian fleet passing through the Straits, the exact nature of the British response to depend on the circumstances. The second was to deny Russian warships the right both to pass through the Suez Canal and to coal at British ports. As it would be difficult to carry out the first proposal without seeming to accuse Russia beforehand of intending to break the Treaty of Paris, Balfour suggested telling the

---

[24] The final destination of the second contingent of reinforcements was undecided. Should Russia not menace India too seriously, the 70,000 might be sent to Manchuria as part of a joint Anglo-Japanese force.

[25] K. Neilson, ' "A Dangerous Game of American Poker": Britain and the Russo-Japanese War', *JSS* 12 (1989), 63–87.

[26] 'Report on the Conclusion Arrived on the 11th February in Reference to Russia and Constantinople', Balfour, 14 Feb. 1903, Cab 4/1/1B.

[27] Balfour to Lansdowne, 19 Jan. 1904, Balfour Papers, Add MSS 49728.

[28] The correspondence in Cab 37/68/11.

[29] 'Memorandum by Mr. Balfour respecting the Russian Black Sea Fleet and the Passage of the Dardanelles', Balfour, 19 Jan. 1904, Cab 37/68/11.

Turkish government instead, confident that the news would 'of course, be at once handed on to the Russian Government'.

Lansdowne did not employ Balfour's devious methods. Instead, the foreign secretary decided to use the situation to Britain's advantage. First, he ensured that Japan knew where Britain stood. He informed Tokyo of Britain's policy about both the Straits and the Suez Canal, arguing that 'an intimation of this sort would have an excellent effect on the Japanese, even if it were to be a *brutum fulmen*.'[30] Lansdowne's adherence to Japan was evident, although he was not going to give the latter any overt support. Clear, too, was Lansdowne's attitude to Russia. Any British action on behalf of Russia had a price: some tangible advantage for Britain.

This was illustrated by the foreign secretary's reaction to an attempt on 18 January by the French foreign minister to extend a 'feeler on behalf of his Russian friends who are dying to get out of the war'.[31] Given that 'the Japanese have distinctly told us that they do not want mediation', Lansdowne responded 'languidly', telling Balfour that his reply would 'depend upon the answer which Benckendorff gives me to the questions which I put to him at our last interview'. This latter point referred to a meeting on 13 January, when the foreign secretary had pressed the Russian ambassador to give an unequivocal answer to the British demands that Russia evacuate Manchuria.[32] The trade-off was plain: without a favourable Russian response to British concerns, no mediation in the Russo-Japanese imbroglio was possible.

This still left some practical matters. On the diplomatic front, Balfour had Lansdowne instruct Scott that the British attitude should be one of uncompromising objection to any 'intimation' that the Russian Black Sea fleet was about to pass the Straits.[33] On 27 January a meeting of the CID considered what to do from a naval point of view if the Russians chose to ignore diplomacy.[34] The two means of directly resisting this move—either to station a fleet at Lemnos and attack the Russians as they emerged from the Black Sea or to put a superior fleet in the eastern Mediterranean and oppose by force of arms any Russian attempt to use the Suez Canal—were both rejected.[35] The former was felt unfeasible because of the unprotected nature of the harbour at Lemnos, its vulnerability to torpedo attacks, and the fact that Britain would appear to be the aggressor. The latter was too dangerous, as the Russian fleet might turn westward and effect a junction with the French fleet.

---

[30] Lansdowne to Selborne, 19 Jan. 1904, Cab 37/68/11.
[31] Lansdowne to Balfour, 18 Jan. 1904, Balfour Papers, Add MSS 49728.
[32] Lansdowne to Scott, confidential disp. 16, 13 Jan. 1904, FO 65/1677.
[33] Balfour to Lansdowne, 19 Jan. 1904, Cab 37/68/11.
[34] Minutes of the 30th meeting of the CID, 27 Jan. 1904, Cab 2/1.
[35] 'Imperial Defence Committee, January 27. Course to be pursued if, during Hostilities between Japan and Russia, the Black Sea Fleet were to force the Dardanelles', Balfour, 28 Jan. 1904, Cab 4/1; Arnold-Forster diary entry 27 Jan. 1904, Arnold Forster Papers, Add MSS 50336.

The course adopted was to follow the Russian fleet through the Suez Canal and shadow its progress eastward. This would prevent any assistance by the French fleet, and would leave the Russian ships, isolated and without adequate coaling facilities, at the mercy of the British. This policy was approved by the Cabinet on 4 February.[36] All now turned on events.

While the Russian and Japanese governments continued to play out what Ian Nish has termed their 'adversarial coda' leading to war, Anglo-Russian relations deteriorated.[37] The Russians were upset about British actions in Tibet, resented the fact that two Russian torpedo-boat destroyers had been ordered out of Malta and believed that the British were counselling the Japanese towards aggression.[38] With regard to the latter point, Scott wrote from Russia that the '[f]eeling is very strong against us here just now as they regard us as playing a double game,—peace & neutrality in our mouths when talking to Russia & other powers & our Minister at Tokio advising & egging on the Japanese to resist all terms offered by Russia & fight her'.[39]

Thus only the timing of the outbreak of hostilities on 8 February was unexpected in London. Three days before, Arnold-Forster had opined that the Japanese breaking off of negotiations 'of course means war', and had conferred with Selborne to ensure a co-ordinated British response.[40] The British were under no illusions as to what a Russo-Japanese war meant for Anglo-Russian relations. 'I am afraid', Sanderson wrote to Scott, 'as you say that we shall be very unpopular', while the British military attaché in Russia argued that, should the war go badly for the Tsarist forces, Russia would advance towards India.[41] While Scott did not share fully his attaché's beliefs, the ambassador felt it certain that Russia would do something to ruffle British feathers.[42] But Scott's views had become irrelevant. Hardinge had been offered the post of ambassador to Russia by Lansdowne on 13 February and had accepted.[43] This adumbrated a more combative British policy; with the 'Edwardian' Hardinge in charge at St Petersburg, no longer would the best possible light be put on every Russian action.

[36] Untitled note by Sandars on a Cabinet meeting, 4 Feb. 1904, Sandars Papers, MS Eng. hist. *c*.748, 31st meeting of the CID, 8 Feb. 1904, Cab 2/1.

[37] Nish, *Russo-Japanese War*, 206–21.

[38] Sanderson to Scott, 27 Jan. 1904, Scott Papers, Add MSS 52299; Curzon to Brodrick, 28 Jan. 1904, Curzon Papers, MSS Eur F111/163; Scott to Lansdowne, disp. 50, 4 Feb. 1904, FO 65/1678.

[39] Scott to Lansdowne, 4 Feb. 1904, Lansdowne Papers, FO 800/115.

[40] Arnold-Forster diary entry, 5 Feb. 1904, Arnold Forster Papers, Add MSS 50336; Sanderson to Scott, 10 Feb. 1904, Scott Papers, Add MSS 52299.

[41] Sanderson to Scott, 10 Feb. 1904, Scott Papers, Add MSS 52299. [Napier's confidential disp. 12, 18 Feb. 1904, in Scott to Lansdowne, disp. 71, 18 Feb. 1904, FO 65/1678.]

[42] Scott to Sanderson, 18 Feb. 1904, Lansdowne Papers, FO 800/115.

[43] Hardinge to Bertie, 14 Feb. 1904, Bertie Papers, FO 800/176; Hardinge to Scott, 16 Feb. 1904, Scott Papers, Add MSS 52302.

Scott's last two months in Russia—he left his post in late April—were extremely unpleasant. This was galling to the ambassador, for he had been very popular in Russian society, and the social boycott of the Embassy offended him deeply.[44] While both Sanderson and Hardinge attempted to soothe Scott's bruised feelings, it was evident that Anglo-Russian relations at a personal level in St Petersburg were not cordial.[45] To compound this, the Russian press carried on an unrelenting attack against Britain.[46] While this was part of a wider-ranging search for scapegoats— 'recriminations are bandied about, & there is a feeling that some one deserves hanging'—being carried on in Russia, it meant that any incidents, however small, would have to be treated carefully lest they have grave repercussions.[47]

Meanwhile, Lansdowne had to ensure that his other diplomatic fences were carefully mended. In the case of France, this was relatively easy, since Delcassé was enthusiastic both to avoid being drawn into the Russo-Japanese conflict and to finalize the Anglo-French discussions.[48] Both of these aims required good Anglo-French relations. Lansdowne not only shared Delcassé's desires, but also felt that the French hoped to bring about an Anglo-Russian *rapprochement*.[49] The problem was Germany. From China, the British minister reported that the Germans were 'exceedingly anti-Japanese', but inclined to follow the 'real German tradition [and] wait until she sees to which side victory inclines, and then join in falling upon the underdog'.[50] At the Foreign Office, there was a belief that the Germans 'are stirring up both the French & the Russian Press against us', and there was a rumour, originating from the British embassy at Vienna, that Wilhelm II had offered Russia support against the other powers.[51]

It was against this background that the CID continued to discuss the defence of India. The subject was seen as intimately linked with the events of the Russo-Japanese conflict. St John Brodrick posited a situation in which Russia would 'put pressure on us on the Afghan frontier at the moment they are intriguing with

[44] Hardinge to Scott, 24 Feb. 1904, Scott Papers, Add MSS 52302; Sanderson to Scott, 24 Feb. 1904, Scott Papers, Add MSS 52299; Scott to Lansdowne, 27 Feb. 1904, Lansdowne Papers, FO 800/140; Hardinge to Bertie, 2 Mar. 1904, Bertie Papers, FO 800/183; and Spring Rice to Ferguson (a friend), 2 Mar. 1904, in S. Gwynn (ed.), *The Letters and Friendships of Sir Cecil Spring Rice* (2 vols; London, 1929), i. 402–6.

[45] Sanderson to Scott, 24 Feb. 1904, Scott Papers, Add MSS 52299; Hardinge to Scott, 24 Feb. 1904, Scott Papers, Add MSS 52302.

[46] Sanderson to Scott, 18 Feb. 1904, Scott Papers, Add MSS 52299.

[47] Scott to Sanderson, 27 Feb. 1904, Lansdowne Papers, FO 800/115; Neilson ' "Dangerous Game" ', 66–7.

[48] Monson (British ambassador, Paris) to Lansdowne, 23 Feb. 1904, Lansdowne Papers, FO 800/126.

[49] Lansdowne to Lascelles, 23 Mar. 1904, Lansdowne Papers, FO 800/129.

[50] Satow (British minister, Peking) to Lansdowne, 25 Feb. 1904, Lansdowne Papers, FO 800/120.

[51] Barrington to Lascelles, 2 Mar. 1904, Lascelles Papers, FO 800/12; Lascelles to Barrington, 4 Mar. 1904, Lansdowne Papers, FO 800/129.

Germany to get their fleet through the Dardanelles', and Lord Roberts, the chief of the general staff, hoped that 'no move will be made by Russia for some time to come, for we are certainly not prepared at present to put a large army in the field'.[52] Possible British countermoves to any Russian aggression were slight; naval opinion doubted whether anything significant could be done.[53] In the meantime, the British considered their options with respect to the issues of belligerent rights and freedom of the sea that the war in the Far East seemed likely to engender.[54]

But, initially, the war caused a paralysis in Anglo-Russian relations. Until events unfolded, the British could do no more than observe and contemplate their options. Particularly important to such contemplations was the Russian reaction to the signing on 8 April of the Anglo-French entente. While the British had not negotiated the entente solely with a mind to its impact on Anglo-Russian relations, several were quick to point out that the new agreement could be used as a standing point from which to approach Russia. This was particularly important, as the Russians believed that Japan would not have gone to war without the British support that St Petersburg imputed to the Anglo-Japanese Alliance. On 13 April Spring Rice wove these disparate threads together in a letter from St Petersburg.[55] While Spring Rice felt that no agreement with Russia 'unless sanctioned by force' was possible, the first secretary argued (in a phrase that Lansdowne marked in the margin of the letter) that the 'next step should be no doubt to use the French arrangement as a stepping stone to some sort of improvement in our relations with Russia'.

Such an idea also had Russian roots. In the course of a discussion in Copenhagen with Edward VII (the latter in the midst of a royal visit), Aleksandr Izvolskii, the Russian ambassador to Denmark (and whose supersession of Lamsdorff as foreign minister was already being bruited), let it be known that 'he belongs to a group in Russia who would like an understanding with England and in fact sees salvation in such a policy'.[56] The King replied that he, too, favoured an improvement in relations between the two countries. In London, Benckendorff informed Lansdowne that Lamsdorff both 'regarded favourably' the Anglo-French entente and felt that it might 'form a useful precedent' for an arrangement between Russia and Britain.[57] All this gave Lansdowne hope that Anglo-Russian relations could be

[52] Brodrick to Curzon, 25 Mar. 1904, Curzon Papers, MSS Eur F111/163; Roberts to Kitchener, secret, 30 Mar. 1904 Kitchener Papers, PRO 30/57/28.

[53] Selborne to Kerr, secret, 1 Apr. 1904; Kerr to Selborne, 2 Apr. 1904, both Selborne Papers 39; Selborne to Balfour, 3 Apr. 1904, Balfour Papers, Add MSS 49707; Selborne to Balfour, 5 Apr. 1904, Selborne Papers 39.

[54] Neilson, '"Dangerous Game"', 67–70.

[55] Spring Rice to Mallet, 13 Apr. 1904, Lansdowne Papers, FO 800/115.

[56] E. Goschen (British minister, Copenhagen) to Lansdowne, 16 Apr. 1904, Lansdowne Papers, FO 800/122.

[57] Lansdowne to Scott, disp. 168A, draft, 19 Apr. 1904, FO 65/1577.

improved in the future.[58] However, the foreign secretary was cautious. When Benckendorff inquired on 22 April as to whether Izvolskii's conversation with Edward VII might bear immediate fruit, Lansdowne told the ambassador that, while the Russo-Japanese War continued, it would be difficult to pursue talks.[59] Lansdowne also rejected Benckendorff's suggestion that the British government 'allay the apprehension' of the Russian government about the intent of the Younghusband expedition to Tibet. The foreign secretary pointed out that statements outlining British policy had already been made on the subject in both the Commons and the Lords. While the French added their voice to this Russian request, Lansdowne preferred to await events.[60]

In Russia, such an attitude was viewed as implicitly anti-Russian. The Russian government quietly, and the Russian public loudly, felt that Britain was taking advantage of Russia's predicament to advance in Tibet and resented Lansdowne's remarks in the House of Lords alleging that the Mürzsteg agreement had not led to any positive results in the Balkans. They believed that the Anglo-French entente meant that France no longer would support Russia on matters where such support might irritate Britain.[61] The initial Russian defeats on the Yalu added to Russia's prickliness. Thus, when Hardinge arrived in St Petersburg on 16 April to take up his post as ambassador, the situation was a difficult one.

None the less, Hardinge encountered a warm personal reception.[62] His close ties to Edward VII and his previous time in Russia ensured that the highest levels of society were cordial to him, reversing the position that had existed the previous two months under Scott. This was important, as it put Hardinge in a position to hear the gossip and rumours that formed the undercurrents of political life in Russia. Lamsdorff, too, was convivial, although the foreign minister soon acquainted Hardinge with Russian grievances concerning Tibet and Macedonia.[63]

Hardinge soon acquainted himself with the realities of the political situation in Russia.[64] The ambassador correctly believed that Nicholas II's principal ministers,

[58] Lansdowne to Lascelles, 18 Apr. 1904, Lansdowne Papers, FO 800/129.
[59] Lansdowne to Scott, disp. 176 secret, 22 Apr. 1904, FO 65/1677; C. H. D. Howard (ed.), *The Diary of Sir Edward Goschen 1900–14* (London, 1980), 85–6; Hardinge to Bertie, 22 Apr. 1904, Bertie Papers, FO 800/176.
[60] Spring Rice (first secretary, St Petersburg) to Lansdowne, 28 Apr. 1904, Lansdowne Papers, FO 800/140.
[61] Spring Rice to Lansdowne, disp. 238, 11 May 1904, FO 65/1680; Spring Rice to Foreign Office, private and secret tel., 12 May 1904; Spring Rice to Lansdowne, 12 May 1904, both Lansdowne Papers, FO 800/140; Lansdowne's remarks in *Parl Debs*, 4th series, vol. 134, cols. 508–15.
[62] Hardinge diary entries, 17 and 19 May 1904, Hardinge Papers, vol. 5; Hardinge to Lansdowne, 25 May 1904, Lansdowne Papers, FO 800/140; Lansdowne to Knollys (Edward VII's private secretary), 25 May 1904, Hardinge Papers, vol. 6.
[63] Hardinge to Lansdowne, disp. 256, 18 May 1904, FO 65/1680.
[64] Hardinge to Lansdowne, 25 May 1904, Lansdowne Papers, FO 800/140; D. M. McDonald, *United Government and Foreign Policy in Russia, 1900–14* (Cambridge, MA, 1992), 31–75.

Lamsdorff, Kuropatkin (the war minister) and Plehve (minister of the interior) were opposed to the war, but that Nicholas was under the influence of what Hardinge termed the Emperor's ' "Council of the Far East" ' headed by Rear Admiral A. M. Abaza, a close ally of A. M. Bezobrazov and a member of Nicholas's personal suite. With the Emperor's regarding the war as a personal crusade and operating without regard to the views of his own ministers, Hardinge realized that it would be difficult to deal officially with any Anglo-Russian matters relating to the Far East. For this reason, Lansdowne's policy of avoiding discussions with Russia during the war was sensible and prudent. For his part, Hardinge hoped to avoid any permanent estrangement between the two countries and, particularly, any shift in Russian policy towards a pro-German stance.[65] To this end, he attempted to ensure that newspapers, both Russian and English, did not write inflammatory articles about Anglo-Russian relations.[66] Further, he warned the Foreign Office that British diplomatic codes were probably compromised by the Russian secret police and initiated efforts to ensure secure communications.

These were precautionary steps. Some matters, however, required immediate decisions. In June and July, the British government found itself with a series of naval problems involving Russia.[67] The issues involved were diverse. The first centred around the Black Sea provisions of the Treaty of Paris. The British refused to accept the contention that the Russian Volunteer fleet—a quasi-official group of merchant ships that could be converted to troop ships and commerce raiders in time of war—should have free passage of the Straits. Equally, the British refused to accept the Russians' unilateral definition of what constituted contraband. The British needed also to decide just how the Suez Canal convention of 1888 should be applied: would Russian warships on the way to the Far East be allowed both to pass and to obtain coal? Further, it was necessary to decide on a course of action should the Russian fleet immured in Port Arthur break out and attempt to seek haven at Wei-hai-wei. And all of this was complicated

---

[65] J. Steinberg, 'Germany and the Russo-Japanese War', *AHR* 75 (1970), 1965–86; D. Geyer, *Russian Imperialism: The Interaction of Domestic and Foreign Policy, 1860–1914*, trans. B. Little (Leamington Spa, 1987), 220–47.

[66] Hardinge diary entry, 29 May 1904, Hardinge Papers, vol. 5; Hardinge to Chirol, 3 June 1904, Sanderson Papers, FO 800/2; Hardinge to Sanderson, 3 June 1904, Lansdowne Papers, FO 800/115. Hardinge failed with *The Times*, see Moberley Bell to Chirol, 8 June 1904; Chirol to Hardinge, 14 June 1904, both Hardinge Papers, vol. 7, but had limited success with the Russian papers; Hardinge to Lansdowne, disp. 285, 9 June 1904; Hardinge to Lansdowne, disp. 330, 2 July 1904, both FO 65/1680.

[67] Neilson, ' "Dangerous Game" ', 70–9; J. W. Coogan, *The End of Neutrality: The United States, Britain and Maritime Rights 1899–1915* (Ithaca, NY, 1981); K. Neilson, ' "The British Empire Floats on the British Navy": British Naval Policy, Belligerent Rights and Disarmament, 1902–9' in B. J. C. McKercher (ed.), *Arms Limitation and Disarmament: Restraints on War, 1899–1939* (New York, 1992), 21–42; M. Allen, 'Rear Admiral Reginald Custance: Director of Naval Intelligence 1899–1902', *MM* 78 (1992), 61–75.

by British fears that Russia would threaten India in order to influence British actions.[68]

While this latter proved to be groundless, the naval concerns did not.[69] The passage of the Straits and Suez Canal by the *Smolensk* and *Petersburg*—two ships of the Volunteer fleet—in early July raised British hackles. But the seizure in the Red Sea of the British steamer *Malacca* by the *Petersburg* on 13 July precipitated a crisis. The British response was rapid and belligerent.[70] On 20 July, Lansdowne informed Benckendorff that the situation was grave and warned him that Britain would, if necessary, take action to deal with it. In St Petersburg, Hardinge gave this message to Lamsdorff both verbally on 19 August and in a written note the following day. In the Cabinet, the government decided on 21 July to take all necessary naval steps to prevent any further Russian attacks on British ships.[71] This carried the threat of war. Hardinge underlined the seriousness of the situation and its significance for Anglo-Russian relations in a letter to Bertie.[72] His letter also revealed the new attitude that Hardinge brought to his post. 'Above all things', the ambassador wrote, 'let us be firm and after the covered threats which I had to make to Lamsdorff yesterday I hope that we shall have a little backbone and not allow these people to bluff us.' An 'Edwardian' policy required courage.

By 28 July, the situation seemed under control, as the Russian government had agreed to release the *Malacca* and several similar naval incidents seemed well on the way to solution.[73] In the interim, however, the British had received news about Russia's internal circumstances that revealed a delicate and difficult situation. On 21 July, Hardinge sent to London a memorandum by Spring Rice outlining the views of Dillon (and, hence, it was assumed, those of Witte) about Russian domestic politics.[74] According to Dillon, Nicholas II was completely under the influence of Bezobrazov, and, among his ministers, listened only to those, like Plehve, who were 'not indisposed to a warlike policy, since it occupies public attention &

---

[68] F. A. Campbell (assistant under-secretary, Foreign Office) to Hardinge, 1 June 1904; Sanderson to Hardinge, 1 June 1904, both Hardinge Papers, vol. 7.

[69] For British contingency planning, 'Estimate of the Forces Required to Oppose Russia Successfully for the Defence of India', H. Mullay (DQMG, Indian Army), 30 June 1904, Roberts Papers, WO 105/42.

[70] Outlined in 'Telegrams Relating to the Actions of Vessels Belonging to the Russian Volunteer Fleet from July 3 to July 23, 1904', 26 July 1904, Selborne Papers, 154; 'Seizure of the "Malacca"', n.s., 8 Aug. 1904, Cab 17/60.

[71] Balfour to the King, 21 July 1904, Sandars Papers, MS Eng. hist. *c*.716. German observations that Britain was quite likely to begin a war against Russia can be seen less as an attempt to export the 'Copenhagen complex' and more as a realistic observation on the serious nature of the Anglo-Russian naval quarrel: J. Steinberg, 'The Copenhagen Complex', in W. Laqueur and G. L. Mosse (eds.), *1914: The Coming of the First World War* (New York, 1966), 30.

[72] Hardinge to Bertie, 21 July 1904, Bertie Papers, FO 800/176.

[73] Hardinge's cumulative diary entry, 28 July 1904, Hardinge Papers, vol. 5.

[74] Hardinge to Sandars, 21 July 1904, Sandars Papers, MS Eng. hist *c*.748.

diminishes the prospect of internal troubles'. The Emperor was seen as afflicted with a sort of religious mania and convinced that he had divine guidance in the war. More ominously, '[t]he idea of a war with England would be much more popular throughout Russia than a war with Japan'.

This reiterated what Dillon had said in England a month earlier, in June, to Balfour's private secretary.[75] Its impact was to reinforce the British belief both that there were divided councils in Russia and that decisions were not being made in a rational fashion. The assassination of Plehve on 28 July only complicated the situation. It was not clear just who was advising Nicholas, and Hardinge had no desire to encourage 'unthinking hotheads' in the Emperor's entourage who advocated drawing Britain into the Russo-Japanese War so that, if Russia were to lose, it would be to a superior combination of opponents rather than to Japan alone.[76] For this reason, Lansdowne noted, while it was important to maintain a firm stand about naval matters, Benckendorff and Lamsdorff should not be treated harshly: 'we must blacken *their* faces as little as possible.'[77]

But while Russian face was being saved, the British had to take precautions and make practical decisions. On 28 July, a 'special' Cabinet was held to consider what to do should the Russian fleet break out from Port Arthur and seek refuge at Wei-hai-wei.[78] It was decided that any Russian ships that should ignore the British warning not to enter port would be disarmed and interned. Five days later, Balfour struck a committee to determine what the British response should be if a Russian warship legally took a British ship as a prize.[79] Such a case was different from those involving the Volunteer fleet; the prime minister hoped that both France and the United States would take a stand on this issue. This was particularly pressing, as there was discontent within British shipping circles over the fact that cargoes were being placed in German ships, as the latter were felt to be relatively immune from Russian depredations.[80] The news that the Russian railroad from Orenburg to Tashkent was within two-and-a-half months of being completed could only have added to the concerns surrounding Anglo-Russian relations.[81]

On 11 August, Balfour decided to take a firm stand. At a Cabinet held that same day, the prime minister outlined his policy. It was, as he told the King 'a strong one'.[82] The reason for adopting such a firm position was the need to impress on

[75] Sandars' memo, 9 June 1904, Sandars Papers, MS Eng. hist. *c*.748.

[76] Hardinge to Lansdowne, 4 Aug. 1904, Lansdowne Papers, FO 800/140.

[77] Lansdowne to Hardinge, 27 July 1904, Lansdowne Papers, FO 800/140.

[78] Balfour to the King, 28 July 1904, Sandars Papers, MS Eng. hist. *c*.716.

[79] Balfour to the King, 2 Aug. 1904, Sandars Papers, MS Eng. hist. *c*.716.

[80] Chirol to Hardinge, 10 Aug. 1904, Hardinge Papers, vol. 7; Lascelles to Lansdowne, 4 Aug. 1904, Lascelles Papers, FO 800/12.

[81] Hardinge to Lansdowne, disp. 380, 2 Aug. 1904, containing Napier's (British military attaché) disp. 49, 31 July 1904, FO 65/1681; Roberts (CGS) to Kitchener (c-in-c, Indian Army), 11 Aug. 1904, Kitchener Papers, PRO 30/57/28.

[82] Balfour to the King, 11 Aug. 1904, Sandars Papers MS Eng. hist. *c*.716.

Russia the seriousness of the situation: 'The Russians are sometimes under the delusion that a *conciliatory* attitude is a *weak* attitude; and that G.[reat] B.[ritain] is prepared to make any concession rather than defend her rights by force. So lamentable a misunderstanding of the real feelings of this Country is a serious menace to good international relations, and the sooner it is dispelled the better.' To ensure that the Russians were aware of the British attitude, both Lansdowne in the Lords and Balfour in the Commons made strong speeches warning Russia that Britain would tolerate no further illegal interference with British trade.[83]

While public attention in Russia was somewhat deflected from serious matters by the birth of an heir apparent on 12 August, Balfour's policy had its desired effect. On 18 August, Hardinge reported that Lansdowne's speech in the Lords had 'impressed these people'.[84] As an added bonus, Lamsdorff's domestic position had been strengthened at the expense of Nicholas's grand ducal advisors who had advocated an aggressive naval policy against neutral shipping. With the American government's officially joining the British in denouncing the Russian policies with respect to contraband, the situation seemed defused.[85] Lansdowne helped this along, offering as an olive branch the fact that the British would not appoint an official representative in Tibet, thus eliminating the Russian contention that Britain was taking advantage of Russia's preoccupation in the Far East to steal a march at Lhassa.[86]

However, the events of June and July had left a dangerous legacy. Feeling in Britain against Russia was high.[87] Thus, when the *Smolensk* stopped British ships in the Indian Ocean on 23 August, the British reaction was sudden and violent. While Lansdowne believed that the incident could be attributed to 'stupidity' on the part of some individual Russian, he instructed Hardinge to make an immediate pro-test.[88] Balfour took immediate steps to head off the impending crisis. Taking advantage of an opportunity to speak to the London Chamber of Commerce about the impact of the Russo-Japanese War on British trade, the prime minister attempt-ed to warn St Petersburg of the gravity of the situation 'without being in any way offensive to the Russian Government'.[89] The only problem, Balfour lamented, was finding the right formula: 'it is hard to estimate the exact amount of menace which the latter [the Russian government] require before they think we mean business.'

[83] *Parl Debs*, 4th series, vol. 140, cols. 154–7, 271–7.

[84] Hardinge to Lansdowne, 18 Aug. 1904, Lansdowne Papers, FO 800/140.

[85] Coogan, *End of Neutrality*, 49.

[86] Hardinge to Lansdowne, 18 Aug. 1904, Hardinge Papers, vol. 6 and reply, 24 Aug. 1904, Lansdowne Papers, FO 800/140.

[87] Chirol to Hardinge, 23 Aug. 1904; Knollys to Hardinge, 24 Aug. 1904, both Hardinge Papers, vol. 7.

[88] Lansdowne to Balfour, 25 Aug. 1904, Balfour Papers, Add MSS 49728.

[89] Balfour to Lansdowne, 25 Aug. 1904, Balfour Papers, Add MSS 49728.

To back up this 'menace', Balfour instructed Britain's intelligence agencies to ascertain the coaling situation for the Russian raiders at French African ports and informed the Indian military authorities to make no secret of their preparations to defend the subcontinent. By 26 August, as Sir George Clarke wrote, 'matters are much tangled & anything can happen'.[90]

By the end of August, and despite the pacific counsel of the first sea lord, Selborne had reached the conclusion that it was necessary to shadow the Russian cruisers.[91] Believing that the Russian navy was deliberately following a policy different than that which the Russian foreign ministry was espousing, Balfour agreed.[92] In the meantime, Lansdowne instructed Hardinge to continue to push at St Petersburg for a clarification of the Russian policy covering the entire gamut of naval issues between the two countries.[93] In London, various means to avoid the continuing friction between the two countries were discussed, but the most promising, the idea of suggesting to Russia that neutral shipping be liable to attack only in certain designated areas, was rejected as providing a precedent that would overly constrict Britain's own actions as a belligerent in any future war.[94] In the end, what was adopted was a policy of 'unostentatious' observation of the *Smolensk* and *Petersburg*, a policy designed both to avoid antagonizing the Russian government and to safeguard British interests.[95] With all Russia depressed by the reverses of the Russian army at Liaoyang and the Baltic fleet preparing to depart for the Far East, Hardinge felt it best to let other issues lie.[96] By the end of September, with the Russian government's coming to accept the British position with regard to contraband, such a policy seemed justified. Only the precipitate action of Younghusband in Tibet, who in defiance of his instructions had signed a treaty making Tibet a virtual British protectorate, seemed to cloud Anglo-Russian relations.[97]

The latter was soon overcome. Lansdowne's denunciation of Younghusband's

---

[90] Clarke to Esher, 26 Aug. 1904, Esher Papers, ESHR 10/34.

[91] Kerr to Selborne, 26 Aug. 1904, Selborne Papers, 41; Selborne to Balfour, 28 Aug. 1904, Balfour Papers, Add MSS 49708.

[92] Balfour to Selborne, 30 Aug. 1904, Selborne Papers, 39.

[93] Lansdowne to Selborne, 31 Aug. 1904, Selborne Papers, 40.

[94] F. A. Campbell (assistant under-secretary, Foreign Office) to Lansdowne, memo, 6 Sept. 1904, Balfour Papers, Add MSS 49728; Kerr to Selborne, 9 Sept. 1904, Selborne Papers, 41; Lansdowne to private secretary, FO, tel., 9 Sept. 1904, Lansdowne Papers, FO 800/141; Lansdowne to Balfour, memo, 30 Sept., Balfour Papers, Add MSS 49728.

[95] Neilson, '"Dangerous Game"', 79; Bertie (acting PUS during Sanderson's illness) to Lansdowne, minute, 19 Sept. 1904, Cab 1/4; Lansdowne to Balfour, 20 Sept. 1904, Balfour Papers, Add MSS 49728.

[96] Hardinge to Lansdowne, disp. 463, 14 Sept. 1904, FO 65/1681; Hardinge to Lansdowne, 15 Sept. 1904, Lansdowne Papers, FO 800/141.

[97] Hardinge to Lansdowne, 27 Sept. 1904; Lansdowne to Hardinge, 4 Oct. 1904, both Lansdowne Papers, FO 800/141; Brodrick to Selborne, 5 Oct. 1904, Selborne Papers, 39; D. Dilks, *Curzon in India* (2 vol.; London, 1969), ii. 92–101.

actions soon restored a semblance of tranquillity between the two countries, and the first three weeks of October were largely uneventful, as all eyes were on the battles in Manchuria. The calm was deceptive. When the Russian Baltic fleet sank a number of British trawlers off the Dogger Bank on the night of 21 October, this precipitated the most severe crisis in Anglo-Russian relations of the Russo-Japanese War. All the anger that Russian naval actions had generated over the previous five months came to the fore, and the two countries came perilously close to war in the course of the next fortnight. Only careful diplomacy, and the eventual Russian willingness to back down, prevented public opinion from pushing Britain into precipitate action against the Russian fleet.

The Dogger Bank incident occurred on a Friday night. News of it reached London only on Sunday evening, and the British response therefore had to wait until 24 October to be formulated.[98] Lansdowne's actions were immediate and comprehensive. Hardinge was told to demand from the Russian government 'an ample apology and complete and prompt reparation as well as security against the recurrence of such intolerable acts'.[99] Meanwhile, Lansdowne asked the Russian chargé d'affaires, Sergei Sazonov, to call at the Foreign Office. The latter apologized for what he termed 'an unfortunate mistake', but refused to make any 'damaging admissions', a position reiterated by Benckendorff the following day when the ambassador returned to the Russian embassy.[100] Lansdowne refused to be deflected, and repeated the demands that he had asked Hardinge to make at St Petersburg, adding that those responsible must be punished.

Privately, there were those in the government who did not want to wait for the diplomatic process to take its course. Balfour himself was in favour of stronger action, but this depended on Britain's naval preparedness. As the prime minister telegraphed to Selborne:

What do you propose to do about outrage in North Sea. My first thoughts are to stop the Russian Fleet at first convenient place and exact explanation and reparation, though granting this to be best course, we can only do it if we have adequate force available on the spot. I should be sorry to see so gross and gratuitous a blunder left to the slow methods of diplomacy. Do sailors think there is any justification for the panic to which it was presumably due?[101]

Balfour's last sentence spoke to a point that had been raised by Sazonov, and which was to become a sticking point in the resolution of the affair. The Russian chargé had suggested that the possible presence on the Dogger Bank of Japanese

[98] Lansdowne to Balfour, 25 Oct. 1904, Balfour Papers, Add MSS 49729.
[99] Lansdowne to Hardinge, tel. 174, 24 Oct. 1904, FO 65/1729.
[100] Lansdowne to Hardinge, disp. 374, 24 Oct. 1904; Lansdowne to Hardinge, disp. 375, 25 Oct. 1904, both FO 65/1729; Benckendorff to Lansdowne, 25 Oct. 1904, Lansdowne Papers, FO 800/141.
[101] Balfour to Selborne, tel., 24 Oct. 1904, Selborne Papers, 39.

torpedo boats, of whose existence in European waters there had been strong rumours in Russia, might have triggered the Baltic fleet's action. While, in the
absence of anything less than absolute proof, Lansdowne had rejected Sazonov's
contention, the question refused to die. And, regardless of the truth of the rumours,
according to Hardinge the nerves of the Russian naval commanders at the time of
the departure of the Baltic fleet had been frayed sufficiently so as 'to render a
collision almost inevitable'.[102]

The real problem was that the Russian government, while expressing its sympathy and promising compensation, refused to regard the incident as anything more
than a regrettable exigency of war. Unable to make contact with the Baltic fleet
directly, and unwilling to make anything more than a token effort to remedy this
situation, the Russians hoped to ignore the entire matter.[103] This was absolutely
unacceptable to the British. Lansdowne spoke twice with Benckendorff on 26
October.[104] The language was menacing. At the first meeting, the foreign secretary
'dwelt upon the need of prompt measures to intercept the [Russian] Fleet. If it were
allowed to continue its journey without calling at Vigo, we might find ourselves at
war before the week was over.' At the second meeting, Lansdowne underlined his
point: should the Russian fleet not stop, he informed Benckendorff, '[i]t was my duty
to tell him that . . . it might be necessary for us to take measures for the purpose of
enforcing them'. With the Channel fleet at Gibraltar and the Home fleet at the Firth
of Forth, the Royal Navy was ideally situated to effect Lansdowne's threat.[105]

On 27 October, the Russian government launched its diplomatic counter-attack.
The Baltic fleet had stopped at Vigo, and its commander, Vice-Admiral Z. P.
Rozhenstvensky, had telegraphed to St Petersburg his version of events.
Rozhenstvensky averred that the Russian fleet had indeed been threatened by
torpedo boats, accused the Hull trawlers of interfering with his line of fire, and
argued that in such circumstances it was only natural that he had not stopped to

---

[102] Hardinge to Lansdowne, tel. 151, 25 Oct. 1904, FO 65/1729. Russian fears of Japanese subversion
were not entirely fanciful; A. Motojiro, *Rakka ryūsui: Colonel Akashi's Report on His Secret Cooperation
with the Russian Revolutionary Parties during the Russo-Japanese War* (Helsinki, 1988), 69–84. I would
like to thank Professor Ian Nish for bringing this to my attention; see also, R. G. Griffith, 'Clandestine
Japanese Activity in the Baltic During the Russo-Japanese War', *Journal of Baltic Studies*, 18 (1987), 71–
8; M. Futrell, *Northern Underground: Episodes of Russian Revolutionary Transport and Communications
through Scandinavia and Finland 1863–1917* (London, 1963); O. K. Fält, 'Collaboration between Japanese Intelligence and the Finnish Underground during the Russo-Japanese War', *Asian Profile*, 4 (1976),
205–38; J. N. Westwood, *Russia Against Japan: A New Look at the Russo-Japanese War* (London, 1986),
140.

[103] Hardinge to Lansdowne, tels. 152 and 153, both 25 Oct. 1904; Hardinge to Lansdowne, disp. 531,
26 Oct. 1904, all FO 65/1729.

[104] Lansdowne to Hardinge, disp. 377, 26 Oct. 1904, FO 65/1729.

[105] Lansdowne to Balfour, 25 Oct. 1904, Balfour Papers, Add MSS 49729; Admiralty to c-in-c,
Channel fleet, tel. 79, 28 Oct. 1904, FO 65/1729.

pick up survivors. Given this, Lamsdorff contended, what more could the Russian government do but express its regrets and offer compensation?[106] Lamsdorff was in an unprecedentedly angry state, and noted that he had 'indisputable proofs' of schemes by Japanese agents to attack the Russian fleet and 'reliable proof' of the arrival in Hull of twenty Japanese officers.[107] Hardinge believed both that Rozhenstvensky's report had been altered before it was shown to him and that it was 'plausible, and yet bristling with doubts', but decided, in the face of Lamsdorff's agitation, not to press the point.[108]

Benckendorff played the same line with Lansdowne.[109] But the foreign secretary was unmoved by Benckendorff's contention that Rozhenstvensky's telegram 'entirely altered' the situation: 'I told Count Benckendorff that the version given by the Admiral would not carry the slightest conviction in this country.' After meeting informally with his Cabinet colleagues, Lansdowne reaffirmed this position to Benckendorff, and insisted that it was 'absolutely necessary' that those responsible for the outrage be left behind at Vigo. Lansdowne's uncompromising rejection of the Russian contention undoubtedly was based primarily on the fact that British naval intelligence stated that Rozhenstvensky's hostile torpedo boats 'had no real existence'.[110] But there were also domestic political considerations. The Unionist government was widely viewed as moribund in 1904, and many of its own back-benchers lent it support simply because they 'regarded its maintenance in office as indispensable for the protection of our Imperial interests'.[111]

Having indignantly stated its case and firmly asserted its innocence, the Russian government then began to seek a compromise that would keep its dignity intact. As the British government did not wish to go to war, this attempt was met with cautious warmth. On 28 October, a solution satisfactory to both sides seemed in the works.[112] In the morning, Benckendorff informed Lansdowne that the Russians would keep the fleet at Vigo until things were resolved. This, the ambassador hoped, would allow Balfour to make a public statement defusing the tension between the two countries. In the afternoon, Benckendorff returned with instructions from Lamsdorff in which the Russian minister agreed to the establishment of an independent commission of enquiry at the Hague. Lansdowne was pleased with

---

[106] Hardinge to Lansdowne, 27 Oct. 1904, Lansdowne Papers, FO 800/141.

[107] Hardinge to Lansdowne, confidential disp. 539, 28 Oct. 1904, FO 65/1739.

[108] Hardinge to Lansdowne, 27 Oct. 1904, Lansdowne Papers, FO 800/141.

[109] Lansdowne to Hardinge, disp. 378, 27 Oct. 1904, FO 65/1729.

[110] Battenberg (DNI) to FO, 27 Oct. 1904; Lansdowne to British representatives in France, Germany, Holland, Denmark, and Sweden, 27 Oct. 1904, both FO 65/1729.

[111] M. Bentley, *Politics Without Democracy 1815–1914* (London, 1984), 305–11; Chirol to Hardinge, 23 Aug. 1904, Hardinge Papers, vol. 7.

[112] Lansdowne to Hardinge, disp. 379, 28 Oct. 1904, FO 65/1729.

this development and, with Benckendorff's approval, drew up a statement for Balfour to read that evening in Southampton.[113] Given subsequent events, the details of this statement were important. The Russian government, Balfour announced that evening, had expressed its regret, had agreed to detain the Russian fleet at Vigo pending an investigation, had promised that no guilty officers would depart, had accepted the idea of an international enquiry at the Hague, had pledged to punish the guilty, and had guaranteed that there would be no repetition of such happenings. With Lamsdorff's exuding cordiality towards Hardinge in St Petersburg and Lansdowne's thanking Benckendorff effusively in London, the Dogger Bank incident seemed settled.[114]

But it had been a close run thing. On 29 October, Lansdowne wrote that as of the evening of 27 October 'it looked to me as if the betting was about even as between peace & war'.[115] Thus, when on 31 October Benckendorff asked for assurances, now that four Russian officers had been put ashore at Vigo, that the Russian fleet would not be detained further, and attempted to wriggle out of the agreed-upon provisions concerning punishment, Lansdowne was infuriated.[116] The Channel fleet was immediately told to continue monitoring the Russians, the latter 'most characteristically . . . trying to minimise the effect of their concessions'.[117] On 1 November, war seemed imminent. In this, a primary concern was that France remain firmly onside, but with the government's domestic credibility on the line, a Russian retreat was the only acceptable solution.[118] Fortunately for all concerned, the situation was defused on 2 November, when it was determined that the Russian government did not reject punishment as such, but would agree to it only when and if culpability were established by the tribunal. At the bottom of the crisis of 31 October was the fact that Benckendorff had inadvertently promised more than Lamsdorff had authorized.[119] But it was indicative both of the tension surrounding the situation and of the general disregard felt for Russian veracity that Russian bad faith was immediately suspected.

Over the course of the next few weeks, the matter dragged on. With the likeli-

---

[113] Lansdowne to Benckendorff, 28 Oct. 1904, FO 65/1729; Lansdowne to Balfour, *c*.28 Oct. 1904, Balfour Papers, Add MSS 49729; Benckendorff to Lansdowne, 28 Oct. 1904, Lansdowne Papers, FO 800/141.

[114] Lansdowne to Benckendorff, 28 Oct. 1904, preceding note; Hardinge to Lansdowne, confidential disp. 539, 28 Oct. 1904, FO 65/1739.

[115] Lansdowne to Hardinge, 29 Oct. 1904, Hardinge Papers, vol. 7.

[116] Lansdowne to Hardinge, disp. 389, dated 31 Oct., but clearly reworked to cover the events of that evening, FO 65/1730.

[117] Admiralty to vice-admiral, Channel fleet, very confidential tel. 385, 31 Oct. 1904, FO 65/1730.

[118] Chirol to Lascelles, 2 Nov. 1904, Lascelles Papers, FO 800/12; Clarke to Esher, 1 Nov. 1904, Esher Papers, ESHR 10/34; Balfour to the King, 3 Nov. 1904, Sandars Papers, Ms Eng. hist. *c*.716; Kerr to Selborne, 3 Nov. 1904, Selborne Papers, 41.

[119] Hardinge corroborated this point; see his letter to Lansdowne, 4 Nov. 1904, Hardinge Papers, vol. 6.

hood of armed conflict between the two countries diminished, the Russians attempted to avoid any provisions in the agreement for the international inquiry that might prove embarrassing.[120] It was not until 25 November that a final text was agreed upon, and the Commission itself did not hold its first meeting until early 1905. But Anglo-Russian relations did not become warmer. In St Petersburg, Hardinge found himself busy defending the embassy from attempts by the Russian secret police to compromise its security, while in London rumours swirled about a Russo-German *rapprochement*.[121] His views probably influenced by Spring Rice's Germanophobe fulminations from St Petersburg, Louis Mallet, Lansdowne's précis writer, noted on 11 November that '[w]e all know that Germany is anxious to see us at loggerheads with Russia' and added that 'the present attitude of the Germans fills me with suspicion'.[122] Only the report of the British military attaché at St Petersburg—back from six weeks inspecting the Russian position in Central Asia—that there was no evidence at all of any immediate Russian threat to India was of much cheer.[123] And this only helped drive the discussions in the CID towards the conclusion that Indian demands for reinforcements against the Russian threat were excessive.

The last month of 1904 was one of relative calm in Anglo-Russian relations. There was ample speculation about the future of the Franco-Russian alliance and the role of Germany in international affairs, but the focus was on the riots and demonstrations in Russia that accompanied attempts at domestic reform.[124] Even the fall of Port Arthur on 2 January 1905 did little but spark the hope that a negotiated peace between Russia and Japan might now honourably occur.[125] However, Hardinge reported that the Russian public, which was not informed of Port

---

[120] Some of the tedious wrangling in Hardinge to Lansdowne, tel. 194, 13 Nov. 1904; Hardinge to Lansdowne, disp. 587, 13 Nov. 1904, both FO 65/1731; Lansdowne to Hardinge, private tel., 14 Nov. 1904, Lansdowne Papers, FO 800/141.

[121] Improved Russo-German relations had been bruited since the early autumn: Clarke to Esher, 6 Sept. 1904, Esher Papers, ESHR 10/34; Chirol to Hardinge, 6 Sept. 1904, Hardinge Papers, vol. 7; Chirol to Lascelles, 7 Sept. 1904, Lascelles Papers, FO 800/12; Balfour to Clarke, 20 Sept. 1904, Balfour Papers, Add MSS 49700; Chirol to Lascelles, 21 Sept. 1904, Lascelles Papers, FO 800/12; Findlay (British agent, Cairo) to Hardinge, private and confidential, 2 Oct. 1904, Hardinge Papers, vol. 7; Chirol to Lascelles, 5 Oct. 1904, Lascelles Papers, FO 800/12; Lansdowne to Hardinge, 19 Oct. 1904, Lansdowne Papers, FO 800/141; Clarke to Esher, 1 Nov. 1904, Esher Papers, ESHR 10/34.

[122] Mallet to Sandars, 1 Nov. 1904; Spring Rice to Mallet, 5 Nov. 1904, both Balfour Papers, Add MSS 49747.

[123] Napier's report 64 secret, 10 Nov. 1904, in Hardinge to Lansdowne, secret disp. 579, 10 Nov. 1904, FO 65/1682.

[124] Hardinge to Lansdowne, very confidential disp. 651, 2 Dec. 1904, FO 65/1682; Monson (British ambassador, Paris) to Lansdowne, 23 Dec. 1904; Lansdowne to Monson, 26 Dec. 1904, both Lansdowne Papers, FO 800/126; Barrington to Lascelles, 28 Dec. 1904, Lascelles Papers, FO 800/12. On the latter: Hardinge to Lansdowne, disp. 665, 8 Dec. 1904; Hardinge to Lansdowne, confidential disps. 694 and 708, 21 and 28 Dec. 1904, all FO 65/1682.

[125] Clarke to Esher, 3 Jan. 1905, Esher Papers, ESHR 10/35.

Arthur's fate until 15 January, favoured pushing on to victory.[126] 'I am having a quieter time now', Hardinge wrote two days later, 'than I have had ever since I have been here. I only hope it will last.'[127]

Hardinge got his wish. Although the events of 'Bloody Sunday' five days later were an international sensation, they had little impact on Hardinge, although Lady Hardinge was fortunate to have passed through St Petersburg just two days before the incident.[128] But there was substantial interest in London in Delcassé's 'great desire' to effect an Anglo-Russian *rapprochement*.[129] Lansdowne was cautious. The foreign secretary wished to ensure that Britain and France kept each other informed about items—such as possible peace terms in the Russo-Japanese War—of mutual interest, but he was not optimistic about an improvement in relations between London and St Petersburg.[130] Keeping in mind his experiences with the Russians over the Dogger Bank affair, Lansdowne wrote to Bertie that:

I am glad you spoke plainly upon the subject of the difficulties of establishing a permanent understanding between Great Britain and Russia. I do not see why such an understanding would be impossible, but it is a very different affair from an understanding with France. The Russian diplomatic currency has become debased and discredited and it will not be easy to restore it to its face value.

With Russia reeling from military defeat and racked with internal disorder, most British statesmen, rather than contemplate any improvement in Anglo-Russian relations, could echo the sentiments expressed by the secretary of state for India, and hope 'that Russia's wings may be clipped for some time to come'.[131]

For the next three months, Hardinge had little to do in St Petersburg beyond reporting on the Russian internal situation. The ambassador was dumbfounded by the fact that Nicholas II remained shut-up at Tsarskoe Selo, completely out of touch with events, and yet determined to carry on the war with Japan.[132] Even the disastrous Russian defeat at Mukden seemed not to disturb the Emperor.[133] With the Russians unwilling to make peace while the Baltic fleet steamed to its doom, Hardinge held a watching brief. On 19 April, the ambassador went on leave. However, by the time that Hardinge returned to St Petersburg on 29 May, much had changed. In the first instance, the Franco-German quarrel over Morocco, initiated by the Kaiser's landing in Tangier on 31 March, had become more

---

[126] Hardinge to Lansdowne, disp. 37, 16 Jan. 1905, FO 65/1698.
[127] Hardinge to Bertie, 17 Jan. 1905, Bertie Papers, Add MSS 63050.
[128] W. Sablinsky, *The Road to Bloody Sunday* (Princeton, 1976).
[129] Bertie to Lansdowne, private and confidential, 17 Jan. 1905, Lansdowne Papers, FO 800/126.
[130] Lansdowne to Bertie, 19 Jan. 1905, Lansdowne Papers, FO 800/126.
[131] Brodrick to Curzon, 26 Jan. 1905, Curzon Papers, MSS Eur F111/164.
[132] Hardinge to Knollys, 1 Mar. 1905, Hardinge Papers, vol. 6.
[133] Hardinge to Sanderson, 15 Mar. 1905, Hardinge Papers, vol. 6.

pronounced, with Delcassé's position being threatened as a result.[134] Second, the final blow to Russian arms had been struck by the Japanese at Tsushima on 27–28 May. Third, the negotiations for the renewal of the Anglo-Japanese alliance had begun to take on serious shape.[135] Finally, the internal situation in Russia had continued to worsen.

All of these things played on one another. There was general belief that the Germans, having failed in their attempt at a *rapprochement* with the Russians, were trying to drive a wedge between Britain and France, taking advantage of Russia's weakened position.[136] As to the renewal of the Anglo-Japanese alliance, the British believed that the alliance needed to be widened in scope, so that, just as the Royal Navy stood with the Imperial Japanese Navy against Russian aggression, the Japanese army would support Britain in India.[137] Such an extension would guarantee the British position without involving enormous costs and increases in manpower. With Russia soon likely to be forced into a peace settlement, it was important that Anglo-Japanese discussions begin quickly, lest the two sets of negotiations interfere with one another. Complicating this was the parlous domestic political state of the Unionist government and the accompanying fear that a Liberal government would pursue a pacifist foreign policy. For those who thought in imperial and balance-of-power terms, time was of the essence. As Chirol wrote to Lascelles: '[i]f they [the Unionist government] can secure a renewal on expanded terms of the A.[nglo]-J.[apanese] alliance & consolidate our relations with France by converting the negative *entente* of last year into a positive one, they will have done a big thing, & averted the most serious dangers with which the accession of the Radicals would threaten the Empire.'[138] Thus, when Hardinge returned to St Petersburg, the relative calm of six weeks earlier had ended.

But the centre of activity was in London, not St Petersburg. Events drove British diplomacy and all was in flux. Delcassé's resignation on 6 June 'produced a very painful impression' in London, where it was generally assumed that the French had 'thrown Delcassé overboard in a mere fit of panic' due to German pressure.[139] With

---

[134] B. J. C. McKercher, 'Diplomatic Equipoise: The Lansdowne Foreign Office, the Russo-Japanese War of 1904–5, and the Global Balance of Power', *CJH* 24 (1989), 327–30.

[135] Nish, *Anglo-Japanese Alliance*, 298–322.

[136] Hardinge to Knollys, 12 Apr. 1905, Hardinge Papers, vol. 6; Bertie to Lansdowne, private and confidential, 30 Apr. 1905, Lansdowne Papers, FO 800/127; Spring Rice to Lansdowne, disp. 296, 6 May 1905, FO 65/1700; Bertie to Lansdowne, 12 May 1905, Lansdowne Papers, FO 800/127.

[137] 'Renewal of the Anglo-Japanese Alliance', C. L. Ottley (DNI), 8 Apr. 1905, Cab 17/67; minutes of the 70th meeting of the CID, 12 Apr. 1905, Cab 2/1; Clarke to Esher, 20 Apr. 1905, Esher Papers, ESHR 10/35; Mallet to Sandars, 20 Apr. 1905, Sandars Papers, MS Eng. hist. *c*.749.

[138] Chirol to Lascelles, 18 Apr. 1905, Lascelles Papers, FO 800/11; Clarke to Esher, 23 July 1905, Esher Papers, ESHR 10/37.

[139] Lansdowne to Bertie, 12 June 1905, Bertie Papers, FO 800/64; Clarke to Esher, 7 June 1905, Esher Papers, ESHR 10/36.

negotiations with Japan underway, Britain could not fail to give support to France, lest the Japanese assume that British sureties were of value only in fair weather. Since the Anglo-Japanese alliance was manifestly anti-Russian, these same negotiations were felt likely to worsen Anglo-Russian relations.[140] But this was balanced by an unexpected effect that the Moroccan crisis had in St Petersburg. British fears of a Russo-German *rapprochement* were lessened by the fact that the Russians regarded Germany's challenge to France in Morocco as resulting from a calculation that France could be bullied now that Russia was temporarily *hors de combat*.[141]

By the beginning of July, peace seemed on the horizon, given that Russia and Japan had accepted the American offer of mediation and preparations were going ahead for a peace conference.[142] But with Lamsdorff ill and the Russian navy—via the *Potemkin*—joining the Russian army in mutinies, there were fears of revolution in Russia.[143] British diplomacy had to content itself with pushing ahead with the Japanese discussions. This action was complicated by the fact that President Roosevelt, failing to comprehend that a Britain engrossed in such discussions could and would not press the Japanese to seek moderate terms, needed to be assured that Britain was not working to prolong the conflict in the Far East.[144] This was enough for a government on its last legs domestically. Balfour's government was beaten in a division in the Commons on 20 July, and came close to resigning. At the behest of Edward VII among others, Balfour decided to remain in office until the crucial issues of foreign policy—the Anglo-Japanese negotiations, the Moroccan crisis, and the peace negotiations at Portsmouth—were resolved.[145]

By the beginning of August, there were new twists. While the Japanese negotiations were nearing completion, the meeting of the Kaiser and Nicholas II at Björkö had begun a raft of speculation about Russo-German relations and the resolution of the Russo-Japanese War.[146] There were suspicions that Russia's increasing reluctance to make peace resulted from whatever assurances the Kaiser

---

[140] Balfour's untitled memo on the renewal of the Anglo-Japanese alliance, 31 May 1905, Cab 1/5.

[141] Hardinge to Lansdowne, confidential disp. 387, 13 June 1905, FO 65/1701.

[142] R. A. Esthus, *Double Eagle and Rising Sun: The Russians and Japanese at Portsmouth in 1905* (Durham, NC, 1988).

[143] Geyer, *Russian Imperialism*, 220–30; R. T. Manning, *The Crisis of the Old Order in Russia: Gentry and Government* (Princeton, 1982), 106–30; J. Bushnell, *Mutiny amid Repression: Russian Soldiers in the Revolution of 1905* (Bloomington, IN, 1985), 44–73.

[144] Bushnell, *Mutiny amid Repressions*, 49–51; Lansdowne to Durand (British ambassador, Washington), 10 July 1905, Lansdowne Papers, FO 800/144; Lansdowne to Balfour, 12 July 1905, Lansdowne Papers, FO 800/116.

[145] R. F. Mackay, *Balfour: Intellectual Statesman* (Oxford, 1985), 212–13; Sandars' memo, 25 July 1905, Sandars Papers, MS Eng. hist. *c.*749.

[146] I. Geiss, *German Foreign Policy 1871–1914* (London, 1976), 103–4; Hardinge to Lansdowne, confidential disp. 474, 25 July 1905, FO 65/1701; Brodrick to Selborne, 27 July 1905, Selborne Papers, 2; Hardinge to Lansdowne, 1 Aug. 1905, Lansdowne Papers, FO 800/141.

may have given to Nicholas. For his part, Lansdowne continued to reassure Roosevelt that Britain was in no way encouraging the Japanese to seek harsh terms.[147] This was a delicate matter. When the Japanese treaty was signed on 12 August, the British requested that it be kept secret until after the Portsmouth Peace Conference, which had opened on 5 August, had concluded. The British felt that secrecy was necessary as the treaty might both offend 'Russian susceptibilities' and be blamed for any failure at Portsmouth.[148]

Despite these concerns, there was no thought of keeping the Anglo-Japanese treaty permanently from the Russians. Hardinge, with an eye to the future of Anglo-Russian relations, made this point to Lansdowne four days after the signing of the new agreement:

The day will sooner or later arrive when an announcement will have to be made and, if there should be no objection, I think it would be a good thing that before the publication is made the Russian Govt. should be told and should be assured of its unaggressive and purely defensive character. If the war is over then we could simultaneously resume the negotiations which you began & which were interrupted by the war, and I feel confident that you would find them [the Russians] easier to deal with than before. Lamsdorff & other Ministers have frequently told me of their determination to come to terms with us as soon as the war is over. The French will naturally do all they can to realise an Anglo-Russian agreement which the Germans will, on the other hand, do all in their power to prevent.[149]

Lansdowne shared Hardinge's opinion. On 3 September, with the Portsmouth settlement four days old, the foreign secretary informed Balfour that Russia and the United States should both be given the text of the Anglo-Japanese renewal.

To Hardinge, Lansdowne was more expansive. The foreign secretary urged his ambassador to attempt to demonstrate to the Russians that the Anglo-Japanese agreement was entirely defensive in nature.[150] And, while the treaty was aimed at Russia, this should not be interpreted as indicating that British policy was inherently anti-Russian

[a]ll measures of precaution, whether they take the shape of military and naval preparations, or, as in this case, of Alliances, must be directed against somebody, and no country has, it seems to me, the right to take offence because another country raises the wall of its back garden high enough to prevent an over-adventurous neighbour or that neighbour's unruly or overzealous agents from attempting to climb over it.

Indeed, Lansdowne told Hardinge to impress upon the Russians that the foreign secretary 'always desired and still desires that we should live on neighbourly terms

---

[147] Lansdowne to Spring Rice, 7 Aug. 1905, Lansdowne Papers, FO 800/116.
[148] Nish *Anglo-Japanese Alliance*, 336–7; Balfour to the King, 3 Aug. 1905, cited, ibid. 336.
[149] Hardinge to Lansdowne, 16 Aug. 1905, Lansdowne Papers, FO 800/141.
[150] Lansdowne to Hardinge, 4 Sept. 1905, Hardinge Papers, vol. 7.

with Russia'. To Benckendorff, Lansdowne made an even more explicit statement. After reiterating the substance of the above, Lansdowne added that the Anglo-Japanese agreement 'contain[ed] nothing to prevent Russia and Great Britain from resuming the friendly examination of those important questions which you and I were discussing when the war so unfortunately interrupted our deliberations'.[151] Clearly, the direction of the future of Anglo-Russian relations lay with the Russian government.

The Russo-Japanese War had a profound effect on Anglo-Russian relations. Russia's defeat brought to an end a decade of Anglo-Russian quarrels in China and the Far East. The defeat of the Russian navy had eliminated one of the components of the two-power standard. And Russia's military setbacks meant that threats to India, while they were still likely to occur, had less force. Although Kitchener continued to trumpet the Russian threat, all agreed that this was now a threat for the future and most accepted as a fact that at present the 'defence of India lies mainly with the F.[oreign] O.[ffice]'.[152] Indeed, the Foreign Office had already aided in the defence of India via the provisions of the renewed Anglo-Japanese alliance. Further, all this had been achieved without Britain's becoming completely estranged from Russia, offering the possibility of a postwar improvement in relations between the two countries.

It was also a vindication of Lansdowne's diplomacy. Both the Anglo-Japanese Alliance and the Anglo-French entente had demonstrated that they could survive a major international crisis. In fact, the Anglo-Japanese Alliance had been such a signal success that it had proved capable of being extended and renewed in the midst of hostilities. The Anglo-French entente had not stood in the way of the Franco-Russian Dual Alliance, and Britain's support for the French over Morocco must have seemed doubly valuable to Paris in the light of Russia's weakened condition and frequent flirtations with Germany. Nor had the British been forced to surrender any ground on a number of contentious issues involving international law and the conventions regarding freedom of the seas and belligerent rights. In the autumn of 1905, the British position was dramatically improved from that of two years before. She could again offer an olive branch to Russia, and offer it from a position of increased strength. The Russian response depended on the view from St Petersburg.

---

[151] Lansdowne to Benckendorff, 8 Sept. 1905, Lansdowne Papers, FO 800/141.

[152] Cf. P. Towle, 'The Russo-Japanese War and the Defence of India', *Military Affairs*, 44 (1980), 111–17; Clarke to Esher, 16 Aug. and 11 Sept. 1905, Esher Papers, ESHR 10/37.

PART III

RECONCILIATION? 1906–1917

9

Forging the Anglo-Russian Convention

THE Treaty of Portsmouth was signed on 5 September 1905. On 31 August 1907, the British and Russians inked the Anglo-Russian Convention. This two-year period was tumultuous. Until the late summer of 1906, Russia was convulsed with internal disorder, a fact that affected both Russia's foreign policy and Britain's policy towards the Tsarist state.[1] Concerned that Russia's unstable domestic situation made negotiations with her uncertain, British diplomacy made haste slowly. Not until the end of May 1906 and Nicolson's arrival as ambassador did any significant moves towards an Anglo-Russian understanding take place, and even these were tentative. Only in September did the serious negotiations begin that led to the Convention a year later.

The Anglo-Russian Convention was the culmination of continuous British attempts to come to a diplomatic understanding with Russia.[2] Why were the negotiations of 1906–7 successful, where earlier efforts were not? The reasons were Russian. The shock of defeat in the Russo-Japanese War led to a complete reassessment of Russian foreign policy, a move personified by the appointment of Izvolskii as foreign minister in May 1906. Given Russia's weaknesses—domestic, financial, and military—a policy of *recueillement* was necessary. Russia mended her diplomatic fences comprehensively. In addition to negotiating the Anglo-Russian Convention, Russia restored good relations with Japan and tightened her relationship with France, all the while attempting to come to an understanding with Germany over the Baltic and with Austria-Hungary in the Balkans.[3]

---

[1] J. Bushnell, *Mutiny Amid Repression: Russian Soldiers in the Revolution of 1905–6* (Bloomington, IN, 1985), R. T. Manning, *The Crisis of the Old Order in Russia: Gentry and Government* (Princeton, 1982); L. Engelstein, *Moscow, 1905: Working-Class Organization and Political Conflict* (Stanford, CA, 1982). On Russian foreign policy, A. V. Ignatev, *Vneshniaia politika Rossii v 1905–7 gg.* (Moscow, 1986); B. J. Williams, 'The Revolution of 1905 and Russian Foreign Policy', in C. Abramsky, *Essays in Honour of E. H. Carr* (London, 1974), 101–25.

[2] R. P. Churchill, *The Anglo-Russian Convention of 1907* (repr. edn.; Freeport, NY, 1972); B. J. Williams, 'Great Britain and Russia, 1905 to the 1907 Convention', in F. H. Hinsley (ed.), *British Foreign Policy under Sir Edward Grey* (Cambridge, 1977), 133–47; and A. F. Ostaltseva, *Anglo-russkoe soglashenie 1907 goda* (Saratov, 1977).

[3] V. A. Marinov, *Rossiia i Iaponiia pered pervoi mirovoi voinoi (1905–14 gody)* (Moscow, 1974), 23–51; J. Long, 'Franco-Russian Relations during the Russo-Japanese War', *SEER* 52 (1974), 213–33; J. P.

But while the principal reasons for improved Anglo-Russian relations emanated from St Petersburg, there were also changed circumstances in London that led towards *rapprochement*. The first was the election of the Liberal government and the appointment of Sir Edward Grey as foreign secretary. Grey favoured better Anglo-Russian relations. Equally, the Liberals' election manifesto had called for reduced military spending and a move towards international arms limitation.[4] Improved relations with Russia helped obviate the need for expenditure on the Indian frontier, and the Second Hague Conference— conveniently called by Nicholas II—promised arms reduction. This helped balance the Radicals' ingrained antipathy towards Russia, and ensured that Grey would have only limited opposition within his own party for a policy of improved relations with Russia. Grey also faced little criticism from the opposition benches. The Unionists, concerned that the Liberals would pursue universal peace at the expense of British security, clung to Grey and the other Liberal Imperialists as a bulwark against the excesses of the Radicals.[5] As long as Grey's diplomacy guaranteed British defence, he found little criticism from Balfour's shadow government.

But this was in the future. In the aftermath of Portsmouth, Lansdowne's first task was to ensure that Anglo-Russian relations were not soured by the announcement of the renewal of the Anglo-Japanese Alliance. In addition, Lansdowne suggested that Anglo-Russian negotiations might resume their prewar status, and encouraged Barings in their loan negotiations with Russia. Progress towards an Anglo-Russian agreement was slow. As Spring Rice pointed out, any negotiations with Russia that appeared even to suggest an anti-German intent stood little chance of success.[6] And, Hardinge warned, the Russian government might consider a

Sontag, 'Tsarist Debts and Tsarist Foreign Policy', *SR* 27 (1968), 529–41; D. W. Spring, 'Russia and the Franco-Russian Alliance, 1905–14: Dependence or Interdependence?', *SEER* 66 (1988), 564–92; J. Steinberg, 'Germany and the Russo-Japanese War', *AHR* 75 (1970), 1965–86; B. F. Oppel, 'The Waning of a Traditional Alliance: Russia and Germany after the Portsmouth Peace Conference', *CEH* 5 (1977), 318–29; I. I. Astafev, *Russko-germanskie diplomaticheskie otnosheniia 1905–11 gg. (ot portsmutskogo mira do potsdamskogo soglasheniia)* (Moscow, 1972), 10–111; P. Luntinen, *The Baltic Question 1903–8* (Helsinki, 1975); F. R. Bridge, 'Izvolsky, Aehrenthal, and the End of the Austro-Russian Entente, 1906–8', *Mitteilungen des österreichischen Staatsarchivs*, 29 (1976), 315–62.

[4] A. J. A. Morris, *Radicalism Against War 1906–14: The Advocacy of Peace and Retrenchment* (Totowa, NJ, 1972); H. S. Weinroth, 'The British Radicals and the Balance of Power, 1902–14', *HJ* 13 (1979), 653–82; A. T. Sidorowicz, 'The British Government, the Hague Peace Conference of 1907, and the Armaments Question' and K. Neilson, ' "The British Empire Floats on the British Navy": British Navy Policy, Belligerent Rights, and Disarmament, 1902–9', both in B. J. C. McKercher, (ed.), *Arms Limitation and Disarmament: Restraints on War, 1899–1939* (Westport, 1992), 1–20, 21–42.

[5] R. Williams, 'Arthur James Balfour, Sir John Fisher and the Politics of Naval Reform, 1904–10', *HR* 60 (1987), 80–99; id., *Defending the Empire: The Conservative Party and British Defence Policy 1899–1915* (New Haven, 1991), 77–233.

[6] Spring Rice to Lascelles, 13 Sept. 1905, Lascelles Papers, FO 800/12.

Russo–German agreement as a counterpoise against the Anglo–Japanese grouping.[7] The need for caution was put clearly on 19 September:

Their [the Russians'] idea of an agreement with us, has always been that they should have everything they wanted with our assistance, or at our expense, & that we should be content with anything we could get out of the remainder. When next we begin a deal with them we may hope that they will be more reasonable. But the problem in the future is whether under new conditions their policy will lose its predominating character of military aggression, & it will be some time before any change in this respect can show itself clearly.[8]

Anglo–Russian discussions would have to await events. The most pressing task for the British was to attempt to read the tea leaves and determine the direction of Russian policy. Thus, close attention was paid to Witte. In France, where he arrived from the United States on 19 September, Witte spent much of his time negotiating with Barings and their French banking associates.[9] This was all to the good for Anglo–Russian relations. A few days later in Berlin, Witte was given a royal welcome by the Kaiser, an occurrence that led to much speculation in diplomatic circles that Witte had become a firm advocate of a Russo–German *rapprochement*. This led to a difference between Witte and Lamsdorff, with the latter, as Spring Rice reported, advising 'caution' and the *Pevcheskii most* advocating that Russia 'temporise between Germany & England and not . . . give the ring to either of them—at least at once'.[10]

By the beginning of October, the British representatives in Russia were convinced that Witte was 'completely collared by the Kaiser'.[11] Hardinge felt that even Lamsdorff was coming under the influence of Witte, who 'makes no effort to conceal his anger' at the signing of the Anglo–Japanese treaty.[12] Witte's ideal' was a 'Russo–German–French understanding directed evidently against England & Japan'.[13] Only the news that Lord Revelstoke himself was travelling to St Petersburg to participate in Barings' loan negotiations held out any hope for better relations.[14] The generally hostile atmosphere at St Petersburg suggested to Lansdowne that no new initiatives towards Russia should be made and that

[7] Hardinge to Lansdowne, 13 Sept. 1905, Hardinge Papers, vol. 6.
[8] Sanderson to Hardinge, 19 Sept. 1905, Hardinge Papers, vol. 7.
[9] Based on Noetzlin to Revelstoke, 20 and 22 Sept. 1905, both Barings Papers, Barings Partners' filing/206; Hardinge to Sanderson, 27 Sept. 1905, Hardinge Papers, vol. 6; Hardinge to Lansdowne, confidential disp. 586, 1 Oct. 1905, FO 65/1703.
[10] Spring Rice to Lascelles, 2 Oct. 1905, Lascelles Papers, FO 800/12.
[11] Spring Rice to Mallet, 4 Oct. 1905, Lansdowne Papers, FO 800/116.
[12] Hardinge to Lansdowne, very confidential disp. 594, 4 Oct. 1905, FO 65/1703.
[13] Hardinge to Lansdowne, 5 Oct. 1905, Hardinge Papers, vol. 6.
[14] Revelstoke to Hardinge, confidential, 5 Oct. 1905; Hardinge to Revelstoke, 8 Oct. 1905; Revelstoke to Hardinge, tel., 12 Oct. 1905, all Barings Papers, Barings Partners' filing/206.

Barings' negotiations be allowed to proceed on their own.[15] Events pushed this policy. By the middle of October, Lamsdorff made it clear that no Anglo-Russian negotiations were possible at the present.[16] Thus, with Benckendorff's holding out the promise of an arrangement with Russia in the future, Lansdowne contented himself with 'reminding the Russians here & at St Petersburg, that we are quite ready to talk to them whenever they feel inclined'.[17]

This was prudent. Unrest in Russia was at fever pitch. On 25 October, Hardinge's scheduled departure from St Petersburg was delayed by a train strike in the capital, and political uncertainty and possible revolution threatened the consummation of Barings' loan negotiations.[18] Even Nicholas II's issuing of the October manifesto, with its promise of an elected Duma, at the end of the month failed to bring calm. In Spring Rice's words, the situation was 'still obscure, and it cannot be said that the danger is over'. The following fortnight underlined this observation. Faced with political uncertainty, the group of bankers that Barings had formed suspended the Russian loan negotiations. Violent mobs smashed property and assaulted Jews throughout Russia. Stead, who had just returned to England from Russia, on 10 November warned of the danger to British nationals in Russia and even suggested that British socialists, inspired by events in Russia, might wreak havoc in London.[19] The unrest had its impact in political circles in Britain. Brodrick's observation that, while the 'unlimited power of shooting and terrorising [of the Russian authorities] seems equal to each emergency as it arises . . . I believe the Imperial family are at last beginning to get a little uneasy, and the end of these upsets *must* affect their credit', spoke not only to the Russian situation, but also to Russian methods.[20]

On 4 December Balfour resigned, and an interim Liberal government took office. This meant a hiatus in Anglo-Russian relations, although Lansdowne had been careful to ensure that several key appointments at the Foreign Office and in the diplomatic service had been made before he left office. With Hardinge's replacing Sanderson as PUS, Nicolson's becoming ambassador to St Petersburg and

---

[15] Lansdowne's minute (17 Oct.) on Hardinge to Lansdowne, confidential disp. 604, 8 Oct. 1905, FO 65/1703.

[16] Hardinge to Lansdowne, very confidential disp. 616, 14 Oct. 1905, FO 65/1703; Hardinge to Lansdowne, 15 Oct. 1905, Hardinge Papers, vol. 6.

[17] Lansdowne to Bertie, 8 Oct. 1905, Lansdowne Papers, FO 800/127; quotation from Lansdowne to Hardinge, 17 Oct. 1905, Hardinge Papers, vol. 7.

[18] Revelstoke to Barings, 25 Oct. 1905, Barings Papers, Barings Partners' filing/206; Engelstein, *Moscow, 1905*, 97–113 and Spring Rice to Lansdowne, disp. 643, 31 Oct. 1905, FO 65/1703. Following quotation from the latter.

[19] Spring Rice to Lansdowne, 9 Nov. 1905; FO to Spring Rice, tel., 10 Nov. 1905, both Lansdowne Papers, FO 800/141; Barrington to Walker (Home Office), 11 Nov. 1905, Lansdowne Papers, FO 800/116.

[20] Brodrick to Selborne, 17 Nov. 1905, Selborne Papers 2.

Grey's taking over at the Foreign Office, all the pieces for an 'Edwardian' policy towards Russia were in place. But, when Grey took office on 11 December, he had several things to contend with before he could turn to Russia. With a 'keen active opponent in my constituency' and the need to familiarize himself with the overall situation, Grey was not being modest when he stated that 'my wheels will drag heavily'.[21] None the less, on 13 December Grey assured Benckendorff that Britain had no intention of taking advantage of Russia's internal difficulties by advancing in Central Asia or elsewhere, provided that Russia did not do so first.[22] Benckendorff's assurances that Russia had no such intentions and the news of further civil unrest in Russia together promised that official Anglo-Russian relations would be quiet.[23] Such news from Russia had several implications, not all of them favourable. Grey worried that, despite Benckendorff's promises, 'enterprising Russian officers in Asia Minor may take advantage of the confusion at St Petersburg to do things on their own account'.[24] Grey also was aware that Russia's domestic turmoil weakened France's position *vis-à-vis* Germany. In such circumstances, Grey noted on 22 December, 'I hope the struggle [in Russia] won't last too long. I want to see Russia re-established in the councils of Europe & I hope on better terms with us than she has yet been.'

The impending Algeciras Conference drove home such concerns. Just before the conference opened, with Russia an uncertain quantity, France asked Britain for a promise of military assistance against Germany should it be required.[25] Grey refused an outright commitment—'[i]f we give any promise of armed assistance', he informed Bertie, 'it must be conditional'—but did authorize staff talks between the two countries. Grey's circumstances were difficult. Although the Russian government had weathered the storm of the armed uprising in Moscow in December, the foreign secretary was inundated with reports detailing the parlous state of Russia's finances and the precarious nature of her domestic stability.[26] Russia's financial indebtedness to France complicated the situation.[27] The Russians wanted a further loan, but the French government was reluctant to provide it, as this would be seen by both the French and Russian liberals as propping up the

---

[21] Grey to Bertie, 13 Dec. 1905, Grey Papers, FO 800/49.

[22] Morley to Minto, 14 Dec. 1905, Morley Papers, MSS Eur D573/1.

[23] Spring Rice's disps. 756–800, 12–22 Dec. 1905, FO 65/1794.

[24] Grey to Spring Rice, 22 Dec. 1905, Spring Rice Papers, FO 800/241.

[25] Bertie to Grey, 15 Jan. 1906, Grey Papers, FO 800/49; J. W. Coogan and P. F. Coogan, 'The British Cabinet and the Anglo-French Staff Talks, 1905–1914: Who Knew What and When Did He Know It?', *JBS* 24 (1985), 110–31.

[26] Hardinge to Grey, disp. 34, 10 Jan. 1906, FO 371/122/2421; Spring Rice to Grey, disp. 60, 16 Jan. 1906, FO 371/122/2427; Spring Rice to Grey, disp. 53, 16 Jan. 1906, FO 371/121/2403; Engelstein, *Moscow, 1905*, 202–25; Bushnell, *Mutiny Amid Repression*, 109–44.

[27] Spring Rice to Grey, 16 Jan. 1906, Grey Papers, FO 800/72.

autocracy.[28] On the other hand, a failure to give a loan might result in the repudiation of Russia's debts, the subsequent collapse of the French money market and the inability of France to withstand German menaces at Algeciras. No wonder Grey longed 'to see Russia re-established in the councils of Europe'.

Throughout January, Grey was constrained by circumstances. Diplomatically, all eyes were on the Algeciras conference. Domestically, the focus was the election. Grey could not pursue a decided policy with respect to the French request for a British military commitment: 'all this must remain in the air till the elections are over: all my colleagues are fighting their own or other election contests and I am alone in London and cannot consult them or get them together.'[29] Grey could only monitor the situation in Russia and prepare the way for the two countries to be on 'better terms'. This required preparing key people for the possibility of an Anglo-Russian *rapprochement*. John Morley, the Liberal secretary of state for India, began one phase of the task on 25 January. Morley wrote to the Indian viceroy, Lord Minto, about a proposed British loan to Persia, warning of the need to avoid giving the impression that Britain was attempting to steal a march on Russia during the latter's difficulties since '[w]e may or may not in the fullness of time find it desirable to come to a general understanding with Russia'.[30] Kitchener, the Indian commander-in-chief, also needed to be persuaded. Sir George Clarke, the secretary to the CID, had started this process at the end of the Russo-Japanese War, arguing that the Russian threat to India was diminished, and, in February and March 1906, three meetings of the CID considered the implications of this fact.[31] These meetings underlined the fact that 'there is a strong feeling that the change in the military position of Russia ought to produce some change in our military policy in India. This feeling will have to be accounted with, and acted upon'.[32]

While Benckendorff began plumping for an Anglo-Russian agreement early in March, before anything could proceed there were matters major and minor to clear up between the two countries.[33] These included the linked issues of anti-Semitic

[28] O. Crisp, 'The Russian Liberals and the 1906 Anglo-French Loan to Russia', *SEER* 39 (1961), 497–511; J. W. Long, 'Organized Protest Against the 1906 Russian Loan', *CMRS* 13 (1972), 24–39.

[29] Grey to Bertie, 15 Jan. 1906, Grey Papers, FO 800/49.

[30] Morley to Minto, 25 Jan. 1906, Morley Papers, MSS Eur D573/1; F. Kazemzadeh, *Russia and Britain in Persia, 1864–1914* (New Haven, 1968), 472–9.

[31] Clarke to Esher, 1 and 11 Sept. 1905, 7 Oct. 1905, Esher Papers, ESHR 10/37; Clarke to Kitchener, 14 Oct. 1905,? Jan. 1906, 5 Jan. 1906, Kitchener Papers, PRO 30/57/34; minutes of 83rd, 84th and 85th meetings of the CID, 1 Feb., 15 Feb. and 9 Mar. 1906, Cab 2/2.

[32] Morley to Minto, 8 Mar. 1906, Morley Papers, MSS Eur D573/1.

[33] Spring Rice to Grey, 26 Jan. and 1 Mar. 1906, Grey Papers, FO 800/72; Grey's remarks at the 85th meeting of the CID, 9 Mar. 1906, Cab 2/2; Grey to Spring Rice, disp. 129, 19 Mar. 1906, in H. Temperley, and G. P. Gooch (eds.), *B[ritish] D[ocuments] on the Origins of the War, 1898–1914]*, (11 vol. in 13; London, 1926–38), iv, doc. 212 (see *BD* hereafter).

activity by the Russian secret police and efforts by the latter to compromise the security of the British embassy in St Petersburg.[34] These potentially divisive matters were largely resolved by the end of March, leaving the way clear for Grey to deal with more substantive issues. One such was India and defence. On 15 March, Morley had written to Minto warning the latter that discussions of Indian defence had 'hitherto been far too parochial' and that future studies had to be made in the context of 'attempt[ing] to look once more in a way at the political and strategical necessities of the Empire as a *whole*'.[35] This was somewhat vague, but later Morley was more specific. The Indian secretary asked Minto to consider 'in a preparatory and provisional way' an Anglo-Russian agreement and '*what would be the terms that you would exact from Russia* as essential to the bargain'.[36] Further, the viceroy was to enquire of Kitchener what the latter deemed necessary for the 'reasonable and practicable safety' of India. The Indian commander-in-chief was warned that the Liberal government was 'committed . . . [to] reductions of expenditures' and that this meant 'there will be a disinclination to accept increases [in military expenditure] in India coinciding with decreases here'.[37] On another military front, the DMO was asked to outline the military aspects to be considered in a possible Anglo-Russian agreement.[38]

There was also a financial dimension. On 17 March Lamsdorff told Barings that the time was now propitious for a renewal of the abandoned loan negotiations.[39] Revelstoke brought this to Grey's attention, and enquired as to the attitude of the British government. The foreign secretary's response was circumspect, but encouraging: 'while from the financial point of view' Grey could not 'take the responsibility of tendering any advice . . . from a political stand-point he would view with satisfaction' Barings' involvement.[40] Such political approval left Revelstoke free to pursue the negotiations. The loan was enmeshed in politics. Édouard Noetzlin, a director of the Banque de Paris et des Pays-Bas and Revelstoke's collaborator in the loan, stated that the French government would allow the loan negotiations to go forward only after the Algeciras conference had ended, no doubt to ensure that the Russians did not waver in their support for France.[41] From St Petersburg, Spring

[34] C. Andrew and K. Neilson, 'Tsarist Codebreakers and British Codes', *INS* 1 (1986), 6–12.

[35] Morley to Minto, 15 Mar. 1906, Morley Papers, MSS Eur D573/1.

[36] Morley to Minto, 23 Mar. 1906, Morley Papers, MSS Eur D573/1, original emphasis.

[37] Clarke to Kitchener, 6 Apr. 1906, Kitchener Papers, PRO 30/57/34.

[38] 'Military Considerations Involved With Regard To An Entente Cordiale Between Great Britain And Russia' Colonel W. R. Robertson, M. O. 2, 20 Mar. 1906, Grey Papers, FO 800/102.

[39] Benckendorff to Revelstoke, 18 Mar. 1906, Barings Papers, Barings Partners' filings/207; Revelstoke to Hardinge, 23 Mar. 1906, enclosing Lamsdorff to Benckendorff, tel., 17 Mar. 1906, FO 371/124/10982 and Grey's undated minute.

[40] Hardinge to Revelstoke, 28 Mar. 1906, Barings Papers, Barings Partners' filings/207.

[41] Noetzlin to Revelstoke, private and confidential, 21 Mar. 1906, Barings Papers, Barings Partners' filing/207.

Rice outlined for Revelstoke the considerable political baggage that the loan carried in Russia.[42]

The end of the Algeciras conference added another political dimension. On 5 March the German government, piqued by its failure over Morocco, forbade German banks and financiers to place the Russian loan on the Berlin market. This had considerable repercussions. Spring Rice noted that the German action, with its implicit repudiation of Witte's pro-German policy, made the latter's resignation 'expected'.[43] In London, Grey found himself bombarded by questions. Revelstoke asked whether the German announcement meant that the British government would change its attitude towards the Russian loan.[44] Both Benckendorff and Paul Cambon, the French ambassador to London, enquired in a similar vein. Grey's response to all three was the same: British policy remained unchanged.[45] Indeed, Grey informed Benckendorff that for Britain to oppose the loan would be 'a very unfriendly act, which I should not think of doing, at the very moment when we had been co-operating so cordially at the Algeciras Conference'. Realizing that this could be interpreted by British Liberals as lending support to the Russian autocracy at the expense of the Russian liberals, Grey carefully kept Campbell-Bannerman abreast of the situation.[46]

While the loan negotiations hung fire and the results of the Russian elections to the First Duma trickled in, little could be done, except to ensure that no misunderstandings arose between Britain and Russia.[47] A close eye also was kept on the personnel of the Russian government. At the end of March, Spring Rice reported that Witte had offered his resignation, possibly as a threat to get his own way, but that the Emperor had refused to accept it 'as it is hard to get anyone to take his place'.[48] Lamsdorff's position was thought shaky, a fact that the British regretted, as the foreign minister was believed to be in favour of improved Anglo-Russian

---

[42] Spring Rice to Revelstoke, confidential, 3 Apr. 1906, Barings Papers, Barings Partners' filing/207.

[43] Spring Rice to Grey, secret tel. 64, 6 Apr. 1906, FO 371/124/11911.

[44] Revelstoke to Grey, 6 Apr. 1906, Barings Papers, Barings Partners' filing/207.

[45] Grey to Revelstoke, 6 Apr. 1906, Barings Papers, Barings Partners' filing/207; Grey to Spring Rice, disp. 163, 6 Apr. 1906, FO 371/124/12483; Grey to Bertie, disp. 204, 6 Apr. 1906, FO 371/124/12335. Quotation from disp. 163.

[46] Grey to Campbell-Bannerman, 6 Apr. 1906, Campbell-Bannerman Papers, Add MSS 52514. The prime minister canvassed his chancellor of the exchequer, and, when Asquith approved of Grey's thinking, Campbell-Bannerman agreed: see the latter's note (7 Apr.) on Asquith to Campbell-Bannerman, 7 Apr. 1906, Grey Papers, FO 800/100.

[47] Grey to Spring Rice, 26 Mar. 1906; Grey to Campbell-Bannerman, 26 Mar. 1906; Spring Rice to Grey, 10 Apr. 1906, all Grey Papers, FO 800/72; Spring Rice to Revelstoke, 8 Apr. 1906, Barings Papers, Barings partners' filing/207; Spring Rice to Ronald Graham, 11 Apr. 1906, FO 371/120/12890; Spring Rice to Grey, tel. 68, 11 Apr. 1906, FO 371/124/12565; Spring Rice to Grey, 12 Apr. 1906, Grey Papers, FO 800/72.

[48] Spring Rice to Grey, 29 Mar. 1906, Grey Papers, FO 800/72; Spring Rice to Grey, disp. 216, 28 Mar. 1906, FO 371/121/11175; Spring Rice to Lascelles, 25 Apr. 1906, Lascelles Papers, FO 800/13.

relations. Lamsdorff's uncertain position meant a cautious foreign policy: in Spring Rice's words, the 'Lamsdorff regime is a regime of frank funk, in which the Foreign Secretary's chief object was not to pledge himself or his government to anything what ever'. The first secretary also was convinced that the 'Germans have vowed his [Lamsdorff's] destruction' and that he soon would be replaced by someone who would follow 'an anti-English game'.[49] Not even the signing of the Russian loan on 16 April ended the paralysis in Anglo-Russian relations. Spring Rice believed that a visit by Edward VII to Russia might induce Nicholas II to authorize the opening of talks. However, the King could not go until there was stability in Russia, lest some incident be 'unpleasant' for him or 'repugnant to public feeling here'.[50] In these circumstances, Grey was loathe to suggest any preliminary terms to Russia, lest 'they . . . be used against us by the next man, and even if they are not, they can lead to nothing till the Tsar is taking a hand & that brings me back to the King's visit'. For the rest of April, the situation was unclear. Witte's resignation remained an open issue until 2 May, when it was accepted.[51] Two days later, Lamsdorff's resignation was reported, an event confirmed on 7 May when Izvolskii agreed to succeed him.[52]

In the meantime, Grey continued to lay the groundwork for Anglo-Russian discussions. On 24 April, Asquith, Morley, and Nicolson, the latter just returned from the Algeciras Conference, met with the foreign secretary.[53] The object was to 'talk freely about possible arrangements with Russia'. While the meeting produced no concrete line of action, it was significant. All agreed that an Anglo-Russian agreement was both important and desirable; however, it was equally obvious that the matter could not be rushed. As Nicolson informed Spring Rice: 'I am having talks—a little desultory & vague—with people here as to a possible arrang[emen]t with Russia—but it seems to me we had better wait to see with whom we have to negotiate.'[54] None the less, other preparations went forward. Morley sent an initial draft of Nicolson's instructions concerning Persia and Afghanistan and a final draft about Tibet to Minto for consideration. Morley adjured the viceroy not to 'argue the question of Russian good faith, whether the Petersburg Government, or its quarrels on the frontier: for present purposes, that good faith is a hypothetical assumption'.[55]

---

[49] Spring Rice to Grey, 12 Apr. 1906, Grey Papers, FO 800/72.

[50] Grey to Spring Rice, 16 Apr. 1906, Spring Rice Papers, FO 800/241.

[51] Spring Rice to Grey, tel. 77, 2 May 1906, FO 371/121/14931.

[52] Spring Rice to Grey, secret tel. 82, 4 May 1906, FO 371/121/15178; Sir A. Johnstone (British minister, Copenhagen) to Grey, tel. 6, 7 May 1906, FO 371/121/15601.

[53] Grey to Nicolson, 19 Apr. 1906, Nicolson Papers, FO 800/338; Nicolson to Spring Rice, 25 Apr. 1906, Spring Rice Papers, FO 800/241.

[54] Nicolson to Spring Rice, 2 May 1906, Spring Rice Papers, FO 800/241.

[55] Morley to Minto, 25 May 1906, Morley Papers, MSS Eur D573/1.

Nicolson arrived in St Petersburg on 28 May, eighteen days after Izvolskii arrived from Copenhagen to take up his post as Russian foreign minister. But, prior to this several things had occurred. First, the Foreign Office's campaign against the continuing efforts by the Russian secret police to compromise the security of the British embassy in St Petersburg finally ended that troublesome matter. Second, there had been far-reaching political changes in Russia. Nicholas II had replaced not only Witte and Lamsdorff, but also the rest of his ministers.[56] The pro-German and reactionary element in this new ministry was both considerable—especially the appointments of Gormykin and Durnovo—and a concern to the British. In addition, there was a new player on the political scene. The First Duma began sitting on 10 May, and its sessions were carefully scrutinized by the British.[57] The relationship between the new, elected body and the Emperor's ministers was the question of the day, and formed part of the turbulent background to Anglo-Russian discussions.

When Nicolson arrived in St Petersburg, his education about Russia began.[58] On 29 May, he met with Izvolskii for the first time, and 'broke ground as to future discussions'.[59] A week later, the ambassador presented his credentials to Nicholas II, informing the Emperor of the British desire to come to an understanding with Russia. The way in which Nicolson approached the subject with both the minister and the sovereign was important, for it reflected the sensitivity of the British government to the situation facing the Russian authorities. Germany was central to this. Russo-German relations had deteriorated during the Russo-Japanese War and this decline was further marked by the actions of the German government during the loan negotiations. But such coolness was not thought likely to be permanent. While the British were not opposed to better relations between Berlin and St Petersburg, London did not wish such an occurrence to be at its expense. This was particularly true with respect to German attempts to enhance their presence in Persia and the Middle East. On 11 May, Grey suggested to Benckendorff that a joint Anglo-Russian loan might be offered to Persia in order to thwart a proposed German loan to the Shah.[60] The foreign secretary also suggested that co-operation between the two countries might be extended to the construction of the Baghdad railway. However, Grey was quick to emphasize that the British would not 'use our

[56] Spring Rice to Grey, disp. 309, 10 May 1906, FO 371/121/16396.

[57] Spring Rice to Grey, 10 and 11 May 1906, both Grey Papers, FO 800/72; Morley to Minto, 18 May 1906, Morley Papers, MSS Eur D573/1; Hardinge to Nicolson, 30 May 1906, Nicolson Papers, FO 800/338.

[58] K. Neilson, ' "My Beloved Russians": Sir Arthur Nicolson and Russia, 1906–16', *IHR* 9 (1987), 521–54.

[59] Nicolson diary entry, 30 May 1906, PRO 30/81/13; Nicolson to Grey, 6 June 1906, Grey Papers, FO 800/72.

[60] Grey to Spring Rice, disp. 213, 11 May 1906, FO 371/125/16301.

friendship with Russia as a lever to create difficulties with Germany, either for Russia or for ourselves'.[61] From Berlin, Lascelles seconded Grey's position: while a Russian agreement would be 'most desirable' for Britain, the ambassador argued that it should not 'exclude good relations with Germany'.[62] Nicolson's initial conversations with Izvolskii and Nicholas moved delicately around the German issue. On the one hand, the ambassador attempted to keep the issues of the Persian loan and the Baghdad railway separate from discussions of any Anglo-Russian agreement. On the other, he was certain that the Russians would discuss the Anglo-Russian talks with the Germans, despite Izvolskii's professions of confidentiality.[63]

But for the next three months, despite Nicolson's opening of discussions on Tibet with Izvolskii on 7 June, only desultory progress was made.[64] This was due almost entirely to events in Russia. The First Duma and the Russian government were unable to find common ground.[65] On 21 July, Nicholas II dissolved the Duma, an event that led to further speculation about Russia's political future.[66] Paralleling the Russian government's quarrel with the Duma was the ongoing violence throughout the country.[67] This had its effect in Britain. On 25 July, Hardinge wrote that 'we fully realise that this [Russian] Govt is not one with which we could make an agreement and you had better go slowly with our negotiations'.[68] Nicolson did not agree with this decision. He felt that a delay would be interpreted by the Russian government as a vote of no confidence and might lead to German advances in Persia.[69] Further, he believed that the autocracy would survive the unrest. His views were not accepted in London. 'But while Russia is on the brink of revolution', Grey wrote on 10 August, 'it is no good going faster in these matters than is

[61] Grey to Nicolson, disp. 237, 23 May 1906, FO 371/125/17967.

[62] Lascelles to Fitzmaurice, 2 June 1906, Lascelles Papers, FO 800/19.

[63] Nicolson diary entry, 29 May 1906, PRO 30/81/13; Nicolson to Grey, 6 June 1906, Grey Papers, FO 800/72.

[64] Nicolson diary entry, 7 June 1906, Nicolson Diary, PRO 30/81/13; Nicolson to Grey, tel. 111, 7 June 1906, *BD*, iv, doc. 224.

[65] G. A. Hosking, *The Russian Constitutional Experiment: Government and Duma, 1907–14* (Cambridge, 1973), 14–24; Manning, *Crisis of the Old Order*, 205–59; A. E. Healy, *The Russian Autocracy in Crisis: 1905–1907* (Hamden, 1976), 132–261.

[66] Nicolson's diary entry, 22 July 1906, Nicolson Papers, PRO 30/81/13; Hardinge to Nicolson, 25 July 1906; Spring Rice to Nicolson, 25 July 1906, both Nicolson Papers, FO 800/338.

[67] Nicolson's diary entries, 10 June, 16 June, 27–29 Jun, 10 July 1906, Nicolson Papers, PRO 30/81/13; Smith (British consul-general, Odessa) to Hardinge, 14 June 1906, FO 371/120/20938; Napier (British military attaché, St Petersburg) to Nicolson, report 41, 17 June 1906, FO 371/126/21440; Nicolson to Grey, disp. 378, 19 June 1906, FO 371/122/21442; Stevens (British vice-consul, Batoum) to Grey, disp. 16, 30 June 1906, FO 371/120/25030; Nicolson to Grey, disp. 421, 4 July 1906, FO 371/122/23119; Nicolson to Grey, disp. 444, 16 July 1906, FO 371/127/24889.

[68] Hardinge to Nicolson, 25 July 1906, Nicolson Papers, FO 800/338.

[69] Nicolson diary entry, 28 July 1906, Nicolson Papers, PRO 30/81/13; Nicolson to Hardinge, 29 July 1906, Nicolson Papers, FO 800/337.

necessary to keep the negotiations alive. I cannot see how things are to come right in Russia till the present organization & machinery of Government is broken up & that can only be done by Revolution.'[70]

But, while little was done in the way of negotiating the Anglo-Russian Convention over the summer of 1906, Anglo-Russian relations were not uneventful. There were four active issues. The first was managing the ongoing Anglo-Russian co-operation on Crete in the aftermath of the civil war on the island.[71] While this often was difficult, the problems were local and unlikely to upset good Anglo-Russian relations generally. The other three issues—the treatment of Jews in Russia, the proposed visit of a squadron of the Royal Navy to Russia, and Nicholas II's dissolution of the Duma—were potentially more explosive. The Radicals within the new Liberal government were fervently anti-Tsarist, and saw all three matters as opportunities to lash out at the Russian autocracy. The pogroms of 1906 led to frequent questions in the House of Commons. While Nicolson and those at the Foreign Office regretted this as it might worsen Anglo-Russian relations, Grey had to deal with the fact that '[Charles] Trevelyan and other radicals have been shouting' about the treatment accorded Russian Jews.[72] Only the end of the parliamentary session and the decline in anti-Semitic activities in Russia brought an end to Grey's trials.

The proposed naval visit to Cronstadt was a similar problem. Both British Radicals and Russian liberals argued that the visit would be a visible act of support for the embattled Russian autocracy.[73] As such, they opposed it. This faced Grey with a conundrum, for cancelling the visit unilaterally would be a rebuke to the Russian government. Matters came to a head on 7 July when Grey was asked in the House of Commons whether the fleet's visit signified the government's approval of the way in which the Tsarist regime was suppressing reform. Grey was rescued on 12 July, when Nicholas II himself suggested (possibly due to Grey's having spoken to Benckendorff about the delicacy of the matter) that the fleet's visit be postponed. The final swipe at Russia by the Radicals was taken as a result of the dissolution of

[70] Grey to Nicolson, 10 Aug. 1906, Grey Papers, FO 800/72.

[71] B. J. C. McKercher, *Esme Howard: A Diplomatic Biography* (Cambridge, 1989), 38–70.

[72] Spring Rice to Nicolson, 27 June 1906, Nicolson Papers, FO 800/338.

[73] Morley to Minto, 22 June 1906, Morley Papers, MSS Eur D573/1; R. P. Maxwell to Nicolson, 23 June 1906; Hardinge to Nicolson, 27 June 1906, both Nicolson Papers, FO 800/338; Nicolson to Hardinge, 1 July 1906, Nicolson Papers, FO 800/337; Nicolson diary entry, 2 July 1906, Nicolson Papers, PRO 30/81/13; Nicolson to Grey, private tel., 2 July 1906 and Grey to Nicolson, tel. 119, both FO 371/126/22462; Chirol to Nicolson, 3 July 1906, Nicolson Papers, FO 800/338; Nicolson to Grey, 5 July 1906, Grey Papers, FO 800/72; answer to Keir Hardie's parliamentary question of 7 July 1906 in FO 371/126/23068; Grey to Nicolson, tel. 134, 10 July 1906, FO 371/126/23536; Nicolson diary entry, 11 July 1906, Nicolson Papers, FO 30/81/13; Nicolson to Grey, tel. 145, FO 371/126/23605; Nicolson to Grey, tel. 146, 12 July 1906, FO 371/126/23658.

the Duma on 22 July. By coincidence, six members of the Duma were in London, attending the fourteenth conference of the Inter-Parliamentary Union. By further coincidence, Campbell-Bannerman was scheduled to welcome the delegates to the opening session of the Union on 23 July. With the Russian situation the talk of the political world, the prime minister felt constrained to address the topic. The result was his only memorable public remark: 'La Douma est morte—Vive la Douma.'[74] While Grey was able to keep the repercussions of this remark to a minimum, the Russian umbrage taken over it showed how delicately placed were Anglo-Russian affairs.

By September, the prospects for a convention were much more propitious. Nicolson felt that the ill-feeling caused by Campbell-Bannerman's speech had dissipated.[75] Further, the ambassador was convinced—contrary to Grey's opinion—that with Stolypin in charge, revolution was no longer likely. Nicolson felt, despite a rash of assassinations and attempted assassinations, a backlash of reaction was likely.[76] Morley had continued to hammer away at Minto's objections to any Anglo-Russian negotiations, and, by early September the Foreign Office was able to send Nicolson draft instructions on Afghanistan that included the revisions insisted upon by the India Office.[77] Finally, with Parliament in recess and no new pogroms in Russia, the public furore over the treatment of Russian Jews subsided. The way was clear for negotiations.

The order of the negotiations—Persia, Afghanistan, and Tibet—was determined by circumstances. A German offer of a loan to Persia was viewed unfavourably both in London and St Petersburg, leading the latter to regard Persia as a first priority.[78] On 17 September, Nicolson had a 'satisfactory talk' with Isvolskii, in which the latter showed a 'readiness to agree to our line as to spheres of interest'.[79] Grey took immediate action, and the British offered to provide both the Russian and British shares of a joint loan to Persia in order to keep the Germans out.[80] Despite this, the Persian negotiations did not go smoothly. The Foreign Office felt that 'Iswolsky is extracting all cards & giving nothing in return', a fact that Nicolson

[74] J. Wilson, *CB: A Life of Sir Henry Campbell-Bannerman* (London, 1973), 535–7; B. Hollingsworth, 'The British Memorial to the Russian Duma, 1906', *SEER* 53 (1975), 539–57.

[75] Nicolson to Hardinge, 29 Aug. 1906, Nicolson Papers, FO 800/337.

[76] Nicolson's diary entries, 25 Aug. and 30 Aug. 1906, Nicolson Papers, PRO 30/81/13; Nicolson to Grey, disp. 565, 29 Aug. 1906, FO 371/122/29746.

[77] Morley to Minto, 15 and 29 Aug. 1906, both Morley Papers, MSS Eur D571/1; 'Afghanistan. Draft Instructions to Sir A. Nicolson', n.d. (but 5 Sept. 1906) and minutes, FO 371/126/30179.

[78] Nicolson to Grey, 12 Sept. 1906, Nicolson Papers, FO 800/337; Nicolson diary entry, 13 Sept. 1906, Nicolson Papers, PRO 30/81/13.

[79] Nicolson diary entry, 17 Sept. 1906, Nicolson Papers, PRO 30/81/13.

[80] Grey to Nicolson, private tel., [18] Sept. 1906, Grey Papers, FO 800/72; Morley to Minto, 20 Sept. 1906, Morley Papers, MSS Eur D573/1.

attributed both to the balkiness of the Russian general staff and to the revolutionary turmoil in Russia.[81] British concern about the stability of the Russian government meant that Grey was willing to let matters proceed slowly.[82] In part, this was unavoidable. For, while Nicolson was 'deep in Persian negotiations' by 10 October, at that time Izvolskii left St Petersburg for three weeks.[83]

While the Russian minister toured the capitals of Western Europe in an attempt to ensure that his negotiations with Britain did not engender another crisis like that in Morocco and result in his sharing Delcassé's fate, Nicolson's discussions came to a halt.[84] In the interim, Nicolson argued that the negotiations should be speeded up when Izvolskii returned, lest German influence and press leaks torpedo the talks.[85] With regard to the former, Nicolson suggested that the Persian settlement should contain a clause forbidding the Persian government from granting concessions to other European powers in any region that impinged on either the Russian or British spheres of influence. But, by the time that Izvolskii returned at the beginning of November, all that had been accomplished was the signing of the joint Anglo-Russian loan to Persia. With Izvolskii's continuing to plead for 'time & patience', Nicolson took the initiative.[86] On 5 November, the ambassador sent a draft proposal of a Persian agreement to Grey.[87] Nicolson's motives reflected his conception of his diplomatic role:

You may think that I am writing the last chapter of our novel before I have concluded the first: but it seems to me that if I could communicate something in the nature of the enclosed document, even at this early stage, I might be able to remove some of his [Isvolskii's] hesitations, and also . . . be of assistance to him in discussing the matter with the opponents of an understanding with us. Moreover it would give me opportunities of pressing him to fill in the gaps.

But even as he did this, Nicolson was not optimistic about the pace of the nego-tiations, for he was fully aware that Izvolskii's domestic opponents would not be easily overcome.[88]

    [81] Nicolson diary entry, 22 Sept. 1906, Nicolson Papers, PRO 30/81/13; Nicolson to Grey, 26 Sept. 1906, Nicolson Papers, FO 800/337.
    [82] Lascelles to Fitzmaurice, 28 Sept. 1906, Lascelles Papers, FO 800/19; Chirol to Lascelles, 2 Oct. 1906, Lascelles Papers, FO 800/13; Grey to Nicolson, 3 Oct. 1906, Nicolson Papers, FO 800/338.
    [83] Nicolson to Lascelles, 10 Oct. 1906, Lascelles Papers, FO 800/13; Nicolson to Hardinge, 11 oct. 1906, Nicolson Papers, FO 800/337.
    [84] Bertie to Grey, 22 Oct. and private and confidential, 25 oct. 1906, Grey Papers, FO 800/49; Tyrrell to Spring Rice, 31 Oct. 1906, Spring Rice Papers, FO 800/241.
    [85] Nicolson to Hardinge, 24 Oct. 1906; Nicolson to Grey, 24 Oct. 1906, Nicolson Papers, FO 800/337.
    [86] Nicolson diary entry, 3 Nov. 1906, Nicolson Papers, PRO 30/81/13.
    [87] Nicolson to Grey, 5 Nov. 1906, Grey Papers, FO 800/72.
    [88] Nicolson to Spring Rice, 7 Nov. 1906, Spring Rice Papers, FO 800/241. Nicolson to Lascelles, 8 Nov. 1906, Lascelles Papers, FO 800/13.

It was Nicolson's awareness of these difficulties that prompted a long letter to Grey on 7 November.[89] Nicolson pointed out that Izvolskii's critics were asking a difficult question: what was Russia getting in the Persian discussions? In the Anglo-French negotiations, Britain had made substantial concessions to France, but Izvolskii 'seemed to doubt if peace and good will were strong enough arguments, or whether the Russian mind was in a mood, generally speaking, to be willing to make sacrifices in order to secure a good understanding with us'. As Britain could not make any 'great concessions' in Central Asia, Nicolson argued that she should be prepared to give something to Russia elsewhere, particularly in the Middle East. Nicolson's suggestion triggered events in London. Hardinge wrote a memorandum on the Dardanelles, outlining its legal status and strategic significance to Britain.[90] Hardinge's conclusion reflected the CID's position of 1903: 'it is evident that it is, if desirable, possible to make an important concession to Russia in relation to the Dardanelles without fundamentally altering the present strategic position in the Mediterranean.'

Here was Nicolson's quid pro quo. Armed with this, Grey wrote to Nicolson authorizing the ambassador to give Izvolskii a modified copy of the draft that Nicolson had proposed earlier.[91] Further, Grey sent a copy of Hardinge's memorandum, but warned Nicolson to let Izvolskii take the initiative: '*it is for him to say what it is he wants.*' The prescience of Nicolson's suggestion was evident later in November when the counsellor at the Russian embassy in London, A. F. Poklevsky-Kozell, told Hardinge that Russian public opinion would require some concession to Russia, and mentioned both the Dardanelles and the Far East as areas where this might occur.[92] Hardinge was careful to tell Poklevsky that Britain would do nothing that might affect the Anglo-Japanese Alliance, but in St Petersburg Izvolskii 'gave a pretty broad hint' that Britain might 'council moderation' to Japan in the Russo-Japanese negotiations that Izvolskii opened late in 1906.[93] While Grey refused to be drawn into the Tokyo–St Petersburg talks, their occurrence relegated the Anglo-Russian talks to second place in Izvolskii's mind until February 1907.[94]

Meanwhile, Minto and Spring Rice continued to fight their rearguard action against the negotiations with Russia. Despite Morley's efforts to reconcile the

[89] Nicolson to Grey, 7 Nov. 1906, Nicolson Papers, FO 800/337.

[90] 'Memorandum respecting the Passage of Russian War Vessels through the Dardanelles and Bosphorus', Hardinge, 16 Nov. 1906, Grey Papers, FO 800/92.

[91] Grey to Nicolson, [*c.*17] Nov. 1906, Nicolson Papers, FO 800/338.

[92] Hardinge to Nicolson, 28 Nov. 1906, Nicolson Papers, FO 800/338.

[93] Nicolson diary entry, 28 Nov. 1906, Nicolson Papers, PRO 30/81/13; Nicolson to Grey, 5 Dec. 1906, Nicolson Papers, FO 800/337. I. H. Nish, *The Anglo-Japanese Alliance: The Diplomacy of Two Island Empires 1894–1907* (London, 1966), 359–60.

[94] Hardinge to Nicolson, 12 Dec. 1906, Nicolson Papers, FO 800/338; Nicolson diary entries, 15 and 16 Dec. 1906, 15 Jan. 1907, Nicolson Papers, PRO 30/81/13; Nicolson to Hardinge, 20 Dec. 1906, Nicolson Papers, FO 800/337; Hardinge to Nicolson, 23 Jan. 1907, Nicolson Papers, FO 800/339.

viceroy to an Anglo-Russian agreement, Minto remained strongly convinced that 'Russian and British interests in Persia are absolutely irreconcilable'.[95] Spring Rice's position was similar, and he tied his opposition to a belief that a Russo-German arrangement over the Baghdad railway was impending.[96] While the minister to Persia's views were shared by several members of the élite, Hardinge felt that Spring Rice was too 'fond' of swallowing 'silly rumours'.[97] With Morley's similar dismissal of Minto's arguments, Anglo-Russian negotiations were not to be deflected on the British side.[98] While the Russo–Japanese talks continued, the Anglo-Russian negotiations did not entirely cease. Nicolson worked on drawing up articles for the discussions about Tibet; Hardinge pushed the India Office to put its views forward about the subject.[99] In preliminary discussions with Izvolskii, Nicolson found that the Russian minister advocated an Anglo-Russian parity in Tibet, a stance that the ambassador found unacceptable.[100] However, by mid-January things were brighter. Izvolskii gave Nicolson a 'preamble to the Thibet convention really clearer & better than mine', failed to bite at Nicolson's 'fly' concerning the Baghdad railway and stopped 'the customary appeal for delay' about Persia.[101] With Benckendorff's being present in Russia to push along the negotiations, Nicolson was optimistic.[102]

Further encouragement came at the end of the month. The Russians created an interdepartmental committee to discuss the issues of the Anglo-Russian negotiations.[103] With Tibet 'practically settled', Nicolson enquired whether Grey wished to put forward the British position about Afghanistan in order to assist the committee and 'strengthen their hands'.[104] This was rejected in London. Hardinge believed that the agreement 'hinge[d] on Persia', and preferred to discover the Russian position on that country before discussing Afghanistan, a view that the India Office shared.[105] On 31 January, Nicolson reported optimistically that a

[95] Minto to Morley, 26 Dec. 1906, Morley Papers, MSS Eur D573/10.

[96] Spring Rice to Nicolson, 11 Jan. 1907, Nicolson Papers, FO 800/339.

[97] Hardinge to Nicolson, 24 Dec. 1906, 8 Jan. 1907, Nicolson Papers, FO 800/338 and 339; Tyrrell to Spring Rice, 18 Feb. 1907, Spring Rice Papers, FO 800/241.

[98] Hirtzel diary entries, 16 and 17 Jan. 1907, Hirtzel Papers, MSS Eur D 1090.

[99] Nicolson diary entry, 16 Dec. 1906, Nicolson Papers, PRO 30/81/13; Hardinge to Nicolson, 24 Dec. 1906, Nicolson Papers, FO 800/338.

[100] Nicolson diary entry, 26 Dec. 1906, Nicolson Papers, PRO 30/81/13; Nicolson to Grey, 2 Jan. 1907, Nicolson Papers, FO 800/337.

[101] Nicolson diary entries, 15 and 16 Jan. 1907, Nicolson Papers, PRO 30/81/13; Nicolson to Grey, 16 Jan. 1907, Grey Papers, FO 800/72.

[102] Nicolson to Hardinge, 17 Jan. 1907, Nicolson Papers, FO 800/337; Nicolson to Grey, tel. 53, 27 Jan. 1907, FO 371/321/3763.

[103] Nicolson to Grey, tel. 13, 28 Jan. 1907, FO 371/320/3227.

[104] Nicolson to Hardinge, 31 Jan. 1907, Nicolson Papers, FO 800/337; Nicolson to Grey, disp. 58, 30 Jan. 1907, FO 371/320/3768.

[105] Hardinge's minute on Nicolson to Grey, tel. 13, 28 Jan. 1907, FO 371/320/3227; India Office to FO, 6 Feb. 1907, FO 371/320/4177.

'better disposition' towards an Anglo-Russian agreement existed in St Petersburg and that 'we only want them to define their zone in Persia: and Afghanistan should present no difficulties'.[106] Nicolson's mood became buoyant in mid-February. He became 'convinced' of Izvolskii's desire to conclude an agreement, a belief reinforced when the Russian interdepartmental committee approved in principle the idea of an understanding.[107] On 19 February, Nicolson reported a very significant breakthrough.[108] Izvolskii announced that the Russians were satisfied about Tibet, and read Nicolson a draft of the Russian terms about Persia. For the British, the key point was that the Russians accepted that Seistan—vital to the defence of India—should be left in the British zone. Having convinced his 'military party' to accept this point, Izvolskii asked that, in turn, Britain abjure building any railways into Afghanistan. Further, Izvolskii wished to exclude Germany from Persia in exchange for Russia and Britain's dropping any opposition to German participation in the Baghdad railway. In Nicolson's view, time was now of the essence. He recommended that the negotiations be pushed along as fast as possible.

His enthusiasm was shared in London. On 22 February, Grey and Hardinge met with Morley and his officials at the India Office to discuss the Russian proposal.[109] 'Our general opinion', Hardinge noted, 'is that it forms a satisfactory basis for settlement & for the first time I see daylight ahead.' Grey was equally optimistic, and congratulated Nicolson on his achievement.[110] When the details of the Russian proposal arrived in London, there was cause for exultation: '[t]he Russian sphere of influence is even less than what George Curzon assigned to them, & there is no question of their coming down to the Gulf.'[111] Persia was seemingly on its way to solution, and on 28 February Nicolson gave Izvolskii the outline of British terms concerning Afghanistan.[112] With the Russo-Japanese negotiations progressing smoothly, there was good cause to hope that a general settlement of Anglo-Russo-Japanese imperial questions in Asia was possible.[113]

Matters did not proceed rapidly. From the beginning of March to the middle of May, Izvolskii did not respond to the British proposals about Afghanistan. There

[106] Nicolson to Hardinge, 31 Jan. 1907, Nicolson Papers, FO 800/337.
[107] Nicolson to Grey, 13 Feb. 1907, Nicolson Papers, FO 800/337; Nicolson to Grey, tel. 24, 17 Feb. 1907, FO 371/320/5221.
[108] Nicolson to Grey, tels. 25 and 26, 19 Feb. 1907, FO 371/320/5665 and 5666 and minutes; detailed in Nicolson to Grey, disp. 98, *BD*, iv, doc. 388.
[109] Hirtzel diary entry, 22 Feb. 1907, Hirtzel Papers, MSS Eur D1090; Morley to Minto, 22 Feb. 1907, Morley Papers, MSS Eur D573/2; Hardinge to Nicolson, 22 Feb. 1907, Nicolson Papers, FO 800/339.
[110] Grey to Nicolson, private tel., 25 Feb. 1907, Grey Papers, FO 800/72.
[111] Hardinge to Lascelles, 26 Feb. 1907, Lascelles Papers, FO 800/13.
[112] Nicolson to Hardinge, 28 Feb. 1907, Grey Papers, FO 800/72.
[113] Morley to Minto, 7 Mar. 1907, Morley Papers, MSS Eur D573/2; Nicolson to Hardinge, 13 Mar. 1907, Nicolson Papers, FO 800/337.

were several reasons for this, including Izvolskii's preoccupation with Japan, the uncertain political situation after the elections to the Second Duma and the distractions provided by preparations for the Second Hague Conference.[114] Another was the attempt to open talks about the Dardanelles.[115] This was suggested by Benckendorff when he returned from Russia, and met little resistance in London. Hardinge felt that without a settlement on the Straits, 'no agreement with Russia can be said to be complete or on a solid basis'.[116] But such negotiations were not without their problems: they would allow Austria and Germany to 'make themselves disagreeable'. And, as Britain required 'a solid "quid pro quo" to make an effect in the shop window . . . we suggested [to Benckendorff] that the R. [ussian] Govt should agree to support the actual status quo in the Persian Gulf'. Grey also favoured negotiations about the Straits, but objected to any idea of tying them to the talks about Central Asia.[117] He wished to conclude the Asiatic agreements first, lest the Straits talks, where Britain expected Russian support in Egyptian matters, prevent a Central Asian settlement. More importantly, Grey was concerned about the impact of Russia's internal situation on British opinion. He was confident that he could complete the Asiatic settlement whatever occurred in Russia, but 'I don't think we could do more, if things were very bad in Russia, for there would be resentment at our choosing this time to make a concession about the Straits'. However, the simple fact that Britain endorsed settling the Straits in Russia's favour resulted in Izvolskii's 'beaming with pleasure'.[118] It was, he told Nicolson, 'a great evolution' in Anglo-Russian relations. Despite Nicolson's fears to the contrary, on 15 April Izvolskii agreed to keep the two negotiations separate.[119]

The negotiations marked time for another month as the Russians prepared their Afghan draft. Even Hardinge, who had often stated that the talks would be long, found this tedious.[120] In London, various opponents of the agreement utilized this time to attempt to reopen other aspects of the negotiations, particularly the de-

[114] Nicolson to Grey, disp. 145, 18 Mar. 1907, FO 371/322/10338; Nicolson to Grey, 11 Apr. 1907, Grey Papers, FO 800/72; Nicolson to Grey, disp. 140, 14 Mar. 1907, FO 371/322/8616; Nicolson to Grey, disp. 149, 21 Mar. 1907, FO 371/322/9659; Nicolson to Grey, disp. 162, 27 Mar. 1907, FO 371/322/10354; Nicolson to Hardinge, 28 Feb. 1907, Grey Papers, FO 800/72; Nicolson diary entry, 10 Mar. 1907, Nicolson Papers, PRO 30/81/13; Nicolson to Hardinge, 25 Apr. 1907, Grey Papers, FO 800/72.

[115] 'Memorandum by Sir Edward Grey', Grey, 15 Mar. 1907, *BD*, iv, doc. 257; Hardinge to Bertie, 18 Mar. 1907, Bertie Papers, FO 800/164.

[116] Hardinge to Nicolson, 19 Mar. 1907, Nicolson Papers, FO 800/339.

[117] Grey to Nicolson, 1 Apr. 1907, Nicolson Papers, FO 800/339.

[118] Nicolson to Grey, 27 Mar. 1907, Nicolson Papers, FO 800/337.

[119] Nicolson to Grey, 11 Apr. 1907, Grey Papers, FO 800/72; Nicolson to Grey, 15 Apr. 1907, Nicolson Papers, FO 800/337.

[120] Hardinge to Nicolson, 2 May 1907, Nicolson Papers, FO 800/339.

marcation of zones of influence in Persia, while Spring Rice continued to voice his discontent with the entire matter.[121] This was resisted, and when Izvolskii communicated his draft on 16 May, the British impression of it was, according to Grey, 'favourable'.[122] By the beginning of June, with all the Russian drafts in hand, the discussions progressing smoothly, the results of Morley's subcommittee on the defence of India seemingly resolving that problem for the indefinite future, and the military details of the second Anglo-Japanese alliance as they pertained to Russia resolved, all seemed set for an quick end to the negotiations.

This did not occur for two reasons. The first was British. The abrupt dissolution of the Duma on 16 June and the subsequent modification of the electoral laws to favour the political right offended many in the Liberal party.[123] With influential Unionists already believing that the government was giving away too much in the negotiations, an unholy alliance between the opposition and the Radicals seemed likely. Since the latter's dislike of Russia was inherent, Grey attempted to buy off the Unionists by getting the Russians to agree to maintain the *status quo* in the Persian Gulf, the position that Lansdowne had adopted in May 1903.[124] Grey's policy helped to create the second, Russian reason for delay. Izvolskii did not wish to accede to this British request, since to do so might offend the Germans, always prickly about anything that could affect the Baghdad railway.[125] Needing a German loan, and with 'the fate of Delcassé, in mind, Izvolskii was chary of reopening the Persian negotiations.[126]

Izvolskii proved immovable.[127] In the end, Grey had to content himself with the Russian minister's agreement that Grey might reiterate Lansdowne's 1903 remark about the Gulf, a move that Morley felt would deal with public opinion.[128] It was Afghanistan that proved to be the final sticking point in the negotiations. The nub of the disagreement was a Russian concern that the British draft let London retain its ability to intervene to ensure that British treaties with the Amir were observed,

[121] Grey to Nicolson, 1 May 1907, and reply, 8 May 1907, both *BD*, iv, docs. 270 and 271; Tyrrell to Spring Rice, 15 May 1907, Spring Rice Papers, FO 800/241; Hardinge to Nicolson, 15 May 1907, Nicolson Papers, FO 800/339; Spring Rice to Chirol, 24 May 1907, in S. Gwynn (ed.), *The Letters and Friendships of Sir Cecil Spring Rice* (2 vols.; London, 1929), ii. 100–1; O'Beirne to Bertie, 28 May 1907, Bertie Papers, FO 800/176.
[122] Nicolson to Hardinge, 16 May 1907, Nicolson Papers, FO 800/337; Hirtzel diary entry, 23 May 1907, Hirtzel Papers, MSS Eur D1090; Grey to Nicolson, private tel., 24 May 1907, Grey Papers, FO 800/72.
[123] Hardinge to Nicolson, 26 June 1907, Nicolson Papers, FO 800/339.
[124] Grey to Nicolson, 6 June 1907, *BD*, iv, doc. 417.
[125] Nicolson to Hardinge, 4 July 1907, Nicolson Papers, FO 800/337.
[126] Nicolson to Hardinge, 4 July 1907, Nicolson Papers, FO 800/337; O'Beirne to Revelstoke, 5 July 1907, Barings Papers, Barings Partners' filing/207.
[127] *BD*, iv, docs. 434–44.
[128] Morley to Minto, 18 July 1907, Morley Papers, MSS Eur D573/2.

whereas St Petersburg would have to forgo any right of intervention in Afghanistan.[129] At the heart of the matter was a Russian fear that Britain might utilize this provision to annexe part of Afghanistan, something that had long concerned Russian military authorities.[130] The irony of this aside, given similar British fears of Russian intentions, the point proved difficult. On 14 July, Nicolson proposed that he return to London to consult with Grey, a suggestion that the foreign secretary accepted.[131] Morley rightly termed the situation a 'crisis', for the careful negotiations of the previous ten months hung in the balance.[132] Nicolson arrived in London on 22 July. For the next three weeks, he conferred with Grey, Morley, and officials from the India and Foreign Offices. During this time, Nicolson solidified his reputation as 'the best man of his day in his own trade'.[133] Morley proved to be Nicolson's main hurdle. The Indian secretary was adamantly opposed either to Russia's gaining an equal right to annexe part of Afghanistan or to Britain's having to consult with Russia before exercising the right to annexe herself.[134] For Morley, such a concession would both lessen Britain's own position and 'arouse . . . [the] suspicions [of the Amir] by admitting the right of a third party to intervene between us'.[135] After several conferences and dinners, Nicolson was able to persuade the government to allow him to return to Russia with, as Morley reported, 'two strings to his bow'.[136] The strings dealt with Morley's concerns: first, as a concession, Russia should not be asked to state explicitly that she would not annexe any part of or intervene in Afghanistan; but, second, in exchange she should agree that the two countries would consult with each other before taking any action. Nicolson had convinced Morley that to reject both of these ideas outright would mean an end to negotiations. What remained was for Nicolson to induce the Russians to agree.

When Nicolson arrived back in St Petersburg on 12 August, he felt 'well equipped' to deal with Izvolskii.[137] The latter seemed 'contented and pleased' with Nicolson's remarks about Afghanistan, but expressed reservations about the Per-

[129] Nicolson to Grey, disp. 358, 3 July 1907, *BD*, iv, doc. 486.

[130] Nicolson to Grey 13 July 1907, *BD*, iv, doc. 490; W. C. Fuller, Jr., *Strategy and Power in Russia 1600–1914* (New York, 1992), 333, 365.

[131] Nicolson to Grey, private tel. and reply, 14, 15 July 1907, Grey Papers, FO 800/72.

[132] Morley to Minto, 18 July 1907, Morley Papers, MSS Eur D573/2; Esher to M. V. Brett, 16 July 1907, in M. V. Brett and Oliver, Viscount Esher, *Journals and Letters of Reginald, Viscount Esher* (4 vols.; London, 1934–8), ii. 241.

[133] Morley to Minto, 2 Aug. 1906, Morley Papers, MSS Eur D573/2.

[134] Hirtzel diary entry, 26 July 1907, Hirtzel Papers, MSS Eur D1070.

[135] Hirtzel diary entry, 29 July 1907, Hirtzel Papers, MSS Eur D1070.

[136] Hirtzel diary entry, 31 July 1907, Hirtzel Papers, MSS Eur D1070; Morley to Minto, 2 Aug. 1907, Morley Papers, MSS Eur D573/2.

[137] Nicolson to Spring Rice, 14 Aug. 1907, FO 800/141.

[138] Nicolson to Grey, 15 Aug. 1907, Grey Papers, FO 800/72.

sian Gulf.[138] However, it was Afghanistan that caused an 'unexpected and serious hitch' in discussions on 25 August.[139] Izvolskii, after consultation with Nicholas II and the other Russian ministers, insisted on having a bit of both 'strings' that Nicolson had brought to Russia. In short, he did not wish to bind Russia to a policy of non-intervention, but wanted Britain to agree to consultation before intervening in Afghanistan. Hurried consultations in London came to the conclusion that this was unacceptable.[140] And, as Morley put it later, all seemed 'gloomy'.[141] However, Nicolson's firm objections won the day. Izvolskii was able to persuade his colleagues that the British declaration not to interfere in or annexe Afghan territory as long as the Amir observed his treaty obligations was a sufficient guarantee of Russia's interests.[142] With this, the British were willing to drop their requirement for a Russian pledge not to intervene in Afghanistan, and the Russians were willing to eschew their demand for consultation. On 29 August, Grey congratulated Nicolson on the 'successful conclusion of these long and difficult negotiations'.[143] Two days later, the Anglo-Russian Convention was signed.

The Convention was the culmination of Grey's efforts since he had become foreign secretary. In a broader sense, it was the culmination of efforts to come to terms with Russia that stretched back at least as far as Rosebery. By concluding it, the British gained a good deal. At the most general and formal level, the century-long Anglo-Russian enmity had been formally ended, although Anglo-Russian rivalry persisted at lower levels. More specifically, the Convention either solved or eased a number of problems. With respect to Persia, the gain was considerable. First, Seistan (whose strategic significance always was in the minds of Indian defence planners) no longer bordered any part of Persia under Russian domination, thus safeguarding the north-west frontier. Second, the Russian sphere in Persia was relatively small. Third, while the Persian Gulf had been left out of the Convention, Grey had gained the agreement of the Russian government to his reiterating Lansdowne's remarks of 1903, and so the *status quo* remained. Finally, the British and Russian governments were to work together to exclude third parties (principally Germany) from gaining concessions in Persia. With respect to Afghanistan, the British had also made substantial gains. The Russians had accepted that Afghanistan was outside their sphere of interest, had conceded not to send its agents into the country, and had agreed to make its representations to the Afghan government via Britain. This latter carried a British responsibility for seeing that Russia's concerns in Afghanistan were dealt with, but that was an acceptable obligation.

[139] Nicolson to Grey, tel. 168, 25 Aug. 1907, *BD*, iv, doc. 506.
[140] Hirtzel diary entries, 26, 28 Aug. 1907, Hirtzel Papers, MSS Eur D1090.
[141] Grey to Nicolson, tel. 161, 26 Aug. 1907, *BD*, iv, doc. 507; Morley to Minto, 28 Aug. 1907, Morley Papers, MSS Eur D573/2.
[142] Nicolson to Grey, 29 Aug. 1907, *BD*, iv, doc. 511.
[143] Grey to Nicolson, private tel., 29 Aug. 1907, Grey Papers, FO 800/72.

10

Alliance Firmed, 1907–1910

THE Anglo-Russian Convention had resulted from the coincidence of two endeavours: Izvolskii's effort to ensure Russian security after the Russo-Japanese War and the long-standing British attempt to come to terms with Russia. Neither was achieved completely by the signing of the Convention. Consequently, after the signing, Izvolskii turned his attention to shoring up Russia's diplomatic position and protecting her most vulnerable points: the Baltic approaches and the Dardanelles. To deal with the former, he opened discussions with Sweden and Germany; to deal with the latter, he began talks with Austria-Hungary.[1] The discussions with Sweden and Germany eventually stalled. The talks with Austria-Hungary resulted in the Russian diplomatic débâcle over the Austro-Hungarian annexation of Bosnia and Herzegovina and increased Izvolskii's anxieties. This 'diplomatic Tsushima' led to his efforts to placate Germany, a process that found its expression in the issue of the Baghdad railway.

For the British, Izvolskii's diplomacy held both promise and peril. If the Anglo-Russian Convention proved beneficial to Russia during Izvolskii's complicated manœuvrings, then Anglo-Russian relations would be secure.[2] However, should Izvolskii conclude that the Convention acted as a barrier to good relations between Russia and the German-speaking powers, then the Anglo-Russian arrangement might be jettisoned. Further, should Izvolskii decide to sacrifice British interests to achieve better Russo-German relations—as the Baghdad railway threatened—then his diplomacy might be menacing. To complicate matters, Britain's own relations with Germany deteriorated during this time, largely as a result of the Anglo-German naval race. This meant that the consequences of a possible Russo-German *rapprochement* grew more serious. Anglo-Russian relations thus became the pivot of Britain's attempts to maintain a favourable global balance of power. For the most part, Grey's policy towards Russia was necessarily reactive, since he could neither compel Anglo-Russian relations to be cordial nor force Russo-German relations to

[1] On the Baltic, see F. Lindberg, *Scandinavia in Great Power Politics* (Stockholm, 1958), 145–264; P. Luntinen, *The Baltic Question 1903–8* (Helsinki, 1975), 120–241.

[2] For a survey, D. W. Sweet and R. T. B. Langhorne, 'Great Britain and Russia', in F. H. Hinsley (ed.), *British Foreign Policy under Sir Edward Grey* (Cambridge, 1977), 236–50.

be distant. It was Izvolskii and his successor's efforts to steer Russian foreign policy between Germany and Britain that determined the nature of Anglo-Russian relations from mid-1907 to the beginning of 1911.

The reception of the Anglo-Russian Convention in both countries was largely favourable.[3] The exceptions to this were the Russian and Indian military authorities, the latter 'quite as militant' as their Russian counterparts in their opposition to the agreement.[4] But their opposition, along with that of such individuals as Curzon, was expected, and had little effect. In the aftermath of his negotiations, and with 'St Petersburg—a social desert', Nicolson found himself 'leading the most quiet of lives'.[5] The ambassador contented himself with keeping a close eye on Izvolskii's efforts to ensure that Russo-German relations did not suffer as a result of the Anglo-Russian Convention.[6] Grey also adopted a watching brief, for he believed that 'Russia needs a period of recuperation and for this it is necessary to be on as good terms as possible with every body; she is assured of this with France by her alliance; she wants to secure it with Germany by a conciliatory policy'. British policy was to ensure that Izvolskii's efforts did not affect British interests and for Britain to remain strong against any German threat.[7]

Izvolskii's attempt to secure the Baltic approaches spoke to both matters. On 12 November Nicolson reported that Russo-German negotiations dealing with the Baltic had begun.[8] As the British had no idea of the nature of the talks, rumours abounded. In general terms, the British did not object to a maintenance of the *status quo* in the Baltic, but were concerned about any abrogation of the terms of the 1856 agreement concerning the Åland Islands and a possible closure of the Baltic to all but Russian and German warships. However, circumstances had changed since the Treaty of Paris.[9] Britain and France were the guarantors of the 1856 agreement, but France was now an ally of Russia, and Britain alone was unable to support Sweden against a Russian demand to fortify the Ålands. Further, the British did not wish to appear unreasonable or to be attempting to isolate the Germans, particularly as a Baltic agreement could be seen as analogous to the Mediterranean agreement that Britain, France, and Spain had signed in May

---

[3] Morley to Minto, 26 Sept. 1907, Morley Papers, MSS Eur D573/2; Hardinge to Nicolson, 2 Oct. 1907, Nicolson Papers, FO 800/340.

[4] Hardinge to Nicolson, 14 Oct. 1907, Nicolson Papers, FO 800/340.

[5] Nicolson to Lascelles, 15 Oct. 1907, Lascelles Papers, FO 800/13.

[6] Nicolson to Grey, disp. 532, 23 Oct. 1907, in H. Temperley and G. P. Gooch (eds.), *B[ritish] D[ocuments on the Origins of the War* 1898–1914*]* (11 vols. in 13; London, 1926–38), iv, doc. 544 and minutes (see *BD* hereafter).

[7] Ibid.; Hardinge to Nicolson, 30 Oct. 1907, Nicolson Papers, FO 800/340.

[8] Hardinge to Nicolson, 12 Nov. 1907, Nicolson Papers, FO 800/340.

[9] Grey to Tweedmouth, 19 Nov. 1907, Grey papers, FO 800/87; Grey to Bertie, 29 Nov. 1907, Grey Papers, FO 800/50.

1907.[10] Thus, in St Petersburg, Nicolson attempted to extract the facts of the negotiations from Izvolskii, while in London, Hardinge outlined the British position to the Russian representatives.[11] Both men took hope from assurances that Russia, whatever her Baltic policy, wished to keep herself out of the German orbit.[12] In fact, Hardinge believed that Russia would 'constantly find herself in conflict with Germany' in the Near East, and that this would redound to the advantage of Anglo-Russian relations.

The British were much too optimistic about Russian policy. In fact, Izvolskii had opened discussions about the Baltic with Germany earlier in the year, during the conversations between Nicholas II and Wilhelm II at Swinemunde in early August, a meeting that had generated much speculation in London about a waning of the Franco-Russian alliance and a waxing of good Russo-German relations.[13] As a result of these negotiations, a Russo-German secret treaty had been signed on 29 October. It guaranteed the *status quo* in the Baltic, thus satisfying Germany's interests, but a separate protocol stipulated that any alteration in the status of the Ålands would not be considered as changing the *status quo*, thus satisfying Izvolskii's aim. The latter's triumph seemed complete: he had secured good relations with Germany at the same time as improving Russia's own naval security. His success was short-lived. Despite Russian assurances that no treaty had been signed with Germany, the British and French soon discovered its existence. At the end of November, Bertie told Grey that he knew 'for certain' that there was a treaty, leading the foreign secretary to set about uncovering its terms.[14] This induced Izvolskii, after consultation with the Germans, to inform the British of the Russo-German discussions, but not of the Russo-German treaty.[15] The matter became more complex the following week. The Germans, suspicious that Izvolskii was playing a double game and anxious to exclude Britain and France from the Baltic, proposed an agreement to the British, paralleling the Russo-German Baltic treaty, designed to guarantee the *status quo* in the North Sea.[16]

Grey's response—to insist that the Baltic and North Sea issues were linked, that

---

[10] K. A. Hamilton, 'Great Britain, France, and the Origins of the Mediterranean Agreements of 16 May 1907', in B. J. C. McKercher and D. J. Moss (eds.), *Shadow and Substance in British Foreign Policy 1895–1939: Memorial Essays Honouring C. J. Lowe* (Edmonton, Alta, 1984), 115–50.

[11] Nicolson to Hardinge, 21 Nov. 1907, Nicolson Papers, FO 800/337; Hardinge to Grey, 23 Nov. 1907, Grey Papers, FO 800/92.

[12] Hardinge to Nicolson, 25 Nov. 1907, Nicolson Papers, FO 800/340.

[13] Hardinge to Bertie, 3 Aug. 1907, Bertie Papers, FO 800/174; Hardinge to Lascelles, 6 Aug. 1907, Lascelles Papers, FO 800/13; O'Beirne to Grey, disp. 407, 10 Aug. 1907, FO 371/326/27686.

[14] Bertie to Grey, private and secret, 28 Nov. 1907 and reply, 29 Nov. 1907, Grey Papers, FO 800/50.

[15] Luntinen, *The Baltic Question*, 147–82.

[16] Lindberg, *Scandinavia in Great Power Politics*, 71–90; Luntinen, *The Baltic Question*, 183–7.

Britain would not discuss either unless the French were consulted, and that Russia should inform France of the Russo-German agreement in the Baltic—reflected the complexity of British interests in the region.[17] The Norwegian declaration of independence from Sweden in 1905 had precipitated a reconsideration of British strategic interests in the Baltic.[18] The British were wary both of any Russo-German combination that made the Baltic a *mare clausum* and of any proposal that would limit British actions there, for these would eliminate any naval lever that Britain might exercise against Germany in the Baltic. For this reason, early in 1907 the British were lukewarm in their support for a treaty guaranteeing Norway's neutrality and territorial integrity without any corresponding assurance that Germany would not be able to seize Denmark. In June, British concerns were magnified when the Russian government attempted to gain general consent for the fortification of the Åland Islands. This, a contravention of one of the conventions of the Treaty of Paris of 1856, would effectively isolate Sweden and make her dependent on Russia. British influence and power in the Baltic would be diminished. As a result, Britain vetoed the draft Norwegian treaty, and agreed instead only to an alternative treaty (signed 2 November 1907) that guaranteed Norway's territorial integrity.

Therefore, Hardinge termed the German proposal about the North Sea 'a feeble attempt to obtain a new grouping of the Northern Powers', and castigated Izvolskii for not keeping the French and British aware of his Baltic negotiations.[19] However, the PUS did not believe that Izvolskii had 'been deceiving us over the Baltic question', instead blaming the Russian minister's inexperience in ' "les grandes affaires" '.[20] Since the British did not object to the maintenance of the *status quo* in the Baltic and were anxious to nurture the Anglo-Russian Convention, they were inclined to give Izvolskii the benefit of the doubt, despite evidence to the contrary concerning his good faith.[21] What concerned them was that Izvolskii had treated the French badly and that Germany was attempting to use the situation to her own ends.[22] None the less, Hardinge saw the general circumstances as working to the

[17] Tyrrell to Grey, 5 Dec. 1907 and Grey's minute, Grey Papers, FO 800/92; Grey to Bertie, 6 Dec. 1907, Grey Papers, FO 800/50.

[18] D. W. Sweet, 'The Baltic in British Diplomacy before the First World War', *HJ* 13 (1970), 454–74; P. Hayes, 'Britain, Germany, and the Admiralty's Plans for Attacking German Territory, 1906–15', in L. Freedman, P. Hayes, and R. O'Neill (eds.), *War, Strategy, and International Politics: Essays in Honour of Sir Michael Howard* (Oxford, 1992), 95–9; Tweedmouth to Grey, 30 Dec. 1907, Grey Papers, FO 800/87. For the German plans, P. M. Kennedy, 'The Development of German Naval Operations Plans against England, 1896–1914', *EHR* 89 (1974), 56–64.

[19] Hardinge to Nicolson, 11 Dec. 1907, Nicolson Papers, FO 800/340.

[20] Hardinge to Nicolson, 24 Dec. 1907, Nicolson Papers, FO 800/340.

[21] Bertie to Hardinge, private and secret tel., 28 Dec. 1907, Grey Papers, FO 800/50.

[22] Grey to Nicolson, 25 Dec. 1907, Grey Papers, FO 800/72; Bertie to Grey, private and secret, 25 Dec. 1907, Nicolson Papers, FO 800/340.

benefit of Britain's relationship with Russia. France's irritation with Russia over the Baltic and German 'intrigues' in Persia were making Russia 'realise at last that we are playing the game in a loyal & straightforward manner, and that they cannot possibly hold their own in Persia & the Middle East without our cooperation'.[23]

During the first four months of 1908, the linked issues of the Baltic, the North Sea, and the Åland Islands continued to cause difficulties. Grey had two goals. First, he wanted to ensure that any North Sea and Baltic agreements made it clear that there was no gap between the two bodies of water, as he feared that any agreement that did not cover the Baltic Straits would be used by Germany to exclude the Royal Navy from the Baltic. Second, he would not allow a settlement about the Ålands to be forced on Sweden by Russia.[24] For the French, the issue was to prevent any Russo-German *rapprochement* to the detriment of the Franco-Russian entente. For Izvolskii, the goal was to find a face-saving compromise to mask the failure of his grand design. On 23 April this was reached. Izvolskii's earlier dropping of the Ålands issue paved the way for all the powers to sign both the Baltic and North Sea agreements guaranteeing the *status quo*. In addition, the two seas were agreed to be contiguous. This satisfied the Admiralty's strategic concerns about keeping the Straits open in peace and promised the necessary legal pretext in war, should Germany violate the agreement, for the British to 'regard ourselves as absolutely free to do what we like & even to ignore the integrity of Norway should we require a naval base on the Norwegian coast'.[25] With this agreement, the Baltic and the Ålands ceased to be an issue in Anglo-Russian relations until the First World War.[26]

Part of Izvolskii's willingness to compromise in the Baltic stemmed from his other diplomatic difficulties. As Hardinge had observed, Russia's position in the Near and Middle East required careful attention. The first problem was the decline of the Austro-Russian condominium in Macedonia.[27] With the Mürzsteg punctuation no longer functioning properly, and with Austria concerned about both Russia's stability and the implications of the Anglo-Russian Convention, the Austrian foreign minister, Baron Alois Aehrenthal, announced in January 1908 that Austria-Hungary would support the building of railway lines in the Sanjak of Novibazar.[28] This was anathema to Izvolskii, for the lines would ensure that

---

[23] Hardinge to Villiers, 7 Jan. 1908, Villiers Papers, FO 800/24.

[24] Sweet, 'The Baltic', 474–7; Luntinen, *The Baltic Question*, 196–235.

[25] Hardinge to Nicolson, 5 Feb. 1908, Nicolson Papers, FO 800/341.

[26] P. Luntinen, 'The Aland Question during the Last Years of the Russian Empire', *SEER* 44 (1976), 557–71.

[27] The following is based on F. R. Bridge, 'Izvolsky, Aehrenthal, and the End of the Austro-Russian Entente, 1906–8', *Mitteilungen des österreichischen Staatsarchivs*, 29 (1976), 315–62 and id., *Great Britain and Austria-Hungary 1906–14* (London, 1972), 80–91.

[28] H. Heilbronner, 'Aehrenthal in Defense of Russian Autocracy', *JfGOE* 17 (1969), 380–96.

Serbia's commercial development would be tied to that of Austria-Hungary to the detriment of Russian-sponsored railway schemes. The result was a 'general onslaught' in Russian newspapers against Izvolskii's foreign policy.[29]

Thus, at the beginning of February 1908, Izvolskii's position was weak: France was annoyed by his flirtation with Germany over the Baltic, Sweden was obdurate in its opposition to his Ålands project, and Austria-Hungary was predatory in the Balkans to the detriment of his domestic popularity. Only Anglo-Russian relations were satisfactory. The British were sympathetic to Izvolskii's pique with Aehrenthal, and wished to co-operate with Russia in the Balkans.[30] Even Curzon's attack on the Anglo-Russian Convention during the debates on its ratification in the House of Lords in early February was useful; it gave Izvolskii timely ammunition against his domestic critics who claimed that he had given up too much to Britain.[31] Nicolson reported that Izvolskii 'chants a paean that our Convention has been signed, & that our relations are so friendly'. Nicolson realized that Izvolskii must perforce continue to work with both Germany and Austria-Hungary, but the ambassador pointed out that the Russian's confidence in them was shaken and that 'in these circumstances M. Iswolsky turns to us'.[32]

The key was Macedonia. Due to Aehrenthal's actions over the Novibazar railway and the later refusal of the ambassadors at Constantinople to proceed with judicial reform (for which Aehrenthal was blamed), the Mürzsteg punctuation was 'as dead as mutton'.[33] In these circumstances, Grey moved carefully to provide what Nicolson called 'a comfortable anchorage' for Izvolskii.[34] On 24 February, the foreign secretary got the agreement of the Cabinet to propose in Parliament that the Powers appoint a governor for Macedonia, a governor whose decrees would be backed by the force of a gendarmerie.[35] The foreign secretary was well aware of the implications of his Macedonian policy for Anglo-Russian relations. He was 'pleased' that 'events are bringing Russia and us together', but felt that public opinion in Britain was still so unused to good relations between the two countries that the relationship required nurturing.[36] Further, the foreign secretary regarded the combination of Britain, France, and Russia as a 'weak one', since France was preoccupied with Morocco and Russia was not yet recovered from the Russo-Japanese War. But, the future might prove different. 'Ten years hence', he told Nicolson, 'a combination of Britain, Russia, and France may be able to dominate Near Eastern

---

[29] Nicolson to Hardinge, 29 Jan. 1908, Nicolson Papers, FO 800/337.
[30] Hardinge to Nicolson, 5 Feb. 1908, Nicolson Papers, FO 800/341.
[31] Nicolson to Hardinge, 12 Feb. 1908, Nicolson Papers, FO 800/337.
[32] Nicolson to Grey, 12 Feb. 1908, Grey Papers, FO 800/73.
[33] Hardinge to Lascelles, 19 Feb. 1908, Lascelles Papers, FO 800/11.
[34] Nicolson to Lascelles, 24 Feb. 1908, Lascelles Papers, FO 800/11.
[35] Asquith to the King, 24 Feb. 1908, Asquith Papers, I/5; *Parl Debs*, 4th ser., vol. 184, 1692–1708.
[36] Grey to Nicolson, 24 Feb. 1908, Nicolson Papers, FO 800/341.

policy; and within that time events will probably make it more and more clear that it is to the interest of Russia and us to work together: but we must go slowly.'

This was wise. For, as Nicolson reported in late February 1908, while the Russian minister was 'vexed and indignant' with Aehrenthal, Izvolskii had 'no desire to brusquely break away from Austria'.[37] Grey's Fabian policy also bore fruit in Britain. His defence of the Anglo-Russian Convention, his utterances about Macedonia, and his Congo policy meant that 'the F.O. is in good favour with all the world'.[38] For this to continue—and such a consideration pertained to the Ålands negotiations, the Russian desire for King Edward to visit Nicholas II, and the Macedonian question—there needed to be no Russian episodes that could disturb British public opinion. As Hardinge told Nicolson: 'public feeling in this country is very strong in favour of the protection of small & weak countries against the big and strong' and there could be 'no pogroms, no withdrawal of Finnish liberty &c'.[39]

Until early March, in order to keep in step with Izvolskii, Grey held back from proposing formally to the powers the idea for a governor and gendarmerie in Macedonia that he had outlined in Parliament on 25 February.[40] While Izvolskii did not favour Grey's idea, the Russian minister found common ground between his own and Grey's proposals.[41] This was the beginning of a series of negotiations that culminated in June at Reval when, during Edward VII's state visit to Nicholas II, Hardinge and Izvolskii reached a compromise on Macedonian reform.[42] This agreement had diplomatic ripples. Aehrenthal, despite a virulent press reaction to the Anglo-Russian settlement, was content to be rid of the Macedonian incubus and pleased that a *rapprochement* between St Petersburg and London pushed Berlin closer to Vienna.[43] In Berlin, the compromise generated further fears of encirclement, and gave fresh impetus to those who wished to carry on the naval race with Britain. Despite the fact that the Young Turk revolution in July 1908 led to the Anglo-Russian agreement on Macedonia being abandoned on 27 July, the very fact that it had been concluded signified the improved relationship between them.

However, the Macedonian imbroglio also helped to generate the circumstances that led to the Bosnian crisis. In the spring of 1908, despite his irritation with Aehrenthal, Izvolskii opened discussions with the Austrian foreign minister.[44]

[37] Nicolson to Grey, 26 Feb. 1908, Grey Papers, FO 800/73.

[38] Sanderson to Nicolson, 3 Mar. 1908, Nicolson Papers, FO 800/341; Morley to Minto, 27 Feb. 1908, Morley Papers, MSS Eur D573/3.

[39] Hardinge to Nicolson, 3 Mar. 1908, Nicolson Papers, FO 800/341.

[40] Nicolson to Grey, 4 Mar. 1908, Grey Papers, FO 800/73.

[41] Nicolson to Grey, 11 Mar. 1908, Nicolson Papers, FO 800/337.

[42] 'Visit to the Emperor of Russia at Reval in June, 1908', Hardinge, 12 Jun. 1908, *BD*, v, doc. 195.

[43] F. R. Bridge, *From Sadowa to Sarajevo: The Foreign Policy of Austria-Hungary, 1866–1914* (London, 1972), 299–301.

[44] Bridge, 'Izvolsky, Aehrenthal', 326–31.

These talks were aimed at patching up the Austro-Russian split caused by the Novibazar railroad, but, by the beginning of July, Izvolskii was pushing a more ambitious project. On 2 July he suggested to Aehrenthal that Russia would accept an Austro-Hungarian annexation of Bosnia, Herzegovina, and the Sanjak in exchange for an endorsement of the opening of the Straits to Russian warships. Aehrenthal's answer was delayed, in part by his own feeling that this was a poor bargain for Austria-Hungary and in part by the Young Turk revolution. However, by mid-August, Aehrenthal had decided that Austria-Hungary would annexe Bosnia and Herzegovina, and saw the Russian proposal as an opportunity to obtain Izvolskii's acceptance with little commitment on Austria-Hungary's part. On 27 August, the final Austro-Hungarian reply to Izvolskii's proposal of 2 July had been formulated. The stage was set for the dramatic events of the autumn.

While this was going on, Anglo-Russian relations were quiet. Grey's position was strong.[45] The troublesome Macedonian question had been resolved diplomatically by the Anglo-Russian agreement, an agreement that had not soured British relations with Austria. The revolution in Turkey found great favour among the Liberal party, eliminating the constant pressure on Grey from parliamentary groups like the Balkan Committee.[46] But the revolt was not an unmixed blessing. Grey was aware that his policy towards the new Turkish regime would necessarily have to be favourable, possibly to the detriment of Anglo-Russian co-operation. As he put it on 8 August: 'The delicate point will presently be Russia—we cannot revert to the old policy of Lord Beaconsfield, we have now to be pro-Turkish without giving rise to any suspicion that we are anti-Russian.'[47] To the delight of the growing number of Germanophobes in the Foreign Office, the general thrust of events seemed to be pushing all the powers towards Britain at the expense of Germany, although moderates like Morley decried this trend.[48]

Nicolson returned to Russia from leave early in August 1908. He was optimistic about Anglo-Russian relations. The ambassador found Izvolskii 'more self confident & firmer generally than when I left in April'.[49] Unaware that much of the change in the Russian foreign minister's attitude stemmed from his anticipation of a diplomatic coup at Constantinople, Nicolson believed that 'unless he [Izvolskii] is

[45] C. J. Lowe and M. L. Dockrill, *The Mirage of Power*, i, *British Foreign Policy 1902–14* (London, 1972), 79–81.

[46] K. G. Robbins, 'Public Opinion, the Press and Pressure Groups', in Hinsley (ed.), *British Foreign Policy*, 85–6.

[47] Cited, J. Heller, *British Policy towards the Ottoman Empire 1908–1914* (London, 1983), 11; see also, M. B. Cooper, 'British Policy in the Balkans, 1908–9', *HJ* 7 (1964), 258–67; Grey to Lowther (British ambassador, Constantinople), 11 Aug. 1908, extract in Grey to Nicolson, 11 Aug. 1908, Nicolson Papers, FO 800/341.

[48] K. Wilson, 'The Question of Anti-Germanism at the British Foreign Office before the First World War', *CJH* 18 (1983), 23–42; Morley to Minto, 10 Aug. 1908, Morley Papers, MSS Eur D573/3.

[49] Nicolson to Grey, 13 Aug. 1908, Nicolson Papers, FO 800/337.

deceiving me he is earnestly desirous of laying Russian foreign policy alongside that of England'. The immediate task that faced Nicolson was settling the problems stemming from the flight of several thousand Afghan tribesmen, the Jamshedis, into Russia in July.[50] This was a matter of some significance, for it spoke directly to the functioning of the Anglo-Russian Convention. Under the latter's terms, Russia was to make all representations to the Amir of Afghanistan via Britain. The British had informed the Amir of this immediately after the Convention had been signed, but the latter had refused to give official sanction to the Convention, an action that had the legal potential to abrogate the Anglo-Russian agreement. If the British were unable to satisfy Russian complaints about the Jamshedis, then St Petersburg might either renounce the Convention formally or take action unilaterally against the Amir, an act which would annul the Convention in practice.[51] Thus the Jamshedis took on a significance far greater than would otherwise have been the case.

The Jamshedi problem took until the end of September 1908 to be resolved, as telegrams and letters flew between the Russian government, the Foreign Office, the India Office, and the government of India. The essential stumbling block was the Amir's refusal to respond to British proddings, but the government of India also was sympathetic to his countercharges that the Jamshedis, with Russian conniv-ance, were using Russian territory as a safe haven from which to launch raids against their tribal opponents in Afghanistan.[52] Whatever the truth of the matter, by the end of August Hardinge was blistering in his condemnation of the Indian government: 'The Govt of India are hopelessly weak and the Ameer has found them out, which makes the situation difficult & even critical. The Viceroy's Coun-cil are an inferior lot of men, while the Viceroy is devoid of brains.'[53] Nicolson's concerns were wider. Should the Convention prove ineffectual in dealing with the Jamshedis, the ambassador worried about the future of the agreement itself.[54] What Nicolson preferred was something in the way of a new Afghanistan Convention with Russia, and he suggested that Hardinge broach this idea with Izvolskii when the latter visited England in October. For the moment, however, the Jamshedi incident approached an end when, on 18 September, the Amir agreed to the repatriation of all but those tribesmen he suspected of fomenting unrest.[55] Four days later, the Russians agreed to allow those of the latter who did not wish to

[50] Benckendorff to Grey, 20 July 1908, FO 371/518/25395 and minutes; O'Beirne to Grey, tel. 123, 20 July 1908, FO 371/518/25728 and minutes.

[51] Nicolson to Grey, private tel., 17 Aug. 1908, FO 371/518/28723.

[52] IO to FO, 31 July 1908, FO 371/518/26669; IO to FO and enclosures, 4 Aug. 1908, FO 371/518/ 27161; Russian embassy to FO, 7 Aug. 1908 and minutes, FO 371/518/27448; Nicolson to Grey, disp. 361, 13 Aug. 1908, FO 371/518/28448; IO to FO, 19 Aug. 1908, Grey to Nicolson, tel. 309, 21 Aug. 1908, both FO 371/518/28949; Nicolson to Grey, tel. 147, 24 Aug. 1908, FO 371/518/29481.

[53] Hardinge to Nicolson, 31 Aug.; 15 Sept. 1908, Nicolson Papers, FO 800/341.

[54] Nicolson to Hardinge, 9 Sept. 1908, Nicolson Papers, FO 800/337.

[55] IO to FO, 18 Sept. 1908, FO 371/518/32377.

return to Afghanistan to stay in Russia.[56] Since the Russians seemed to be disposed to act as if the assent of the Amir to the Convention was irrelevant to its functioning, Nicolson concluded that the Jamshedi incident was 'almost closed'.[57]

While this Afghan border incident occupied British attention, Izvolskii was embarking on a much more ambitious project. At the beginning of September, he had conversations at Carlsbad with Count Berchtold, the Austro-Hungarian ambassador to Russia. In them, and during similar talks later with Berchtold and Aehrenthal at Castle Buchlau on 16 September, Izvolskii accepted in principle the Austrian reply of 27 August.[58] In turn, he was both informed of Austria-Hungary's intention to annexe Bosnia and Herzegovina in early October and given Aehrenthal's assurance that Austria-Hungary would then look favourably on the Russian desires concerning the Straits. With agreement in hand, Izvolskii resumed his tour of Europe, hoping to lay the foundations for a European conference to follow in the wake of the annexation. Indeed, Izvolskii hoped to use such a conference to do more than secure the Straits. He hoped to present Russia as the defender of the Balkan states and even of Turkey against Austria-Hungary's rapacity to the benefit of his own domestic popularity, a fact that the final, equivocal Russian reply to the Austro-Hungarian memorandum underlined.

When Izvolskii arrived in Paris on 4 October, he discovered that events had begun to compress his timetable. Bulgaria's intention to declare its independence from the Ottoman Empire on 5 October was common knowledge in the French capital, and Austria-Hungary had leaked to the French government the fact of its impending annexation of Bosnia and Herzegovina. This meant that Russia would have difficulty posing as the protector of the Balkans and would appear as an accomplice of Austria-Hungary's. Certainly Bertie, to whom Izvolskii pleaded his innocence in Paris, felt that the Russian 'did not quite tell me the truth, the whole truth, and nothing but the truth' about Russia's complicity.[59] This was countered by Nicolson's assertion that Izvolskii's only fault was being 'a little yielding in his opposition, and a little too discursive in examining compensations' in discussions with Aehrenthal, but the Russian faced a sceptical audience when he arrived in London on 9 October.[60]

In conversation with Grey the next day, Izvolskii urged the need for a conference to discuss the Bosnian crisis.[61] He attempted to play on British concerns by emphasizing the 'critical' need to demonstrate the value of the Convention to its

[56] Nicolson to Grey, tel. 171, 22 Sept. 1908, FO 371/518/32909.
[57] Nicolson to Hardinge, 24 Sept. 1908, Nicolson papers, FO 800/337.
[58] Bridge, 'Aehrenthal and Izvolsky', 331–8 and apps.
[59] Bertie to Grey, disp. 380, 4 Oct. 1908, *BD*, v, doc. 293.
[60] Nicolson to Grey, 8 Oct. 1908, Grey Papers, FO 800/73.
[61] Grey to Nicolson, 14 Oct. 1908, *BD*, v, doc. 379.
[62] Hardinge to Bertie, 12 Oct. 1908, Bertie Papers, FO 800/180.

opponents in St Petersburg. He argued that his own dismissal, and that of Stolypin, would follow should he be sent 'back empty-handed to Russia' and that this would 'be playing the game of the reactionaries who . . . are very anxious to do what they can to upset our Convention with Russia'.[62] Hardinge noted cynically of this argument that 'it struck me very forcibly that he was thinking more of his own position than of anything else'. On the morning of 12 October Grey brought Izvolskii's proposals before the Cabinet.[63] That body favoured the idea of a European conference, with an eye to providing Turkey with compensation for annexation of Bosnia and Herzegovina and Bulgaria's declaration of independence, but rejected Izvolskii's idea that the Straits be opened to Russian warships, despite Grey and Asquith's acceptance of this point. Without some sort of reciprocal gain for Britain and with a fear that Russian warships might pass into the Mediterranean, attack British shipping and then retire to safety within the Black Sea, the time was judged 'highly inopportune' to raise the matter. As the British attitude to a change in the *status quo* at the Straits during the negotiations of the Anglo-Russian Convention the previous year had been so encouraging to Russian aspirations, it was not surprising that Izvolskii 'went away thoroughly miserable' when the Cabinet's decision was relayed to him that afternoon.[64]

But not for long. That evening, Grey held a private dinner at his house for Morley, Izvolskii, and Benckendorff. At it, the Russian minister suggested that the Straits be opened in peacetime to the warships of all the riparian states of the Black Sea and that, in the case of war between Russia and another state, the latter should have equal access to the Black Sea. This reciprocity Hardinge termed a 'shop-window ware', since it 'is already a settled principle of naval warfare with us' that the Royal Navy would not enter the Black Sea unless Turkey were an ally.[65] However, the PUS believed that the Cabinet would probably approve Izvolskii's proposal since reciprocity could be more easily sold to a public that did not 'understand these strategical considerations'. Izvolskii was careful to tie his new offer to another British interest: the maintenance of the Anglo-Russian Convention. With the Jamshedi issue still on everyone's mind, the Russian minister's assurance that 'whether the Amir gave his formal adhesion or not, the Russian Government would treat the Convention as a valid instrument' was an alluring prospect.[66]

On 13 October, Grey held a formal dinner for the Russian minister at the Foreign Office. This was a bipartisan affair, designed to impress Izvolskii with the unanimity of British policy towards Russia, and was attended by such Unionist

[63] Asquith to the King, 12 Oct. 1908, Asquith Papers I/5.
[64] Hardinge to Nicolson, 13 Oct. 1908, *BD*, v, doc. 372.
[65] Ibid.
[66] Morley to Minto, 14 Oct. 1908, Morley Papers, MSS Eur D573/3.

luminaries as Balfour and Lansdowne in addition to Liberal ministers.[67] It was a measure of Izvolskii's desperation and of his lack of understanding of the British political system that he cornered Balfour at dinner and 'was extraordinarily insistent, and behaved like a plenipotentiary arguing at a Congress, than one talking to another at a social gathering'.[68] Izvolskii outlined to the former prime minister the views that he had expressed the previous evening, and added two threatening notes: that British opposition to his plans would both strengthen the anti-British party in Russia and provide support for those in Russia who advocated an attack on Turkey. Balfour quickly passed on these remarks to Asquith and Grey. The next day, Grey outlined Izvolskii's new proposals to the Cabinet.[69] That body welcomed the Russian's statement that the Convention remained in force regardless of the Amir's attitude. And, as Hardinge had anticipated, the Cabinet accepted in principle Izvolskii's ideas about the Straits, although raising the matter was still deemed 'highly inconvenient'.[70] As for the naval implications of Izvolskii's plan, Asquith was clear: 'I attach very little *strategic* value—so far as we are concerned—to the maintenance of the existing restrictions: and this is the opinion of our naval and military advisers.' Despite Swedish fears that a change at the Dardanelles might presage changes in the Baltic to Stockholm's disadvantage, the British naval position was decided.[71]

While Izvolskii must have been disappointed by the fact that Barings delayed bringing out a Russian loan that the foreign minister was helping to negotiate, his trip to London provided optimism about a favourable resolution of the Bosnian crisis.[72] Since British political opinion generally expected a European conference to settle the Balkan crisis, and was not opposed to a change in the *status quo* at the Straits, Izvolskii's position had improved.[73] And, despite the fact that many of the élite had not been impressed personally by Izvolskii, Grey believed that the visit was 'most favourable to good relations with Russia'.[74] But, Grey's policy in the Balkan crisis was necessarily complicated.[75] On the one hand, the foreign secretary could not afford to support the demands of Russia's client, Serbia, for compensa-

[67] Brodrick to Selborne, 6 Nov. 1908, Selborne Papers 3.

[68] Balfour to Asquith, 14 Oct. 1908, Asquith Papers I/11.

[69] Asquith to the King, 14 Oct. 1908, Asquith Papers I/5.

[70] Asquith to Balfour, 15 Oct. 1908, Asquith Papers I/11; Balfour to Lansdowne, ? [but likely 15 or 16] Oct. 1908, Balfour Papers, Add MSS 49729.

[71] Spring Rice (British Minister, Stockholm) to Cromer, 1 Nov. 1908, Cromer Papers, FO 633/14.

[72] Revelstoke to Noetzlin, very confidential, 15 and 17 Oct. 1908; Revelstoke to Hope, confidential, 14 Nov. 1908, all Barings Papers, Barings Partners' filing/209.

[73] Lansdowne to Balfour, 15 Oct. 1908, Balfour Papers, Add MSS 49729; Esher diary entry, 15 Oct. 1908, Esher Papers, ESHR 2/11.

[74] Morley to Minto, 14 Oct. 1908, Morley Papers, MSS Eur D573/3; Lansdowne to Balfour, 15 Oct. 1908, Balfour Papers, Add MSS 49729; Grey to Nicolson, 26 Oct. 1908, Nicolson Papers, FO 800/341.

[75] Heller, *British Policy towards the Ottoman Empire*, 9–23; Cooper, 'British Policy in the Balkans', 264–5.

tion too strongly lest he appear unsympathetic to the new constitutional regime in Turkey. On the other hand, for the sake of good Anglo–Russian relations, he did not wish to 'cold shoulder' Russia over the matter.[76] Unaware that Izvolskii's support for Serbia was only a small part of the Russian minister's manœuvrings, Grey's first priority was to help resolve the general crisis. Here, knowing 'how far' Izvolskii would support Serbian demands would 'be useful'.

Discovering this was not easy. Nicolson saw Izvolskii on 31 October, and the latter expressed himself 'much perplexed' by the situation.[77] Three days later, Nicolson had an audience with Nicholas II. At Grey's direction, the ambassador praised Izvolskii's efforts in London, and assured the Emperor of Britain's desire to co-operate with Russia in resolving the Balkan crisis.[78] Nicolson came away from the audience convinced of three things: that Izvolskii's position was safe, that Nicholas was 'loyally and sincerely determined' to act with Britain, and that support for close relations with Britain was growing in Russia.[79] However, what Nicolson did not perceive was the fact that Russian policy was essentially an effort at damage control. While Nicholas was 'incensed' by Aehrenthal's efforts to saddle Izvolskii with the responsibility for the annexation, this emotion resulted from having been bested by the Austrian rather than from a belief, as Nicolson assumed, that Izvolskii had been 'misled and indeed tricked'. For Nicholas had full knowledge of Izvolskii's negotiations with Aehrenthal in September.[80] Although the Tsar had been unhappy that the interests of the Balkan Slavs were to be sacrificed, he had noted in discussions on Izvolskii's negotiations that 'I fully understand that the annexation [of Bosnia and Herzegovina] is even advantageous to us, and I entirely approve the system of guarantees and compensations proposed by Alexander Petrovich [Izvolskii].'[81] However, Bulgaria's precipitate declaration of independence and Aehrenthal's intimations of Russian complicity in the annexation had wrecked the Russian policy. Russia could no longer pretend that her actions in the Balkans were those of the good Samaritan and that the gain of the Straits in any European conference was purely fortuitous. Coupled with this was a decline in Izvolskii's support in Russia. Stolypin and Kokovtsov were outraged at his actions, since Russia was unprepared for and could not afford war in support of Izvolskii's risky policy.[82] They lobbied Nicholas to adopt the policy advocated by public

---

[76] Grey to Nicolson, 10 Oct. 1908, Grey Papers, FO 800/73.

[77] Nicolson to Grey, private tel., 31 Oct. 1908, Grey Papers, FO 800/73.

[78] Grey to Nicolson, tel., 570, 2 Nov. 1908, FO 371/519/38424.

[79] Nicolson to Grey, 4 Nov. 1908, Grey Papers, FO 800/73.

[80] Bridge, 'Izvolsky, Achrenthal', 335–6.

[81] Reported in Charykov (assistant Russian foreign minister) to Izvolskii, 21–22 Sept. 1908, cited in Bridge, 'Aehrenthal, Izvolsky', 353.

[82] D. M. McDonald, *United Government and Foreign Policy in Russia 1900–14* (Cambridge, MA, 1992), 136–9.

opinion in Russia: disinterested support for the Balkan states without any thought
of compensation for Russia at the Straits. With his and Izvolskii's policy collapsing,
Nicholas II transformed his frustration at being balked into anger at Aehrenthal,
and attempted to play the aggrieved party. There was a sharp, unintended irony to
Nicolson's remark after his audience on 3 November that Nicholas was 'a very
straightforward honourable man'.[83]

Russian discomfort at being caught in an awkward position was reinforced by
events. In early November, following the publishing of Wilhelm II's indiscreet
'interview' in the *Daily Telegraph* on 28 October, a Franco-German spat occurred
in Casablanca.[84] There were suspicions that the ferocity of the German response
was a 'red herring drawn across the track of the Emperor's "interview" ', but they
were mixed with concerns that Germany might be taking advantage of the Balkan
situation to humiliate France and, indirectly, Russia.[85] On 5 November, Izvolskii
asked Nicolson what Britain would do if Germany were to attack France; the linked
nature of the Bosnian and Casablanca crises was underlined on 10 November when
Benckendorff asked Grey what Britain would do if Germany were to support
Austria in the Balkans.[86] Grey's response was guarded, but he suggested that
Britain would probably have supported France in the Casablanca incident and that
Britain would 'naturally be against the aggressor in any war'. While this was
hopeful for Izvolskii, the fact that the uncertain political situation had caused the
loan negotiations with France (in which Barings was involved) to collapse no doubt
reinforced his anger with Aehrenthal and drove home the fact that Russia was
largely impotent.[87] Further, Izvolskii's own position had been diminished. At a
meeting of the Russian Council of Ministers on 7 November, Izvolskii had attempted to defend his policy, but Stolypin and Kokovtsov had clipped his wings.[88]
In future, foreign policy would not be made by Izvolskii working separately from
the other ministers.

Russia's financial and military ability to go to war was of keen interest to the

[83] Nicolson to Villiers, 5 Nov. 1908, Villiers Papers, FO 800/22.

[84] G. E. Silberstein, 'Germany, France and the Casablanca Incident 1908–9: An Investigation of a
Forgotten Crisis', *CJH* 11 (1976), 331–54; E. W. Edwards, 'The Franco-German Agreement on
Morocco', *EHR* 78 (1963), 483–513; M. B. Hayne, *The French Foreign Office and the Origins of the
First World War* 1898–1914 (Oxford, 1993), 181–2; T. F. Cole, 'The *Daily Telegraph* Affair and its
Aftermath: The Kaiser, Bülow and the Reichstag, 1908–9', in J. C. G. Röhl and N. Sombart (eds.),
Kaiser Wilhelm II: New Interpretations: The Corfu Papers (Cambridge, 1982), 249–68; K. A. Lerman,
The Chancellor as Courtier: Bernhard von Bülow and the Governance of Germany 1900–9 (Cambridge,
1990), 221–7.

[85] Esher diary entry, 5 Nov. 1908, Esher Papers, ESHR 2/11; Haldane (secretary of state for war) to
his mother, 6 Nov. 1908, Haldane Papers, MS 5980.

[86] Nicolson to Grey, 5 Nov. 1908; Grey to Nicolson, 10 Nov. 1908, both Grey Papers, FO 800/73.

[87] Revelstoke to Hope, confidential, 14 Nov. 1908, Barings Papers, Barings Partners' filing/209.

[88] McDonald, *United Government and Foreign Policy*, 141–5.

British, since Russia's Balkan policy was felt to hinge on it.[89] Colonel Guy Wyndham, the British military attaché in Russia, felt that Russia would be formidable on the defensive, but an unknown quantity on the offensive.[90] His views were thought optimistic at the Foreign Office, and were somewhat discounted. As to Russia's finances, although revenues were rising rapidly enough to meet ordinary expenditure, the funds necessary both to pay off Russia's 1904 loan and to refurbish the army and navy could come only from further foreign borrowing.[91] As the availability of such loans were necessarily influenced by the international situation, Russia was in a cleft stick: she could play a big role in the Balkans if her finances were strong; however, her finances would be strong only if the Balkan problems were resolved. This meant that British and Russian policies towards the Balkans should not have diverged. Both countries favoured Bulgaria's and Austria's paying some sort of compensation to Turkey. However, Russia's support for Serbia's territorial claims surpassed any British commitment to Belgrade, since Izvolskii's 'Balkan policy is regarded as a failure; and the Servian case will be treated as a test case, by which to judge whether he will succeed or not in retrieving the faults of Russian diplomacy'.[92] None the less, Grey was willing to work closely with Izvolskii, and early in February 1909 strongly supported the Russian minister's successful attempt to end the Bulgar–Turk imbroglio.[93] For Hardinge, this was epochal: 'It is really astonishing', he told Nicolson self-satisfiedly, 'what a development there has been of the Anglo-Russian *entente* in the form of our co-operation in the Balkans, though, after all, it is only what those who have studied the question have known for years must inevitably be its outcome.'[94]

While Izvolskii appreciated Grey's support, the strength of the Anglo-Russian bond was soon tested over Serbia.[95] Early in January 1909 Aehrenthal had convinced the Austro-Hungarian governments to compensate Turkey for the annexation, thus eliminating that contentious issue.[96] But, ominously, the Austro-Hungarian chief of staff, Conrad von Hötzendorf, had been assured by his German counterpart on 21 January that an Austro-Hungarian attack on Serbia

[89] Nicolson to Grey, 18 Nov. 1908, Grey Papers, FO 800/73.

[90] Wyndham's report (19 Nov.) in Nicolson to Grey, disp. 530, 19 Nov. 1908, FO 371/519/40798 and minutes; Nicolson to Grey, disp. 541, 26 Nov. 1908, FO 371/519/42551 and minutes.

[91] O'Beirne to Revelstoke, confidential, 3 Dec. 1908, Barings Papers, Barings Partners' filing/211; O'Beirne memo (n.d.), in Nicolson to Grey, disp. 566, 3 Dec. 1908, FO 371/518/42575; O'Beirne memo (30 Nov.), in Nicolson to Grey, disp. 568, 3 Dec. 1908, FO 371/519/42577 and minutes.

[92] Nicolson to Grey, 21 Jan. 1909, Grey Papers, FO 800/73.

[93] Grey to Nicolson, 2 Feb. 1909, Grey Papers, FO 800/73.

[94] Hardinge to Nicolson, 2 Feb. 1909, Nicolson Papers, FO 800/342.

[95] Nicolson to Grey, 10 Feb. 1909, Nicolson Papers, FO 800/337.

[96] Bridge, *Sadowa to Sarajevo*, 312–13.

would be supported by Germany against any Russian intervention.[97] With the Russian general staff's advising him that Russia was in no position to go to war, Izvolskii needed what support he could garner from both Britain and France.[98] British policy was not based on assumptions of Russian supineness. Although he knew that French support for Russia was unlikely, Nicolson continued to advise Grey that should Austria-Hungary attack Serbia 'the probabilities are now that *Russia would actively intervene.*'[99] Since the ambassador assumed that Britain would be able to do little in such circumstances, he hoped for a conference as 'the only hope of preserving the peace'.[100]

This was a fond hope, since Austria-Hungary continued to reject any compromises that Serbia put forward, despite the fact that these compromises had been urged upon Serbia by Russia and supported by Britain.[101] By 10 March, both Grey and Izvolskii had come to the conclusion that Austria-Hungary would not be satisfied except with a complete acceptance of its own position.[102] Nicolson continued to contend that Russia might resist any Austro-Hungarian action against Serbia by force of arms, but he was aware that the persistence of domestic unrest in Russia—some 2,835 people had been executed by the government in the three years ending 30 October 1908—made the government fearful that revolution might ensue.[103] On 9 March the Duma passed a bill for large increases in military expenditure, but the debate underscored Russia's military unpreparedness. The warning by the leader of the Octobrists, Aleksandr Guchkov, that 'Russia's patience [concerning the Balkans] could not last for ever' was patriotic and prophetic, but an admission of weakness.[104] For the British, the only bright light was that Izvolskii 'appreciates the genuineness of our support during the present crisis. It has been perfectly loyal which is more than can be said for the attitude of the French.'[105]

The precipitate surrender of the Russian government to the German ultimatum of 23 March, which brought an end to the Bosnian crisis, shook the British belief that Anglo-Russian relations would improve as a result of events in the Balkans.

---

[97] N. Stone, 'Moltke-Conrad: Relations Between the Austro-Hungarian and German General Staffs, 1919–14', *HJ* 9 (1966), 207.

[98] W. C. Fuller, Jr., *Strategy and Power in Russia 1600–1914* (New York, 1992), 420–1.

[99] Nicolson to Grey, 24 Feb. 1909, Grey Papers, FO 800/73, original emphasis.

[100] Nicolson to Hardinge, 25 Feb. 1909, Nicolson Papers, FO 800/337.

[101] Nicolson to Grey, tel. 106, 27 Feb. 1909, *BD*, v, doc. 619; Grey to Nicolson, tel. 254, 27 Feb. 1909, *BD*, v, doc. 621; Grey to Nicolson, disp. 84, 1 Mar. 1909, *BD*, v, doc. 635; Nicolson to Grey, disp. 142, 3 Mar. 1909, *BD*, v.

[102] Grey to Nicolson, 3 Mar. 1909, Nicolson Papers, FO 800/342; Nicolson to Grey, 10 Mar. 1909, Grey Papers, FO 800/73.

[103] Nicolson to Grey, 10 Mar. 1909, Grey Papers, FO 800/73; Nicolson to Grey, disp. 161, 11 Mar. 1909, FO 371/726/9777 and minutes.

[104] Nicolson to Grey, disp. 157, 10 Mar. 1909, FO 371/726/9773; J. F. Hutchinson, 'The Octobrists and the Future of Imperial Russia as a Great Power', *SEER* 50 (1972), 220–37.

[105] Hardinge to Nicolson, 15 Mar. 1909, Nicolson Papers, FO 800/342.

Although Hardinge had become convinced that Izvolskii had signed a compromising agreement at Buchlau, he and Nicolson were dumbfounded and dismayed by the Russian collapse.[106] Nicolson, admitting that he might be 'pursuing nightmares', envisioned a regrouping of the powers, with France and Russia gravitating towards Germany out of weakness and with Britain being isolated. For him, the proper precaution was to make the Anglo-Russian entente 'nearer to the nature of an alliance' in order to counter those in Russia who would now argue that Russia's security demanded closer Russo-German relations.[107] Hardinge believed that Russian anger with Germany was too strong to permit such an occurrence; however, he advocated the need for a stronger foreign minister than Izvolskii. Grey, too, saw less dramatic consequences and favoured less dramatic action.[108] For him, Russia now had Bulgaria's support and the goodwill of the other Slavs who were frightened by the bullying attitude of the Central Powers. Russia needed political reform, both to regain her strength and to become a more acceptable British ally. Britain's policy was to keep 'in touch so that our diplomatic action may be in accord and in mutual support'.

In practice, the British attempted to determine the actual nature of the Russian response to their diplomatic débâcle. The first consequence, the removal of General A. F. Rediger as minister of war and his replacement by General V. A. Sukhomlinov, was seen as mostly favourable, especially at it was accompanied by a pledge by the Octobrists to support further defence expenditure.[109] It was the careers of Izvolskii and Stolypin that drew closest scrutiny. In Nicolson's mind, their fates were linked.[110] Quite separate from the Bosnian crisis, Stolypin's position was under attack over his attempt to create a Russian naval general staff.[111] The ambassador argued that if Izvolskii were replaced by I. L. Goremykin, then Stolypin must surely fall, 'as the two could not possibly work together'. Given the inherent strength of the pro-German elements in Russia and Goremykin's own leanings, this would mean that 'our entente is doomed'.[112] When Nicolson reported that Izvolskii's dismissal was imminent, London's reaction was swift. Given that

---

[106] Hardinge to Nicolson, 15 Mar. 1909, Nicolson Papers, FO 800/342; Nicolson to Grey, 24 Mar. 1909, *BD*, v, doc. 764; Hardinge to Nicolson, 30 Mar. 1909, Nicolson Papers, FO 800/342.

[107] For the nuances, see Nicolson to Hardinge, 3 Apr. 1909, Nicolson Papers, FO 800/337.

[108] Grey to Nicolson, 2 Apr. 1909, Nicolson Papers, FO 800/342.

[109] Nicolson to Grey, disp. 201, 27 Mar. 1909, FO 371/728/12076; Nicolson to Grey, disp. 213, 2 Apr. 1909, FO 371/726/13592; cf. Nicolson to Grey, disp. 230, 8 Apr. 1909, FO 371/726/13608.

[110] Nicolson to Grey, 8 Apr. 1909; Nicolson to Hardinge, 3 Apr. 1909, both Nicolson Papers, FO 800/337; Nicolson to Grey, disp. 223, 7 Apr. 1909, FO 371/726/13601. The subsequent two quotations are from the former.

[111] E. Chmielewski, 'Stolypin and the Russian Ministerial Crisis of 1909', *CSS* 4 (1967), 1–38; G. Hosking, *The Russian Constitutional Experiment: Government and Duma, 1907–14* (Cambridge, 1973), 74–105.

[112] Hosking, *Russian Constitutional Experiment*, 74–105; this view was common, see Hardinge to Goschen, 20 Apr. 1909, Hardinge Papers, vol. 17.

the dismissal would be 'regarded as another Delcassé incident & as a change to Germanophil policy in foreign affairs', Nicolson was instructed to lobby Nicholas II on Izvolskii's behalf.[113] Nicolson agreed, but pointed out that the 'real danger' was Stolypin's removal, since his leaving would sweep away Izvolskii in any case.[114] At an audience on 14 March, Nicolson praised Stolypin, defended Izvolskii against the Emperor's mild criticisms, and laid stress on the importance of maintaining cordial Anglo-Russian relations.[115] Nicolson also emphasized both Britain's loyalty to the Anglo-Russian understanding and naval strength, the latter in order to remind Nicholas of the value of Britain's friendship.[116]

This naval episode should be seen in the light of outside events. Austria-Hungary had just announced that she would build four Dreadnoughts, a move that Hardinge, since the new construction would force Britain to divert capital ships from the North Sea to the Mediterranean, termed a 'thanks offering' to Germany for her support in the Bosnian crisis.[117] This had strategic implications for the heated debates in London over building estimates for the Royal Navy.[118] Hardinge felt that the Austro-Hungarian action would 'knock out entirely the little Navy people in the Cabinet'.[119] But, while the Radicals lost their struggle to limit the number of Dreadnoughts built to four, they won a partial victory in foreign policy. This took the form of an injunction forbidding the use of the term 'Triple Entente' in official correspondence.[120] While Hardinge termed this 'trifling', it was symptomatic both of the Radicals' dislike of being associated with Russia on ideological grounds and of their belief that good Anglo-Russian relations offended Germany.[121]

This embedded Anglo-Russian relations firmly in Liberal politics, and faced Grey with an awkward dilemma. During Nicolson's audience with Nicholas II, the latter had hinted that Anglo-Russian relations should become closer and take the form of an alliance. Nicolson advised this strongly. However, as Hardinge informed Nicolson confidentially, such a move was politically 'impossible' with the Liberals in power.[122] But, should Grey not take up the Emperor's hint, this would strength-

---

[113] Nicolson to Grey, private tel., 7 Apr. 1909, Grey Papers, FO 800/73; Hardinge to Nicolson, private tel., 8 Apr. 1909, FO 371/729/13412.

[114] Nicolson to Hardinge, private tel., 9 Apr. 1909, FO 371/729/13989.

[115] Nicolson to Grey, disp. 239 confidential, 14 Apr. 1909, FO 371/729/15520 and minutes.

[116] Ibid.; Nicolson to Grey, 19 Apr. 1909, Nicolson papers, FO 800/337.

[117] Hardinge to Nicolson, 12 Apr. 1909, Nicolson papers, FO 800/342.

[118] A. J. Marder, *From the Dreadnought to Scapa Flow*, i, *1904–1914: The Road to War* (London, 1961), 159–71.

[119] Ibid., and see Esher diary entry, 15 Apr. 1909, Esher Papers, ESHR 2/12.

[120] Hardinge to Nicolson, 30 Apr. 1909, *BD*, ix, doc. 7.

[121] Hardinge to Lowther, 18 May 1909, Lowther Papers, FO 800/193; O'Beirne to Nicolson, n.d. (but late Apr. 1909), Nicolson Papers, FO 800/342.

[122] Hardinge to Nicolson, 12 Apr. 1909, Nicolson Papers, FO 800/342.

en the hand of those in St Petersburgh who preferred closer Russo-German relations. In these circumstances, Hardinge attempted to square the circle. In a long memorandum, written with an eye on the convictions of his political masters, the PUS discussed Britain's options should she be asked to support Russia in a war against Germany and Austria-Hungary.[123] Hardinge's memorandum assumed a number of things: Nicolson's concern that the Russian ministry would be reactionary and pro-German, that Germany would support Austria-Hungary in all circumstances and vice versa, that Germany planned on using her fleet to 'obtain a position of predominance in Europe', and that the combination of France and Russia was at present too weak to run the risk of war with the Central Powers. In any European crisis, Hardinge believed that Russia would have to come to terms with the Central Powers and that France, abandoned by Russia, would seek a similar accommodation.

The clear implication was that Britain held the balance and that she should throw her weight behind the Franco-Russian grouping. However, in a politic fashion Hardinge noted that Russia's government was too reactionary for the British public to accept an alliance and that the public also was too unaware of Germany's aggressive intentions to accept an Anglo-Russian alliance as an unpleasant necessity. In these circumstances, Britain could either remain isolated or come to terms with Germany. The latter Hardinge termed a 'more serious and more insidious danger', since an agreement by which Britain would remain benevolently neutral in a European conflict involving Germany would allow the latter to consolidate her power in Europe and then turn against Britain. Thus Britain should chose isolation, albeit isolation based upon naval strength. Hardinge added, however, that 'the Russia of the future will be liberal' and that such a Russia would be acceptable in any coalition to counter a German drive for European hegemony. A Russian alliance, however attractive to Nicolson, was relegated to an uncertain morrow.

The British kept their eyes firmly on Stolypin. The latter saw Nicholas II on 5 May as the crisis over the naval staff bill reached its climax.[124] While the Emperor noted his intention to veto the bill, Stolypin was persuaded to stay. At the Foreign Office, Mallet viewed the result of this and the Bosnian imbroglio as positive: 'As M. Stolypin & M. Isvolsky remain, we have done extremely well out of the recent crisis & our position is a strong one'. With both Nicholas II and Stolypin 'cordially in favour' of maintaining good Anglo-Russian relations, this conclusion was under-

---

[123] 'Memorandum by Sir Charles Hardinge on the Possibility of War'. The version found in *BD*, v, app. III, is dated [? April 1909], but a slightly different typed version, corrected by Hardinge is dated 4 May 1909 and found in FO 371/733/41171. For Hardinge's shaping his remarks, Hardinge to Nicolson, 12 May 1909, Nicolson Papers, FO 800/342.

[124] Nicolson to Grey, disps. 292 and 293, 7 May 1909, FO 371/729/18277, 18278 and minutes.

standable. The real problem remained the political acceptability of Russia.[125] Nicholas II's forthcoming visit to Cowes continued to draw fire from the Radicals, leading Hardinge to note that the Liberals were 'dreadfully weak kneed about the tail of their supporters'.[126] Nicolson deprecated their complaints, for he argued that political interaction between the two countries was supported strongly by Russian liberals and that to oppose such occurrences was to encourage reaction in Russia. His views were deliberately circulated to the Cabinet to underline this point, and support was given to Pares's efforts to arrange a visit of Duma members to Britain.[127] Grey realized the need to maintain political support for his Russian policy, and was not above commissioning Nicolson to provide reports from Russia showing improvements in civil liberties there and to circulate such reports to the Cabinet.[128]

While all eyes were on the exchange of royal pleasantries at Cowes in early August, the focus of Anglo-Russian relations was moving out of the Balkans and into Persia and Mesopotamia.[129] The 1907 Convention had regularized the position of the British and Russians in Persia, but it had not stabilized the country. The ongoing struggle for supremacy between the Shah, Mohammad Ali, and the Majlis (the Persian parliament) erupted into civil war in mid-1908, with Ali's being forced to abdicate in July 1909. British policy had been cautious, attempting to work with the Russians but at the same time refusing to support the Shah.[130] Grey was required by both parliamentary pressure from his own party and the dictates of his own political beliefs to support the constitutionalist movement in Persia.[131] Thus, early in 1909, much to Izvolskii's annoyance, the British refused to participate in a joint Anglo-Russian loan to Persia until the Shah was willing to grant a constitution.[132] The ongoing Bosnian crisis overshadowed the differences between the two countries over Persia, but Russia's sending of troops to Tabriz in late April to

[125] Nicolson to Grey, disp. 313, 16 May 1909, FO 371/729/19347 and minutes; Nicolson to Hardinge, 19 May 1909, Nicolson Papers, FO 800/337.
[126] Hardinge to Nicolson, 9 June 1909, Nicolson Papers, FO 800/342.
[127] Hardinge to Nicolson, 25 May 1909, Tyrrell to Nicolson, 26 May 1909, both Nicolson Papers, FO 800/342; Sanderson to Tyrrell, 4 June 1909, H. Montgomery (Grey's précis writer) to Grey, 5 June 1909, both Grey Papers, FO 800/93.
[128] Grey to Nicolson, private tel., 8 June 1909, Grey Papers, FO 800/73; O'Beirne to Grey, disp. 444, 23 July 1909, FO 371/732/28888.
[129] D. McLean, *Britain and Her Buffer State: The Collapse of the Persian Empire, 1890–1914* (London, 1979), 73–105; F. Kazemzadeh, *Russia and Britain in Persia, 1864–1914* (New Haven, 1968), 510–80; S. A. Cohen, *British Policy in Mesopotamia 1903–1914* (London, 1976), 94–195; B. C. Busch, *Britain and the Persian Gulf, 1894–1914* (Berkeley, 1967), 348–83.
[130] I. Klein, 'British Intervention in the Persian Revolution, 1905–9', *HJ* 15 (1972), 731–52; McLean, *Britain and Her Buffer State*, 73–104.
[131] D. McLean, 'English Radicals, Russia, and the Fate of Persia 1907–13', *EHR* 93 (1978), 338–42.
[132] Hardinge to Nicolson, 20 Jan. 1909, Nicolson Papers, FO 800/342; Nicolson to Hardinge, 11 Feb. 1909, Nicolson Papers, FO 800/337.

protect Russian nationals there injected a rancorous element into Anglo-Russian relations.[133] By the beginning of June, Nicolson was promising to give Izvolskii 'no peace' until the Russian troops were withdrawn.[134]

But, the Persian issue was tied up with matters of Imperial defence and power politics. British plans to defend their interests in Persia were posited around uncontested naval control of the Persian Gulf.[135] Linked to this was the issue of strategic railways. There was an Anglo-Russian moratorium on the building of railways in Persia that dated from 1889.[136] Railways posed two threats: to the British, who suspected that the Russians would use the lines to advance militarily, and to the Russians, who feared that British commercial competition in Persia would drive out Russian merchants. However, by the beginning of the century, it became clear that lines were likely to be built into the region with or without British and Russian participation, and this introduced a greater threat: the spectre of German involvement in Mesopotamia and the Gulf region. In 1902, a German consortium gained a concession for a line to Baghdad. To reach its ultimate goal, Basra and the Gulf, the consortium required more money, and the British were asked to participate. Lansdowne favoured joining the Germans, since this would ensure Britain some measure of influence in the project. Opposition in the Cabinet and adverse public opinion thwarted Lansdowne's desire, and the British withdrew from the scheme.[137] When the matter was briefly reconsidered in 1906, the CID concluded that it was not in Britain's best interest that the Baghdad line be built; however, if it were to be constructed, then Britain should attempt to see that the portion of the line from Baghdad to Basra was under either British or international control.[138] This view was reiterated in March 1907 by a committee appointed by Grey to study the matter.[139]

The signing of the Anglo-Russian Convention changed the British view, as co-operation with Russia against Germany in Middle Eastern railway matters became more attractive. A subcommittee of the CID met in March 1908 to consider the entire matter.[140] While the government of India continued to oppose any linking of

---

[133] Nicolson to Hardinge, 11 Mar. 1909, Nicolson Papers, FO 800/337.

[134] Nicolson to Hardinge, 2 June 1909, Nicolson Papers, FO 800/337.

[135] 'The Military Requirements of the Empire as Affected by the Defence of India', Morley, 1 May 1907, Cab 16/2, pp. 15–17.

[136] J. S. Galbraith, 'British Policy on Railways in Persia, 1870–1914', *MES* 25 (1989), 480–505.

[137] R. M. Francis, 'The British Withdrawal from the Baghdad Railway Project in April 1903', *HJ* 16 (1973), 168–78.

[138] Minutes of the 92nd meeting of the CID, 26 July 1906, Cab 2/2.

[139] 'Report [of the Baghdad Railway Committee]', R. P. Maxwell, R. Ritchie, W. H. Clark, W. Tyrrell, Alwyn Parker, 26 Mar. 1907, Cab 37/87/36. The committee's conclusions are discussed in Hardinge to Lowther (British Ambassador, Constantinople), 29 June 1909, Hardinge Papers, vol. 17.

[140] 'Report and Proceedings of a Sub-Committee of the Committee of Imperial Defence on the Baghdad Railway, Southern Persia and the Persian Gulf', Morley, 26 Jan. 1909, Cab 6/4/102D.

Russian lines with British lines on military grounds, the Foreign Office saw the matter in wider terms. As a result, the British suggested to the Russians that the latter build a trans-Persian line from Julfa to Teheran and hence to Mohammerah and the Gulf, the latter portion to be built by the British.[141] Further, the British reiterated the view that they had put forward to the Russians in 1906 and had repeated to the Germans in November 1907: that discussions concerning railway lines should be pursued *à quatre*, that is, among Britain, France, Germany, and Russia, rather than *à deux*.[142] The Russians agreed to the British proposal, but discovered that the British were in favour only of earmarking the routes at present because of the fears of the government of India to contemplate any linkage of systems. With the coming of the Bosnian crisis, the Baghdad railway issue faded into the background.

In July 1909, the matter was raised again. Grey informed the Russian chargé d'affaires that British policy remained unchanged, and pressed the Russians 'to make up their minds . . . with regard to the Baghdad Railway'.[143] This was complicated by Anglo-German relations. In that same month, the Germans offered a naval agreement to the British as the preliminary for a general Anglo-German arrangement.[144] The trade-offs became clear in the course of the autumn of 1909. In the Middle East, the British would abandon their opposition to a rise in the Turkish customs—money which would be used to finance the Baghdad railway—and give up their efforts to obtain a concession for a rival line from the Gulf to Baghdad up the Tigris. In exchange, the Germans would agree to the British having at least a 50 per cent control of the line from Baghdad to the Gulf. But, this Middle Eastern deal was only agreeable to the Germans if the British would accept the wider Anglo-German arrangement, which was based on reciprocal neutrality should either party be involved in a war with a third power or powers.

The British kept the Russians informed about the Baghdad railroad discussions with Germany.[145] Initially, Izvolskii remained indifferent to them, but, when the British appeared to take seriously the German offer for discussions *à deux*, the Russian minister reacted angrily.[146] Grey was conciliatory, and by the beginning of

---

[141] D. W. Spring, 'The Trans-Persian Railway Project and Anglo-Russian Relations, 1909–14', *SEER* 54 (1976), 60–2; Hardinge to Nicolson, 17 Mar. 1908, Hardinge to Nicolson, 1 Apr. 1908; Hardinge to O'Beirne, 22 July 1908, all Hardinge Papers, vol. 13.

[142] 'Memorandum for Communication to M. Isvolski', FO, confidential, 27 Nov. 1906; 'Note of a Private Conversation between Sir Edward Grey and Mr. Haldane on November 14, 1907', FO, 14 Nov. 1907; 'Memorandum respecting the Baghdad Railway', FO, 3 July 1908, all *BD*, vi, docs. 241, 62, 266.

[143] Grey to O'Beirne, 9 July 1909, Grey Papers, FO 800/73.

[144] D. W. Sweet, 'Great Britain and Germany, 1905–11', in Hinsley (ed.), *British Foreign Policy*, 227–33.

[145] Nicolson to Grey, 7 Oct. 1909, Grey Papers, FO 800/73; Hardinge to Nicolson, 12 Oct. 1909, Hardinge Papers, vol. 17.

[146] Nicolson to Grey, 19 Nov. 1909, Grey Papers, FO 800/73.

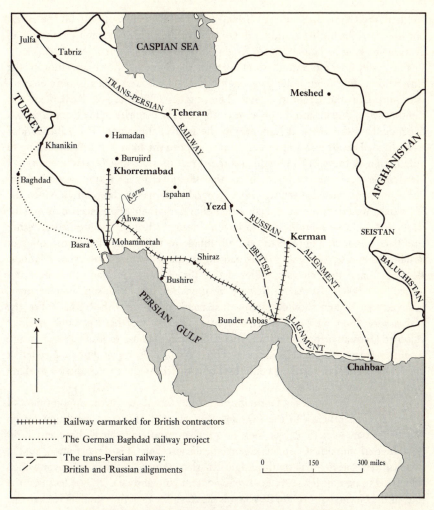

MAP 10.1 Railway projects in Persia and the Gulf

December 1909, Izvolskii was 'quite rational' about the subject: the British hoped that he would be satisfied by an agreement 'earmarking' the future lines connecting the Russian and Indian systems.[147] As always, the fears of the Indian military authorities were the sticking point for the British.[148] Nicolson found this galling,

[147] Nicolson to Hardinge, 1 Dec. 1909, Hardinge Papers, vol. 16; Hardinge to Goschen, 8 Dec. 1909, Hardinge Papers, vol. 17.
[148] Hardinge to Nicolson, 5 Jan. 1910, Nicolson Papers, FO 800/343.

and believed that a 'half-hearted' friendship with Russia would offend the latter, but there was little that could be done.[149] With the British election paralysing all decision-making in January 1910, Anglo-Russian relations remained static.

The result of the election, while not directly changing the composition of the élite who made foreign policy, was significant.[150] Only 275 Liberals were elected, two more than the Unionists' total. The number of Radicals in Parliament was significantly reduced, and the government's working majority in the Commons was dependent on the votes of Labour and the Irish Nationalists. The Liberals also were divided about how to proceed with respect to the House of Lords, leading to a reduction in the party's morale and the threat of a possible second election. In Hardinge's view, this weakness meant that the government would be unlikely to come to terms with Germany, either generally or over naval matters, since the Unionists would never accept such a policy and their acquiescence would be necessary for any *rapprochement* to have meaning.[151] Equally, it meant that other countries might be tempted to take advantage in the realm of foreign policy of Britain's domestic turmoil.[152] This had implications for Anglo-Russian relations. Both Hardinge and Nicolson believed that the ongoing German offers were de-signed to weaken the Anglo-Russian relationship, and Nicolson, in particular, believed that Britain should attempt to strengthen the tie with Russia.[153] For the ambassador, there were two linked concerns. The first was that Russia might draw closer to Germany; the second was that Russia might chose to profit from a future Anglo-German conflict. Hardinge accepted Nicolson's views, but believed that good Anglo-Russian relations could best be ensured by the two countries working closely together in Persia.[154]

In these circumstances, a German protest in March against the appointment of several French officials to the Persian ministry of finance as a condition for an Anglo-Russian loan to Persia took on greater importance than the event itself warranted. 'I think the Germans mean to be disagreeable', Hardinge fumed, 'and to do what they can to break up the Anglo-Russian entente, in the same way in which they tried to demolish the Anglo-French entente in Morocco.'[155] The fact that the tone of the German protest to Russia was much stiffer than the parallel German one

[149] Nicolson to Hardinge, 12 Jan. 1910, Hardinge Papers, vol. 20; Hardinge to Nicolson, 18 Jan. 1910, Nicolson Papers, FO 800/343.

[150] For the results, see N. Blewett, *The Peers, the Parties and the People: The British General Elections of 1910* (Toronto, 1972); G. L. Bernstein, *Liberalism and Liberal Politics in Edwardian England* (London, 1986), 115–18.

[151] Hardinge to Nicolson, 1 Feb. 1910, Nicolson Papers, FO 800/343.

[152] Hardinge to Goschen (British ambassador, Berlin), 15 Mar. 1910, Hardinge Papers, vol. 21.

[153] Nicolson to Hardinge, 9 Feb. 1910, Hardinge Papers, vol. 20.

[154] Hardinge to Nicolson, 15 Feb. 1910, *BD*, ix, pt. 1, doc. 111.

[155] Hardinge to Barclay (British minister, Teheran), 15 Mar. 1910 Hardinge Papers, vol. 21. Grey shared this view; Grey to Nicolson, 18 Mar. 1910, *BD*, ix, pt. 1, doc. 140.

made in London, was seen as having several implications. The first was that Izvolskii could be bluffed; the second was that his position would thus be weakened further, leading to his replacement.[156] Over the next month, the British kept a close eye on Izvolskii and tried to determine the exact reasons both for the German protest and for its peremptory tone.[157] In mid-April, Nicolson had an audience with Nicholas II at which the ambassador emphasized the need for Britain and Russia to work together in Persia.[158]

The matter stood there until late May, at which time Izvolskii proposed that Britain and Russia put forward a common line towards Germany with respect to all railway negotiations.[159] Hardinge was pleased by this, despite noting the practical difficulties involved in tripartite negotiations. But any such negotiations also would be complicated further by changing appointments. At the beginning of June, Hardinge was made viceroy of India and Nicolson, in London for George V's coronation, was selected to replace him as PUS. Thus, it was not until mid-July, when Nicolson returned to Russia to clear up affairs before becoming PUS, that Izvolskii's proposal could have been discussed fully.[160] That it was not was due to Izvolskii's own circumstance. On 21 July, he intimated to Nicolson that he would soon resign as foreign minister and be replaced by Sergei Sazonov, an appointment which Nicholas II confirmed at Nicolson's farewell audience on 5 August.[161] With Nicolson's not taking up his new position until late September, with Sazonov's requiring time to familiarize himself with his new office, and with Morley's resigning as secretary of state for India in mid-September, Anglo-Russian relations came to a standstill.

The last three months of 1910 ended this fugue, largely due to a change in Russian policy. When Sazonov came to office he decided that Russia could not afford to pursue a policy that constantly placed her in opposition to Germany.[162] A

---

[156] Untitled minutes by Mallet and Hardinge, [?] Mar. 1910, Grey Papers, FO 800/93; Hardinge to Nicolson, 15 Mar. 1910, Hardinge Papers, vol. 21.

[157] Nicolson to Hardinge, 23 Mar. 1910, Hardinge Papers, vol. 20; Hardinge to Nicolson, 29 Mar. 1910, Hardinge Papers, vol. 21; Nicolson to Grey, 6 Apr. 1910, Grey Papers, FO 800/73.

[158] Grey to Nicolson, private tel., 13 Apr. 1910, Grey Papers, FO 800/73; Nicolson to Hardinge, 20 Apr. 1910, Hardinge Papers, vol. 20; Hardinge to Nicolson, 26 Apr. 1910, Nicolson Papers, FO 800/343.

[159] O'Beirne to Hardinge, 2 June 1910, Hardinge Papers, vol. 20; Hardinge to O'Beirne, 6 June 1910, Hardinge Papers, vol. 21.

[160] Nicolson to Grey, 13 July 1910, Grey Papers, FO 800/73.

[161] Nicolson to Grey, 21 July 1910; Nicolson to Grey, private and confidential tel., 5 Aug. 1910, both Grey Papers, FO 800/73.

[162] I. I. Astafev, *Russko-germanskie diplomaticheskie otnosheniia 1905–11 gg. (ot portsmutskogo mira do potsdamskogo soglasheniia)* (Moscow, 1972), 219–48, esp. 241–2; A. S. Avetian, *Russko-germanskie diplomaticheskie otnosheniia nakanune pervoi mirovoi voiny 1910–1914* (Moscow, 1985), 66–82; Kazemzadeh, *Britain and Russia*, 593–97; J. A. Head, 'Public Opinions and Middle Eastern Railways: The Russo-German Negotiations of 1910–11', *IHR* 6 (1984), 28–47.

meeting at Potsdam of Nicholas II and Wilhelm II and their foreign ministers in November 1910 resulted in a *rapprochement* between the two countries, although a final agreement between them was not signed until August 1911. In it, the quarrel over the Baghdad railway was resolved: Russia would drop her opposition to the Baghdad railway and would agree to connect it to her own Persian line. In exchange, the Germans would neither support Austria-Hungary in any Balkan adventure nor build any railway lines into Persia and the Caucasus.

All this was not revealed to the British. Sazonov disingenuously stated that Germany would not support Austria-Hungary in the Balkans should Vienna ignore Russia's programme for the 'maintenance of the *status quo* in the Balkans and the pacific development of the minor states'.[163] While Nicolson, particularly in light of the ongoing Anglo–German naval discussions, suspected Berlin of attempting to fracture the entente, he was confident that Russia would not abandon Britain.[164] This opinion was shaken in December 1910. While Sir George Buchanan, Nicolson's replacement in St Petersburg, found Sazonov seemingly pro-British, there were undercurrents that were disturbing.[165] When Sazonov showed Buchanan the draft terms of Potsdam as they concerned railway concessions, it was clear at the Foreign Office that the Russians were determined to deal with the Middle Eastern lines 'without paying the slightest attention to our interests'. This sense of abandonment was reinforced by Buchanan's audience with the Tsar and a meeting with Stolypin.[166] Stemming from Potsdam, Buchanan found two beliefs current: that British opposition to the Russian trans-Persian line demonstrated that Russia got nothing out of the Anglo-Russian Convention, and that improved Russo-German relations in the Middle East would promote an Anglo–German naval agreement.

Grey moved quickly to erase this misconception. On 15 December he informed Benckendorff that Britain did not oppose the trans-Persian line, but did have some strategic reservations.[167] As to the Baghdad railway, the British still preferred that any final solution, although bilateral negotiations were acceptable, should be satisfactory to Britain, France, Germany, and Russia. But, with respect to the notion that improved Russo-German relations might lead to an Anglo–German naval understanding, there was indignation at the Foreign Office. Mallet thought it important to inform the Russians of what the last two years of talks, with

[163] Nicolson to Hardinge, 30 Nov. 1910, Hardinge Papers, vol. 92.

[164] Ibid.; Nicolson to Goschen, 26 Oct. and 22 Nov. 1910, both Nicolson Papers, FO 800/334.

[165] Buchanan to Nicolson, 10 Dec. 1910, Nicolson Papers, FO 800/344; Buchanan to Grey, disp. 482, 9 Dec. 1910, *BD*, x, pt. 1, doc. 617; Buchanan to Grey, disp. 483 secret and enclosures, 10 Dec. 1910, *BD*, x, pt. 1, doc. 618 and the minute by Norman.

[166] Grey to Hardinge, 18 Dec. 1910, Hardinge Papers, vol. 92; Buchanan to Grey, disp. 494, 18 Dec. 1910, FO 371/1213/46 and minutes.

[167] Grey to Buchanan, disp. 314 secret, 15 Dec. 1910, *BD*, x, pt. 1, doc. 621.

Germany's demand for British neutrality in a Continental war, suggested were Berlin's true intentions:

We are all anxious to come to an agreement with Germany on this question [the Baghdad railway], but our efforts have been snubbed at Berlin. Germany does not care about agreements of that kind. She has told us what sort of political agreement she wants & her proposals would be far from agreeable to Russia or France &, if accepted by us, would have a very disturbing effect on the balance of Power in Europe.[168]

This, too, was Nicolson's interpretation. Early in 1911, he warned Grey that Germany intended to use Potsdam to 'rearrange the European groupings'.[169]

Unlike his advisers, Grey did not reject the possibility of reaching an accord with Germany. Nor did he feel that Anglo-Russian relations would necessarily suffer from such an occurrence. On 7 January, he told Buchanan that he was 'delighted' that Russia and Germany were now on good terms, 'so long as that it is not allowed to make a breach between her [Russia] and us'.[170] The foreign secretary also stated that Britain would respond positively to German attempts to be 'on good terms', but only if they could be obtained without making a 'barrier between ourselves and Russia, or France'. Although Sazonov responded on 22 January with assurances that the Russian negotiations with Germany in no way implied that Russia's adherence to the entente had weakened, this was not taken at face value in London.[171] While Sazonov's sincerity was not questioned, it was generally felt that he had been overmatched and had conceded too much. However, the British still did not know exactly what had been agreed, and at the end of January 1911, Nicolson could profess that he was 'still very much puzzled to what actually did take place at Potsdam'.[172]

But one thing was clear by early 1911. The great expectations of the Anglo-Russian Convention held in 1907 had not been realized. The record was mixed. In some ways Anglo-Russian relations had improved a good deal, particularly in the aftermath of the Bosnian crisis. A particular instance was India, where the urgency had been removed from concerns about defence. But co-operation was still at arm's length, especially in Persia, and there was little warmth between the two countries. This was not Grey's fault. The foreign secretary was anxious to make Anglo-Russian relations as cordial as possible, but domestic and international circumstances worked against him. At home, Grey faced the unrelenting opposition of the

---

[168] Mallet's minute (n.d.) on Buchanan to Grey, disp. 494, 18 Dec. 1910, FO 371/1213/46.
[169] Nicolson to Grey, untitled memo, 2 Jan. 1911, Grey Papers, FO 800/93.
[170] Grey to Buchanan, 7 Jan. 1911, Grey Papers, FO 800/74.
[171] Buchanan to Grey, private tel., 22 Jan. 1911, Grey Papers, FO 800/74.
[172] Nicolson to Cartwright (British ambassador, Vienna), 23 Jan. 1911, Nicolson Papers, FO 800/347.

Radicals in his own party towards anything suggesting a closer relationship with Russia. Abroad, Grey had to deal with German diplomacy. Here, there were two different, but related issues. The first was Germany's endeavours, alternately threatening and cajoling, to sunder Russia from France and Britain. The second was her attempt, supported in Britain by the Radicals, to induce Britain to agree to naval arms limitation, but always within the context of a general political agreement that would isolate Britain in Europe. And, while Grey could offer Britain's friendship to Russia, he could not force her to accept it. Russia's policy was driven by concerns about security, and Germany could offer Russia at least as much in this regard as could Britain. In 1907, the Russians had seemed to opt for Britain. At Potsdam, they had hedged their bets. The future direction of Anglo-Russian relations was uncertain.

11

Alliance Under Fire, 1911–1914

ANGLO-RUSSIAN relations were strained from the Potsdam conference to the outbreak of war in 1914. The working of the Anglo-Russian Convention in Persia was the most obvious difficulty between the two countries, but it was only a symptom of deeper problems. The British had two concerns about Russia. The first was that, as Russia recovered from the effects of the Russo-Japanese War, the Tsarist state would grow more aggressive in Central Asia. The second was that Russia would gradually dissociate herself from both the Anglo-Russian Convention and the Franco-Russian alliance and reach a *rapprochement* with Germany. Despite these worries, Grey's foreign policy was not driven by a fear of the consequences of Russia's actions. Instead, Grey pursued an even-handed policy of trying to reach acceptable accommodations with all the powers, a policy in which the search for *détente* with Germany was not believed to be antithetical to close Anglo-Russian co-operation.

The first six months of 1911 were a quiet period in Anglo-Russian relations, but a time full of speculation about their nature and the general course of European diplomacy. The British view was that the Russians had 'put their foot in it' at Potsdam.[1] While Sazonov had assured Buchanan subsequently that Russia did not contemplate any rearranging of the European alliance structures, the British were not convinced. Nicolson felt that the Russian was 'completely hypnotized by Berlin', a view also current in Paris.[2] This led to a certain duality in British policy. On the one hand, the British were apprehensive that too-intimate Russo-German relations would cause a collapse of Anglo-Russian amity. On the other, Grey hoped for friendly Russo-German relations as part of his belief that cordial relations were possible throughout Europe. This was a fine line, and the difficulties of it were exemplified by the British attitude in the first half of 1911 towards the ongoing Russo-German negotiations over railway construction in Persia. The British had offered to advance part of the money necessary to build the Russian section of line

[1] Grant Duff diary entry, 20 Jan. 1911, Grant Duff Papers; Chirol to Hardinge, 20 Jan. 1911, Hardinge Papers, vol. 92; Buchanan to Grey, 26 Jan. 1911, Grey Papers, FO 800/74.

[2] Buchanan to Grey, private tel., 22 Jan. 1911, Grey Papers, FO 800/74; Nicolson to Lowther, 6 Feb. 1911; Bertie to Nicolson, 8 Feb. 1911, both Nicolson Papers, FO 800/347.

expressly to prevent the Germans from becoming involved in Persia, but London was also concerned that any collapse of the Russo-German talks would be blamed on Britain.[3] Sazonov's frequent changes of position—he oscillated between contending that Russia would never allow the Germans to participate in Persian railways and stating that Russia could not prevent it—made determining British policy all the more difficult.[4]

Other circumstances also contributed to a growing uncertainty about the commitment of Russia to the Anglo-Russian Convention and to the maintenance of good Anglo-Russian relations. Some were personal, temporary, and relatively unimportant. Grey took a short leave from the Foreign Office in February (Morley acted in his stead) because of the death of his brother. Sazonov was absent from the *Pevcheskii most* (his assistant, A. A. Neratov deputized for him) from March to near the end of 1911 because of illness.[5] As a result, Anglo-Russian relations necessarily marked time. Domestic political events in both countries also intruded. In Britain, in addition to the simmering debate over the powers of the Lords, the Radical members of the Cabinet attacked the naval estimates as being extravagant and overtly anti-German, and insisted on the creation of a Cabinet committee to oversee foreign affairs, especially the arms-limitation negotiations with Berlin.[6] In Russia, Stolypin's grip was shaken when his attempts to introduce local self-government in some portions of the empire created political deadlock, the so-called Western *zemstvo* crisis.[7] As a result, in March Stolypin was reported (wrongly) to have resigned. This, coupled with attacks on Sazonov's foreign policy in the Duma, led the British to fear that both men would be replaced and that the new cabinet would be 'more conservative & consequently more inclined to Berlin'.[8] This uncer-

[3] Nicolson to Buchanan, 17 Jan. 1911, Nicolson Papers, FO 800/347; Buchanan to Nicolson, 8 Feb. 1911, in H. Temperley and G. P. Gooch (eds.), *B[ritish] D[ocuments] on the Origins of the War* 1898–1914*] (11 vols. in 13; London, 1926–38), x, pt. 1, doc. 681 (see *BD* hereafter); Nicolson to Buchanan, 14 Feb. 1911, Nicolson Papers, FO 800/342.

[4] Buchanan to Grey, tel. 39, secret, 16 Feb. 1911, *BD*, x, pt. 1, doc. 690 and minutes; Grant Duff diary entry, 22 Feb. 1911, Grant Duff Papers.

[5] Grey to Crewe, 5 Feb. 1911, Crewe Papers, C/17; Chirol to Hardinge, 10 Feb. 1911, Hardinge Papers, vol. 92; Buchanan to Grey, private tel., 9 Mar. 1911, Grey Papers, FO 800/74; Buchanan to Grey, disp. 6, 21 Mar. 1911, FO 371/1214/10950.

[6] Sanderson to Pares, 29 Jan. 1911, Pares Papers, 61; Chirol to Hardinge, 17 Feb. 1911, Hardinge Papers, vol. 92; Nicolson to Goschen, 28 Feb. 1911, Nicolson Papers, FO 800/347; Nicolson to Hardinge, 2 Mar. 1911, Hardinge Papers, vol. 92; Asquith to the King, 9 Mar. 1911, Asquith Papers, I/6; Hardinge to Bertie, 5 Apr. 1911, Bertie Papers, FO 800/180.

[7] Ia. A. Avrekh, 'Vopros o zapadnom zemstve i bankrotstvo Stolypina', *IZ* 70 (1961), 61–112; E. Chmielewski, 'Stolypin's Last Crisis', *CSS* 3 (1964), 95–126; R. Edelman, *Gentry Politics on the Eve of the Russian Revolution: The Nationalist Party 1907–17* (New Brunswick, NJ, 1980), 116–26; D. M. McDonald, *United Government and Foreign Policy in Russia, 1900–14* (Cambridge, MA., 1992), 161–3; Buchanan to Grey, tel. 59, 20 Mar. 1911, FO 371/1214/10270; Buchanan to Nicolson, 23 Mar. 1911, Nicolson Papers, FO 800/348; Buchanan to Grey, disp. 69, 23 Mar. 1911, FO 371/1214/11048.

[8] Nicolson to Grey, memo, 21 Mar. 1911, Grey Papers, FO 800/93.

tainty contributed to the fear that Germany was on the verge of destroying the existing groupings in Europe to her own advantage.[9]

The Moroccan crisis of 1911 must be set in these circumstances.[10] In April, well before the *Panther* anchored off Agadir, Nicolson was convinced that German diplomacy was determined to 'smash up' the Triple Entente and 'to isolate France as much as possible'.[11] A month later, Bertie feared that the French, believing that British support for France was lukewarm, might give way to the Germans in the same fashion as the Russians had done at Potsdam.[12] Nicolson worried that the continuing naval arms limitation discussions with Germany might land Britain 'in the same difficulties in which Russia found herself after the Potsdam meeting', since their success depended on 'a general political understanding' with Germany to the detriment of the Triple Entente and their failure would lead to German charges that Britain had rejected 'pacific and amicable proposals'.[13] Thus the *Panthersprung* on 1 July seemed to pose a general challenge to Britain's diplomacy and to threaten her position in Europe. Tyrrell summed it up on 21 July: the 'German move' was designed 'to test the Anglo–French *entente*. It should be viewed from that point of view alone!'[14] Tyrrell, who believed that France had pursued a 'stupid and dishonest' policy in Morocco, none the less felt that Britain must give France the same unequivocal support that Germany had given Austria-Hungary over Bosnia in 1909. But Grey found it difficult to convince his Cabinet colleagues of this point. On 19 July, the Cabinet was willing to propose only a conference over Morocco and unwilling to make a German entrance into Morocco a *casus belli*.[15] In the midst of industrial disputes and the Lords crisis, the Cabinet would not contemplate European war over Morocco.[16]

This attitude seemed justified when, during the next several weeks, the Moroccan crisis abated temporarily. Nicolson was 'pleasantly surprised' that Lloyd George and Churchill, hitherto advocates of appeasing Germany, had stood firm during the episode. This looked promising for a foreign policy along the lines

[9] Bertie to Hardinge, 16 Mar. 1911, Bertie Papers, FO 800/174; Goschen (British ambassador, Berlin) to Hardinge, 28 Mar. 1911, Hardinge Papers, vol. 92; Hardinge to Nicolson, 29 Mar. 1911, Nicolson Papers, FO 800/348; Haig (British chief of staff, India) to Kiggell (director of staff duties, WO), 5 Apr. 1911, Kiggell Papers, I/7.

[10] My account of the crisis is based on J-C. Allain, *Agadir 1911: Une crise impérialiste en Europe pour la conquête de Maroc* (Paris, 1976); K. A. Hamilton, *Bertie of Thame: Edwardian Ambassador* (London, 1990), 214–47; M. L. Dockrill, 'British Policy during the Agadir Crisis of 1911', in F. H. Hinsley (ed.), *British Foreign Policy Under Sir Edward Grey* (Cambridge, 1977), 271–87.

[11] Nicolson to Hardinge, 19 Apr. 1911, Hardinge Papers, vol. 92.

[12] Bertie to Nicolson, private and confidential, 14 May 1911, Nicolson Papers, FO 800/348.

[13] Nicolson to Hardinge, 19 May 1911, Hardinge Papers, vol. 92.

[14] Tyrrell to Hardinge, 21 July 1911; Nicolson to Hardinge, 5 July 1911, both Hardinge Papers, vol. 92.

[15] Asquith to the King, 19 July 1911, Asquith Papers I/6.

[16] For the former, Asquith to the King, 11 Aug. 1911, Asquith Papers, I/6.

preferred by the PUS.[17] But there were other, less comforting, occurrences. Prior to the CID meeting called for 23 August to discuss the military ramifications of the crisis, Brigadier-General Sir Henry Wilson, the DMO, told Grey that the latter's 'amazing theory that Russia was a governing factor' in the European military situation was incorrect.[18] While Wilson's opinion was not a disinterested one—that DMO had a known 'perfect obsession' in favour of British intervention on the Continent, an intervention that a powerful Russia would make less necessary—his views could not be discounted totally.[19] Their effect was undoubtedly reinforced at the meeting itself, when Lloyd George was informed of the 'actual comparative military weakness of Russia'.[20] Equally disquieting for advocates of the necessity of good Anglo-Russian relations was the fact that the Russian support for France during the crisis initially seemed lukewarm, causing Nicolson to lament that many now had 'the impression that Russia could not be counted on with absolute certainty to afford any military assistance to her Ally'.[21] Although Russia's subsequent declarations were firm and the crisis ended with the signing of the Franco-German treaty of 4 November 1911, the Moroccan episode suggested that the German challenge to the existing diplomatic order would not necessarily be met by a united, powerful Triple Entente.[22] Stolypin's death on 19 September simply added to the uncertainty concerning the future direction of Russia's foreign policy.

From September until mid-1912, Grey and his foreign policy were under attack.[23] Within the Cabinet, there was a protest against the implications, which the CID meeting of 23 August had highlighted, of the military talks with France.[24] Outside the Cabinet, there was a growing public clamour over Persia. There were

[17] Nicolson to Hardinge, 27 July 1911, Nicolson Papers, FO 800/349; Nicolson to Hardinge, 17 Aug. 1911, Hardinge Papers, vol. 92; B. B. Gilbert, 'Pacifist to Interventionist: David Lloyd George in 1911 and 1914: Was Belgium an Issue?', *HJ* 28 (1985), 863–84.

[18] Wilson diary entry, 9 Aug. 1911, Wilson Papers; 'amazing' was omitted in the published version: see C. E. Callwell, *Field-Marshal Sir Henry Wilson Bart., G.C.B., D.S.O.: His Life and Diaries* (2 vols.; London, 1927), i. 98–9; S. R. Williamson, Jr., *The Politics of Grand Strategy: Britain and France Prepare for War, 1904–14* (pbk. edn.; London, 1990), 187–92; J. Gooch, *The Plans of War: The General Staff and British Military Strategy c.1900–16* (London, 1974), 289–92.

[19] Hankey (assistant secretary, CID) to McKenna (first lord of the admiralty), 15 Aug. 1911, Hankey Papers, HNKY 7/3.

[20] Grant Duff diary entry, 25 Aug. 1911, Grant Duff Papers; 114th meeting of the CID, 23 Aug. 1911, Cab 2/2.

[21] Nicolson to Buchanan, 12 Sept. 1911, Nicolson Papers, FO 800/350; Bertie to Grey, 6 Jan. 1912, Grey Papers, FO 800/53; D. Lieven, *Russia and the Origins of the First World War* (London, 1983), 38.

[22] L. A. Neiman, 'Franko-russkie otnosheniia vo vremia marokkanskogo krizisa 1911 g.', *Frantsuzskii ezhegodnik* (1969), 65–91; Nicolson to Hardinge, 14 Sept. 1911, Nicolson Papers, FO 800/350; Grey to Asquith, 13 Sept. 1911, Asquith Papers, I/13.

[23] J. A. Murray, 'Foreign Policy Debated: Sir Edward Grey and his Critics, 1911–12', in L. P. Wallace and W. C. Askew (eds.), *Power, Public Opinion, and Diplomacy: Essays in Honor of Eber Malcolm Carroll by his Former Students* (Freeport, NY, 1959), 140–71.

[24] Asquith to the King, 2 and 16 Nov. 1911, Asquith Papers, I/6; M. V. Brett and Oliver, Viscount Esher (eds.), *Journals and Letters of Reginald Viscount Esher* (4 vols.; London, 1938), iii. 74.

several foci for this unrest. In the summer of 1911, W. Morgan Shuster, an American appointed by the Persian parliament (the Majlis) to act as Persia's treasurer general in order to reform the country's finances, attempted to hire Major Charles Stokes, the British military attaché in Teheran, as the head of a Persian treasury gendarmerie.[25] The Russian government immediately protested against this move, arguing that it was a violation of the Anglo-Russian Convention. Shuster attempted to swing British public opinion to his side through interviews with *The Times*' correspondent. Embroiled in the Moroccan crisis, and unwilling to threaten good Anglo-Russian relations over a matter as trivial as Stokes' appointment, on 19 August Grey effectively squashed Shuster's plan by forbidding Stokes's resigning to take up the post. While what Nicolson termed the 'wretched question' of Stokes dragged on into October, Grey's action had taken the fire from it.[26]

More serious was the Russian objection to Shuster and his efforts to reform Persian finances. Early in October 1911, Shuster ordered the seizure of the property of a brother of Mohammed Ali (the former Shah and a Russian client).[27] The immediate Russian protest against this and a threat to occupy northern Persia in retaliation raised concern at the Foreign Office, where Nicolson argued that a collapse of the Anglo-Russian understanding would be 'disastrous to our foreign policy'.[28] At the beginning of November there was a brief hope that the Russians had withdrawn their threat as a result of Grey's informing them of the tremendous strain that an occupation would place on good Anglo-Russian relations, but this hope was short-lived.[29] On 11 November, the Russian government renewed its threat against the Majlis.[30]

This crisis came at an unfortunate time for Grey. With his management of foreign policy already under attack from within the Cabinet, the Russian ultimatum increased the clamour for a public discussion of foreign policy.[31] Nicolson expressed his fervent hope that, in order to ease the pressure on the foreign secretary, the Persian imbroglio would be resolved before Grey's statement in the House on 27 November.[32] Nicolson's hope was unfulfilled, but Grey's speech was not de-

---

[25] F. Kazemzadeh, *Russia and Britain in Persia, 1864–1914* (New Haven, 1968), 586–91.

[26] Nicolson to Buchanan, 12 Sept. 1911, Nicolson Papers, FO 800/350.

[27] Kazemzadeh, *Russia and Britain*, 613–15.

[28] Nicolson to Barclay, 24 Oct. 1911; Nicolson to O'Beirne, 25 Oct. 1911, both Nicolson Papers, FO 800/351.

[29] O'Beirne to Nicolson, 2 Nov. 1911, Nicolson Papers, FO 800/351.

[30] Reported a day earlier: O'Beirne to Grey, 10 Nov. 1911, Grey Papers, FO 800/74.

[31] D. McLean, 'English Radicals, Russia, and the Fate of Persia 1907–13', *EHR* 93 (1978), 342–7; Murray, 'Foreign Policy Debated', 144–53; A. J. A. Morris, *Radicalism Against War 1906–14: The Advocacy of Peace and Retrenchment* (Totowa, NJ, 1972), 251–81; K. Robbins, *Sir Edward Grey: A Biography of Lord Grey of Fallodon* (London, 1971), 251–4.

[32] Nicolson to Buchanan; Nicolson to Barclay (British minister, Teheran), 21 Nov. 1911, both Nicolson Papers, FO 800/352.

signed to placate his critics.[33] The thrust of it was that the Moroccan crisis had resulted from Germany's actions and that Britain had 'no intention of swerving from the agreement with Russia' over Persia.[34] While this speech was strongly supported by the bulk of the Unionists (with the notable exception of Curzon), and certainly by the Foreign Office, it failed to placate Grey's Liberal critics outside the Cabinet.[35] Grey took immediate steps to ensure that his speech also was not misinterpreted by the Russians as indicating that Britain was indifferent to Russian actions in Persia.[36] More informally, Tyrrell suggested that Bernard Pares write to his friends in Russia, outlining the British objections to Tsarist policy in Persia.[37] In Cabinet, Grey explained to his colleagues that, while Russia's policy in Persia was 'inconsiderate & tactless', the Russian insistence that Shuster be removed was 'not unreasonable'.[38] This policy satisfied neither Grey's critics nor those, like Nicolson, who wished for closer Anglo-Russian ties, but it reflected what was politically possible and appeared to mollify the Russians.[39]

In fact, there were hints that the Russians wished to expand the nature of the Convention.[40] But events in Persia meant that any reconsideration would have to wait. On 20 December the Majlis accepted the Russian ultimatum, and four days later Shuster was dismissed.[41] But an incident between Russian troops and the local population at Tabriz on 20 December inflamed public opinion both in Russia and Britain.[42] Grey had no intention of changing his Russian policy: he felt that 'if the [Anglo-Russian] Agreement were to go, everything would be worse for us and Persia. So I stake every thing upon pulling the Agreement through all difficulties'.[43] However, public opinion needed to be courted. Here, events were fortuitous. In January 1912, a group of prominent Englishmen, led by Pares, travelled to Russia to reciprocate the 1909 visit by select members of the Duma. Since the impending

[33] *Parl Debs*, 27 Nov. 1911, 5th ser., 32, 152–65.

[34] Grant Duff diary entry, 1 Dec. 1911, Grant Duff Papers.

[35] A. J. A. Morris, *The Scaremongers: The Advocacy of War and Rearmament 1896–1914* (London, 1984), 302–5; Esher to O. M. B., 28 Nov. 1911, in Brett and Esher (eds.) *Journals and Letters of Viscount Esher*, iii. 74–5; Nicolson to Stamfordham, 29 Nov. 1911 and Nicolson to Goschen, 5 Dec. 1912, both Nicolson Papers, FO 800/352; Chirol to Hardinge, 6 Dec. 1912, Hardinge Papers, vol. 92.

[36] Grey to Benckendorff, 1 Dec. 1911; Grey to Buchanan, private tel., 2 Dec. 1911; Buchanan to Grey, 4 Dec. 1912. all Grey Papers, FO 800/74; Nicolson to Buchanan, 5 Dec. 1911, *BD*, x, pt. 1, doc. 898.

[37] Pares to Nicolson, 5 Dec. 1911, Nicolson Papers, FO 800/352.

[38] Asquith to the King, 8 Dec. 1912, Asquith Papers, I/6.

[39] Buchanan to Grey, private tel., 12 Dec. 1911, Grey Papers, FO 800/74; Kazemzadeh, *Russia and Britain*, 636–8.

[40] Buchanan to Grey, 28 Dec. 1911, Grey Papers, FO 800/74.

[41] Kazemzadeh, *Russia and Britain*, 642–4.

[42] Buchanan to Grey, 28 Dec. 1911 and reply, 2 Jan. 1912, Grey Papers, FO 800/74; Chirol to Hardinge, 28 Dec. 1911, Hardinge Papers, vol. 92.

[43] Grey to Hardinge, 28 Jan. 1912, Grey Papers, FO 800/94.

visit had attracted great attention in Russia, and in the hope of improving public relations between the two countries, much care was taken with selecting the delegation.[44] What Hardinge termed the 'pilgrimage of love' turned out to be 'an unqualified success from start to finish'.[45] In fact, Buchanan reported from St Petersburg that it had 'served to create a friendly feeling towards England such as has never before existed in this country'.[46] Coincidentally, January saw the publication of the first 'Russian Number' of *The Times*, a special issue devoted to promoting an awareness of Russia in Britain. Its 'entirely enthusiastic' reception in Russia promised to help offset the Russian belief that the Anglo-Russian Convention operated to Russia's detriment in Persia.[47]

But these favourable occurrences only helped to balance the ongoing assault on Grey's policy. The public fulminations of the Persia Committee led Buchanan to note that 'it is useless for me to go on trying to win the confidence and friendship of the Russians, if all my work is to be undone by speeches such as [those made by] Arthur Ponsonby and his friends'.[48] Buchanan's task was not eased by Shuster, who, fresh from his dismissal in Persia, spoke in England at the end of January 1912 denouncing Russia's policy in Persia.[49] Nicolson might feel that the agitation against Grey's Russian policy was 'largely based upon ignorance', an opinion shared by some junior diplomats, but such opposition remained a political fact of life.[50] And, in combination with the attacks on Grey's handling of British policy towards Germany, it meant that the foreign secretary had at least to appear to assuage his critics. This was in part accomplished by sending Lord Haldane to Berlin to carry on the informal negotiations on naval arms limitation begun by Albert Ballin and Sir Ernest Cassel, respectively the head of the Hamburg-Amerika Shipping Line and a prominent British banker.[51] Opening negotiations with Berlin, particularly by such informal means, had its opponents: Sir Edward Goschen, the

[44] Nicolson to Hardinge, 20 Dec. 1911, Nicolson Papers, FO 800/352; Buchanan to Grey, 28 Dec. 1911, Grey Papers, FO 800/74; Chirol to Hardinge, 28 Dec. 1911, Hardinge Papers, vol. 92; Asquith to Grey, 3 Jan. 1912, Grey Papers, FO 800/100.

[45] Hardinge to Chirol, 24 Jan. 1912, Hardinge Papers, vol. 92; Buchanan to Grey, disp. 31, 31 Jan. 1912, FO 371/1465/5071.

[46] Buchanan to Nicolson, 8 Feb. 1912, Nicolson Papers, FO 800/353.

[47] Wilton to Northcliffe (owner of *The Times*), Northcliffe Papers, Add MSS 62253; Tyrrell to Chirol, 31 Jan. 1912, Grey Papers, FO 800/106.

[48] Buchanan to Nicolson, 24 Jan. 1912, Nicolson Papers, FO 800/353.

[49] Nicolson to Buchanan, 30 Jan. 1912, Nicolson Papers, FO 800/353.

[50] Nicolson to Buchanan, 17 Jan. 1912, Nicolson Papers, FO 800/353; E. Howard (British consul-general, Berne) to his brother, 1 Feb. 1912, Howard Papers, DHW 4/Family/13.

[51] R. T. B. Langhorne, 'Great Britain and Germany, 1911–1914', in Hinsley (eds.), *British Foreign Policy*, 288–314; Asquith to the King, 3 Feb. 1912, Asquith Papers, I/6; S. E. Koss, *Lord Haldane: Scapegoat for Liberalism* (New York, 1969), 71–94; L. Cecil, *Albert Ballin: Business and Politics and Imperial Germany 1888–1918* (Princeton, 1967), 182–90.

British ambassador to Berlin, noted that doing so 'makes me sick: and Nico [Nicolson] more so'.[52]

Grey continued, however, simultaneously to work towards better Anglo–Russian relations. First, he accepted Sanderson's advice that a Blue Book on Persian affairs would help to disarm his domestic critics.[53] Second, he adopted Buchanan's suggestion that King George V thank Nicholas II personally for the hospitality offered the Pares' delegation and that the Foreign Office should utilize the opportunity to open further discussions about Persia.[54] Buchanan, armed with the details of the Haldane mission (in order to assure the Russians that no Anglo–German agreement to their disadvantage was contemplated), had an audience with the Emperor on 23 February.[55] The result was encouraging. Nicholas II spoke strongly in favour of good Anglo–Russian relations, and deprecated German attempts to reform the Turkish armed forces as unfavourable to Russia. Further, he expressed the hope that close co-operation between London and St Petersburg could continue in Persia, but noted that Russia would side with the Slavic states in the Balkans against any Turkish aggression. Mallet and Nicolson were pleased by both the anti-German and pro-British tenor of Nicholas' remarks, especially in the context of the Haldane mission. By March, with 'a complete lull as regards Persia', the Cabinet preoccupied with the coal strike and the Haldane talks not progressing, there was optimism among those who preferred the Anglo–Russian Convention to improved Anglo–German relations.[56]

In April, events moved dramatically. By the middle of the month, the Haldane mission had been judged a failure, but all was not sweetness and light in Anglo–Russian relations. The shelling of a shrine at Meshed by Russian troops on 31 March led to another flurry of British complaints about Russia's activities.[57] As usual, they were met by a mixture of indignation and denial. With Sazonov's own

---

[52] Goschen diary entry, 5 Feb. 1912, in C. H. D. Howard (ed.), *The Diary of Edward Goschen 1900–14* (London, 1980), 259; Bertie to Nicolson, 11 Feb. 1912, Nicolson Papers, FO 800/353; Chirol to Hardinge, 15 Feb. 1912, Hardinge Papers, vol. 92.

[53] Sanderson to Hardinge, 26 Jan. 1912, Hardinge Papers, vol. 92; Buchanan to Grey, private tel. and reply, both 20 Feb. 1912, Grey Papers, FO 800/74; Buchanan to Nicolson, 22 Feb. 1912, Nicolson Papers, FO 800/354.

[54] Buchanan to Nicolson, 8 Feb. 1912, *BD*, ix, pt. 1, doc. 548.

[55] Buchanan to Nicolson, 17 Feb. 1912, private tel.; Nicolson to Buchanan, 18 Feb. 1912, private tel., both *BD*, vi, docs. 519, 520; Buchanan to Grey, disp. 66, secret, 24 Feb. 1912 and minutes, *BD*, ix, pt. 1, doc. 553.

[56] Buchanan to Nicolson, 7 Mar. 1912, Nicolson Papers, FO 800/354; Chirol to Hardinge, 1 and 15 Mar. 1912, Hardinge Papers, vol. 92; Nicolson to Buchanan, 26 Mar. 1912 and Hardinge to Nicolson, 12 Mar. 1912, Nicolson Papers, both FO 800/354; Bertie to Nicolson, 28 Mar. 1912, *BD*, vi, doc. 556; Langhorne, 'Great Britain and Germany', 290–300.

[57] Kazemzadeh, *Russia and Britain*, 664–8; Grey to Buchanan, 3 Apr. 1912, Grey Papers, FO 800/74; Buchanan to Nicolson, 4 Apr. 1912, Nicolson Papers, FO 800/356; Buchanan to Grey, 13 and 18 Apr. 1912, both Grey Papers, FO 800/74.

position under attack by Witte and, in any case, with the Russians becoming rather bored by British protestations, there was no concrete response to the British protests. In its absence, the British fell back upon their general beliefs about the nature of Russian government. London assumed that the problem originated with the lack of control that the Russian government exercised over its consuls in Persia; to think otherwise would have meant both that the Anglo-Russian Convention was incapable of resolving the Persian imbroglio and that the Russian government was not committed to observing the agreement. The first would have vitiated British policy since 1907; the second would run counter to long-standing assumptions about Russia. Nicolson put the view of these who chose to accept Russia's good faith clearly: Russia was 'occasionally a somewhat difficult partner to work with, but we must submit to these little difficulties sooner than permit a dissolution of the partnership'.[58] The reasoning behind this thinking was clear; to abandon the Anglo-Russian Convention would end any British influence on Russian behaviour in Central Asia and also affect the European situation.

The linkage between the two was manifest. On 18 April, in the wake of the Haldane mission, Paul Cambon, the French ambassador to London, approached Nicolson about a tightening of the Anglo-French entente.[59] By the beginning of May, Cambon had expanded on this idea.[60] According to the French ambassador, the Russians had proposed a Russo-French naval convention, and he explained that the French government instead preferred a tripartite naval arrangement involving Britain. This French trial balloon underlined the face that the definition of the entente needed clarification. 'It is clear', Nicolson wrote to Grey about Cambon's proposal, 'that we shall very shortly have to decide our future policy in regard to our relations with France & Russia. It is evident that we shall probably be asked if we intend to take a more active part than hitherto in mutual assistance.' Bertie opined from Paris that Britain had to give some assurances to France about security 'unless we prefer to run the risk of being stranded in splendid isolation'.[61] But Cambon's suggestion was a potential political bombshell, as the events of the previous autumn had shown, and Grey was careful to keep both Asquith and the Cabinet informed of the French proposal.

The proposal also played into the British debate on naval policy.[62] In March 1912, Winston Churchill, the first lord of the admiralty, had suggested that most

[58] Nicolson to Hardinge, 18 Apr. 1912, Hardinge Papers, vol. 92.

[59] J. F. V. Keiger, *France and the Origins of the First World War* (London, 1983), 106–13; Nicolson to Goschen, 23 Apr. 1912, Nicolson Papers, FO 800/355.

[60] Outlined in Nicolson to Grey, confidential, 4 May 1912, Grey Papers, FO 800/94, with minutes by Grey (5 May) and Asquith (6 May), which are referred to below.

[61] Bertie to Nicolson, private and confidential, 9 May 1912, Nicolson Papers, FO 800/356.

[62] K. Neilson, ' "Greatly Exaggerated": The Myth of the Decline of Great Britain before 1914', *IHR* 13 (1991), 702–4.

naval units be withdrawn from the Mediterranean. The strategic arguments about this aside, at the Foreign Office there were strong objections about the political effect of withdrawal.[63] All negative consequences could be avoided, Nicolson argued, if Britain and France had a definite naval agreement that committed France to 'safeguard our interests in the Mediterranean'. Nicolson was so convinced of the need to maintain Britain's Mediterranean strength that he preferred not to represent the Foreign Office at a meeting of the CID in early July if Grey felt otherwise.[64] Such an attitude was part and parcel of Nicolson's long-standing belief in the need for the entente to take on the nature of a formal alliance, and was just as much what Grey wanted to avoid. At the CID, Grey proposed a compromise, wherein Britain's naval (and hence diplomatic) strength in the Mediterranean was maintained without recourse to either greatly increased naval estimates or formal alliance with France.[65] Nicolson fully understood Grey's position and the political reasons for it, but, after the announcement of the Franco-Russian naval convention (signed 16 July), the PUS reiterated that a tripartite agreement would be the best guarantee of Britain's naval position.[66] With his health poor and his advice seemingly unpalatable to Grey, Nicolson departed for six weeks leave at the beginning of August with thoughts of resignation as PUS in his mind.[67]

In July and August, the centres of Anglo-Russian relations were events in Persia and preparations for Sazonov's visit to England in September. Tied into both was debate about the construction of the trans-Persian railway, where Curzon continued to fulminate about the dangers to Indian security, much to the irritation of both the Russians and the Foreign Office.[68] But much more important was the discussion about what position the British should take over Persia generally. By the end of July, Grey was beginning to acknowledge, albeit regretfully, that the restoration of Mohammed Ali might be the only solution to the existing chaos.[69] Sazonov was reported to want both Britain and Russia to have 'a free hand to take what measures we thought best for the protection of our interests in our

    [63] Nicolson to Grey, 6 May 1912 and 'Effect of a British Evacuation of the Mediterranean on Questions of Foreign Policy', Eyre Crowe, 8 May 1912, both Nicolson Papers, FO 800/357.
    [64] Nicolson to Grey, 30 June 1912, Nicolson Papers, FO 800/357.
    [65] Minutes of the 117th meeting of the CID, 4 July 1912, Cab 2/2; Robbins, *Grey*, 261–2.
    [66] Nicolson to Grey, 4 Aug. 1912, Grey Papers, FO 800/94.
    [67] Mallet to Hardinge, 27 July 1912, Hardinge Papers, vol. 92; Nicolson to Grey, 14 Aug. 1912, Grey Papers, FO 800/94.
    [68] D. W. Spring, 'The Trans-Persian Railway Project and Anglo-Russian Relations, 1909–14', *SEER* 54 (1976), 70–1; Chirol to Hardinge, 17 July 1912; Hardinge to Curzon, 12 Aug. 1912, both Hardinge Papers, vol. 92; Buchanan to Nicolson, 27 July 1912 and reply 30 July, both Nicolson Papers, FO 800/358.
    [69] Grey to Buchanan, 27 July 1912, Grey Papers, FO 800/74.

respective spheres of influence'.[70] With Sazonov due in London on 20 September *en route* to Balmoral, Grey needed to determine British policy. 'To make ready for Sazonov', Grey met with Crewe, Asquith, and Morley on 19 September, with the latter predicting that Persia would certainly be a 'terribly awkward corner' for the government.[71] This prediction had two roots. The first came from those like Hardinge who feared an expanded Russian control of northern Persia for its effect on Indian security; the second from Grey's fellow Liberals, some of whom feared that a partition of Persia would 'split the Liberal party'.[72]

Grey certainly hoped to avoid the latter. As he told C. P. Scott, apropos Persia, on the eve of the conversations: 'if there is one thing more than another that I have striven to secure during the last seven years it is that we shall not incur any increase of Imperial liabilities.'[73] Though true, this remark was intended primarily to pacify Liberal opinion. Grey was fully aware that the Anglo-Russian Convention needed overhaul, and that this might involve Britain's taking on responsibility for more of Persia.[74] After three days of talks with Sazonov at Balmoral, Grey was not 'under the illusion that we have solved the Persian difficulty'.[75] In fact, he felt it likely that 'partition is the only alternative to collapse', but argued that 'if so collapse must come first & even then may be preferred to partition'. This was for political reasons, as were Grey's efforts to drive home to Sazonov the impact of Russian actions on British domestic politics.[76] However, Grey did not fail to take note of several points raised by Sazonov that might be used for British advantage in the eventuality that revision of the Anglo-Russian Convention become necessary.[77] But, at the end, while Balmoral had been useful, much remained unresolved, and Crewe's assessment—'*Persia* is really a knot that cannot be untied, do what we will'—was an accurate one.[78]

Nor did Sazonov get the accolades in Russia from his trip that had seemed likely

---

[70] Buchanan to Grey, 8 Aug. 1912, Grey Papers, FO 800/74.

[71] Grey to Crewe, 8 Sept. 1912, Crewe Papers, C/17; Morley to Esher, secret, Esher Papers, ESHR 10/31. Quotations from the latter.

[72] Hardinge to Sanderson, 12 Sept. 1912; Hardinge to Chirol, 26 Sept. 1912, both Hardinge Papers, vol. 92; J. D. Goold, ' "Old Diplomacy": The Diplomatic Career of Lord Hardinge, 1910–22', Ph.D. thesis (Cambridge University, 1976), 47–51; C. P. Scott to Grey, 20 Sept. 1912, Grey Papers, FO 800/111.

[73] Grey to Scott, 21 Sept. 1912, Grey Papers, FO 800/111.

[74] Nicolson to Granville (British counsellor, Berlin), 24 Sept. 1912, Nicolson Papers, FO 800/358.

[75] This and the next quotation from Grey to Nicolson, 27 Sept. 1912, Nicolson Papers, FO 800/358; and see 'Conversations between M. Sazonov and Sir Edward Grey at Balmoral on Tuesday, September 24 and following days', Grey, 25 Sept. 1912, *BD*, ix, pt. 1, doc. 803.

[76] Grey to Crewe, 24 Sept. 1912, Crewe Papers, C/17.

[77] Grey to Crewe, 26 Sept. 1912, Crewe Papers, C/17.

[78] Crewe to Esher, 4 Oct. 1912, Esher Papers, ESHR 10/31.

beforehand.[79] Instead, the worsening Balkan situation that was to culminate in the outbreak of hostilities between the Ottoman Empire and a Bulgar-Greek-Serb-Montenegran coalition on 18 October, led to attacks on Sazonov and speculation that he would be replaced by Witte.[80] The foreign minister was chastised both for not getting a revision of the Anglo-Russian Convention and for not finding a solution to the Balkan puzzle while in Britain.[81] Britain was portrayed as being pro-Turkish for the sake of the peace of Moslem India. Faced with a barrage of complaint and a public outburst of pan-Slav fervour, Sazonov immediately placed Russian support behind the coalition and began to lobby for support from France and Britain.[82] The British appreciated his circumstances, although Grey was quite aware that the policy that Sazonov now espoused in Russia was not what he had advocated at Balmoral.[83] In addition to a certain mild amusement about this, in British eyes (and quite accurately) Russia had been the driving force behind the Serbo-Bulgar alliance, which was felt to have been the catalyst for the war.[84] However, Sazonov's veiled threat that a failure of Britain and France to support Russia would lead to the collapse of the Triple Entente, struck a chord in London.[85]

The crisis offered Nicolson yet another opportunity to trumpet the value of the Anglo-Russian understanding and the need both to maintain and, preferably, to enhance it. While he had little sympathy for Sazonov's predicament, the PUS observed to Buchanan that a 'serious breach' with Russia would be 'most disastrous'.[86] 'I do not disguise from myself', the PUS went on, 'that this understanding [with Russia] is of more vital interest to us than it is to Russia.' In support of this, he trotted out the familiar arguments: first, that, without restraints and security provided by the Convention, Russia could do what she liked in Central Asia and the Far East to Britain's detriment; second, that Britain's policy in Europe of supporting France against Germany would not be sustainable without Russia. Grey, how-

[79] Cf. Buchanan to Grey, disp. 290, 26 Sept. 1912, FO 371/1471/40862 and Buchanan to Grey, 3 Oct. 1912, tel. 350, *BD*, ix, pt. 1, doc. 775; Buchanan to Grey, disp. 299, 6 Oct. 1912, FO 371/1470/42418.

[80] A. Rossos, *Russia and the Balkans: Inter-Balkan Rivalries and Russian Foreign Policy 1908–1914* (Toronto, 1981), 33–69; Buchanan to Nicolson, 17 Oct. 1912, Nicolson Papers, FO 800/359.

[81] Buchanan to Grey, disp. 301, 9 Oct. 1912, *BD*, ix, pt. 1, doc. 811 and minutes.

[82] Buchanan to Grey, private and secret tel., 22 Oct. 1912, Grey Papers, FO 800/74; Bax-Ironside (British minister, Sofia) to Nicolson, 17 Oct. 1912, Nicolson Papers, FO 800/359.

[83] Grey to Buchanan, 21 Oct. 1912, Grey Papers, FO 800/74.

[84] Nicolson to Hardinge, 18 Apr. 1912; Nicolson to Lowther (British ambassador, Constantinople), 29 Apr. 1912; O'Beirne to Nicolson, 16 May 1912, all Nicolson Papers, FO 800/355; Cartwright (British ambassador, Vienna) to Nicolson, 4 July 1912; O'Beirne to Nicolson, 11 July 1912, both Nicolson Papers, FO 800/357; E. C. Thaden, *Russia and the Balkan Alliance of 1912* (University Park, PA, 1965), 58–98.

[85] Buchanan to Grey, private and secret tel., 22 Oct. 1912, Grey Papers, FO 800/74.

[86] Nicolson to Buchanan, 22 Oct. 1912, *BD*, ix, pt. 2, doc. 57.

ever, reacted cautiously. Instead of offering Sazonov unconditional support, the foreign secretary supported the idea of mediation and reform, a response that seemed to satisfy Sazonov, if not the Russian public.[87]

What Grey preferred in the Balkan struggle was to play the honest broker and help arrange a negotiated settlement.[88] To achieve this aim, Grey wished to work closely with Germany, no doubt to avoid another Bosnian crisis.[89] However, he was careful to ensure that Russian interests were given full consideration. This was particularly important in regard to the fate of Constantinople. On 2 November, Sazonov informed Grey that 'Constantinople & district . . . must either remain Turkish [or] become Russian and that Russia would regard any attempt made by another Power to take permanent possession of them as a casus belli'.[90] Grey promptly replied that Britain stood by her position of 1908, despite Bertie's belief that the French hoped that London would 'put the skids on the Russian coach' as regards to war aims.[91] War aims also concerned the British Cabinet. Serbia's demand for an Adriatic port raised concerns about a possible war between the Triple Alliance and Russia: the Cabinet wished Grey to council both St Petersburg and Berlin to avoid discussions of such aims until the cessation of hostilities.[92]

With this political reality in mind, Grey's policy was to call upon the powers to reach a settlement, at the same time as trying to ensure that this did not lead to a collapse of the Anglo-Russian Convention. This became more difficult in mid-November, as Russia's policy became more pro-Serbian, and as both Russia and Austria-Hungary made ominous military preparations.[93] Sazonov's inquiry as to what Britain's action would be in the case of a war between Russia and Austria-Hungary, thus resulted in Grey's response being 'naturally and necessarily . . . the evasive one'.[94] For Nicolson, the likely result of this was that many in Russia would question the value of the Convention and that Sazonov could conveniently blame any future Russian backdown on Britain's lack of support.[95]

[87] Grey to Buchanan, private tel., 23 Oct. 1912; Buchanan to Grey, private tel., 24 Oct. 1912, both Grey Papers, FO 800/74; Buchanan to Grey, disp. 322, 30 Oct. 1912, *BD*, ix, pt. 2, doc. 78; Buchanan to Nicolson, 31 Oct. 1912, Nicolson Papers, FO 800/359.

[88] Robbins, *Grey*, 264–9; R. J. Crampton, 'The Balkans, 1909–14', in Hinsley (ed.), *British Foreign Policy*, 256–70.

[89] R. J. Crampton, *The Hollow Detente: Anglo-German Relations in the Balkans 1911–1914* (London, 1979), 55–74.

[90] Buchanan to Grey, private tel., 2 Nov. 1912, Grey Papers, FO 800/74.

[91] Crampton, 'The Balkans', 260; Bertie to Grey, 7 Nov. 1912, Grey Papers, FO 800/53.

[92] Asquith to the King, 9 Nov. 1912, Asquith Papers, I/6.

[93] McDonald, *United Government and Foreign Policy*, 184–7; A. V. Ignatev, *Russko-angliiskie otnosheniia nakanune pervoi mirovoi voiny (1908–14 gg)* (Moscow, 1962), 151–5; S. R. Williamson, Jr., *Austria-Hungary and the Origins of the First World War* (London, 1991), 132–3.

[94] Nicolson to Buchanan, 19 Nov. 1912, *BD*, ix, pt. 2, doc. 238.

[95] Nicolson to Goschen, 19 Nov. 1912, Nicolson Papers, FO 800/360; Nicolson to Hardinge, 21 Nov. 1912, Hardinge Papers, vol. 92.

At the end of November, Russian pressure on Britain for support diminished. This was the result of a quarrel between Sazonov and Kokovtsov on the one hand and the Russian minister of war, V. A. Sukhomlinov on the other, with the latter favouring a Russian mobilization and the former pair opposing it.[96] Nicholas II's decision to support his civilian ministers took some of the fire out of the situation. This was short-lived. On 2 December, the German chancellor, Theodore von Bethmann Hollweg, spoke to the Reichstag affirming that Germany would support Austria-Hungary in a war with Russia.[97] While this was received with surprising calm in Russia, in Britain it was regarded as a repeat of the German action of March 1909.[98] The British response was firm: Grey informed Lichnowsky, the German ambassador to London, that Russia would not give way and Haldane informed the Germans that British neutrality in a war of aggression was not likely.[99] While this provoked the Kaiser's fury and led to the famous 'war council' of 8 December, the official German response was to continue to support Grey's call for an international settlement.

The way to that settlement began on 17 December, with the initial meeting of the ambassadors in London, and culminated in the signing of the Treaty of London on 30 May 1913. Grey's efforts to ensure a fair settlement enhanced his reputation, and brought an end to much of the Radicals' criticism that had dogged his diplomacy in the previous two years.[100] When this was combined with the success of the ongoing Anglo-German negotiations about Portuguese colonies, it appeared as if Grey had succeeded in squaring the circle by being on good terms with all of the Great Powers simultaneously.[101] However, the path between the opening of the Conference and the signing of the Treaty was a tortuous one. For Anglo-Russian relations, the key aspect was Russia's championing of both Serbia's efforts to obtain access to the Adriatic and Montenegro's attempt to get the town of Scutari. These points were particularly important, for, when Russia had agreed to submit the

[96] McDonald, *United Government and Foreign Policy*, 185–6.
[97] The following is based on I. Geiss, *German Foreign Policy 1871–1914* (London, 1976), 141–5; Crampton, *Hollow Detente*, 73–4.
[98] Buchanan to Grey, private tel., 5 Dec. 1912; Buchanan to Nicolson, private tel., 7 Dec. 1912, both Grey Papers, FO 800/74.
[99] See K. Wilson, 'The British *Démarche* of 3 and 4 December 1912: H. A. Gwynne's Note on Britain, Russia and the First Balkan War', *SEER* 62 (1984), 552–9 for the event. I have found no evidence that substantiates the interpretation that Wilson puts on the actions of Grey and Haldane.
[100] Morris, *Radicalism Against War*, 355–9.
[101] The discussions with Germany over the Portuguese colonies soon soured, R. T. B. Langhorne, 'Anglo-German Negotiations Concerning the Future of the Portuguese Colonies', *HJ* 16 (1973), 361–87 and J. D. Vincent-Smith, 'The Anglo-German Negotiations over the Portuguese Colonies in Africa, 1911–14', *HJ* 17 (1974), 620–9, despite the success in negotiating equitable territorial allotments, P. H. S. Hatton, 'Harcourt and Solf: the Search for an Anglo-German Understanding thruogh Africa, 1912–14', *ESR* 1 (1971), 123–45.

former issue to the London Conference, there had been an outbreak of public indignation in St Petersburg claiming that Sazonov's diplomacy was ineffectual.[102] The British had to be careful not to push Russia too hard.[103]

As the Conference struggled to find solutions in the face of possible hostility between Russia and Austria-Hungary, there was considerable discussion over the future of Anglo-Russian relations. This centred around the difference of opinion between Tyrrell and Nicolson as to how firm Britain could be with Russia. In April 1913, Tyrrell believed that improved relations with Germany meant that Britain could 'therefore take a somewhat firmer line with Russia without compromising the *Entente*'.[104] For Tyrrell, it was Russia's 'cynical selfishness' with respect to Persia that most threatened good Anglo-Russian relations. Nicolson saw the matter differently. Always an adherent of good relations with Russia, the PUS's views of the necessity for them had been strengthened early in 1913 by persistent reports of Russia's increased military strength.[105] Nicolson and Hardinge both remembered the endless problems that had occurred with Russia before the signing of the Convention, and viewed the latter as the best, although imperfect, means of maintaining good relations between the two states.[106] And Nicolson was certain that Germany was playing a double game: attempting to improve relations with both Britain and Russia in the hope of driving a wedge between them, all the while increasing Germany's own military strength.[107] This difference of views did not mean that British policy was hopelessly divided, for it is easy to overstate the differences between Tyrrell and Nicolson. Both advocated maintaining the entente with Russia. Tyrrell simply wished to put the British concerns about Persia to Russia both more firmly and more frankly and did not want, as he believed Nicolson desired, to 'leave the Russians to pipe the tune and us to dance to it'.[108] While Grey might have found Tyrrell's advice, which promised a greater latitude for British diplomacy, more congenial, the foreign secretary certainly had no intention of ending the Anglo-Russian Convention. Instead, Grey spent a fortnight in

---

[102] Buchanan to Nicolson, 24 Dec. 1912, Nicolson Papers, FO 800/361.

[103] Buchanan to Nicolson, 28 Dec. 1912, *BD*, ix, pt. 2, doc. 303; Nicolson's minute (n.d.) on Buchanan to Grey, tel. 1, 1 Jan. 1913, *BD*, ix, pt. 2, doc. 431.

[104] Chirol to Hardinge, 18 Apr. 1913, Hardinge Papers, vol. 93. This letter significantly modifies Chirol's earlier (10 Apr. in ibid.) report to Hardinge of Tyrrell's position.

[105] Nicolson to Goschen, 21 Jan. 1913, Nicolson Papers, FO 800/362; Nicolson to Grey, memo, 24 Feb. 1913, *BD*, ix, pt. 2, doc. 656; Nicolson to Goschen, 11 Mar. 1913, Nicolson Papers, FO 800/364; Grant Duff diary entry, 15 Mar. 1913, Grant Duff Papers.

[106] Hardinge to Chirol, 30 Apr. 1913, Hardinge Papers, vol. 93.

[107] Nicolson to Buchanan, 25 Feb. 1913, *BD*, ix, pt. 2, doc. 660; Nicolson to Lowther (British ambassador, Constantinople), 4 Mar. 1913, Lowther Papers, FO 800/193; Nicolson to Goschen, 8 Apr. 1913, Nicolson Papers, FO 800/365.

[108] Chirol to Hardinge, 23 May 1913, Hardinge Papers, vol. 93.

Scotland 'fishing, and enjoying himself with all the zest of a schoolboy', hopeful that the Balkan crisis had been defused.[109]

The approach of a successful conclusion to the London conference allowed Grey to turn his attention to Persia.[110] Since the beginning of 1913, a subcommittee of the CID had been studying a proposal put forward by a Franco-Russo-British consortium, the Société d'Études, for a link between the proposed Russian trans-Persian line and the Indian railway system.[111] The conclusions of the subcommittee underscored a fundamental difference between the Foreign Office and the other departments, particularly the Indian military representatives. The latter were concerned about the strategic implications of the junction and opposed it. The former were concerned that if the British representatives withdrew from the project they would be replaced (possibly by Germans) and, more importantly, that Anglo-Russian relations would deteriorate. The Indian government, to Hardinge's intense irritation, would accept only a Russian line going from Teheran to Bunder Abbas, and would not agree to a linkage from there to Karachi.[112] For the Russians, this option was unacceptable, and they made it clear that only an acceptance of the Société's proposal would indicate that there was any value to the Anglo-Russian Convention. The outbreak of the Second Balkan War on 29 June and the subsequent dealings with the details of its settlement delayed discussion of this impasse until 1914, but it was not surprising that Nicolson noted at the beginning of July 1913 that there were issues in Anglo-Russian relations that 'cause me some little anxiety'.[113]

This was the context in which Tyrrell had advocated taking a firmer line with Russia. His ideas gained some support from Sir George Buchanan in May 1913. While the ambassador was home on leave, he drafted a memorandum dealing with the entire spectrum of Anglo-Russian relations.[114] This memorandum, which was seen by Asquith and discussed by Grey and Crewe with Buchanan, called for Britain to make several things clear to the Russians.[115] First, Grey should inform them that British public opinion was 'not yet ripe' for the connection of railway lines in Persia and would also determine whether Britain would support Russia in a European war against Germany. In order to make the latter possible, the Russians

[109] Sanderson to Hardinge, 25 Apr. 1913, Hardinge Papers, vol. 93; Grey to Nicolson, 16 Apr. 1913, Nicolson Papers, FO 800/365.

[110] Nicolson to Buchanan, 6 May 1913, Nicolson Papers, FO 800/366.

[111] Spring, 'Trans-Persian Railway', 74–8; summarized in 'Quetta-Seistan Railway', Austen Chamberlain (secretary of state for India), 4 Aug. 1916 and 'The Nushki-Seistan Railway. Note by the Secretary', Hankey (secretary, CID), 17 Aug. 1916, Cab 6/4/107-D and 109-D.

[112] Hardinge to Chirol, 12 June 1913; Hardinge to Nicolson 22 July 1913, both Hardinge Papers, vol. 93.

[113] Nicolson to Hardinge, 2 July 1913, Nicolson Papers, FO 800/367.

[114] 'Memorandum by Sir G. Buchanan on Anglo-Russian Relations', 19 May 1913, FO 371/1745/24413.

[115] Grey to Crewe, 20 May 1913 and reply (21 May), Crewe Papers, C/17.

must make things 'easier' for Britain in Persia. That could be achieved by outlining their respective interests in the neutral zone and by letting both countries (within clearly defined limits) take 'such measures as they may deem necessary' in their own zones. More generally in Asia, Russia needed to acknowledge Britain's 'predominant influence' in Tibet, while Britain would make a reciprocal bow to Russia's position in Mongolia. Finally, the 'general character' of the Convention might be broadened by adding that the two governments would consult and might collaborate for their 'respective interests and for the maintenance of European peace'. With Sazonov in favour of 'a secret revision of our agreement' and notwithstanding numerous Anglo-Russian differences, there seemed a good possibility of a redefinition of the Convention.[116]

From July to December 1913, Anglo-Russian relations centred around the debris resulting from the Second Balkan War. For Britain, the preferred policy was to maintain the Ottoman Empire as much as possible, however difficult that might be, for the benefit of British interests.[117] Much of this was achieved by the signing of a series of railway agreements that finally brought an end to, among other things, the vexed question of how near the Gulf German participation in the Baghdad railway should extend, while the Turks also agreed to a delineation of the Turko-Persian frontier.[118] But the Baghdad railway settlement upset both the Russians, who feared that any German penetration into the Gulf would necessarily affect Russian trade adversely, and Hardinge, who saw the railway agreements generally as a prelude to the 'partition of Asiatic Turkey' to the detriment of the interests of British India.[119]

These were issues of some import, but did not have the same impact as did the appointment in the autumn of 1913 of Lieutenant-General Otto Liman von Sanders to be commander of both the German military mission in Turkey and the Turkish First Army Corps at Constantinople.[120] Sazonov interpreted the appointment as a direct challenge to the Russian position, and stated that it 'would afford a test of the real value [to Russia] of the Triple Entente'.[121] Grey was not willing to see the matter

---

[116] Buchanan to Nicolson, 26 June 1913, *BD*, ix, pt. 2, doc. 1089.

[117] Asquith to the King, 9 July 1913, Asquith Papers, I/7; J. Heller, *British Policy Towards the Ottoman Empire 1908–14* (London, 1983), 72–111.

[118] M. Kent, 'Constantinople and Asiatic Turkey, 1905–14', in Hinsley (ed.), *British Foreign Policy*, 152–5; D. McLean, 'British Finance and Foreign Policy in Turkey: The Smyrna-Aidin Railway Settlement 1913–14', *HJ* 19 (1976), 521–30; A. Parker to Hardinge, 29 July 1913, Hardinge Papers, vol. 93.

[119] A. Bodger, 'Russia and the End of the Ottoman Empire', in M. Kent (ed.), *The Great Powers and the End of the Ottoman Empire* (London, 1984), 90–2; Hardinge to Chirol, 4 Sept. 1913, Hardinge Papers, vol. 93.

[120] U. Trumpener, 'Liman von Sanders and the German-Ottoman alliance', *JCH* 1 (1966), 179–92; Heller, *British Policy*, 111–16; Bodger, 'Russia and the End of the Ottoman Empire', 94–5.

[121] O'Beirne to Grey, disp. 375, 9 Dec. 1913, *BD*, x, pt. 1, doc. 412.

in this light, arguing that the appointment was not worthy of being a *casus belli*.[122] Despite this, Buchanan was very concerned early in January 1914 that, if Sazonov was unable to get the Germans to agree to a face-saving compromise, the Russian foreign minister would force the issue.[123] In that case, if the British response was that no support would be given Russia, 'the Anglo-Russian understanding would be a thing of the past'. The Russian belief that the von Sanders mission was an attempt to get a 'veiled protectorate' over the Straits imbued the matter with more significance than its appearance suggested. However, the British stood firm, and a compromise settlement was reached.

During January, Sazonov returned to the attack about the trans-Persian line. This raised again the matter of the nature of Anglo-Russian Convention, the topic that dominated Anglo-Russian relations until the outbreak of war.[124] The crux of the matter was whether the Anglo-Russian Convention was merely what had been negotiated in 1907—a limited settlement of matters in Central Asia and a general lessening of tension between traditional enemies—or the first step toward a full-scale alliance. Opinions varied. Nicolson preferred the latter, but realized that domestic political realities precluded any such arrangement.[125] Hardinge supported the PUS, but was unwilling to see India's interests compromised over matters concerning either defence or the position of Tibet.[126] Tyrrell and Eyre Crowe, who had taken over the Eastern Department late in 1913 when Mallet had become British ambassador to Constantinople, wanted to maintain the Convention, but wished to take a firmer line with Russia, particularly over Persia.

Sazonov found the endless suspicions of the Indian government about the trans-Persian line and the reticence of Britain to support Russia generally galling. Early in February, his displeasure boiled over in a conversation with Buchanan.[127] Sazonov berated the British for refusing ever to 'take any action in which the Triple Alliance would not join', called for the Triple Entente to be converted into a formal alliance and suggested that if those who opposed the trans-Persian line were always to decide British policy then it would be better to admit it and 'wait until Lord Curzon and those who shared his views were dead before reviving the scheme.' Nicolson passed on Sazonov's blast to Grey, and the foreign secretary's response to it made clear the general line of his policy towards Russia.[128] Grey pointed out that,

[122] See Grey's remarks on Crowe's memo (29 Dec. 1913), *BD*, x, pt. 1, doc. 452 and on Nicolson's minute on Buchanan to Grey, disp. 6, 8 Jan. 1914, *BD*, x, pt. 1, doc. 465.

[123] Buchanan to Crowe, 8 Jan. 1914, FO 371/2090/3140.

[124] Spring, 'Trans-Persian Railway', 79–81; Nicolson to Hardinge, 15 Jan. 1914, D. W. Sweet and R. T. B. Langhorne, 'Great Britain and Russia, 1907–14', in Hinsley (ed.), *British Foreign Policy*, 252–5.

[125] Nicolson to Goschen, 10 Feb. 1914, Nicolson Papers, FO 800/372.

[126] Goold, ' "Old Diplomacy" ', 53–7.

[127] Buchanan to Nicolson, 5 Feb. 1914, Nicolson Papers, FO 800/372.

[128] Grey to Buchanan, 11 Feb. 1914, Grey Papers, FO 800/74.

given the strategic objections to the juncture of the trans-Persian and Indian lines, the British position that there 'should at least be certain strategic safeguards as to the route by which the line is to approach the Indian frontier' was a compromise not unreasonably urged upon me'. With respect to Persia generally, Grey noted that he had swallowed Russia's actions in the north because they were consistent with 'the spirit' of the Anglo-Russian Convention, for Russia possessed a predominant position there before 1907. However, the ongoing Russian military occupation and the consequent deterioration of the British position in the south of Persia, made 'public opinion here sensitive'. As to the wider issues of policy, Grey was unwilling to be towed in the Russian wake. Britain would not involve herself in any matter in which 'British interests are not greatly concerned'.

This was firm, but not unfriendly. However, before Buchanan could inform Sazonov of Grey's remarks, domestic Russian politics intruded. In February, Kokovtsov was removed as chairman of the council of ministers and replaced by Goremykin. Despite their differences about policy towards Russia, Crowe and Nicolson were united in their belief that this appointment was a bad one for good Anglo-Russian relations, and Grey was 'very much preoccupied at the internal situation in Russia and the vacillating policy of the Russian Govt in foreign affairs'.[129] This preoccupation was no doubt also fuelled by rumours that Goremykin would both dismiss Sazonov and surround himself with reactionary (and often pro-German) ministers whose influence on Nicholas II would be unfavourable to Britain.[130] The ministerial change was considered likely to presage a more robust Russian foreign policy, and this belief was underlined by the press war that broke out between Germany and Russia in March 1914.[131] The cause of this contretemps was the hostile German reaction to the Russian decision to increase the permanent peacetime strength of the Russian army from 1.3 million men to 1.75 million men, the so-called great programme.[132] The British were well aware of this expansion, and it was widely believed that it marked the complete recovery of Russia's military strength from the post-1905 low.[133]

[129] Memo, Bertie, 16 Feb. 1914, Bertie Papers, FO 800/188; the minutes by Crowe (12 Feb.), Nicolson (n.d.) and Grey (n.d.) on Buchanan to Grey, tel. 46, 11 Feb. 1912, FO 371/2091/6329.

[130] Minute, Lancelot Oliphant (clerk, Eastern Department, FO), 16 Feb. 1914, FO 371/2091/8357; Nicolson to de Bunsen (British ambassador, Vienna), 16 Feb. 1914, Nicolson Papers, FO 800/372; Buchanan to Grey, 18 Feb. 1914, Grey Papers, FO 800/74.

[131] Nicolson to de Bunsen, 2 Mar. 1914, Nicolson Papers, FO 800/373; Goschen to Grey, disp. 95, 6 Mar. 1914, *BD*, x, pt. 2, doc. 518; Buchanan to Grey, tel. 64, 6 Mar. 1914, FO 371/2092/10035; Buchanan to Grey, disp. 67, 11 Mar. 1914, FO 371/2092/11628; Buchanan to Grey, disp. 75, 18 Mar. 1914, *BD*, x, pt. 2, doc. 528.

[132] B. W. Menning, *Bayonets Before Bullets: The Imperial Russian Army, 1861–1914* (Bloomington, IN, 1992), 233–4.

[133] Knox (British military attaché, St Petersburg) to Buchanan, disp. L, 19 Mar. 1914, secret, WO 106/1039 and minutes.

The growth of Russian strength was also a further push towards coming to a solution with respect to the trans-Persian railway matter. On 19 March, an interdepartmental committee met to discuss the matter, in an effort to help end what Nicolson termed Britain's policy of 'drifting rather aimlessly about' with respect to Persia.[134] The new British proposal still did not accept the linkage of the trans-Persian and Indian systems, and the Russians rejected it as a result. By the beginning of April, there were mixed signs of the British about the Russian view of the future of relations between the two countries. Sazonov was complaining of Britain's perpetual distrust of Russia, Witte (supported by a number of prominent German-ophiles) had made public remarks questioning the value of Anglo-Russian friendship and proposing a Russo-German arrangement, but Nicholas II had suggested that Britain and Russia should join together in a defensive alliance.[135] Fortunately for the British (although they were unaware of the fact), Witte's remarks proved to have no weight, for Nicholas II had decided to follow a strong pro-entente policy. This decision was manifested on 17 April, when the French chargé d'affaires in London suggested that, during a forthcoming trip to the French capital, Grey should discuss with the French and Russians 'as to enlarging the scope of the Anglo-Russian understanding either by transforming it into a defensive alliance or by coming to some naval convention'.[136] This idea had been inspired by Sazonov, but there was no doubt that it also found great favour in Paris.[137]

On 23 April, with rumours circulating in the Russian press about the renegotiation of the Anglo-Russian relationship, Grey agreed at Paris to the opening of Anglo-Russian naval talks and to inform Russia of the nature of the Anglo-French discussions concerning naval and military matters.[138] Grey was careful to hedge the agreement with the usual caveats that the talks would commit Britain to nothing in advance: as he informed Bertie, they 'could not amount to very much, but it would be something'. Following the discussions in Paris, Grey repeated this position to Benckendorff, and took the entire matter before the Cabinet on 13 May, where that body 'warmly approved' the foreign secretary's remarks.[139] With agreement in

---

[134] Spring, 'Trans-Persian Railway', 79–80; Nicolson to Buchanan, 24 Mar. 1914, Nicolson Papers, FO 800/373.

[135] Buchanan to Grey, disp. 93, 31 Mar. 1914, FO 371/2092/15087 and minutes; Buchanan to Nicolson, 2 Apr. 1914, Nicolson Papers, FO 800/373; Buchanan to Grey, disp. 100, secret, 3 Apr. 1914, *BD*, x, pt. 2, doc. 537 and minutes; McDonald, *United Government and Foreign Policy*, 199–204.

[136] Untitled memo, secret, Nicolson, 17 Apr. 1914, FO 371/2092/17370 and Grey's undated minute.

[137] Untitled memo, Bertie, 24 Apr. 1914, Bertie Papers, Add MSS 63032.

[138] Nicolson to Buchanan, 21 Apr. 1914, Nicolson Papers, FO 800/373; untitled memo, Bertie, 27 Apr. 1914, Bertie Papers, Add MSS 63032; Buchanan to Grey, disp. 116, 24 Apr. 1914, FO 371/2092/18564; Grey to Bertie, disp. 249, secret, *BD*, x, pt. 2, doc. 541. The following quotation is from the latter.

[139] Grey to Buchanan, 7 May 1914, Grey Papers, FO 800/74; Asquith to the King, 14 May 1914, Asquith Papers, I/7.

principle that the Anglo-Russian naval talks would go forward, Grey turned his attention to Central Asia.

Here the going was not smooth. On 5 May, the British had communicated the details of a draft convention between Britain, China, and Tibet to Sazonov.[140] This agreement effectively changed the Anglo-Russian Convention with respect to Tibet, and Buchanan was charged by Nicolson to 'endeavour to persuade' Sazonov to agree to it. The Russian minister was not impressed: at the end of May, he rejected the tripartite agreement, and warned Britain of Russia's 'predominant position' in the north of Persia.[141] This had been anticipated; earlier in May, Grey had told Crewe that 'the expected but dreaded break down in Persia seemed imminent.[142] Early in June, Buchanan reported that he had 'never seen Sazonov so angry' as about public opinion in Britain and its attitude towards Russia's actions in Persia.[143]

The time had come for a complete examination of the workings of the Anglo-Russian Convention with regard to Persia. On 10 June, Grey spoke to Benckendorff about the matter, and instructed Buchanan to do likewise with Sazonov.[144] Opinions as to the direction of the negotiations were varied. In India, Hardinge was opposed to any change in the Convention or to the neutral zone, but wanted Britain to lease some islands at the mouth of the Persia Gulf.[145] Nicolson was reconciled to the idea of partition, for Persia was unable to establish domestic stability herself and Britain was similarly unable to create calm in the south.[146] The contrast between strong Russian action in the north and weak British action in the south was leading to the neutral zone's moving towards Russia, to Britain's detriment. Crowe's opinion was similar to Nicolson's: the acting head of the Eastern Department was convinced that the Convention was not functioning properly in Persia and that a definite settlement—including the possibility of partition—of the boundaries between the two states was a necessity.[147] Grey, however, had to walk a careful line. Due to a leak, on 11 June he had been forced to answer a question in the House of Commons about the nature of the Anglo-Russian naval talks, and the foreign secretary did not wish to keep the issue in the public eye, lest it inflame his Radical critics, always suspicious of autocratic

[140] Nicolson to Buchanan, 5 May 1914, Nicolson Papers, FO 800/374.
[141] Buchanan to Nicolson, 28 May 1914, Nicolson Papers, FO 800/374 and Morley's minute (15 June).
[142] Grey to Crewe, 11 May 1914, Crewe Papers, C/17.
[143] Buchanan to Nicolson, 11 June 1914, Nicolson Papers, FO 800/374.
[144] Grey to Buchanan, disp. 217, 10 June 1914, *BD*, x, pt. 2 and enclosure.
[145] Hardinge to Chirol, 11 June 1914, Hardinge Papers, vol. 93.
[146] Nicolson to Hardinge, 11 June 1914, Hardinge Papers, vol. 93; Nicolson to Buchanan, 16 June 1914, Nicolson Papers, FO 800/374.
[147] Sweet and Langhorne, 'Great Britain and Russia', 253–5; Crowe to Howard (British minister, Stockholm), 27 June 1914, Howard Papers, DHW 4/Official/18.

Russia.[148] Further, Grey had to consider the ongoing negotiations with China over Tibet, since to sign the proposed agreement without Russia's agreement would 'blow the 1907 [Anglo-Russian] Convention to pieces, and we [Nicolson and Grey] are both of us rather unwilling to take so drastic a measure'.[149]

Despite these problems, Anglo-Russian relations seemed moving forward. On 24 June, Buchanan had an audience with Nicholas II.[150] The tone was friendly. With respect to Persia, the Emperor favoured partition. He also proposed that naval discussions begin immediately, with the hope that they could be completed when Prince Louis of Battenberg, the Tsar's relative and British first sea lord, visited Russia in August.[151] During the audience, Sazonov noted that he would 'like to see the naval question, the Tibetan question and the Persian question all settled together by the beginning of August', a suggestion which Nicholas supported. Clearly it was time to move forward, and on 8 July Grey commissioned Sir George Clerk to draw up a memorandum outlining a British proposal to Russia concerning the future of Persia.[152] While this was going on, Buchanan continued to press Sazonov about Persia. On 9 July the Russian foreign minister suggested that public concern in Britain about Russia's actions in Persia might be allayed by a tripartite agreement between Russia, Britain, and Japan in which each would guarantee the others' Asiatic holdings.[153] This proposal was warmly received by Nicolson, and, before Grey could take it to the Cabinet, repeated by Sazonov on 19 July.[154] A day later, Grey noted that he was 'personally attracted' to Sazonov's proposal and that he would take it to Asquith and the Cabinet, 'as soon as the Parliamentary & Irish situation' gave them time to consider the matter.[155] On 21 July, Clerk submitted his memorandum on Persia, but Balkan events overtook any potential implementation of its recommendations.

The repercussions of the assassination at Sarajevo intruded into Anglo-Russian relations only slowly. During the July crisis, Grey had followed the policy of close collaboration with Germany that had worked so successfully during the first Balkan

[148] 'Sir Edward Grey's Statement in the House of Commons, 11 June 1914', *BD*, x, pt. 2, doc. 548; Goschen to Grey, disp. 215, 23 May 1914, FO 371/2092/23647 and Crowe's minute (28 May); Grey to Buchanan, 10 June 1914, Grey Papers, FO 800/74.

[149] Nicolson to Buchanan, 30 June 1914, Nicolson Papers, FO 800/374; Grey to Crewe, 18 June 1914, Crewe Papers, C/17.

[150] Buchanan to Grey, disp. 192, 25 June 1914, *BD*, x, pt. 2, doc. 553.

[151] See also Battenberg to Nicolson, 23 May 1914, Nicolson Papers, FO 800/374.

[152] The memo is printed in K. Wilson, 'The Struggle for Persia: Sir G. Clerk's Memorandum of 21 July on Anglo-Russian Relations in Persia', *Proceedings of the 1988 International Conference on Middle Eastern Studies*, 290–334.

[153] Buchanan to Nicolson, 9 July 1914, Nicolson Papers, FO 800/375.

[154] Nicolson to Buchanan, 14 July 1914, Nicolson Papers, FO 800/375; Buchanan to Grey, private and secret tel., 19 July 1914, Grey Papers, FO 800/74.

[155] Grey to Buchanan, private tel., 20 July 1914, Grey Papers, FO 800/74.

crisis.[156] It was not until 24 July, when Buchanan informed Grey of Russia's hope that Britain would 'express strong reprobation' at Austria-Hungary's ultimatum to Serbia, that much thought seems to have been given to Russia outside of the negotiations about Persia.[157] Predictably, both Crowe and Nicolson felt that Britain should make a firm stand, the former because 'our interests are tied up with those of France and Russia in this struggle'; the latter because 'our attitude during the crisis will be regarded by Russia as a test'. Not surprisingly, given the fact that discussions of Persia and Central Asia had dominated Anglo-Russian relations for the past six months, Nicolson's view was reiterated by Buchanan, who informed Grey that 'if we fail her [Russia] now we cannot hope to maintain that friendly co-operation with her in Asia that is of such vital importance to us'.[158] These views were repeatedly urged upon Grey during the next ten days, but their impact is uncertain since the foreign secretary remained largely aloof from his advisers at the Foreign Office and the issue of war or peace was decided in the Cabinet.[159] There was some reflection of them, however, when Grey made his dramatic speech in the House of Commons on 3 August, at which time the foreign secretary briefly alluded to the fact that if Britain remained neutral in the war the ententes with France and Russia would be at an end, regardless of the outcome of hostilities.[160]

The impact of Russia in that venue and on the British decision to go to war is a contentious point.[161] On the one hand, Keith Wilson argues that Britain went to war to protect her interests in Asia from the consequences of standing aloof from the war—in short that the maintenance of good Anglo-Russian relations was the determining factor in Grey's advocacy of war. On the other hand, Zara Steiner believes that Grey attempted to pursue an even-handed policy, but in the final

---

[156] Z. Steiner, *Britain and the Origins of the First World War* (London, 1977), 221; M. G. Ekstein and Z. Steiner, 'The Sarajevo Crisis', in Hinsley (ed.), *British Foreign Policy*, 397–410.

[157] Buchanan to Grey, disp. 166, 24 July 1914, *BD*, xi, doc. 101 and the minutes by Crowe and Nicolson. My account of the following ten days follows the outline in Steiner, *Britain and the Origins*, 221–41.

[158] Buchanan to Grey, disp. 169, 25 July 1914, very confidential, *BD*, xi, doc. 125.

[159] Nicolson to Buchanan, 28 July 1914, *BD*, xi, doc. 239; Crowe's minute on Bertie to Grey, tel. 95, 30 July 1914, *BD*, xi, doc. 318; Crowe to Grey, memo, 31 July 1914, Grey Papers, FO 800/94; Nicolson to Grey, memo, 1 Aug. 1914, Grey Papers, FO 800/94; Buchanan to Grey, tel. 202, 2 Aug. 1914, *BD*, xi, doc. 490; Buchanan to Nicolson, 3 Aug. 1914, *BD*, xi, doc. 665. Good recent accounts of the final days of diplomacy can be found in S. J. Valone, ' "There Must Be Some Misunderstanding": Sir Edward Grey's Diplomacy of August 1, 1914', *JBS* 27 (1988), 405–24 and M. Brock, 'Britain Enters the War', in R. J. W. Evans and H. Pogge von Strandmann (eds.), *The Coming of the First World War* (Oxford, 1988), 145–78.

[160] *Parl Debs*, 5th ser., 65, 1809–27.

[161] Cf. Steiner, *Britain and the Origins*, 242–57 and two works by K. Wilson, *The Policy of the Entente: Essays on the Determinants of British Foreign Policy*, 1904–14 (Cambridge, 1985), 74–84, 95–9, 115–20; 'Imperial Interest in the British Decision for War, 1914: The Defence of India in Central Asia', *RIS* 10 (1984), 189–203.

12

Alliance in Action, 1914–1917

BRITISH policy in the war had four main pillars: keeping the coalition intact and functioning smoothly, supplying the Allies with money and arms, maintaining the supremacy of the Royal Navy and its command of the seas, and ensuring Britain a dominant postwar position by winning the peace.[1] Russia was involved to a greater or lesser extent in all four.[2] First, Russia was one of Britain's two (later three) principal allies, and it was always necessary to consider her preferences in all inter-Allied military discussions. Considerations of the Eastern front had a considerable impact on British military planning. Second, due to the unexpected length of the war, Britain had to act as Russia's banker and armourer to an extent never contemplated before 1914. Third, while direct Anglo-Russian naval co-operation was slight, consisting mainly of British submarines acting in the Baltic, Britain had to ship supplies to Russia by sea. This latter activity was often the subject of contention between the two allies, and tied to arguments concerning whether Britain was providing as much in the way of supplies and monies as the Tsarist state required. Finally, Russia was a critical factor when British war aims were considered, for there was a strong belief that Britain must not win the war for the benefit of Petrograd (as St Petersburg became at the outbreak of war). Considerations of the relationship, particularly with respect to defence, between the expected postwar territorial positions of Britain and Russia were an important aspect of British thinking during the war. When discussing the functioning of the Anglo-Russian alliance, each of these pillars needs to be considered separately, but before doing so, there are some general points that require examination.

The expanded nature of the Anglo-Russian relationship during the war, and the exigencies of the war itself, led to an expansion in the membership of the British élite.[3] The experiences that the new members brought to the élite were diverse. Those who became involved in Anglo-Russian relations with respect to finance and

---

[1] These themes are identified by D. French in *The Strategy of the Lloyd George Coalition 1916–18* (forthcoming, Oxford University Press) and his 'The Meaning of Attrition, 1914–16', *EHR* 103 (1988), 386.

[2] K. Neilson, *Strategy and Supply: The Anglo-Russian Alliance 1914–17* (London, 1984) provides a detailed account of the relationship and an extended bibliography.

[3] Neilson, *Strategy and Supply*, 1–42.

supply had no knowledge of Russia beyond that of an ordinary educated Briton. This was not so on the military side. The three men most responsible for policy were Lord Kitchener of Khartoum, the secretary of state for war until his death in June 1916; General Sir William Robertson, the chief of the imperial general staff (CIGS) from December 1915 to March 1918, and General Sir Douglas Haig, the commander-in-chief of the British Expeditionary Force (BEF) from December 1915 to the end of the war. Each had experience of Russia. Kitchener and Haig had each been chief of staff in India, the former from 1902 to 1909; the latter from 1909 to 1911. While in India, Kitchener was a strong opponent of the negotiations for the Anglo-Russian Convention, believing that military, not diplomatic strength was the proper means of defending the subcontinent.[4] Cognizant of Russian strength, during the war Kitchener believed that Petrograd was essential to the Allies' victory, and he shaped his policy accordingly.[5] Before 1914, Haig shared Kitchener's belief in the Russian threat to India, and denigrated Hardinge's 'blind belief' in Russia as a reliable partner to help keep German influence at bay in Persia.[6] During the war, however, Haig paid scant attention to the Eastern front, keeping his gaze firmly on Flanders. Not so Robertson. While working in the intelligence department at the War Office from 1900 to 1907, Robertson had been head of the divisions (Foreign and Indian from 1901 to 1904 and MO 2 from 1904 to 1907) responsible for Russia. As such, he had helped carry out a number of war games, including one contemplating a possible Anglo-Russian conflict.[7] Even in the aftermath of the Russo-Japanese War, MO 2 retained a belief in the capabilities of the Russian army.[8] As CIGS during the war, then, Robertson was quick to appreciate the need to co-ordinate British military efforts with those of Russia and to consider the wider aspects of coalition warfare.

The British also needed to portray Russia as an acceptable ally.[9] A carefully

[4] G. H. Cassar, *Kitchener: Architect of Victory* (London, 1977), 139–41; Morley to Minto, 3 Oct. 1906, Morley Papers, MSS Eur D573/2; Chirol to Lascelles, 2 Oct. 1906, Lascelles Papers, FO 800/13; Chirol to Nicolson, 27 Oct. 1907, Nicolson Papers, FO 800/340.

[5] K. Neilson, 'Kitchener: A Reputation Refurbished?', *CJH* 15 (1980), 207–27.

[6] Haig to Kiggell, 5 Apr. 1911, Kiggell Papers I/8.

[7] Sir W. Robertson, *From Private to Field-Marshal* (London, 1921), 91, 134–6; T. G. Fergusson, *British Military Intelligence, 1870–1914* (London, 1984), 204–6.

[8] 'The Military Resources of the Russian Empire', General Staff, WO, 1907, WO 33/419; cf. P. Towle, 'The Russo-Japanese War and the Defence of India', *Military Affairs*, 44 (1980), 111–17.

[9] The following is based on K. Neilson, ' "Joy Rides"?: British Intelligence and Propaganda in Russia, 1914–17', *HJ* 24 (1981), 885–906; M. L. Sanders, 'Wellington House and British Propaganda during the First World War', *HJ* 18 (1975), 119–46; M. L. Sanders, 'British Film Propaganda in Russia, 1916–18', *Historical Journal of Film, Radio and Television*, 3 (1983), 117–29; D. G. Wright, 'The Great War, Government propaganda and English "Men of Letters" 1914–16', *Literature and History*, 7 (1978), 70–100; M. L. Sanders and P. M. Taylor, *British Propaganda during the First World War, 1914–18* (London, 1982), ch. 3; H. W. Kock, 'Das britische Russlandbild im Spiegel der britischen Propaganden 1914–18', *Zeitschrift für Politik*, 27 (1980), 71–96.

orchestrated campaign to achieve this end was begun in September 1914. Through a judicious combination of subsidized publications, censorship of the news, and the controlled issuance of information, Russia's public image was refurbished. Great emphasis was placed on the endurance and courage of the Russian peasantry, and, by extension, the strength of the Russian army. The advances in Russian parliamentary government since 1906 were given prominence, and the nature of the autocracy played down. It was implied that Russia was moving inevitably down the same road that had led to parliamentary democracy in Britain. To dispel any rumours about 'Cossack outrages', Bernard Pares was sent to Russia by the Foreign Office, and British propaganda films were shown in Russia in 1916 and 1917 in order to convince the Tsarist state of Britain's contribution to the war. At the Foreign Office, any criticisms of Russia's actions with respect to human rights at home and her treatment of Finns and Poles were suppressed.[10] With the voice of the Radicals largely muted by the war, Russia was being remade in the popular, if not the official mind.[11]

I

Ensuring the smooth functioning of the Anglo-Russian alliance was complicated. Until October 1914, all that could be done to ensure co-operation was diplomatic in nature. During August, Sazonov strove to expand the alliance by drawing in the Balkans states and Italy.[12] On 5 September, at Russian insistence, Britain, France, and Russia signed the Pact of London, which guaranteed that no member of the entente would sign a separate peace.[13] In all this, Grey's role was secondary; while the British were enthusiastic about the search for allies, the foreign secretary did not wish to cramp Sazonov's style in a region where Russian power and Russian military successes counted for more than anything Britain could do.[14] In any case, during August and the first half of September, when the fate of France hung in the balance, Anglo-Russian military co-operation was scant.

[10] K. Neilson, '"My Beloved Russians": Sir Arthur Nicolson and Russia, 1906–16', *IHR* 9 (1987), 549.
[11] This prefigured the efforts in the Second World War to portray the Soviet Union as a suitable ally; P. M. H. Bell, *John Bull and the Bear: British Public Opinion, Foreign Policy and the Soviet Union 1941–5* (London, 1990).
[12] C. J. Smith, Jr., *The Russian Struggle for Power, 1914–17* (New York, 1956), 21–42, 135–84; W. W. Gottlieb, *Studies in Secret Diplomacy during the First World War* (London, 1957), 39–48, 66–73; W. A. Renzi, *In the Shadow of the Sword: Italy's Neutrality and Entrance into the Great War, 1914–15* (New York, 1987), 88–97.
[13] D. Stevenson, *The First World War and International Politics* (Oxford, 1988), 110, 118.
[14] Asquith to the King, 11 and 20 Aug. 1914, Asquith Papers I/7; C. J. Lowe and M. L. Dockrill, *The*

After the Marne, however, the British fought on the Western front with one eye on the Eastern campaign. During October, there was concern that Russia might focus her war effort against Austria-Hungary, allowing Germany to attempt to invade Britain with troops brought from the East.[15] While Churchill argued that the Royal Navy could prevent all but a raid, the Cabinet was convinced that the two fronts were 'interdependent', and emphasized the need for full and complete communication between the two allies.[16] The events of November drove home the linked nature of the two theatres. When Turkey entered the war, Grey was quick to reiterate the position, made clear in 1908 and 1912, that Russia had a special claim to Constantinople and the Straits. He did so in order to ensure that Russian forces were not deflected away from the main European theatres and towards the Ottoman empire.[17] The importance of preventing such a move was evident. Sir John French, the commander of the BEF, wrote on 15 November that '[t]he fact is that everything now *depends on Russia*—we can hold on here without much difficulty but are not strong enough . . . to take a vigorous offensive'.[18]

From December 1914 through February 1915, the British looked for a new strategy to win the war.[19] The failure of either the French army or the Russian 'steamroller' to effect a rapid victory meant that Britain had to ensure the stability of the alliance if victory were to be had. With grumblings in Russia about the British fighting to the last drop of Russian blood and rumours of a possible separate peace between Germany and the Tsarist state, the British needed to obtain accurate information about her ally's strength and intentions and to reassure Russia that Britain would provide as much material support as possible.[20] In the last two weeks

Mirage of Power (3 vols; London, 1972), ii. 169–72, 183–6; C. J. Lowe, 'The Failure of British Diplomacy in the Balkans', *CJH* 4 (1969), 77–82.

[15] D. French, *British Strategy and War Aims: 1914–16* (London, 1986), 42–6; Churchill to Grey, 25 Sept. 1914, Grey Papers, FO 800/88; Grey to Buchanan, tel., 4 Oct. 1914, FO 371/2095/55811; minutes of 129th meeting of the CID, 7 Oct. 1914, Cab 2/3; Kitchener to Grey, 15 Oct. 1914, FO 371/2095/59975.

[16] Churchill to Kitchener, 19 Oct. 1914, Kitchener Papers, PRO 30/57/72; Asquith to the King, 22 Oct. 1914, Asquith Papers, I/7; Neilson, *Strategy and Supply*, 48–9. There was later concern about invasion: Hankey to Esher, 20 Nov. 1914, Hankey Papers, HNKY 4/6.

[17] Neilson, *Strategy and Supply*, 49–51; Untitled memo, Bertie, 18 Dec. 1914, Bertie Papers, Add MSS 63035.

[18] French to Stamfordham, 15 Nov. 1914, cited, R. Holmes, *The Little Field-Marshal Sir John French* (London, 1981), 253, original emphasis.

[19] French, *British Strategy*, 56–77.

[20] L. L. Farrar, Jr., *Divide and Conquer: German Attempts to Conclude a Separate Peace, 1914–18* (Boulder, CO, 1978), 9–13; R. Sh. Ganelin, 'Storonniki separatnogo mira s Germaniei v tsarskoi Russii' in E. V. Tarle (ed.), *Problemy istorii mezhdunarodnykh otnoshenii* (Leningrad, 1972), 126–32; Buchanan to Nicolson, 10 Dec. 1914, Nicolson Papers, FO 800/376; Kitchener to Grey, 20 Dec. 1914, Grey Papers, FO 800/102; Grey to Buchanan, tel., 21 Dec. 1914, Grey Papers, FO 800/74.

of December, British military and political figures repeatedly discussed these matters, both inside and outside the newly created War Council.[21]

The strategic discussions of January 1915 reflected the problems of coalition warfare.[22] Kitchener had to balance the desire of both the commander of the BEF, Sir John French, and the French government to have British reinforcements sent to the Continent against his own worries about home defence in the eventuality of a stalemate or a Russian defeat on the Eastern front.[23] This was complicated by two facts: that Kitchener's relations with the French were poor and that Paris suspected both the sincerity of Britain's commitment to the Western front and the extent of Russia's ambitions in the Balkans.[24] The compromise solution was the Dardanelles campaign, which was seen originally as a project with the potential to defeat the Turks, to create a Balkan bloc against the Central Powers and to aid in the opening of the Straits.[25] Two added advantages were that the campaign could be abandoned without any real losses and that it would permit Kitchener to keep his last strategic reserve, the 29th Division, in England to await the outcome of events on the Eastern front.[26] Thus it was not until 10 March, when the Russian front had stabilized, that Kitchener sent the 29th Division to the Mediterranean.

On 1 May, the Central Powers launched a big offensive against the Russians.[27] For the next four months, the Russians retreated. This, and the failure of the British offensive at Neuve Chapelle, forced Kitchener's hand. He believed that a breakthrough against entrenched German positions was unlikely and that it was better to keep back as many British resources as possible in order to assure Britain the dominant voice at the end of the war, but had to commit troops to France in order to prevent the collapse of the coalition.[28] At a conference with the French at Calais on 6 July Kitchener reluctantly agreed to send further troops to France in order to buttress both French and Russian morale. The continued

[21] Neilson, *Strategy and Supply*, 58–62; French, *British Strategy*, 63–8.

[22] In addition to French and Neilson cited in the previous note, W. J. Philpott, 'Kitchener and the 29th Division: A Study in Anglo-French Strategic Relations, 1914–15', *JSS* 16 (1993), 382–8.

[23] Neilson, 'Kitchener', 212–17.

[24] Ibid.; R. Holmes, 'Sir John French and Lord Kitchener', in B. Bond (ed.), *The First World War and British Military History* (Oxford, 1991), 113–39; G. H. Cassar, *The French and the Dardanelles: A Study of Failure in the Conduct of War* (London, 1971), 34–40; D. Dutton, 'The Balkan Campaign and French War Aims in the Great War', *EHR* 94 (1979), 100–1.

[25] The literature is introduced and analysed in E. M. Spiers, 'Gallipoli', in Bond (ed.), *The First World War*, 165–88.

[26] Neilson, 'Kitchener', 214–18; Philpott, 'Kitchener and the 29th Division', 387–92.

[27] N. Stone, *The Eastern Front 1914–17* (London, 1975), 165–93.

[28] The rest of this paragraph is based on French, 'Attrition', 394–5; Philpott, 'Kitchener and the 29th Division', 396–402; Neilson, 'Kitchener', 218–23; R. Williams, 'Lord Kitchener and the Battle of Loos: French Politics and British Strategy in the Summer of 1915', in L. Freedman, P. Hayes, and R. O'Neill (eds.), *War, Strategy, and International Politics: Essays in Honour of Sir Michael Howard* (Oxford, 1992), 126–30; Neilson, *Strategy and Supply*, 94–7.

deterioration of French morale in July and the fall of Warsaw at the beginning of August led Kitchener to tell Asquith on 17 August that no more reinforcements should be sent to the Dardanelles. An offensive in France was 'necessary to relieve pressure on Russia and keep the French Army and people steady'.[29] At the Dardanelles Committee (as the War Council had become) three days later, Kitchener informed his colleagues of the need to support Britain's allies by joining in an offensive in France and that it was necessary to make war 'as we must, and not as we should like to do'.[30]

The failure of the Loos offensive in September meant that the British now had to determine a new policy for 1916. The choices were either a continuation of efforts in the Balkans—at the Dardanelles, Salonika, or elsewhere—or a greater commitment to the Western front. Russia was central to this decision, but it was a different Russia that faced the British. In September, as the Eastern front stabilized, Nicholas II took personal command of the Russian army at the front both to ensure his own position and to effect better co-ordination of the Russian war effort.[31] Nicholas then prorogued the Duma, and followed this with a purge of his liberal ministers, including the minister of agriculture, A. M. Krivoshein, whom the British had hoped would replace Goremykin.[32] Only the retention of Sazonov, whose own dismissal had been rumoured, kept alive British hopes for a liberal Russia in the future.[33]

Despite this, the war needed to be won. Supporters of a Balkan campaign argued that providing supplies to the Russians would allow a Russian force to be despatched to aid the Serbs and act in conjunction with an Anglo-French force operating out of Salonika.[34] Grey also explored the possibility of solving the Mediterranean situation by means of a separate peace with Turkey, but one that would deny Russia Constantinople in the postwar. This was met with predictable Russian hostility, and the idea was dropped.[35] It did, however, spur the Russians into proposing joint military action, of the sort outlined above, in aid of

---

[29] Kitchener to Asquith, draft, 17 Aug. 1915, Kitchener MSS, WO 159/7; Cassar, *French and the Dardanelles*, 163–71; J. K. Tanenbaum, *General Maurice Sarrail 1856–1929: The French Army and Left-Wing Politics* (Chapel Hill, NC, 1974), 53–63.

[30] Meeting of the Dardanelles Committee, 20 Aug. 1915, Cab 42/3/16.

[31] R. Pearson, *The Russian Moderates and the Crisis of Tsarism 1914–17* (London, 1977), 28–64; V. S. Diakin, *Russkaia burzhuaziia i tsarsim v gody pervoi mirovoi voiny* (Leningrad, 1967), 72–127.

[32] Buchanan to Grey, tel., 25 Aug. 1915, FO 371/2455/119748 and minutes; Buchanan to Grey, tel., 1 Oct. 115, FO 371/2454/141732 and minutes.

[33] K. Neilson, 'Wishful Thinking: The Foreign Office and Russia 1907–17', in B. J. C. McKercher and D. J. Moss (eds.), *Shadow and Substance in British Foreign Policy 1895–1939: Memorial Essays Honouring C. J. Lowe* (Edmonton, Alta, 1984), 162–3.

[34] Neilson, *Strategy and Supply*, 116–20.

[35] Grey to Buchanan, private and secret tel., 16 Nov. 1915; Buchanan to Grey, private and secret tel., 17 Nov. 1915 and minutes, both Grey papers, FO 800/75; 'Gallipoli', Balfour, 19 Nov. 1915, Robertson Papers I/9/29.

the Serbs.[36] The French, for internal political reasons also supported a substantial commitment at Salonika, and the combined Allied pressure proved too much for the British.[37] Despite their own belief that Salonika should be abandoned, early in December 1915 the British deferred to the wishes of their allies, and the expeditionary force at Salonika was retained.[38]

The Allied plan for the 1916 campaign was determined at a conference held at Chantilly on 6–8 December 1915.[39] The Russians, feeling that they had borne the brunt of German attacks in 1915, demanded that the Allies agree to come to the aid of any member of the entente that was subjected to a German attack in 1916.[40] Beyond that, it was agreed that the British, Russians, and Italians should engage in preliminary attacks in the West, while a concerted offensive by all the Allies would begin in the summer. Although there were those in Britain who objected to this approach, arguing that a policy of attrition would require so much manpower as to cripple British industries and economic power, arguments concerning the need to maintain the unity of the alliance were decisive.[41]

The German attack at Verdun in February 1916, their own version of attrition, upset the Allied plans.[42] Ironically, the Russians suddenly found themselves called upon to rescue the French. The result was the failed offensive at Lake Narotch in March 1916, followed by a blanket Russian refusal to attempt further large attacks until they felt themselves completely ready.[43] The end of the Russian steamroller meant that the British would have to come to the rescue. Robertson, appointed CIGS in December 1915, argued at the War Committee on 3 May, that Britain could best aid France and Russia by an offensive in the West, and dismissed other venues (the Balkans, the Middle East, and so on) as impracticable.[44] With the distinction between a limited offensive to aid Verdun and a full-scale attack de-

---

[36] Untitled memoradum given to Sir John Hanbury Williams (British representative at *Stavka*—the Russian military headquarters), 22 Nov. 1915, Robertson Papers I/9/33; V. A. Emets, 'Pozitsiia Rossii i ee soiuznikov v voprose o pomoshchi Serbii oseniu 1915 g.', *IZ* 75 (1965), 132–6.

[37] D. Dutton, 'The Union Sacrée and the French cabinet crisis of October 1915', *ESR* 8 (1978), 411–24; Cassar, *French and the Dardanelles*, 231–5; Tanenbaum, *Sarrail*, 80–3.

[38] Meeting of the War Committee, 1 Dec. 1915, Cab 42/6/1; D. Dutton, 'The Calais Conference of December 1915', *HJ* 21 (1978), 143–56; Neilson, *Strategy and Supply*, 121–2, 124–5; Selborne to Balfour, 27 Nov. 1915, Balfour Papers, Add MSS 49708; Balfour to Selborne, 29 Nov. 1915, Selborne Papers 1; Selborne to Kitchener, 2 Dec. 1915, Kitchener Papers, PRO 30/57/80.

[39] French, *British Strategy*, 164–5; Neilson, *Strategy and Supply*, 122–4.

[40] I. I. Rostunov, *Russkii front pervoi mirovoi voiny* (Moscow, 1976), 279–82.

[41] French, 'Attrition', 398–400; K. Grieves, *The Politics of Manpower, 1914–18* (Manchester, 1988), 20–4.

[42] L. L. Farrar, 'Peace Through Exhaustion: German Diplomatic Motivations for the Verdun Campaign', *Revue Internationale d'Histoire Militaire*, 8 (1972–5), 477–94.

[43] Stone, *Eastern Front*, 222–31.

[44] Meeting of the War Committee, 3 May 1916; 'Military assistance for Russia', Robertson, both Cab 42/13/2.

signed to kill the maximum number of Germans blurred by Robertson and Haig, the British moved inexorably towards the Somme.[45] Further, Robertson continued to fend off proposals, both Russian and French, during May and June for attacks in the Balkans, arguing that British efforts must be concentrated on preparing for the joint Allied offensive against Germany in the summer.[46]

The unexpected success of what was originally intended to be a subsidiary Russian offensive against Austria-Hungary (the so-called Brusilov offensive, begun 4 June 1916) and the impact of the Somme offensive had the effect of bringing Rumania into the war on the side of the entente.[47] This widened the Eastern front, created new pressures for an expansion of the Balkan theatre and generated British optimism that, despite a concern that Russia was becoming more reactionary and possibly pro-German, the war could soon be won.[48] Rumania's entry also generated efforts to curtail the sending of more British troops to France. David Lloyd George, the secretary of state for war, who was the principal advocate of finding a way around the strategic deadlock in the West, proposed instead that the Allied forces at Salonika should combine with the Russians and Rumanians for joint attack against Bulgaria.[49] Robertson and Haig both moved to solidify military opinion against such a proposal. With General M. V. Alekseev, the Russian chief of staff, and General J. J. C. Joffre, the French commander, both opposed to a Balkan offensive, the matter collapsed.

But the Salonikan front refused to die. By October, both the Russians and the French, albeit for different reasons, had changed their minds and were pressing for it to be reinforced. For the Russians, it was the military and foreign policy situations that had altered. Rumania's entrance into the war had been rapidly followed by Rumania's military collapse, an event that necessitated an extension of Russia's front and threatened the entire southern flank.[50] Equally, the Russians were concerned that the change of governments in Greece might lead to Russia's having to forego the acquisition of Constantinople. For the French, it was the political reality of having to appear to provide as much support as possible for General Sarrail, the commander of the Salonika front and a darling of the French left.[51] The British were well aware of both these circumstances.[52] The determining factor that led to

[45] French, 'Attrition', 400–2.

[46] Neilson, *Strategy and Supply*, 150–2; French, *British Strategy*, 200–5.

[47] G. E. Torrey, 'Rumania and the Belligerents 1914–16', *JCH* 1 (1966), 171–92; id., 'The Rumanian Campaign of 1916: Its Impact on the Belligerents', *SR* 39 (1980), 27–43.

[48] French, *British Strategy*, 205–11; Grey to Crewe, 22 July 1916 and reply (24 July), both Crewe Papers, C/17; Hardinge to Buchanan, 21 July 1916, Hardinge Papers, vol. 23; Hankey diary entry, 21 Aug. 1916, Hankey Papers, HNKY 1/1.

[49] Neilson, *Strategy and Supply*, 152–6.

[50] Stone, *Eastern Front*, 272–81.

[51] Tanenbaum, *Sarrail*, 128–40.

[52] Meeting of the War Committee, 24 Oct. 1916, Cab 42/22/5.

the British sending an extra division to Salonika was the fact that the Russians insisted on treating Salonika as a 'main theatre'.[53]

Robertson hoped to reverse this decision at the inter-Allied military conference at Chantilly, which opened on 15 November 1916, and to insist instead on the primacy of the Western front for Britain.[54] However, British opinion was divided. Grey was deeply concerned about events in Russia. A report sent him by Major-General G. M. W. Macdonogh, the director of military intelligence (DMI) noted that '[t]he situation in Russia is not such as to inspire confidence', and Nicholas's dismissal of several of his ministers and their replacement by those thought to be pro-German reactionaries was deemed ominous.[55] There were persistent reports from Stockholm that Russia and Germany were discussing a separate peace.[56] Thus, at Chantilly and at Paris, where a parallel conference of Allied politicians was held, Robertson found himself blocked. Although the military leaders decided that the focus for the 1917 campaign should be the main (Eastern and Western) fronts, the political conference decided that the matter should be reconsidered at a meeting of the Allies in Petrograd. Robertson found himself having to fight off an attempt to send him to Russia, an attempt he regarded as a ploy to remove him from the decision-making process in London.[57]

If Robertson were to achieve his aims, they would have to be agreed to at Petrograd. The Petrograd Conference, held from 30 January to 20 February 1917, did not fulfil the CIGS's wish.[58] The focus of the conference was munitions, but its military and political discussions resolved none of the matters that had been discussed at Chantilly. This resulted from the events that had occurred in the interim between the two conferences. First, the fall of the Asquith government at the beginning of December 1916 brought Lloyd George to power.[59] The new prime minister was committed to finding an alternative to the Western front, and his voice could not be ignored. At a conference in Rome in early January, Lloyd George

[53] Robertson to Joffre, 27 Oct. 1916, Haig Papers, 109; Robertson to Haig, 25 Oct. 1916, Haig Papers, 108.

[54] Robertson to Joffre, 27 Oct. 1916 and reply, 3 Nov. 1916, Haig Papers, 109; Robertson to Haig, 4 Nov. 1916, Robertson Papers I/22/88.

[55] 'The Situation in Russia', Macdonogh, 30 Oct. 1916, Macdonogh Papers, WO 106/1511; Hardinge to Bertie, 14 Nov. 1916, Bertie Papers, FO 800/178; Buchanan to Grey, 5 Dec. 1916, Cab 1/21/33; Pearson, *Russian Moderates*, 115–23.

[56] Howard to Hardinge, confidential, 7 Oct. 1916, Howard Papers, DHW 5/6; Howard to Buchanan, 11 Oct. 1916, Howard Papers, DHW 4/Official/8.

[57] Hankey to Robertson, 9 Nov. 1916, Hankey Papers, HNKY 4/8; Hankey to Robertson, 10 Nov. 1916, secret and personal, Hankey Papers, HNKY 6/8. Robertson to Haig, 10 Nov. 1916, Robertson Papers, I/22/89; Haig to Kiggell, Kiggell Papers, II/6.

[58] Neilson, *Strategy and Supply*, 225–48; the proceedings are in 'Procès verbaux, Petrograd', Cab 28/2 IC 16.

[59] J. Turner, *British Politics and the Great War: Coalition and Conflict 1915–18* (New Haven, 1992), 124–51.

pressed for both an increase at Salonika and reinforcements for the Italian front.[60] Second, the replacement of Joffre as French commander-in-chief by General Robert Nivelle resulted in an end to French demands for a Salonika offensive, since Joffre's removal had been based on Nivelle's promise of a decisive victory in France. Third, the Russians, suspicious that the decisions at Chantilly had been designed to throw the brunt of the fighting in 1917 on their shoulders, continued to press for a greater commitment to the Balkans and decided to focus their own military effort against Austria-Hungary.[61] Thus the Conference concluded that the Anglo-French force would act on the defensive at Salonika, that there would be no Russian offensive in Rumania, and that the Nivelle offensive would not be matched by a Russian offensive in the East.[62] The unanimity of Chantilly had broken down, and no new consensus had emerged.

The abdication of Nicholas II less than a month after the close of the Petrograd Conference brought an end to Britain's relationship with Tsarist Russia, and ushered in a new era of relations with the successor Provisional Government. After Nicholas left the throne, the nature of the impact of Russia on British military planning changed. Russia went from being an ally potentially capable of winning the war, to being an ally of dubious value whose very commitment to the Allied cause was suspect. Over the eight months that marked the life span of the Provisional Government, British policy towards Russia was ambivalent. The British attempted to sustain the Provisional Government in the hope that, in the long run, it would be able to field a credible military force on the Eastern front. However, as early as the end of March 1917, the British had decided that any military help from Russia in that year would be slight.[63] As a result, Russia was shunted to a side-track, given consideration in only two circumstances: first, when it appeared that Russia might launch an offensive; second, when it appeared that Russia might collapse totally. Co-operation had become resuscitation.

II

The financial and economic aspects of the Anglo-Russian alliance were as complicated and contentious as were the purely military aspects of the relationship. Prior

---

[60] 'Conclusions of a conference of the Allies, held at the Consulta, Rome on the 5th, 6th and 7th January 1917', n.s., n.d., Cab 28/2 IC 15.

[61] Rostunov, *Russkii front*, 332–8; 'Letter from Lieut. Gen. Dessino to the Chairman of the War Cabinet', K. N. Dessino (Russia's military representative to Britain), 22 Dec. 1916, Cab 17/180; 18th meeting of the War Cabinet, 26 Dec. 1916, Cab 23/1.

[62] V. A. Emets, 'Petrogradskaia konferentsiia 1917 g. i Frantsiia', *IZ* 83 (1969), 23–37.

[63] K. Neilson, 'The Breakup of the Anglo-Russian Alliance: The Question of Supply in 1917', *IHR* 3 (1981), 62–75; L. P. Morris, 'The Russians, the Allies and the War, February–July 1917', *SEER* 50 (1972), 29–48.

to 1914, Britain had no plans to bankroll or to supply Russia. In a war generally felt likely to be short, this would not be necessary; in any case, Britain had no obligation to join the Franco-Russian struggle against the Central Powers.[64] This situation ended in August 1914. By the middle of that month, an inter-Allied body, the Commission Internationale de Ravitaillement (CIR) was set up at the prompting of the French government, in order to co-ordinate the purchase of war *matériel*. On 22 September, the Russians joined the CIR, beginning three years of Anglo-Russian co-operation (and conflict) with respect to supply.[65]

The need for co-operation was manifest. The Russian government was purchasing supplies both in America and in Britain (especially from Vickers), and the result of uncoordinated buying was to drive up prices.[66] This was complicated by the fact that many Russian government departments, particularly the Main Artillery Department of the Ministry of War, refused to work through the CIR, believing it to be corrupt.[67] Inter-Allied finance had its own problems. During the autumn of 1914, the Russians attempted to solve their financial problems by means of large loans from private banks in Britain and the United States.[68] In mid-October, the British lent Russia £20 millions, and negotiations for a further loan of £40 millions began in December. The negotiations were difficult, because the British expected the Russians to borrow the money at a commercial rate, and, in addition, to secure the loan by shipping gold to Britain. This latter resulted from the fact that Britain was responsible for arranging the credit for Allied purchasing abroad, and this credit depended on maintaining the value of sterling. However, the Russians viewed the British insistence on the need to ship gold as an insult and as evidence that the British did not appreciate the magnitude of the Russian war effort. Despite this basic divergence of views, there were some successes with respect to financial co-operation. On 4–5 February 1915, the Allies met to discuss this problem at Paris.[69] The British and French agreed to back a Russian loan of £100 millions, to be raised in London and Paris. France and Russia agreed each to provide Britain with £12 millions in gold to maintain British credit in the United States.

[64] L. L. Farrar, Jr., *The Short War Illusion* (Santa Barbara, CA, 1974); T. Wilson, 'Britain's "Moral Commitment" to France in August 1914', *History*, 64 (1979), 380–90.

[65] 'Commission Internationale de Ravitaillement. Constitution and Function', n.s., n.d.; 'C.I.R. Establishment and Function', R. F. H. Duke (secretary, CIR), n.d., both Mun 5/7/170/25/; K. Burk, *Britain, America and the Sinews of War 1914–18* (London, 1985), 44–5.

[66] Spring Rice (British ambassador, Washington) to Grey, tel. 73, urgent, 9 Oct. 1914, FO 371/2224/57870; Wintour (the Director of Army Contracts, WO) to Law (controller, commercial and consular affairs, FO), 30 Oct. 1914, FO 368/1087/66260; Wyldbore Smith (director, CIR) to J. A. C. Tilley (FO), 2 Feb. 1915, FO 371/2447/13198.

[67] The minutes on FO 368/1077/44234 and Blair's (assistant British military attaché, Russia) despatch LXV, 23 Jan. 1915, WO 106/989. For the problems generally, D. W. Graf, 'Military Rule Behind the Russian Front, 1914–17: The political Ramifications', *JfGOE* 22 (1974), 390–411.

[68] A. L. Sidorov, *Finansovoe polozhenie Rossii gody pervoi mirovoi voiny* (Moscow, 1960), ch. 1; Stone, *Eastern Front*, 153–6; Neilson, *Strategy and Supply*, 54–7.

[69] Neilson, *Stragegy and Supply*, 66–8.

By 1915, it was apparent that the war would not end quickly. The British moved to ensure better co-operation among the Allies with respect to purchase in the United States by signing an agreement making J. P. Morgan & Company the sole purchasing agent in the United States for the British government.[70] Through the offices of the CIR, this made Morgans the official purchaser for the entente in America. However, the Russians refused to be constrained completely, and continued to purchase in the United State outside regular channels.[71] None the less, the Russians made an effort to put their administrative house in better order by sending to Britain a new purchasing mission, headed by General Timchenko-Ruban of the Engineering Department of the Russian War Office.[72] The new arrivals created the Russian Government Committee (RGC), whose brief was to improve the co-ordination of Russian purchasing both in Britain and abroad.[73] The RGC was independent of the CIR, but many of its members also served on the latter body, thus ensuring reasonable co-operation between the two bodies. In May 1915, two representatives of the Main Artillery Department, Major-General E. K. Hermonious and Colonel N. Beliaev, were sent to Britain in the hope of easing some of the administrative tangle.

The Russian retreat in May 1915 had political as well as military ramifications. Many in Russia used the fact of the munitions shortages that were widely blamed for Russia's defeats as an opportunity to berate the Tsarist government for incompetence and to demand political reform.[74] This endowed Anglo-Russian dealings about munitions with a political significance beyond their impact on military matters. For Kitchener, with his weather eye on the Eastern front, something needed to be done. In May, he sent his personal representative, Colonel W. E. Ellershaw, to Russia in an attempt to improve Anglo-Russian co-operation about the purchase of military supplies. In the middle of that month, Ellershaw and the Russian commander-in-chief, the Grand Duke Nicholas Nikolaevich, signed an agreement giving Ellershaw the right to purchase abroad for the Russian army.[75] To follow up this initiative, Kitchener created the Russian Purchasing Committee (RPC) at the War Office, a body composed of members from the War Office, the

---

[70] Burk, *Sinews of War*, 15–22.

[71] Wyldbore Smith to Tilley, 2 Feb. 1915, FO 371/2447/12198; Burk, *Sinews of War*, 47; Neilson, *Strategy and Supply*, 190–1, 205–7.

[72] A. L. Sidorov, 'Missiia v Angliiu i Frantsiiu po voprosu snabzheniia Rossii predmetami vooruzheniia', *Istoricheskii arkhiv*, 4 (1949), 351–86.

[73] D. S. Babichev, 'Deiatelnost Russkogo pravitelstvennogo komiteta v Londone v gody pervoi mirovoi voiny (1914–17)', *IZ* 57 (1956), 276–92.

[74] T. D. Krupina, 'Politicheskii krizis 1915 g. i sozdanie osobogo sobeshchaniia po oborone', *IZ* 83 (1969), 58–75; L. H. Siegelbaum, *The Politics of Industrial Mobilization in Russia, 1914–17* (London, 1983), 24–84; Pearson, *Russian Moderates*, 39–65.

[75] Hanbury Williams (British military representative, *Stavka*) to Kitchener, 19 May 1915, Kitchener Papers, PRO 30/57/67.

newly created Ministry of Munitions and the CIR.[76] The supply of munitions for Russia thus became a personal project for Kitchener, but the fact that the procurement process itself was divided between the RPC, the CIR and the Ministry of Munitions meant that there were inevitable bureaucratic impediments to the smooth functioning of the Anglo-Russian co-operation.

Another impediment was the situation in the Untied States. In May 1915, Major-General A. V. Sapozhnikov had been sent to New York by the Russian government to set up a body, the Russian Purchasing Committee, designed to act as a parallel body to the RGC in London.[77] Sapozhnikov read his brief to mean that he could purchase outside the framework provided by the CIR and Morgans, and in July 1915, Hermonious and Ellershaw travelled to New York in an attempt to resolve all the problems involving independent Russian buying in the United States.[78] In an attempt to put the entire issue of the Allied purchase of munitions in the United States on a more rational footing, they were soon joined in New York by D. A. Thomas, a representative of the Ministry of Munitions. However, this intention aside, it was contracts placed by Hermonious and Ellershaw that helped to trigger an exchange-rate crisis that threatened Allied credit in the United States.

The outcome was another inter-Allied finance conference, at Boulogne on 20 August. Here, the British and French each agreed to keep $200 millions in gold available to send to the United States in order to bolster Allied credit. The Russians balked at such a contribution, but the British were firm as to its necessity. This reflected wider British concerns. At meetings of the War Policy Cabinet Committee, which had been established to consider Britain's resources and the future conduct of the war, both the chancellor of the excheque, Reginald McKenna, and the president of the board of trade, Walter Runciman, emphasized that the British had to choose between putting a large army in the field and continuing to finance and supply their allies.[79] In these circumstances, the British demanded fuller Anglo-Russian co-operation with respect to finance, and refused to grant further credits until this was arranged. After difficult negotiation, the result was the Anglo-Russian Treasury Agreement of 30 September 1915.[80]

The Treasury Agreement was a milestone. The Russians were granted a credit of £25 millions per month for the following year, the money to be used to pay for existing contracts in Britain, the United States, and the British Empire. New purchases, up to the value of £4.5 millions per month, could be made, but only if

---

[76] Great Britain, *History of the Ministry of Munitions* (12 vols.; London, 1920–4), ii, pt. VIII, 10–12.

[77] Knox (British military attaché Russia) to MO 3 (WO), disp. T, 22 Apr. 1915, WO 106/1057.

[78] Neilson, *Strategy and Supply*, 103–7; Burk, *Sinews of War*, 63–8.

[79] Runciman's testimony (19 Aug. 1915), Cab 37/132/1 and McKenna's testimony (23 Aug. 1915), Cab 37/133/9; French, *British Strategy*, 122–3.

[80] The conference is outlined in Sidorov, *Finansovoe polozhenie*, 259–76; the text of the agreement is in T 172/255.

the Russians adhered to the provisions of the annexe to the Treasury Agreement, which meant working through the RGC, the RPC and the CIR. In return the Russians had to commit £40 millions worth of gold to the Bank of England. The outflow of gold threatened to weaken the ruble, so that the British also agreed to help the Russian government expand its fiduciary issue by providing some £200 millions worth of credit upon which new paper money could be issued. But this seemingly comprehensive agreement foundered on the continued Russian purchasing of goods outside its provisions.[81] Some British officials advocated taking a firmer line with the Russians, but the realities of the situation were clear.[82] With Russia's military co-operation needed in the Balkans and elsewhere, any endeavour to force the Russians to adhere too closely to the Treasury Agreement would be counter-productive, for the Russians would resent the attempt and ignore it when they chose. And, if the British cut off Russian credit, the result might well be an end to an effective Russian war effort on the Eastern front.

This line was adopted by the Russians at the inter-Allied munitions conference in London held from 23 November to 1 December 1915.[83] Admiral A. I. Rusin, the Russian representative, put forward extravagant demands, side-stepped any attempt to centralize Allied purchasing to the diminishment of Russia's ability to buy independently, and intimated that only the fulfillment of his maximum demands could ensure a significant military contribution by the Russians in 1916. This conference, which paralleled the military and political gatherings held at the same time at Chantilly and Paris, underlined the Russian insistence that her sanguinary sacrifices of 1915 be recognized by the Allies in concrete form. In France, the Russians insisted on the principle that all the Allies would support whichever one was attacked by the Central Powers; in London, the Russians insisted on the need to give Russia's economic needs a high priority.

The Russian demands were complicated by matters of transport. Since the closure of the Black Sea in November 1914, Allied supplies going to Russia did so by one of three routes: via Vladivostok, via Archangel, and overland through Norway and neutral Sweden.[84] Britain had been central to this since the beginning

---

[81] Outlined in 'War Office Russian Buying Commission', confidential memo, Booth (Ministry of Munitions), 9 Nov. 1915, Black Papers, Mun 5/533; 'Memorandum of Conference held in Director of Army Contracts' room on the 14th Oct. 1915, to consider the interpretation of the British-Russian Financial Agreement', n.s., 14 Oct. 1915, Mun 7/149.

[82] 'Note on memorandum on munitions contracts for the Allies', n.s. (but Hanson, the director of army contracts, WO), n.d. (*c*.20 Nov. 1915), Mun 7/149.

[83] Neilson, *Strategy and Supply*, 129–33; 'Conference between Representatives of the Allied Governments', n.s., each day noted separately, Mun 5/5068.

[84] Swedish transshipment had its own problems: K. Neilson and B. J. C. McKercher, ' "The Triumph of Unarmed Force": Sweden and the Allied Blockade of Germany, 1914–17', *JSS* 7 (1984), 178–99.

of the war, primarily through the firm of R. Martens.[85] By the end of 1915, Martens was unable to provide sufficient tonnage for Russia, and the Tsarist government asked the British to provide the necessary bottoms. The debate over whether this could be done, and how much the Russians required, paralleled the debates over Russian purchasing and finances. The Russians assumed that the British could provide an unlimited amount of transport, while the British demanded that the Russians pare their requirements to the minimum and put the essential items in order of priority.[86] Further, the British believed that many of the supplies shipped to Russia via the White Sea would be wasted, since the Russians lacked the means to move goods from the ports there to the front.[87] Since there was a shortage of tonnage for all Allied needs, Russia's requests were treated in that global context. It was the Russian debacle at Lake Narotch that decided matters. Fearful that Russia would not make a sizeable military contribution in 1916 unless she received sufficient supplies from abroad, the British allotted extra shipping to the White Sea routes.[88] On 5 May 1916, after tedious negotiations, the Admiralty agreed both to provide sufficient tonnage for the 1916 shipping season and to co-ordinate all transport efforts (including the on- and off-loading of ships) in the White Sea.[89]

By July 1916, there was a need for a thorough reconsideration of all matters involving Anglo-Russian finance and supply. This was done in London, from 13 to 16 July.[90] The issues were those that had led to deadlock in November 1915. The Russians demanded vast amounts of supplies and money and tied their provision to the continuance of the Russian war effort; the British called for the Russians to put their needs in order of priority and insisted that shortages precluded the granting of all of Russia's wishes. The result was an uneasy compromise. The British gave the Russians further credit amounting to £25 millions per month for the next six

[85] C. E. Fayle, *History of the Great War Based on Official Documents by Direction of the Historical Section Committee of Imperial Defence: Seaborne Trade* (3 vols.; London, 1920–4), ii. 122–5; E. W. Haig (of R. Martens) to FO, 30 June 1915, FO 368/1494/88343; A. L. Sidorov, *Ekonomicheskoe polozhenie Rossii v gody pervoi mirovoi voiny* (Moscow, 1973), 295–7.

[86] Neilson, *Strategy and Supply*, 177–81.

[87] Stone, *Eastern Front*, 157–8; reports 3, 18, and 20 of Admiral Phillimore (the Admiralty's liaison officer in Russia), 20 Oct. 1915, Feb. 1916 and 17 Mar. 1916, all ADM 137/1389.

[88] 'The Ignoring of the Freight Problem on the Part of the Russians', WO, 3 Feb. 1916, Cab 1/23/13; meeting of the War Cabinet, 8 Mar. 1916, Cab 42/10/3; 'Report of Shipping Control Committee', n.s., 31 Mar. 1916, Cab 37/144/46; Hankey to C. Jones (secretary to the shipping control committee), 11 Apr. 1916, Cab 17/182; meeting of the War Cabinet, 28 Apr. 1916, Cab 42/12/12.

[89] 'Memorandum of Agreement between the Russian and British Governments as to the Necessary Procedure to be Established in order to Ensure Transport of Munitions to Russia', signed by Benckendorff and Grey, 5 May 1916, Layton Papers, Mun 4/372; M. A. Stoliarenko, 'Anglo-russkie soglashe-niia o severnykh portakh Rossii v gody pervoi mirovoi voiny', *Vestnik Leningradskogo Universiteta*, 16 (1961), 46–58.

[90] The proceedings of the conference are in Mun 4/5068.

months and an immediate grant of £63 millions for military orders, with a further £63 millions forthcoming in the autumn on the understanding that Russia should hold ready £40 millions worth of gold for shipment to Britain. In addition, further administrative improvements were made to the machinery of Anglo-Russian purchase.[91] This latter was particularly necessary, since, after Kitchener's death in June, the War Office's RPC was dismantled, with most of its personnel being transferred to the Ministry of Munitions, where a new body, the Russian Supply Committee (RSC), was created.[92]

All these issues were debated again at the end of the 1916 campaign. The inter-Allied supply conference, held in London 8–10 November, held no surprises.[93] The Russian calls for supplies clearly exceeded the transport available to move them. However, the British were not alone in opposing the Russian demands. The French insisted that their needs were an equal priority, leaving the British to adjudicate the competing claims. The decision reflected two things: the increase in Britain's productive capacity and a general judgement on the future course of the war. As the British productive capacity for munitions was greater than it had been a year earlier, they were more sympathetic to the Russian requests. This still left the issue of how to transport munitions to Russia, and here the British decision to give Russia much of what she demanded resulted from a belief that the Eastern front offered the best chance of Allied success in 1917. British manpower could better be employed in producing munitions for the Allies and goods for export so as to pay for the needs of war than in attacking the German lines in Flanders.

The Petrograd Conference was the last attempt during the war to resolve all matters regarding Anglo-Russian finance and supply. That it failed to do so reflected the mutually exclusive nature of the British and Russian views concerning these matters. When the sessions on supply opened, the Russians put forward the view that their ports had the ability to handle some 9.5 million tons during the 1917 shipping season.[94] This was more than double what the British believed possible. Arguments over the matter resulted in the Russians threatening that their military effort in 1917 depended on the supplies being shipped, and the British reiterating that there was a need for establishing priorities and weeding out non-essential items. As to finance, Russian requests for a new loan were rejected, but an agreement signed 27 October 1916 that provided Russia with monthly credits was extended for 1917, provided Russia continued to ship the gold that was due to the

[91] See the agreement signed by P. Bark (Russian finance minister) and Grey, 14 July, Mun 4/4866; 'Protocol', signed by Bark, Ribot (French minister of finance) and McKenna, 15 July 1916, T 172/385.
[92] 'Russian Government Supplies', confidential, n.s., 27 June 1916, Mun 4/6254.
[93] 'Summary of the Proceedings of the Inter-Ally Munitions Conference Held in London November 8th, 9th and 10th 1916', n.s., n.d., Mun 4/5068.
[94] 'Conférence des Allies à Petrograd. Commission de Ravitaillement', 1st session, 30 Jan. 1917, Cab 28/2 IC 16(B).

British.[95] The decisions of the Petrograd Conference were never implemented. The military collapse of the Tsarist state in the aftermath of the March revolution resulted in a British fear that supplies sent to Russia either would never be utilized against the Central Powers or, worse, would fall into enemy hands. Thus, supplies for Russia were doled out sparingly, as the competing requests for these supplies from other allies and from the British forces themselves were given a higher priority in the effort to win the war.[96] However, despite Russian charges that Britain provided too little, between August 1914 and the autumn of 1917 more than 5 million tons of supplies were shipped to Russia.[97]

III

Anglo-Russian relations during the war were mainly concerned with winning the war. However, the British did not intend to win the war for the benefit of Russia. This view, albeit for widely differing reasons, was shared by those on the Liberal left and by those concerned with Britain's postwar imperial situation and the balance of power in Europe.[98] Thus, there existed a 'war within the war', one in which Britain struggled to ensure that she would win the peace and emerge from the hostilities in a position to defend her worldwide interests against all comers, including a triumphant Russia.

The first issue involved in this struggle was the matter of Constantinople and the Straits. Given the long history of this subject, Grey was not surprised when Sazonov raised the issue informally at the beginning of September 1914.[99] However, Grey, no doubt following the precedent of the Balkan Wars, did not wish to pursue the matter of war aims until the outcome of the war itself was clear, since this would have meant potentially divisive discussions with her allies.[100] Events conspired to force a decision on the British sooner than they preferred. Throughout August and September, there was great concern about the reliability of Britain's Moslem subjects in Egypt and India. With German agents working hard to create

---

[95] Neilson, *Strategy and Supply*, 202–4; 237–8.

[96] Neilson, 'Breakup of the Anglo-Russian Alliance', 62–75.

[97] Fayle, *Seaborne Trade*, iii. 33.

[98] L. S. Jaffe, *The Decision to Disarm Germany: British Policy towards Postwar German Disarmament, 1914–1919* (London, 1985), 45–50.

[99] W. A. Renzi, 'Who Composed "Sazonov's Thirteen Points"? A Re-Examination of Russia's War Aims of 1914', *AHR* 88 (1983), 347–57; Buchanan to Nicolson, 13 Sept. 1914, Nicolson Papers, FO 800/375.

[100] C. J. Smith, Jr., 'Great Britain and the 1914–15 Straits Agreement with Russia: The British Promise of November 1914', *AHR* 70 (1965), 1021–5; V. H. Rothwell, *British War Aims and Peace Diplomacy 1914–18* (Oxford, 1971), 18–22.

disaffection, there were fears of a Holy War against Britain and concerns about the security of Egypt and the Persian Gulf.[101] The closure of the Straits by the Turks on 26 September heightened tensions between the two states, and Indian Army troops were despatched to Bahrein to ensure the security of British interests in the Gulf.[102] But it was the attack on Odessa and Sevastopol by the Turkish fleet on 29 October that precipitated matters. With Russia and the Ottoman empire now at war, the British had little option but to follow suit on 5 November. As discussed above, throughout October, the British had been concerned that Russia might concentrate her military effort against Austria-Hungary, thus freeing German troops either for a raid against Britain or for a powerful offensive in the West.[103] With another front beckoning, and one that offered the glittering prize of Constantinople, the British fear that the Russian steamroller might be diverted away from Berlin grew stronger. Since the die was cast with Turkey, the scramble was on for the legacy of the Ottoman empire. Grey no longer had to act cautiously lest Moslem opinion be affected adversely. Thus, in order to keep Russia firmly focused against Germany, he promised the Russians that Constantinople and the Straits would be theirs in any postwar settlement and announced a British protectorate over Egypt.[104]

Still, Grey was reluctant to discuss British desiderata until the Dardanelles campaign and the negotiations surrounding the possible entry of Greece and Italy into the war made it unavoidable. The Russians were highly suspicious of the British decision to try and force the Straits.[105] Sazonov feared either that Britain might take Constantinople for herself or that Russia's claim to that city might be bargained away in an effort to bring Italy and the Balkan neutrals into the war. The result was the formal promise to Russia of Constantinople and the Straits decided at the War Council on 10 March.[106] At that meeting, Grey emphasized the need to promise Russia Constantinople so as to 'remove Russian suspicions as to our

---

[101] D. French, 'The Dardanelles, Mecca and Kut: Prestige as a Factor in British Eastern Strategy, 1914–16', *WS* 5 (1987), 50–3; J. Heller, 'Sir Louis Mallet and the Ottoman Empire: The Road to War', *MES* 12 (1976), 3–45.

[102] S. A. Cohen, 'The Genesis of the British Campaign in Mesopotamia, 1914', *MES* 12 (1976), 119–32.

[103] Grey to Buchanan, 4 Oct. 1914, FO 371/2095/55811.

[104] Bertie to Grey, private and confidential, 12 Nov. 1914, Bertie Papers, FO 800/177; Neilson, *Strategy and Supply*, 49–50; G. Paget, 'The November 1914 Straits Agreement and the Dardanelles–Gallipoli Campaign', *AJPH* 33 (1987), 254–5; A. L. Macfie, 'The Straits Question in the First World War, 1914–18', *MES* 19 (1983), 49–52.

[105] Smith, *Russian Struggle*, 188–98; S. Sazonov, *Fateful Years: 1909–16: The Reminiscences of Serge Sazonov* (London, 1928), 255–6; Lowe and Dockrill, *Mirage of Power*, ii. 169–83; Macfie, 'Straits Question', 53–8.

[106] Buchanan to Grey, tel. 249, 4 Mar. 1915, Cab 37/125/19; Hankey diary entries, 4, 5, 6, 9, 10 Mar. 1915, Hankey Papers, HNKY 1/1; Meeting of the War Council, 3 Mar. 1915, Cab 42/2/3; meeting of the War Council, 10 Mar. 1915, Cab 42/2/5.

attitude and to get rid of the Russian objections to the participation of other nations' at the Dardanelles. Although there were those who subsequently felt that Grey had been 'bluffed' by Sazonov, there was no doubt that fears of Russia's possibly marking a separate peace determined Grey's policy.[107] While Grey's remarks were decisive in determining British policy, they also triggered a discussion of the consequences of this promise. Balfour thought it 'injurious to our interests to allow Russia to occupy a position on the flank of our route to India', but allowed that it might be necessary given the exigencies of the war. Kitchener, his views no doubt shaped by his prewar time as British Agent in Egypt, shared Balfour's fears, and insisted on the need for Britain to take Alexandretta, for '[w]ith Russia in Constantinople, France in Syria, and Italy in Rhodes, our position in Egypt would be untenable if any other Power held Alexandretta'. While Asquith deflected further discussion, it was evident that the entire issue of the inheritance of the Ottoman legacy would need thorough discussion. In the interim, Grey informed Sazonov on 11 March that Britain agreed to the Russian demand only reluctantly, that Russia should no longer object to the participation of other states in the Dardanelles campaign, and that Constantinople should remain an entrepôt for south-east Europe and the Straits should be open to merchant shipping.[108] And, while precise British desiderata had not yet been formulated, one of them would involve a 'revision of [the] Anglo-Russian Agreement about Persia recognizing [the] present neutral sphere as a British sphere'. If the Ottoman Empire were to be dismembered in Russia's favour, then Britain must use the opportunity to solve the long-standing problems with Russia in Persia, an idea to which the Russians agreed.[109]

The result of the War Council of 10 March was a committee, chaired by the former British ambassador to Vienna, Maurice de Bunsen.[110] The committee met in April and May 1915, with a mandate to determine British desiderata in Turkey in Asia. Its discussions made clear the British concerns about the postwar strategic position. The preliminary positions had been staked out in the aftermath of the War Council meeting of 10 March. Kitchener expanded on his call for a British base at Alexandretta.[111] Noting that 'at some future date, we may find ourselves at

---

[107] Untitled memo, Bertie, 30 Oct. 1915, Bertie Papers, Add MSS 63039.

[108] Grey to Buchanan, tel. 43, private and secret, 11 Mar. 1915, Cab 37/126/3.

[109] Buchanan to Grey, tel. 54, private and secret, 13 Mar. 1915, Cab 37/126/5.

[110] Rothwell, *British War Aims*, 26–8; A. S. Klieman, 'Britain's War Aims in the Middle East in 1915', *JCH* 3 (1968), 237–51; M. Kent, 'Asiatic Turkey, 1914–16', in F. H. Hinsley (ed.), *British Foreign Policy Under Sir Edward Grey* (Cambridge, 1977), 444–5; 'British Desiderata in Turkey in Asia: Report: Proceedings, and Appendices of a Committee Appointed by the Prime Minister', May 1915, de Bunsen, Cab 27/1. (Hereafter, 'De Bunsen Committee')

[111] 'Alexandretta and Mesopotamia', secret, Kitchener, 16 Mar. 1915, Cab 24/1/G-12; J. Nevakivi, 'Lord Kitchener and the Partition of the Ottoman Empire, 1915–16', in K. Bourne and D. C. Watt (eds.), *Studies in International History* (London, 1967), 316–29.

enmity with Russia, or with France, or with both in combination', he argued that Britain required Alexandretta as a counterweight to protect Egypt. However, he added that Alexandretta was most significant for the defence of Mesopotamia, since it could provide a railway terminus for the Baghdad railway and link the British position in the Gulf to the Mediterranean. This argument was backed by the Admiralty.[112] Asserting that the Mediterranean was 'the centre of world politics', the Admiralty insisted on the need to acquire Alexandretta 'as a counterpoise to the new weight that Russia is acquiring' in that sea. This need was furthered by the new naval dependence on oil supplies: the Russian fleet operating out of Constantinople would have Russia's petroleum reserves at her back; the British fleet operating out of Alexandretta could be backed by Britain's petroleum reserves in Mesopotamia. The Admiralty also opposed the possibility of Alexandretta's being held by any other naval power, particularly France, since this, too, would threaten Britain's naval position in the eastern Mediterranean.[113] The former first sea lord, Admiral A. K. Wilson, was even more pessimistic. He rejected the CID's opinion of 1903 that ceding the Straits and Constantinople to Russia would not affect the naval balance in the Mediterranean (a precedent that Maurice Hankey, the secretary to the War Council, had brought forward).[114] Instead, he stated that a Russian acquisition of Constantinople combined with the advances in submarine technology since 1903 meant that a 'hostile Russia . . . could make our communication through the Mediterranean with Egypt and India almost impossible'. Indeed, Wilson believed that only 'friendly relations and close co-operation with Russia in the affairs of Asia' could prevent a postwar Anglo-Russian arms race 'far in excess of anything that we have undergone with Germany'. This pessimism lasted at the Admiralty until at least the autumn of 1916, when that body argued that Russia's possession of Constantinople and the Straits necessitated both a British acquisition of some of the islands 'between Crete and the mainland' and a 'redistribution of our naval strength in the Mediterranean'.[115]

Similar views were reiterated to the de Bunsen committee. On 13 April, the director of military operations (DMO), Major-General Sir Charles Callwell, charged the committee not to forget that 'in the future was the possibility of a war with Russia'.[116] Callwell argued that if Britain were to acquire Basra, then the need to have a defensible frontier to the north would also require the taking of the

---

[112] 'The War: Alexandretta and Mesopotamia', Admiralty, 17 Mar. 1915, Cab 24/1/G-13.

[113] 'Alexandretta: Its Importance as a Future Base', Admiral H. B. Jackson (employed on special duties, Admiralty), 15 Mar. 1915, Cab 24/1/G-15.

[114] See 'Russia and Constantinople: Note by the Secretary', Hankey, 1 Mar. 1915, Cab 24/1/G-11; 'Russia and Constantinople: Remarks by Admiral of the Fleet Sir A. K. Wilson on Paper G-11', Wilson, 15 Mar. 1915, Cab 24/1/G-17; Hankey diary entry, 17 Mar. 1915, Hankey Papers, HNKY 1/1.

[115] 'Note on the Possible Terms of Peace by the First Sea Lord of the Admiralty', Admiral H. B. Jackson, 12 Oct. 1916, Cab 29/1/P-8.

[116] De Bunsen Committee, 2nd meeting, 13 Apr. 1915, Cab 27/1.

vilayets of Baghdad and Mosul. Since in the case of war with Russia it would be impossible to send reinforcements from India to Mesopotamia, it was essential that Britain acquire a port on the Mediterranean and link it by rail to the Gulf in order to be able to transport reserves from Britain to Mesopotamia as quickly as possible. This was support for the earlier arguments about the need for Alexandretta, but Callwell, cognizant of the likely objections of Paris to Britain's taking a port earmarked as a likely French acquisition, stated that Haifa would be an adequate terminus.[117] The Admiralty reluctantly agreed, for while Haifa was as not as promising a naval base as was Alexandretta, it was sufficient as a port at which to disembark troops and supplies and could be turned into a 'submarine and destroyer base'. Much more important was to ensure that a pipeline was built from the Gulf to the Mediterranean in order to ensure that oil supplies for the Mediterranean fleet were secure.[118] The taking of this much territory meant that Britain would have a long frontier with Russia, stretching from the Russian sphere of influence in Persia to eastern Turkey, but if France could be induced to take the hinterland of Alexandretta, a helpful buffer zone between British and Russian territories could be created.[119] Getting the French and Russians to agree to such an idea, and squaring this with British promises to the Arabs was another matter, but the security of the Empire against Russia was the key issue.[120]

Here, Persia was vital. After entering the war, the Turks had sent troops into western Persia, raising concerns either that the Persians would join the Central Powers or that German influence would become paramount in Persia. There were strained relations between Russian troops in the north of Persia and the Persian government. In this situation, both Nicolson and Hardinge were inclined to overlook any Russian transgressions against the 1907 Convention, while Grey assured Sazonov that Britain and Russia could discuss, without prejudice, Persia after the war.[121] Sazonov's reply was to deprecate Britain's 'inveterate suspicion' of Russian actions and to note that, if Britain wanted a bigger sphere in Persia, he would accept such a solution.[122] An immediate gap emerged between Grey's advisers and the foreign secretary. Both Eyre Crowe and George Clerk argued that Britain

---

[117] The French objections were well known, see French, *British Strategy*, 81–2; D. Dutton, 'The Balkan Campaign', 102–5. For French fears about Russia's postwar position in the Mediterranean, see Bertie's memo of a conversation with the Cambon brothers, 16 Mar. 1915, Bertie Papers, Add MSS 63037.

[118] De Bunsen committee, 3rd meeting, 15 April 1915, testimony of Rear-Admiral E. J. W. Slade, Cab 27/1; H. Mejcher, 'Oil and British Policy towards Mesopotamia, 1914–18', *MES* 8 (1972), 377–91.

[119] De Bunsen Committee, 'Report', 11; Lowe, *Mirage of Power*, ii. 219–21.

[120] E. Kedourie, 'Cairo and Khartoum on the Arab Question, 1915–18', *HJ* 7 (1964), 280–97; French, *British Strategy*, 146–8; B. Westrate, *The Arab Bureau: British Policy in the Middle East, 1916–20* (University Park, PA, 1992), 79–100.

[121] Nicolson to Hardinge, 31 Dec. 1914; Hardinge to Nicolson, 6 Jan. 1915, both Hardinge Papers, vol. 93; Grey to Buchanan, tel. 11, 4 Jan. 1915, FO 371/2427/937.

[122] Buchanan to Grey, tel. 38, 11 Jan. 1915, FO 371/2427/4030 and minutes.

should take advantage of this opening and enter into discussions with Russia aimed at a renegotiation of the Anglo-Russian Convention. Grey was adamant in his refusal to do so: 'During the war', he informed Sazonov, 'the Persian question does not exist for me apart from its effect on the war.'[123] Sazonov's acceptance of this point meant that the matter rested there until the negotiations over Constantinople began.[124]

When it was decided to include Persia as part of Britain's desiderata, Nicolson seized on this as an opportunity to end the problems that had plagued Anglo-Russian relations. The PUS hoped that 'practically the whole of the neutral zone' should become British, despite the fact that this would make the Russian and British spheres 'coterminous'.[125] Hardinge agreed, and suggested that, once Russia had what she desired in the Near East and Britain had what she wanted in Mesopotamia and Persia, a 'definite treaty of alliance' between the two countries could be effected, since there would be no more reason for discord between them.[126] But, viewed from the perspective of defence, should the millennium in Anglo-Russian relations not occur, the British position in Mesopotamia would have been much improved by the acquisition of the neutral zone. With the head of the Gulf in British hands, with Russia's zone in Persia not bordering on Britain's new acquisitions in Mesopotamia, and with a secure terminus on the Mediterranean for a railway, British fears about the security of Seistan and the Gulf would be much alleviated. However, despite the tacit Russian acceptance of the Persian solution, it was never implemented. The German-inspired Persian uprising in the summer of 1915 meant that Britain and Russia were forced to co-operate as best they could against the revolutionary forces, regardless of spheres of influence.[127] After the Russian revolution in March 1917 largely brought an end to Russian assistance, the British moved unilaterally to secure their imperial interests in Persia.[128]

The British were also concerned about the postwar position of Russia in Europe. The optimism generated by Rumania's entry into the war and the Allied successes of the summer of 1916 led to a discussion of war aims in which Russia figured large.[129] The principal matter was to maintain the balance of power in Europe by ensuring that the defeat of the Central Powers did not result in the creation of a

---

[123] Grey to Buchanan, tel. 67, 18 Jan. 1915, FO 371/2427/4030.

[124] Buchanan to Grey, tel. 91, 21 Jan. 1915, FO 371/2427/9062.

[125] Nicolson to Hardinge, 11 Mar. 1915, Hardinge Papers, vol. 93.

[126] Hardinge to Nicolson, 8 Apr. 1915, Hardinge Papers, vol. 93.

[127] Buchanan to Grey, tel. 1135, 10 Aug. 1915, FO 371/2428/110252; Buchanan to Grey, tel. 1136, 10 Aug. 1915, FO 371/2428/110253.

[128] F. Stanwood, 'Revolution and the "Old Reactionary Policy": Britain in Persia, 1917', *JICH* 6 (1978), 144–65; B. Schwarz, 'Divided Attention: Britain's Perception of a German Threat to Her Eastern Position in 1918', *JCH* 28 (1993), 103–22.

[129] Jaffe, *Decision to Disarm Germany*, 42–60; French, *British Strategy*, 210–16.

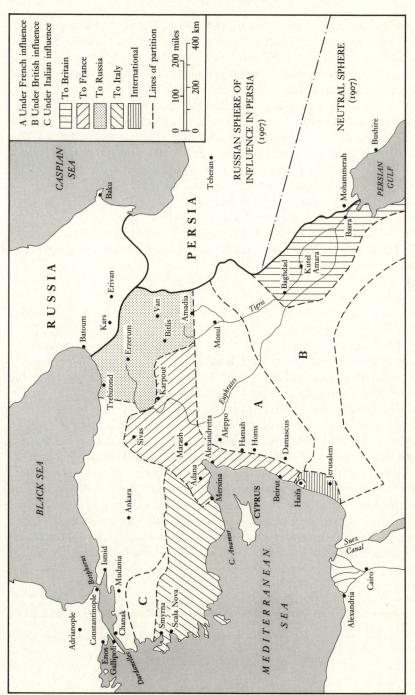

MAP 12.1 The partition of Asiatic Turkey

Europe (particularly eastern Europe) dominated by Russia. As Robertson noted, unless there was a strong 'Central European' power that was 'Teutonic', the only alternative would be one that 'would lean towards Russia'.[130] For that reason, Robertson wished to maintain Germany as a powerful land power, while weakening her as a naval threat to Britain. The Foreign Office took a similar stand, pointing out that if Russia incorporated all of Poland into the Russian empire after the war, '[t]he Western Allies might very properly take exception' since this would bring the Russian boundary too close to Berlin and Vienna.[131] For this reason, both the War Office and Foreign Office preferred the creation of a semi-autonomous Poland. Only Balfour pointed out that Poland likely would not act as an effective buffer between Russia and Germany and that, if it did, the result would be to 'divert her [Russian] interests towards the Far East' to Britain's detriment.[132] 'The more Russia is made a European rather than an Asiatic Power,' Balfour concluded, 'the better for everybody.' The First World War might have been touted as 'the war to end all wars', but the British were not convinced that it was likely to bring an end to Anglo-Russian enmity.

IV

The nature of the Anglo-Russian alliance during the First World War was determined by the events of the war itself. Britain and Russia shared a common goal—the defeat of the Central Powers—and Britain shaped her strategy within the confines of the Allied coalition with careful reference to Russia and the Eastern front. Initially, the British expected the Russian 'steamroller' to be the decisive element on land and anticipated that their own contribution to the war would be mainly naval and economic. As the war became one of long duration and one that tested the economic and financial sinews of all the combatants, the Russians expected the British to be able to provide an unlimited amount of money and supplies to the Russian cause. Neither the British nor the Russian hopes were attained. The Russian army performed well, but the nature of the war—one that involved increased firepower and necessitated trench warfare—did not permit a rapid victory. The British provided substantial amounts of money and *matériel* for Russia, but the competing demands of the other allies (and Britain herself) meant that not all of Russia's extravagant needs could be met.

---

[130] 'Peace Terms', General Staff (Robertson), 31 Oct. 1916, Cab 29/1/P-4.

[131] 'Suggested Basis for a Territorial Settlement in Europe', R. Paget and W. Tyrrell (FO), 7 Aug. 1916, Cab 29/1/P-5.

[132] 'The Peace Settlement in Europe: Memorandum by Mr. Balfour', Balfour, 4 Oct. 1916, Cab 29/1/P-7.

None the less, when looked at from the perspective of the pre-1914 Anglo-Russian relationship, the functioning of the Anglo-Russian alliance was surprisingly smooth. Prior to the war, Britain and Russia had made no plans for either military or naval collaboration, and economic and financial co-operation was not even considered. In addition, the two countries were divided by long-standing imperial differences, particularly over the way in which the Anglo-Russian Convention operated in Persia. These problems were largely overcome. While there were differences between the two allies about military strategy, these differences were no greater than those between, say, either Britain and France or France and Russia. And, these differences reflected the dissimilar natures of the Western and Eastern fronts just as much as they did any irreconcilable arguments over the proper way to conduct the war. With regard to Salonika in particular, the British were sensitive to Russia's interests and were willing to subordinate their own strategic vision to the smooth functioning of the alliance. In the economic and financial war, Britain gave Russia full consideration, but in a war where too many customers chased too few goods, there was bound to be disappointment.

While Britain both required and valued Russia as an ally in the First World War that did not mean that the interests of the two were completely congruent. Grey co-operated closely with Sazonov in attempts to acquire more allies for the entente, and was willing to cede Constantinople and the Straits to Russia in order to assure her wholehearted and continued participation in the war, but he and the rest of the British élite were unwilling to accord Russia a dominant postwar position globally at the expense of Great Britain. In this respect, the Anglo-Russian relationship remained as uneasy as it had been before the war, despite the probable solution of the Persian imbroglio. And, had the Tsarist state managed to outlast the war, Britain and Russia would have found themselves sharing a long and unstable boundary in Persia and the Middle East: as much a source of potential discord as the north-west frontier had been prior to 1907. Thus, at the end of Nicholas II's reign, the future of Anglo-Russian relations looked much as it had when Nicholas came to the throne. Despite the Anglo-Russian alliance during the First World War, the bear and the whale remained allies of a kind.

Conclusion

We have not a friend in Europe, and I believe that the main cause of the dislike of foreign countries of Great Britain is, that we are like an octopus with gigantic feelers stretching out all over the habitable world, and constantly interrupting and preventing foreign nations from doing that which we in the past have done ourselves.[1]

(Lord George Hamilton, 1899)

STUDIES dealing with British foreign and defence policy before 1914 suffer from a basic flaw. While well researched and well argued, they are based on the fundamental assumption that Britain was destined to go to war with Germany in 1914. This tendency to read history backwards—in effect, to have the White Queen's memory—has led to a misunderstanding of events. The effect has been not only to exaggerate the impact that Germany had on British policy, but also to underplay the influence of other states. As a result, the historical literature centres on Anglo-German relations and considers other dimensions of British policy too much in this Anglo-German context. To remedy this distortion, Britain's relations with other states need to be regarded more independently. In particular, and for the reasons outlined below, Britain's relations with Russia need to be given more prominence.

In 1894, Russia was Britain's most persistent and formidable opponent. The principal global powers, Britain's and Russia's interests clashed worldwide, nearly everywhere the 'feelers' of the 'octopus' of the British Empire reached.[2] Since at least the 1820s, Russia had posed a threat to British India, a threat that grew apace after 1860 as Russia expanded into Central Asia. In the Far East, Russian activities in China (and the building of the trans-Siberian railway) challenged Britain's commercial interests. In the Near East, Russia's persistent efforts to solve the Eastern question to her own satisfaction had led to the Crimean War and the crisis of 1878. The Russian army was the biggest in Europe, if not the most efficient, and the Russian navy, combined with that of Russia's newly acquired ally, France, was the yardstick against which the Royal Navy's two-power standard was measured. When it is remembered that Tsarist Russia, widely regarded as the bastion of reaction and repression, was seen as the greatest ideological challenge to liberal

---

[1] Hamilton to Curzon, 2 Nov. 1899, Curzon Papers, MSS Eur F111/144.
[2] An argument could, of course, be made for France. However, the French empire was neither as large nor as secure as the empires possessed by Britain and Russia.

Europe, Russia's claim to the mantle of being Britain's most implacable foe seems evident.

The effect of Russia on British policy before 1914 was different from that of any other power. This singularity sprang from the peculiar nature of the two states. Britain and Russia were the book ends of Europe, in but not of the Continent. Each, to an extent not possessed by other powers, had the luxury of withdrawing— Britain behind the Channel; Russia behind the barrier created by sheer distance— from European affairs, and neither had an effective means of striking a direct blow at the other.[3] Since Russia affected Britain both on the Continent and imperially, considerations of her were vital to Britain's defence and foreign policy. But this contention needs both amplification and qualification. Anglo-Russian relations in Europe were always pursued in the context of the relations between the Great Powers generally. Therefore, Britain always had allies or potential allies when dealing with Russia about Continental issues.[4] However, Anglo-Russian relations outside Europe were a different matter. In China, Anglo-Russian affairs involved the other European powers only marginally, and Britain was unlikely to be able to garner any assistance from them to deal with Russia. Indeed, as the events from 1895 to 1898 in the Far East demonstrated, Russia was at least as likely to gain European support in rivalries outside the Continent as was Britain. The Anglo-Russian quarrel on the north-west frontier of India made this point even more manifest. If Britain were to oppose Russia on the subcontinent, she would do so without the benefit of allies and with only her own resources. And, as the Boer War demonstrated, the other powers might threaten to use the opportunity caused by an imperial distraction to create difficulties for Britain elsewhere.

However, this is not to posit the false dichotomy that Britain's European and extra-European dealings with Russia were separate. In fact, this sort of 'geographical' approach to Anglo-Russian relations has led to a fundamental under-estimation of the significance of Russia for British policy. In the period from 1895 to 1902, for example, Russia was the common factor in British policy with respect to China, Japan, the Ottoman Empire, and Persia, in addition to being both a principal influence on British naval policy and the chief concern in discussions of the defence of India. Further, in the deliberations concerning whether to accept the German blandishments for an Anglo-German alliance, considerations of Russia were central. Given the fact that histories dealing with foreign policy, imperial history, and defence policy are generally put into separate compartments, the ubiquity of Russia for British policy has been obscured. It was not obscured for the

---

[3] See the illuminating discussion of the Anglo-Russian relationship from 1815 to 1848 in P. W. Schroeder, 'Did the Vienna Settlement Rest on a Balance of Power?', *AHR* 97(1992), 683–706. I believe that much of Schroeder's argument holds true until the 1890s.

[4] The underlying assumption of D. French, *The British Way in Warfare 1688–2000* (London, 1990).

British élite, who realized that the Tsarist empire constituted the single most persistent and long-term threat to Britain and the Empire.

The qualification 'long-term' is significant. The burgeoning economic, military, and naval strength of Germany, combined with the belligerence of German diplomacy, made the Reich an extremely important short-term threat to Britain's security after about 1906. However, despite some minor clashes over colonial issues, Germany, with the possible exception of efforts to extend her influence in the Middle East and Persia, posed no direct threat to the British Empire. The German danger was essentially a challenge to the *status quo* in Europe. And, any such challenge generated its own opposition among the other Great Powers. In short, expansionist Germany was not only a problem for Britain, but also for the rest of the Great Powers. Thus, Britain's European position was strong and flexible, since her support was coveted by those powers who sought to contain Germany.

British policy towards Russia also needs to be set in the context of the changing international situation after about 1870. The rise of Germany in Europe and Japan in the Far East produced international problems for Britain that were qualitatively different from those that existed earlier in the nineteenth century. While not all foreign policy matters after 1870 were new—for example, the Eastern Question remained a central issue until the First World War—how Britain dealt with them had to reflect the new realities of power and circumstance. For the sake of analysis, the two different sets of problems may be termed 'Victorian' and 'Edwardian', and may be seen as paralleling the division between 'Victorians' and 'Edwardians' within the British policy-making élite. Given that the rise of Germany and Japan occurred while Victoria was still vigorously on her throne, these terms might seem misleading. However, since the two revisionist powers did not present their challenge (albeit for varying reasons) to the *status quo* until near the end of Victoria's rule, the distinction is not completely anachronistic. How, then, did the new 'Edwardian' situation affect Britain's policy towards Russia?

In one sense, the simple answer is that it did not. Since Anglo-Russian enmity was both dangerous and expensive, Britain always hoped to find an acceptable accommodation with Russia, and the new circumstances did not change this goal. However, in specific terms, and regarding both the means that Britain could employ and the opportunities presented to her, the 'Edwardian' period was entirely different from the 'Victorian'. Japan's rise in the Far East was particularly fortuitous for Britain. First, the Anglo-Japanese alliance provided Britain with a cheap and effective means of countering Russia's expansion into China, with little danger that Britain's commitment to Japan would involve any but a limited increase in British responsibilities. Second, the Russo-Japanese War was a disaster for Russia, both on the battlefield and at home, and led to a thorough re-examination of Russia's foreign policy. The new Russian policy was extremely favourable for

Britain; the Russians decided to accept the olive branch that Britain had extended continuously in the previous decade. The result was the Anglo-Russian Convention of 1907 and a temporary end to nearly a century of Anglo-Russian hostility.

In Europe, the 'Edwardian' situation was a mixed blessing. On the one hand, a powerful and restless Germany believed to be intent on establishing its hegemony in Europe was a threat to Britain, particularly when the Reich chose to challenge the naval supremacy, which underpinned Britain's position as a Great Power. On the other hand, Germany's aggressive policy was a catalyst for change in the foreign policies of the other Great Powers. After Fashoda, the French realized that being simultaneously on bad terms with both Britain and Germany was an untenable position, and began the complicated manœuvrings that were to result in the signing of the Entente Cordiale in 1904. The fact that the Germans chose to provoke a quarrel over Morocco with Russia's ally France at the very time when Russia was weakened by the Russo-Japanese War angered and humiliated the Russians, and helped to drive the Tsarist state away from a possible postwar realignment with Germany and towards the Anglo-Russian Convention. Thus, the 'Edwardian' situation permitted Britain to transform her contentious relations of 1894 with France and Russia into the more cordial ententes existing after 1907.

The foregoing should not suggest that this was a German-driven British foreign policy, or that defence policy was shaped by Britain's inability to defend her interests independently.[5] Rather, the Anglo-Russian relationship was the dominant long-term determinant of both British policies and was determined largely by its own dynamics, independent of Anglo-German relations. It is vital to remember the essential continuity of the policies followed by Rosebery, Kimberley, Salisbury, Lansdowne, and Grey towards Russia. Since Britain was pursuing a policy of accommodation with Russia long before Germany was perceived as a threat to Britain, it seems illogical to argue that the Anglo-Russian Convention was in any way a derivative of the rise of the Anglo-German antagonism. Without the White Queen's ability to remember the future, there is no reason to interpret British policy before 1914 as being directed towards creating a bloc designed to counter German aspirations in Europe.

This brings us to the need to reconsider the foreign policy of Sir Edward Grey. Recent attempts to paint a Machiavellian face on Grey have contended that the foreign secretary pursued a devious and duplicitous policy.[6] As part of this, the traditional view that Grey concluded an entente with Russia in order to curb

[5] I have argued for Britain's strength elsewhere: ' "Greatly Exaggerated": The Myth of the Decline of Great Britain before 1914', *IHR* 13(1991), 695–725. For a compelling discussion of Britain's economic and financial strength, see P. J. Cain and A. G. Hopkins, *British Imperialism: Innovation and Expansion 1688–1914* (London, 1993), especially 466–73.

[6] K. Wilson, 'Grey', in id. (ed.), *British Foreign Secretaries and Foreign Policy: From Crimean War to First World War* (London, 1987), 172–97.

Germany has been thrown out. Instead, it is argued that *fear* of Russia drove British policy, and that Grey (and his advisers at the Foreign Office) constructed an artificial German menace to make an Anglo-Russian *rapprochement* palatable to both the Liberal party and the general public.[7] A derivative of this argument is that Britain went to war in 1914, not out of a need to check Germany's bid for European hegemony, but rather out of a fear that not to support Russia would result in the latter's threatening Britain's Asiatic empire.[8] This argument contains fundamental truths, but is flawed in both emphasis and interpretation. British foreign and defence policy was determined by considerations of Russia to a degree previously unappreciated. However, the British were not *afraid* of Russia, despite the ongoing concerns about the defence of India. Rather, Russia was the most persistent *concern* of the British élite, because Russia's threat to Britain would have to be met solely out of British resources and because Britain was relatively powerless to strike a direct and decisive blow against Russia. For this reason the British consistently attempted to reach some sort of accommodation with the empire of Nicholas II. Equally, the German threat to Britain was not invented. German foreign policy, from at least 1898 to 1914, was designed to establish German hegemony in Europe. British attempts to find common ground with Germany over foreign policy issues—in the period from 1898 to 1901 and again from 1909 to 1912—foundered on the fact that the price of accommodation was to accept Germany's dominant position on the Continent. At bottom, it was Grey's unwillingness to risk Germany's achieving this aim that led to Britain's entry into the war. Finally, and derivatively, Britain did not go to war in 1914 because of fears for Central Asia. A German army, followed by a Germany navy moored in the Low Countries, was a much more immediate concern to Britain's existence than any action that Russia might take on the north-west frontier should Britain remain aloof from the war.

The ambivalent nature of the Anglo-Russian alliance during the First World War was fitting, for it reflected the nature of the relationship that had existed for the previous twenty years. Throughout the reign of Nicholas II, Britain eyed Russia warily. But, the British position was not an aggressive one. Despite the wishes of the advocates of imperial expansion, Britain had no territorial aspirations that threatened Russian interests. Indeed, Britain made concerted and genuine efforts to come to terms with Russia. The difficulty in doing so reflected the fact that Britain could not force Russia to agree to an accommodation acceptable to both sides. Only events—the repercussions of the Russo-Japanese War—provided the

---

[7] K. Wilson, *The Policy of the Entente: Essays on the Determinants of British Foreign Policy, 1904–14* (Cambridge, 1985), 74–7, 100–20.

[8] K. Wilson, 'Imperial Interests in the British Decision for War, 1914: the Defence of India in Central Asia', *RIS* 10 (1984), 189–203.

Bibliography

I. MANUSCRIPT SOURCES

All papers are held in the Public Record Office, Kew, unless otherwise noted.

1. Records of Departments of State

Admiralty

Adm 137 Historical Section: 1914–1918 War Histories

Cabinet Office

Cab 1	Miscellaneous Records
Cab 2	CID: Minutes
Cab 3	Home Defence Memoranda (CID)
Cab 4	Miscellaneous Memoranda (CID)
Cab 5	Colonial Defence Memoranda (CID)
Cab 6	Indian Defence Memoranda (CID)
Cab 16	CID Ad hoc Subcommittees of Enquiry: Proceedings and Memoranda
Cab 17	Correspondence and Miscellaneous Papers (CID)
Cab 21	Registered Files
Cab 23	Minutes to 1939
Cab 24	Memoranda to 1939
Cab 27	Committees: General Series to 1939
Cab 28	Allied (War) Conferences
Cab 29	Peace Conference and Other International Conferences
Cab 37	Photographic copies of Cabinet Papers
Cab 42	Photographic copies of the Papers of War Council, Dardanelles Committee and War Committee

Foreign Office

FO 65	General Correspondence: Russia
FO 368	General Correspondence: Commercial
FO 371	General Correspondence: Political

Ministry of Munitions

Mun 4	Records of the Central Registry
Mun 5	Historical Records
Mun 7	Ministry of Munitions: Files transferred to War Office

Public Record Office

PRO 30	Documents acquired by gift, deposit or purchase

Treasury

T 170	Bradbury Papers
T 172	Chancellor of the Exchequer's Office: Miscellaneous papers

War Office

WO 32	Registered Papers, Central Series
WO 106	Directorate of Military Operations and Intelligence

2. Private Papers

Asquith	Bodleian Library, Oxford
Arnold-Forster	British Library
Ardagh	PRO 30/40
Balfour	British Library
Barings	Barings Archives, 8 Bishopsgate, London
Bertie	British Library
	FO 800/159–91
Black	Mun 4/327, 452–575
Clive	The Liddell Hart Centre for Military Archives, King's College, London
Crewe	Cambridge University Library
Cromer	FO 633/1–43
Curzon	India Office Library
Esher	Churchill College Archives Centre, Cambridge
Grant Duff	Imperial War Museum, London
Grey	FO 800/35–113
Haig	National Library of Scotland
Haldane	National Library of Scotland
Hamilton	India Office Library
Hankey	Churchill College Archives Centre, Cambridge
Hardinge	Cambridge University Library
Hicks Beach (St Aldwyn)	Gloucestershire Record Office
Hirtzel	India Office Library
Howard	Cumbria County Record Office

Kiggell	Liddell Hart Centre for Military Archives, King's College, London
Kimberley	National Library of Scotland
Kitchener	PRO 30/57; WO 159
Lansdowne	FO 800/115–46
Lascelles	FO 800/6–20
Lowther	FO 800/193
Macdonogh	WO 106/1510–16
Midleton (St John Brodrick)	PRO 30/67
Morley	India Office Library
Nicolson	FO 800/336–81; PRO 30/81/1–17
Northcliffe	British Library
O'Conor	Churchill College Archives Centre, Cambridge
Pares	School of Slavonic and East European Studies, London
Ponsonby	Bodleian Library, Oxford
Roberts	WO 105
Robertson	Liddell Hart Centre for Military Archives, King's College, London
Rosebery	National Library of Scotland
Salisbury (3rd Marquis)	Hatfield House
Sandars	Bodleian Library, Oxford
Sanderson	FO 800/1–2
Scott	British Library
Selborne	Bodleian Library, Oxford
Spring Rice	FO 800/241–42
Sydenham (Clarke)	British Library
Vickers	Cambridge University Library
Villiers	FO 800/22–24
Wilson	Imperial War Museum

II. PRINTED SOURCES

1. Official Histories and Collections of Documents

FAYLE, C. E., *History of the Great War Based on Official Documents by Direction of the Historical Section Committee of Imperial Defence. Seaborne Trade* (3 vols.; London, 1920–24).

TEMPERLEY, H., and GOOCH, G. P. (eds.), *British Documents on the Origins of the War, 1898–1914* (11 vols. in 13; London, 1926–38).

GREAT BRITAIN, *History of the Ministry of Munitions* (12 vols.; London, 1920–4).

2. Memoir Material and Biographies

ABRIKOSSOW, D. I., *Revelations of a Russian Diplomat* (Seattle, 1964).

BEAUMONT, SIR H., 'Diplomatic Butterfly', unpublished manuscript, n.d., Imperial War Museum.

BOYCE, D. G. (ed.), *The Crisis of British Power: The Imperial and Naval Papers of the Second Earl of Selborne, 1895–1910* (London, 1990).

BRETT, M. V., and OLIVER, VISCOUNT ESHER (eds.), *Journals and Letters of Reginald Viscount Esher* (4 vols; London, 1938).

BROCK, M., and BROCK, E. (eds.), *H.H. Asquith: Letters to Venetia Stanley* (Oxford, 1982).

BRUCE, H. J., *Silken Dalliance* (London, 1946).

—— *Thirty Dozen Moons* (London, 1949).

BUCHANAN, SIR G., *My Mission to Russia and Other Diplomatic Memories* (2 vols.; London, 1923).

BUCHANAN, M., *The Dissolution of an Empire* (London, 1932).

BURTON, D. H., *Cecil Spring Rice: A Diplomat's Life* (London, 1990).

BUSCH, B. C., *Hardinge of Penshurst: A Study in the Old Diplomacy* (Hamden, 1980).

CALLWELL, C. E., *Field-Marshal Sir Henry Wilson Bart., G.C.B., D.S.O.: His Life and Diaries* (2 vols.; London, 1927).

CASSAR, G. H., *Kitchener: Architect of Victory* (London, 1977).

CECIL, L., *Albert Ballin: Business and Politics in Imperial Germany 1888–1918* (Princeton, 1967).

CHIROL, Sir V., *Fifty Years in a Changing World* (London, 1927).

DAYER, R. A., *Finance and Empire: Sir Charles Addis 1871–1945* (New York, 1988).

DILKS, D., *Curzon in India* (2 vols.; London, 1969).

DUTTON, D., *Austen Chamberlain: Gentleman in Politics* (Bolton, 1985).

GOOLD, J. D., ' "Old Diplomacy": The Diplomatic Career of Lord Hardinge, 1910–22', Ph.D. thesis (Cambridge University, 1976).

GWYNN, S. (ed.), *The Letters and Friendships of Sir Cecil Spring Rice: A Record* (2 vols.; London, 1929).

HAMILTON, K., *Bertie of Thame: Edwardian Ambassador* (London, 1990).

HARDINGE, A., *A Diplomatist in Europe* (London, 1927).

HARDINGE, C., *My Indian Years, 1910–16* (London, 1948).

—— *Old Diplomacy* (London, 1947).

HAYTER, SIR W., *A Double Life* (London, 1974).

HENDERSON, SIR N., *Water Under the Bridges* (London, 1945).

HICKS BEACH, LADY VICTORIA, *Life of Sir Michael Hicks Beach, Earl St Aldwyn* (2 vols.; London, 1932).

HOLMES, R., *The Little Field-Marshal Sir John French* (London, 1981).

HOWARD, C. H. D. (ed.), *The Diary of Edward Goschen 1900–14* (London, 1980).

JENKINS, R., *Asquith* (2nd edn.; London, 1978).

JOHNSON, B. C. (ed.), *Tea and Anarchy! The Bloomsbury Diary of Olive Garnett 1890–3* (London, 1989).

JUDGE, E. H., *Plehve: Repression and Reform in Imperial Russia 1902–4* (Syracuse, NY, 1983).

KARSAVINA, T., *Theatre Street* (New York, 1931).

KENNEDY, K. H., *Mining Tsar: The Life and Times of Leslie Urquhart* (London, 1986).

KOSS, S. E., *John Morley at the India Office* (New Haven, 1969).

—— *Lord Haldane: Scapegoat for Liberalism* (New York, 1969).

LENSEN, G. (ed.), *Korea and Manchuria Between Russia and Japan 1895–1904: The Observations of Sir Ernest Satow British Minister Plenipotentiary to Japan (1895–1900) and China (1900–6)* (Tallahassee, 1966).

LERMAN, K. A., *The Chancellor as Courtier: Bernhard von Bülow and the Governance of Germany 1900–9* (Cambridge, 1990).

LETLEY, E., *Maurice Baring: A Citizen of Europe* (London, 1991).

LIEVEN, D., *Nicholas II: Emperor of All the Russias* (London, 1993).

LOCKHART, R. H. B., *British Agent* (New York, 1933).

MACKAY, R. F., *Balfour: Intellectual Statesman* (New York, 1985).

MCKERCHER, B. J. C., *Esme Howard: A Diplomatic Biography* (Cambridge, 1989).

MARTEL, G., *Imperial Diplomacy: Rosebery and the Failure of Foreign Policy* (Kingston, Ont., 1986).

MORRIS, A. J. A., *Sir Charles Trevelyan 1870–1958: Portrait of a Radical* (New York, 1977).

NABOKOFF, C., *Ordeal of a Diplomat* (London, 1921).

NAPIER, H. D., *The Experiences of a Military Attaché in the Balkans* (London, 1923).

NEWTON, Lord., *Lord Lansdowne* (London, 1929).

ONSLOW, Earl of, *Sixty-Three Years: Diplomacy, the Great War and Politics, with Notes on Travel, Sport and Other Things* (London, 1944).

PARES, B., *A Wandering Student* (Syracuse, NY, 1948).

ROBBINS, K., *Sir Edward Grey: A Biography of Lord Grey of Fallodon* (London, 1971).

ROBERTSON, Sir. W., *From Private to Field-Marshal* (London, 1921).

RÖHL, J. C. G., and SOMBART, N. (eds.), *Kaiser Wilhelm II: New Interpretations: The Corfu Papers* (Cambridge, 1982).

SAZONOV, S., *Fateful Years, 1909–16: The Reminiscences of Serge Sazonov* (London, 1928).

SENESE, D., *S. M. Stepniak-Kravchinskii: The London Years* (Newtonville, MA, 1987).

SPIERS, E. W., *Haldane: An Army Reformer* (Edinburgh, 1980).

SPINNER, Jr., T. J., *George Joachim Goschen: The Transformation of a Victorian Liberal* (London, 1973).

TILLEY, Sir J., *London to Tokyo* (London, 1942).

TREVELYAN, G. M., *Grey of Fallodon* (London, 1948).

WATERS, W. H. -H., *'Secret and Confidential': The Experiences of a Military Attaché* (London, 1926).

WILSON, J., *CB: A Life of Sir Henry Campbell-Bannerman* (London, 1973).

WITTE, S. I., *The Memoirs of Count Witte*, trans. and ed. S. Harcave (London, 1990).

III. PRINTED SECONDARY WORKS

1. Books

ABRAMSKY, C. (ed.), *Essays in Honour of E. H. Carr* (London, 1974).

ADAMS, R. J. Q., and POIRIER, P. P., *The Conscription Controversy in Great Britain, 1900–18* (London, 1987).

ALDER, G. J., *British India's Northern Frontier 1865–95* (London, 1963).

ALLAIN, J. -C., *Agadir 1911: Une crise impérialisme en Europe pour la conquête de Maroc* (Paris, 1976).

ANDERSON, M. S., *Britain's Discovery of Russia 1553–1815* (London, 1958).

—— *The Eastern Question 1774–1923: A Study in International Relations* (London, 1966).

ANDREW, C., *Théophile Delcassé and the Making of the Entente Cordiale* (London, 1969).

ASTAFEV, I. I., *Russko-germanskie diplomaticheskie otnosheniia 1905–11 gg. (ot portsmutskogo mira do potsdamskogo soglasheniia)* (Moscow, 1972).

AVETIAN, A. S., *Russko-germanskie diplomaticheskie otnosheniia nakanune pervoi mirovoi voiny 1910–14* (Moscow, 1985).

BALLHATCHET, K., *Race, Sex and Class under the Raj: Imperial Attitudes and Policies and Their Critics, 1793–1905* (London, 1980).

BARING, M., *Landmarks of Russian Literature* (London, 1910).

BARROS, J., *The Åland Islands Question: Its Settlement by the League of Nations* (New Haven, 1960).

BEASLEY, W. G., *Japanese Imperialism 1894–1945* (Oxford, 1987).

BECKETT, I., and Gooch, J. (eds.), *Politicians and Defence: Studies in the Formulation of British Defence Policy 1845–1970* (Manchester, 1981).

BELL, P. M. H., *John Bull and the Bear: British Public Opinion, Foreign Policy and the Soviet Union 1941–5* (London, 1990).

BENTLEY, M., *Politics Without Democracy 1815–1914* (London, 1984).

BERNSTEIN, G. L., *Liberalism and Liberal Politics in Edwardian England* (London, 1986).

BLAKE, LORD, and CECIL, H. (eds.), *Salisbury: The Man and his Policies* (London, 1987).

BLEWETT, N., *The Peers, the Parties and the People: The British General Elections of 1910* (Toronto, 1972).

BOND, B. (ed.), *The First World War and British Military History* (Oxford, 1991).

BOURNE, K., and WATT, D. C. (eds.), *Studies in International History* (London, 1967).

BRIDGE, F. R., *From Sadowa to Sarajevo: The Foreign Policy of Austria-Hungary, 1866–1914* (London, 1972).

—— *Great Britain and Austria-Hungary 1906–14* (London, 1972).

BULLEN, R. (ed.), *The Foreign Office 1782–1982* (Frederick, MD, 1984).

BURK, K., *Britain, America and the Sinews of War 1914–18* (London, 1985).

BUSCH, B. C., *Britain and the Persian Gulf, 1894–1914* (Berkeley, 1967).

BUSHNELL, J., *Mutiny Amid Repression: Russian Soldiers in the Revolution of 1905–6* (Bloomington, IN, 1985).

CAIN, P. J., and Hopkins, A. G., *British Imperialism: Innovation and Expansion 1688–1914* (London, 1993).

CAMPBELL, A. E., *Great Britain and the United States 1895–1903* (London, 1960).

CAMPBELL, C. S., *Anglo-American Understanding, 1898–1903* (Baltimore, 1957).

CASSAR, G. H., *The French and the Dardanelles: A Study of Failure in the Conduct of War* (London, 1971).

CHURCHILL, R. P., *The Anglo-Russian Convention of 1907* (repr. edn.; Freeport, NY, 1972).

CLARKE, I. F., *Voices Prophesying War, 1763–1984* (London, 1966).

Cohen, S. A., *British Policy in Mesopotamia 1903–14* (London, 1976).

CONRAD, J., *The Secret Agent* (London, 1907).

—— *Under Western Eyes* (London, 1947; first pub. 1911).

COOGAN, J. W., *The End of Neutrality: The United States, Britain and Maritime Rights 1899–1915* (Ithaca, NY, 1981).

CRAMPTON, R. J., *The Hollow Detente: Anglo-German Relations in the Balkans 1911–14* (London, 1979).

CROSS, A. G. (ed.), *The Russian Theme in English Literature from the Sixteenth Century to 1980: An Introductory Survey and a Bibliography* (Oxford, 1985).

—— (ed.), *Russia Under Western Eyes 1517–1815* (London, 1971).

DAKIN, D., *The Greek Struggle in Macedonia 1897–1913* (Thessalonika, 1966).

DALY, J. C. K., *Russian Seapower and 'The Eastern Question', 1827–41* (London, 1991).

DAVIS, L. E., and HUTTENBACK, R. A., *Mammon and the Pursuit of Empire: The Political Economy of British Imperialism, 1860–1912* (Cambridge, 1986).

DIAKIN, V. S., *Russkaia burzhuaziia i tsarism v gody pervoi mirovoi voiny* (Leningrad, 1967).

—— *Samoderzhavie, burzhuaziia i dvorianstvo, 1907–11 gg.* (Leningrad, 1978).

DILKS, D. (ed.), *Retreat from Power: Studies in Britain's Foreign Policy of the Twentieth Century*, i, *1906–39* (London, 1981).

DILLON, E. J., *The Eclipse of Russia* (London, 1918).

D'OMBRAIN, N., *War Machinery and High Policy: Defence Administration in Peacetime Britain 1902–14* (London, 1973).

EDELMAN, R., *Gentry Politics on the Eve of the Russian Revolution: The Nationalist Party 1907–17* (New Brunswick, NJ, 1980).

EDWARDS, E. W., *British Diplomacy and Finance in China, 1895–1914* (Oxford, 1987).

EKSTEINS, M., *The Rites of Spring: The Great War and the Birth of the Modern Age* (Toronto, 1989).

ENGELSTEIN, L., *Moscow, 1905: Working-Class Organization and Political Conflict* (Stanford, CA, 1982).

ESTHUS, R. A., *Double Eagle and Rising Sun: The Russians and Japanese at Portsmouth in 1905* (Durham, NC, 1988).

EVANS, R. J. W., and POGGE VON STRANDMANN, H. (eds.), *The Coming of the First World War* (Oxford, 1988).

FARRAR, JUN., L. L., *Divide and Conquer: German Attempts to Conclude a Separate Peace, 1914–18* (Boulder, CO, 1978).

—— *The Short War Illusion* (Santa Barbara, CA, 1974).

FERGUSSON, T. G., *British Military Intelligence, 1870–1914* (London, 1984).

FERRIER, J. -L., (ed.), *Art of Our Century: The Chronicle of Western Art 1900 to the Present*, trans. W. Glanze (New York, 1989).

FERRIS, J. R., *Men, Money, and Diplomacy: The Evolution of British Strategic Foreign Policy, 1919–26* (Ithaca, NY, 1989).

FINK, C., HULL, I. V. and KNOX, M. (eds.), *German Nationalism and European Response, 1890–1945* (Norman, OK, 1985).

FREEDMAN, L., Hayes, P., and O'Neill, R. (eds.), *War, Strategy, and International Politics: Essays in Honour of Sir Michael Howard* (Oxford, 1992).

FRENCH, D., *British Economic and Strategic Planning 1905–15* (London, 1982).

—— *British Strategy and War Aims: 1914–16* (London, 1986).

—— *The British Way in Warfare 1688–2000* (London, 1900).

—— *The Strategy of the Lloyd George Coalition 1916–18* (forthcoming, Oxford).

FRIEDBERG, A. L., *The Weary Titan: Britain and the Experience of Relative Decline, 1895–1905* (Princeton, 1988).

FRIEDGUT, T. H., *Iuzovka and Revolution*, i, *Life and Work in Russia's Donbass, 1869–1914* (Princeton, 1989).

FULLER, Jr., W. C., *Strategy and Power in Russia 1600–1914* (New York, 1992).

FUTRELL, M., *Northern Underground: Episodes of Russian Revolutionary Transport and Communications through Scandinavia and Finland 1863–1917* (London, 1963).

GAINER, B., *Alien Invasion: The Origins of the Aliens Act of 1905* (New York, 1972).

GATRELL, P., *The Tsarist Economy 1850–1917* (London, 1986).

GEISS, I., *German Foreign Policy 1871–1914* (London, 1976).

GEORGIEV, V. A., N.S. Kiniapina, M.T. Panchenkova, and V.I. Sheremet, *Vostochnyi vopros vo vneshnei politike Rossii* (Moscow, 1978).

GEYER, D., *Russian Imperialism: The Interaction of Domestic and Foreign Policy, 1860–1914* trans. B. Little (Leamington Spa, 1987).

GIRAULT, R., *Emprunts russes et investissements français en Russie, 1887–1914* (Paris, 1973).

GLEASON, J. H., *The Genesis of Russophobia in Great Britain* (Cambridge, MA, 1950).

GLEIG, C., *When All Men Starve: Showing How England Hazarded her Naval Supremacy, and the Horrors which Followed the Interruption of her Food Supply* (New York, 1898).

GOOCH, J., *The Plans of War: The General Staff and British Military Strategy c.1900–16* (London, 1974).

GOTTLIEB, W. W., *Studies in Secret Diplomacy during the First World War* (London, 1957).

GREAVES, R. L., *Persia and the Defence of India 1884–92: A Study in the Foreign Policy of the Third Marquis of Salisbury* (London, 1959).

GREGORY, P. R., *Russian National Income, 1885–1913* (Cambridge, 1982).

GRENVILLE, J. A. S., *Lord Salisbury and Foreign Policy: The Close of the Nineteenth Century* (London, 1964).

GRIEVES, K., *The Politics of Manpower, 1914–18* (Manchester, 1988).

GRIFFITH, G. *The Angel of the Revolution: A Tale of the Coming Terror* (London, 1893).

—— *The Outlaws of the Air* (London, 1897).

GUROFF, G., and CARSTENSEN, F. V. (eds)., *Entrepreneurship in Imperial Russia and the Soviet Union* (Princeton, 1983).

HAMILTON, C. I., *Anglo-French Naval Rivalry 1840–70* (Oxford, 1993).

HATTON, R., and ANDERSON, M. S. (eds.), *Studies in Diplomatic History: Essays in Memory of David Bayne Horn* (London, 1970).

HAYNE, M. B., *The French Foreign Office and the Origins of the First World War 1898–1914* (Oxford, 1993).

HEALY, A. E., *The Russian Autocracy in Crisis, 1905–7* (Hamden, 1976).

HELLER, J., *British Policy towards the Ottoman Empire 1908–14* (London, 1983).

HENTY, G. A., *Condemned as a Nihilist: A Story of Escape from Siberia* (New York, 1897).

HINSLEY, F. H. (ed.), *British Foreign Policy Under Sir Edward Grey* (Cambridge, 1977).

HOLMES, C., *Anti-Semitism in British Society, 1876–1939* (New York, 1979).

HOSKING, G. A., *The Russian Constitutional Experiment: Government and Duma, 1907–14* (Cambridge, 1973).

HÖLZLE, E., *Die Selbstentmachtung Europas: Das Experiment des Friedens vor und im Ersten Weltkrieg* (Göttingen, 1975).

HOUGHTON, W. A., *The Victorian Frame of Mind 1830–70* (New Haven, 1973).

HOWARD, C. H. D., *Splendid Isolation: A Study of Ideas Concerning Britain's International Position and Foreign Policy During the Later years of the Third Marquis of Salisbury* (London, 1967).

HOWARD, M., *The Continental Commitment: The Dilemma of British Defence Policy in the Era of Two World Wars* (London, 1972).

HYNES, S., *The Edwardian Turn of Mind* (Princeton, 1968).

IGNATEV, A. V., *Vneshniaia politika Rossii v 1905–7 gg.* (Moscow, 1986).

IGNATEV, I. V., *Russko-angliiskie otnosheniia nakanune pervoi mirovoi voiny (1908–14 gg)* (Moscow, 1962).

INGRAM, E., *The Beginning of the Great Game in Asia, 1828–34* (Oxford, 1979).

—— *Commitment to Empire: Prophecies of the Great Game in Asia 1797–1800* (Oxford, 1981).

—— *In Defence of British India: Great Britain in the Middle East, 1775–1842* (London, 1984).

JAFFE, L. S., *Decision to Disarm Germany: British Policy towards Postwar German Disarmament, 1914–19* (London, 1985).

JELAVICH, B., *The Ottoman Empire, the Great Powers, and the Straits Question 1870–87* (Bloomington, IN, 1973).

JOLL, J., *1914: The Unspoken Assumptions* (London, 1967).

JONES, R. A., *The British Diplomatic Service 1815–1914* (Waterloo, Ont., 1983).

KAZEMZADEH, F., *Russia and Britain in Persia, 1864–1914* (New Haven, 1968).

KEIGER, J. F. V., *France and the Origins of the First World War* (London, 1983).

KENNEDY, P., *The Realities Behind Diplomacy: Background Influences on British External Policy, 1865–1980* (London, 1981).

—— *The Rise and Fall of British Naval Mastery* (London, 1976).

—— *The Rise and Fall of the Great Powers* (New York, 1987).

—— *The Rise of the Anglo-German Antagonism 1860–1914* (London, 1980).

KENT, M. (ed.), *The Great Powers and the End of the Ottoman Empire* (London, 1984).

KING, F. H. H., *The History of the Hongkong and Shanghai Banking Corporation*, ii, *The*

Hongkong Bank in the Period of Imperialism and War, 1895–1918: Wayfoong, the Focus of Wealth (Cambridge, 1988).

—— (ed.), *Eastern Banking: Essays in the History of the Hongkong and Shanghai Banking Corporation* (London, 1983).

LACQUEUR, W. and MOSSE, G. L. (eds.), *1914: The Coming of the First World War* (New York, 1966).

LAMBERT, A., *The Crimean War: British Grand Strategy, 1853–56* (Manchester, 1990).

LAMBI, I. N., *The Navy and German Power Politics, 1862–1914* (London, 1984).

LANGER, W. L., *The Diplomacy of Imperialism 1890–1902* (2nd edn.; New York, 1968).

LE QUEUX, W., *The Great War in England in 1897* (London, 1894).

—— *Secrets of the Foreign Office: Describing the Doings of Duckworth Drew, of the Secret Service* (London, 1903).

LEBZELTER, G. C., *Political Anti-Semitism in England 1918–39* (London, 1978).

LIEVEN, D., *Russia and the Origins of the First World War* (London, 1983).

—— *Russia's Rulers under the Old Regime* (New Haven, 1989).

LINDBERG, F., *Scandinavia in Great Power Politics* (Stockholm, 1958).

LOWE, C. J., *The Reluctant Imperialists* (2 vols.; London, 1967).

—— *Salisbury and the Mediterranean 1886–96* (London, 1965).

—— and Dockrill, M. L., *The Mirage of Power* (3 vols.; London, 1972).

LUNTINEN, P., *The Baltic Question 1903–8* (Helsinki, 1975).

MCDONALD, D. M., *United Government and Foreign Policy in Russia 1900–14* (Cambridge, MA, 1992).

MCKAY, J. P., *Pioneers for Profit: Foreign Entrepreneurship and Russian Industrialization 1885–1913* (Chicago, 1970).

MCKERCHER, B. J. C. (ed.), *Arms Limitation and Disarmament: Restraints on War, 1899–1939* (New York, 1992).

—— and Moss, D. J. (eds.), *Shadow and Substance in British Foreign Policy 1895–1939: Memorial Essays Honouring C. J. Lowe* (Edmonton, Alta., 1984).

MCLEAN, D., *Britain and Her Buffer State: The Collapse of the Persian Empire, 1890–1914* (London, 1979).

MCNEILL, W. H., *The Pursuit of Power: Technology, Armed Force, and Society since A.D. 1000* (Chicago, 1982).

MALOZEMOFF, A., *Russian Far Eastern Policy 1881–1904: With Special Emphasis on the Causes of the Russo-Japanese War* (Berkeley, 1958).

MANNING, R. T., *The Crisis of the Old Order in Russia: Gentry and Government* (Princeton, 1982).

MARDER, A. J., *The Anatomy of British Sea Power* (London, 1942).

—— *From the Dreadnought to Scapa Flow* (5 vols.; London, 1961–70).

MARINOV, V. A., *Rossiia i Iaponiia pered pervoi mirovoi voinoi (1905–14 gody)* (Moscow, 1974).

MATTHEW, H. C. G. *The Liberal Imperialists: The Ideas and politics of a Post-Gladstonian Élite* (London, 1973).

MELCHIORI, B. A., *Terrorism in the Late Victorian Novel* (London, 1985).

MENNING, B. W., *Bayonets Before Bullets: The Imperial Russian Army, 1861–1914* (Bloomington, IN, 1992).

MERRIMAN, H. S., *Prisoners and Captives* (London, 1891).

—— *The Sowers* (New York, 1968; first pub. 1895).

MILLER, M. A. *The Russian Revolutionary Emigres 1825–70* (Baltimore, 1986).

MITCHELL, B. R., *European Historical Statistics 1750–1970* (London, 1978).

MONGER, G., *The End of Isolation: British Foreign Policy 1900–7* (London, 1963).

MORRIS, A. J. A., *Radicalism Against War 1906–14: The Advocacy of Peace and Retrenchment* (Totowa, NJ, 1972).

—— *The Scaremongers: The Advocacy of War and Rearmament 1896–1914* (London, 1984).

MOSSE, W. E., *The European Powers and the German Question 1848–71: With Special Reference to England and Russia* (New York, 1981; first pub. London, 1958).

MOTOJIRO, A., *Rakka ryūsui: Colonel Akashi's Report on His Secret Cooperation with the Russian Revolutionary Parties during the Russo-Japanese War* (Helsinki, 1988).

MUNIMITSU, M., *Kenkenroku: A Diplomatic Record of the Sino-Japanese War*, trans. and ed., G. M. Berger (Tokyo, 1982).

NASSIBIAN, A., *Britain and the Armenian Question 1915–23* (London, 1984).

NEILSON, K., *Strategy and Supply: The Anglo-Russian Alliance 1914–17* (London, 1984).

—— and HAYCOCK, R. G. (eds.), *Men, Machines & War* (Waterloo, Ont., 1988).

—— and MCKERCHER, B. J. C. (eds.), *Go Spy the Land: Military Intelligence in History* (New York, 1992).

NICOLSON, H., *Sir Arthur Nicolson, Bart. First Lord Carnock: A study in the Old Diplomacy* (London, 1930).

NISH, I., *The Anglo-Japanese Alliance: The Diplomacy of Two Island Empires 1894–1907* (London, 1966).

—— *The Origins of the Russo-Japanese War* (London, 1985).

OL', P. V., *Foreign Capital in Russia*, trans. G. Jones and G. Gerenstain (New York, 1983).

ORBELL, J., *Baring Brothers & Co., Limited: A History to 1939* (London, 1985).

OSTALTSEVA, A. F., *Anglo-russkoe soglashenie 1907 goda* (Saratov, 1977).

PARES, B., *Russia and Reform* (London, 1907).

PEARSON, R., *The Russian Moderates and the Crisis of Tsarism 1914–17* (London, 1977).

PELCOVITS, N. A., *Old China Hands and the Foreign Office* (2nd edn.; New York, 1969).

PLATT, D. C. M., *Britain's Investment Overseas on the Eve of the First World War* (London, 1986).

—— *Foreign Finance in Continental Europe and the United States, 1814–70* (London, 1984).

PORTER, A. N., *The Origins of the South African War: Joseph Chamberlain and the Diplomacy of Imperialism 1895–9* (Manchester, 1980).

PORTER, B., *The Origins of the Vigilant State: The London Metropolitan Special Branch before the First World War* (London, 1987).

—— *The Refugee Question in Mid-Victorian Politics* (Cambridge, 1979).

PRIESTLEY, J. B., *The Edwardians* (London, 1970).

QUESTED, R. K. I., *The Russo-Chinese Bank: A Multinational Financial Base of Tsarism in China* (Birmingham, 1977).

—— '*Matey' Imperialists? The Tsarist Russians in Manchuria 1895–1917* (Hong Kong, 1982).

RANFT, B. (ed.), *Technical Change and British Naval Policy 1860–1939* (London, 1977).

READING, D. K., *The Anglo-Russian Commercial Treaty of 1734* (New Haven, 1938).

RENZI, W. A., *In the Shadow of the Sword: Italy's Neutrality and Entrance into the Great War, 1914–15* (New York, 1987).

RHODES JAMES, R., *The British Revolution: British Politics, 1880–1939* (2 vols.; London, 1976).

ROBSON, R. (ed.), *Ideas and Institutions of Victorian Britain: Essays in Honour of George Kitson Clark* (London, 1967).

ROSE, J., *The Edwardian Temperament 1895–1919* (Athens, OH, 1987).

ROSSOS, A., *Russia and the Balkans: Inter-Balkan Rivalries and Russian Foreign Policy 1908–14* (Toronto, 1981).

ROSTUNOV, I. I., *Russkii front pervoi mirovoi voiny* (Moscow, 1976).

ROTHWELL, V. H., *British War Aims and Peace Diplomacy 1914–18* (Oxford, 1971).

SABLINSKY, W., *The Road to Bloody Sunday* (Princeton, 1976).

SANDERS, M. L. and TAYLOR P. M., *British Propaganda during the First World War, 1914–18*, (London, 1982).

SARKISSIAN, A. O. (ed.), *Studies in Diplomatic History and Historiography in Honour of G. P. Gooch* (London, 1961).

SCHURMAN, D. M., *The Education of a Navy: The Development of British Naval Strategic Thought, 1867–1914* (Chicago, 1965).

—— 'Imperial Defence 1868–87: A Study in the Decisive Impulses Behind the Change from "Colonial" to "Imperial" defence', Ph.D. thesis (Cambridge, University, 1955).

SEARLE, G. R., *The Quest for National Efficiency: A Study in British Politics and British Political Thought, 1899–1914* (Oxford, 1971).

SHANNON, R. T., *Gladstone and the Bulgarian Agitation, 1876* (London, 1963).

SHATSILLO, K. F., *Russkii imperializm i razvitie flota nakanune pervoi mirovoi voiny (1906–14)* (Moscow, 1968).

SIDOROV, A. L., *Ekonomicheskoe polozhenie Rossii v gody pervoi mirovoi voiny* (Moscow, 1973).

—— *Finansovoe polozhenie Rossii v gody pervoi mirovoi voiny (1914–17)* (Moscow, 1960).

SIEGELBAUM, L. H., *The Politics of Industrial Mobilization in Russia, 1914–17* (London, 1983).

SLATTER, J. (ed.), *From the Other Shore: Russian Political Emigrants in Britain, 1880–1917* (London, 1984).

SMITH, JR., C. J., *The Russian Struggle for Power, 1914–17* (New York, 1956).

SPIERS, E. W., *The Army and Society 1815–1914* (London, 1980).

STAFFORD, D., *The Silent Game: The Real World of Imaginary Spies* (Toronto, 1988).

STANKSY, P., *Ambitions and Strategies: The Struggle for the Leadership of the Liberal Party in the 1890s* (Oxford, 1964).

STEINER, Z., *Britain and the Origins of the First World War* (London, 1977).

—— *The Foreign Office and Foreign Policy 1898–1914* (Cambridge, 1969).

STEVENSON, D., *The First World War and International Politics* (Oxford, 1988).

STONE, N., *The Eastern Front 1914–17* (London, 1975).

SUMIDA, J. T., *In Defence of Naval Supremacy: Finance, Technology and British Naval Policy, 1899–1914* (London, 1989).

TANENBAUM, J. K., *General Maurice Sarrail 1856–1929: The French Army and Left-Wing Politics* (Chapel Hill, NC, 1974).

TARLE, E. V. (ed.), *Problemy istorii mezhdunarodnykh otnoshenii* (Leningrad, 1972).

TAYLOR, A. J. P., *The Troublemakers: Dissent over Foreign Policy 1792–1939* (Harmondsworth, 1985).

THADEN, E. C., *Russia and the Balkan Alliance of 1912* (University Park, PA, 1965).

Times, The, The History of The Times: The Twentieth Century Test 1884–1912 (New York, 1947).

TOLF, R. W., *The Russian Rockefellers: The Saga of the Nobel Family and the Russian Oil Industry* (Stanford, CA, 1976).

TRACY, L., *The Final War* (New York, 1896).

TREBILCOCK, C., *The Vickers Brothers: Armaments and Enterprise, 1854–1914* (London 1977).

TURNER, J., *British Politics and the Great War: Coalition and Conflict 1915–18* (New Haven, 1992).

VERNER, A., *The Crisis of Autocracy: Nicholas II and the 1905 Revolution* (Princeton, 1990).

VOYNICH, E. L., *Olive Latham* (Philadelphia, 1904).

WALLACE, L. P. and ASKEW, W. C. (eds.), *Power, Public Opinion, and Diplomacy: Essays in Honor of Eber Malcolm Carroll by his Former Students* (Freeport, NY, 1959).

WARK, W. K. (ed.), *Spy Fiction, Spy Films, and Real Intelligence* (London, 1991).

WATT, I. (ed.), *Conrad: The Secret Agent: A Casebook* (London, 1973).

WATT, D. C., *Personalities and Politics: Studies in the Formulation of British Foreign Policy in the Twentieth Century* (London, 1965).

—— *What About the People? Abstractions and Reality in History and the Social Sciences* (London, 1983).

—— *Succeeding John Bull: America in Britain's Place 1900–75* (Cambridge, 1984).

WESTRATE, B., *The Arab Bureau: British Policy in the Middle East, 1916–20* (University Park, PA, 1992).

WESTWOOD, J. N., *Russia Against Japan: A New Look at the Russo-Japanese War* (London, 1986).

WILLAN, T. S., *The Muscovy Merchants of 1555* (Manchester, 1953).

WILLIAMS, R., *Defending the Empire: The Conservative Party and British Defence Policy 1899–1915* (New Haven, 1991).

WILLIAMSON, JR., S. R., *Austria-Hungary and the Origins of the First World War* (London, 1991).

—— *The Politics of Grand Strategy: Britain and France Prepare for War, 1904–14* (paperback edn.; London, first pub. Cambridge, MA, 1969).

WILSON, K., *Empire and Continent: Studies in British Foreign Policy from the 1880s to the First World War* (London, 1987).

—— *The Policy of the Entente: Essays on the Determinants of British Foreign Policy, 1904–14* (Cambridge, 1985).

—— (ed.), *British Foreign Secretaries and Foreign Policy: From Crimean War to First World War* (London, 1987).

WORMER, K., *Grossbritannien, Russland und Deutschland: Studien zur britischen Weltreichpolitik am Vorabend des Ersten Weltkriegs* (Munich, 1980).

YAPP, M., *Strategies of British India: Britain, Iran and Afghanistan 1798–1850* (Oxford, 1980).

YOUNG, L. K., *British Policy in China 1895–1902* (Oxford, 1970).

Yuzawa, T. and UDAGAWA, M. (eds.), *Foreign Business in Japan before World War II* (Tokyo, 1990).

ZIEGLER, P., *The Sixth Great Power: Barings, 1762–1929* (London, 1988).

2. Articles

ADAMS, R. J. Q., 'The National Service League and Mandatory Service in Edwardian Britain', *Armed Forces & Society*, 12 (1985), 53–74.

ALDER, G. J., 'India and the Crimean War', *JICH* 2 (1973), 15–37.

ALLEN, M., 'Rear Admiral Reginald Custance: Director of Naval Intelligence 1899–1902', *MM* 78 (1992), 61–75.

ANDERSON, E., 'The Role of the Crimean War in the Baltic', *Scandinavian Studies*, 41 (1969), 263–75.

ANDREW, C. and NEILSON, K., 'Tsarist Codebreakers and British Codes', *INS* 1 (1986), 6–12.

AVREKH, A. IA., 'Tretia Duma i nachalo krizisa treteiunskoi sistemy (1908–9)', *IZ* 53 (1955), 50–109.

—— 'Vopros o zapadnom zemstve i bankrotstvo Stolypina', *IZ* 70 (1961), 61–112.

BABICHEV, D. S., 'Deiatelnost Russkogo pravitelstvennogo komiteta v Londone v gody pervoi mirovoi voiny (1914–17)', *IZ* 57 (1956), 276–92.

BAILES, H., 'Patterns of Thought in the Late Victorian Army', *JSS* 4 (1981), 29–45.

—— 'Technology and Tactics in the British Army, 1866–1900', in Neilson and Haycock (eds.), *Men, Machines, & War*, 21–48.

BARKAI, H., 'The Macro-Economics of Tsarist Russia in the Industrialization Era: Monetary Developments, the Balance of Payments and the Gold Standard', *JEH* 33 (1973), 339–71.

BARTLETT, C. J., 'The Mid-Victorian Reappraisal of Naval Policy', in Bourne and Watt (eds.), *Studies in International History*, 189–208.

BAYLEN, J. O., 'Madame Olga Novikov: Defender of Imperial Russia, 1880–1900', *Historia*, 1 (1951), 133–56.

—— 'Madame Olga Novikov, Propagandist', *ASEER* 10 (1951), 255–71.

—— 'The Tsar and the British Press: Alexander III and the *Pall Mall Gazette*, 1888', *EEQ* 15 (1982), 425–39.

—— 'W. T. Stead and the Russian Revolution of 1905', *CJH* 2 (1967), 45–66.

—— 'W. T. Stead, Apologist for Imperial Russia, 1870–80' *Gazette: International Journal for Mass Communications Studies*, 6 (1960), 281–97.

BECKETT, I. F. W., 'Edward Stanhope at the War Office 1887–92', *JSS* 5 (1982), 278–307.

—— 'H. O. Arnold-Forster and the Volunteers', in Beckett and Gooch (eds.), *Politicians and Defence*, 47–68.

—— 'The Stanhope Memorandum of 1888: A Reinterpretation', *BIHR* 57 (1984), 240–7.

BEELER, J. F., 'A One Power Standard? Great Britain and the Balance of Naval Power, 1860–80', *JSS* 15 (1992), 548–75.

BERNSTEIN, G. L., 'Sir Henry Campbell-Bannerman and the Liberal Imperialists', *JBS* 23 (1983), 105–24.

BODGER, A., 'Russia and the End of the Ottoman Empire', in Kent (ed.), *The Great Powers and the End of the Ottoman Empire*, 76–110.

BOLSOVER, G. H., 'Izvol'sky and the Reform of the Russian Ministry of Foreign Affairs', *SEER* 63 (1985), 21–40.

BOYLE, T., 'The Liberal Imperialists, 1892–1906', *BIHR* 52 (1979), 48–82.

BRAILEY, N., 'Sir Ernest Satow, Japan and Asia: The Trials of a Diplomat in the Age of High Imperialism', *HJ* 35 (1992), 115–50.

BRANCOVAN, C. E., 'Grand Duke Nikolay Mikhailovic on the Ministerial and Parliamentary Crisis of March–April 1911: Five Letters to Frédéric Masson', *OSP*, NS, 6 (1973), 66–81.

BRIDGE, F. R., 'Izvolsky, Aehrenthal and the End of the Austro-Russian Entente, 1906–8', *Mitteilungen des österreichischen Staatsarchivs*, 29 (1976), 315–62.

BROCK, M., 'Britain Enters the War', in R. J. W. Evans, and H. Pogge von Strandmann (eds.), *The Coming of the First World War* (Oxford, 1988), 145–78.

BROCK, P., 'Joseph Cowen and the Polish Exiles', *SEER* 32 (1953), 52–69.

—— 'Polish Democrats and English Radicals 1832–62: A Chapter in the History of Anglo-Polish Relations', *JMH* 25 (1953), 139–56.

BUZARD, J., 'A Continent of Pictures: Reflections on the "Europe" of Nineteenth-Century Tourists', *PMLA* 108 (1993), 30–44.

CARSTENSEN, F. V., 'Foreign Participation in Russian Economic Life: Notes on British Enterprise, 1865–1914', in Curoff and Carstensen (eds.), *Entrepreneurship in Imperial Russia and the Soviet Union*, 140–58.

CECIL, L., 'William II and his Russian "Colleagues" ', in Fink et al. (eds.), *German Nationalism and European Response*, 1890–1945, 95–134.

CHALLIS, N. and DEWEY, H. W., 'The Blessed Fools of Old Russia', *JfGOE* 22 (1974), 1–11.

CHMIELEWSKI, E., 'Stolypin and the Russian Ministerial Crisis of 1909', *CSS* 4 (1965), 1–38.

—— 'Stolypin's Last Crisis', *CSS* 3 (1964), 95–126.

CLENDENNING, P. H., 'William Gomm: A Case Study of the Foreign Entrepreneur in Eighteenth Century Russia', *JEEH* 6 (1977), 533–48.

COCKFIELD, J., 'Germany and the Fashoda Crisis', *CEH* 16 (1983), 256–75.

COHEN, S. A., 'The Genesis of the British Campaign in Mesopotamia, 1914', *MES* 12 (1976), 119–32.

COLE, T. F., 'The *Daily Telegraph* affair and its aftermath: the Kaiser, Bülow and the Reichstag, 1908–9', in Röhl and Sombart (eds.), *Kaiser Wilhelm II*, 249–68.

CONACHER, J. B., 'The Asian Front in the Crimean War and the Fall of Kars'. *JASHR* 58 (1990), 169–87.

COOGAN, J. W. and COOGAN, P. F., 'The British Cabinet and the Anglo-French Staff Talks, 1905–1914: Who Knew What and When Did He Know It?', *JBS* 24 (1985), 110–31.

COOPER, M. B., 'British Policy in the Balkans, 1908–9', *HJ* 7 (1964), 258–67.

CORNFORD, J. P., 'The Parliamentary Foundations of the Hotel Cecil', in Robson (ed.), *Ideas and Institutions of Victorian Britain*, 268–311.

CORP, E. T., 'The Problem of Promotion in the Career of Sir Eyre Crowe, 1905–20', *AJPH* 28 (1982), 236–49.

—— 'Sir Eyre Crowe and the Administration of the Foreign Office, 1906–14', *HJ* 22 (1979), 443–54.

—— 'Sir William Tyrrell: The *Eminence Grise* of the British Foreign Office, 1912–15', *HJ* 25 (1982), 697–708.

COSGROVE, R. A., 'The Career of Sir Eyre Crowe: A Reassessment', *Albion*, 4 (1972), 193–205.

CRAMPTON, R. J., 'The Balkans, 1909–14', in Hinsley (ed.), *British Foreign Policy Under Sir Edward Grey*, 256–70.

CRISP, O., 'The Russian Liberals and the 1906 Anglo-French Loan to Russia', *SEER* 39 (1961), 497–511.

—— 'The Russo-Chinese Bank: An Episode in Franco-Russian Relations', *SEER* 52 (1974), 197–212.

CROSS, A. G., 'British Knowledge of Russian Culture (1698–1801)', *Canadian-American Slavic Studies*, 13 (1979), 412–35.

—— 'Introduction', in id. (ed.), *The Russian Theme in English Literature from the Sixteenth Century to 1980*, 1–82.

—— 'Introduction', in id. (ed.), *Russia Under Western Eyes 1517–1815*, 13–47.

DOCKRILL, M. L., 'British policy during the Agadir Crisis of 1911', in Hinsley (ed.), *British Foreign Policy Under Sir Edward Grey*, 271–87.

DOUGLAS, R., 'Britain and the Armenian Question, 1894–7', *HJ* 19 (1976), 113–33.

DUNAE, P. A., 'Boy's Literature and the Idea of Empire, 1870–1914', *VS* 24 (1980), 105–21.

DUNNING, C., 'James I, The Russia Company, and the Plan to Establish a Protectorate Over North Russia', *Albion*, 21 (1989), 206–26.

DUTHIE, J. L., 'Pragmatic Diplomacy or Imperial Encroachment? British Policy towards Afghanistan, 1874–9', *IHR* 5 (1983), 475–95.

—— 'Pressure From Within: The "Forward" Group in the India Office During Gladstone's First Ministry', *JAH* 15 (1981), 36–72.

—— 'Sir Henry Creswicke Rawlinson and the Art of Great Gamesmanship', *JICH* 11 (1983), 253–74.

—— 'Some Further Insights into the Working of Mid-Victorian Imperialism: Lord

Salisbury, the "Forward" Group and Anglo-Afghan Relations: 1874–8', *JICH* 8 (1980), 181–208.

DUTTON, D., 'The Balkan Campaign and French War Aims in the Great War', *EHR* 94 (1979), 97–113.

—— 'The Calais Conference of December 1915', *HJ* 21 (1978), 143–56.

—— 'Unionist Politics and the Aftermath of the General Election of 1906: A Reassessment', *HJ* 22 (1979), 861–76.

—— 'The Union Sacrée and the French Cabinet Crisis of October 1915', *ESR* 8 (1978), 411–24.

EDWARDS, E. W., 'The Franco-German Agreement on Morocco', *EHR* 78 (1963), 483–513.

EKSTEIN, M. G. and STEINER, Z., 'The Sarajevo Crisis', in Hinsley (ed.), *British Foreign Policy under Sir Edward Grey*, 397–410.

ELLENBERGER, N. W., 'The Souls and London "Society" at the End of the Nineteenth Century', *VS* 25 (1982), 133–60.

EMETS, V. A., 'Petrogradskaia konferentsiia 1917 g. i Frantsiia', *IZ* 83 (1969), 23–37.

—— 'Pozitsiia Rossii i ee soiuznikov v voprose o pomoshchi Serbii oseniu 1915 g.' *IZ* 75 (1965), 122–46.

ESTHUS, R. A., 'Nicholas II and the Russo-Japanese War', *RR* 40 (1981), 396–411.

FAIRBANKS, Jr., C. H., 'The Origins of the *Dreadnought* Revolution: A Historiographical Essay', *IHR* 13 (1991), 246–72.

FAIRLIE, S., 'Shipping in the Anglo-Russian Grain Trade, to 1870: Part One', *Maritime History*, 1 (1971), 158–75.

—— 'Shipping in the Anglo-Russian Grain Trade, to 1870: Part Two', *Maritime History*, 2 (1972), 31–45.

FALKUS, M. 'Aspects of Foreign Investment in Tsarist Russia', *JEEH* 8 (1979), 5–36.

FÄLT, O. K., 'Collaboration Between Japanese Intelligence and the Finnish Underground during the Russo-Japanese War', *Asian Profile*, 4 (1976), 205–38.

FARRAR, Jr., L. L., 'Peace Through Exhaustion: German Diplomatic Motivations for the Verdun Campaign', *Revue Internationale d'Histoire Militaire*, 8 (1972–5), 477–94.

FERRIS, J., 'Lord Salisbury, Secret Intelligence, and British Policy toward Russia and Central Asia, 1874–8', in Neilson and McKercher (eds.), *Go Spy the Land*, 115–52.

FRANCIS, R. M., 'The British Withdrawal from the Baghdad Railway Project in April 1903', *HJ* 16 (1973), 168–78.

FRASER, P., 'Unionism and Tariff Reform: The Crisis of 1906', *HJ* 5 (1962), 149–66.

FRENCH, D., 'The Dardanelles, Mecca and Kut: Prestige as a Factor in British Eastern Strategy, 1914–16', *WS* 5 (1987), 45–61.

—— 'The Edwardian Crisis and the Origins of the First World War', *IHR* 4 (1982), 207–21.

—— 'The Meaning of Attrition, 1914–16', *EHR* 103 (1988), 385–405.

FRIEDBERG, A. L., 'Britain Faces the Burdens of Empire: The Financial Crisis of 1901–5', *WS* 5 (1987), 15–37.

FRITZINGER, L. B., 'Friends in High Places: Valentine Chirol, *The Times*, and Anglo–German Relations, 1892–6', *Victorian Periodicals Review*, 21 (1988), 9–14.

GALBRAITH, J, S., 'British Policy on Railways in Persia, 1870–1914', *MES* 25 (1989), 480–505.

GALTON, D., 'The Anglo-Russian Literary Society', *SEER* 48 (1970), 272–82.

GANELIN, R. Sh., 'Storonniki separatnogo mira s Germanaiei v tsarskoi Rossii', in Tarle (ed.), *Problemy istorii mezhdunarodnykh otnoshenii*, 126–55.

GATRELL, P., 'After Tsushima: Economic and Administrative Aspects of Russian Naval Rearmament, 1905–13', *EconHR*, 2nd ser., 43 (1990), 255–70.

—— 'Industrial Expansion in Tsarist Russia, 1908–14', *EconHR*, 2nd ser., 35 (1982), 99–110.

GILBERT, B. B., 'Pacifist to Interventionist: David Lloyd George in 1911 and 1914: Was Belgium an Issue?', *HJ* 28 (1985), 863–84.

GILLARD, D. R., 'Salisbury', in Wilson, (eds.), *British Foreign Secretaries and Foreign Policy*, 119–37.

—— 'Salisbury and the Indian Defence Problem, 1885–1902', in Bourne and Watt (eds.), *Studies in International History*, 236–48.

GOLDSTEIN, E. R., 'Vickers Limited and the Tsarist Regime', *SEER* 58 (1980), 561–71.

GOOCH, J., 'Haldane and the "National Army" ', in Beckett and Gooch (eds.), *Politicians and Defence*, 69–86.

GOOLD, J. D., 'Lord Hardinge and the Mesopotamia Expedition and Inquiry, 1914–17', *HJ* 19 (1976), 919–45.

—— 'Lord Hardinge as Ambassador to France, and the Anglo-French Dilemma over Germany and the Near East, 1920–2', *HJ* 21 (1978), 913–37.

GORDON, M. R., 'Domestic Conflict and the Origins of the First World War: The British and German Cases', *JMH* 46 (1974), 191–226.

GRAF, D. W., 'Military Rule Behind the Russian Front, 1914–17: The Political Ramifications', *JfGOE* 22 (1974), 390–411.

GRANT, R., 'The Society of Friends of Russian Freedom (1890–1917): A Case Study in Internationalism', *Journal of the Scottish Labour History Society*, 3 (1970), 3–24.

GREGORY, P. R. and SAILOR, J., 'Russian Monetary Policy and Industrialisation, 1861–1913', *JEH* 36 (1976), 836–51.

GRIFFITH, R. G., 'Clandestine Japanese Activity in the Baltic During the Russo-Japanese War', *Journal of Baltic Studies*, 18 (1987), 71–8.

GUTZKE, D. W., 'Rosebery and Campbell-Bannerman: The Conflict over Leadership Reconsidered', *BIHR* 54 (1981), 241–50.

HAMBURG, G. M., 'The London Emigration and the Russian Liberation Movement: The Problem of Unity, 1889–1897', *JfGOE* 25 (1977), 321–39.

HAMILTON, C. I., 'Anglo-French Seapower and the Declaration of Paris', *IHR* 4 (1982), 166–90.

—— 'Naval Power and Diplomacy in the Nineteenth Century', *JSS* 3 (1980), 74–88.

—— 'The Royal Navy, *la Royale*, and the Militarisation of Naval Warfare, 1840–70, *JSS* 6 (1983), 182–212.

—— 'Sir James Graham, the Baltic Campaign and War-Planning at the Admiralty in 1854', *HJ* 19 (1976), 89–112.

HAMILTON, K. A., 'Great Britain, France, and the Origins of the Mediterranean Agreements of 16 May 1907', in McKercher and Moss (eds.), *Shadow and Substance in British Foreign Policy 1895–1939*, 115–50.

HARGREAVES, J. D., 'Lord Salisbury, British Isolation and the Yangtze Valley, June–September 1900', *BIHR* 30 (1957), 62–75.

HARRISON, W., 'The British Press and the Russian Revolution of 1905–7', *OSP*, NS, 7 (1974), 75–96.

—— 'Mackenzie Wallace's View of the Russian Revolution of 1905–7'. *OSP*, NS, 4 (1971), 73–82.

HATTON, P. H. S., 'Harcourt and Solf: The Search for an Anglo-German Understanding through Africa, 1912–14', *ESR* 1 (1971), 123–45.

HAYES, P., 'Britain, Germany, and the Admiralty's Plans for Attacking German Territory, 1906–15', in Freedman et al. (eds.), *War, Strategy, and International Politics*, 95–116.

HEAD, J. A., 'Public Opinions and Middle Eastern Railways: The Russo-German Negotiations of 1910–11', *IHR* 6 (1984), 28–47.

HEILBRONNER, H., 'Aehrenthal in Defense of Russian Autocracy', *JfGOE* 17 (1969), 380–96.

—— 'An Anti-Witte Diplomatic Conspiracy, 1905–1906: The Schwanebach Memorandum', *JfGOE* 14 (1966), 347–61.

HELLER, J., 'Sir Louis Mallet and the Ottoman Empire: The Road to War', *MES* 12 (1976), 3–45.

HENRIKSON, A. K., 'The Geographical "Mental Maps" of American Foreign Policy Makers', *International Political Science Review*, 1 (1980), 496–530.

HILEY, N., 'Decoding German Spies: British Spy Fiction, 1908–18', in Wark (ed.), *Spy Fiction, Spy Films, and Real Intelligence*, 55–79.

HOARE, J. E., 'Komundo-Port Hamilton', *Asian Affairs*, 17 (1986), 298–308.

HOLLINGSWORTH, B., 'The British Memorial to the Russian Duma, 1906', *SEER* 53 (1975), 539–57.

—— 'The Society of Friends of Russian Freedom: English Liberals and Russian Socialists, 1890–1917', *OSP*, NS, 3 (1979), 45–64.

HOLMES, R., 'Sir John French and Kitchener', in Bond (ed.), *The First World War and British Military History*, 113–39.

HOPKINS, A. G., 'Accounting for the British Empire', *JICH* 16 (1988), 234–47.

—— 'The Victorians and Africa: A Reconsideration of the Occupation of Egypt, 1882', *Journal of African History*, 27 (1987), 363–91.

HUTCHINSON, J. F., 'The Octobrists and the Future of Imperial Russia as a Great Power', *SEER* 50 (1972), 220–37.

JEFFERSON, M. M., 'Lord Salisbury and the Eastern Question, 1894–7', *SEER* 39 (1960), 44–60.

—— 'Lord Salisbury's Conversations with the Tsar at Balmoral, 27 and 29 September 1896', *SEER* 39 (1960), 216–22.

JEFFERY, K., 'The Eastern Arc of Empire: A Strategic View 1850–1950', *JSS* 5 (1982), 531–45.

JELAVICH, B., 'British Means of Offence Against Russia in the Nineteenth Century', *RH* 1 (1974), 119–35.

—— 'Great Britain and the Russian Acquisition of Batum, 1878–86', *SEER* 48 (1970), 44–66.

JENSEN, R. B., 'The International Anti-Anarchist Conference of 1898 and the Origins of Interpol', *JCH* 16 (1981), 323–47.

JONES, D. R., 'Nicholas II and the Supreme Command: An Investigation of Motives', *Sbornik*, 11 (1985), 47–83.

KAPLAN, H. H., 'Observations on the Value of Russia's Overseas Commerce with Great Britain during the Second Half of the Eighteenth Century', *SR* 45 (1986), 85–94.

—— 'Russia's Impact on the Industrial Revolution in Great Britain during the Second Half of the Eighteenth Century: The Significance of International Commerce', *Forschungen zur osteuropäischen Geschichte*, 29 (1981), 7–59.

KEDOURIE, E., 'Cairo and Khartoum on the Arab Question', 1915–18', *HJ* 7 (1964), 280–97.

KELLY, J. B., 'Salisbury, Curzon and the Kuwait Agreement of 1899', in Bourne and Watt (eds.), *Studies in International History* (London, 1967), 249–90.

KENNEDY, P. M., 'The Development of German Naval Operations Plans Against England, 1896–1914', *EHR* 89 (1974), 48–76.

—— 'German World Policy and the Alliance Negotiations with England, 1897–1900', *JMH* 45 (1973), 602–25.

—— 'The Influence and Limitations of Sea Power', *IHR* 10 (1988), 2–17.

KENT, M., 'Asiatic Turkey, 1914–16', in Hinsley (ed.), *British Foreign Policy Under Sir Edward Grey*, 436–51.

—— 'Constantinople and Asiatic Turkey, 1905–14', in Hinsley (ed.), *British Foreign Policy Under Sir Edward Grey*, 148–64.

KIERNAN, V. G., 'Diplomats in Exile', in Hatton and Anderson (eds.), *Studies in Diplomatic History*, 301–21.

KIMBALL, A., 'The Harassment of Russian Revolutionaries Abroad: The London Trial of Vladimir Burtsev in 1898', *OSP*, NS, 6 (1973), 48–65.

KING, D. J. S., 'The Hamburg Branch: The German Period, 1899–1920', in F. H. H. King (ed.), *Eastern Banking*, 517–45.

KINIAPINA, N. S., 'Borba Rossii za otmenu ogranichitelnykh uslovii parizhskogo dogovora 1856 goda', *VI* 8 (1972), 35–51.

KLEIN, I., 'British Intervention in the Persian Revolution, 1905–9', *HJ* 15 (1972), 731–52.

KLIEMAN, A. S., 'Britain's War Aims in the Middle East in 1915', *JCH* 3 (1968), 237–51.

KOCH, H. W., 'Das britische Russlandbild im Spiegel der britischen Propaganden 1914–18', *Zeitschrift für Politik*, 27 (1980), 71–96.

KRUPINA, T. D., 'Politicheskii krizis 1915 g. i sozdanie osobogo sobeshchaniia po oborone', *IZ* 83 (1969), 58–75.

KUTOLOWSKI, J, F., 'Polish Exiles and British Public Opinion: A Case Study of 1861–62', *CSP*, 21 (1979) 45–65.

—— 'Victorian Provincial Businessmen and Foreign Affairs: The Case of the Polish Insurrection, 1863–64', *Northern History*, 21 (1985), 236–58.

LAMBERT, A., 'Preparing for the Russian War: British Strategic Planning, March 1853–March 1854', *WS* 7 (1989), 15–39.

LANGHORNE, R. T. B., 'Anglo-German Negotiations Concerning the Future of the Portuguese Colonies, 1911–14', *HJ* 16 (1973), 361–87.

—— 'Great Britain and Germany, 1911–14', in Hinsley (ed.), *British Foreign Policy Under Sir Edward Grey*, 288–314.

LIEVEN, D., 'Bureaucratic Authoritarianism in Late Imperial Russia: The Personality, Career and Opinions of P. N. Durnovo', *HJ* 26 (1983), 391–402.

—— 'Pro-Germans and Russian Foreign Policy 1890–1914', *IHR* 2 (1980), 34–54.

LONG, J. W., 'Franco-Russian Relations during the Russo-Japanese War', *SEER* 52 (1974), 213–33.

—— 'Organized Protest Against the 1906 Russian Loan', *CMRS* 13 (1972), 24–39.

LOWE, C. J., 'The Failure of British Diplomacy in the Balkans', *CJH* 4 (1969), 73–100.

LUNTINEN, P., 'The Åland Question during the Last Years of the Russian Empire', *SEER* 44 (1976), 557–71.

MCDERMOTT, J., 'The Revolution in British Military Thinking from the Boer War to the Moroccan Crisis', *CJH* 9 (1974), 159–77.

MACFIE, A. L., 'The Straits Question in the First World War, 1914–18', *MES* 19 (1983), 43–74.

MCKERCHER, B. J. C., 'Diplomatic Equipoise: The Lansdowne Foreign Office, the Russo-Japanese War of 1904–5, and the Global Balance of Power', *CJH* 24 (1989), 299–339.

MCLEAN, D., 'British Finance and Foreign Policy in Turkey: The Smyrna–Aidin Railway Settlement 1913–14', *HJ* 19 (1976), 521–30.

—— 'English Radicals, Russia, and the Fate of Persia 1907–13', *EHR* 93 (1978), 338–52.

—— 'The Foreign Office and the First Chinese Indemnity Loan, 1895', *HJ* 16 (1973), 303–21.

—— 'A Professor Extraordinary: E. G. Browne and His Persian Campaign 1908–13', *HJ* 21 (1978), 399–408

MAGILL, L. M., 'Joseph Conrad: Russia and England', *Albion*, 3 (1971), 3–8.

MAHAJAN, S., 'The Defence of India and the End of Isolation: A Study in the Foreign Policy of the Conservative Government, 1900–5', *JICH* 10 (1982), 168–92.

MANN, T., 'Joseph Conrad's *The Secret Agent* (1926)', in Watt (ed.), *Conrad: The Secret Agent*, 99–112.

MARSDEN, A., 'Salisbury and the Italians in 1896', *JMH* 40 (1968), 91–117.

MARSH, P., 'Lord Salisbury and the Ottoman Massacres', *JBS* 11 (1972), 63–84.

MEJCHER, H., 'Oil and British Policy towards Mesoptomia, 1914–1918', *MES* 8 (1972), 377–91.

MORREN, D. G., 'Donald Mackenzie Wallace and British Russophilism, 1870–1919', *CSP* 9 (1967), 170–83.

MORRILL, D. L., 'Nicholas II and the Call for the First Hague Conference', *JMH*, 46 (1974), 296–313.

MORRIS, L. P., 'The Russians, the Allies and the War, February–July 1917', *SEER* 50 (1972), 29–48.

MOSER, T. C., 'An English Context for Conrad's Russian Characters: Sergey Stepniak and the Diary of Olive Garnett', *Journal of Modern Literature*, 11 (1984), 3–44.

MOSSE W. E., 'The End of the Crimean System: England, Russia and the Neutrality of the Black Sea, 1870–1', *HJ* 4 (1961), 164–90.

—— 'Public Opinion and Foreign Policy: the British Public and the War-Scare of November 1870', *HJ* 6 (1963), 38–58.

MUNTING, R., 'Ransomes in Russia: An English Agricultural Engineering Company's Trade with Russia to 1917', *EconHR*, 2nd ser., 31 (1978), 257–69.

MURFETT M. H., 'An Old Fashioned Form of Protectionism: the Role Played by British Naval Power in China from 1860–1941', *American Neptune*, 50 (1990), 178–91.

MURRAY, J. A., 'Foreign Policy Debated: Sir Edward Grey and his Critics, 1911–12', in Wallace and Askew (eds.), *Power, Public Opinion, and Diplomacy*, 140–71.

NEILSON, K., 'The Breakup of the Anglo-Russian Alliance: The Question of Supply in 1917', *IHR* 3 (1981), 62–75.

—— ' "The British Empire floats on the British Navy": British Naval Policy, Belligerent Rights and Disarmament, 1902–9', in McKercher (ed.), *Arms Limitation and Disarmament*, 21–42.

—— ' "A Dangerous Game of American Poker": Britain and the Russo-Japanese War', *JSS* 12 (1989), 63–87.

—— ' "Greatly Exaggerated": The Myth of the Decline of Great Britain before 1914', *IHR* 13 (1991), 695–725.

—— ' "Joy Rides"?: British Intelligence and Propaganda in Russia, 1914–17', *HJ* 24 (1981), 885–906.

—— 'Kitchener: A Reputation Refurbished?', *CJH* 15 (1980), 207–27.

—— ' "My Beloved Russians": Sir Arthur Nicolson and Russia, 1906–16', *IHR* 9 (1987), 521–54.

—— 'Russian Foreign Purchasing in the Great War: A Test Case', *SEER* 60 (1982), 572–90.

—— 'Tsars and Commissars: W. Somerset Maugham, *Ashenden* and Images of Russia in British Adventure Fiction, 1890–1928', *CJH* 27 (1992), 475–500.

—— 'Watching the "Steamroller": British Observers and the Russian Army before 1914', *JSS* 8 (1985), 199–217.

—— 'Wishful Thinking: The Foreign Office and Russia, 1907–17', in McKercher and Moss (eds.), *Shadow and Substance in British Foreign Policy 1895–1939*, 151–80.

—— and McKercher, B. J. C., ' "The Triumph of Unarmed Force": Sweden and the Allied Blockade of Germany 1914–17', *JSS* 7 (1984), 178–99.

NEIMAN L. A., 'Franko-russkie otnosheniia vo vremia marokkanskogo krizisa 1911 g.', *Frantsuzskii ezhegodnik* (1969), 65–91.

NEVAKIVI J., 'Lord Kitchener and the Partition of the Ottoman Empire, 1915–16', in Bourne and Watt (eds.), *Studies in International History*, 316–29.

NISH I. H., 'Naval Thinking and the Anglo-Japanese Alliance 1900–4', *Keio Hogaku Kenkyu*, 56 (1983), 5–14.

—— 'The Royal Navy and the Taking of Wei-hai-wei, 1898–1905', *MM* 54 (1968), 39–54.

OPPEL, B., 'The Waning of a Traditional Alliance: Russia and Germany after the Portsmouth Peace Conference', *CEH* 5 (1977), 318–29.

OREL, H., 'English Critics and the Russian Novel: 1850–1917', *SEER* 33 (1955), 457–69.

PAGET, G, 'The November 1914 Straits Agreement and the Dardanelles–Gallipoli Campaign', *AJPH* 33 (1987), 253–60.

PALMER, A. W., 'Lord Salisbury's approach to Russia 1898', *OSP*, NS, 6 (1955), 102–14.

PARTRIDGE, M., 'Alexander Herzen and the English Press', *SEER* 36 (1958), 454–70.

—— 'Alexander Herzen and the Younger Joseph Cowen, M. P. Some Unpublished Material', *SEER* 41 (1962), 50–63.

PERRINS, M., 'The Armored Cruiser *Riurik* and Anglo-Russian Naval Co-operation 1905–9', *Defense Analysis*, 8 (1992), 173–8.

—— 'The Council for State Defence 1905–9: A Study in Russian Bureaucratic Politics', *SEER* 58 (1980), 370–98.

PHELPS, G., 'The Early Phases of British Interest in Russian Literature', *SEER* 36 (1958), 418–33.

—— 'The Early Phases of British Interest in Russian Literature', *SEER* 38 (1960), 415–30.

PHILPOTT W. J., 'Kitchener and the 29th Division: A Study in Anglo-French Strategic Relations 1914–15', *JSS* 16 (1993), 375–407.

POLLARD, S., 'Capital Exports, 1870–1914: Harmful or Beneficial?' *EconHR*, 2nd ser., 38 (1985), 489–514.

PORTER, A. N., 'The Balance Sheet of Empire, 1850–1914', *HJ* 31 (1988), 685–99.

—— 'Lord Salisbury, Foreign Policy and Domestic Finance, 1860–1900', in Blake and Cecil (eds.), *Salisbury*, 148–84.

PORTER, B., ' "Bureau and Barrack": Early Victorian Attitudes towards the Continent', *VS* 27 (1984), 407–33.

PRESTON, A., 'The Eastern Question in British Strategic Policy During the Franco-Prussian War', *Historical Papers* (Canadian Historical Association), 55–88.

—— 'Frustrated Great Gamesmanship: Sir Garnet Wolseley's Plans for War against Russia, 1873–80', *IHR* 2 (1980), 239–65.

—— 'Sir Charles Macgregor and the Defence of India, 1857–87', *HJ* 12 (1969), 58–77.

RAMM, A., 'Lord Salisbury and the Foreign Office', in Bullen (ed.), *The Foreign Office 1782–1982*, 46–65.

RANFT, B., 'Parliamentary Debate, Economic Vulnerability, and British Naval expansion, 1860–1905', in Freedman, Hayes, and O'Neill (eds.), *War, Strategy, and International Politics*, 75–93.

—— 'The Protection of British Seaborne Trade and the Development of Systematic Planning for War, 1860–1906', in id. (ed.), *Technical Change and British Naval Policy 1860–1939*, 1–22.

RENZI, W. A., 'Who Composed "Sazonov's Thirteen Points"? A Re-Examination of Russia's War Aims of 1914', *AHR* 88 (1983), 347–57.

ROBBINS, K. G., 'Public Opinion, the Press and Pressure Groups', in Hinsley (ed.), *British Foreign Policy under Sir Edward Grey*, 70–88.

ROLLO, P. J. V., 'Lord Lansdowne', in Wilson (ed.), *British Foreign Secretaries and Foreign Policy*, 159–71.

ROSENBAUM, A., 'The Manchurian Bridgehead: Anglo-Russian Rivalry and the Imperial Railways of North China, 1897–1902', *MAS* 10 (1976), 41–64.

SALT, J., 'Britain, the Armenian Question and the Cause of Ottoman Reform: 1894–6', *MES* 26 (1990), 308–28.

SANDERS, M. L., 'British Film Propaganda in Russia 1916–18', *Historical Journal of Film, Radio and Television*, 3 (1983), 117–29.

—— 'Wellington House and British Propaganda during the First World War', *HJ* 18 (1975), 119–46.

SARKISSIAN, A. O., 'Concert Diplomacy and the Armenians, 1890–6', in id. (ed.), *Studies in Diplomatic History and Historiography in Honour of G. P. Gooch*, 48–75.

SATRE, L. J., 'St John Brodrick and Army Reform', *JBS* 15 (1976), 117–39.

SAUNDERS, D., 'Stepniak and the London Emigration: Letters to Robert Spence Watson, 1887–90', *OSP*, NS, 13 (1980), 80–93.

—— 'Vladimir Burtsev and the Russian Revolutionary Emigration (1880–1905)', *ESR* 13 (1983), 39–62.

SCHROEDER, P. W., 'Did the Vienna Settlement Rest on a Balance of Power?', *AHR* 97 (1992), 683–706.

SCHURMAN, D. M., 'The Imperial Crisis of 1878', unpublished paper.

SCHWARZ, B., 'Divided Attention: Britain's Perception of a German Threat to her Eastern Position in 1918', *JCH* 28 (1993), 103–22.

SENESE, D., 'Felix Volkovsky in London, 1890–1914', *Immigrants and Minorities*, 2 (1983), 67–78.

SHATSILLO, K. F., 'Inostrannyi kapital i voenno-morskie programmy Rossii nakanune pervoi mirovoi voiny', *IZ* 69 (1961), 72–100.

—— 'O disproportsii v razvitii vooruzhennykh sil Rossii nakanune pervoi mirovoi voiny (1906–1914 gg.)', *IZ* 83 (1969), 123–36.

SHPAYER-MAKOV, H. 'Anarchism in British Public Opinion 1880–1914', *VS* 31 (1988), 487–516.

—— 'The Reception of Peter Kropotkin in Britain 1886–1917', *Albion*, 19 (1987), 373–90.

SIDOROV, A. L., 'Missiia v Angliiu i Frantsiiu po voprosu snabzheniia Rossii predmetami vooruzheniia', *Istoricheskii arkhiv*, 4 (1949), 351–86.

—— 'Otnosheniia Rossii s soiuznikami i innostranye postavki vo vremia pervoi mirovoi voiny 1914–17 gg.', *IZ* 15 (1945), 128–79.

SIDOROWICZ, A., 'The British Government, the Hague Peace Conference of 1907 and the Armaments Question', in McKercher (ed.), *Arms Limitation and Disarmament*, 1–20.

SILBERSTEIN G. E., 'Germany, France and the Casablanca Incident 1908–9: An Investigation of a Forgotten Crisis', *CJH* 11 (1976), 331–54.

SLATTER, J., 'Stepniak and the Friends of Russia', *Immigrants and Minorities*, 2 (1983), 33–49.

SMITH, Jr., C. J., 'Great Britain and the 1914–1915 Straits Agreement with Russia: The British Promise of November 1914', *AHR* 70 (1965), 1015–34.

SMITH S. R. B., 'Public Opinion, the Navy and the City of London: The Drive for British Naval Expansion in the Late Nineteenth Century', *WS* 9 (1991), 29–50.

SONTAG, J. P., 'Tsarist Debts and Tsarist Foreign Policy', *SR* 27 (1968), 529–41.

SPIERS, E. M., 'Gallipoli', in Bond (ed.), *The First World War and British Military History*, 165–88.

—— 'Haldane's Reform of the Regular Army: Scope for Revision', *BJIS* 6 (1980), 69–81.

SPRING, D. W., 'Russia and the Franco-Russian Alliance, 1905–14: Dependence or Interdependence?', *SEER* 66 (1988), 564–92.

—— 'The Trans-Persian Railway Project and Anglo-Russian Relations, 1909–14', *SEER* 54 (1976), 60–82.

STANWOOD, F., 'Revolution and the "Old Reactionary Policy": Britain in Persia, 1917', *JICH* 6 (1978), 144–65.

STEINBERG, J., 'The Copenhagen Complex', in Laqueur and Mosse (eds.), *1914: The Coming of the First World War* (New York, 1966), 21–44.

—— 'Germany and the Russo-Japanese War', *AHR* 75 (1970), 1965–86.

STEINER, Z., 'Elitism and Foreign Policy: The Foreign Office in the Great War', in McKercher and Moss (eds.), *Shadow and Substance in British Foreign Policy 1895–1939*, 19–56.

—— 'Great Britain and the Creation of the Anglo-Japanese Alliance', *JMH* 31 (1959), 27–36.

STEPHAN, J. J., 'The Crimean War in the Far East', *MAS* 3 (1969), 257–77.

STOLIARENKO, M. A., 'Anglo-russkie soglasheniia o severnykh portakh Rossii v gody pervoi mirovoi voiny', *Vestnik Leningradskogo Universiteta*, 16 (1961), 46–58.

STONE, N., 'Moltke-Conrad: Relations Between the Austro-Hungarian and German General Staffs, 1909–14', *HJ* 9 (1966), 201–28.

STRACHAN, H., 'Soldiers, Strategy and Sebastopol', *HJ* 21 (1978), 303–325.

SUN, E-T. Z., 'The Lease of Wei-hai-Wei', *PHR* 19 (1950), 277–83.

SWEET, D. W., 'The Baltic in British Diplomacy before the First World War', *HJ* 13 (1970), 454–74.

—— 'Great Britain and Germany, 1905–11', in Hinsley (ed.), *British Foreign Policy Under Sir Edward Grey*, 216–35.

—— and Langhorne, R. T. B., 'Great Britain and Russia, 1907–14', in Hinsley (ed.), *British Foreign Policy under Sir Edward Grey*, 236–55.

THOMPSTONE, S., 'Ludwig Knoop, "The Arkwright of Russia" ', *Textile History*, 15 (1984), 45–73.

THORNTON, A. P., 'Afghanistan in Anglo-Russian Diplomacy, 1869–73', *Cambridge Historical Journal*, 11 (1954), 204–18.

TORREY, G., 'Indifference and Mistrust: Russian–Romanian Collaboration in the Campaign of 1916', *Journal of Military History*, 57 (1993), 279–300.

—— 'Rumania and the Belligerents, 1914–16', *JCH* 1 (1966), 171–92.

—— 'The Rumanian Campaign of 1916: Its Impact on the Belligerents', *SR* 39 (1980), 27–43.

TOWLE, P., 'The Russo-Japanese War and the Defence of India', *Military Affairs*, 44 (1980), 111–17.

TREBILCOCK, C., 'British Armaments and European Industrialization, 1890–1914', *EconHR*, 2nd ser., 26 (1973), 254–72.

—— 'British Multinationals in Japan, 1900–41: Vickers, Armstrong, Nobel, and the Defense Sector', in Yuzawa and Udagawa (eds.), *Foreign Business in Japan before World War II*, 89–100.

TRUMPENER, U., 'Liman von Sanders and the German-Ottoman Alliance', *JCH* 1 (1966), 179–92.

TUCKER, A., 'The Issue of Army Reform in the Unionist Government, 1903–5', *HJ* 9 (1966), 90–100.

TURNBULL, D., 'The Defeat of Popular Representation, December 1904: Prince Mirskii, Witte, and the Imperial Family', *SR* 48 (1989), 54–70.

VALONE, S. J., ' "There Must Be Some Misunderstanding": Sir Edward Grey's Diplomacy of August 1, 1914', *JBS* 27 (1988), 405–24.

VINCENT-SMITH, J. D., 'The Anglo-German Negotiations over the Portuguese Colonies in Africa, 1911–14', *HJ* 17 (1974), 620–9.

WARMAN, R., 'The Erosion of Foreign Office Influence in the Making of Foreign Policy', *HJ* 15 (1972), 133–59.

WARTH, R. D., 'Before Rasputin: Piety and the Occult at the Court of Nicholas II', *Historian*, 476 (1985), 323–37.

WATT, D. C., 'The Nature of the foreign-policy-Making Élite in Britain', in id., *Personalities and Politics*, 1–15.

WEINROTH, H. S., 'British Radicals and the Balance of Power, 1902–14', *HJ* 13 (1970), 653–82.

—— 'Left-Wing Opposition to Naval Armaments in Britain before 1914', *JCH* 6 (1971), 93–120.

WILLIAMS, B. J., 'The Approach to the Second Afghan War: Central Asia during the Great Eastern Crisis, 1875–8', *IHR* 2 (1980), 216–38.

—— 'Great Britain and Russia, 1905 to the 1907 Convention', in Hinsley (ed.), *The Foreign Policy of Sir Edward Grey*, 133–47.

—— 'The Revolution of 1905 and Russian Foreign Policy', in Abramsky (ed.), *Essays in Honour of E. H. Carr*, 101–25.

WILLIAMS, R., 'Arthur James Balfour, Sir John Fisher and the Politics of Naval Reform, 1904–10', *HR* 60 (1987), 80–99.

—— 'Lord Kitchener and the Battle of Loos: French Politics and British Strategy in the Summer of 1915', in Freedman, Hayes, and O'Neill (eds.), *War, Strategy, and International Politics*, 117–32.

WILSON, K., 'The Anglo-Japanese Alliance of August 1905 and the Defending of India: A Case of the Worst Scenario', *JICH* 21 (1993), 334–56.

—— 'The British *Démarche* of 3 and 4 December 1912: H. A. Gwynne's Note on Britain, Russia and the First Balkan War', *SEER* 62 (1984), 552–9.

—— 'British Power in the European Balance, 1906–14', in Dilks (ed.), *Retreat from Power*, i, 1906–39, 21–41.

—— 'Constantinople or Cairo: Lord Salisbury and the Partition of the Ottoman Empire 1886–97', in id. (ed.), *Empire and Continent*, 1–30.

—— 'Grey', in id. (ed.), *British Foreign Secretaries and Foreign Policy: From Crimean War to First World War* (London, 1987), 172–97.

—— 'Imperial Interests in the British Decision for War, 1914: The Defence of India in Central Asia', *RIS* 10 (1984), 189–203.

—— 'The Question of Anti-Germanism at the British Foreign Office before the First World War', *CJH* 18 (1983), 23–42.

—— 'Sir Eyre Crowe on the Origin of the Crowe Memorandum of 1 January 1907', *BIHR* 55 (1983), 238–41.

—— 'The Struggle for Persia: Sir G. Clerk's Memorandum of 21 July on Anglo-Russian Relations in Persia', *Proceedings of the 1988 International Conference on Middle Eastern Studies*, 290–334.

WILSON, T., 'Britain's "Moral Commitment" to France in August 1914', *History*, 64 (1979), 380–90.

WRIGHT, D, G., 'The Great War, Government Propaganda and English "Men of Letters" 1914–16', *Literature and History*, 7 (1978), 70–100.

ZHILIN, A., 'Bolshaia programma po usileniiu russkoi armii', *VIZ* 16 (1974), 90–7.

ZUCKERMAN, F. S., 'Political Police and Revolution: The Impact of the 1905 Revolution on the Tsarist Secret Policy', *JCH* 27 (1992), 279–300.

—— 'Vladimir Burtsev and the Tsarist Political Police in Conflict, 1907–14', *JCH* 12 (1979), 193–219.

Index